PEUGEOT
106, 205, 206, 306
WORKSHOP MANUAL

by
Ivor Carroll, Bob Cooke, Lindsay Porter, Jim Tyler

Every care has been taken to ensure that the material in this book is correct. However, should any matter not be clear after reading this book, you are advised to consult your nearest franchised Peugeot dealer. Liability cannot be accepted for damage, loss, accidents or injury, due to failure to follow instructions or to consult expert advice if this is required.

Ring this number to find your nearest Peugeot dealer in the UK – 0845 200 1234.

CONTENTS

CHAPTER 1:	Facts & Figures		**CHAPTER 9:**	Ignition, Fuel, Exhaust
CHAPTER 2:	Safety First!		**CHAPTER 10:**	Electrical, Dash, Instruments
CHAPTER 3:	Getting Through the Annual Test		**CHAPTER 11:**	Steering, Suspension
CHAPTER 4:	Workshop Top Tips!		**CHAPTER 12:**	Brakes
CHAPTER 5:	Servicing		**CHAPTER 13:**	Bodywork
CHAPTER 6:	Engine		**CHAPTER 14:**	Interior, Trim
CHAPTER 7:	Transmission, Clutch		**CHAPTER 15:**	Wiring Diagrams
CHAPTER 8:	Cooling Systems			

FACT FILE

'LEFT' AND 'RIGHT' SIDES OF THE CAR

- Throughout this manual, we refer to the 'left' and 'right' sides of the car. They refer to the sides of the car that you would see if you were sitting in the driver's seat, looking forward.

First published in 2001 by:
Porter Publishing Ltd.
The Storehouse • Little Hereford Street
Bromyard • Hereford • HR7 4DE • England

Tel: 01885 488 800
Fax: 01885 483 012
www.portermanuals.com

© Copyright Lindsay Porter and Porter Publishing Ltd, 2001.

All rights reserved. No part of this publication may be reproduced, stored in a retrieval system, or transmitted in any form including electronic, electrical, mechanical, optical, photocopying, recording or by any other means without prior written permission of the publisher. All enquiries should be addressed to the publisher at the address shown on this page.

British Library Cataloguing in Publication Data.
A catalogue record for this book is available from the British Library.

ISBN 1-899238-45-X

Series Editor: Lindsay Porter
Layout and Typesetting: Pineapple Publishing, Worcester
Printed in England by The Trinity Press, Worcester

CHAPTER 1: FACTS & FIGURES

Please read **Chapter 2, Safety First** before carrying out any work on your car.

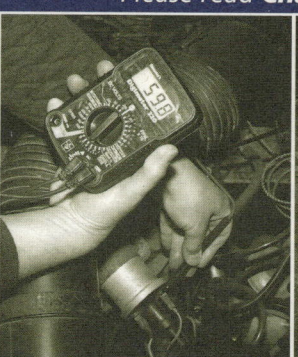

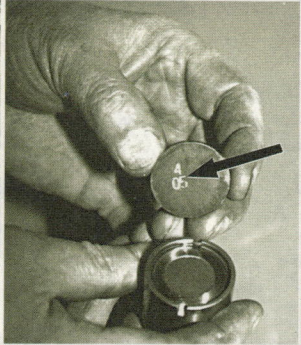

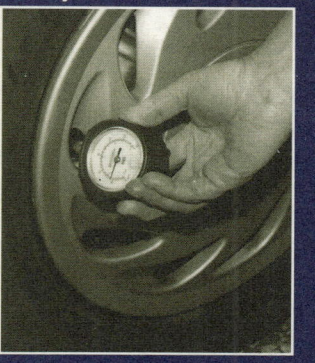

This chapter provides you with all the information you will need about your car, especially in connection with servicing and repairing it. First, you'll need to identify the engine type. If you don't know it already, see **Chapter 6, Engine**.

Before buying parts, be sure to take your vehicle's chassis and engine numbers with you – **Part G: Identification Numbers** in this chapter.

CONTENTS

	Page No.		Page No.
Part A: Major Milestones	1-2	**Part E:** Repair Data	1-9
Part B: Vital Statistics	1-4	**Part F:** Torque Wrench Settings	1-11
Part C: Capacities	1-6	**Part G:** Identification Numbers	1-12
Part D: Service Data	1-7		

IMPORTANT NOTE:
→ Many detail changes have taken place over the years, and there have been many different Special Editions and Options available.
→ The following information will be true of most cases but can only be taken as a general guide.

→ Peugeot's quoted torque settings and other information sometimes vary between publications. The figures shown here are the latest available to us.
→ If in any doubt, consult your local Peugeot dealer for confirmation.

CHAPTER 1 Facts & Figures

1-1

Part A: Major Milestones

106

October 1991: 106 3-door hatchbacks launched with petrol engine.
→ 1.1 and 1.4 models available with optional catalytic converter.
→ All with 5-speed transmission except XN which has 4-speed.
→ Anti-roll bars fitted to XR, XT and XSi models.
→ 1.4 XSi has sporty appearance driving lamps, alloy wheels and sports seats.

February 1993: 5-door models launched.

October 1993: 1.4 XTD diesel version launched and ABS brakes available on all models.

June 1994: New 1.5D models with 1527cc diesel engines launched.

August 1994: 1.6 injection models introduced and some versions now fitted with alarm and immobiliser.

June 1996: 'New', revised version of 106 introduced:
→ Bodyshell said to be stronger than original.
→ New front-end styling, tailgate, rear lights and high-level brake light.
→ New multi-point petrol injection fitted.
→ Diesel versions now fitted with anti-roll bars.

November 1996: 3-speed automatic transmission and GTi versions introduced.

April 1998: Cosmetic range updates including (to some models) driver's side airbag, power assisted steering, remote central locking and other detail improvements.

205

September 1983: 205 introduced in 5-door body style only. Petrol engines designated XV, XW and XY, all with chain-driven over-head camshaft in capacities of 954cc, 1124cc and 1360cc respectively.
→ The 4- or 5-speed transmission formed an integral part of the engine block, being placed beneath the crankcase and sharing lubrication with the engine.
→ Diesel engine available in XUD 1700cc form, with separate transmission.
→ Various trim options available over whole range.

April 1984: GTI model introduced with 1580cc XU5-type engine using a belt-driven camshaft, separate 5 speed gearbox and alloy wheels as standard, in a new 3-door hatchback body style.

October 1984: Three door body style made available in all configurations (not just GTI) and all such models designated 'X' series.

June 1985: Van bodied model introduced with option of petrol or diesel engine.

April 1986: Automatic transmission introduced as option, but only available with 1580cc engine.
→ Cabriolet CTI also introduced, fitted with single-point fuel-injected 1580cc XU5 engine.
→ GTI engine uprated to 115 bhp.

September 1986: Launch of 1905cc XU9 engine fitted to GTI, replacing smaller XU5 unit (not available in UK until January 1987) along with rear disc brakes and modified 'sports' suspension.

December 1987: Range revised, changes including uprated 1.0, 1.1 and 1.4 litre engines designated 'TU', new MA-type 5-speed transmission introduced for whole range except fuel-injected, diesel and automatic models.

June 1988: 1.4 litre Cabriolet introduced, designated CJ, with carburetor-equipped engine.

August 1990: 1.6 litre Cabriolet now fitted with electric hood (optional on 1.4 litre).

October 1991: 1.8 litre turbo-diesel engine introduced, but only in three-door body style; Cabriolet versions now fitted with catalytic converter - also available on 1.1 and 1.4 litre fuel-injected engines.

June 1994: Special 3- and 5-door 'Mardi Gras' editions launched in 1.1, 1.6 Auto., 1.8 diesel and turbo-diesel types.

September 1994: Mardi Gras models now adopted as standard range.

August 1995: All models begin phasing out, but still available into 1996.

December 1995: Model officially discontinued. Some 1996 vehicles registered.

206

October 1998: All-new 206 launched in UK.

June 1999: GTi version launched with 2-litre 137 bhp engine, anti-lock brakes and sports trim inside and out.

December 1999: Diesel versions with 2.0 HDi engines introduced – not covered by this manual.

June 2000: The one millionth 206 is produced. Models built in France, England, Argentina and Brazil.

October 2000: 206 Coupe-Cabriolet launched with electrically retractable rigid roof.

306

April 1993: 306 range launched in 5-door, petrol, hatchback, form.
→ All models with rear drum brakes except XT with rear disks.
→ ABS anti-lock brakes optional on all models.
→ Rev. counter and alarm/immobilser fitted to all models except XN.

June 1993: 1.9 diesel engine versions launched in UK and 4-speed auto. transmission available on XT 1.8 petrol models.

May 1994: 2-litre Cabriolet launched with electric soft-top and high specification levels.

October 1994: Saloon (sedan) versions launched, similar to existing hatchback models.
→ All models now with airbag, RDS audio, immobiliser/alarm with remote locking, split folding rear seat.

July 1996: GTi-6 launched in UK with 16v 2-litre engine and 6-speed manual transmission.
→ Roadster version of convertible also launched, similar to Cabriolet with colour-matched removable hard top.

April 1997: 306 receives minor range revisions.
→ New style front-end with 406-type headlights and grille, larger bumpers in body colour, new instrument panel inside vehicle.
→ All models with sunroof or air conditioning except 306 L.

October 1997: Estate version launched in UK similar in most respects to equivalent hatchbacks.

February 1998: Large number of small revisions introduced including automatic screen wipers and other detail changes.

November 1998: Special Edition 2.0 Rallye 3-door hatchback launched.

June 1999: Range revision with many cosmetic changes such as new dashboard and interior trim details, new lights and other exterior trim details.
→ Passenger-side airbag now fitted as standard on some versions.
→ 306 D Turbo now fitted with HDi common rail diesel engine – not covered by this manual.

June 2001: 306 petrol versions discontinued.
→ Replaced by new 307 model.
→ 306 diesels and Cabriolet continue in production.

December 2001: 306 diesel versions scheduled to be discontinued.

Part B: Vital Statistics

Wheels and Tyres

We include here an example of current provision by Dunlop for Peugeot vehicles. There have been many changes throughout the life of the model range and if you have bought an older model the original specification may have been replaced. We suggest that you check with your Dunlop Tyre station for the correct provision.

MODEL	RIM WIDTH & TYPE	RADIAL TUBELESS TYRES	TYRE PRESSURES (cold): first figure = bar; second = p.s.i. FRONT	REAR
106				
XN/XR (1.1)	4.5 B13	145/70 R13T	2.1/31	2.1/31
XR (1.4), XT	5.0 B13	155/70 R13T	2.2/32	2.2/32
	5.0 J13	165/65 R13T	2.2/32	2.2/32
Xsi	5.5 J14	175/60 R14H	2.2/32	2.2/32
205				
XE-GL	4.5 B13	135 SR13	2.0/29	2.1/31
XL-GL-XR-GR	4.5 B13	145 SR13	1.9/28	2.1/31
XS-XT-GT SR-AUTO	5.0 J13	165/70 SR13	1.7/25	1.9/28
XA-XRA	4.5 B13	145 SR13	1.9/28	2.6/38
CTi-GTi	5.0 B13	185/60 HR14	2.0/29	2.0/29
GTi 1.9	5.5 J14	185/55 VR15	2.0/29	2.0/29
206				
D	5.0 J14	175/65 R14T	2.4/35	2.4/35
XAD	5.0 B13	175/70 R13T	2.5/36	2.5/36
306				
1.1, 1.4, XR 1.6, XT 1.6, XT 1.8, XSi, S16	5.0 B13	165/70 R13	2.2/32	2.2/32

Weights

All weights in kg. All sizes in mm. NB All dimensions when car unladen.
NB Maximum load capacity = (Maximum Laden Weight) minus (Unladen Weight).
Exact unladen weight will vary with model. Refer to the VIN plate, the owner's handbook and, if necessary, a Peugeot main dealer for details.
The figures quoted below give examples of the ranges likely to be encountered

Maximum roof load:
106: 40 kg
205: 50 kg
306: 75 kg

Maximum weight on towball, when fitted – 50 kg.

Tow Limits. These will vary with each model and will depend on anticipated gradients and altitudes. We recommend that you refer to your Peugeot dealer for full details.

MODEL	UNLADEN WEIGHT	MAX. LADEN LADEN WEIGHT	TOW LIMITS WITHOUT BRAKES	WITH BRAKES
106	760-860	1200-1300	380-430	500-700
205	740-935	1140-1240	370-405	800-900
206				
Petrol Engines	985-1100	1405-1525	485-550	1100 except 1.1 = 700
Diesel Engines	1084-1145	1525-1585	540-570	1100
306	1020-1170	1480-1665		900-1000

Dimensions (typical)

MODELS	OVERALL LENGTH	OVERALL WIDTH	WHEEL BASE	FRONT TRACK	REAR TRACK	HEIGHT
106	3564	1590	2385	1380	1300	1369
205	3705	1572	2420	1350	1300	1372-1389
Variations						
Base/Gl/Ge/Van		1562				
Cabriolet		1589		1392	1328	
SR/GT				1364	1314	
1.6GTi				1392	1328	
1.9GTi				1383	1344	
206	3822	1673	2442	1443	1434	1435
306						
Hatch-back	3995	1692	2580	1462	1435	1380
Saloon	4240					

Part C: Capacities

All fluid figures are given in litres.
➜ Manufacturers constantly improve specifications and recommend own brands.
➜ Refer to your main dealer if you are in any doubt.

ENGINE OIL: Multi-grade SAE 10W/40 or 5W/40 such as Castrol GTX Magnatec.

MANUAL TRANSMISSION AND FINAL DRIVE: Pre-1988 Integrated engine/gearbox SAE 10W/40
From 1988 Gear Oil BV 75W80

AUTOMATIC TRANSMISSION: ATF to API GL5/Dexcron Type II

POWER ASSISTED STEERING: Use ATF as above.

BRAKE FLUID: Brake Fluid Dot 4 SAE J1703

COOLING SYSTEM: Important Note. Do not mix different colour or specification coolants.
Porcor TM 108, Glysantin G33, Revkogel 2000 are advised.

FUEL TANK:
106: 45
205: 50
206: 50
306: 60

COOLANT CAPACITY INC. HEATER:
106: 6.0
106 Variation: 5.5 (1.6 TU5 engine)

205
1.0/1.1	5.8
1.4 (TU)	5.8
1.4 (XY7)	6.0
1.4 (XY8)	5.6
1.6/1.9 GTi	6.7
1.6 (XU5)	8.5
1.8/1.9 Diesel	8.3

206
All models	7.0
Except DW engines	8.2

306
1.1/1.4	6.5
1.6	7.0
1.8	7.5
2.0 to 1997	7.0
2.0 from 1997	7.6
1.8/1.9D	9.0

ENGINE OIL CAPACITY:
106: 3.5
106 Variation: 4.8 (1.6D VJ engine)

205
1.0 (XV)	4.5
1.1 (XW)	4.5
1.1 (TU)	3.5
1.4 (TU)	3.5
1.4 (XY7)	5.0
1.4 (XY8)	5.0
1.4 (TU3S)	4.0
1.6/1.9 GTi	5.0
1.6 (XU5)	5.5
1.8/1.9 Diesel	5.0
1.9 Diesel from 1993	4.5 from 1993

206
All models	3.2
Except DW engines	4.75

306
1.1/1.4/1.6	3.5
1.8	4.9
2.0	5.0
1.8D	5.0
1.9D	4.2

TRANSMISSION:
Manual: All models: 2.0
Except
206 Diesel: 1.9
306 1.8 (XU7 engine): 1.8

Automatic: All models: 2.4 litres (drain and refill).
Except
206 Diesel: 3.0 (plus 2.0 litres if Torque converter drained)

BRAKE FLUID: It is recommended that the brake fluid is changed every two years. Inevitably there will be some additional loss in bleeding but 1 litre of fluid should cover the job on most models.

Part D: Service Data

Engine

FIRING ORDER: 1-3-4-2

DIESEL INJECTION ORDER: 1-3-4-2

IGNITION TIMING in degrees Before Top Dead Centre - BTDC: At specified rpm

Engines have considerable variations. Check these guide figures with the manufacturer with particular reference to the engine designation and the year.

106	Degrees	RPM
1.0 (TU9)	8	700
1.1 (TU1)	8	700
1.1l (TU1)	8	850
1.4 (TU3,2)	8	750

ALL OTHER ENGINES: Not adjustable.

206 and 306: None of these engines are adjustable.

205	Degrees	RPM
1.0 (XV8)	6	650
1.0 (TU9)	8	700
1.1 (XW7)	6	650
1.1 (TU1)	8	800
1.1i (TU1M)	8	900 (up to 1992)
1.4 (XY7)	8	650
1.4 (XY6)	10	900
1.4 GT (XY8)	2	950 (up to 1984)
	8	850 (from 1984)
1.4 XS/GT (TU3S)	8	750
1.4 (TU3)	8	750
1.4 (TU3CP)	4	700
1.4 (TU3ACLC)	4	800
1.4i (TU3M)	8	900
1.6 (XU5)	10	900
1.6 GTi	6	700 (up to 1984)
	10	850 (from 1985)
1.6 CTi/GTi	10	700
1.9I (XU9)	10	900
1.9 GTi (XU9JA)	5	700

ALL OTHER ENGINES: Not adjustable

SPARK PLUG TYPES AND GAPS

Engine	Champion	Gap (mm)	Alternative Equipment
106			
1.0/1.0i/1.1/1.1i	C10YCC	0.8	Eyquem RFC42LS
1.1i (from 1997)	RC8DMC	0.8	Eyquem FR7KDC
1.4 TU3	RC9YCC	0.8	Eyquem RFC42LS
1.4i TU3 (KDY)	RC9YCC	0.8	Eyquem RFC42LS
1.4i TU3 (KF2)	RC7YCC	0.8	Eyquem FC62LS
1.4i TU3 (K6B), (KDX)	RC7BMC	0.8	Eyquem RFC58LSP
1.4i TU3 (KFX)	RC8DMC	0.9	Eyquem FR7KDC
1.6i	RC8DMC	1.0	Eyquem FR7KDC
205			
Most models	RS9YCC	0.8	Eyquem RFC42LS
			Eyquem FC52LS
			Bosch F7DCOR
			Bosch FR7DCO
			Bosch H7DC (GAP 0.6)
Exceptions			
1.0 (TU9)	C10YCC	0.8	Eyquem RFC42LS
1.4 GT/1.6GTi	S7YCC	0.8	Bosch H6DC (GAP 0.6)
1.4I XS/GT	RC7YCC	0.8	Eyquem FC62LS
1.6/1.6GTi/CTi	RC7YCC	0.8	Bosch F7DCOR
206			
1.1i/1.4i	RS9YCC	1.0	Eyquem RFC52LS
1.6i	RC7BMC	1.0	Eyquem RFC58LSP
306			
1.1i	C10YCC	0.8	Eyquem RFC42LS

1.4i/1.8i	RS9YCC	1.0		Eyquem RFC52LS
1.6i	RC7BMC	1.0		Eyquem RFC58LSP
1.8i (from 1997)		0.9		Eyquem RFC422LZ2E
2.0i	RC7YCC	0.8		Eyquem FC62LS

Diesel Engines (Glow Plugs)

	Champion	Bosch
106		
1.4	CH147	0 250 202 001
1.6	CH168	0 100 226 188
205		
All models	CH68	0 001 110 017
206		
1.9	CH185	0 281 003 009
306		
1.8/1.9	CH68	0 250 201 019
1.9 Turbo	CH163	0 250 201 033

IDLE SPEED: (RPM) and EMISSIONS in volume percentages or ppm (parts per million).
NA = Not adjustable

	Idle Speed	CO	CO_2	O_2	HCppm
Carburated engines	700	1.25-1.35	13-16	0.5-2.0	300
Variations					
106					
1.4	750	1.5			
205					
1.0/1.1(XW7)	600-700	0.8-1.5			
1.1 (TU1)	850	0.5-1.0			
1.4 (TU3K1A)	700-800	0.8-1.5			
1.4 (TU3K1D)	850	0.5			
1.4 (TU3K1G)	800	0.8-1.5			
1.4 (TU3K2D)	750	1.5			
1.4 (XY6B)	850-950	0.8-1.5	10		
1.4 (XY7)	600-700	1.0-2.0			
1.4GT (XY8)	900-1000	1.5-2.5			
1.4 XG/GT	750	1.0			
1.6	900	0.5-1.5			
Cat + fuel injection	N/A	N/A	14.5-16	0.1-0.5	300
Variations					
106					
1.4i (TU3 K6B)		0.5-1.5	13-16	0.5-2.0	300
1.6i/GTi			10		
306					
1.1i/1.4i/1.6i/1.8I			10		
205					
1.4 (TU3 KAY)	850				
1.6 GTi	900	1.0	13-16	0.5-2.0	300
1.6 GTi/CTi	950	1.0	13-16	0.5-2.0	300
1.9i	900				
1.9 GTi	950	1.5	13-16	0.5-2.0	300
1.9 GTi+cat	850-950				

Part G: Identification Numbers

All manufacturers change the parts they use on the production line, often with startling frequency. The only way of ensuring that the parts you buy are the right ones for the vehicle is to take the vehicle's Vehicle Identification Number (VIN) and engine number with you when buying spares.

There are three main numbers you will need to know in order to buy parts and touch-up paint for a vehicle, and there is other useful information to be found:
➜ 1. VIN
➜ 2. Engine number
➜ 3. Paint code (and other) numbers

SECTION 1: VIN (VEHICLE IDENTIFICATION NUMBER)

The VIN is the vehicle's internationally unique number and tells your parts supplier exactly which model and year the vehicle is. Quote the VIN whenever you buy spares for the vehicle.

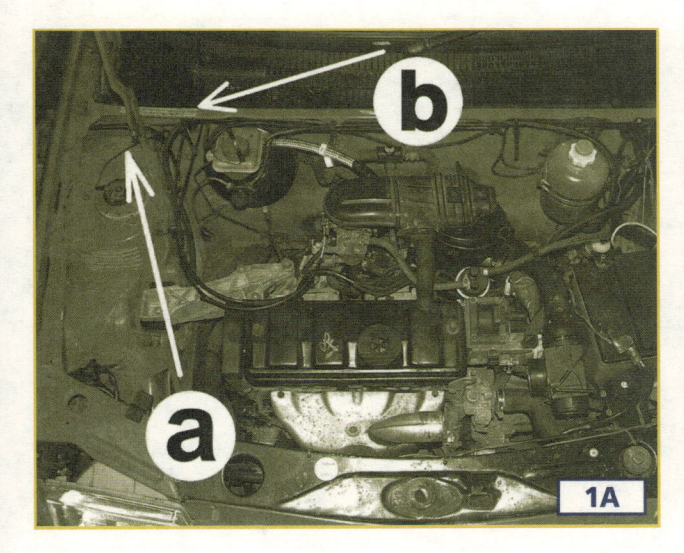

❒ **1B: 106 MODELS:** The VIN is stamped on a plate (**a**) positioned on the front shut-panel.
➜ The VIN is also stamped onto the bodyshell at manufacture and is found on the bulkhead/firewall panel (**b**) in the position shown.
➜ **LATER MODELS:** The VIN may also be visible through the lower corner of the front screen.

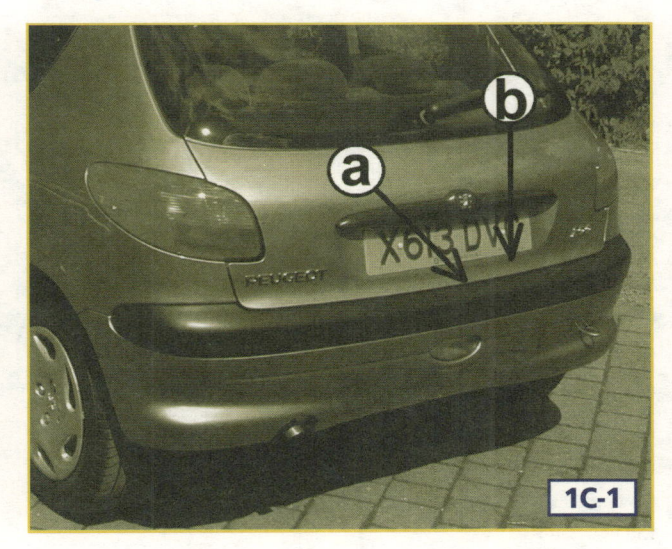

❒ **1A: 205 MODELS:** The VIN is stamped on a plate (**a**) positioned on top of the right-hand inner-wheelarch, in the engine bay. The number should be the same as that shown on the vehicle documents.
➜ Look for the second number (the third box) down on the plate.
➜ The VIN is also stamped onto the bodyshell at manufacture and is found on the bulkhead/firewall panel (**b**) just in front of the air intake grille, and just behind the VIN plate as shown.

❒ **1C-1: 206 MODELS:** The VIN plate is inside the luggage bay, facing the front of the vehicle, just beneath the tailgate latch (position **a**).
➜ The number is also stamped on to the bodywork, on the top face of the tailgate shut panel (position **b**).

Part F: Torque Wrench Settings

Key to Engine Types and Sizes

- A: TU engines
- B: TU (Cast engine)
- C: XU engines
- D: XU
- E: XUD engines.
- F: XUD Variants
- G: XV/XW/XY engines
- H: XV etc.Variants
- I: TUD(K9).
- J: TUD(VJ)

Engine	A	B	C	D	E	F	G	H	I	J
Main bearing cap, bolt										
Stage 1	20	20	Horizontal 25		15	35	36		20	20
Stage 2	45 deg	49 deg	Vertical 54		60 or 90 deg	70	51		44 deg	50 deg
Cylinder head bolts										
Stage 1	20	20	60	60	30	20	50	60	60	40
Stage 2	240 deg	120 deg	20 + 120 deg	100 deg	60 70	60	77	20	Slack	260 deg
Stage 3		120 deg	Run engine 15mins	100 deg	slack + 60 120 deg	180 deg (X7)		300 deg	20	
Stage 4			Wait 120 mins	100 deg	Run engine 10 mins	220 deg (X9)			160 deg	
Stage 5			20 + 120 deg		Wait 150 mins				160 deg	
					Slack + 70					
Big end Bolts										
Stage 1	20	38	40		40		36		20	18
Stage 2	40		slack		Slack				40	37
Stage 3			20 + 70 deg		20 + 70 deg					
Stage 4										
Flywheel/Driveshaft bolts					50		60			65
Clutch to flywheel	15		25							15
Crankshaft pulley	100		110		40		140		110	100
Stage 2					60 deg					
Camshaft sprocket bolt	80		80		35		74			80
Cam/rocker cover bolt	5		10				7		7	20
Timing chain/belt cover	8				12		7		8	
Timing chain/belt tensioner	23		15		18		7		15	
Oil pump to crankcase fixing, bolt	8		20		13		7		9	
Sump bolts	8		20		19		12		8	
	auto	man								
Engine to transmission	35	40	46						35	
Inlet manifold	8		20							
Exhaust manifold	5		20							
Water pump bolts			15		12		13			
Thermostat housing	8		15				15			
Spark plugs /glow plugs	28				25		18		22	25

KEY:

Number only = torque in Nm.

deg = degrees of rotation, using an angular torque gauge.

mins = waiting time or amount of time to run engine.

CRANKSHAFT END FLOAT:	0.07-0.27	0.07-0.32	0.07-0.27	0.07-0.27	0.07-0.27	0.07-0.27	0.07-0.27	0.07-0.27

Valve Gear

INLET VALVE HEAD SIZE:	34.8	34.7	37	36.7	36.8	36.8 / 40 from 1994	41.6	N/A
EXHAUST VALVE HEAD SIZE:	27.8	27.7	29.5	29.2	29.4	29.4 / 32.95 fr.1994	34.5	N/A

Part E: Repair Data

Dimensions in mm unless stated otherwise

Engine 'bottom end'

		XU7 1761cc	XU9 1905cc	XU10 1998cc	TUD5 (VJ) 1527	TUD3 (K9) 1360	XUD7 1765cc	XUD9 1905cc
BORE:		83	83	86	71.8	75	80	83
STROKE:		81	88	86	76.5	77	88	88
PISTON SIZES:								
Petrol	Diesel:							
Size 1:	A		82.953-82.967	82.721-82.139		74.935-74.945	79.922-79.938	82.984-82.939
Size 2:	B		82.963-82.977			74.945-74.955		
Size 3:	C		82.973-82.987			74.955-74.965		
Oversize:	1st Rebore:		82.721-82.739				79.952-79.968	83.13-83.139 / 83.43-83.439 / 83.73-83.739

*Piston size not relevant for these engines - new pistons supplied as matching sets with cylinder liners.

PISTON RING END GAP:							
TOP:	0.3-0.5	0.3-0.5	0.3-0.5		0.20-0.40	0.20-0.40	0.20-0.40
SECOND:	0.3-0.5	0.3-0.5	0.3-0.5		0.15-0.35	0.15-0.35	0.15-0.35
BOTTOM:	0.3-0.5	0.3-0.5	0.3-0.5		0.25-0.5	0.10-0.30	0.10-0.30
CRANK MAIN JOURNAL DIAMETER:		59.98-60.0			49.965-49.981	59.881-60.0	59.881-60.0
RE-GRIND UNDERSIZE:							
CRANK, BIG-END DIAMETER:		49.98-50			44.975-44.991	49.984-50.0	49.984-50.0
RE-GRIND UNDERSIZE:							
MAIN BEARING CLEARANCE:			0.038-0.069				
MAIN BEARING UNDERSIZES:		59.68-59.71			49.665-49.681	59.681-59.7	59.681-59.7
BIG-END BEARING CLEARANCE:				0.025-0.05			
BIG-END BEARING UNDERSIZES:		49.68-49.72			44.675-44.691	49.681-49,7	49.681-49,7
THRUST WASHER THICKNESSES AVAILABLE:							
CRANKSHAFT END FLOAT:						0.07-0.32	0.07-0.32

Valve Gear

INLET VALVE HEAD SIZE:	N/A	41.6		37	35.5		38.6
EXHAUST VALVE HEAD SIZE:	N/A	35.5		31.55	30.55		33

VALVE CLEARANCES (mm) (Check when engine cold)	Inlet	Exhaust
All Petrol engines	0.20	0.40
Except		
205 engines coded XV/XW/XY/X6	0.10	0.25
106 1.6 GTi (TU5NFX)	HYDRAULIC – NOT ADJUSTABLE	
306 2.0i 16v (XU10RFY)	HYDRAULIC – NOT ADJUSTABLE	
All Diesel engines	0.15	0.30

Other Settings
CLUTCH ADJUSTMENT (Pedal Travel)
106 and 205: 135-145mm
206: Not adjustable
306: Adjustable only on early 1.1/1.4/1.6 models: 131-141

BRAKE DISC PAD MINIMUM THICKNESS:
All models: 2.0 mm.

BRAKE SHOE FRICTION LINING MINIMUM THICKNESS:
205 models: 1.0 mm
All other models: 1.5 mm.

Part E: Repair Data

Dimensions in mm unless stated otherwise

Engine 'bottom end'

		XV8 954cc	TU9 954cc	XW7 1124cc	TU1 1124cc	XY7 1360cc	TU3 1360cc	XU5 1580cc	TU5 1587cc
BORE:		70	70	72	72	75	75	83	78.5
STROKE:		62	62		69	77	77	73	82
PISTON SIZES:									
Petrol:	Diesel:								
Size 1:	A	N/A	See Chapter 9*	69.96-69.97	N/A	71.93-71.95	N/A	74.94-74.96	82.953-82.967	78.445-78.47
Size 2:	B			69.97-69.98		71.94-71.96		74.95-74.97	82.963-82.977	
Size 3:	C			69.98-69.99		71.95-71.97		74.96-74.98	82.973-82.987	
Oversize:	1st Rebore:								78.84-78.855

*Piston size not relevant for these engines - new pistons supplied as matching sets with cylinder liners.

	XV8	TU9	XW7	TU1	XY7	TU3	XU5	TU5
PISTON RING END GAP:								
TOP:		0.25-0.45		0.25-0.45		0.3-0.5	0.25-0.45	0.3-0.5
SECOND:		0.25-0.45		0.25-0.45		0.3-0.5	0.45-0.75	0.3-0.5
BOTTOM:		0.3-0.5		0.3-0.5		0.3-0.5	0.2-0.5	0.3-0.5
CRANK MAIN JOURNAL DIAMETER:	49.965-49.981	49.965-49.981	49.965-49.981	49.965-49.981	49.965-49.981	49.965-49.981	59.98-60.0	49.965-49.981
RE-GRIND UNDERSIZE:	0.3		0.3		0.3			
CRANK, BIG-END DIAMETER:	44.975-44.991	37.992-38.008	44.975-44.991	44.975-44.991	44.975-44.991	44.975-44.991	44.99-45.0	44.975-44.991
RE-GRIND UNDERSIZE:	0.3		0.3		0.3			
MAIN BEARING CLEARANCE:		0.023-0.083		0.01-0.036		0.01-0.036		0.01-0.036
MAIN BEARING UNDERSIZES:		49.665-49.681		49.665-49.681	49.665-49.681	49.665-49.681	59.68-59.71	49.665-49.681
BIG-END BEARING CLEARANCE:		0.025-0.05		0.025-0.05		0.025-0.05		0.025-0.05
BIG-END BEARING UNDERSIZES:		36.992-37.008		44.675-44.691	44.675-44.691	44.675-44.691	44.67-44.69	44.675-44.691
THRUST WASHER THICKNESSES AVAILABLE:		2.3		2.3		2.3	2.3	
		2.4		2.4		2.4	2.35	
		2.45		2.45		2.45	2.4	
		2.5		2.5		2.5	2.45	
							2.5	

1C-2: 206 MODELS: The VIN is also visible through the front screen, adjacent to the wiper arm - position shown.

306 MODELS: The VIN plate is inside the luggage bay, facing the front of the vehicle, just beneath the tailgate latch (illustration *1C-, position* a).

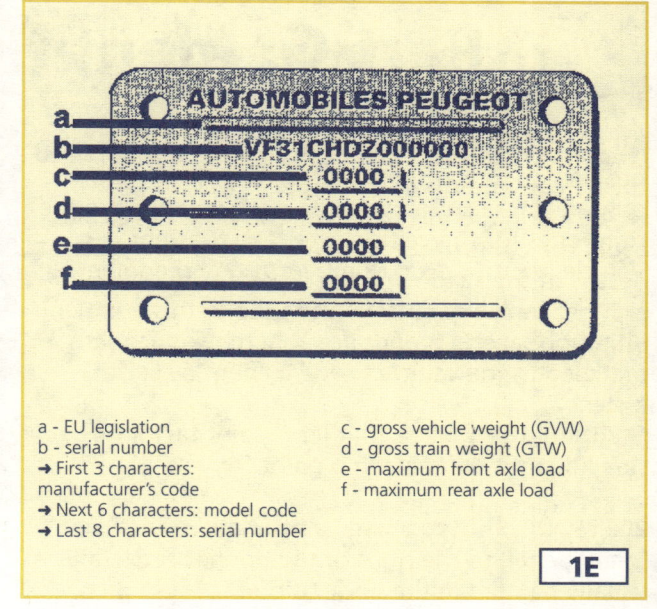

a - EU legislation
b - serial number
➔ First 3 characters: manufacturer's code
➔ Next 6 characters: model code
➔ Last 8 characters: serial number
c - gross vehicle weight (GVW)
d - gross train weight (GTW)
e - maximum front axle load
f - maximum rear axle load

1E: ALL LATER MODELS: On all later models, this is what the numbers on the VIN plate stand for.

SECTION 2: ENGINE NUMBER

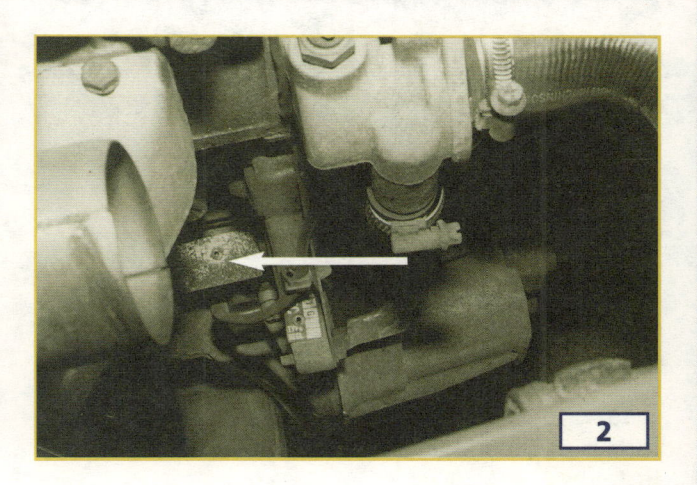

1D: The number is also stamped on to the bodywork, on the top face of the upper inner-wheelarch panel, in the engine bay, in the position shown.
➔ **LATER MODELS:** The VIN may also be visible through the lower corner of the front screen.

2: The engine number (arrowed) will be found on the front of the engine block, at the joint with the gearbox (on all but XU-type engines), embossed onto one of two aluminium plates. The engine number is on the non-printed plate.
➔ On XU engines the plate is found on the right-hand end of the engine, next to the cam-belt cover.
➔ Some 205 engines may have the prefix G1, 2 or 3 - these are related to the XU, XV and XY engines respectively.

CHAPTER 1   Part G

1-13

SECTION 3: PAINT CODE (AND OTHER) NUMBERS

If you need an exact paint colour match, you'll need the vehicle's paint code number.
→ Although the VIN plate will carry the basic colour code, the paint/trim code plate will contain precise details of the shade and the type of trim fitted.
→ Most aerosol paints won't relate to this number, although several brands are able to produce cans matched to the vehicle's code colour, to special order.
→ Alternatively, have your local paint factor mix a small quantity of matching paint for you.

205 MODELS: The number is situated on the front 'slam' panel, to the right of the bonnet catch, and is usually painted in the body colour.

☐ **STEP 3B-2: LATER 106 AND 206 MODELS:** On the inside of the driver's door shut panel, there should be a label showing the paint code number and the tyre pressures.

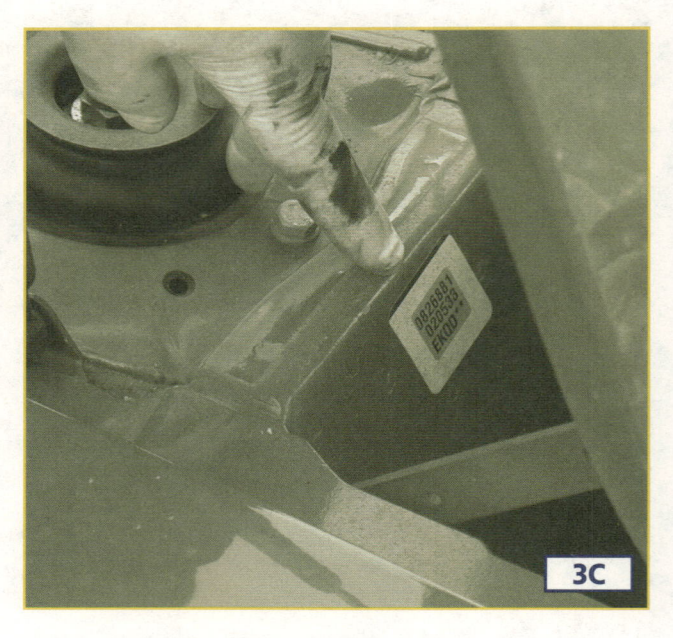

☐ **3B-1: 106 AND 206 MODELS:** The four-letter paint-code is painted on to the left-hand front suspension turret.
→ The other number is a code reference number.

☐ **STEP 3C: 306 MODELS:** The paint code is on a stuck-on label on the rear of this panel, inside the engine bay.

CHAPTER 2: SAFETY FIRST!

Please read this chapter before carrying out any work on your car.

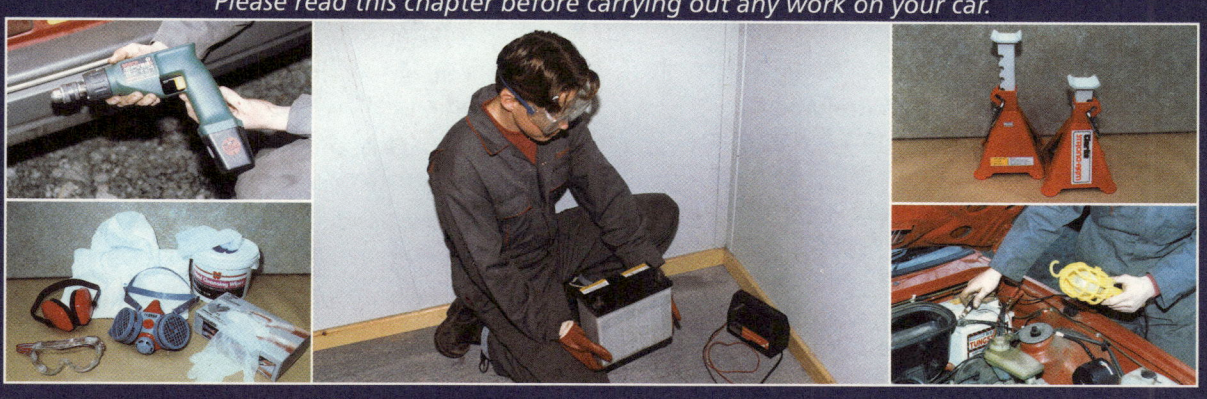

You must always ensure that safety is the first consideration in any job you carry out. A slight lack of concentration, or a rush to finish the job quickly can easily result in an accident, as can failure to follow the precautions outlined in this manual.

Be sure to consult the suppliers of any materials and equipment you may use, and to obtain and read carefully any operating and health and safety instructions that may be available on packaging or from manufacturers and suppliers.

GENERAL

RAISING THE VEHICLE SAFELY

• ALWAYS ensure that the vehicle is properly supported when raised off the ground. Don't work on, around, or underneath a raised vehicle unless axle stands or hoist lifting pads are positioned under secure, load bearing underbody areas. If the vehicle is driven onto ramps, the wheels remaining on the ground must be securely chocked to prevent movement.

• NEVER work on a vehicle supported on a jack. Jacks are made for lifting the vehicle only, not for holding it off the ground while it is being worked on.

❏ **1:** ALWAYS ensure that the safe working load rating of any jack, hoist or lifting gear used is sufficient for the job, and that lifting gear is used only as recommended by the manufacturer.

• NEVER attempt to loosen or tighten nuts that require a lot of force to turn (e.g. a tight oil drain plug) with the vehicle raised, unless it is safely supported. Take care not to pull the vehicle off its supports when applying force to any part of the vehicle. Wherever possible, initially slacken tight fastenings before raising the vehicle off the ground.

• ALWAYS wear eye protection when working under the vehicle and when using power tools.

• Follow the instructions in **Chapter 4** entitled ***Using a Trolley Jack***.

WORKING ON THE VEHICLE

• ALWAYS seek specialist advice from a qualified technician unless you are justifiably confident about your ability to carry out each job. Vehicle safety affects you, your passengers and other road users.

❏ **2:** DON'T lean over, or work on, a running engine unless it is strictly necessary, and keep long hair and loose clothing well out of the way of moving mechanical parts.

• Note that it is theoretically possible for fluorescent striplighting to make an engine fan appear to be stationary - double check whether it is spinning or not! This is the sort of error that happens when you're really tired and not thinking straight. So...

• ...DON'T work on a vehicle when you're over tired.

• ALWAYS work in a well ventilated area and don't inhale dust - it may contain asbestos or other harmful substances.

• NEVER run an engine indoors, in a confined space or over a pit.

• REMOVE your wrist watch, rings and all other jewellery before doing any work on the vehicle - and especially when working on the electrical system.

CHAPTER 2 Safety First!

- DON'T remove the radiator or expansion tank filler cap or other openings when the cooling system is hot, or you may get scalded by escaping coolant or steam. Let the system cool down first and even then, if the engine is not completely cold, cover the cap with a cloth and gradually release the pressure.
- NEVER drain oil, coolant or automatic transmission fluid when the engine is hot. Allow time for it to cool sufficiently to avoid scalding you.
- ALWAYS keep antifreeze, brake and clutch fluid away from vehicle paintwork. Wash off any spills immediately.
- TAKE CARE to avoid touching any engine or exhaust system component unless it is cool enough not to burn you.

RUNNING THE VEHICLE

- NEVER start the engine unless the gearbox is in neutral (or 'Park' in the case of automatic transmission) and the parking brake is fully applied.
- NEVER run a vehicle fitted with a catalytic converter without the exhaust system heat shields in place.
- TAKE CARE when parking vehicles fitted with catalytic converters. The 'cat' reaches extremely high temperatures and any combustible materials under the car, such as long dry grass, could be ignited.

PERSONAL SAFETY

- NEVER siphon fuel, antifreeze, brake fluid or other potentially harmful liquids by mouth, or allow contact with your skin. Use a suitable hand pump and wear gloves.
- BEFORE undertaking dirty jobs, use barrier cream on your hands as a protection against infection. Preferably, wear suitable gloves.
- WEAR IMPERVIOUS GLOVES - disposable types are ideal - when there is a risk of used engine oil or any other harmful substance coming into contact with your skin.

❑ 3: Wurth produce a huge range of workshop products, including the safety-related items shown here.

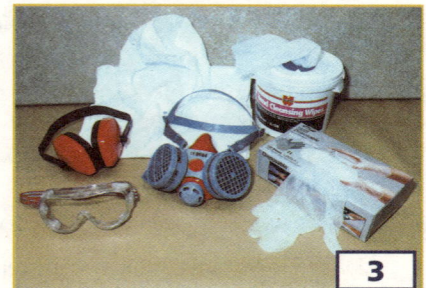

- WIPE UP any spilt oil, grease or water off the floor immediately.
- MAKE SURE that spanners/wrenches and all other tools are the right size for the job and are not likely to slip. Never try to 'double-up' spanners to gain more leverage.

- SEEK HELP if you need to lift something heavy which may be beyond your capability. Don't forget that when lifting a heavy weight, you should keep your back vertical and straight and bend your knees to avoid injuring your back.
- NEVER take risky short-cuts or rush to finish a job. Plan ahead and allow plenty of time.
- BE METICULOUS and keep the work area tidy - you'll avoid frustration, work better and lose less.
- KEEP children and animals well away from the work area and from unattended vehicles.
- ALWAYS tell someone what you're doing and have them regularly check that all is well, especially when working alone on, or under, the vehicle.

HAZARDS

FIRE!

- Petrol (gasoline) is a dangerous and highly flammable liquid requiring special precautions. When working on the fuel system, disconnect the vehicle battery earth (ground) terminal whenever possible and always work outside, or in a very well ventilated area. Any form of spark, such as that caused by an electrical fault, by two metal surfaces striking against each other, by a central heating boiler in the garage 'firing up', or even by static electricity built up in your clothing can, in a confined space, ignite petrol vapour causing an explosion. Take great care not to spill petrol on to the engine or exhaust system, never allow any naked flame anywhere near the work area and don't smoke.

❑ 4: There are several types of fire extinguisher. Take advice from your accredited supplier to make sure that you have the right type for workshop use. Note that water fire extinguishers are not suitable for workshop or automotive use.

PRESSURE

- DON'T disconnect any pipes on a fuel injected engine or on an ABS braking system without releasing residual pressure. The fuel or brake fluid may be under very high pressure - sufficient to cause serious injury. Remember that many systems retain high pressure for sometime after last use. If necessary seek specialist advice.

FUMES

• Vapour which is given off by petrol (gasoline) and many solvents, thinners, and adhesives is potentially very harmful and under certain conditions can lead to unconsciousness or even death, if inhaled. The risks are increased if such fluids are used in a confined space so always ensure adequate ventilation. Always read the supplier's instructions and follow them with care.

• Never drain petrol (gasoline) or use solvents, thinners, adhesives or other toxic substances in an inspection pit. It is also dangerous to park a vehicle for any length of time over an inspection pit. The fumes from even a slight fuel leak can cause an explosion when the engine is started.

MAINS ELECTRICITY

❑ 5: Avoid the use of mains electricity when working on the vehicle, whenever possible. Use rechargeable tools and a DC inspection lamp, powered from a remote 12V battery - both are much safer. However, if you do use mains-powered equipment, ensure that the appliance is connected correctly to its plug, that where necessary it is properly earthed (grounded), and that the fuse is of the correct rating for the appliance. Do not use any mains powered equipment in damp conditions or in the vicinity of fuel, fuel vapour or the vehicle battery. Always use an RCD (Residual Current Device) circuit breaker with mains electricity. Then, if there is a short, the RCD circuit breaker minimises the risk of electrocution by instantly cutting the power supply.

IGNITION SYSTEM

• Never work on the ignition system with the ignition switched on, or with the engine being turned over on the starter, or with the engine running.

❑ 6: Touching certain parts of the ignition system, such as the HT leads, distributor cap, ignition coil etc., can result in a severe electric shock or physical injury as a hand is pulled sharply away. Voltages produced by electronic ignition systems are sometimes very high indeed and could prove fatal, particularly to people with cardiac pacemaker implants. Consult your vehicle's handbook or main dealer if in any doubt.

COOLING FAN

• On many vehicles, the electric cooling fan can switch itself on even with the ignition turned off. This is especially likely after driving the vehicle immediately before turning off, after which heat rises to the top of the engine and turns the fan on, suddenly and without warning. If you intend working in the engine bay, it's best to do so when the engine is cold, to disconnect the battery, or keep away from the fan, if neither of these are possible.

BATTERY

• Never cause a spark, smoke, or allow a naked light near the vehicle's battery, even in a well ventilated area. Highly explosive hydrogen gas is given off as part of the charging process.

• Battery terminals should be shielded, since a spark can be caused by any metal object touching the battery's terminals or connecting straps.

• IMPORTANT NOTE: Before disconnecting the battery earth (ground) terminal read the relevant information in **Chapter 10** regarding saving computer and radio settings. When using a battery charger, switch off the power supply before the battery charger leads are connected or disconnected. If the battery is not of the 'sealed-for-life' type, loosen the filler plugs or remove the cover before charging. For best results the battery should be given a low rate trickle charge. Do not charge at an excessive rate or the battery may burst. Always wear gloves and goggles when carrying or when topping up the battery. Acid electrolyte is extremely corrosive and must not be allowed to contact the eyes, skin or clothes. If it does, wash with copious amounts of water. Seek medical advice if necessary

BRAKES AND ASBESTOS

• Obviously, a vehicle's brakes are among its most important safety related items. ONLY work on your vehicle's braking system if you are trained and competent to do so. If you have not been trained in this work, but wish to carry out the jobs described in this manual, we strongly recommend that you have a garage or qualified mechanic check your work before using the vehicle.

• Whenever you work on the braking system: i) wear an efficient particle mask; ii) wipe off all brake dust from the brakes after spraying on a proprietary brand of brake cleaner (never blow dust off with compressed air); iii) dispose of brake dust and discarded shoes or pads in a sealed plastic bag; iv) wash your hands thoroughly after you have finished working on the brakes and certainly before you eat or smoke; v) replace shoes and pads only with asbestos-free shoes or pads. Note that asbestos brake dust can cause cancer if inhaled; vi) always replace brake pads

CHAPTER 2 Safety First!

and/or shoes in complete 'axle' sets - never replace them on one wheel only.

BRAKE FLUID

• Brake fluid absorbs moisture rapidly from the air and this can cause brake failure. Never use a previously opened container of brake fluid.

ENGINE OIL

• Always wear disposable plastic or rubber gloves when draining the oil from your engine. i) Note that the drain plug and the oil are often hotter than you expect. ii) There are very real health hazards associated with used engine oil. Use barrier cream on your hands and try not to get oil on them. Always wear impermeable gloves and wash hands with hand cleaner soon after carrying out the work. Keep oil out of the reach of children; iii) NEVER, EVER dispose of old engine oil into the ground or down a drain.

PLASTIC MATERIALS

• Be aware of dangers in the form of poisonous fumes, skin irritants, and the risk of fire and explosion. Do not allow resin or 2-pack filler or adhesive hardener to come into contact with skin or eyes. Read carefully the safety notes supplied on the can, tube or packaging.

FLUOROELASTOMERS

• Fluoroelastomers are commonly used for oil seals, wiring and cabling, bearing surfaces, gaskets, diaphragms, hoses and 'O' rings. If they are subjected to temperatures greater than 315 degrees Celcius, they will decompose and can be potentially hazardous. Some decomposition may occur when a car has been in a fire or has been dismantled with the assistance of a cutting torch.

• According to the Health and Safety Executive, "Skin contact with this liquid or decomposition residues can cause painful and penetrating burns. Permanent irreversible skin and tissue damage can occur". Damage can also be caused to eyes or by the inhalation of fumes created as fluoroelastomers are burned or heated.

• After a vehicle has been exposed to fire or high temperatures:

1. Do not touch blackened or charred seals or equipment.
2. Preferably, don't handle parts containing decomposed fluoroelastomers, but if you must do so, wear goggles and PVC (polyvinyl chloride) or neoprene protective gloves while doing so. Never handle such parts unless they are completely cool.

3. Contaminated parts, residues, materials and clothing, including protective clothing and gloves, should be disposed of by an approved contractor to currently applicable national or local regulations. Oil seals, gaskets and 'O' rings, along with contaminated material, must not be burned.

WORKSHOP

• Always have a fire extinguisher of the correct type at arm's length when working on anything flammable. If you do have a fire, DON'T PANIC. Direct the extinguisher at the base of the fire.

• NEVER use a naked flame in the workplace.

❐ 7: KEEP your inspection lamp well away from any source of flammable materials.

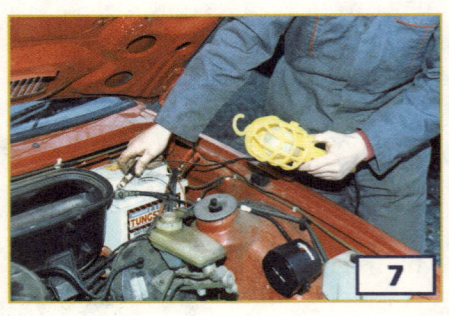

• NEVER use petrol (gasoline) to clean parts. Use only a proprietary degreaser.

• NO SMOKING. There's a risk of fire or of transferring dangerous substances to your mouth.

• BE METHODICAL in everything you do, use common sense, and think of safety at all times.

ENVIRONMENT FIRST!

• The used oil from the sump of just one car can cover an area of water the size of two football pitches, cutting off the oxygen supply and harming swans, ducks, fish and other river life.

❐ 8: When you drain your engine oil - don't oil the drain! Pouring oil down the drain will cause pollution. It is also an offence.

• Don't mix used oil with other materials, such as paint and solvents, because this makes recycling difficult.

• Take used oil to an oil recycling bank. Telephone FREE in the UK on 0800 663366 to find the location of your nearest oil bank, or contact your local authority recycling officer.

CHAPTER 3: GETTING THROUGH THE ANNUAL TEST

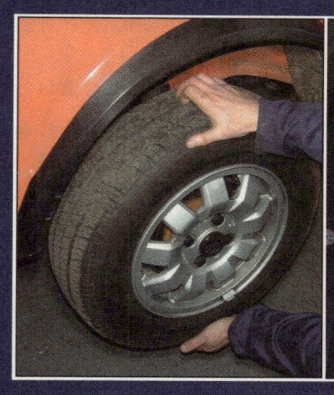

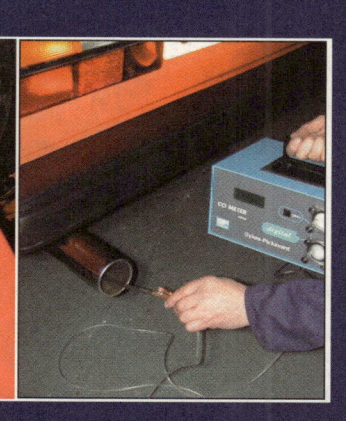

This chapter relates mostly to the UK where vehicles need to pass the 'MoT' test but also has relevance for those in other countries with a similar annual test. Obviously, you won't be able to examine your car to the same degree of thoroughness as the MoT testing station. But you can reduce the risk of being among the four out of 10 who fail the test first time!

The checks shown below are correct for the MoT Test in the UK at the time of writing but they do tend to become stricter! Your local testing station will have the latest information. DON'T BE TURNED AWAY! The vehicle, when presented for test, must be reasonably clean. Testing Stations can refuse to test vehicles that are very dirty and have excessive mud on the underside.

CONTENTS

	Page No.		Page No.
Part A: Inside the Vehicle	3-1	**Part C:** Under the Vehicle	3-3
Part B: Outside of Vehicle	3-3	**Part D:** Exhaust Emissions	3-5

Part A: Inside the Vehicle

STEERING WHEEL AND COLUMN

☐ 1: Try to move the steering wheel towards and away from you and then from side to side. There should be no appreciable movement or play. Check that the steering wheel is not loose on the column and that there are no breaks or loose components on the steering wheel itself.

☐ 2: Lightly grip the steering wheel between thumb and finger and turn from side to side. Vehicles with a steering rack: free play should not exceed approximately 13 mm (0.5 in.), assuming a 380 mm (15 in.) diameter steering wheel. Vehicles fitted with a steering box: free play should not exceed approximately 75 mm (3.0 in.), assuming a 380 mm (15 in.) diameter steering wheel.

☐ 3: If there is a universal joint at the bottom of the steering column inside the vehicle, check for movement. Place your hand over the joint while turning the steering wheel to-and-fro a little way with your other hand. If ANY free play can be felt, the joint must be replaced.

☐ 4: Steering security and locking devices (where fitted) must be in working order.

ELECTRICAL EQUIPMENT

☐ 5: With the ignition turned ON, ensure that the horn works okay.

☐ 6: Check that the front wipers work.

☐ 7: Check that the screen washers work.

☐ 8: Check that the internal warnings for the indicator and hazard warning lights work okay. When ABS brakes are fitted: Make sure that there is an ABS warning light that illuminates and that the lamp follows the correct sequence.

CHECKS WITH AN ASSISTANT

☐ 9: Check that the front and rear side lights and number plate lights work and that the lenses and reflectors are secure, clean and undamaged.

CHAPTER 3 Getting Through the Annual Test

❏ 10: Check the operation of the headlights and check that the lenses are undamaged. The reflectors inside the headlights must not be tarnished, nor must there be condensation inside the headlight.

❏ 11: Turn on the ignition and check the direction indicators, front and rear, and the side markers.

❏ 12: Check that the hazard warning lights operate on the outside of the vehicle and at the internal warning light.

❏ 13: Check that the rear fog light/s, including the warning light inside the vehicle, all work correctly.

❏ 14: Check that the rear brake lights work correctly.

❏ 15: Operate the brake lights, side lights and each indicator in turn, then all at the same time. None should affect the operation of the others.

SAFETY FIRST!

• Follow the Safety information in *Chapter 2, Safety First!* but bear in mind that the vehicle needs to be even more stable than usual when raised off the ground.

• There must be no risk of it toppling off its stands or ramps while suspension and steering components are being pushed and pulled in order to test them.

FRONT SCREEN AND MIRRORS

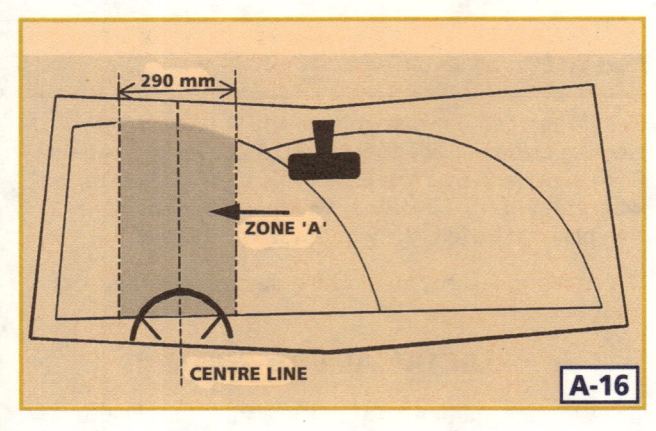

[Diagram: Front screen showing 290 mm ZONE 'A' and CENTRE LINE — A-16]

❏ 16: In zone 'A' of the front screen, no items of damage larger than 10 mm in diameter will be allowed. In the rest of the area swept by the screen wipers, no damage greater than 40 mm in diameter will be allowed, nor should stickers or other obstructions encroach on this area.

❏ 17: Check that the exterior mirror on the driver's side is in good condition.

❏ 18: There must be one other mirror in good condition, either inside the vehicle or an external mirror on the passenger's side.

BRAKES

❏ 19: You cannot check the brakes properly without a rolling road brake tester but you can carry out the following checks:

❏ 20: Pull on the parking brake. It should be fully ON before the lever reaches the end of its travel.

❏ 21: Knock the parking brake lever from side to side and check that it does not then release itself.

❏ 22: Check the security of the parking brake lever mountings and check the floor around them for rust or splits.

❏ 23: Check that the front brake pedal is in good condition and that, when you take hold of it and move it from side to side, there is not too much play.

❏ 24: Push the footbrake down hard with your foot. If it creeps slowly down towards the floor, there is probably a problem with the master cylinder. Release the pedal, and after a few seconds, press down again. If the pedal feels spongy or it travels nearly to the floor, there is air in the system or another dangerous fault with the brakes.

❏ 25: Check the servo unit (when fitted) as follows: Pump the brake pedal several times then hold it down hard. Start the engine. As the engine starts, the pedal should move down slightly. If it doesn't the servo or the vacuum hose leading to it may be faulty.

SEAT BELTS AND SEATS

❏ 26: Examine all of the seat belt webbing (pull out the belts from the inertia reel if necessary) for cuts, fraying or deterioration.

❏ 27: Check that each inertia reel belt retracts correctly.

❏ 28: Fasten and unfasten each belt to ensure that the buckles work correctly.

❏ 29: Tug hard on each belt to ensure that the inertia reel locks, and inspect the mountings, as far as possible, to ensure that all are okay.

[Image A-29: person tugging on seat belt]

IMPORTANT NOTE: Checks apply to rear seat belts as much as to front ones.

❏ 30: Make sure that the seat runners and mountings are secure and that all back rests lock in the upright position.

DOORS AND DOOR LOCKS

❏ 31: Check that doors latch securely when closed and that they can be opened and closed from both outside and inside the vehicle.

3-2

Part B: Outside of Vehicle

ELECTRICAL EQUIPMENT

See *Part A: Inside the Vehicle* for checks on the operation of the electrical equipment.

❏ 1: Examine the wiper blades and replace those that show any damage.

VEHICLE IDENTIFICATION NUMBERS (VIN)

❏ 2: The VIN (or chassis number on older vehicles) must be clearly displayed and legible.

❏ 3: Number (licence) plates must be secure, legible and in good condition with correct spacing between letters and numbers which must be of correct size and style.

BRAKING SYSTEM

❏ 4: Inside the engine bay inspect the master cylinder, servo unit (if fitted), brake pipes and mountings. Look for corrosion, loose fitting or leaks.

STEERING AND SUSPENSION

❏ 5: While still in the engine bay, have your assistant turn the steering wheel lightly from side to side and look for play in steering universal joints or steering system mountings and any other steering connections.

❏ 6: If the vehicle is fitted with power steering, check the security and condition of the steering pump, hoses and drivebelt, in the engine bay.

❏ 7: While your assistant turns the steering wheel more vigorously from side to side, place your hand over each track rod end in turn and feel for playing. Inspect all of the steering linkages, joints and attachments for wear.

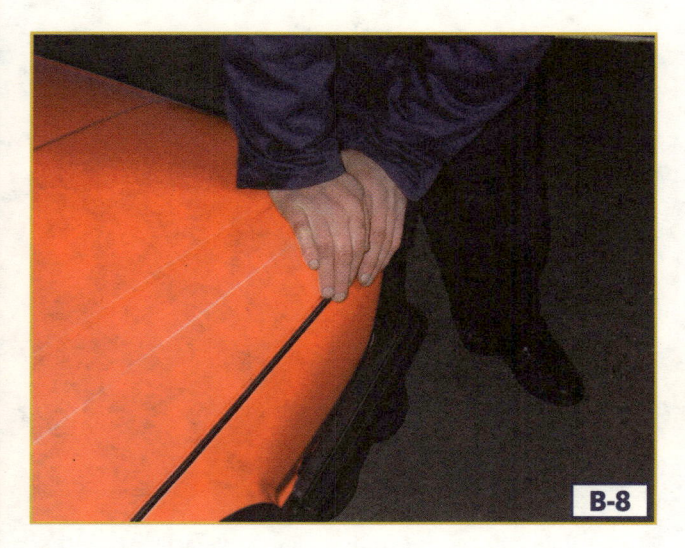

B-8

❏ 8: Go around the vehicle and 'bounce' each corner of the vehicle in turn. Release at the lowest point and the vehicle should rise and settle in its normal position without continuing to 'bounce' of its own accord. If not, a shock absorber is faulty. Always renew in 'axle' pairs or sets.

BODYWORK STRUCTURE

❏ 9: Any sharp edges on the external bodywork, caused by damage or corrosion will cause the vehicle to fail.

❏ 10: Check all load bearing areas for corrosion. Open the doors and check the sills inside and out, above and below. Any corrosion in structural metalwork within 30 cm (12 in.) of seat belt mounting, steering and suspension attachment points will cause the vehicle to fail.

WHEELS AND TYRES

B-11

❏ 11: To pass the test, the tread must be at least 1.6 mm deep throughout a continuous band comprising the central three-quarters of the width of the tread. The Tread Wear Indicators (TWI) will tell you when the limit has been reached, on most tyres. (They are not coloured on 'real' tyres!)

IMPORTANT NOTE: Tyres are past their best, especially in wet conditions, well before this point is reached! (Illustration courtesy of Dunlop)

❏ 12: Check that the front tyres match and that the rear tyres match each other - in terms of size and type but not necessarily make. They must be the correct size for the vehicle and the pressures must be correct.

❏ 13: With each wheel off the ground in turn, check the inside and the outside of the tyre wall for cuts, lumps and bulges and check the wheel for damage. Note that tyres deteriorate progressively over a period of time and if they have degraded noticeably, replace them.

Part C: Under the Vehicle

You will need to support the front of the vehicle off the ground with the rear wheels firmly chocked in both directions.

❏ 1: Have your helper turn the steering from lock to lock and check that the steering turns smoothly and that the brake hoses or pipes do not contact the wheel, tyre or any part of the steering or suspension.

CHAPTER 3 Getting Through the Annual Test

3-3

❏ 2: Particular attention should be paid to evidence of corrosion at the steering rack or steering box fixing points.

❏ 3: Have your assistant hold down the brake pedal firmly. Check each brake flexible hose for bulges or leaks. Inspect all the rigid brake pipes underneath the front of the vehicle for corrosion, damage or leaks and also look for signs of fluid leaks at the brake calipers. Rigid fuel pipes also need to be checked for corrosion, damage or leaks.

❏ 4: At each full lock position, check the steering rack rubber gaiters for splits, leaks or loose retaining clips.

❏ 5: Check the track rod end dust covers to make sure they are in place and are not split.

❏ 6: Inspect each constant velocity joint gaiter - both inners and outers - for splits or damage. You will have to rotate each wheel to see the gaiters all the way round.

❏ 7: Check all of the suspension rubber mountings, including the anti-rollbar mountings (when fitted). Take a firm grip on each shock absorber in turn with both hands and try to twist the damper to check for deterioration in the top and bottom mounting bushes.

❏ 8: Check that the shock absorbers are not corroded, that the springs are in good condition and that there are no fluid leaks down the body of the shock absorber. Renew if necessary

❏ 9: Check the front of the exhaust for corrosion and secure fixing at manifold and mounting points.

C-10

❏ 10: Grasp each wheel at 12 o'clock and 6 o'clock positions and try rocking the wheel.
FRONT WHEELS: Look for movement at suspension ball joints, suspension and steering mountings. Repeat while grasping each wheel at 3 o'clock and 9 o'clock.
ALL WHEELS: At the wheel bearing, look for movement between the wheel and hub.

❏ 11: Spin each wheel and check for noise or roughness in the wheel bearing and binding in either the wheel bearing or the brake.

❏ 12: If you suspect wear at any of the suspension points, try levering with a screwdriver to see whether or not you can confirm any movement in that area.

❏ 13: Vehicles fitted with other suspension types such as hydraulic suspension, torsion bar suspension etc. need to be checked in a way that is relevant to the system, with the additional point that there must be no fluid leaks or damaged pipes on vehicles with hydraulic suspension.

❏ 14: Inspect the rear springs for security at their mounting points and for cracks, severe corrosion or damage.

❏ 15: Check the rear shock absorbers in the same way as the checks carried out for the fronts.

❏ 16: Check all rear suspension mounting points, including the rubbers to any locating rods or anti-roll bar that may be fitted.

❏ 17: Check all of the flexible and rigid brake pipes and the fuel pipes just as for the front of the vehicle.

❏ 18: Have your assistant press down firmly on the brake pedal while you check the rear brake flexible hoses for bulges, splits or other deterioration.

❏ 19: Check the fuel tank for leaks or corrosion. Remember also to check the fuel filler cap - a correctly sealing filler cap is a part of the MoT test.

❏ 20: Examine the parking brake mechanism. Frayed or broken cables or worn mounting points, either to the bodywork or in the linkage will all be failure points.

❏ 21: Check each of the rear wheel bearings as for the fronts.

❏ 22: Spin each rear wheel and check that neither the wheel bearings nor the brakes are binding. Pull on and let off the parking brake and check once again to make sure that the parking brake mechanism is releasing.

SAFETY FIRST!
- Only run the car out of doors.
- Beware of burning yourself on a hot exhaust system!

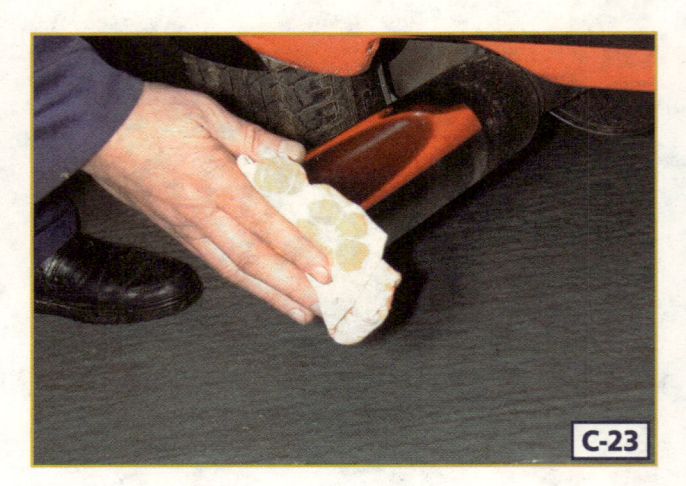

C-23

❏ 23: While you are out from under the vehicle, but with the rear end still raised off the ground, run the engine. Hold a rag over the end of the exhaust pipe and listen for blows or leaks in the system. You can then get back under the vehicle and investigate further if necessary.

☐ 24: Check the exhaust system mountings and check for rust, corrosion or holes in the rear part of the system.

☐ 25: Check the rear brake back plate or calipers (as appropriate) for any signs of fluid leakage.

Part D: Exhaust Emissions

TOP TIP!

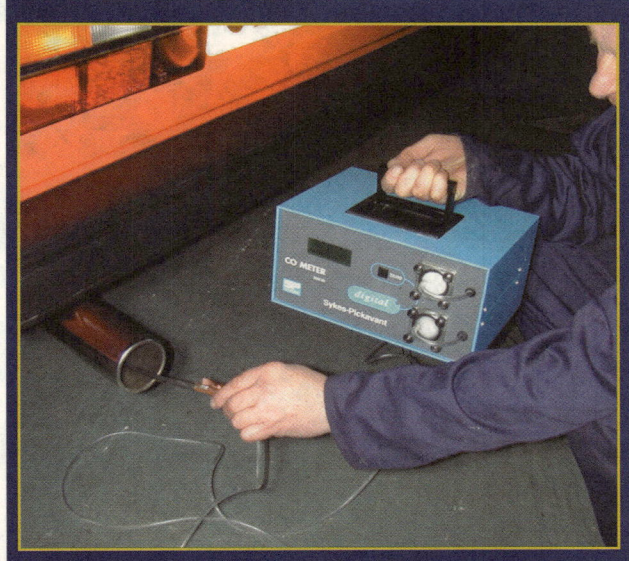

- This is a Sykes-Pickavant CO meter.
- If you don't own a CO meter, you could have your testing station carry out the emission part of the test first so that if it fails, you don't waste money on having the rest of the test carried out.

FACT FILE

FACT FILE: VEHICLE EMISSIONS

The information shown here applies, at the time of writing, to the UK. For information applicable to other territories, or for later amendments, check with the relevant local testing authorities.

PETROL/GASOLINE ENGINED VEHICLES WITHOUT CATALYSER

Vehicles first used before 1 August 1973 - visual smoke check only.

Vehicles first used between 1 August 1973 and 31 July 1986 - 4.5% carbon monoxide and 1,200 parts per million, unburned hydrocarbons.

Vehicles first used between 1 August 1986 and 31 July 1992 - 3.5% carbon monoxide and 1,200 parts per million, unburned hydrocarbons.

PETROL/GASOLINE ENGINED VEHICLES FITTED WITH CATALYTIC CONVERTERS

Vehicles first used from 1 August 1992 (K-registration - on, in the UK)

- All have to be tested at an MoT Testing Station specially equipped to handle vehicles fitted with catalytic converters whether or not the vehicle is fitted with a 'cat'.
- Required maxima are - 3.5% carbon monoxide and 1,200 parts per million, unburned hydrocarbons. There will be a further check to make sure that the catalyst is in working order.

TOP TIP!

- Because 'cats' don't work properly at lower temperatures, ensure that the engine is fully warm!

DIESEL ENGINES' EMISSIONS STANDARDS

- IMPORTANT NOTE: The diesel engine test puts a lot of stress on the engine. It is IMPERATIVE that the vehicle's engine is in good condition before you take it in for the MoT test. The tester is entitled to refuse to test the vehicle if he feels that the engine is not in serviceable condition.

Vehicles first used before 1 August, 1979
- Engine run at normal running temperature; engine speed taken to around 2,500 rpm (or half governed max. speed, if lower) and held for 20 seconds. FAILURE, if engine emits dense blue or black smoke for next 5 seconds, at tick-over.

Vehicles first used on or after 1 August, 1979
- After checking engine condition, and with the engine at normal running temperature, the engine will be run up to full revs between three and six times to see whether the engine passes the prescribed smoke density test. (2.5k for non-turbo vehicles; 3.0k for turbo diesels. An opacity meter probe will be placed in the vehicle's exhaust pipe.) Irrespective of the meter readings, the vehicle will fail if smoke or vapour obscures the view of other road users.

MULTI-FUEL VEHICLES

- Vehicles which run on more than one fuel (eg petrol and LPG) will normally be tested on the fuel they are running on when presented for test.
- There is a slight difficulty with LPG vehicles and unless the testing station analyser has the facility for conversion, the mechanic will have to do a calculation. The machine is set to measure propane, but LPG power gives out hexane. The analyser will have a 'PEF' number shown. This is used as follows: 'propane' reading ÷ PEF no. = hexane value.

CHAPTER 3 Getting Through the Annual Test

3-5

CHAPTER 4: WORKSHOP TOP TIPS!

Please read Chapter 2 Safety First! before carrying out any work on your car.

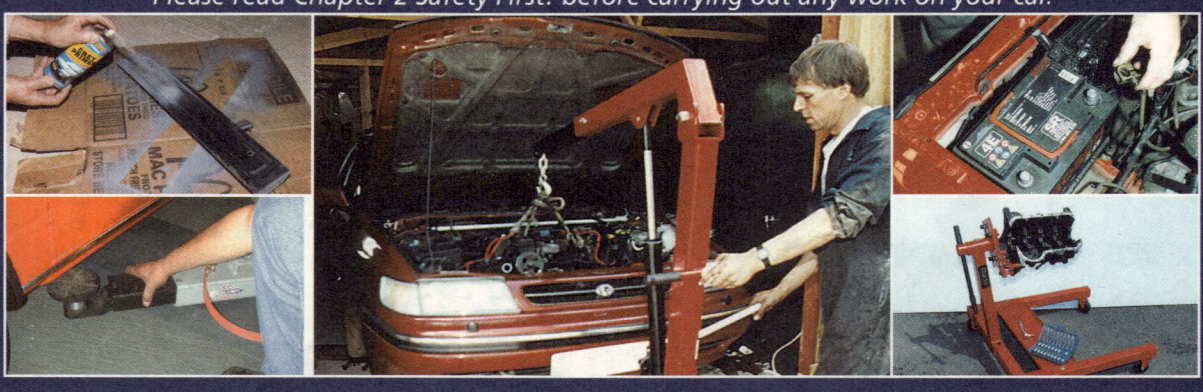

Here are a few *Top Tips!* to help keep things running well in the workshop.

1: DON'T LOSE IT! Buy sandwich bags and store small items in them, in groups, as they are removed. Keep the bags in a box or boxes, and keep the box/es in the vehicle if you have to go off and do something else. If you leave stuff lying around you'll lose some of it - right?

LOOK ON THE BRIGHT SIDE! Don't always assume the worst. That misfire - could it be the ECU? Highly unlikely, so try all the small stuff first. Engine running faults in particular are caused, 90% of the time, by failures in simple components such as spark plugs, leads, loose terminals and so on. So don't be a pessimist!

DON'T BE A BLUEBOTTLE! Work methodically; don't whizz around from one thing to another. Make a resolution to finish one thing before starting the next - even when you hit a tough patch, work through it! You'll finish jobs more quickly and you'll lose less stuff!

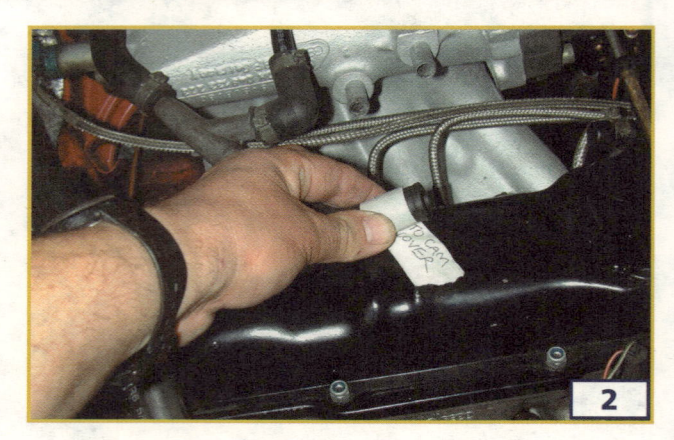

2: LABEL IT! Even in a manual like this, it isn't possible to cover every possible variation of wiring and pipework layout. If you assume that you WON'T remember how every single part goes back together - you'll almost certainly be right! Use tags of masking tape stuck on the ends of all removed connections, and label or number the matching parts. You'll save ages when it's time for reassembly!

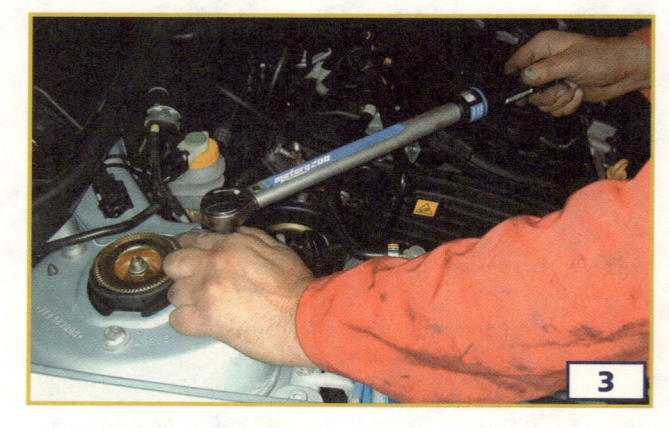

3: TIGHTEN RIGHT! Under-torquing and over-torquing threaded fixings is all too common. Some mechanics pride themselves on being able to judge the correct torque 'by feel'. They can't! Yes, they can get closer than a raw amateur, but the demands of modern components leave no room for guessing.

➔ Under-torqued fixings can come loose, or allow components to 'work' or chaff; over-torqued fixings can be even worse and can fail catastrophically or distort essential parts. Always check that threads run freely, and use a torque wrench!

❏ **4: KEEP TORQUING! Sykes-Pickavant** advise that their torque wrenches - and it actually applies to all makes - will read accurately for much longer if backed-off to the ZERO position before putting away, after each use.

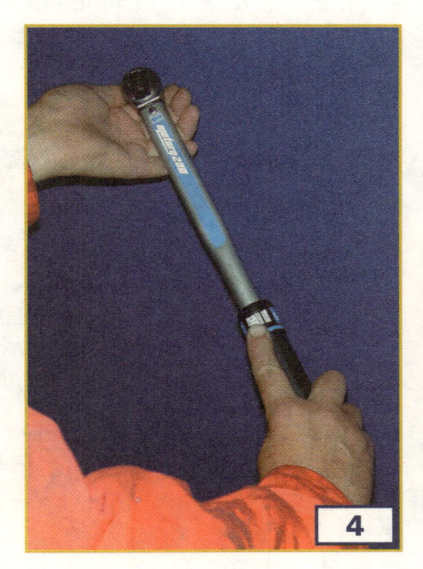

CHOOSING AND USING A HOIST

The best way of raising a vehicle off the ground - almost essential if you intend making your living or part of your income from working on vehicles - is to use a hoist. There are several types available, and the pros and cons are explained here by leading vehicle hoist manufacturer, **Tecalemit**:

➔ **FOUR POST:** This type of hoist is the least expensive, it's stable and capable of taking the greatest weights, but it's also the least versatile. With a post in each corner, the vehicle is driven onto ramps which raise the whole of the vehicle off the ground. The ramps do get in the way and the suspension is compressed by the weight of the vehicle. This restricts access in the wheel wells. On the other hand, it is possible to use a cross-beam from which you can jack specific parts of the vehicle - essential when vehicle testing. A four-post hoist is also useful if it's essential to raise a dangerously rusty vehicle off the ground.

➔ **TWO POST:** A post each side of the vehicle each carries two legs. The legs are swung so that a foot on the end of each leg is positioned under each end of the vehicle's body, usually under the normal jacking points. The great thing about these hoists is that they are 'wheels free' - the wheels and suspension hang down, providing almost ideal access to the underside of the vehicle. A two-post hoist should never be used on a vehicle that is dangerously rusty, because it will be raised on body parts which may collapse if the corrosion is very severe.

➔ **SINGLE POST:** This type has a single post, and swing-out legs reaching right under the vehicle. The advantage gained from the 'loss' of a post is offset by the intrusion of the extra-long support legs. The legs impede under-car access; the second post of a two-post hoist doesn't.

➔ **OUR CHOICE:** Without hesitation, we fitted a **Tecalemit** two-post hoist into the Porter Manuals workshop. Excellent service life from this famous-name manufacturer, and easy access for our mechanics, authors and photographers have made the hoist a wise choice!

❏ **5:** The legs can only be swung into position when they are fully lowered. They are extended, as necessary and aligned beneath the lifting points of the main body tub of the vehicle. As soon as they begin to raise off the ground, the legs are locked into position.

❏ **6:** Access to the vehicle's underside is ideal and, because there are no ramps - and no depressions in the floor, as is often the case with 4-post hoists - there is plenty of room to drive another vehicle beneath the one on the hoist for overnight storage.

❏ **7:** These **Tecalemit** hoists can run from 3-phase or 1-phase electrics, and can be fitted with a converter to enable a domestic level of current supply to power the hoist. In such cases, there will be a momentary delay while the converter builds up the power to the level required.

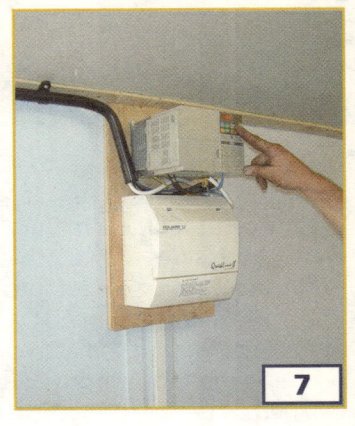

CHAPTER 4 Workshop Top Tips!

4-2

❏ **8A:** When a vehicle is raised on a hoist, it's perfectly safe, PROVIDED that the hoist has received its regular maintenance check by the suppliers. The **Tecalemit** two-post hoist is raised by screw threads and the legs are locked immovably when the motor is not being operated.

TOP TIP!

❏ **8B:** • Put a piece of tape on the post when you've established your best working height.
• Now you can raise the vehicle with the legs lined up with this mark every time!

RAISING THE VEHICLE - SAFELY!

Read this section in conjunction with the essential safety notes in *Chapter 2, Safety First!*

For those who don't have access to a pro. hoist:
➔ NEVER work beneath a vehicle held solely on a jack, not even a trolley jack. The safest way of raising a vehicle may be to drive one end of it up onto a pair of ramps. Sometimes, however, there is no alternative but to use axle stands because of the nature of the work being carried out.
➔ Do not jack-up the vehicle with anyone on board, or when a trailer is connected (it could pull the vehicle off the jack).
➔ Pull the parking brake on and engage first (low) gear.
➔ WHEELS ON THE GROUND SHOULD BE CHOCKED AFTER THE VEHICLE HAS BEEN RAISED, SO THAT THE VEHICLE CANNOT MOVE.

USING RAMPS

Make absolutely certain that the ramps are parallel to the wheels of the vehicle and that the wheels are exactly central on each ramp. Always have a helper watch both sides of the vehicle as you drive up.
➔ Wrap a strip of carpet into a loop around the first 'rung' of the ramps and drive over the doubled-up piece of carpet on the approach to the ramps. This prevents the ramps from skidding away, as they are inclined to do, as the vehicle is driven on to them.

➔ Drive up to the end 'stops' on the ramps but never over them!
➔ Apply the parking brake firmly and put the vehicle in first or reverse gear (or 'P' in the case of auto).
➔ Chock both wheels remaining on the ground, both in front and behind so that the vehicle can't move in either direction.

USING A TROLLEY JACK

On many occasions, you will need to raise the vehicle with a trolley jack - invest in one if you don't already own one. Ensure that the floor is sufficiently clear and smooth for the trolley jack wheels to roll as the vehicle is raised and lowered, otherwise it could slip off the jack.
➔ Before raising the vehicle, ENSURE THAT THE PARKING BRAKE IS OFF AND THE TRANSMISSION IS IN NEUTRAL. This is so that the vehicle can move as the jack is raised.
➔ Reapply brake and place in gear after the raising is complete and chock each wheel to prevent vehicle movement.
➔ Always remember to release brake and gear and remove chocks before lowering again.

❏ **9:** Axle stands also need to be man enough for the job. These inexpensive **Clarke** stands have an SWL of 3 tonnes. Make sure that the axle stands will each be placed beneath a reinforced part of the body, suitable for jacking from, or a main suspension mounting. Never place the jack or axle stand under a moving suspension part.

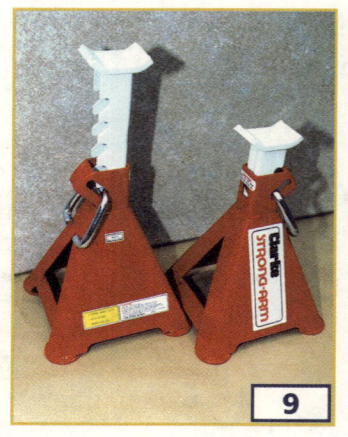

SAFETY FIRST!

• Whenever you're working beneath a vehicle, have someone primed to keep an eye on you!

• If someone pops out to see how you are getting on at regular intervals, it could be enough to save your life!

• Be especially careful when applying force to a spanner or when pulling hard on anything, when the vehicle is supported off the ground.

• It is all too easy to move the vehicle so that it topples off the axle stand or stands.

TOOLS AND EQUIPMENT

This section shows some of the tools and equipment that we have used while working on the vehicles that have been photographed for this manual.

You'll never have a complete set of tools; there will always be something else that you need! But over the years, if you buy equipment a little at a time, as you need it, you will accumulate a surprisingly large range.

When buying tools, it certainly pays to shop around. Tools that you won't need to use regularly, such as an impact screwdriver or a rubbing block for use with abrasive paper can be picked up for a song.

When it comes to larger and more expensive and specialised items, it pays to stick to a known maker rather than to take a chance with an apparently cheap tool whose make you may never have heard of.

❐ **10:** The **Clarke** 'Strong-Arm' engine hoist has the added advantage of being able to be folded into a really small space for storage.

❐ **11:** This engine stand, from the same manufacturer, is remarkably inexpensive. The engine is held at a comfortable working height and can be turned through 360 degrees. Recommended!

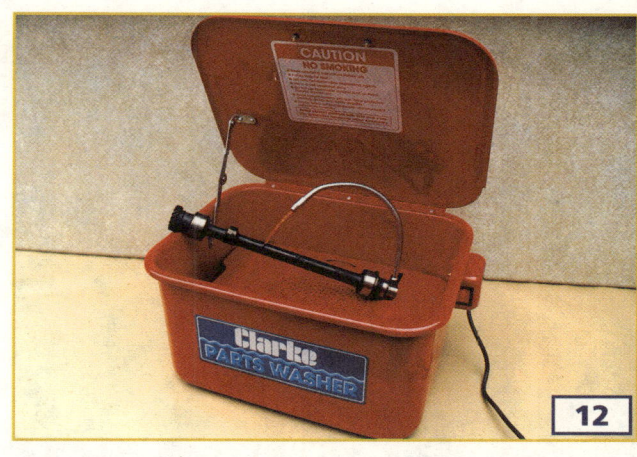

❐ **12:** When you've stripped components down, the most effective way of getting them clean is with a parts washer, this one from **Clarke** again.

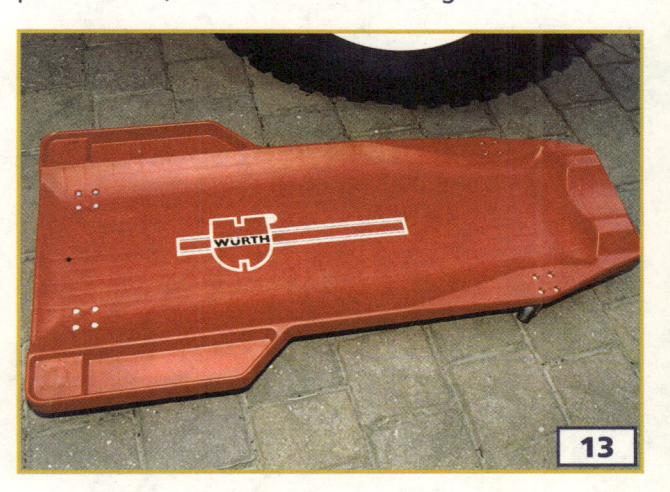

❐ **13:** Sliding beneath the vehicle will be a hundred times easier with a good quality car crawler, such as this plastic moulded crawler from **Wurth**.

❐ **14:** Another tool that you can scarcely do without is a compressor. At the bottom end of the range, both in terms of price and performance, is a compressor such as the **Clarke** Monza. This tiny compressor will power a spray gun sufficiently for 'blowing-in' a panel and you'll also be able to inflate tyres and carry out all sorts of other lightweight jobs.

CHAPTER 4 Workshop Top Tips!

4-4

CHAPTER 4 Workshop Top Tips!

☐ **15:** A compressor such as this 60 c.f.m. unit is the smallest needed by the serious amateur or semi-pro.. It won't run larger air tools, except in shorter bursts, but it's fine for the air wrench, for instance.

☐ **16:** The Air Kit 400 provides a very useful and remarkably low-cost set of basic air tools capable of being powered by even the smaller compressors. Clockwise from top-left:
→ The engine cleaner gun works much better than a brush.
→ The spray gun is basic but effective.
→ Air hose is suitable for all smaller compressors.
→ Wear goggles when using the invaluable air duster.
→ Double-check tyre pressures with a hand-held gauge when using this tyre inflator and gauge.

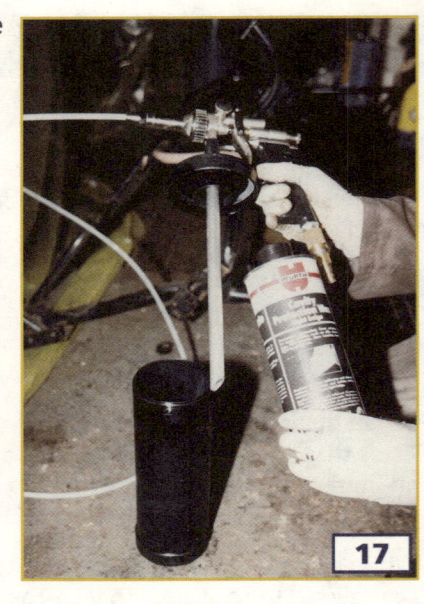

☐ **17:** Another use to which you will be able to put your compressor is spraying cavity protection wax. This **Wurth** injection gun is dual-purpose. It takes disposable **Wurth** screw-on canisters and also has its own large separate canister for injecting any protection wax that you may want to use 'loose'. Hand-powered and cheap-and-cheerful injectors simply don't atomise the protection wax or blast it far enough into nooks and crannies to be useful.

☐ **18:** Another invaluable tool is an angle grinder. This is the **Bosch** PWS7-115. This piece of equipment is perfect for using with grinding and cutting discs but, when used with this twisted-wire brush (available from bodyshop suppliers), scours paint and rust off steel in seconds. Always wear goggles and gloves with this tool.

☐ **19:** Another power tool which has a lot of domestic uses as well as being invaluable when working on a vehicle is something like the Jet 3000 Power Washer. It's a marvellous tool for removing mud, oil, grease and grim before stripping down body or mechanical parts and it is also extremely useful around the outside of the house.

4-5

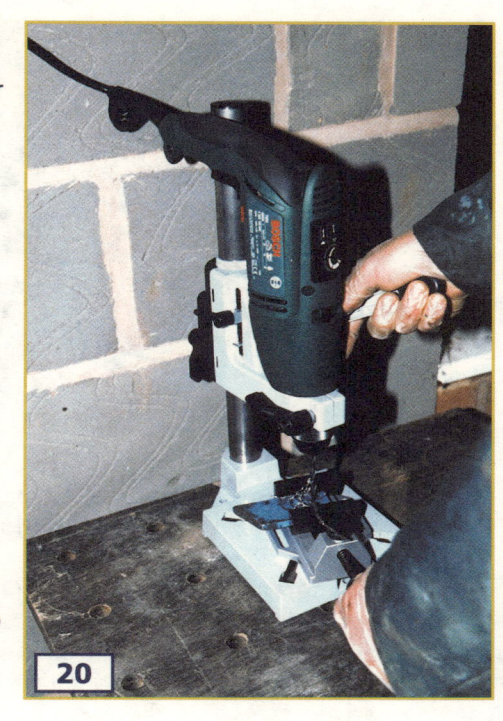

❏ 20: If your budget – or workshop space – won't run to a stand-alone pillar drill, the **Bosch** drill stand will turn your mains-power drill (this is the **Bosch** PSB with powerful 750W motor) into a perfectly adequate light-user version. The same company also offer the hand vice which is an essential piece of equipment for gripping small pieces.

❏ 21: Aerosol cans of paint are extremely useful for small items, such as this number plate backing plate, mainly because there's no cleaning up to do afterwards. For large areas, aerosol is prohibitively expensive and you won't find the depth of paint or the quality as good as you would get from a spray gun. There's always a place for aerosol, however, and the **Hycote** range includes all the various types of primer and finish coats that you could want, as well as offering a range of mix-and-match aerosol paints which are mixed to the shade you need.

❏ 22: There is a wide range of tool boxes and chests available from **Sykes-Pickavant**. They're made of tough heavy gauge steel, are lockable, and contain separate 'filing cabinet' type drawers for tool storage. Most of the units are stackable.

❏ 23. Increasingly, the kind of work described in this manual requires the use of special tools. **Sykes-Pickavant** produce a complete range of regular workshop tools and equipment and also special tools for most purposes.

❏ 24. An air wrench can save a heck of a lot of time on dismantling and reassembly – although you should always finish off with a torque wrench, where appropriate. The **Clarke** 3/8 in. drive is 'wieldy' enough for engine bay work while the 1/2 in. drive wrench and sockets will cope with most heavy duty jobs. Note the flexible 'tail' we add to each tool to protect the female connector on the air line.

CHAPTER 4 Workshop Top Tips!

4-6

Chapter 4 Workshop Top Tips!

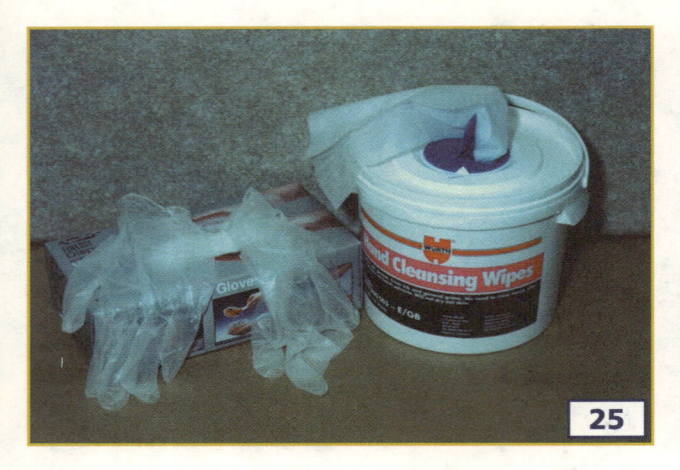

25: You'll need hand cleaner - the sort with granules shifts heavy grease best. **Wurth** also produce these hand wipes - useful if you need to touch upholstery in the middle of a job - and packs of disposable gloves.

26: Wurth produce a huge range of workshop products including electrical connectors and that wonderful 'shrink-fit' wire insulation tubing – slide it on, heat it up, and it 'shrinks' into place and can't come unwrapped.

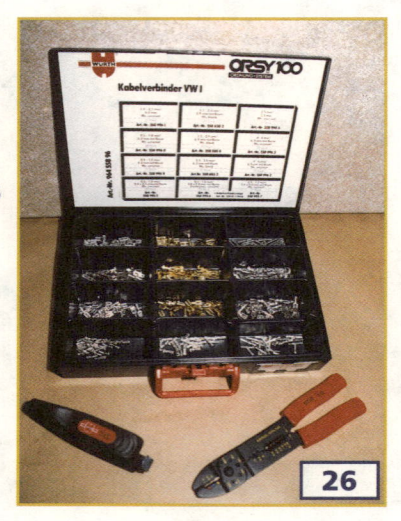

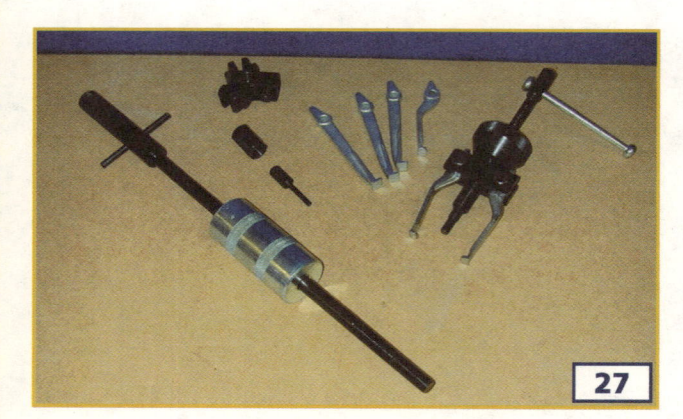

27: It's sometimes necessary to use pullers to remove 'stuck' bearings or other interference fit items. This **Sykes-Pickavant** set includes a variety of arm sizes and types, and a slide hammer to supplement the usual screw-type puller.

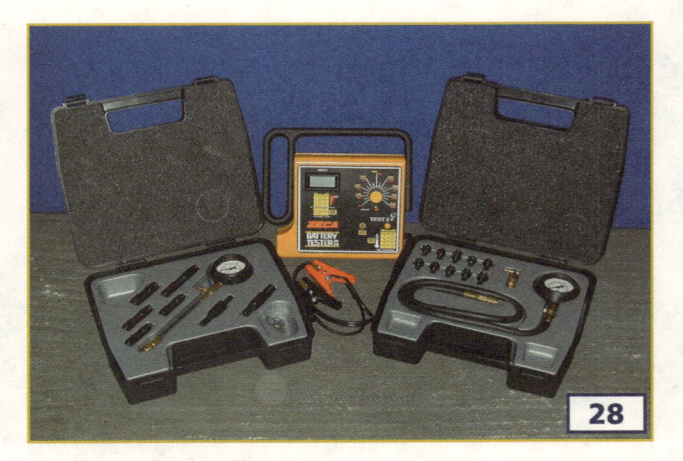

28: With these three **Sykes-Pickavant** kits, you can check (from left to right) many of the engine's most basic functions:
→ Cylinder compression tester - essential for a whole range of mechanical diagnostics, without the need for engine dismantling. Different testers are available for Diesel engines with their very high compression pressures.
→ Battery tester - essential for eliminating or confirming the battery as a source of problems.
→ Oil pressure tester. When combined with the cylinder compressions tester, this is capable of providing virtually a complete picture of the 'inner health' of any engine.

29: Last in this Chapter, but first job before carrying out vehicle dismantling: disconnect the battery! Beware of radio sets, alarms and ECUs that need a continuous electricity supply. See **Chapter 10, Electrical, Dash, Instruments** on preserving a battery feed.

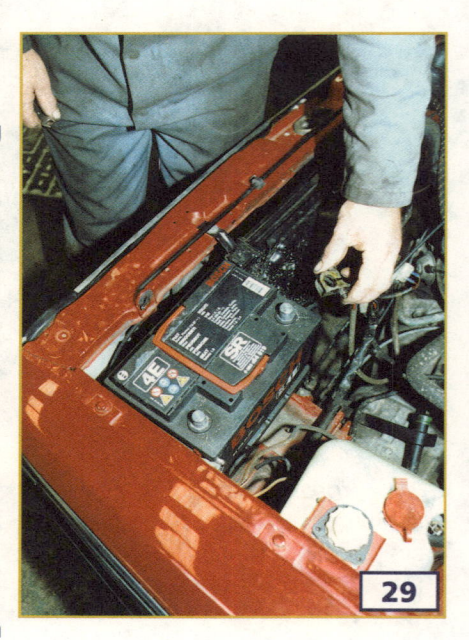

4-7

CHAPTER 5: SERVICING

Please read Chapter 2 Safety First before carrying out any work on your car.

SAFETY FIRST!

• Please read the whole of *Chapter 2, Safety First!* before carrying out any of the work described here.

HOW TO USE THIS CHAPTER

Note that:
→ Each letter code tells you the Service Interval.
→ Look the code up in the Service Intervals Key.
→ Each Service Job has a Job number.
→ IMPORTANT NOTE: Each service should be carried out at EITHER the recommended mileage OR the recommended time interval, whichever comes first.

SERVICE INTERVALS: KEY

A - Every week, or before every long journey.
B - Every 6 months, or 5,000 miles.
C - Every year or 10,000 miles.
D - Every 2 years, or 20,000 miles.
E - Every 3 years, or 30,000 miles.
F - Every 4 years, or 40,000 miles
G - Every 80,000 miles

Job	Description	Interval
JOB 1:	ENGINE OIL - check level.	A
JOB 2:	COOLING SYSTEM - check level.	A
JOB 3:	HYDRAULIC FLUID - check level.	A
JOB 4:	BATTERY - check electrolyte level.	A
JOB 5:	SCREEN/HEADLIGHT WASHER FLUID AND WASHERS - check level, aim jets.	A
JOB 6:	TYRES - check pressures and condition (road wheels).	A
JOB 7:	LIGHTS - check/change bulbs.	A
JOB 8:	SERVICE INTERVAL INDICATOR - reset, when fitted *After every 6-month service.	B*
JOB 9:	ENGINE OIL AND FILTER – change.	C
JOB 10:	VALVE CLEARANCES - check/adjust.	D
JOB 11:	CAMSHAFT DRIVE BELT - check.	C
JOB 12:	CAMSHAFT DRIVE BELT - renew.	F
JOB 13:	COOLING SYSTEM HOSES - check.	C
JOB 14:	COOLANT - replace.	F
JOB 15:	RADIATOR - clean.	E
JOB 16:	WATER PUMP - check.	B
JOB 17:	TRANSMISSION OIL - check.	B
JOB 18:	TRANSMISSION OIL - renew.	F
JOB 19:	DRIVE SHAFT GAITERS - check.	B
JOB 20:	CLUTCH ACTION - check.	B
JOB 21:	SPARK PLUGS - check.	C
JOB 22:	SPARK PLUGS - renew.	E
JOB 23:	CB POINTS/DWELL ANGLE - check/set.	C
JOB 24:	CONTACT BREAKER POINTS - renew.	D
JOB 25:	IGNITION TIMING - check (earlier vehicles only).	D
JOB 26:	AUXILIARY DRIVE BELT/S - check.	B
JOB 27:	IDLE SPEED AND EMISSIONS - check, adjust.	C
JOB 28:	FUEL PIPES - check.	B
JOB 29:	EXHAUST SYSTEM AND MOUNTINGS - check.	B
JOB 30:	AIR CLEANER ELEMENT - renew.	D
JOB 31:	AIR INTAKE CONTROL VALVE - check.	D
JOB 32:	DIESEL ENGINES FUEL FILTER - drain.	B
JOB 33:	FUEL FILTER - renew.	D
JOB 34:	DIESEL GLOW PLUGS - check/clean.	D
JOB 35:	FRONT AND REAR WHEEL BEARINGS – check.	C
JOB 36:	STEERING AND SUSPENSION - check.	B
JOB 37:	STEERING RACK GAITERS - check.	B
JOB 38:	STEERING BALL JOINTS - check.	C
JOB 39:	SUSPENSION JOINTS AND BUSHES - check.	C
JOB 40:	SHOCK ABSORBER ACTION - check.	C
JOB 41:	POWER STEERING FLUID – check.	A
JOB 42:	WHEEL NUTS/BOLTS - check.	B
JOB 43:	FRONT BRAKE PADS - check.	B
JOB 44:	REAR BRAKE SHOES/PADS - check.	C
JOB 45:	PARKING BRAKE ADJUSTMENT - check.	C
JOB 46:	BRAKE PIPES - check.	B
JOB 47:	BRAKE FLUID - renew. *Not mileage related	D*
JOB 48:	SEATBELTS AND SEATBELT MOUNTINGS - check operation and security.	B
JOB 49:	SEAT MOUNTINGS - check.	B
JOB 50:	SPARE TYRE - check.	B
JOB 51:	FRONT SCREEN WIPERS - check.	A
JOB 52:	HORN - check.	C
JOB 53:	LOCKS, CHECK STRAPS AND HINGES - lubricate.	B
JOB 54:	ALARM SENDER UNIT BATTERIES - renew.	C
JOB 55:	ROAD TEST AND FINAL CHECK - after every service.	

CHAPTER 5 Servicing

FACT FILE
ENGINE BAY LAYOUTS

- There are very many different layouts – these are typical of most.
- Not all of the components shown are fitted to all vehicles.

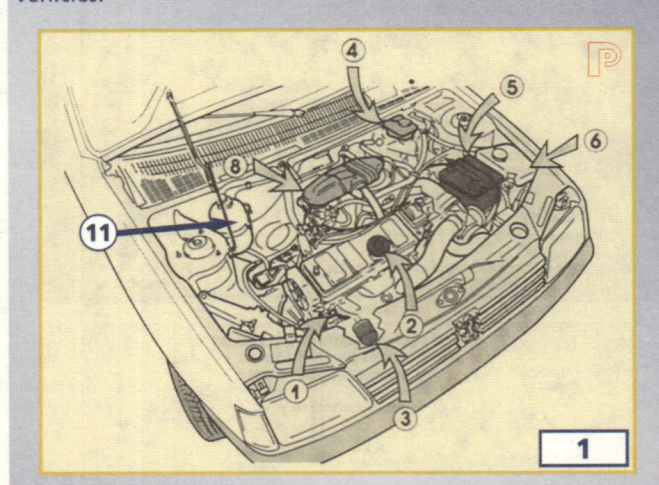

☐ **ILLUSTRATION 1:** 205 TU engine.

☐ **ILLUSTRATION 2:** 106.

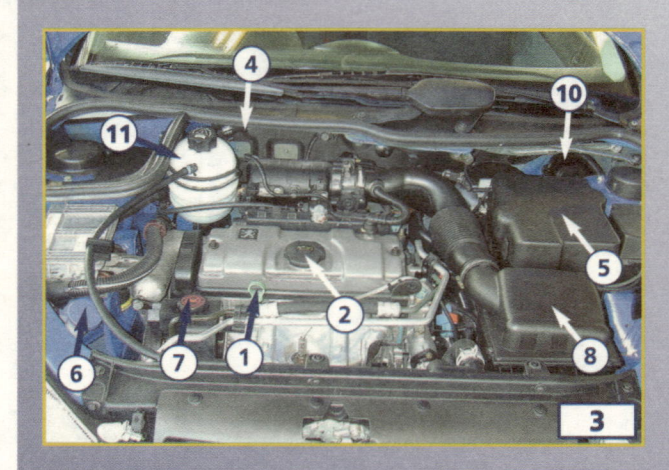

☐ **ILLUSTRATION 3:** 206 Petrol.

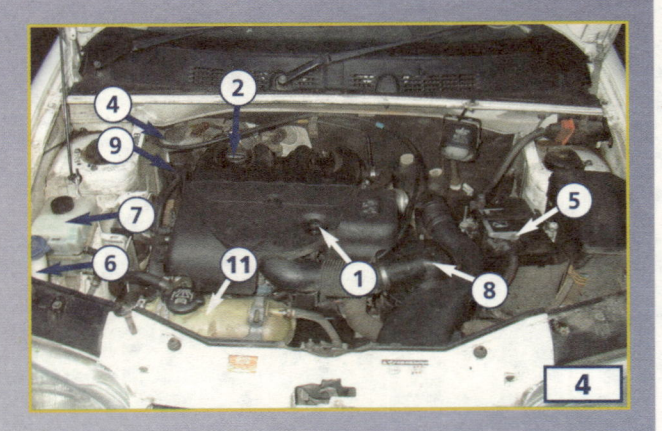

☐ **ILLUSTRATION 4:** 206 D (Van).

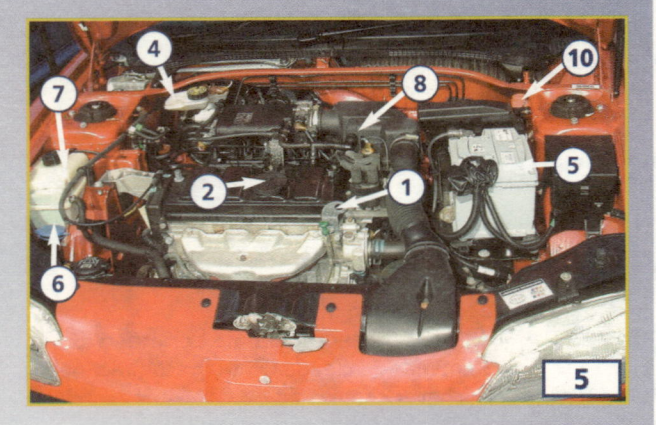

☐ **ILLUSTRATION 5:** 306 Petrol, 1.8 and 2.0.

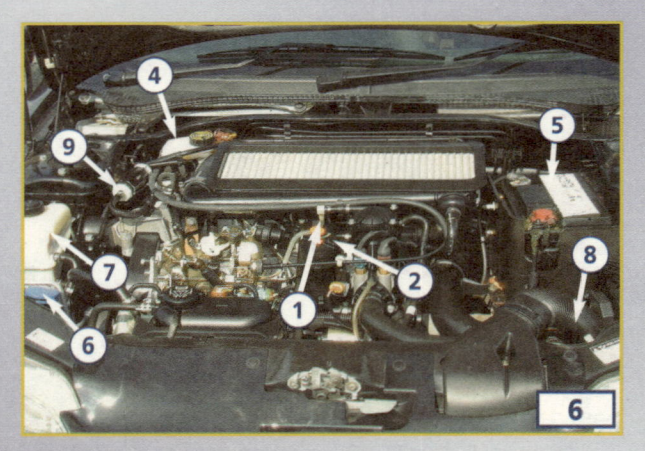

☐ **ILLUSTRATION 6:** 306 TD.

1 – engine oil dipstick
2 – engine oil filler cap
3 – engine oil filter cartridge
4 – brake fluid reservoir/master cylinder
5 – battery
6 – screen wash reservoir
7 – power steering fluid reservoir (if applicable)
8 – air cleaner housing
9 – fuel filter
10 – fuel cut-off inertia switch (if applicable)

JOB 1: ENGINE OIL - *check level.*

Make sure the vehicle is on level ground when you check the dipstick.

☐ **1: XV, XW AND XY ENGINES:** The dipstick is positioned towards the front of the engine behind the air filter housing.
➜ **XU ENGINES:** It is behind and to the top of the engine as you face the front of the vehicle.
➜ **TU AND DIESEL ENGINES:** It is at the front of the engine.

See *Job 9* for filler cap locations.
➜ Just over half a litre, will raise the level from the 'MIN' to the 'MAX' mark.
➜ On all models, check the ground over which the vehicle has been parked for evidence of oil or other fluid leaks.

JOB 2: COOLING SYSTEM - *check level.*

SAFETY FIRST!

• Only remove the header tank or reservoir cap WHEN THE SYSTEM IS COLD.

☐ **2:** Top up as necessary.

JOB 3: HYDRAULIC FLUID - *check level.*

If necessary, top up the level to the 'MAX' mark on the side of the reservoir.
➜ Wipe the top clean before removing the cap and be careful not to damage the wiring.

☐ **3:** Check the brake fluid level warning light.
➜ With the parking brake off - chock the wheels first and place the transmission in first gear (or 'P' in the case of an automatic) - and the ignition switched on, lift the reservoir cap and its float clear of the fluid.
➜ The warning light on the dash should light up.

JOB 4: BATTERY - *check electrolyte level.*

IMPORTANT NOTE: You can't, of course, check the level in a 'sealed for life' battery!
➜ Check the fluid level, and for corrosion around the terminals.
➜ Wash white 'fur' off with hot water.
➜ Protect terminals with petroleum jelly or (better still) proprietary terminal fluid. It's best not to use grease!

JOB 5: SCREEN/HEADLIGHT WASHER FLUID AND WASHERS - *check level, aim jets.*

Check the screenwash fluid lever reservoir and top up if necessary.

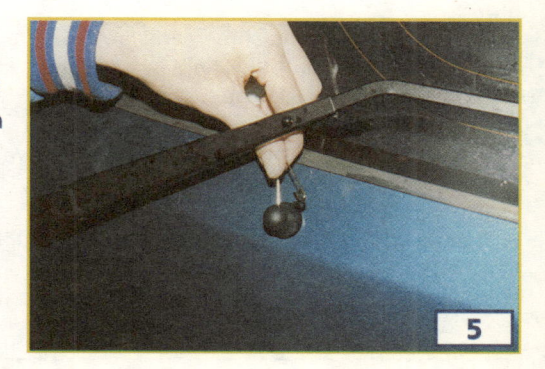

☐ **5:** On most models, if the screen washer jets are not properly aimed, they can be adjusted with a pin.
If one of the jets is blocked, it can usually be freed with a piece of thin wire.

JOB 6: TYRES - *check pressures and condition (road wheels).*

Pressures should be checked when the tyres are cold - they warm up when a vehicle is driven.
➜ Make sure the tread depth exceeds the legal minimum and look for any signs of uneven wear or damage such as cuts, bulges or objects embedded in the tyres.

CHAPTER 5 Servicing Jobs 7-9

TOP TIP!
- If a tyre is worn more on one side than another, it probably means that the suspension or steering is out of adjustment but could be symptomatic of suspension damage.
- If a tyre is worn more in the centre or on both edges, it could mean that tyre pressures are wrong.
- See Chapter 3: The Annual Test for a more detailed explanation of tyre wear and legal limits.

JOB 7: LIGHTS - check/change bulbs.

See **Chapter 10, Electrical, Dash, Instruments** for bulb replacement information.

JOB 8: SERVICE INTERVAL INDICATOR - reset, when fitted.

On later models, you can reset the service interval warning indicator as follows:

☐ **8:** Locate the trip meter button on the dash - 206 position, arrowed.
➔ Turn ignition OFF and hold in the trip button.
➔ Turn ignition ON and immediately release trip button. (If the trip button is held in for 10 secs. after turning the ignition ON, the service interval meter will be reset to zero.)
➔ You can now scroll through the service interval mileages shown until the one that corresponds to the vehicle's next service appears.
➔ Press and hold the trip button in - display will flash - and hold in until flashing stops.
➔ Release the button, turn off the ignition and the resetting is complete.

JOB 9: ENGINE OIL AND FILTER – change.

☐ **9A:** This is the location of the oil drain plug on the majority of these engines.
➔ **ENGINES WITH FLAT SUMP PAN:** The drain plug is on the underside of the 'tea-tray'.

☐ **9B:** Be ready to reposition your bowl - the angle of 'spurt' changes as the oil flows out of the sump!

☐ **9C:** Remember to use a new drain plug washer - not tapered-plug types

SAFETY FIRST!
- DON'T pour the old oil down the drain - it's both illegal and irresponsible.
- Your local council waste disposal site will have special facilities for disposing of it safely.
- Moreover, don't mix anything else with it, as this will prevent it from being recycled.

☐ **9D:** Use a strap or chain wrench to remove the filter.

☐ **9E: XV, XW AND XY ENGINES:** The filter (arrowed) is on the upper face of the engine.
➔ Place rags and a drip tray to catch the inevitable oil spill as the filter is removed.

☐ **9F:** Apply clean engine oil to the rubber sealing ring to prevent it buckling as the filter is screwed home.

5-4

❏ **9G:** When the sealing ring contacts the face on the engine, tighten it a further three-quarters of a turn - by hand only.

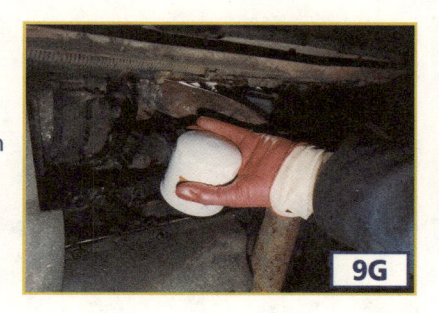

❏ **9H:** Pour in fresh oil - slowly so that it doesn't spurt back.

> **FACT FILE**
> **FILLER CAP LOCATIONS**
> ➔ **XV, XW and XY ENGINES:** The oil cap is located at the top of a 'filler tube' fitted to the valve cover at the rear of the engine - the cap is a simple push-fit.
> ➔ **XU PETROL AND XUD DIESEL ENGINES:** The cap is located towards the centre of the engine bay - the dipstick passes through it - and is released by the two spring clips
> ➔ **TU-SERIES ENGINES:** The filler cap is located on the valve cover and is a 'twist-off', bayonet-type.

JOB 10: VALVE CLEARANCES - *check/adjust.*

See *Chapter 6, Engine*.

JOB 11: CAMSHAFT DRIVE BELT - *check.*

Check the timing belt for damage, cracking or fraying. Replace if any is found.
➔ See also, *Chapter 6, Engine*.

JOB 12: CAMSHAFT DRIVE BELT - *renew.*

See *Chapter 6, Engine*.

JOB 13: COOLING SYSTEM HOSES - *check.*

❏ **13.** Check all the coolant and heater hoses for security and leaks.
➔ Squeeze the larger hoses, and with the smaller hoses, bend the straights and straighten the bends. Listen for cracking sounds, which tell you that the hose is brittle and needs replacing.

JOB 14: COOLANT - *replace.*

See *Chapter 8: Cooling System*.

JOB 15: RADIATOR - *clean.*

> **TOP TIP!**
> • As the radiator picks up most of its debris from the air flowing in from the front, the best way to clear any which is inside the fins is to blow it out from the back.
> • We don't recommend blasting the core with high pressure compressed air as this could damage it.

JOB 16: WATER PUMP - *check.*

Leaks usually start in a small way and, if you spot one in time...
➔ On engines where the water pump is visible, look out for tell-tale coolant dribbles beneath the area of the pump.
➔ If leaks are found, check pump for wear and replace immediately if necessary. See *Chapter 8, Cooling System*.

JOB 17: TRANSMISSION OIL - *check.*

> **SAFETY FIRST!**
> • The following checks have to be carried out with the engine hot and running. The vehicle must be out of doors because of dangerous exhaust fumes.
> • Make sure that hair, jewellery and loose clothing cannot become caught by moving parts.
> • Do not touch any part of the electrical system.
> • Take care not to be burnt by the hot engine.

❏ **17A:** Remove the plug (all types, when fitted - see below) using a plug removal tool.
➔ The level is correct when oil dribbles from the plug-hole, so if oil is apparent, refit the plug.

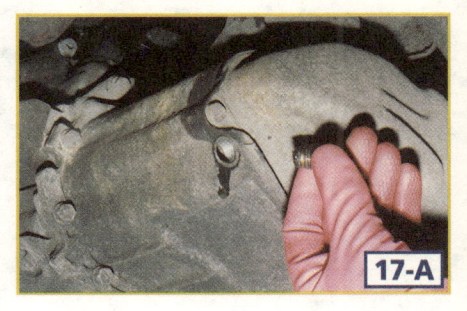

CHAPTER 5 Servicing Jobs 10-17

5-5

CHAPTER 5 Servicing Job 18

17B: Top-up, if required, with the recommended lubricant

TOP TIP!
- The vehicle has to be level to obtain an accurate reading, so ramps or axle stands are not suitable
- The plug can usually be reached from under the front of the vehicle while it is on the ground or, on certain models, from above, inside the engine bay.

MANUAL TRANSMISSION

FACT FILE
TRANSMISSION TYPES
- **FITTED TO XV, XW AND XY ENGINES (TYPE BH):** Gearbox located beneath engine; both units 'share' engine oil. Checking engine oil level also checks 'transmission oil'.
- **XU AND DIESEL ENGINES, 205 TO 1989 (TYPE BE1 GEARBOX):** No facility for checking level between oil changes.
- **XU AND DIESEL ENGINES FROM 1989 (TYPE BE3 GEARBOX):** The combined filler/level plug on this gearbox is situated at the rear of the right-hand end-plate of the gearbox - it is readily accessible from inside the right-hand wheel arch. Check and top-up as for MA type described below.
- **TU ENGINED MODELS (MA TYPE GEARBOX):** This gearbox type has a combined filler/level plug, and also a drain plug.

AUTOMATIC TRANSMISSION

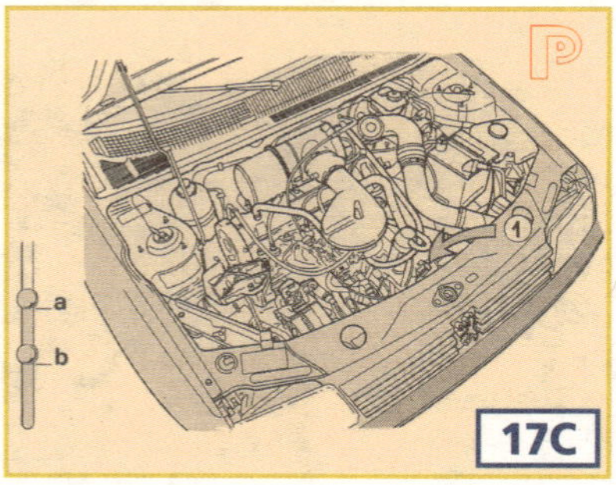

17C: Check level with engine at normal running temperature and WITH the engine running.
→ Keep hands, hair and clothes away from ignition and electrical components.
→ With the vehicle on level ground, apply the parking brake and put gear selector in 'P' (Park).
→ Remove dipstick (position 1), wipe with a clean tissue

and top up with auto. transmission fluid (ATF) if necessary.
→ Point (a) indicates maximum; (b) the minimum levels.

TOP TIP!
- Dark brown or black ATF suggests a worn transmission unit.

JOB 18: TRANSMISSION OIL - renew.

This is not part of all Peugeot's modern service schedules but common sense suggests that fresh lubricant will allow components to last longer.

MANUAL TRANSMISSION

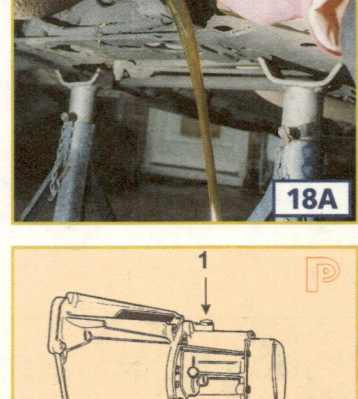

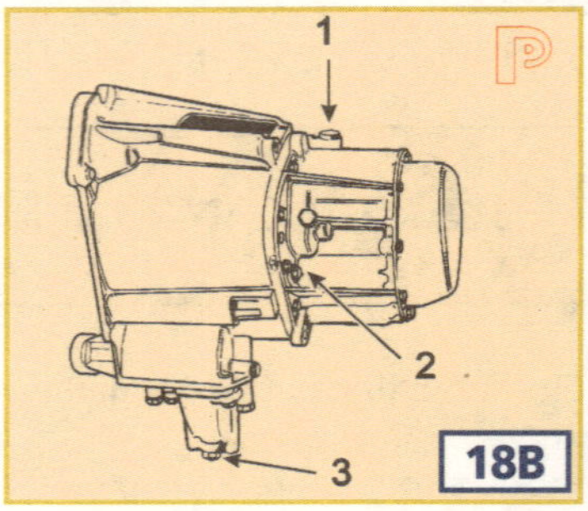

18A: MA-TYPE: Position a container beneath and remove the drain plug from the gearbox; allow several minutes for the oil to drain completely. Some drain plugs are fitted with a magnet to collect any swarf (metal particles) that may be suspended in the oil - clean it off with a rag.

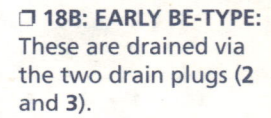

18B: EARLY BE-TYPE: These are drained via the two drain plugs (2 and 3).
→ Refill through the combined filler/vent plug (1) on top of the transmission casing.

18C: LATER BE-TYPE: This is the location (arrowed) of the single drain plug.

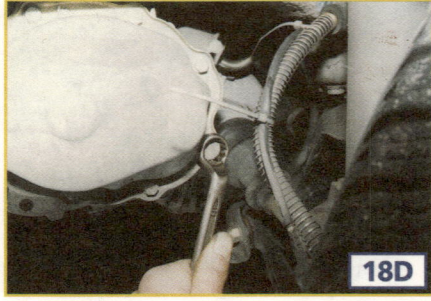

18D: BE-TYPES FROM 1986: Fill through the filler plug, reached through the left-side wheelarch.

5-6

> **TOP TIP!**
> • If there is no drain plug fitted to the transmission casing:
> • With a driveshaft gaiter removed, tip the vehicle by raising just one side with a trolley jack, and drain as much oil as possible.

AUTOMATIC TRANSMISSION

❏ **18E:** Drain both the transmission sump pan and differential via the drain plugs (arrowed).
➝ Refill through the dipstick tube, in the engine bay, using a small-bore tube on the ATF container.

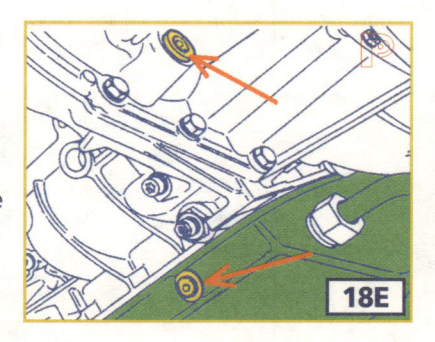

JOB 19: DRIVE SHAFT GAITERS - *check.*

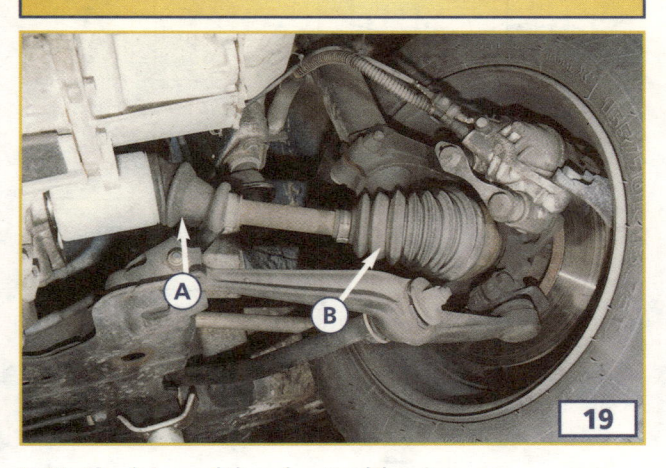

❏ **19:** Check inner (A) and outer (B) gaiters
➝ If any splits are found, replace the gaiters - see **Chapter 11, Steering, Suspension**.

JOB 20: CLUTCH ACTION - *check.*

❏ **20:** If the pedal action feels jerky, 'dry' or heavy, try lubricating the pivots and self-adjusting mechanism located at the top of the pedal with Castrol DWF or releasing fluid.
➝ If the fault persists, the clutch cable probably needs replacing if not a hydraulic clutch - see **Chapter 7: Transmission, Clutch**.

JOB 21: SPARK PLUGS - *check.*

❏ **21:** On engines where spark plugs are recessed, you'll need an extension bar.

> **TOP TIP!**
> • If a plug gets tighter as you turn it, there's every possibility that it is cross threaded. Once out, it probably won't go back in again.
> • If the threads can't be cleaned up with a thread chaser, you will have to add a thread insert to the cylinder head.

JOB 22: SPARK PLUGS - *renew.*

Renew the spark plugs irrespective of apparent condition.

JOB 23: CB POINTS/DWELL ANGLE - *check/set.*

See **Chapter 9, Ignition, Fuel, Exhaust**.

> **TOP TIP!**
> • Remove the spark plugs.
> • Apply the parking brake, select second gear and support the right-hand front wheel off the ground - use an axle stand.
> • Now, you can easily turn the engine by turning the road wheel is turned by hand.

JOB 24: CONTACT BREAKER POINTS - *renew.*

JOB 25: IGNITION TIMING - *check.*

See **Chapter 9, Ignition, Fuel, Exhaust**.

JOB 26: AUXILIARY DRIVE BELT/S - *check.*

See **Chapter 6, Part A** for information on checking and adjusting belts

JOB 27: IDLE SPEED AND EMISSIONS - *check, adjust.*

See **Chapter 9, Fuel, Ignition and Exhaust** for all engine types.

CHAPTER 5 Servicing Jobs 19-27

5-7

CHAPTER 5 Servicing Jobs 28-36

JOB 28: FUEL PIPES - check.

☐ **28:** Make a physical check of all pipework and connections.
➜ Bend all flexible brake hoses to show up signs of cracking rubber - if any are found, the hose should be replaced as soon as possible.
➜ Hoses should also be free from bulges or chafing marks.

JOB 29: EXHAUST SYSTEM AND MOUNTINGS - check.

☐ **29:** Check all the connections and rubber mountings.

TOP TIP!
• If you suspect a leak but it's location isn't obvious, hold a piece of board so that it blocks off the tailpipe. Under pressure, the leak should be more noisy, enabling you to track down its position.

JOB 30: AIR CLEANER ELEMENT - renew.

☐ **30:** Remove the top of the air cleaner housing - undo nuts or clips, depending on model.
➜ Lift out the element and replace it with a new one.
➜ On fuel injected petrol and later diesel engined vehicles, the air cleaner element is larger and is inside a box at the end of the air inlet trunking.

JOB 31: AIR INTAKE CONTROL VALVE - check.

CARBURETOR MODELS: Check the operation of the valve by observing the flap through the end of the intake, first with the engine cold, then when it has reached operating temperature.
➜ If the valve fails to open when the engine is started, check the vacuum pipe from the inlet manifold to the vacuum capsule for signs of splitting or other damage.
➜ Otherwise, you may need to replace the capsule.

JOB 32: DIESEL ENGINES FUEL FILTER - drain.

Drain the fuel filter to remove water. See *Chapter 9, Ignition, Fuel, Exhaust.*

JOB 33: FUEL FILTER - renew.

PETROL AND DIESEL ENGINES: See *Chapter 9, Fuel, Ignition and Exhaust.*

JOB 34: DIESEL GLOW PLUGS - check/clean.

Unscrew each glow plug in turn - see *Chapter 10: Electrical, Dash, Instruments* and clean the carbon off the end with proprietary carburetor cleaner.

JOB 35: FRONT AND REAR WHEEL BEARINGS – check.

In order to check for wear, rock the wheel about its centre, feeling for excess bearing play. Also, try spinning each wheel - as far as you can, with driven wheels - feeling for rough rotation.

TOP TIP!
• If a wheel bearing is worn, you will normally hear a noise on the outer, loaded bearing when cornering.

JOB 36: STEERING AND SUSPENSION - check.

☐ **36:** Raise each front wheel just clear of the ground.
➜ Put a pry bar under the wheel and try to lever it upwards.
➜ Free play suggests wear in suspension

bushes or strut.
→ Check the springs for obvious breaks or sagging.
→ Check tie bar bushes for cracking, softness or wear.

JOB 37: STEERING RACK GAITERS - *check.*
JOB 38: STEERING BALL JOINTS - *check.*

See **Chapter 11, Steering, Suspension**.

JOB 39: SUSPENSION JOINTS AND BUSHES - *check.*

❑ 39: Test the inner suspension arm bush by levering. There should be only a just-perceptible amount of movement.
→ Check all rubber bushes and mountings for distortion, splits or perishing.

JOB 40: SHOCK ABSORBER ACTION - *check.*

See **Chapter 3: The Annual Test** for shock absorber tests.

JOB 41: POWER STEERING FLUID – *check.*

The power steering fluid reservoir cap is fitted with a short dipstick to its underside - the markings relate to the minimum fluid level either when hot (upper mark) or cold (lower mark).
→ If necessary top-up with the recommended fluid.
→ Clean around the cap before unscrewing it, so that no dirt or grit enters the reservoir which could damage the components.

JOB 42: WHEEL NUTS/BOLTS - *check.*

❑ 42: To 'torque' the wheel nuts/bolts correctly, first slacken each nut or bolt and check that the threads aren't stiff or corroded, then tighten with the wrench.

JOB 43: FRONT BRAKE PADS - *check.*
JOB 44: REAR BRAKE SHOES/PADS - *check.*

See **Chapter 12, Brakes**.

JOB 45: PARKING BRAKE ADJUSTMENT - *check.*

Apply the parking brake. It should lock at between 2 and 4 clicks. If more or less than these figures, the parking brake must be adjusted as described in **Chapter 12, Brakes**.

JOB 46: BRAKE PIPES - *check.*

❑ 46: Make a physical check of all pipework and connections. Renew pipework which is rusty.
→ Bend all flexible brake hoses to show up signs of cracking rubber - if any are found, the hose should be replaced as soon as possible.
→ Hoses should also be free from bulges or rubbing marks.

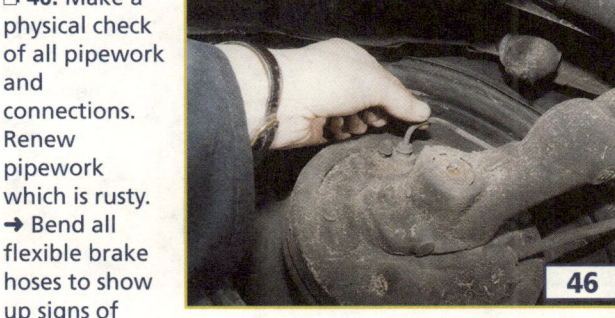

TOP TIP!
• Work out of doors with the car safely supported off the ground - see **Chapter 2, Safety First!**
• Have an assistant press down hard on the brake pedal while you inspect each flexible brake hose in turn.
• If any bulges appear, the hose/s need replacing.

JOB 47: BRAKE FLUID - *renew.*

If this job is not carried out at the recommended interval, it can result in brakes which fail without warning. See **Chapter 12, Brakes**

JOB 48: SEATBELTS AND SEATBELT MOUNTINGS - *check operation and security.*

❑ 48: Examine seatbelts for signs of damage, such as abrasion, cuts, contamination or frayed stitching.
→ Where inertia-reel seatbelts are fitted, pull the belts out as far as they will go and make sure they fully retract.
→ Make sure the seatbelt anchorage points are secure and the retaining bolts are tight.
→ On older vehicles you should make sure that there is no body corrosion which would weaken the seatbelt mountings.

SAFETY FIRST!
• Some vehicles are fitted with seatbelt pre-tensioners. Special safety precautions are need when this type of seatbelt is being removed or refitted - see **Chapter 14, Interior, Trim**.

JOB 49: SEAT MOUNTINGS - check.

Check the seats:
→ For secure mounting, by trying to rock them.
→ The seat adjustment mechanism.
→ That the folding seat backs lock securely in the upright position.

JOB 50: SPARE TYRE - check.

TOP TIP!
- You should inflate the spare tyre to the maximum pressure recommended for high speed or load running.
- Just carry a tyre pressure gauge and, if you have a puncture, let some air out if necessary.

JOB 51: FRONT SCREEN WIPERS - check.
JOB 52: HORN - check.
JOB 53: LOCKS, CHECK STRAPS AND HINGES - lubricate.

☐ **53:** Apply silicone grease or aerosol spray to the jaws of the lock catches in the edges of the doors, tailgate and bonnet.
→ Grease hinges and check straps at each door.
→ Apply graphite lock lube. to the keyholes of locks. Oil tends to attract dirt.

JOB 54: ALARM SENDER UNIT BATTERIES - renew.

JOB 55: ROAD TEST AND FINAL CHECK - after every service.

☐ **55:** Before you can claim to have 'finished' working on the vehicle, you must check it and test it. If you are not a qualified mechanic, we strongly recommend having someone who is a properly qualified mechanic inspect all of the vehicle's safety-related items before using it on the road.

→ **WARM-UP:** Run the vehicle for several minutes before setting out then turn off, check fluid levels and check underneath for leaks.
→ **STEERING:** Check that the steering moves freely in both directions and that the vehicle does not 'pull' one way or the other when driving in a straight line - but do bear in mind the effect of the camber on the road.
→ **BRAKES:** Make sure that the brakes work effectively, smoothly and without the need for 'pumping'. There should be no juddering or squealing.
→ **'PULLING'** Check that the vehicle does not 'pull' from one side to the other when you brake firmly from around 40 mph. (Don't cause a skid and don't try this if there is any risk of having an accident.)
→ **CLUTCH OPERATION:** Make sure the clutch pedal operates smoothly and the clutch engages without juddering.
→ **ENGINE PERFORMANCE:** Make sure the engine is operating satisfactorily under load and on the over-run.
→ **TRANSMISSION:** Make sure the gear changes are smooth, and the transmission appears to be working normally
→ **INSTRUMENTS:** Must work and indicate correctly.

CHAPTER 6: ENGINE

Please read **Chapter 2 Safety First** before carrying out any work on your car.

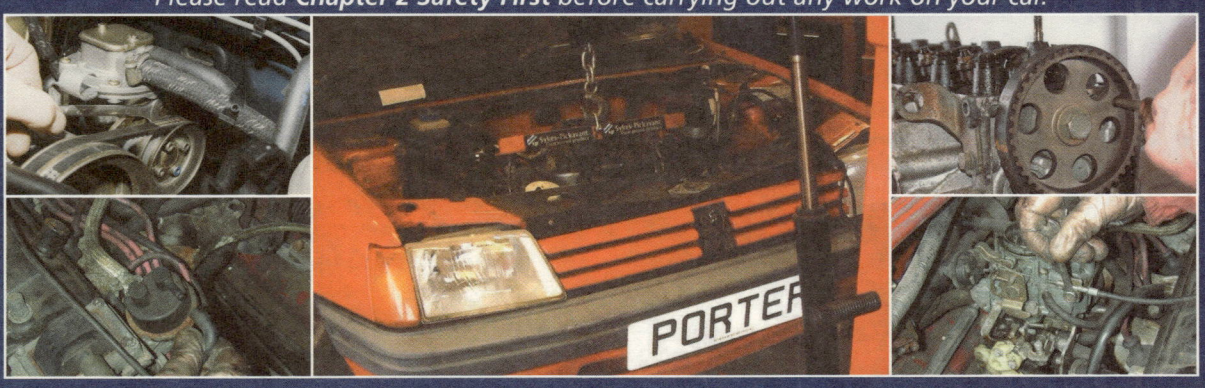

Part A: General Procedures	6-1	**Part G:** Cylinder Head Overhaul	6-39
Part B: Which Engine is Which?	6-12	**Part H:** Cylinder Head Refitting	6-46
Part C: Timing Belt or Chain - Inspection, Adjustment, Replacement	6-15	**Part I:** Engine and Transmission - Removal, Separation, Refitting	6-53
Part D: Auxilairy Drive Belts	6-27	**Part J:** Engine Block - Dismantling, Rebuilding	6-63
Part E: Valve Clearance (Valve Lash) - Adjustment	6-30	**Part K:** Engine/Transmission Mounting - Replacement	6-79
Part F: XV, XW, XY Engines - Cylinder Head Removal	6-34		

Part A: General Procedures

CONTENTS

	Page No.		Page No.
JOB 1: SAFETY FIRST!	6-1	**JOB 10:** EXHAUST AND INLET VALVES - *grinding in*.	6-5
JOB 2: CYLINDER HEAD BOLTS – *tightening, undoing*.	6-2	**JOB 11:** ENGINE – *lifting, moving*.	6-6
JOB 3: OHC ENGINE BEARING CAPS - *removing*.	6-2	**JOB 12:** CRANKSHAFT BEARINGS, CONNECTING ROD BEARINGS – *removing*.	6-7
JOB 4: CYLINDER HEAD GASKETS.	6-2	**JOB 13:** PISTON RINGS - *fitting*.	6-8
JOB 5: GASKET SEALANT.	6-2	**JOB 14:** PISTONS – *removing, refitting*.	6-8
JOB 6: 'STUCK' CYLINDER HEAD - *freeing*.	6-3	**JOB 15:** ENGINE COMPONENTS – *checking, measuring for wear*.	6-9
JOB 7: CYLINDER HEAD - *lifting, fitting*.	6-3	**JOB 16:** REASSEMBLING ENGINE COMPONENTS - *lubrication*.	6-10
JOB 8: CYLINDER HEAD AND COMBUSTION CHAMBERS.	6-3	**JOB 17:** REASSEMBLING ENGINE COMPONENTS - *clearances*.	6-11
JOB 9: EXHAUST AND INLET VALVES AND GUIDES – *removing, replacing*.	6-4		

See *Part B: Which Engine is Which?* for an explanation of the engine types referred to here.

Many of the skills you will use in rebuilding an engine will be common to all engines. So, to save you time and help the job go more smoothly, those skills are shown right here!

JOB 1: SAFETY FIRST!

Be sure to read and follow the advice in *Chapter 2, Safety First!* before carrying out work on your vehicle. In particular, pay attention to the advice on fuel safety - remember that petrol/gasoline is highly explosive and that there are almost always leaks when disconnecting fuel system components on the engine.

In addition, remember that major components may be heavy enough to cause injury if not lifted correctly. See *Job 11* for further important information.

JOB 2: CYLINDER HEAD BOLTS - *tightening, undoing.*

If you get this wrong, you could easily distort the cylinder head – the aluminium heads of Peugeot engines can relatively easily be distorted. NEVER remove the head while there is still heat in the engine.

❏ **STEP 1:** The general rule is to **undo** the outer fixings first, working inwards in a regular, spiral pattern. And to **tighten** the inner ones first, working evenly and diagonally outwards in the reverse order. HOWEVER - Peugeot advise different procedures for different engines. MOST IMPORTANT: Don't guess! ALWAYS remove and tighten in the order specified in the relevant section of this manual.

JOB 3: OHC ENGINE BEARING CAPS - *removing.*

TOP TIP!

❏ **STEP 1:** • The camshaft of XU, XUD and TUD engines is held down by three or five bearing caps.
• If they aren't numbered, mark them with a centre punch – it's *essential* that they aren't mixed up.
• Because of the tension in the valve springs, the caps have to be loosened gradually.
• You can speed things up by leaving two of the caps tight - such as numbers 2 and 3 in a five-cap set-up - while completely removing the other caps.
• Now the two remaining caps can be removed. Loosen each nut a turn at a time to gradually release the pressure from the valve springs.

JOB 4: CYLINDER HEAD GASKETS.

❏ **STEP 1:** NEVER re-use a cylinder head gasket – if you do, it will almost certainly blow, particularly as most Peugeot head gaskets are of the 'self-vulcanising' type, which seal themselves to the cylinder block and head on first use, with engine heat. Fit the new one with the word TOP, HAUT or OBEN (for German-made gaskets), or sometimes the part number facing **upwards**.

❏ **STEP 2: DIESEL ENGINES:** You will have to select the correct gasket thickness because the volume of the combustion chamber is a lot more critical on diesel engines. The correct procedure for each type of engine is shown in the relevant section of this manual.

JOB 5: GASKET SEALANT.

➜ Do NOT use gasket paste on a cylinder head gasket.
➜ Neoprene (compressible 'rubber') gaskets do not normally need gasket paste. If necessary use silicone sealant.

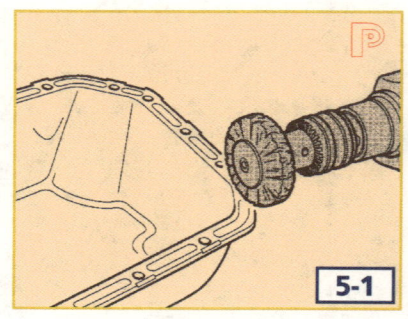

❏ **STEP 1:** When a joint has to be sealed, make sure that you clean off all of the old sealant first. On a pressed steel sump, use a wire brush.

You can use a flat scraper on a cylinder block. In the case of aluminium cylinder blocks take great care not to dig the scraper in, and don't use a power tool of any sort.

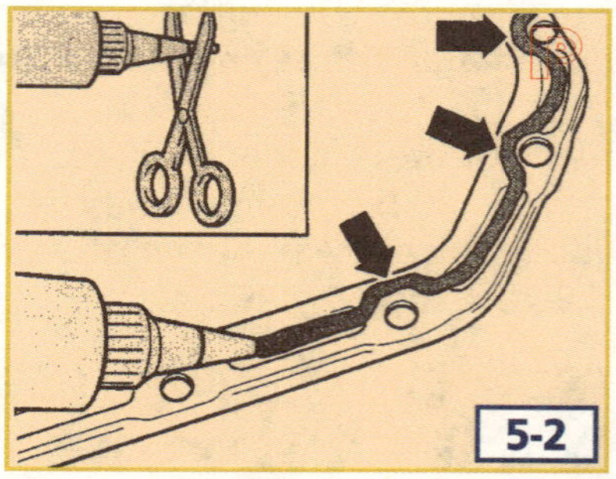

❏ **STEP 2:** Apply silicone sealing compound as follows:
➜ Cut off the nozzle on the sealant tube to give the approximate size of bead that you may need. In the case of a sump, it is usually about 3 mm.
➜ Apply the bead about 2 to 3 mm thick.
➜ Apply the bead in an unbroken line, going around the *inner* sides of the sump bolt holes.

JOB 6: 'STUCK' CYLINDER HEAD - *freeing*.

IMPORTANT NOTE: This following advice applies ONLY to solid-block (non wet-liner) type engines. On engines that have separately inserted cylinders in an open design of crankcase, the cylinder head must ONLY be removed in the manner described in the relevant section detailing cylinder head removal.

On solid-block, cast iron engines, even after all the bolts have been removed, it is sometimes difficult to remove a 'stuck' cylinder head. You must NEVER lever between the mating faces of the head and block. Instead:

→ Look for protrusions or strong brackets on both head and block against which you may be able to lever.
→ Try turning the engine over on the starter motor with spark plugs in place but ignition or diesel injector pump disconnected, so that the engine can't start. The compression created may shift the head.

IMPORTANT NOTE: ONLY TRY THIS ON SOLID BLOCK CAST IRON ENGINES!

→ Extra leverage can be applied by leaving the manifolds in place and pulling on them.
→ You can sometimes use a large, soft-faced mallet on a solid protrusion on the head to try to shock it free. Take very great care not to hammer anywhere that can cause damage.

JOB 7: CYLINDER HEAD – *lifting, fitting*.

When the engine is still installed, a cylinder head may (depending on type) be a dangerously heavy component to lift, because of the need to reach into the engine bay. It's best to have someone help you to lift it away.

TOP TIP!

□ STEP 1: • When refitting a cylinder head held down with bolts rather than studs fitted in the block – and if there are no alignment dowels fitted by the manufacturer - you may have difficulty in aligning the bolt holes in the gasket with those in the head - and if they're not aligned, you won't be able to screw the bolts into the block. Cont...

TOP TIP!

Continued...
• Make a pair of guides out of two old cylinder head bolts, or two pieces of plain steel bar of a size that will just slide into the threads in the block.
• If using old bolts, cut the heads off with an angle grinder and slot the ends so that you can use a screwdriver to remove them.
• Fit the bolts, or the bars, slide the gasket over them, followed by the cylinder head, so that all holes are aligned.
• You can now fit some of the 'proper' bolts before removing the guides.

JOB 8: CYLINDER HEAD AND COMBUSTION CHAMBERS.

□ STEP 1: The cylinder head can be checked for distortion by use of a straight edge and feeler gauge. At the same time, check for excessive corrosion. If you are in doubt, or if the old gasket had blown, have the cylinder head refaced by your Peugeot agent or engine specialist.

IMPORTANT NOTE: On diesel engines, don't pass the straight edge over the swirl chambers, as these may be raised relative to the head mating face.

□ STEP 2: Clean excessive carbon deposits from the crowns of the pistons without damaging the surface of the aluminium.

TOP TIP!

• If the engine is worn and you don't intend overhauling it at this stage, we strongly advise that you don't scrape the carbon from the piston crowns. It can help preserve compression pressures.

JOB 9: EXHAUST AND INLET VALVES AND GUIDES – *removing, replacing*.

VALVE REPLACEMENT

☐ **STEP 1:** With some of these engines, you will need to use a valve-spring compressor with an extension jaw to reach into the recessed valve spring area in the head.

☐ **STEP 2:** Remove the cam followers and valve clearance adjusting shims (XU, XUD and TUD engines only), taking care to maintain their original positions for re-assembly.

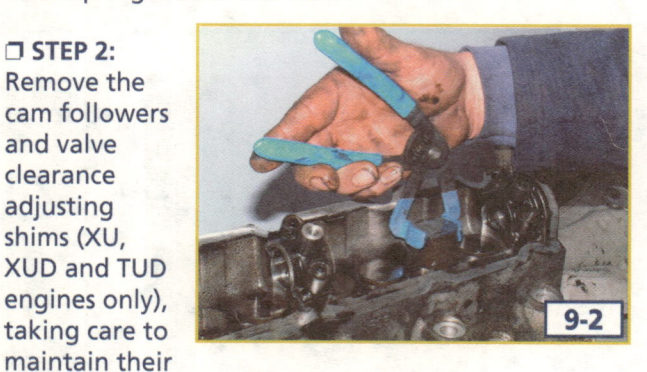

☐ **STEP 3:** Give each valve a sharp tap with a hammer to free the top spring plate from the valve. You could place a socket spanner over the plate to avoid striking the end of the valve stem.

☐ **STEP 4:** Compressing the valve springs so that you can reach in and remove the collets from around the heads of the valves.

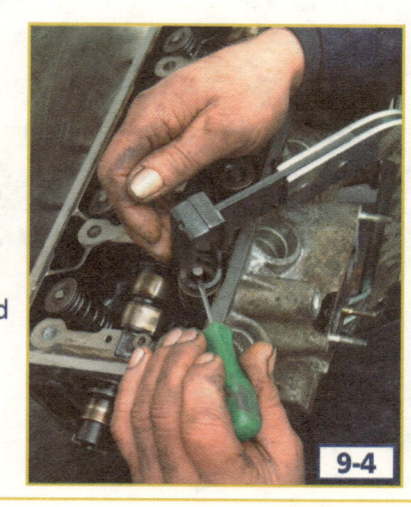

☐ **STEP 5:** Slowly and carefully open the spring compressor tool to release the pressure of the valve spring, and remove the upper spring seat...

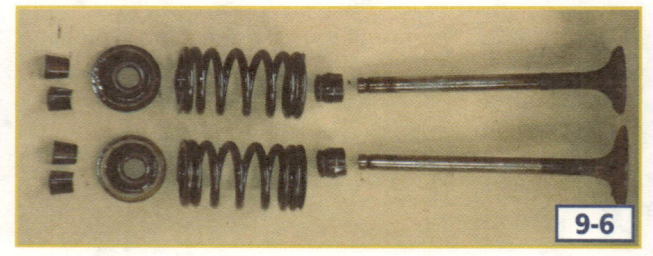

☐ **STEP 6:** ...followed by the springs.

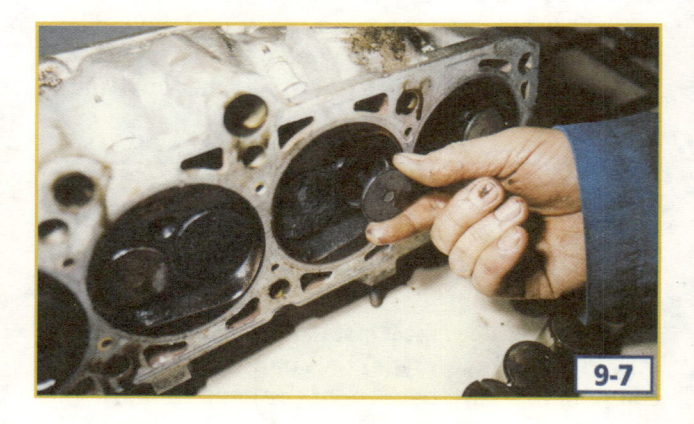

☐ **STEP 7:** Slide out the valves, removing any rubber valve seals and discard the old seals; new ones must be used on re-assembly.

TOP TIP!

- The valves should slide freely out of their guides.
- Any resistance may be caused by a build up of carbon, or a slight burr on the stem where the collets engage.
- This can usually be removed by careful use of fine wet-or-dry paper, allowing you to withdraw the valves without scoring their guides.
- Keep the valves in their correct order by wrapping a numbered piece of masking tape around each stem.

❑ **STEP 8:** Once all the valves have been removed, clean them up ready for inspection. Remove the carbon deposits with a wire brush and degrease the rest. Exhaust valves are prone to burning at their heads, as are their valve seats in the cylinder head.

TOP TIP!

• Check the height of the valve springs against new ones if possible, but if not, compare them with each other.
• If any are shorter than the others, play safe and replace the complete set. They are bound to have suffered fatigue which could cause premature valve failure.

❑ **STEP 9:** To install valves, start from one end. Lubricate a valve stem with fresh engine oil and slide it in to its guide.

❑ **STEP 10:** Locate a new valve stem seal over the stem of the valve and push down into contact with the guide. Push the seal onto its seat using a suitable metal tube.

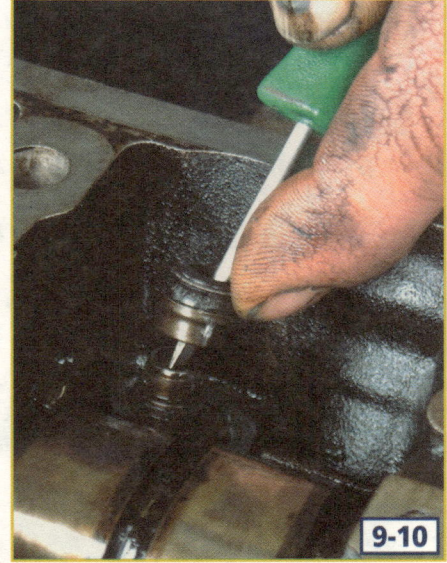

TOP TIP!

❑ **STEP 11:** • Wrap a short length of insulating tape around the collet grooves at the end of each valve stem.
• This will protect the new valve seals from damage as you slide them over the valve stems.
• When you have pushed the new seal firmly onto the top of the valve guide, remove the tape.

❑ **STEP 12:** Refit the spring seat.

❑ **STEP 13:** Position the spring and the spring cap.

❑ **STEP 14:** Re-apply the valve spring compressor and compress the springs enough to allow you to engage the split collets in the stem grooves. Note that the type of collets, the spring caps and the valves must match each other.

TOP TIP!

• Grease the grooves so that the collets will 'stick' in place.
• Collets are easily fitted by 'sticking' the backs of them onto the end of a screwdriver with some grease and feeding them into position.

❑ **STEP 15:** Carefully release the spring compressor and check that the collets are correctly located. Tap the end of each stem with a hammer to bed them all in.

❑ **STEP 16:** Fit the remaining valves.

JOB 10: EXHAUST AND INLET VALVES - *grinding in.*

TOP TIP!

• Before grinding-in the valves, clean the tops of the valve heads back to shiny metal.
• Now the sucker on the end of your valve grinding stick won't keep falling off when you grind-in the valves!

❑ **STEP 1:** Check for valve guide wear:
→ Lift each valve until the end of the stem is level with the top of the valve guide.
→ Attempt to move the head from side to side.
→ If you feel any noticeable play then you may need new guides.
→ This is a job that has to be carried out by your Peugeot dealer or engine rebuild specialist, who will also have the experience to confirm whether or not wear is acceptable, as well as the special tools needed to replace the valve guides.

TOP TIP!

• Modern petrol engines, with hardened valve seats, are not capable of having valves ground in the traditional way, except to remove the smallest of blemishes. If anything more is needed, take the valves and cylinder head to your dealer and have the valves and seats recut to the correct angle by machine.

☐ **STEP 2:** A power-operated valve grinder, such as this Wurth tool, attaches to the electric drill and makes valve grinding on engines with hardened valve seats a more practicable proposition.

☐ **STEP 3:** Apply a small quantity of coarse grinding paste evenly around the valve seat. Use a valve grinding stick tool with a suction cup slightly smaller than the valve face.

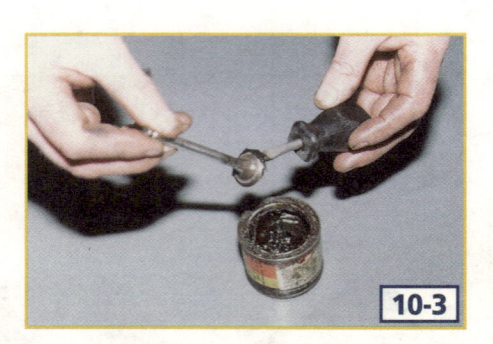

☐ **STEP 4:** Apply a dab of moisture and press the suction pad firmly onto the valve head. Lower the valve stem into the guide and, holding the grinding stick firmly between the palms of your hand, rub back and forth to give rotary grinding action while pressing gently down into the valve seat.

IMPORTANT NOTE: Absolutely NO paste must find its way into the guide, as this will rapidly wear the guide.

Lift the valve regularly to redistribute the cutting paste around the contact area. When you can feel the paste wearing thin remove the valve, wipe the surfaces clean and check the contact surface on valve and seat. You must aim to achieve a complete, narrow ring of grey around the valve seat and valve face. If there are any blemishes still in the surface then more coarse paste will be needed. Once a complete ring has been obtained, clean off the coarse paste and finish off with fine paste. Finally, thoroughly remove all traces of cutting paste from the valves and head.

TOP TIP!
- A narrow contact band means high pressure on the seat and longer valve life.
- A wide contact band reduces the contact pressure and induces early valve seat burning.

☐ **STEP 5:** Now repeat this operation on the remaining valves.

☐ **STEP 6:** Wash the whole cylinder head again using paraffin (kerosene) and an old brush, making sure that all traces of grinding paste are removed, then dry off. Use compressed air if available.

SAFETY FIRST!
- Treat compressed air with respect. Always wear goggles to protect your eyes.
- Never allow the airline nozzle near any of the body apertures.

JOB 11: ENGINE – *lifting, moving.*

☐ **STEP 1:** Always use suitable lifting equipment, such as the Clarke Strongarm hydraulic engine hoist we show being used. Hire one from a tool-hire specialist if you don't own one. Most ceiling/roof structures are not strong enough to bear the weight of having lifting gear suspended from them, without being suitably reinforced.

The weakest part of the lifting gear used to lift and lower an engine is often the connection to the engine itself. It's best not to use ropes because they can stretch and slip. Ideally, you should make up a solid lifting eye which can be fixed to the engine at one or more cylinder head-to-block bolts.

Alternatively, buy a piece of strong steel chain - one with welded links, not open links which could pull apart - and bolt it down to two suitable locations on the engine. The hook on your lifting gear should be of the type that can be snapped closed and can be fitted to the lifting eye or chain on the engine.

If you intend removing the engine while leaving the transmission in place, you will need to make up a suitable bridge, supported on each side of the engine bay and with a vertical chain or rod taking the weight of the otherwise unsupported engine-end of the transmission unit.

When moving major engine and/or transmission components around the workshop, use a sufficiently strong trolley. Make sure that the weight of such components cannot fall on to hands, feet or any other parts of the body.

JOB 12: CRANKSHAFT BEARINGS, CONNECTING ROD BEARINGS – *removing*.

❏ **STEP 1:** Check that all the connecting rods and their big-end bearing caps are marked with matching numbers, starting from the timing cover end. Make sure that the markings tell you which way round they go. If there are no marks there, use 'dots' of typists' correction fluid on clean metal, or add centre-punch marks.

12-1

12-2

❏ **STEP 2:** If you are to refit the same pistons, and they do not have a direction marking on the crown (which is rare), mark them to show their position and which way round they face.

❏ **STEP 3:** Undo the securing bolts and remove the caps, keeping them in their correct order.

12-3

TOP TIP!

12-4

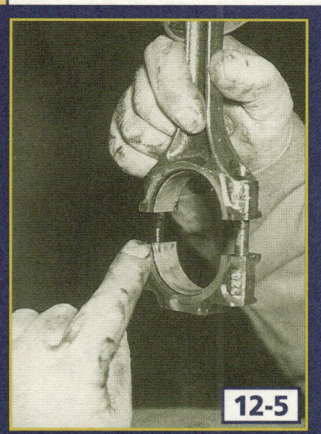

12-5

❏ **STEP 4:** • Inspect the top of each cylinder bore - there may be a small ring of carbon build-up which can make it difficult to remove the pistons. If so, scrape it carefully away.
• Use a hammer handle to tap the piston/connecting rod assemblies carefully out of the bores.

❏ **STEP 5:** ...keeping them in the correct order and keep the matching conrods and bearing caps together.

❏ **STEP 6:** Check that all crankshaft main bearing caps are correctly marked, starting from the timing cover end. Undo and remove them, keeping them in the correct order.

TOP TIP!

• A narrow contact band means high pressure on the seat and longer valve life.
• A wide contact band reduces the contact pressure and induces early valve seat burning.

CHAPTER 6 Part A Jobs 13-14

TOP TIP!

☐ **STEP 7:**
- If any of the caps are difficult to remove, lever the bolt holes with a bar, or a pair of bars - or a pair of fixing bolts, and tap carefully with a hammer.
- Bearing shells are best removed by sliding them out with your thumbs, pushing the tab-end out first.
- DON'T try to lever them out - it won't work!

☐ **STEP 8:** Retrieve the thrust washers from each side of the centre main bearing cap.

☐ **STEP 9:** When lifting the crankshaft clear of the cylinder block, look out for 'stray' bearing shells or thrust washers falling into the block.

JOB 13: PISTON RINGS - *fitting*.

☐ **STEP 1:** Make sure that the bores and pistons are clean, then fit the rings, preferably using a piston ring spreader. Make sure the rings are fitted with the word 'TOP' facing upwards.

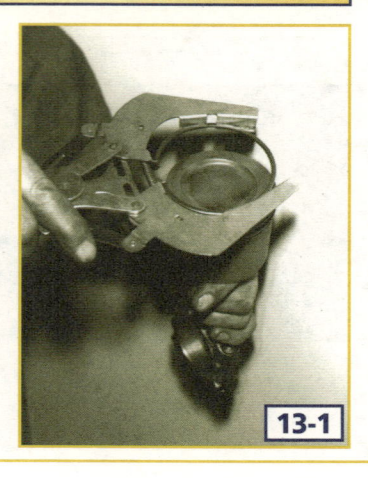

☐ **STEP 2:** If you don't have access to a piston ring spreader, work the rings down a little at a time, using a feeler gauge or gauges to bridge the gaps. Piston rings are very brittle, very easy to break and are expensive to replace!

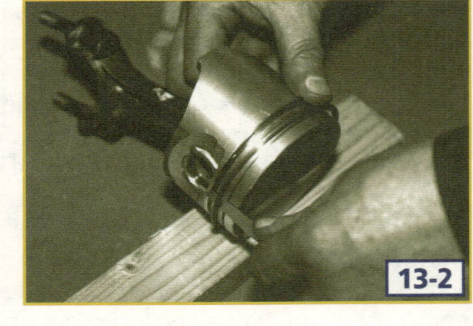

☐ **STEP 3:** Fit the piston rings with their gaps disposed at equal intervals round the piston circumference and lubricate them well.

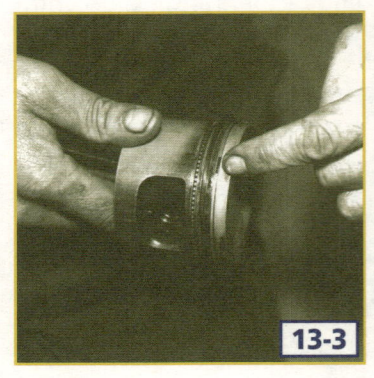

JOB 14: PISTONS – *removing, refitting*.

Pistons may be held to connecting rods by different methods - see relevant section of manual. However, refitting a piston into its cylinder bore is always as described here:

TOP TIP!

- Wrap insulation tape, or a short piece of plastic tube, over each conrod thread, so that it cannot damage the crank as it goes in.

☐ **STEP 1:** Locate a ring clamp over the piston rings and tighten enough to close the ring gaps, but not too tight! Lubricate the rings so that they compress and slide easily within the clamp.

☐ **STEP 2:** Position the assembly in its correct bore with the connecting rod identification marks facing each other and also so that the complete piston/conrod assemblies face the right way.

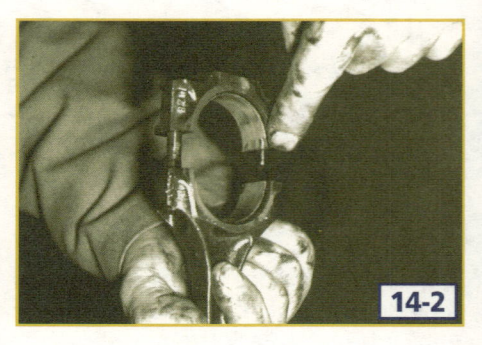

6-8

☐ **STEP 3:** With the ring clamp touching the cylinder block, use a hammer shaft to carefully tap the piston through and into the bore.

14-3

> **TOP TIP!**
> • Turn the crankshaft so that the journal for the connecting rod you are working on is at bottom dead-centre. Now the connecting rod will line up with its crank journal.

☐ **STEP 4:** Locate the upper half of the big end shell bearing in the conrod, making sure that the mating surfaces are clean. Lubricate the crankpin and the big-end shell and draw the conrod down the bore so that the big end locates with the crankpin. Fit the other half of the big-end shell to the bearing cap and lubricate. Offer the cap to the connecting rod and make sure that the numbers match. Screw in the fixing bolts and tighten progressively to the correct torque.

14-4

JOB 15: ENGINE COMPONENTS – *checking, measuring for wear.*

GENERAL

All parts must be thoroughly cleaned before inspection. Keep them in the right order for re-assembly in case they are to be re used. Check each component as follows:

CYLINDER BLOCK

☐ **STEP 1:** Look for any cracks or evidence of gas or water blow-by on both sides of the gasket, on the cylinder head and in the block casting, particularly at bolt holes and between cylinders. Note that certain all-aluminium engines covered by this manual do not have a conventional solid cylinder block, but instead have an open aluminium crankcase into which steel cylinders (liners) are placed.

15-1

☐ **STEP 2:** Check the bores as follows:
→ Check for score marks, caused by burned pistons or broken rings.
→ Check for a wear ridge just below the top of the bore where the top piston ring ends its travel.
→ If you have access to a suitable internal micrometer, measure the bores at the points shown. Otherwise, ask your engine specialist to measure the bores for wear if there is any evidence of a wear ridge.

15-2

☐ **STEP 3:** Assuming the bores to be in reasonable condition, it is sometimes possible to 'glaze bust' the bores and fit new piston rings. If not, the cylinders will have to be rebored, though it should be noted that all-aluminium engines with separate cylinder 'liners' cannot have their liners rebored, and a new set of liners and pistons needs to be bought.

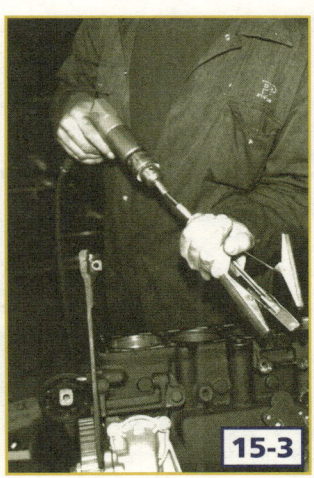

15-3

> **TOP TIP!**
> ☐ **STEP 4:** You can't check for bore ovality like this, but you can gain a good idea of overall wear:
> • Push each piston ring squarely into the cylinder until it is about 15 mm from the bottom edge where no wear will have taken place.
> • Measure the ring gap with a feeler gauge.
> • Now carry out the same check on the most badly worn parts of the bore and see how much wear has taken place.

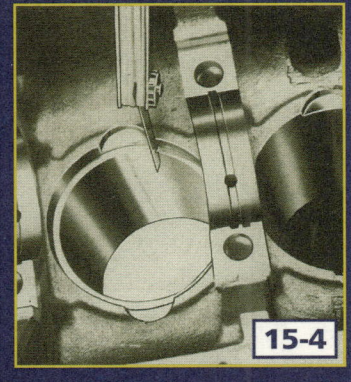

15-4

CHAPTER 6 Part A Job 15

6-9

☐ **STEP 5:** You will need a suitably large external micrometer to measure the pistons. Check about 15 mm from the bottom of the skirt.

☐ **STEP 6:** Check the piston ring clearances with a set of feeler gauges.

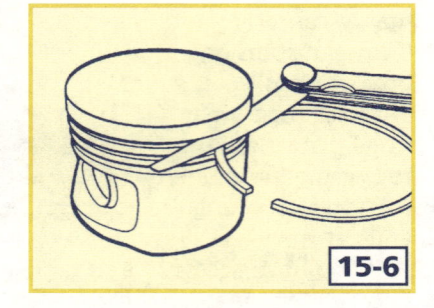

CRANKSHAFT

☐ **STEP 7:** Check the main journals and crankpins:
➜ for any signs of wear ridges round the circumference or scoring of the surface.
➜ for ovality, using a suitable micrometer, although the precision Vernier gauge shown here will give an excellent guide.

☐ **STEP 8:** Check the shell bearings, which should have an even, dull grey finish, like the ones shown here.

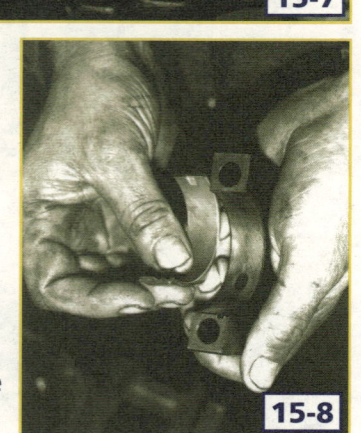

☐ **STEP 9:** If the leaded layer is scored or has worn through to the copper coloured backing, or if the crankshaft has any of the previously mentioned faults, the crankshaft should be reground by your specialist who will also supply the new shell bearings and thrust washers.

☐ **STEP 10:** Check the crankshaft end float by using a feeler gauge between the thrust washer and the crankshaft.

☐ **STEP 11:** If an engine is being rebuilt, a new oil pump should be fitted as a matter of course. However, if you are checking a stripped engine to see how badly worn it is, include the oil pump in those checks. Any scoring of the oil pump rotors, or the bore in which they run, is unacceptable, and will cause a lowering of engine oil pressure. If any such wear is evident, renew the complete oil pump.

CAMSHAFT

Check the following:

☐ **STEP 12:** Check each cam lobe for wear, which can be quite rapid once started. If you replace the camshaft, fit new followers as well.

☐ **STEP 13:** Cam followers (or rockers) should also be checked, particularly where they contact the cam lobe.

☐ **STEP 14:** Check all camshaft bearings and their corresponding surfaces in the housing for a smooth, shiny surface without wear ridges.

JOB 16: REASSEMBLING ENGINE COMPONENTS - *lubrication*.

If you start a rebuilt engine up 'dry', severe damage may be caused well before the engine oil has had time to circulate. Metal-to-metal surfaces will 'pick up' and rubber seals will be torn out.

You should keep an oil can with fresh engine oil in it next to you while you are reassembling an engine.

Alternatively, you can use purpose-made assembly lubricant. But DON'T use a friction-reducer meant for adding to engine oil. It may prevent the engine from bedding in properly.

❏ **STEP 1:** Apply copious amounts of lubricant to every rotating, rubbing and oil seal surface as the assembly takes place. You CAN'T over-lubricate!

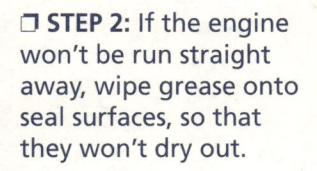

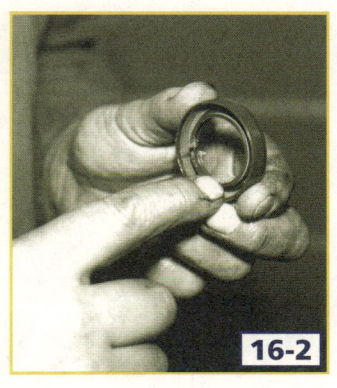

❏ **STEP 2:** If the engine won't be run straight away, wipe grease onto seal surfaces, so that they won't dry out.

❏ **STEP 3:** Fill the oil pump housing with as much fresh engine oil as it will take, so that the pump itself is lubricated and so that it delivers fresh oil to the engine as quickly as possible.

Before starting the engine, fit a fully charged battery and crank the engine over with spark plugs (or diesel pre-heaters) removed, so that the engine will spin rapidly without starting and without putting strain on the bearings. Turn the engine on the starter for around 30 seconds to circulate oil to the bearings, before starting up.

SAFETY FIRST!

• Make sure that it is safe to spin the engine with HT leads disconnected on your particular engine.
• Some ignition systems may suffer damage if not first completely disconnected.
• Take care not to cause injury from uncontrolled high tension sparks.

JOB 17: REASSEMBLING ENGINE COMPONENTS - *clearances*.

Specific assembly details are given in the relevant section of this manual, but it's well worth pointing out some general information, especially with regard to fitting the crankshaft bearings:

IMPORTANT NOTES: The following points should be regarded as essential and not optional!
• You should change the oil pump when carrying out an engine overhaul.
• All bearings, shells, piston rings and ALL seals that bear on moving parts MUST be copiously lubricated with fresh engine oil as the engine is being reassembled.

• Work ONLY in clean conditions, with clean components and clean hands.
• Re-assemble in the reverse order of the dismantling procedure and take note of the following steps which will help you carry out a smooth operation.

❏ **STEP 1:** Make sure you have all the necessary gaskets, available from your Peugeot dealership in complete sets.

TOP TIP!

• If the centre main bearing has separate thrust washers, apply grease to the smooth side of the thrust washers and 'stick' them in position each side of the centre main bearing, before lowering the crank into position.

❏ **STEP 2:** Make sure all bearing seats are perfectly clean and locate the shells so that their tabs engage with the slots. Once lubricated, a shell can be placed on a journal and pushed around into its correct position.

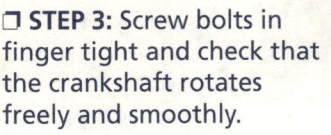

❏ **STEP 3:** Screw bolts in finger tight and check that the crankshaft rotates freely and smoothly.

❏ **STEP 4:** Tighten each bolt evenly and progressively until the specified torque setting is reached. Check after tightening EACH bearing that the crankshaft rotates smoothly. If it doesn't, remove the bearing cap and shells and investigate as follows:
➔ Check that there is no dirt or debris under a bearing shell – the most likely cause.
➔ The next most likely cause is that there has been a build up of carbon on the rim of a seating and/or cap. Scrape off any that is present.
➔ Check that the shells supplied are the right size for any machining that may have been carried out.

❏ **STEP 5:** The checks described in *Step 4* will only tell you if a bearing is too tight; it won't tell you if one is too loose.

Part B: Which Engine is Which?

CONTENTS

	Page No.		Page No.
JOB 1: UNDERSTAND ENGINE TYPES.	6-12	JOB 2: UNDERSTAND CYLINDER HEAD TYPES.	6-13

JOB 1: UNDERSTAND ENGINE TYPES.

There's no point in talking exclusively about individual Peugeot vehicle models covered by this manual, because very similar engines are used across different models. There are five broad engine types fitted to the vehicles covered here, all of four-cylinder, overhead camshaft design. These are known as the XV, XW, XY type, the XU (petrol) and XUD (diesel) type, the TU (petrol) and TUD (diesel) type. Note that the illustrations show the position of the engine identification numbers, which include the exact engine type, and the engine build code.

IMPORTANT NOTE: In several of the following drawings, the locations of the engine type number (**1**) and the engine serial number (**2**) are shown.

XV, XW, XY PETROL ENGINES

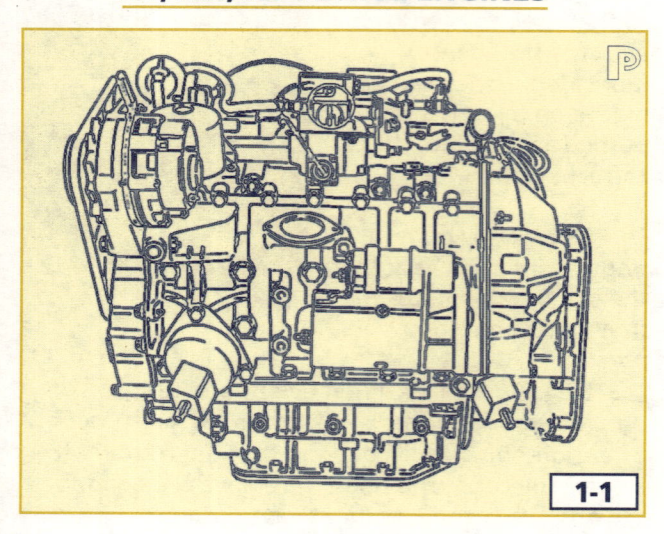

1-1

☐ **STEP 1:** The smaller engines from 954cc, through 1124cc, to 1360cc. These engine capacities are shared with the TU series engines, which replaced the 'X' family towards the end of the Eighties. The 'X' family engines have a unique layout and are characterised by being all-aluminium with a chain-driven camshaft, and mounted at an acute angle (almost 'lying down') in the engine bay. They are equipped with a gears-in-sump manual transmission that uses an idler-gear train to pass drive from engine to transmission. These engines have rocker-type screw-adjustable tappets.

TU PETROL ENGINES

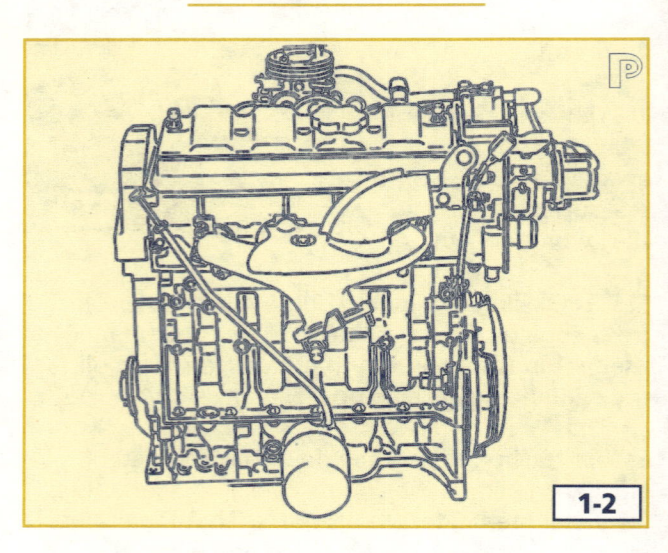

1-2

☐ **STEP 2:** Mounted vertically, unlike the XV, XW, XY family, the TU comes in capacities of 954cc, 1124cc, 1294cc, 1360cc and 1587cc. All but the 1587cc version are all-aluminium, where the crankcase (block) is of the open type with 'wet' cylinder liners inserted. The 1587cc TU engine has a conventional cast iron cylinder block. Camshaft drive on all is by toothed belt, and these engines have rocker-type screw-adjustable tappets.

XU PETROL ENGINES

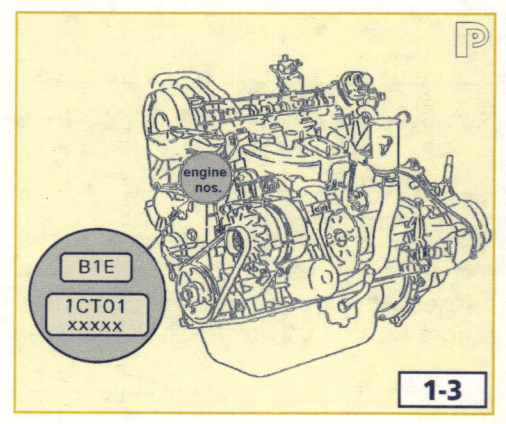

☐ **STEP 3:** Generally larger petrol engines of 1580cc, 1761cc, 1905cc and 1998cc, with aluminium block, 'wet' cylinder liners and cylinder head on all but the 1998cc. This largest XU engine uses a conventional cast iron block with no separate bore liners. All types have a toothed belt type camshaft drive, and shim-adjustable bucket-type tappets acted on directly by the overhead camshaft.

1-3

TUD DIESEL ENGINES

☐ **STEP 4:** These are diesel versions of the TU petrol engines, in two capacities – 1360cc and 1527cc. They are of all aluminium 'wet' liner construction, using separate cylinder liners in an open crankcase. Camshaft drive is by toothed belt, and the tappets are shim-adjustable buckets, acted on directly by the overhead camshaft.

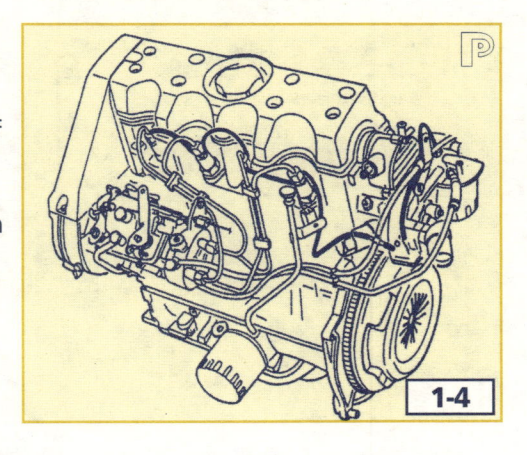

1-4

XUD DIESEL ENGINES

☐ **STEP 5:** These are diesel versions of the XU petrol engines, in two capacities – 1769cc and 1905cc – both available in turbocharged and non-turbocharged guises. They are of cast iron block, aluminium alloy cylinder head construction, with camshaft drive by toothed belt, and bucket-type shim-adjustable tappets acted on directly by the overhead camshaft.

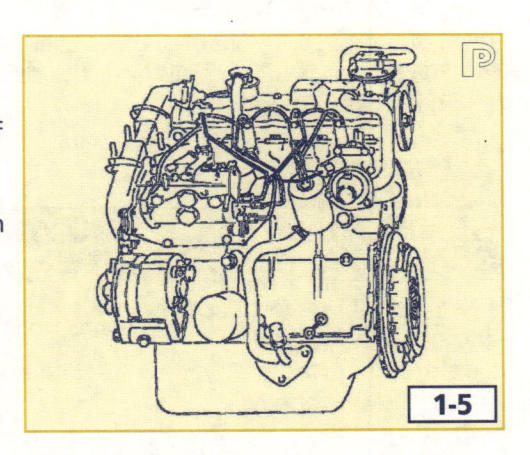

1-5

JOB 2: UNDERSTAND CYLINDER HEAD TYPES.

All engines have overhead camshafts (OHC) and can have one of two basic types of cylinder head:

HEAD WITH SCREW-ADJUSTED VALVES

This is the type of cylinder head fitted to the XV, XW, XY series petrol engines (in the 205) and to the TU petrol engines used across various models.
→ The camshaft runs in bearings formed in the head casting, and a rocker shaft assembly is fitted above it.
→ Exhaust and inlet manifolds are on the opposite sides of the head, and the distributor is horizontal – fitted on the end of the head.

HEAD WITH SHIM-ADJUSTED VALVES

→ This is the type of cylinder head fitted to the XU petrol and TUD diesel engines used across various models.
→ The camshaft runs in lower bearings formed in the head casting, and upper bearings that are separate caps bolted to the head.
→ The camshaft acts directly on bucket type tappets positioned over the valves. On the TUD diesel engine the adjustment shims for setting valve clearances are sited on top of the bucket tappets, while on the XU petrol they are between the buckets and the valve stems.
→ On XU engines the distributor is horizontal – fitted to the end of the head.

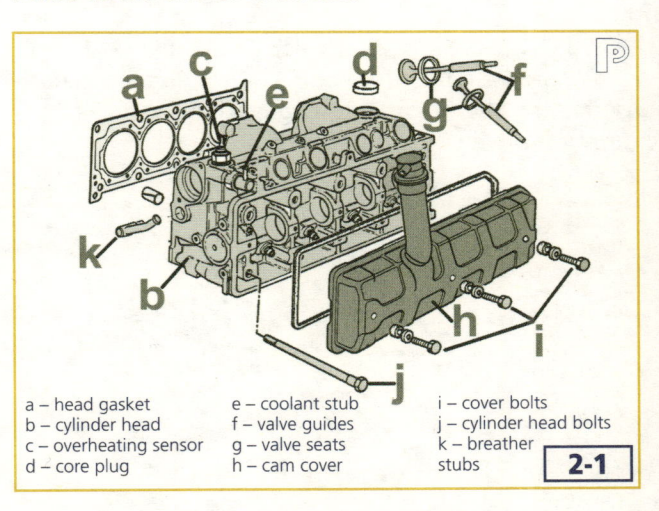

2-1
a – head gasket
b – cylinder head
c – overheating sensor
d – core plug
e – coolant stub
f – valve guides
g – valve seats
h – cam cover
i – cover bolts
j – cylinder head bolts
k – breather stubs

☐ **ILLUSTRATION 1: XV, XW, XY ENGINE CYLINDER HEAD:** This is the cylinder head of 1.0-litre to 1.4-litre petrol engines used in the 205 until 1988. XV, XW, XY engines have the camshaft driven by chain.

☐ **ILLUSTRATION 2: TU ENGINE CYLINDER HEAD:** This is the cylinder head of 1.0-litre to 1.4-litre petrol engines used in the 106 and 205 from 1988, and the 1.1 to 1.6-litre petrol engines used in the 306 from 1993, and the 206. TU engines have the camshaft driven by toothed belt.

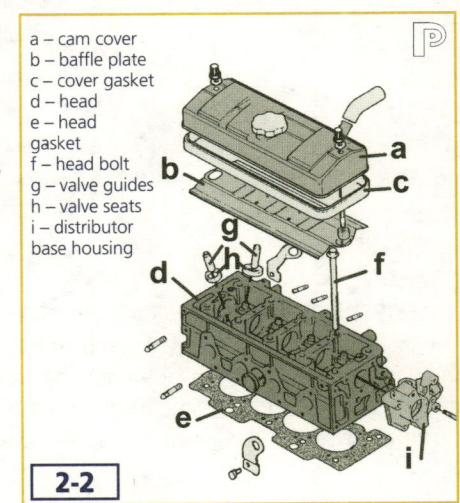

2-2
a – cam cover
b – baffle plate
c – cover gasket
d – head
e – head gasket
f – head bolt
g – valve guides
h – valve seats
i – distributor base housing

CHAPTER 6 Part B Job 2

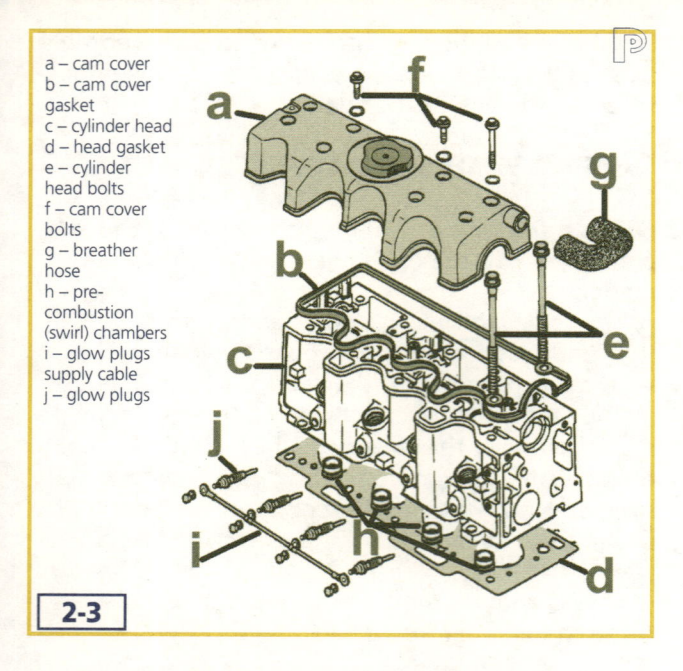

Illustration 2-3 labels:
- a – cam cover
- b – cam cover gasket
- c – cylinder head
- d – head gasket
- e – cylinder head bolts
- f – cam cover bolts
- g – breather hose
- h – pre-combustion (swirl) chambers
- i – glow plugs supply cable
- j – glow plugs

ILLUSTRATION 3: TUD ENGINE CYLINDER HEAD: This is the cylinder head of 1.4 and 1.5-litre diesel engines used in the 106 range. TUD engines have the camshaft driven by toothed belt.

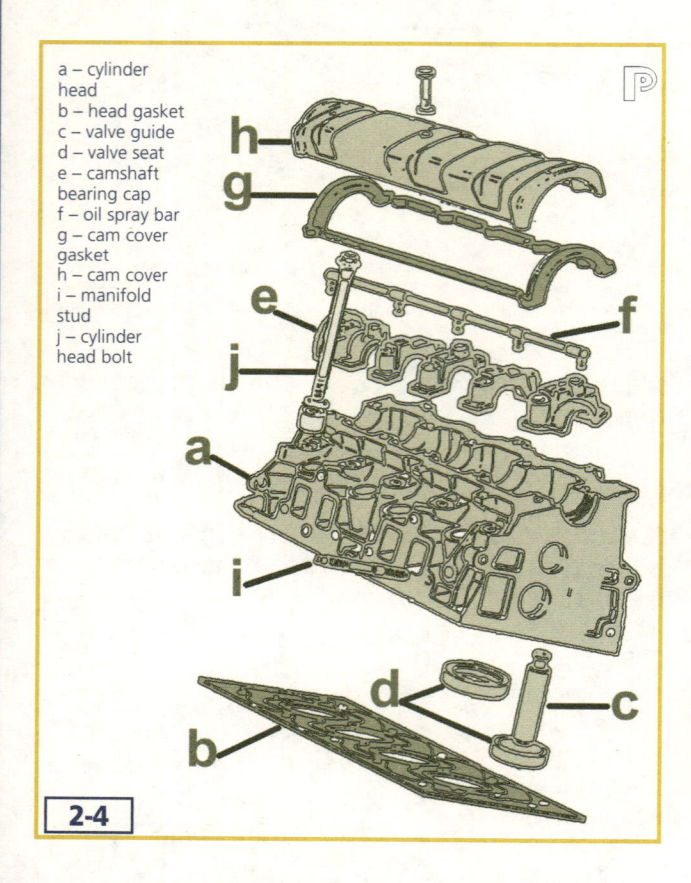

Illustration 2-4 labels:
- a – cylinder head
- b – head gasket
- c – valve guide
- d – valve seat
- e – camshaft bearing cap
- f – oil spray bar
- g – cam cover gasket
- h – cam cover
- i – manifold stud
- j – cylinder head bolt

ILLUSTRATION 4: XU ENGINE CYLINDER HEAD: This is the cylinder head of 1.6 and 1.9-litre petrol engines used in the 205 range, as well as that of the 8-valve engines of 1.8 and 2.0-litre engines used in the 306. XU engines have the camshaft driven by toothed belt.

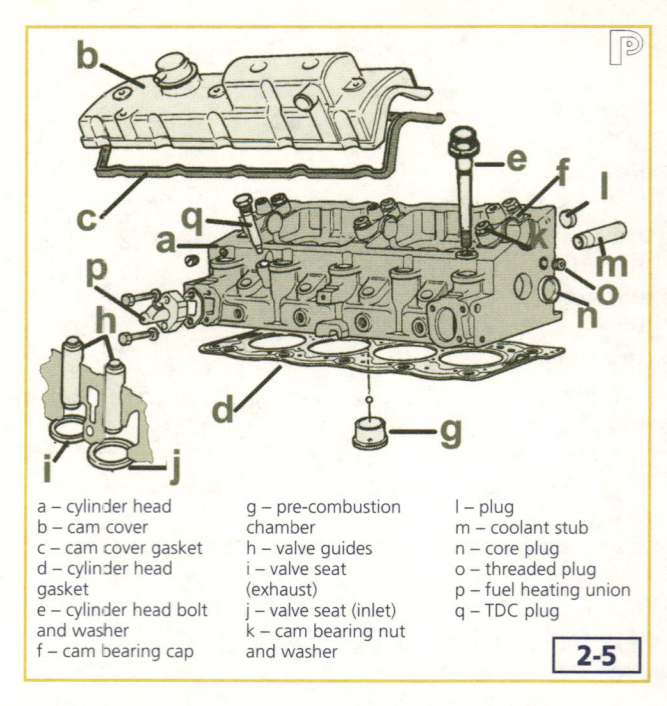

Illustration 2-5 labels:
- a – cylinder head
- b – cam cover
- c – cam cover gasket
- d – cylinder head gasket
- e – cylinder head bolt and washer
- f – cam bearing cap
- g – pre-combustion chamber
- h – valve guides
- i – valve seat (exhaust)
- j – valve seat (inlet)
- k – cam bearing nut and washer
- l – plug
- m – coolant stub
- n – core plug
- o – threaded plug
- p – fuel heating union
- q – TDC plug

ILLUSTRATION 5: XUD ENGINE CYLINDER HEAD: This is the cylinder head of the 1.8 and 1.9-litre turbo and non-turbo diesel engines used in the 205 and 306 ranges. XUD engines have the camshaft driven by toothed belt.

FACT FILE
GENERAL CYLINDER HEAD REMOVAL INFORMATION!

- The cylinder head can be removed with the engine in the vehicle.
- Before removing the cylinder head, make sure the engine is stone cold.
- Undo the cylinder head bolts strictly in the order laid out in the relevant section.
- These precautions help to prevent cylinder head distortion.
- The new cylinder head gasket should stay in its packaging until required, to avoid contamination by oil or grease.

SAFETY FIRST!

- Disconnect both battery leads, negative (-) terminal first.

6-14

Part C: Timing Belt or Chain
Inspection, Adjustment, Replacement
CONTENTS

	Page No.		Page No.
JOB 1: CAMSHAFT TIMING BELT - *check*.	6-15	**JOB 4:** VALVE TIMING	
JOB 2: CAMSHAFT TIMING BELT		– *locking camshaft and crankshaft*.	6-23
– *replacement, adjustment (engine in vehicle)*.	6-16	**JOB 5:** XV, XW, XY ENGINES, TIMING CHAIN	
JOB 3: TIMING BELT		– *replacement*.	6-25
– *replacement, adjustment (engine out)*.	6-23		

See *Part B: Which Engine is Which?* for an explanation of the engine types referred to here.
➔ Note that the XV, XW, XY series engines have a chain driven camshaft and so do not required scheduled timing belt checks or replacement.
➔ For signs of timing chain wear on stripdown, see *Part A: General Procedures*.

JOB 1: CAMSHAFT TIMING BELT - *check*.

It is ESSENTIAL that the camshaft drive belt is renewed at the recommended interval. See the *Service Interval Chart* at the start of *Chapter 5, Servicing*. If the belt breaks, the valves may collide with the pistons, causing serious engine damage. At the very least, the engine will immediately stop running. *Job 2: Camshaft timing belt - replacement and adjustment* explains how to carry out the work.

SAFETY FIRST!

• Disconnect the battery negative (-) earth/ground terminal. See *Chapter 10, Electrical, Dash, Instruments, Fact File: Disconnecting the Battery* BEFORE doing so!
• Make sure that you have the code for the radio (if coded) before disconnecting.

❑ **STEP 1: CURSORY INSPECTION:** Detach any hoses that are secured to the timing belt cover, then unclip or unscrew the top of the camshaft belt outer cover and pull it away. Examine the belt for wear. This inspection will only show severe damage.

❑ **STEP 2:** In order to examine the belt properly, you will have to remove the cover. If there is any cracking, or if the toothed side appears worn, or any 'teeth' are missing, replace the belt straight away.

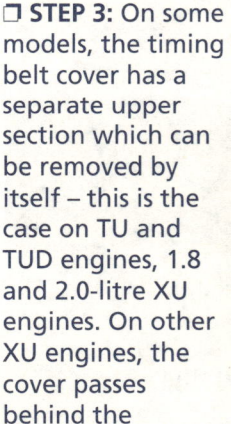

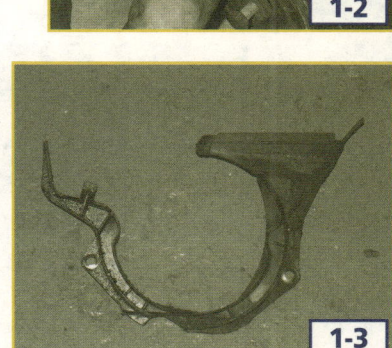

❑ **STEP 3:** On some models, the timing belt cover has a separate upper section which can be removed by itself – this is the case on TU and TUD engines, 1.8 and 2.0-litre XU engines. On other XU engines, the cover passes behind the crankshaft pulley. If you have to remove the crank pulley, on some models – namely those that do not have a removeable access panel under the right-hand wheelarch, it is necessary to disconnect the right-hand engine mountings and lower the engine - supporting it on a trolley jack - so that the bottom pulley can be unbolted and removed, after first removing the auxiliary drive belt - V-shaped on some, a flat ribbed belt on others.

❑ **STEP 4:** If the belt is in good condition, it may still need re-tensioning.
➔ **EITHER:** Check that you can twist the belt through approximately 90 degrees (45 degrees for diesels) at the

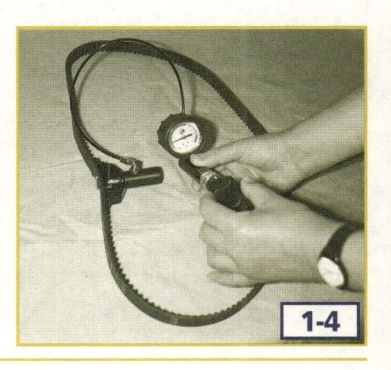

centre of its longest 'run' between camshaft sprocket and crankshaft sprocket, using only the strength of fingers and thumb.
→ **OR:** Use the correct tool, such as this Sykes-Pickavant tension checking tool – used with the belt *in situ*, of course! If necessary, slacken the adjuster fixing nut and re-adjust as shown in *Job 2*.

| JOB 2: | CAMSHAFT TIMING BELT – *replacement, adjustment (engine in vehicle).* |

On all engines, the cam belt should be renewed at the recommended interval. If it breaks, the engine will suffer total failure and could be catastrophically damaged.

SAFETY FIRST!

• Disconnect the battery negative (-) earth/ground terminal. See *Chapter 10, Electrical, Dash, Instruments, Fact File: Disconnecting the Battery* BEFORE doing so!
• Make sure that you have the code for the radio (if coded) before disconnecting.

TOP TIP!

• We recommend that, if an engine has been standing for two years or more, you should replace the belt as a matter of course, because it will be prone to early failure.

IMPORTANT NOTE: Avoid potential major problems by following this advice:
→ In some engines – and certainly all the diesel engines - the valves will collide with the pistons if the camshaft/s is/are turned while the engine is set to Top Dead Centre (TDC).
→ To avoid risk of damage, the camshaft/s should NEVER be replaced (or turned if already in place) while the pistons are at TDC.
→ Always turn the engine in the normal direction of rotation when aligning shafts prior to belt removal.

Section A: TU petrol engines.

NOTE: 206 models are fitted with an engine undershield held by four peripheral bolts and four peripheral screws. The undershield should be removed before carrying out the following work.

❑ **STEP A1:** Slacken the alternator and remove the external belt(s). Remove the alternator (if necessary - certain models). See *Part D: Auxiliary Drive Belts*.

❑ **STEP A2:** Undo the retaining bolts and remove the timing belt upper cover (a). Detach any wiring/hoses from the timing belt centre cover, then remove the retaining bolts from the centre cover and lift off the cover.

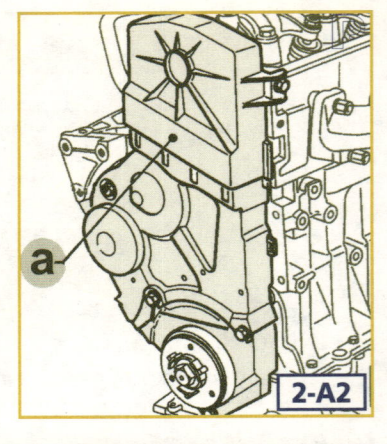

2-A2

❑ **STEP A3:** Undo the three crankshaft pulley retaining bolts (arrowed), and remove the pulley, making a note of which way round it fits.

2-A3

→ Note that on some models access is made easier via an under-wheelarch access panel.
→ Remove the retaining bolts of the timing belt lower cover (between one and three, depending on model), and withdraw the cover over the crankshaft nose.

TOP TIP!

• As the timing belt of the TU engine also drives the water pump, it is advisable to check the condition of the pump when renewing the belt.
• Feel for up and down movement of the pump sprocket (bearing wear) and look for evidence of coolant leaks from behind the sprocket.
• If you have difficulty gaining access to the crankshaft pulley and the lower sections of the timing belt cover, you may find it helps to disconnect the right-hand side engine mountings and lower the engine - supporting it on a trolley jack - so that the bottom pulley can be unbolted and removed, after first removing the auxiliary drive belt - V-shaped on some; a flat ribbed belt on others.

❑ **STEP A4:** Set the camshaft and crankshaft to the 'locked' position - see *Job 4*.

IMPORTANT NOTE: The crankshaft and camshaft must not be turned independently of each other, or the valves may collide with the pistons.

❑ **STEP A5:** Slacken the central retaining nut of the timing belt tensioner wheel.
→ Now identify the square recess (arrowed) in the tensioner body.

❑ **STEP A6:** Use a square-section shaft inserted in the square recess in the tensioner to rotate the tensioner (clockwise) and relieve belt tension.
→ You can now lock the tensioner in this position by retightening the central nut.

❑ **STEP A7:** Slide the timing belt carefully off the sprockets and take care not to rotate any of the toothed pulleys.

❑ **STEP A8:** Slide on the new timing belt, making sure that any direction arrows marked on the belt indicate the normal direction of rotation (clockwise) of the engine.
→ Item (**a**) is the tensioner, moved out of the way.
→ Item (**b**) is the camshaft locking pin.

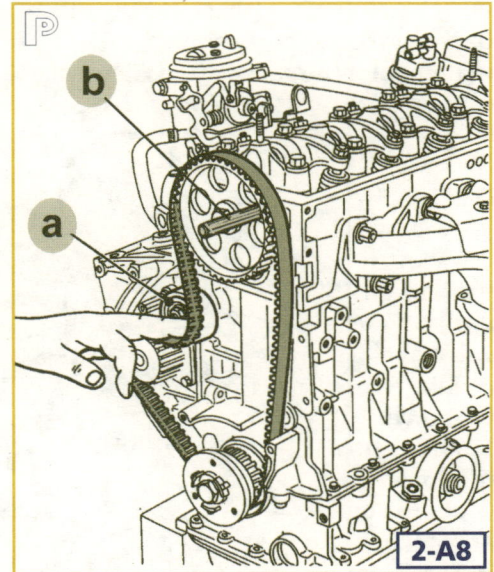

TOP TIP!

• Fitting the belt almost invariably means that a sprocket or sprockets have to move slightly away from the precise position on their alignment marks, so that the teeth on the belt can slide on to the teeth on the sprockets. This is normal - nothing to worry about!

❑ **STEP A9:** Make sure that all the slack in the new belt is between the water pump and camshaft sprockets (and that the run between camshaft and crankshaft sprockets is taut) then tension the belt by undoing the tensioner centre nut and swinging the tensioner pulley anti-clockwise against the belt to take up all slack…
→ **EITHER:** until you can only just turn the belt through 90 degrees, using thumb and forefinger, half way along the run of belt between camshaft and crankshaft sprockets. Tighten the centre nut.
→ **OR:** use the correct tool, such as the Sykes-Pickavant tension checking tool shown in *Job 1, Step 4*.
→ This illustration shows the correct Peugeot tool (**a**) with a 1.5 kg weight (**b**) correctly tensioning the belt as the nut is retightened.
→ In all cases, the crank- and camshaft locking pins are removed before adjusting.

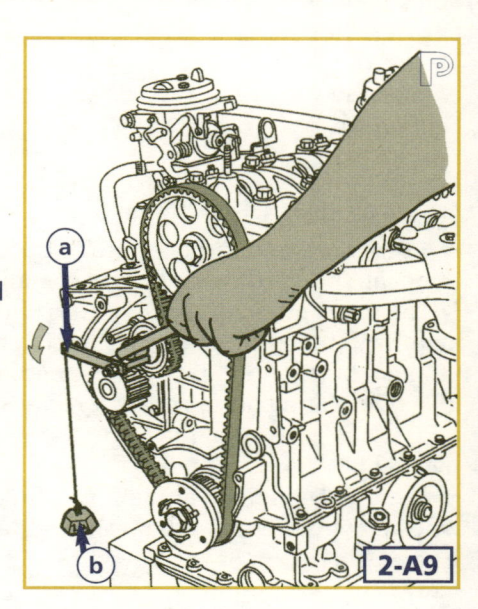

❑ **STEP A10:** To settle the new timing belt into position, rotate the crankshaft through two whole revolutions and recheck/reset the tension.

❑ **STEP A11:** Replace the timing belt covers and other components removed earlier.

TOP TIP!

• If there is a growling noise which rises and falls with the engine speed, the belt tension may be too tight.

Section B: TU diesel engines.

☐ **STEP B1:** The job of belt replacement and adjustment is as given for TU petrol engines (see *Section A*), but with the following important differences:

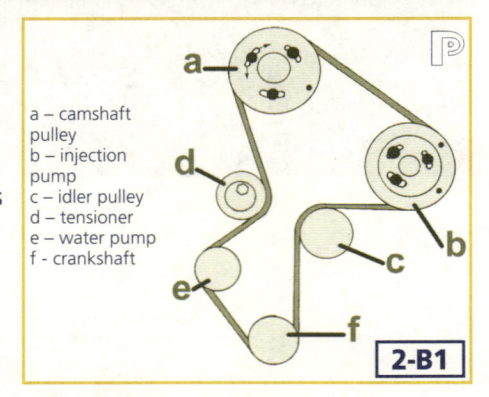

a – camshaft pulley
b – injection pump
c – idler pulley
d – tensioner
e – water pump
f – crankshaft

2-B1

➔ There are three sprockets to lock prior to belt removal, the third being that of the injection pump.
➔ The injection pump sprocket has two holes which align with holes in the pump sprocket backplate.
➔ 8 mm bolts or drill bits can be used for locking the injection pump and camshaft sprockets, while a 6 mm bolt or bit is required to do the same job at the flywheel.
➔ Some TUD-engined models have an under-wheelarch rubber plug that can be levered loose to give access to one of the timing belt centre-cover screws.
➔ Correct timing belt tension on the TUD diesel is even more critical than on the TU petrol engine. If you do not have special tooling for this, and you are relying on the 'belt-twist' test previously mentioned, the amount of twist acceptable (gauged halfway between the camshaft and injection pump sprockets) should be 45 degrees.
➔ IMPORTANT NOTE: If the TUD diesel has its belt tension tested 'by hand' in this way, then the vehicle should only be driven gently at low revs, and straight to a dealer or specialist who can verify and if necessary, correct the tension, using the requisite Peugeot special tool.

TOP TIP!

• As the diesel engine can be more difficult to rotate, due to its higher compression, it helps to remove the glow plugs from the engine first - see *Chapter 9, Ignition, Fuel, Exhaust*.

Section C: XU petrol engines.

☐ **STEP C1:** Slacken the alternator adjustment bolts and remove the external belt(s).
➔ Remove the alternator (if necessary, certain models) and, if fitted, unbolt the external belt tensioner device - see *Part D: Auxiliary Drive Belts*.

☐ **STEP C2:** If your vehicle has an under-wheelarch access panel, remove this, and push the radiator bottom hose away from the crankshaft pulley, lodging it under the sump.

☐ **STEP C3:** If the vehicle has no access panel, support the right-hand end of the engine with a trolley jack (use wood between jack pad and engine to avoid damage).
➔ Detach the right-hand side upper engine mounting (three nuts retaining right-hand engine mounting bracket, one nut retaining bracket to mounting rubber, and three bolts retaining bracket to engine and cylinder head – see *Steps C5A* and *C5B*). You can now, when ready, lower the right-hand side of the engine/transmission unit on the jack, to gain access to the crankshaft pulley.

☐ **STEP C4:** Unbolt/unclip and remove the timing belt cover sections (**c** and **d**).
➔ Note that there are differing designs of timing cover assembly used on the XU series petrol engines.
➔ On later engines, there is a thrust washer (**e**) beneath the lower cover (**d**).
➔ Item (**a**) is the camshaft locking pin; (**b**) is the belt tensioner.

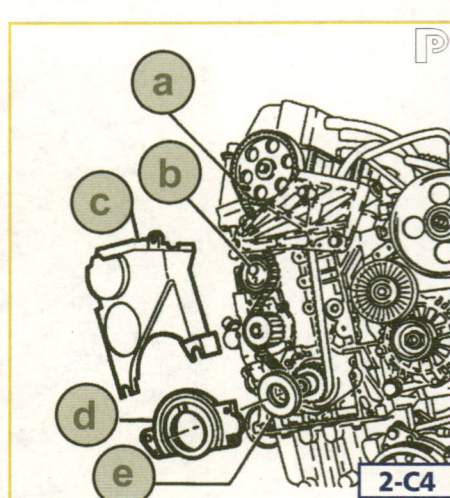

2-C4

☐ **STEP C5A:** Set the camshaft to the 'locked' position - see *Job 4*.
➔ Take note of the type of timing belt tensioner fitted to your engine.
➔ This is the earlier type with spring plunger roller...

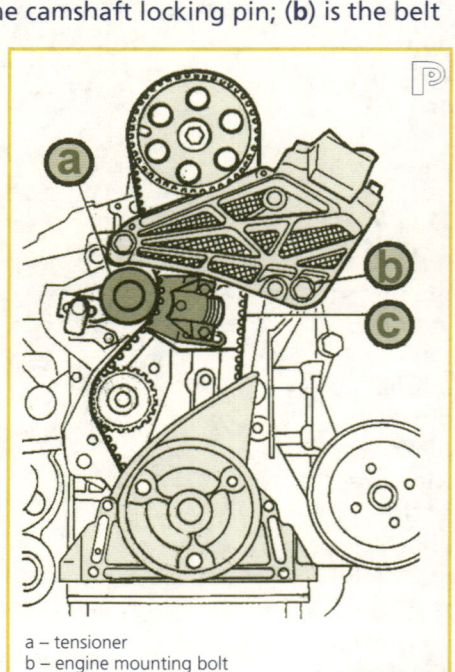

a – tensioner
b – engine mounting bolt
c – timing belt

2-C5A

❏ **STEP C5B:** ...and this is the later, off-centre roller type.

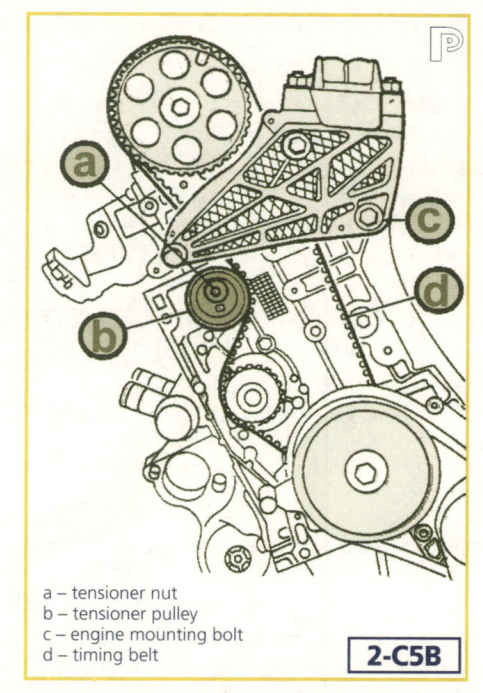

a – tensioner nut
b – tensioner pulley
c – engine mounting bolt
d – timing belt

2-C5B

❏ **STEP C6:** Working underneath the clutch housing, undo the bolts that secure the metal clutch inspection plate to the bellhousing, and remove the plate.
→ Now jam the starter ring-gear teeth against a bellhousing boss using a very large screwdriver, to prevent the engine from turning.
→ Using a suitable socket, undo the crankshaft pulley centre bolt, withdraw the pulley and bolt, and collect the Woodruff key, which keys the pulley to the crankshaft nose.
→ If the crankshaft pulley is difficult to withdraw, this is most likely because of corrosion between pulley and crankshaft nose. A two- or three-legged puller will be needed to coax the pulley off.

MODELS WITH SPRING-PLUNGER TENSIONER

❏ **STEP C7:** Loosen the two retaining nuts at top and bottom of the tensioner plunger body - see *2-C5A*.

❏ **STEP C8:** Loosen the tensioner cam locknut (b), located at the rear of the cylinder block flange (which juts out from the rear side of the cylinder block).
→ Use a spanner on the squared-end (a) of the tensioner cam adjustment shaft (jutting out from rear side of cylinder block flange) to rotate the cam until it fully compresses the tensioner spring, then retighten the adjuster locknut.

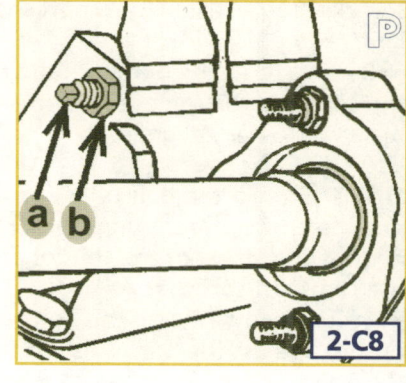

MODELS WITH OFF-CENTRE ROLLER TENSIONER

❏ **STEP C9:** Loosen the tensioner roller nut (see illustration *2-A5*) to take tension off the belt.

BOTH TENSIONER TYPES

IMPORTANT NOTE: The crankshaft and camshaft must not be turned or the valves may collide with the pistons.

> **TOP TIP!**
> • As the timing belt of the XU engine also drives the water pump, it is advisable to check the condition of the pump when renewing the belt, feeling for up and down movement of the pump sprocket (bearing wear) and looking for evidence of coolant leaks from behind the sprocket.

❏ **STEP C10:** Slide the timing belt carefully off the sprockets – see illustration *2-A7*.

MODELS WITH SPRING-PLUNGER TENSIONER

❏ **STEP C11:** Slide the new belt onto the crankshaft sprocket first, then refit the crankshaft pulley, and check (using the locating rods - see *Job 4*) that the crankshaft is still in the correct position, as previously set.

❏ **STEP C12:** These lines are timing marks that line up with corresponding dot-punch marks on the camshaft and crankshaft

CHAPTER 6 Part C Job 2

6-19

sprocket respectively (camshaft shown in illustration).

→ Be sure to fit the belt with the arrows indicating the correct direction of rotation and with the timing marks (arrowed) aligned.

❑ **STEP C13:** Fit the belt fully: first around the outside of the water pump sprocket, then its back against the inside of the tensioner roller, then on to the camshaft sprocket.

→ You can now release the belt tensioner so that it pushes against the belt. This is done by slackening the adjuster cam locknut and rotating the cam (see illustration *2-C8*) to allow the tensioner spring to expand.

→ Retighten the adjuster locknut, and also tighten the top and bottom nuts of the tensioner body.

TOP TIP!

- Fitting the belt almost invariably means that a sprocket or sprockets have to move slightly away from the precise position on their alignment marks, so that the teeth on the belt can slide on to the teeth on the sprockets. This is normal - nothing to worry about!

❑ **STEP C14:** Withdraw the locating rods used for locking the sprockets, then rotate the crankshaft fully by two revolutions, using a socket and drive on the crankshaft pulley centre bolt. This will settle the belt and tensioner.

❑ **STEP C15:** Loosen the tensioner body top and bottom nuts (illustration *2-C5, item A*), then retighten them. Now turn the crankshaft further in the correct direction of rotation until the holes in and behind the camshaft sprocket (illustration *2-C12*) and crankshaft pulley, previously used for locking the shafts (see *Job 4*), are in alignment.

→ Try passing the locating rods through again. If they will not go through, because of out-of-alignment, remove the timing belt, and start the belt refitting procedure again.

❑ **STEP C16:** Peugeot advise that the new belt should be run-in and retensioned before refitting the timing cover sections, as follows.

→ You should tighten the crankshaft pulley bolt to the correct torque, then temporarily refit the external drive belt, ensuring it is correctly tightened.

→ Keeping well clear of all moving parts, start the engine and run it until it reaches full operating temperature. Stop the engine and allow it two hours' cooling time.

❑ **STEP C17:** Turn the crankshaft so that it is at Top Dead Centre, with the No. 1 cylinder on the firing stroke. Loosen then retighten the tensioner body top and bottom nuts to ensure a 'fine adjustment' of belt tensioning.

❑ **STEP C18:** Remove the external drive belt and the crankshaft pulley, refit the timing belt covers, refit and retorque the crankshaft pulley, then refit the external drive belt, ensuring it is adjusted to the correct tension. Reconnect all other components, removed or disconnected earlier.

MODELS WITH OFF-CENTRE ROLLER TENSIONER

❑ **STEP C19:** Follow *Steps C11* and *C12*.

❑ **STEP C20:** Make sure the camshaft sprocket is locked.

❑ **STEP C21:** When aligned, you should insert an 8 mm or 10 mm drill bit or bolt, depending on model, through the sprocket and into a hold in the cylinder head, then turn the tensioner roller in an anti-clockwise direction to push against the belt and take all slack out of it.

→ In this position, tighten the roller securing nut to hold this belt tension.

❑ **STEP C22:** Make sure that all the slack in the belt is between the camshaft and crankshaft sprockets (i. e. that the run between camshaft and crankshaft sprockets is taut) then tension the belt by undoing the tensioner centre nut and swinging the tensioner pulley anti-clockwise against the belt to take up all slack…

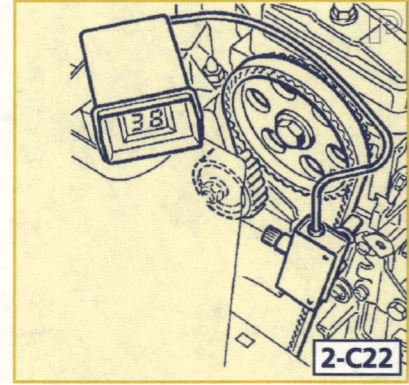

→ **EITHER:** Until you can only just turn the belt through 90 degrees, using thumb and forefinger, half way along the run of belt between camshaft and crankshaft sprockets.

→ **OR:** Use the correct tool, such as the Peugeot SEEMTRONIC device shown here on the tautest run of the belt. Alternatively, use the Sykes-Pickavant tension checking tool - see illustration *2-A9*.

→ If necessary, slacken the adjuster fixing nut and re-adjust and finally, tighten the centre nut.

❑ **STEP C23:** Refit the crankshaft pulley and re-insert the relevant locating rod (see *Job 4*) to confirm that alignment is still correct.

❑ **STEP C24:** Remove the locating rods from the crankshaft pulley and camshaft sprocket, and rotate the crankshaft through two whole revolutions in the normal direction of rotation (clockwise) then again check that the locating rods can be inserted in the crankshaft pulley and the camshaft sprocket. If not, remove the belt and recommence the refitting procedure.

☐ **STEP C25:** If alignment is correct, remove the locating rods and again check the timing belt tension, midway between camshaft and crankshaft sprockets. If it is not as it should be, reset the tension.

☐ **STEP C26:** Remove the crankshaft pulley, refit the timing belt covers, refit and retorque the crankshaft pulley, then refit the external drive belt, ensuring it is adjusted to the correct tension. Reconnect all other components removed or disconnected earlier.

TOP TIP!
- If there is a growling noise which rises and falls with the engine speed, the belt tension may be too tight.

Section D: XUD diesel engines.

NOTE: The job of belt replacement and adjustment is similar to that given for XU petrol engines – see *Section C* - but with the following important differences:
➔ There are three shafts to lock prior to belt removal, the third being that of the injection pump.
➔ Its sprocket has two holes which align with holes in the pump sprocket backplate, and 8 mm bolts or drill bits can be used for locking the injection pump and camshaft sprockets, while an 8 mm bolt or bit is required at the flywheel.

TOP TIP!
- As the diesel engine can be difficult to rotate, due to its higher compression, it helps to remove the glow plugs from the engine first - see *Chapter 9, Ignition, Fuel, Exhaust*.

☐ **STEP D1:** Remove the under-wheelarch panel (arrowed) to give access to the engine crankshaft pulley (205 model shown).

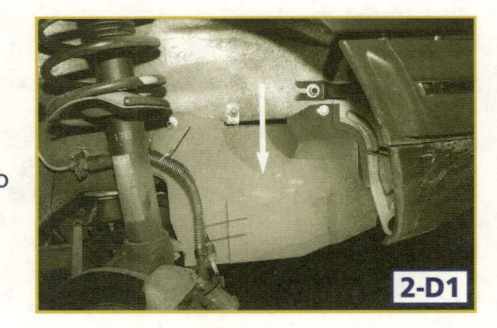

☐ **STEP D2:** If it is in the way, detach and push the radiator bottom hose away from the crankshaft pulley, lodging it under the sump (205 model shown).

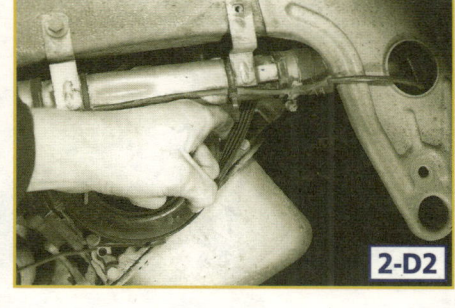

☐ **STEP D3:** Slacken the alternator and remove the external belt(s).
➔ Remove the alternator (if necessary, certain models) and, if there is one, unbolt the external belt tensioner device - see *Part D: Auxiliary Drive Belts*.

☐ **STEP D4:** Working underneath the clutch housing, undo the bolts that secure the metal clutch inspection plate to the bellhousing, and remove the plate.
➔ Now jam the starter ring-gear teeth against a bellhousing boss using a very large screwdriver, to prevent the engine from turning.
➔ Using a suitable socket, undo the crankshaft pulley centre bolt, withdraw the pulley and bolt, and collect the Woodruff key (if it is loose) which keys the pulley to the crankshaft nose.
➔ If the crankshaft pulley is difficult to withdraw, this is most likely because of corrosion between pulley and crankshaft nose. A two- or three-legged puller will be needed to coax the pulley off (see illustration *2-C6*).

☐ **STEP D5:** Undo the bolts securing the bottom timing cover - the thin moulding that sits around the crankshaft sprocket (one bolt arrowed) - and withdraw the cover.

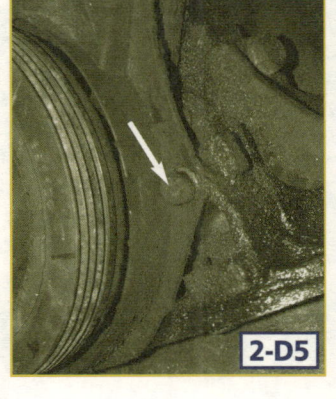

☐ **STEP D6:** Support the right-hand end of the engine with a trolley jack (use wood between jack pad and engine to avoid damage), detach the right-hand side upper engine mounting.
➔ Three nuts retaining right-hand engine mounting bracket.
➔ One nut retaining bracket to mounting rubber.

➜ Three bolts retaining the bracket to engine and cylinder head.

☐ **STEP D7:** Flip off the large spring catches securing the periphery of the timing belt covers, and the single similar catch down to the left and below the belt tensioner roller (see illustration *2 D-12*)

➜ Use pliers to pull upwards the spring retainer (just above crank pulley) that holds together the two main sections of the timing cover.
➜ Slip the covers off the pedestal above this retainer.
➜ Note that later covers do not have this single spring retainer, but instead have the covers located by two central pedestals.
➜ Remove the two timing belt covers.

☐ **STEP D8:** If necessary, lower the right-hand side of the engine/transmission unit on the jack, to improve access to the region of the crankshaft pulley, and set the camshaft and crankshaft to the 'locked' position - see *Job 4*.

☐ **STEP D9:** Slacken the bolt and nut on the belt tensioner roller bracket.
➜ The nut (**a**) is the bracket pivot, and the bolt (**b**) is a clamp bolt that secures the tensioner's position, and thus the belt tension.

☐ **STEP D10:** You can now insert a 3/8 in. square drive (from a small socket set) into the square opening at the top of the tensioner bracket, and use this to oppose tensioner spring pressure and rotate the bracket and roller in an anti-clockwise direction, away from the belt.
➜ The illustration shows the vertical plunger and spring within the mounting casting (see *2-D12*, arrowed), against which the tensioner acts.
➜ Tighten the bracket clamp bolt to secure the tensioner assembly in this position.

☐ **STEP D11:** Slide the timing belt off its sprockets and withdraw it from the engine.

☐ **STEP D12:** Note the arrow markings on the new timing belt - they indicate the direction of rotation of the engine, and so the fitted direction of the belt.
➜ This illustration shows correct location of the belt.
➜ Fit the new timing belt with the direction-of-rotation arrows on the belt facing the right way.
➜ Fit the belt in this order:
➜ over the crankshaft sprocket
➜ over the roller under the injection pump sprocket
➜ over the water pump sprocket
➜ then with its back on the tensioner roller
➜ over the injection pump sprocket (half pushed on)
➜ over the camshaft sprocket.
➜ At all times keep the various runs of the belt pulled tight.

TOP TIP!

• The belt is a very tight fit over the camshaft sprocket, and only half-pushing it on to the injection pump sprocket allows sufficient slack to just feed it on to the camshaft sprocket.
• Once in place, push it fully on to the injection pump sprocket.

☐ **STEP D13:** Hold the belt tensioner bracket against spring pressure, using the 3/8-inch drive, then slacken the bracket clamp bolt. Now slowly allow the tensioner assembly to move against the belt, under its spring pressure. Tighten the clamp bolt.

☐ **STEP D14:** Remove the previously inserted locating rods from the flywheel, injection pump sprocket and camshaft sprocket, then turn the crankshaft by two complete turns in its normal direction of rotation (clockwise).

☐ **STEP D15:** Slacken the tensioner bracket clamp bolt, then retighten it, and also tighten the bracket pivot nut.

→ Recheck the alignment of the flywheel, injection pump sprocket and camshaft sprocket using the locating rods – see *Job 4*.
→ If they cannot be aligned, remove the timing belt and recommence the refitting procedure.

❏ **STEP D16:** You can now refit the timing belt covers, reposition the lower radiator hose, refit and re-torque the crankshaft pulley.
→ Re-attach and tighten the upper engine mounting, then refit the external drive belt, ensuring it is adjusted to the correct tension.
→ Reconnect all other components removed or disconnected earlier.

| JOB 3: | TIMING BELT – *replacement, adjustment (engine out)*. |

The process is the same as the one followed when renewing the cam belt when the engine is in the vehicle, but certain procedures, such as disconnecting engine mountings etc., can obviously be ignored.

ALL ENGINES

When fitting a cam belt as part of an engine build, it is MOST IMPORTANT that the crankshaft, camshaft (and if a diesel, the injection pump) are locked in their correct positions, as fully detailed under *Job 4*. Otherwise serious engine damage will result.
→ Don't re-use an already used belt. It will be more prone to break once removed - renew!

| JOB 4: | VALVE TIMING – *locking camshaft and crankshaft*. |

FACT FILE
SETTING THE CAMSHAFT SPROCKET:

IMPORTANT NOTE: Avoid potential major problems by following this advice:
→ On most engines, the valves will collide with the pistons if the camshaft is turned while the engine is set to Top Dead Centre (TDC).
→ To avoid risk of damage, the camshaft should NEVER be replaced (or turned if already in place) while the pistons are at TDC.
→ Timing location holes are provided at the flywheel and the camshaft sprocket on the TU engine, and additionally at the injection pump sprocket of the TUD diesel engine. On the XU petrol engines, location holes are provided at the camshaft sprocket and crankshaft pulley, while on the XUD diesel

Section A: TU petrol engines.

❏ **STEP A1:** Turn the crankshaft in the correct direction of rotation (clockwise) until the timing location hole in the camshaft sprocket (arrowed) is in alignment with the corresponding recess in the cylinder head.
→ This occurs when the sprocket hole is at the 2 o'clock position.

❏ **STEP A2:** You should now be able to insert a 6 mm drill bit or bolt through the hole (arrowed) in the cylinder block flange (transmission end of engine) and into the corresponding recess in the engine flywheel.
→ You will find it easier to gain access to this hole if you first unbolt and withdraw the starter motor.
→ It is normal to need to 'jiggle' the crankshaft slightly to locate the drill bit or bolt.

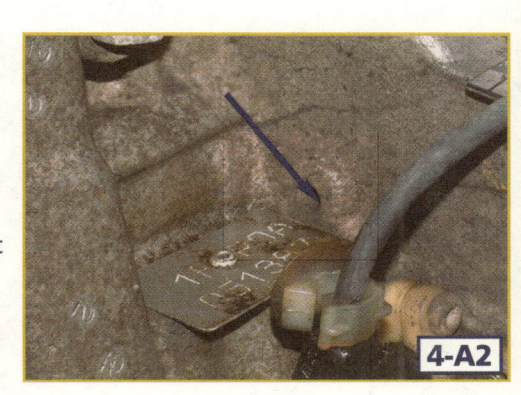

engine these are at the flywheel, the camshaft sprocket and the injection pump sprocket.
→ These holes are used to lock the camshaft and crankshaft respectively in their correct positions before timing belt removal. This is done by passing a drill bit or bolt of the correct diameter through the sprocket or pulley and into a corresponding recess in the engine, or through a hole in the cylinder block-to-transmission mating flange, and into the flywheel.
→ Once the shafts are locked in this way, and the timing belt is removed, they must remain locked until the replacement belt has been fitted.

❏ **STEP A3:** Insert a 10 mm drill bit or bolt through the camshaft-sprocket hole (at 2 o'clock).
➜ The crankshaft and camshaft are now safely locked and ready for belt removal.

Section B: TUD diesel engines.

❏ **STEP B1:** Turn the crankshaft in the correct direction of rotation (clockwise) until the timing location hole in the camshaft sprocket is in alignment with the corresponding recess in the cylinder head.
➜ This occurs when the sprocket hole is at the 4 o'clock position.

❏ **STEP B2:** You should now be able to insert a 6 mm drill bit or bolt through the hole provided in the cylinder block flange (transmission end of engine) and into the corresponding recess in the engine flywheel (see illustration *4-A2*). It is normal to need to 'jiggle' the crankshaft slightly to locate the drill bit or bolt. You will find it easier to gain access to this hole if you first unbolt and withdraw the starter motor.

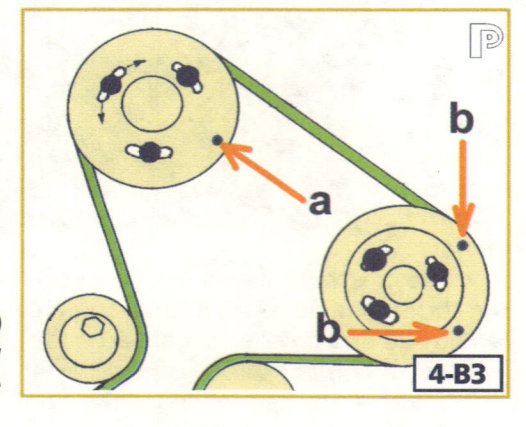

❏ **STEP B3:** Insert an 8 mm bolt through the camshaft-sprocket hole at about 4 o'clock (**a**) and screw it into the sprocket backplate.
➜ Similarly, insert two 8 mm bolts into the two holes provided on the injection pump sprocket (**b**) and screw them into the backplate behind the sprocket.
➜ The crankshaft, camshaft and injection pump are now safely locked ready for belt removal.

Section C: XU petrol engines.

❏ **STEP C1:** Turn the crankshaft in the correct direction of rotation (clockwise) until the timing location hole in the camshaft sprocket is in alignment with the corresponding recess in the cylinder head. This occurs when the sprocket hole is approximately at the 7 o'clock position.

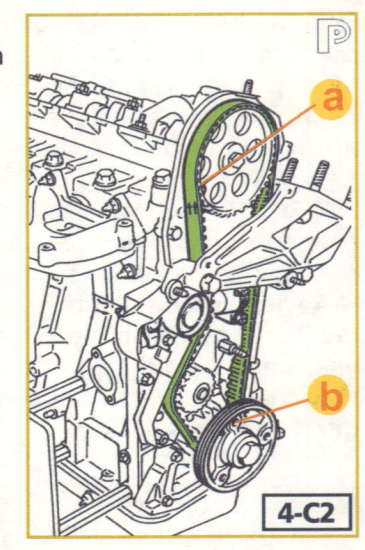

❏ **STEP C2:** You should now be able to insert a 10 mm drill bit or bolt (8 mm – 1.8 and 2.0-litre engines) through the smallest hole (**b**) in the crankshaft pulley, and into the recess in the cylinder block.
➜ It is normal to need to 'jiggle' the crankshaft slightly to locate the drill bit or bolt.
➜ Insert a 10 mm drill bit or bolt (8 mm – 1.8 and 2.0-litre engines) through the camshaft-sprocket hole (**a**) (at approximately 7 o'clock).
➜ The crankshaft and camshaft are now safely locked ready for belt removal.

Section D: XUD diesel engines.

❏ **STEP D1:** Turn the crankshaft in the correct direction of rotation (clockwise) until the timing location hole in the camshaft sprocket is in alignment with the corresponding recess in the cylinder head.
➜ This occurs when the sprocket hole is approximately at the 4 o'clock position.
➜ The two holes provided at the injection pump sprocket should now also be in alignment with their corresponding holes in the sprocket backplate.

❏ **STEP D2:** You should now insert an 8 mm drill bit through the hole provided in the cylinder block flange (transmission end of engine, adjacent to starter motor) and into the corresponding recess in the engine flywheel.
➜ You will find it easier to gain access to this hole if you first unbolt and withdraw the starter motor.
➜ It is normal to need to 'jiggle' the crankshaft slightly to locate the drill bit or bolt.
➜ The proper, cranked Peugeot tool is shown, so shaped to allow insertion with the starter motor in place.

☐ **STEP D3:** Insert an 8 mm bolt (arrowed) through the camshaft-sprocket hole and screw it into the sprocket backplate.

☐ **STEP D4:** Similarly, insert two 8 mm bolts (arrowed) into the two holes provided on the injection pump sprocket, and screw them into the backplate behind the sprocket.
➔ The crankshaft, camshaft and injection pump are now safely locked ready for belt removal.

JOB 5: XV, XW, XY ENGINES, TIMING CHAIN – *replacement*.

☐ **STEP 1:** Disconnect the battery negative (-) earth/ground terminal. See *Chapter 10, Electrical, Dash, Instruments, Fact File: Disconnecting the Battery* BEFORE doing so!

☐ **STEP 2:** Support the weight of the engine (towards right-hand/timing chain end) with a trolley jack, using a piece of wood between jack pad and engine/transmission.
➔ You can now loosen the nuts of the right-hand engine mounting (arrowed), situated towards the bottom of the timing cover.

☐ **STEP 3:** Unscrew/unclip and remove the right-hand under-wheelarch access shield.

☐ **STEP 4:** Lift the engine sufficiently to clear the chassis leg and suspension components, then loosen the crankshaft pulley nut (arrowed).
➔ To do this you will need to lock the engine: this is best achieved by removing the starter motor and jamming the flywheel ring gear teeth with a large screwdriver.

☐ **STEP 5:** Remove the alternator drive belt - see *Part D: Auxiliary Drive Belts*.

☐ **STEP 6:** Disconnect and remove the fuel pump from the top edge of the timing cover - but ONLY after reading the relevant notes in *Chapter 2, Safety First!*.

☐ **STEP 7:** Disconnect the spark plug leads, undo the rocker cover retaining bolts, and lift off the cover.

☐ **STEP 8:** Remove the right-hand engine mounting bracket, then undo all the securing bolts from the periphery of the timing cover.
➔ Carefully coax off the cover – but do not lever between the cover and its mating face at the engine.
➔ Retrieve the fuel pump pushrod from the top of the timing cover.

☐ **STEP 9:** Temporarily refit the crankshaft pulley nut in order to turn the crankshaft.
➔ Use the positions of these sprockets and chain, arranged off the vehicles, as a guide.
➔ Turn the crankshaft until the timing marks (arrowed) on the timing chain and the camshaft and crankshaft sprockets are lined up as shown.
➔ The marked chain links should appear as bright or painted links.

☐ **STEP 10:** Remove the gear (**a**) from the crankshaft nose – the one that meshes with the larger oil pump drive gear. Retrieve the Woodruff key (that keys the gear to the crankshaft) if it is loose.

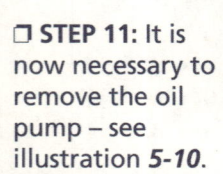

☐ **STEP 11:** It is now necessary to remove the oil pump – see illustration **5-10**.
→ The pump body can be unbolted from the engine by passing a suitable Allen key through the openings (**b**) in the pump sprocket (**c**), and undoing the retaining bolts - see illustration **5-10**.

☐ **STEP 12:** Lock the camshaft sprocket from rotation, by passing a rod through one of the sprocket holes, but don't allow the rod to damage the mating surface of the cylinder head – protect it first.

☐ **STEP 13:** Now undo the camshaft sprocket bolt and withdraw the cam that operates the fuel pump pushrod from behind the camshaft sprocket bolt head.

☐ **STEP 14:** With a small screwdriver, turn the adjuster on the chain tensioner body to allow the tensioner pad to withdraw towards the body, then lock the pad in this position with the adjuster.

☐ **STEP 15:** Lift off the camshaft sprocket and chain, and remove the chain.

☐ **STEP 16:** Fit the new chain over the camshaft sprocket, with the bright links aligned either side of the sprocket mark - see illustration **5-9**.
→ Refit the sprocket to the camshaft, taking care to align the Woodruff key in the camshaft with the slot inside the camshaft sprocket.

☐ **STEP 17:** Refit the fuel pump cam to the end of the camshaft, then refit and torque-tighten the camshaft sprocket retaining bolt.

☐ **STEP 18:** Position the chain over the crankshaft sprocket, with the bright links and sprocket dot mark still correctly aligned - see illustration **5-9**.

☐ **STEP 19:** Turn the chain tensioner adjuster so that the tensioner pad comes out against spring pressure and tensions the chain - see illustration **5-14**.

☐ **STEP 20:** Refit the oil pump and tighten its retaining bolts. Refit the oil pump drive gear to the crankshaft nose, ensuring the Woodruff key is in place.

☐ **STEP 21:** Position the timing chain cover retaining bolt that is nearest to the water pump pulley, in its hole in the timing cover.
→ Clean the mating faces if necessary, fit a new timing cover gasket, and offer up the timing cover to the engine, screwing in that retained bolt first.
→ Fit and tighten evenly all the remaining cover bolts.

☐ **STEP 22:** There is a bracket (arrowed) that fits beneath one of the bolt heads, and prevents the main cooling hose from contacting the water pump pulley – make sure this goes back where it came from.

☐ **STEP 23:** Slice off the top loop of the gasket, where it protrudes above the timing cover, it is not needed.

☐ **STEP 24:** Refit the fuel pump pushrod and fuel pump (using a new gasket), the rocker cover (new gasket), starter motor, alternator belt and engine mounting, and reconnect the necessary wiring, hoses and air ducting.

Part D: Auxiliary Drive Belts

CONTENTS

	Page No.
JOB 1: DRIVE BELT/S – check/adjust, replace.	6-27

See *Part B: Which Engine is Which?* for an explanation of the engine types referred to here.

JOB 1: DRIVE BELT/S - check, adjust, replace.

VERSIONS WITH AIR CONDITIONING

SAFETY FIRST!

• DO NOT open the pressurised pipework on the air conditioning system.

• The air conditioning system contains pressurised gas and specialist equipment is needed to extract it. It is illegal to discharge the gas to the atmosphere.

• The gas used in air conditioning systems is extremely harmful to the environment and may cause injury to the person carrying out the work if released in an uncontrolled manner.

• If air conditioning units are in the way of carrying out other work such as auxiliary belt replacement, whenever possible move units to one side with pipes still attached.

NOTE: For replacement of auxiliary belt(s) follow the instructions given for belt tension adjustment, and slacken the existing belt sufficiently to remove it from its pulleys. Fit the new belt and set its tension as detailed later.

IMPORTANT NOTES:
• Flat, ribbed belts should be checked for condition, as for V belts.
• Before removing the ribbed belt, mark the direction of rotation with a felt pen or typists' correction fluid.
• When installing a flat belt, ensure that the ribs are correctly seated in the grooves in the pulley. On some models, certain pulleys are wider than the ribbed belt and in those cases, it is MOST IMPORTANT that the belt is seated centrally in the pulley with an equal number of 'spare' grooves on each side of the belt.
• If belt tension adjustment is effected at the alternator, loosen ALL the alternator fixing and pivot bolts before attempting to adjust the tension. Retighten them all after adjustment is complete.
• Some 306 and 206 models are equipped with an automatic sprung belt tensioner. With these there is no need to check or adjust belt tension.

CHECK CONDITION, TENSION OF BELT/S

☐ **STEP 1:** Check the belt or belts, and if there are any signs of cracking, 'polishing', fraying or severe wear on the inner face/s, replace the belt/s.

FACT FILE
AUXILIARY DRIVE BELT LAYOUTS

XV, XW, XY SERIES ENGINES
• The alternator and V-belt belt tension adjuster are on the top-side of the engine. Access for checking and adjustment is therefore from inside the engine bay, from above the vehicle.
• The drive belt of the XV, XW, XY engines also drives the engine's water pump.

TU AND XU SERIES ENGINES, INCLUDING EARLY XUD DIESELS
• The alternator belt is positioned low on the left-side of the engine, and is usually of the flat, ribbed 'Poly-Vee' type.

• Access to it is gained from beneath the right-hand wheelarch, once the plastic access panel has been removed. In some cases, it may be useful to unclip/unscrew (depending on type) and temporarily relocate the major coolant hose that runs in front of the crankshaft pulley.

TU, TUD, XU AND XUD ENGINES:
• On some the alternator drive may also be used to drive the power steering pump.
• On most diesel engines (though not the early ones) adjustment is made from inside the engine bay.
• Where two drivebelts are fitted (usually because there is an air conditioning pump), both driven from the crankshaft pulley, it is obviously necessary to remove the outer belt in order to remove the inner belt.

❑ **STEP 2:** Each belt should deflect by 13 mm (XV, XW, XY engines) or by 6 mm on others, when firm thumb pressure is applied to the longest 'run' of each belt between the pulleys.

❑ **STEP 3:** The belt of the brake vacuum pump fitted to XUD models should have no more than 5 mm deflection midway along its longest run.

→ Too little tension and the belt might slip; too much, and belt and bearing wear will increase.
→ A new belt may only require a deflection of 2 mm, however. Try it again later, once it has bedded in.

ADJUST BELT TENSION

IMPORTANT NOTES:
• Belt tension should only be adjusted when the engine is cold.
• After adjustment, run the engine for 15 to 30 seconds, to allow the belt to bed-in, then check again.
• Experienced mechanics claim that belts often go slack when the engine heats up, producing belt squeal.
• If this happens on your vehicle, adjust the belt again when the engine is hot. Wear industrial leather gloves and long-sleeved overalls and take very great care not to burn yourself on the hot engine or exhaust.

❑ **STEP 4: EARLIER (XV, XW, XY) ENGINES:** These engines have a simple sliding arrangement for the alternator adjustment.
→ Slacken the alternator mounting bolts/nuts (two arrowed) and lever the alternator away from the engine until the belt tension is correct - take very great care not to damage the alternator body.
→ Retighten the bolts.

❑ **STEP 5: XU, XUD ENGINES:** Much the same instruction applies, although there is a tension adjuster screw that can be screwed inwards or outwards to adjust belt tension, instead of levering the alternator. All alternator mounting bolts/nuts must be slackened first.

❑ **STEP 6: TU, TUD ENGINES:** There is also a tension adjuster screw (arrowed), accessible from under the wheelarch.
Again, all alternator mounting bolts/nuts must first be slackened.

❑ **STEP 7: TU, XU, XUD ENGINES:** Some of these, equipped with power steering and/or air conditioning, are equipped with a tensioning pulley arrangement (4) that is manually adjusted – as opposed to the automatic, sprung type that does not need intervention.
→ With this type, adjustment is carried out by slackening the pinch bolts (**2** and **3**) with a suitable Allen key (access from beneath wheelarch).
→ Then screw in the end-bolt (**1**) to tighten the belt, or backing it off to slacken it. Remember to retighten the pinch bolts.

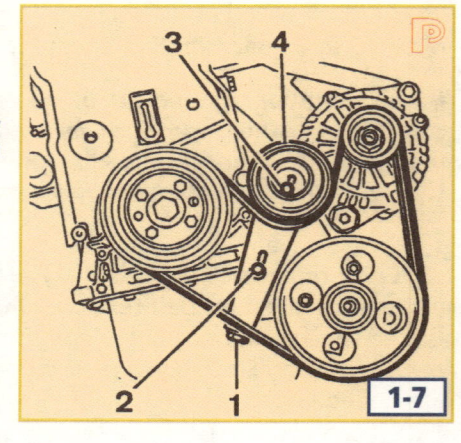

DIESEL VACUUM PUMP DRIVE BELT

❑ **STEP 8: XUD DIESEL ENGINE:** The vacuum pump is mounted at the left-hand (transmission) end of the cylinder head, and is driven by belt from a pulley on the rear of the camshaft. 
➜ To adjust, slacken the clamp bolt, then push the pump backwards to tension the belt.
➜ Tighten the clamp bolt when the correct tension is reached.

AIR CONDITIONING AND POWER STEERING BELT INSTALLATIONS

❑ **STEP 9: TU, XU, AND XUD ENGINES:** There are several variations of auxiliary belt and tensioner arrangement used when power steering and/or air conditioning are fitted.
➜ See *Fact File: Air Conditioning/Power Steering Belts* to identify the type fitted to the vehicle you are working on.

FACT FILE

AIR CONDITIONING/POWER STEERING BELTS

❑ **TYPE A: POWER STEERING WITH NO AIR CONDITIONING:** Tension by manual roller (1)

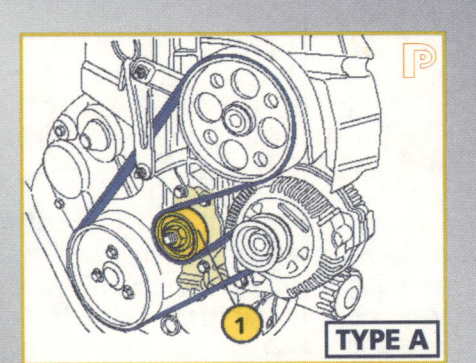

❑ **TYPE B: AIR CONDITIONING WITH NO POWER STEERING:** Tension by manual roller (1) - see also *Type F*.

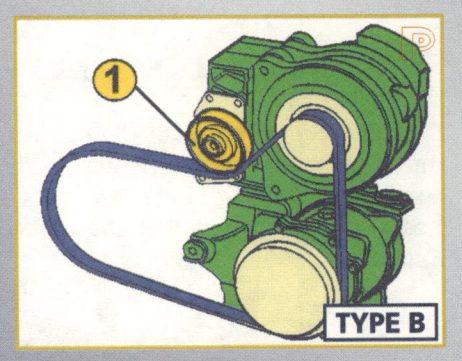

❑ **TYPE C: AIR CONDITIONING AND POWER STEERING:** Tensioned automatically by roller (2).

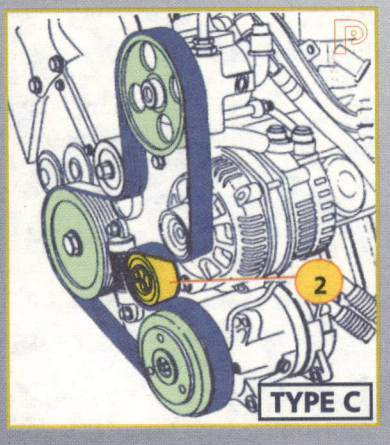

❑ **TYPE D: AUTOMATIC TENSIONER:** To release tension, use 3/8 in. drive in square hole in back-bracket of roller to oppose spring, then lock bracket of roller (2) in this position using 6 mm drill bit through hole in centre of bracket.

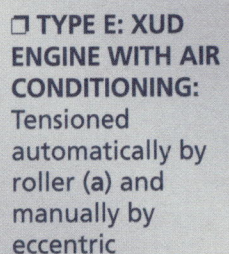

❑ **TYPE E: XUD ENGINE WITH AIR CONDITIONING:** Tensioned automatically by roller (a) and manually by eccentric roller (b).

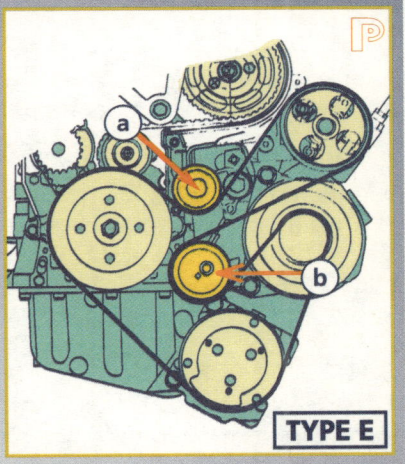

❑ **TYPE F: TENSIONER ROLLER:** To adjust roller (3), slacken locknut (1) and turn central Torx-type adjuster (2).

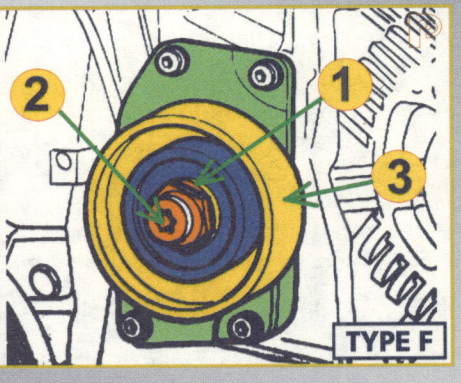

STEP 10: This is the typical air conditioning pump installation, shown on the TU petrol engine
→ Remove the bolts (arrowed) when moving the air conditioning pump.

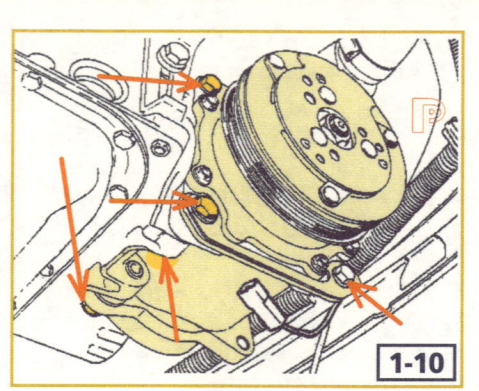

1-10

STEP 11: This shows the air conditioning pump alignment mounting bolt.
→ When refitting it, make sure the slotted end of the bolt (4) faces the pulley end of the pump.
→ Fine alignment of the pulley and belt can be achieved by adjusting dimension (X) with this adjuster bolt.

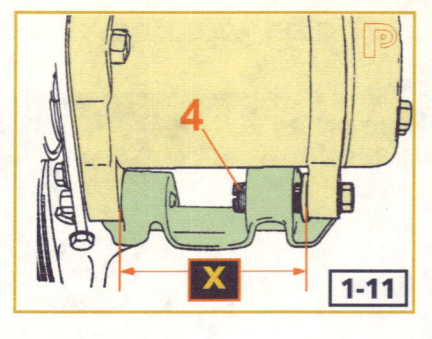

1-11

Part E: Valve Clearance (Valve Lash) Adjustment

CONTENTS

	Page No.
JOB 1: VALVE CLEARANCE – *checking, adjustment*.	6-30

See *Part B: Which Engine is Which?* for an explanation of the engine types referred to here.

IMPORTANT NOTE: You should ALWAYS check the valve clearances with the engine cold. This means that the engine should not have run for at least six hours.

FACT FILE
VALVE OPERATION TYPES

There are two basic types of valve operation on engines fitted to the models described here:

ROCKER-TYPE
• Fitted only to XV, XW, XY and TU engines.
→ They are conventional cast rockers on a rocker shaft, with a locknut and screw adjuster at the valve end of the rocker, for determining tappet clearance (valve clearance).

BUCKET TAPPETS
• These are fitted to XU, XUD and TUD engines.
• The camshaft operates directly on 'buckets' over each valve stem.

XU AND XUD
• There is a shim of calibrated thickness between the valve stem and the under-side of the bucket: this determines the tappet clearance (valve clearance).

TUD ENGINE
• Clearance is dictated by a similar shim, but in this case located between the top of the bucket and the underside of the cam. The advantage of this design is that the shim can be swapped for one of a different size without having to remove the camshaft (as is the case for the XU and XUD engines).

JOB 1: VALVE CLEARANCE – *checking, adjustment.*

Peugeot are quite rare in not specifying a valve clearance check at any service interval. Their thinking is that you should only need to adjust the valve clearances if there is a problem with engine operation, such as excessive valve-gear noise, rough running or loss of cylinder compression.

ALL ENGINES

☐ **STEP 1:** Remove the air cleaner assembly (on models where this is in the way of the camshaft cover) taking care to detach each of the pipes and hoses connected to it. See *Chapter 9, Ignition, Fuel, Exhaust*.

☐ **STEP 2:** On TUD engines, remove the top section of the cam belt cover.

1-2

☐ **STEP 3:** On XV, XW, XY engines, remove the oil filler/breather cap from the rocker cover.

☐ **STEP 4:** On XUD Turbodiesel engines, remove the intercooler – see *Chapter 9, Ignition, Fuel, Exhaust*.

☐ **STEP 5:** On XUD non-turbo engines with large plastic intake air chamber mounted over the top of the engine, remove this chamber.

☐ **STEP 6:** On all engines, disconnect any hoses or wiring from the camshaft/rocker cover.

☐ **STEP 7:** Remove the nuts or bolts (arrowed) holding the camshaft/rocker cover in place, taking care to collect any washers, and take the cover off.

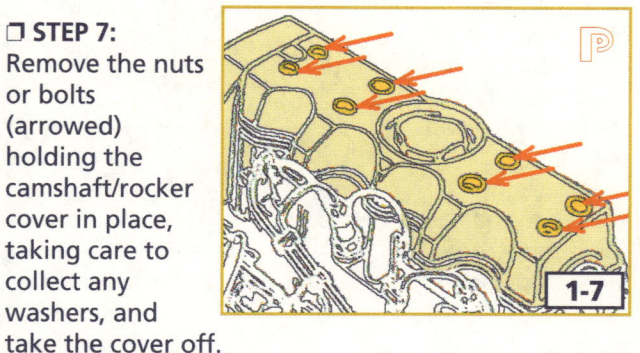

→ IMPORTANT NOTE: The camshaft cover of the TUD engine has eight retaining bolts, and some are of different length, so take note of their positions.

> **TOP TIP!**
> • If the camshaft cover sticks - which it frequently does - DON'T lever the cover or you could easily damage the cover or the gasket, which is sometimes of the re-useable neoprene-type.
> • Work the cover free, carefully.

☐ **STEP 8:** On TU engines, remove the spacer from each of the two cam cover studs (1), and withdraw the oil distribution plate (2).

☐ **STEP 9A:** On XU, XUD and TUD engines the valve clearance is measured directly beneath the cam and must be checked when the high point of the cam (arrowed) is pointing away from the cam follower.

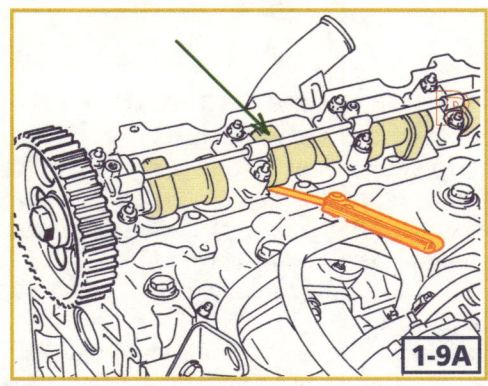

☐ **STEP 9B:** This is the bucket tappet-type, but the same principle applies to the rocker-type tappet.

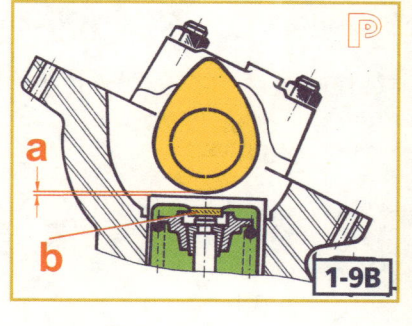

→ The measurement (**a**) is between the top of the 'bucket' and the camshaft.

→ Position (**b**) shows the location of the shims.

ROCKER TYPES (XV, XW, XY AND TU)

> **TOP TIP!**
> • Remember that recommended clearances for inlet and exhaust valves differ. See Chapter 1, Facts and Figures.
> • When measuring a valve clearance, a feeler gauge blade of the correct thickness should be passed between the bucket and cam, or valve stem and rocker. Correct clearance is indicated by a fairly tight, but smooth passage of the blade.
> • XV, XW, XY ENGINES: Counting from the timing chain end, the exhaust valves are: 1, 3, 5, 7, and the inlet valves are 2, 4, 6, 8.
> • TU ENGINES: Counting from the timing belt end, the exhaust valves are: 2, 4, 6, 8, the inlet valves are 1,3,5,7.

XV, XW, XY ENGINES

☐ **STEP 10:** Use a spanner on the crankshaft pulley bolt (arrowed) to turn the engine clockwise until the rockers on valves 1 and 2 are 'rocking' - that is, when the two valves are moving in opposition, with one just closing and the other just opening.

→ Note that No. 1 cylinder is that nearest the transmission end of the engine, and that the cylinders and valves number out towards the left.

→ Follow the sequence below – inlet valves are marked 'In' and exhaust valves 'Ex'.

VALVES ROCKING	VALVES TO ADJUST
1 In – 2 Ex	7 In – 8 Ex
5 In – 6 Ex	3 In – 4 Ex
7 In – 8 Ex	1 In – 2 Ex
3 In – 4 Ex	5 In – 6 Ex

Adjust clearances as described in *Step 11*.

TU ENGINES

☐ **STEP 11:** A different sequence applies to these engines:
➡ TWO valves are checked/adjusted while only ONE valve is open, that is, when fully depressed by the rocker arm.

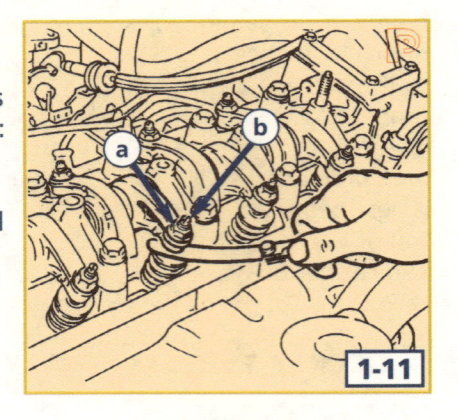

➡ Note that the exhaust valves are at the front of the cylinders, the inlets at the rear; No. 1 cylinder is at the transmission end of the engine.

VALVES ROCKING	VALVES TO ADJUST
1 Ex	3 In - 4 Ex
3 Ex	4 In – 2 Ex
4 Ex	2 In – 1 Ex
2 Ex	1 In – 3 Ex

➡ If adjustment is required, slacken the locknut (*1-11, item a*) with a spanner and turn the adjuster screw (*1-11, item b*) until the blade is a firm fit, then tighten the locknut while holding the screw in position with the screwdriver.
➡ Check the gap afterwards, as it can reduce as the locknut is tightened.
➡ When satisfied the gap is correct, rotate the engine using a spanner on the crankshaft pulley bolt, to the next step of the given sequence.

BUCKET TAPPETS – XU, XUD, TU ENGINES

☐ **STEP 12:** Check the valve clearances. If any are 'out' the relevant shims will have to be changed.
➡ Try different feeler gauge thicknesses until you find one that's a tight sliding fit between cam and follower - see illustration *1-9A*.
➡ Make a written note of each clearance, starting with No. 1 at the timing belt end of the engine.
➡ If a clearance is outside the tolerances shown in *Chapter 1, Facts and Figures*, the relevant shim will have to be changed.
➡ New shims are available from your Peugeot dealer.
➡ This work is fully described below.

TOP TIP!

☐ **STEP 13:** • Remember that recommended clearances for inlet and exhaust valves differ. See Chapter 1, Facts and Figures.

☐ **STEP 14:** On XU and XUD engines it is necessary to remove the camshaft in order to change clearance shims. See *Part G, Job 5*.

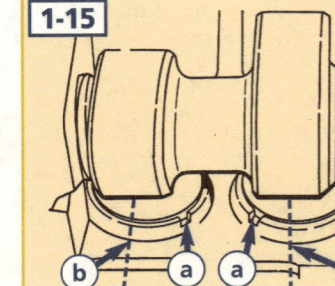

☐ **STEP 15:** On the TUD engine, if a shim is to be replaced, turn the engine so that the relevant cam is facing away from the shim.
➡ Rotate the bucket so that its cut-out notches (a) are positioned at a right angle to the camshaft axis (positions b).
➡ Lever down the bucket against the valve spring, using a suitable screwdriver(s) acting on the raised edge of the bucket, and push out the shim.
➡ Take care not to slip and scratch any valve-gear components.

TOP TIP!

• If you want to give it a try, you will find it extremely difficult to a) persuade the lever to stay on the thin edge of the tappet (lifter), and b) just as difficult to free and remove the shim.
• It could be worth a try if there is only one shim to change. However, *Step 16-on* describes our recommended alternative way of changing shims on the TUD engine.

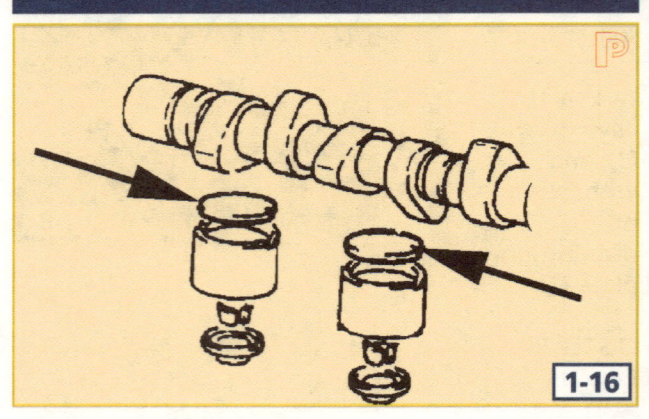

☐ **STEP 16: ALL BUCKET TYPES:** The following assumes that you don't have the luxury of a full set of shims (arrowed) in your garage. But if you follow the following stages, go out and buy the shims you need from your Peugeot dealer and fit them yourself, the clearances should be correct:
➡ **a.** Make up a table, like the one shown on page 6-33.
➡ **b.** Measure each valve clearance, pushing, or attempting to push in various sizes of feeler gauge until you find the right one.
➡ **c.** You can now fill in the first column of the table, writing down all the 'Actual Clearance' figures you

measure. You can also fill in the second column, using the information given in **Chapter 1, Facts & Figures** for your particular engine.

→ **d.** Write down the difference you will need to achieve the correct figure. (Go for the 'mid-point' when a 'plus or minus' figure is given. In other words, 45 mm plus or minus 5 mm, means 40 to 50 mm: use 45 as your 'target'.)

Valve	Actual Clearance	Required Clearance	Difference	Old Shim size	Required Shim size	New Clearance
No 1	.38 mm	.45 mm ±.05 mm	.07 mm too small			
No 1 Inlet	.26 mm	0.25 mm ±0.05 mm	Within tolerance			
No 2 Exhaust	.48 mm					

...and so on:-

FACT FILE
SHIM AVAILABILITY

• Valve clearance shims for the XU petrol engine are available in thicknesses between 2.225 mm and 3.550 mm, in increments of 0.025 mm.
• Valve clearance shims for the XUD diesel engine are available in thicknesses between 2.425 mm and 3.550 mm, in increments of 0.075 mm.
• Valve clearance shims for the TUD diesel engine are available in thicknesses between 3.20 mm and 4.90 mm, in increments of 0.025 mm.

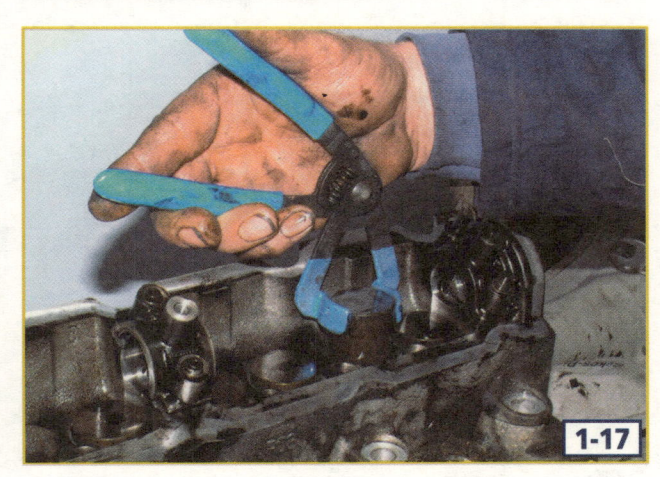

☐ **STEP 20:** The thickness of a shim is engraved on it in mm (arrowed).
→ If this marking is worn away, you will have to measure the thickness with a metric micrometer.
→ On the TUD engine, be sure to fit the shim with the marking facing down.

☐ **STEP 21:** Refit/reconnect all detached parts.
→ Be sure to use a new gasket when the camshaft cover is replaced, unless it is of the neoprene type, in which case it will only need replacing if it is damaged.

1-20

☐ **STEP 17:** Remove the camshaft - see **Part G, Job 5** - and the bucket tappets.
→ Take out each shim and write down its thickness in the 'Old Shim' column.
→ The thickness should be shown on the shim; if invisible you will need to measure the shim with a micrometer.

☐ **STEP 18:** You can now calculate the figure required to reach the recommended figure. If you need to achieve a different clearance, you will have to replace an existing shim.

☐ **STEP 19:** Reassemble the camshaft and check that the figures are correct.

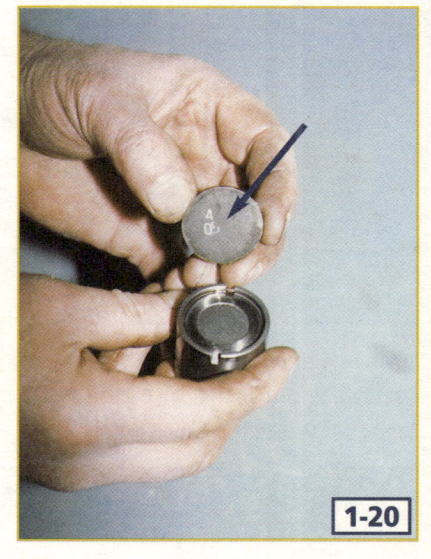

1-17

1-21

TOP TIP!

• Where a clearance is too small, even with the thinnest shim in position, the valves should be removed and the stem ground just sufficiently to make the correction.
• The work must be done with the correct engineering equipment, keeping the valve stem end square and retaining a smooth finish.

CHAPTER 6 Part E Job 1

6-33

Part F: XV, XW, XY Engines Cylinder Head Removal

CONTENTS

	Page No.
JOB 1: XV, XW, XY ENGINES' CYLINDER HEAD – *removal*.	6-34
JOB 2: TU, TUD, XU, XUD ENGINES' CYLINDER HEAD – *removal*.	6-36

Refer to **Part B, Which Engine is Which?** for exploded diagrams of each of the cylinder head types covered here.

JOB 1: XV, XW, XY ENGINES' CYLINDER HEAD – *removal*.

IMPORTANT NOTE: This series of engine is constructed very differently from the other types covered in this manual. One essential difference is that these engines are mounted in the engine bay almost lying down, with the rocker cover facing the bulkhead. This makes the job of cylinder head removal complicated and difficult.

• With the use of Peugeot special tool No. 7.0132, for holding up the camshaft sprocket and chain when these are disconnected from the camshaft, it is perfectly feasible to remove the cylinder head in situ.

• However, as this tool is not generally available to the public, and it is very difficult to gain access to the piston crowns for decoking anyway, we strongly recommend that the entire power unit is removed from the vehicle for head removal.

• *Job 1*, below includes tackling cylinder head removal in situ, with the relevant Peugeot special tool. Cylinder head removal with engine removed is similar, but without the (obvious!) need for using the special tool.

☐ **STEP 1:** Before dismantling, disconnect the battery negative (-) earth/ground terminal. See **Chapter 10, Electrical, Dash, Instruments, Fact File: Disconnecting the Battery** BEFORE doing so!

☐ **STEP 2:** Remove all components of the air intake/filtration system, including warm air ducting from the exhaust, and disconnect the throttle cable and – if fitted – choke cable.

☐ **STEP 3:** Remove the fuel pump and its pushrod.

☐ **STEP 4:** Drain the cooling system – see **Chapter 8, Cooling System**.

☐ **STEP 5:** Disconnect all cooling hoses between vehicle body and power unit, and disconnect, and plug, any fuel hoses to/from the vehicle body and carburettor.

☐ **STEP 6:** Disconnect all wiring between the vehicle body and the cylinder head.

☐ **STEP 7:** Detach the exhaust front downpipe from the exhaust manifold (from beneath the vehicle).

☐ **STEP 8:** Select neutral gear then, from underneath the vehicle, disconnect the gearchange linkage – see **Chapter 7, Transmission, Clutch**.

☐ **STEP 9:** Slacken the left-hand engine mounting nuts (arrowed) - situated under the battery tray - sufficiently to allow the mounting to drop a little. But DON'T remove the nuts!

☐ **STEP 10:** Remove the distributor and spark plug leads.

☐ **STEP 11:** Disconnect the brake servo hose from the inlet manifold.

☐ **STEP 12:** Detach the right-hand rear engine mounting from the subframe (two bolts), and lever the engine upwards, wedging it in position with a suitably sized piece of wood.
→ **IMPORTANT NOTE:** Take care not to allow the moving engine to damage the radiator.

☐ **STEP 13:** Remove the rocker cover.
→ Then turn the engine (using a socket on the crankshaft pulley nut) until the slot in the sprocket end of the camshaft points upwards.
→ Now remove the plastic cover from the ignition timing opening (at the flywheel housing) and turn the crankshaft further until the flywheel timing mark is in line with the Top Dead Centre mark on the external plate – see **Chapter 9, Ignition, Fuel, Exhaust**.

☐ **STEP 14:** Unbolt and remove the camshaft-end access plate from the timing cover (two bolts), then, using a suitable size of hex-headed drive, remove the camshaft sprocket securing bolt (arrowed) from the end of the camshaft.
→ **IMPORTANT NOTE:** Make sure the sprocket does not come off the end of the camshaft.

☐ **STEP 15:** Slacken the four timing chain cover upper bolts (which secure the cover to the cylinder head).
→ Then undo the cylinder head bolts in the order shown.

☐ **STEP 16:** The cylinder head bolts on these engines screw into nuts in open channels on the sides of the crankcase (arrowed). Be sure to collect the nuts, or they will be lost!

☐ **STEP 17:** Lift off the rocker shaft assembly.
→ If there is not sufficient clearance between engine and vehicle body, you may find it beneficial to leave some head bolts in the rocker assembly when lifting it off.

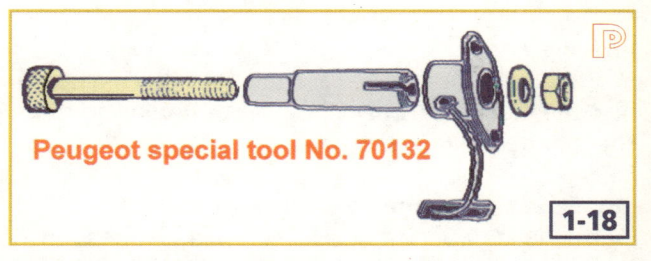

Peugeot special tool No. 70132

☐ **STEP 18:** Working at the camshaft sprocket-end of the engine, slacken the single bolt that secures the camshaft thrust fork, and slide the fork away from the camshaft.
→ At this stage it is necessary to support the camshaft sprocket with Peugeot special tool No. 70132, to prevent the sprocket from dropping into the timing case, and the chain tensioner from taking up all chain slack, thus preventing the sprocket and chain from being retrieved.
→ The special tool passes into the end the camshaft sprocket, and also bolts to the bolt holes of the (removed) camshaft access plate.

❑ **STEP 19:** With the camshaft sprocket supported by the tool (arrowed), withdraw the camshaft from the sprocket.

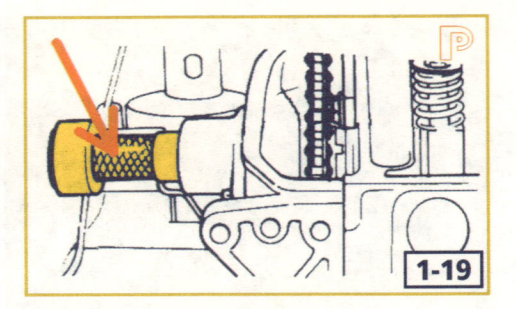

1-19

❑ **STEP 20:** Remove the four bolts, previously slackened (see *Step 15*) which secure the timing cover to the cylinder head.

IMPORTANT NOTE: The cylinder head must not be pulled directly off the crankcase, as this will cause the cylinder liners to be pulled with it, thus breaking their bottom seals. Once the seals are broken, an engine overhaul is needed.

❑ **STEP 21:** To prevent the cylinder lines from being pulled off with the head, the cylinder head must be swivelled to break the head gasket seal.

1-21

→ In order to allow swivelling, one of the two locating rings (arrowed) - one at each end of front side of block - which locate the head, must be tapped down into the crankcase, so allowing the head to pivot around the remaining locating ring.
→ Locate the hole at one corner of the flywheel-end of the head – in it you will see a sprung-steel locating ring.
→ Use a suitable drift to carefully tap this ring down into the crankcase, but only as far as it takes to clear the cylinder head.

❑ **STEP 22:** Swivel the head to break the seal made by the head gasket. If necessary, use a soft-headed mallet at the flywheel end, to encourage the head to move.
→ With the head loosened, carefully remove it, taking care not to dislodge the cylinder liners.

❑ **STEP 23:** It is now necessary to secure the cylinder liners to prevent their bottom seals from being broken.

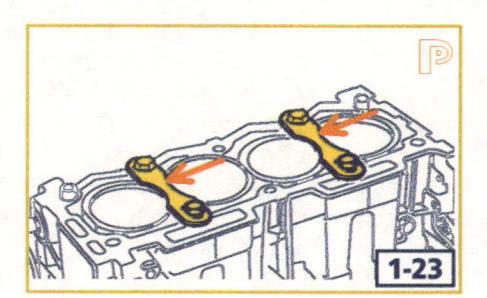

1-23

→ The correct method involves using these Peugeot liner clamps (arrowed). Alternatively, clamping can be achieved using the cylinder head bolts and nuts, large washers to overlap crankcase and liners, and some suitable spacer tubing to take up the height of the missing cylinder head.

❑ **STEP 24:** Remove all traces of the cylinder head gasket from both block and head.
→ Scrape off carbon deposits with a wooden or aluminium scraper, taking care not to gouge the aluminium surface of the head or crankcase.
→ Stuff rags into all openings in the cylinder head to stop debris dropping into them.
→ Clean excessive carbon deposits from the crowns of the pistons without damaging the surface of the aluminium.

TOP TIP!
• If the engine is worn and you don't intend overhauling it at this stage, we strongly advise that you leave the piston crowns alone. The carbon on them can actually help preserve compression pressures when the engine is near the point of needing an overhaul.
• An aerosol gasket remover spray will help to remove pieces of stuck-on gasket.

❑ **STEP 25:** The cylinder head can be checked for distortion by use of a straight edge and feeler gauge. At the same time, check for excessive corrosion.

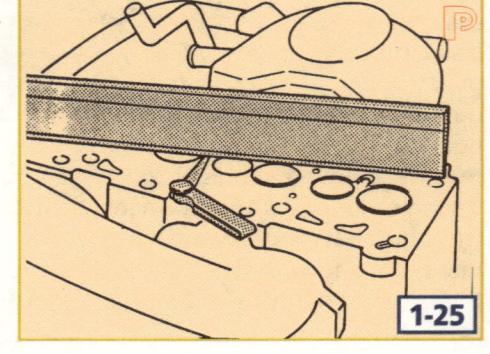

1-25

TOP TIP!
• It pays to have the cylinder head refaced before refitting to greatly reduce the risk of the cylinder head blowing after being refitted.

JOB 2: TU, TUD, XU, XUD ENGINES' CYLINDER HEAD – *removal*.

IMPORTANT NOTE: 206 models are fitted with an engine undershield held by four peripheral bolts and four peripheral screws. The undershield should be removed before carrying out the following work.

❒ **STEP 1:** Before dismantling, disconnect the battery negative (-) earth/ground terminal. See *Chapter 10, Electrical, Dash, Instruments, Fact File: Disconnecting the Battery* BEFORE doing so!

❒ **STEP 2:** Remove the camshaft drive belt - see *Part C: Timing Belt - Inspection, Adjustment, Replacement*.

❒ **STEP 3:** Disconnect, drain or remove the following items (refer to the relevant sections of this manual):
➔ Drain off the coolant into a suitable container and dispose of it responsibly.
➔ Remove the air filter and housing, air chamber (some diesels with the chamber over the head) and all associated air and vacuum lines, including warm air ducts, and EGR valve and lines, if applicable.
➔ **PETROL ENGINES:** Disconnect and remove the HT leads from the spark plugs and also all other connections to the distributor. If the engine is catalyst-equipped, disconnect the wiring to the exhaust system Lambda sensor.
➔ **DIESEL ENGINES:** Disconnect the glow plugs electrical supply, the injector pipes from the injectors (slacken the pipes at the injection pump end too) and the fuel feedback hoses - but ONLY after reading the relevant *Safety First!* notes.
➔ **TURBODIESEL ENGINES:** Disconnect the fittings to the turbocharger but leave the turbo connected to the exhaust manifold and downpipe and remove them together later on.
➔ Note that the turbocharger has a small oil supply line that runs beneath it and connects to the block with a banjo union: it is easily forgotten and easily damaged.
➔ Remove the manifold nuts and bolts and withdraw the manifold from the engine, but leave the exhaust manifold/turbocharger in the car, still connected to the exhaust system.
➔ This will make the head lighter and easier to lift, but it is important to support the exhaust manifold assembly with wire to avoid straining the exhaust system and turbo oil pipes.

❒ **STEP 4:** Disconnect the fuel line at the engine-end and plug the fuel line.

❒ **STEP 5:** Disconnect the throttle cable, and choke cable if fitted. If the diesel engine has a cable running from a waxstat device at the thermostat housing, to the injection pump, disconnect it.
➔ Remove the carburetor or fuel injection system.
➔ Remove all coolant hoses and any oil lines to the cylinder head and its components.
➔ Label and detach all remaining electrical connections to the head and its components. Be aware that there may be wires not connected to the cylinder head that are nonetheless supported by brackets on it.

❒ **STEP 6: ALL MODELS EXCEPT TURBODIESEL:** Detach the exhaust downpipe from the manifold.

❒ **STEP 7: XU PETROL ENGINES:** Loosen the rear lower engine mounting through-bolt and nut.
➔ Also remove the nut retaining the right-hand engine mounting.

❒ **STEP 8: XU PETROL ENGINES:** Place a trolley jack, with a protective piece of wood positioned between the jack pad and the engine, and raise the engine by a little way, then remove the two bolts that retain the right-hand engine mounting bracket to the engine. Lower the engine.

❒ **STEP 9: TU AND TUD ENGINES:** Detach the bracket that secures the oil dipstick tube to the cylinder head (TU engine shown in illustration).
➔ On 2.0-litre XU petrol engines, detach the oil dipstick tube from the inlet manifold.
➔ Other XU engines may have a dipstick tube attachment to the left-hand end of the cylinder head.

TOP TIP!

☐ **STEP 10:** • **ALL ENGINES:** You may wish to remove the inlet manifold at this stage, because it is a large component and it may get in the way.

☐ **STEP 11:** • **ALL ENGINES EXCEPT TURBODIESEL:** If you 'crack' the exhaust manifold nuts at this stage, but leave the manifold in place for now, you will find it easier to lift the head off the block, and easy to undo any stubborn fixing nuts later.

☐ **STEP 12: XUD DIESEL ENGINES:** Undo the camshaft sprocket bolt and remove the sprocket.
→ Remove the four fixing bolts (arrowed) and take the right-hand engine mounting bracket (a) from the engine.
→ Hold the bracket against the upward pressure of the belt tensioner coil spring (b) as the last bolt comes out.
→ Carefully relieve the pressure, salvaging the tensioner plunger (c) and coil spring as you remove the bracket.

☐ **STEP 13: XUD DIESEL ENGINES:** Unbolt and remove the timing belt tensioner (arrowed).
→ Remove the bolt that retains the engine front plate to the fuel injection pump mounting bracket.
→ Remove the bolt and nut retaining the front plate and alternator mounting bracket.
→ Free the front plate.

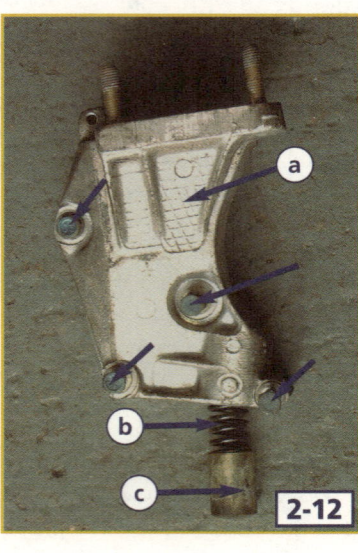

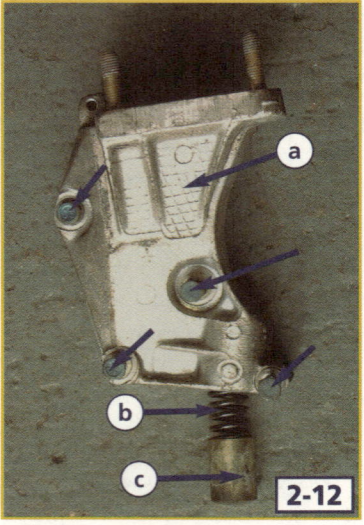

☐ **STEP 14A: XU AND XUD ENGINES:** Slacken the cylinder head bolts progressively, a small amount at a time, so as to de-stress the head as evenly as possible, in the sequence to that shown.

☐ **STEP 14B:** Some XU and XUD engines head bolts have special Torx heads, requiring a Torx T55 socket bit for their removal.
→ Note that the XU petrol and XUD turbodiesel engine have spacers under some bolt heads – make a note of their positions so that they can be replaced correctly.

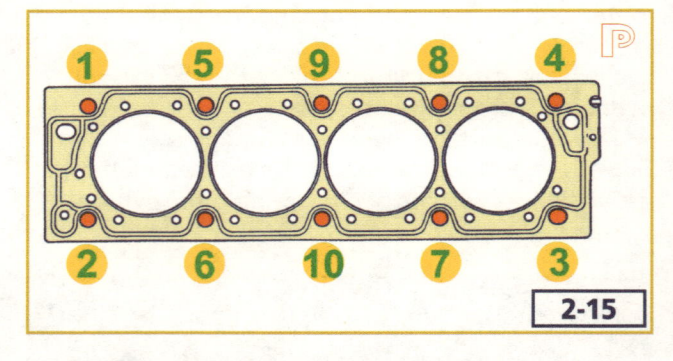

☐ **STEP 15: TU AND TUD ENGINES:** As *Step 14* except follow the sequence shown here.

☐ **STEP 16:** Using two head bolts (a) pushed partly into the two front-end cylinder head bolt holes, attempt to

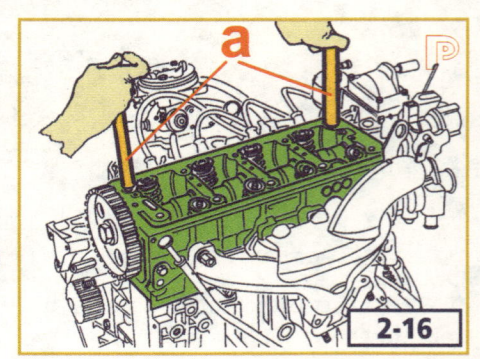

tilt/rock the cylinder head forward, so that it breaks its gasket seal progressively from back to front of the crankcase.
➜ **TU, XU AND TUD ENGINES WITH 'WET' CYLINDER LINERS:** This will avoid accidentally pulling up the liners with the head, which will break their bottom seals and necessitate an engine overhaul.
➜ **XUD DIESEL ENGINE:** This method helps to free the head-to-block locating dowels.

TOP TIP!

• Do not use a wedge to break the seal that often occurs between cylinder head and block.
• Extra leverage can be gained by lifting and rocking carefully on the manifolds, if they are still fitted.

☐ **STEP 17:** TU, TUD AND XU 'WET LINER' ENGINES: It is now necessary to secure the cylinder liners to prevent their bottom seals from being broken.
➜ The proper Peugeot cylinder liner clamps (**a**) are shown here in use.
➜ Items (**b**) are the cylinder head locating pegs.
➜ Alternatively, this can be done using the cylinder head bolts and nuts, some large washers to overlap crankcase and liners, and some suitable spacer tubing to take up the height of the missing head.
➜ Without such a precaution, only clean the cylinder liner mating surfaces with very great care, and DO NOT, at any cost, attempt to rotate the crankshaft, as this will unseat the liners.

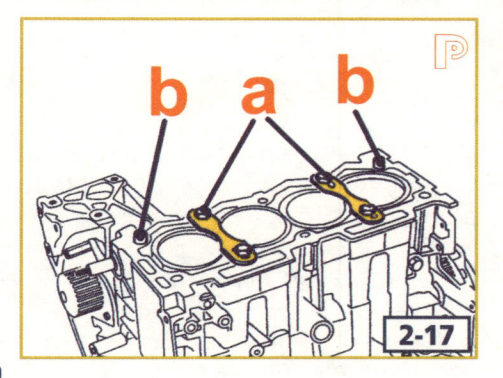

☐ **STEP 18:** Remove all traces of the cylinder head gasket from both block and head.
➜ Scrape off carbon deposits with a wooden or aluminium scraper, taking care not to gouge the aluminium surface of the head.
➜ Stuff rags into all openings in the cylinder head to stop debris dropping into them.
➜ Clean excessive carbon deposits from the crowns of the pistons without damaging the surface of the aluminium.

TOP TIP!

• If the engine is worn and you don't intend overhauling it at this stage, we strongly advise that you leave the piston crowns alone. The carbon on them can actually help preserve compression pressures when the engine is near the point of needing an overhaul.
• An aerosol gasket remover spray will help to remove pieces of stuck-on gasket.

☐ **STEP 19:** The cylinder head can be checked for distortion, at the angles shown, by use of a straight edge and feeler gauge. At the same time, check for excessive corrosion.

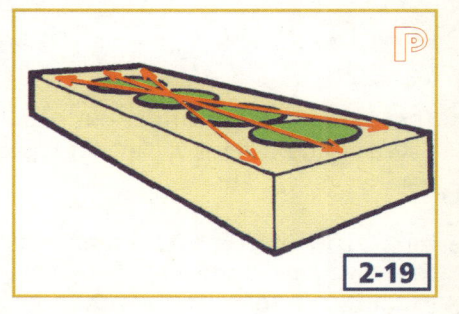

TOP TIP!

• It pays to have the cylinder head refaced before refitting to greatly reduce the risk of the cylinder head blowing after being refitted.
• This advice does not apply to the Diesel engines though, because of their high compression and different construction. If these are distorted, you will have to renew the cylinder head.

Part G: Cylinder Head Overhaul

	Page No.
JOB 1: READ THIS FIRST! - *applies to all types.*	6-40
JOB 2: CAMSHAFT, XV, XW, XY ENGINE - *removing, replacement.*	6-42
JOB 3: CAMSHAFT, TU ENGINE - *removing, replacement.*	6-42
JOB 4: CAMSHAFT, TUD ENGINE - *removing, replacement.*	6-43
JOB 5: CAMSHAFT, XU, XUD ENGINES - *removing, replacement.*	6-43
JOB 6: ROCKER SHAFT (XV,XW,XY & TU) - *overhaul.*	6-44
JOB 7: VALVES - *removing, reworking, refitting.*	6-45
JOB 8: VALVE GUIDES – *replacement.*	6-45
JOB 9: SWIRL CHAMBER (DIESEL ENGINES) – *removing, replacement.*	6-45
JOB 10: CYLINDER HEAD - *re-assembly.*	6-46

See **Part A: General Procedures** for further general information on working on the cylinder head.
➡ See **Part B: Which Engine is Which?** for an explanation of the engine types and for exploded diagrams of each of the cylinder head types covered here.

TOP TIP!

- Cylinder head components are not necessary interchangeable between engines, even though they may apparently be identical.
- If you need to replace any head components - particularly the camshaft - it is most important that you check with your Peugeot dealer or specialist to ensure that you replace like with like.

JOB 1: READ THIS FIRST! - *applies to all types*.

Section A: Which Valve Gear?

There are great similarities but detail differences between the various valve gear types fitted to the engines covered here.

IMPORTANT NOTE: Before dismantling any part of the valve gear, undo all nuts/bolts securing inlet and exhaust manifolds, and remove the manifolds from the head.
- Keep the nuts/bolts in the correct order (if there are any size differences) together with any washers and spacers.

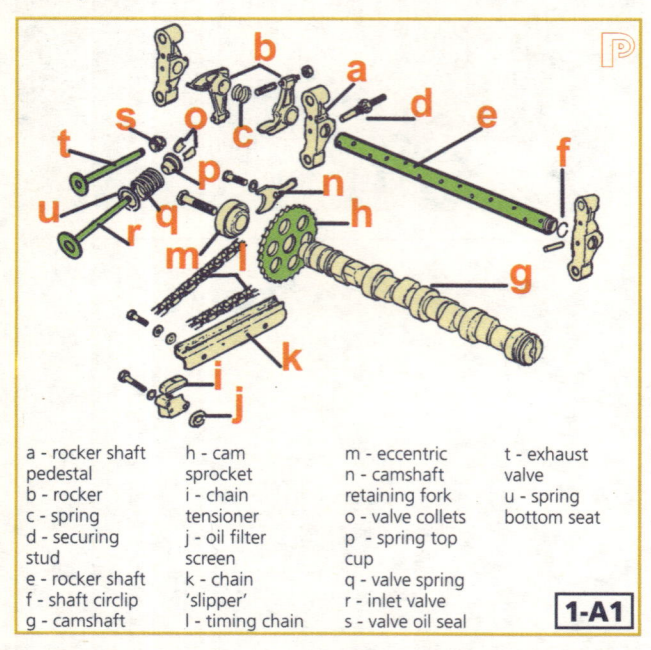

a - rocker shaft pedestal	h - cam sprocket	m - eccentric	t - exhaust valve
b - rocker	i - chain tensioner	n - camshaft retaining fork	u - spring bottom seat
c - spring	j - oil filter screen	o - valve collets	
d - securing stud	k - chain 'slipper'	p - spring top cup	
e - rocker shaft	l - timing chain	q - valve spring	
f - shaft circlip		r - inlet valve	
g - camshaft		s - valve oil seal	

❏ **ILLUSTRATION A1: XV, XW, XY PETROL ENGINES:** This is the OHC rocker-type valve gear fitted to all of these petrol engines - from 1.0 litre to 1.4, and fitted with a cylinder head-mounted distributor.

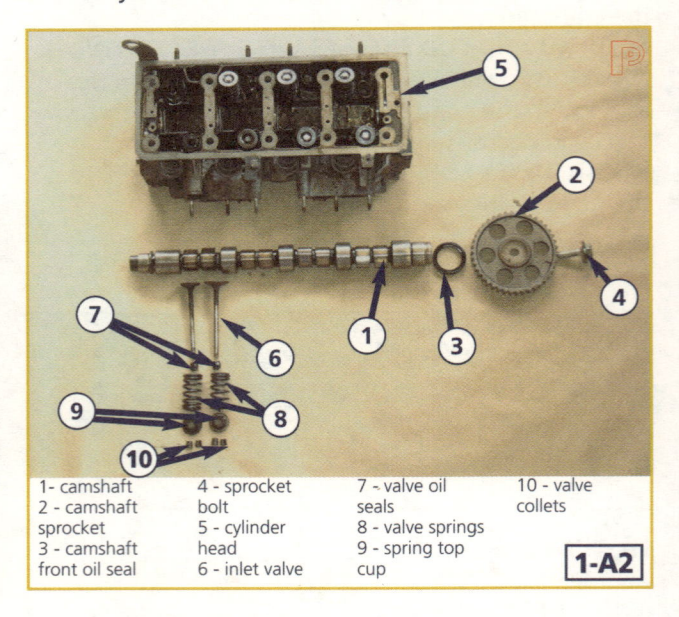

1- camshaft	4 - sprocket bolt	7 - valve oil seals	10 - valve collets
2 - camshaft sprocket	5 - cylinder head	8 - valve springs	
3 - camshaft front oil seal	6 - inlet valve	9 - spring top cup	

❏ **ILLUSTRATION A2: TU PETROL ENGINES:** This is the OHC rocker-type valve gear fitted to the TU petrol engines that took over from the XV, XW, XY series in 1988.
➡ Capacities are 1.0, 1.1 and 1.4 litres, and there are 8 valves.
➡ A larger (1.6-litre) version was eventually also added, to the 306 range.

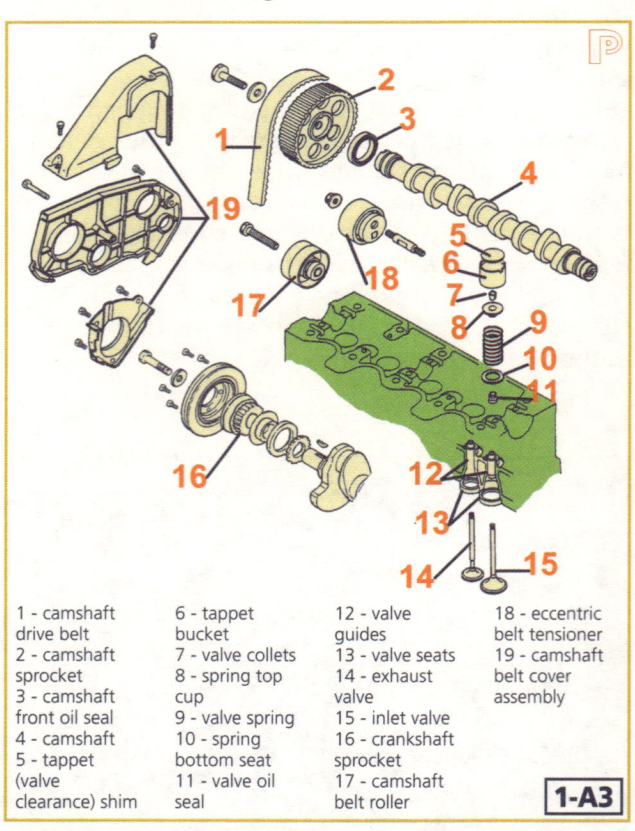

1 - camshaft drive belt	6 - tappet bucket	12 - valve guides	18 - eccentric belt tensioner
2 - camshaft sprocket	7 - valve collets	13 - valve seats	19 - camshaft belt cover assembly
3 - camshaft front oil seal	8 - spring top cup	14 - exhaust valve	
4 - camshaft	9 - valve spring	15 - inlet valve	
5 - tappet (valve clearance) shim	10 - spring bottom seat	16 - crankshaft sprocket	
	11 - valve oil seal	17 - camshaft belt roller	

❏ **ILLUSTRATION A3: TUD DIESEL ENGINES:** This is the direct-acting OHC valve gear fitted to the TUD diesel engines of 1.4 and 1.5 litres.

➜ The TUD Diesel engine's valve gear is essentially very similar to those of the XU and XUD engines, but the cylinder head has a swirl chamber for each cylinder.

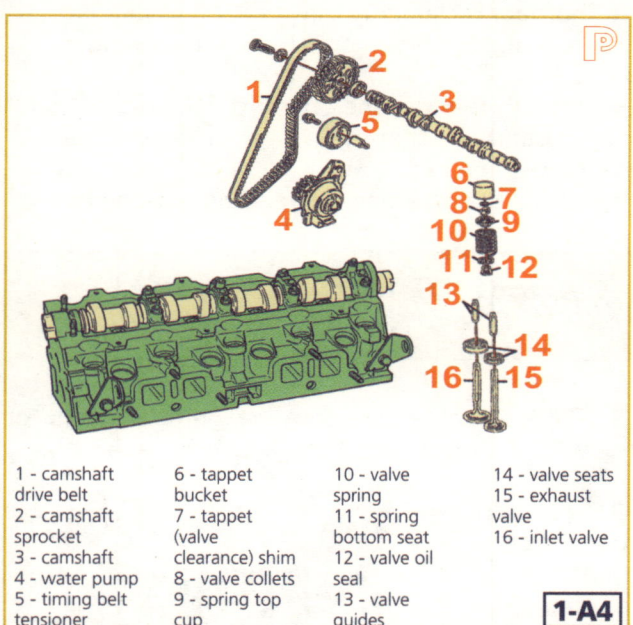

1 - camshaft drive belt
2 - camshaft sprocket
3 - camshaft
4 - water pump
5 - timing belt tensioner
6 - tappet bucket
7 - tappet (valve clearance) shim
8 - valve collets
9 - spring top cup
10 - valve spring
11 - spring bottom seat
12 - valve oil seal
13 - valve guides
14 - valve seats
15 - exhaust valve
16 - inlet valve

1-A4

❒ **ILLUSTRATIONS A4: XU PETROL ENGINES:** This is the direct-acting OHC valve gear fitted to the XU petrol engines that come in capacities of 1.6, 1.8 litres, 1.9 and 2.0 litres with 8 valves.
➜ Timing belt configurations vary between models.

1 - camshaft
2 - camshaft sprocket
3 - vacuum pump pulley
4 - cylinder head
5 - camshaft bearing caps
6 - tappet (valve clearance) shim
7 - tappet bucket
8 - valve springs
9 - spring top cups
10 - inlet valve
11 - exhaust valve
12 - valve collets

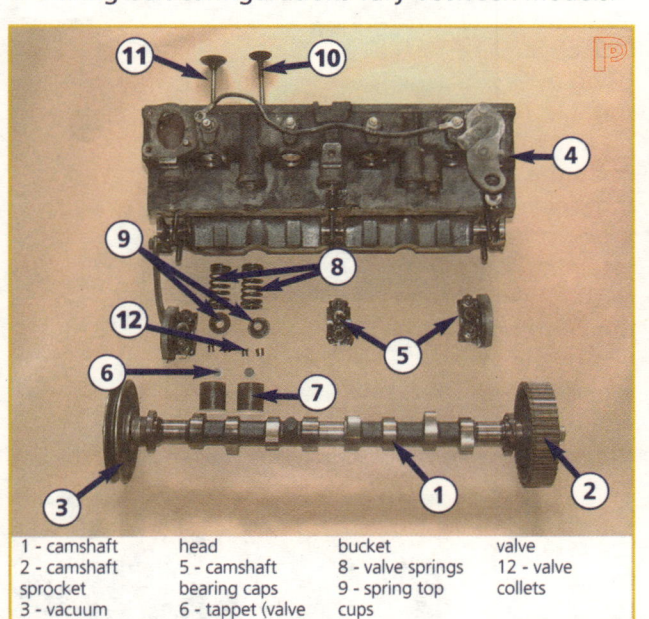

1-A5

❒ **ILLUSTRATION A5: XUD DIESEL ENGINES:** This is the direct-acting OHC valve gear fitted to the XUD diesel engines of 1.8 and 1.9 litres.
➜ The XUD Diesel engine's valve gear is essentially very similar to that of the TUD and XU engines, but the cylinder head has a swirl chamber for each cylinder.

Section B: Common procedures.

This Section consists of important information which is applicable to all of the cylinder heads and valve gear covered in this manual. It should be followed in conjunction with the type of cylinder head that you are working on.

TOP TIP!

• Before dismantling any part of the valve gear, undo all nuts/bolts securing inlet and exhaust manifolds, and remove the manifolds from the head.
• Keep the nuts/bolts in the correct order (if there are any size differences) together with any washers and spacers.

❒ **STEP B1:** If you use a cylinder head stand, such as this Sykes-Pickavant stand, it makes the unit easier to work on.

1-B1

TOP TIP!

❒ **STEP B2:** • If you need to check the end-float in the camshaft bearings, do so before removing the camshaft from the head.
• Measure the camshaft endfloat (free axial movement) using feeler gauges between the fork and the camshaft, or between a bearing and cam edge.
• The acceptable endfloat range is 0.07 to 0.16 mm.

❒ **STEP B3:** Inspect the camshaft:
➜ Look for dull, worn spots at the lobe points and look for damage to the bearing surfaces.
➜ Any problems with the camshaft could be due to poor oil circulation.
➜ Check that the cylinder head oilways are clear and renew the camshaft if necessary.

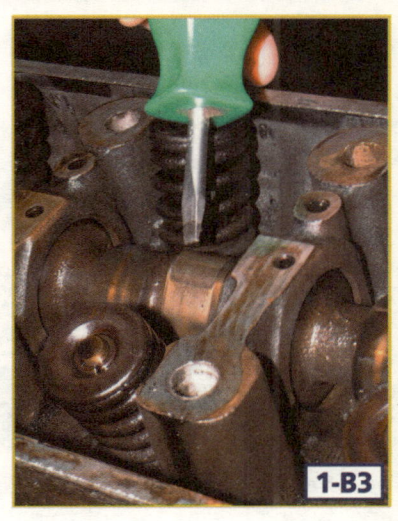

1-B3

CHAPTER 6 Part G Job 1

6-41

☐ **STEP B4:** When you come to remove the camshaft sprocket, you will find that the sprocket bolt will be very tight. To prevent the camshaft from turning:
→ Push a bar through the sprocket hole (**a**) and rest it on the top face of the cylinder head.
→ Place padding between bar and head so that the cylinder head isn't damaged.
→ You can now loosen the sprocket nut (**b**) - you will often need to use an extra-long 'breaker' bar.

JOB 2: CAMSHAFT, XV, XW, XY ENGINE – *removing, replacement*.

☐ **STEP 1:** If not already removed, take the distributor from the end of the cylinder head, but mark its position on the head first, so that it can be refitted to give the same ignition timing.

☐ **STEP 2:** Remove the camshaft retaining fork from the end of the head - similar location to *Job 3, Step 3*.
→ Slacken the clamp bolt and slide the fork in its elongated slot until it is clear of the camshaft groove.

☐ **STEP 3:** Lever out the camshaft oil seal (opposite to cam sprocket end - position arrowed).
→ Carefully slide the camshaft out of the cylinder head from the oil seal-end, taking great care not to damage the camshaft bearings with the edges of the cam lobes.

☐ **STEP 4:** When refitting the camshaft:
→ Drift a new camshaft oil seal flush into the recess at the end of the head.
→ Thoroughly clean the camshaft, oil its bearing journals and the bearing surfaces in the cylinder head.
→ Carefully re-insert the camshaft, taking great care not to damage either the oil seal, or the camshaft bearings.
→ Engage the retaining fork and tighten the bolt.

JOB 3: CAMSHAFT, TU ENGINE – *removing, replacement*.

☐ **STEP 1:** Unbolt and remove the ignition distributor - see *Job 2, Step 1* - and the ignition coil assembly.

☐ **STEP 2:** Lift the rocker shaft assembly from the head.
→ If it is tight, ease it off its locating dowels.

☐ **STEP 3:** Using a suitable Torx bit and driver, undo the bolt that secures the camshaft retaining fork to the distributor-end of the cylinder head, and detach the fork.

☐ **STEP 4:** Tap the retaining fork end of the camshaft, using a soft-headed mallet (and a drift, if necessary) so that the camshaft (**a**) emerges from the opposite end of the cylinder head, taking the front oil seal (**b**) with it.

❐ **STEP 5:** When refitting the camshaft:
→ Drift a new camshaft oil seal flush into the recess at the end of the head.
→ Thoroughly clean the camshaft, oil its bearing journals and the bearing surfaces in the cylinder head.
→ Carefully re-insert the camshaft, taking great care not to damage either the oil seal, or the camshaft bearings.
→ Engage the retaining fork and tighten the bolt.

JOB 4: CAMSHAFT, TUD ENGINE – *removing, replacement.*

❐ **STEP 1:** Support the cylinder head on the bench. If not already removed, take off the brake vacuum pump from the end of the cylinder head (two bolts and washers).

❐ **STEP 2:** The three camshaft bearing caps should have position numbers cast on them.
→ If not, mark each one with an identification, as it is imperative that they are refitted to the same locations, and that they are not refitted the wrong way round.

❐ **STEP 3:** Evenly slacken the camshaft bearing nuts in a progressive manner, so that the valve spring compression is gently released across the length of the head. Remove the nuts and lift off the bearing caps.

❐ **STEP 4:** Lift out the camshaft, complete with oil seal on one end.

❐ **STEP 5: NEW CAMSHAFT:** If you are going to be fitting a new camshaft, it is important that you set the valve clearances at this stage – see *Part E: Valve Clearance/Valve Lash – Checking, Adjustment.*

RE-ASSEMBLY

❐ **STEP 6:** Thoroughly clean the camshaft and the tappet shims, which are operated by the camshaft.
→ Oil the shims, the camshaft bearing journals and cams, and lower the camshaft into position.

❐ **STEP 7:** Clean and oil the bearing surfaces of the camshaft bearing caps, and the bearing surfaces in the cylinder head.

❐ **STEP 8:** Apply a little sealant to the flanges of the two end caps where they bear against the ends of the head, at the points where they will house the camshaft oil seals.

❐ **STEP 9:** Lower the camshaft into place.
→ Position the caps over their studs in the correct numerical order - facing the right way round - and loosely fit their retaining nuts.
→ Progressively tighten the bearing cap nuts until all the caps are seated, then progressively tighten all the nuts to the correct torque – see *Chapter 1, Facts and Figures.*

❐ **STEP 10:** Fit a new camshaft oil seal: lubricate it, then drift it in squarely, using a suitable socket over the camshaft nose, until it is fully seated against its shoulder in the cylinder head.

JOB 5: CAMSHAFT, XU, XUD ENGINES – *removing, replacement.*

This Job deals with both petrol (XU) and diesel (XUD) engines.

❐ **STEP 1: PETROL ENGINES:** Mark the position of the distributor on the cylinder head, so that it can be refitted to give the same ignition timing.

❐ **STEP 2A:** Remove, from the transmission end of the cylinder head:
→ **EITHER - DIESEL:** The brake vacuum pump (XUD - arrowed).

❐ **STEP 2B: OR - PETROL:** The ignition distributor (earlier XU - a), or the ignition coil module (later XU) - see *Chapter 9, Ignition, Fuel, Exhaust.*

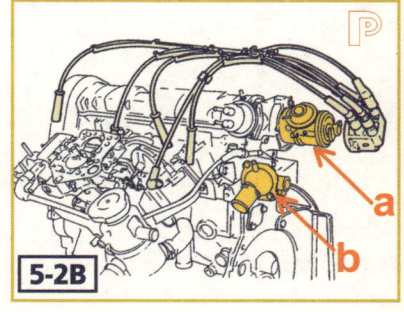

❐ **STEP 3:** Loosen the upper bolt which retains the thermostat housing (*5-2B*) to the left-hand end of the head. Withdraw the bolt and sealing washer.

❏ **STEP 4:** Carefully lever the camshaft oil spray bar (arrowed - petrol engine only) from the camshaft bearing caps, and put to one side, retaining its sealing O-rings.

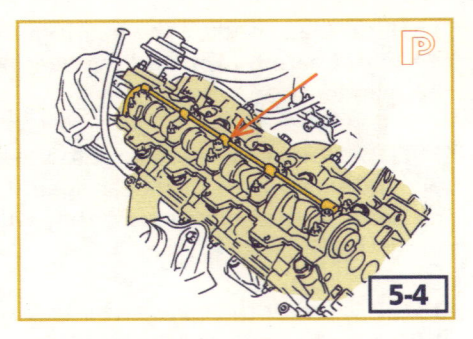

5-4

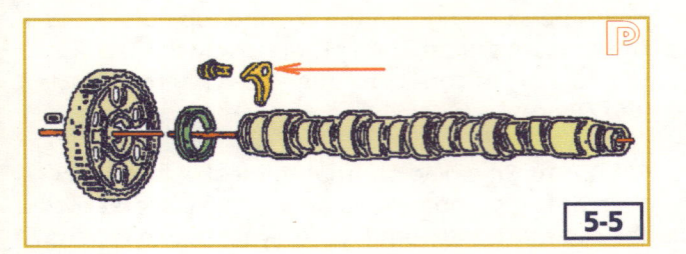

5-5

❏ **STEP 5:** Where one is fitted, withdraw the camshaft retaining fork (arrowed), by first undoing its clamp bolt with an Allen key.
➜ Note that not all XU, XUD engines have a retaining fork.

❏ **STEP 6:** Take off the bearing caps nuts (locations arrowed) and bearing caps and remove the camshaft - see *Job 4, Steps 3 to 5*, bearing in mind that some XU and XUD engines have FIVE camshaft bearing caps.

5-6

❏ **STEP 7: NEW CAMSHAFT:** If you are going to be fitting a new camshaft, it is important that you set the valve clearances at this stage – see *Part E: Valve Clearance/Valve Lash – Checking, Adjustment*.

RE-ASSEMBLY

❏ **STEP 8:** Follow *Job 4, Steps 6-on*.

❏ **STEP 9: ENGINES WITH CAMSHAFT RETAINING FORK:** Refit the fork at the end of the cylinder head and tighten the clamp bolt.

❏ **STEP 10: XU ENGINES:** Check the condition of the camshaft oil spray bar O-rings, and renew, if necessary. Oil the O-rings and push the spray bar back into place in the camshaft bearing caps.

JOB 6: ROCKER SHAFT - XV, XW, XY, TU ENGINES - *overhaul*.

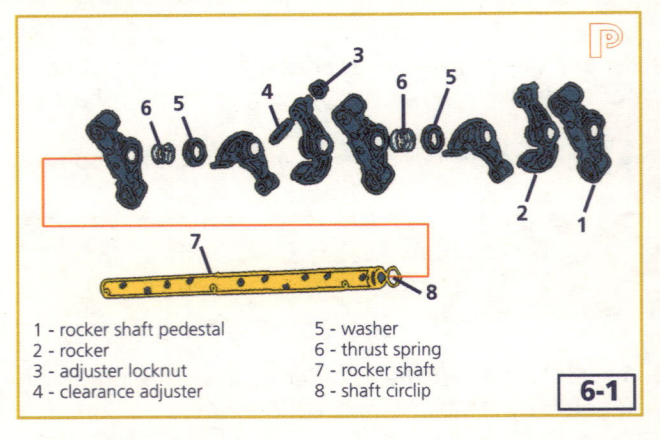

6-1

1 - rocker shaft pedestal
2 - rocker
3 - adjuster locknut
4 - clearance adjuster
5 - washer
6 - thrust spring
7 - rocker shaft
8 - shaft circlip

❏ **STEP 1:** Dismantle the rocker shaft assembly by levering the retaining shaft circlip from the right-hand end of the rocker shaft, using a small, thin-bladed screwdriver.

❏ **STEP 2:** Slide the pedestal, spring (and cup washer - TU engine only) and rockers in turn from the shaft, keeping them in strict order, and continue with the next sets of components.

TOP TIP!

❏ **STEP 3:** • The last pedestal will not slide off, as it is secured to the shaft by the rocker cover retaining stud in its top, and a grub screw.
• If you need to remove it, slacken the grub screw.
• Tightening two nuts against each other on the stud, then use a spanner to 'undo' the lower one, unscrewing the stud from the pedestal.

INSPECTION OF COMPONENTS: Look for the following:
➜ Severe ridging of the shaft.
➜ Excessive side play of the rockers on the shaft, when rockers are twisted.
➜ Wear on the rocker pads where they run against the cams.
➜ The ends of the valve clearance adjuster screws.

❏ **STEP 4:** Clean, lubricate and re-assemble the rocker shaft assembly in the reverse order of removal.
➜ Ensure that rockers and pedestals face the correct directions.

JOB 7: VALVES - removing, reworking, refitting.

→ The components fitted to the vehicles covered here are entirely conventional. See *Part A: General Procedures* for how to carry out the work covered in this Job
→ See *Job 1* for exploded drawings of the various cylinder head types featured here.

☐ **STEP 1:** IMPORTANT NOTE: When re-assembling, lubricate the bearing surfaces of the bucket tappets with copious quantities of fresh engine oil and place them back in position over their respective valves.
→ Don't forget that each bucket should have the correct size of valve clearance shim underneath it (XU, XUD engines) or on top of it (TUD engine).
→ See *Part E, Valve Adjust.*

JOB 8: VALVE GUIDES – replacement.

If you accept the risk of damaging and ruining perfectly new valve guides, it is sometimes possible to replace them without the use of specialist equipment.

☐ **STEP 1:** Use a thread tap to make a thread inside each old guide.

☐ **STEP 2:** Screw a bolt (**a**) into the guide (**b**) and drift the guide (via the end of the bolt) out of the head. This drift is an old threaded stud – anything that slides inside the guide will do.

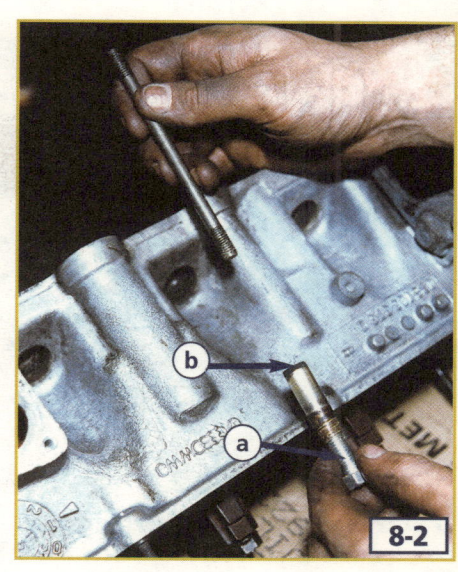

☐ **STEP 3:** Place another (smaller) bolt in the new guide. Drift down onto the bolt head, protecting the guide.
→ Make sure all guides are driven into the correct depth – compare new with old.

☐ **STEP 4:** Ream out the new guides with the correct size of hand reamer, using plenty of cutting fluid.

JOB 9: SWIRL CHAMBER (DIESEL ENGINES) – removing, replacement.

If the swirl chambers are burned or badly carbonated, they will need to be replaced.

☐ **STEP 1:** Unscrew and remove all of the injectors and glow plugs, to prevent damage.

☐ **STEP 2:** Insert a drift into the injector opening and drive the swirl chamber out.

☐ **STEP 3:** Clean the swirl chamber housing in the cylinder head, scraping out any carbonated material.

☐ **STEP 4:** Use a mallet to drive each new swirl chamber into position, making sure that the locating guide and groove are correctly located.

STEP 5: The swirl chamber (arrowed) must project by no more than 0.03 mm - use a dial gauge to check this. If projection is greater:
→ Remove the swirl chamber again and make absolutely certain that the housing is clean.
→ Alternatively, try fitting different swirl chambers into different positions, in case there are small manufacturing variations.
→ As a last resort, take the cylinder head to a machine shop and have it machined so that the swirl chamber projection is okay.

JOB 10: CYLINDER HEAD - *re-assembly*.

STEP 1: Refit the camshaft and camshaft oil seal – see *Jobs 2 to 6*.

STEP 2: After fitting the camshaft to the head, make sure it turns freely (accepting that on those engines with bucket-type tappets, the camshaft will be acting against the valve springs).
→ If there is any reason to suspect undue tightness in the camshaft bearings, check to see if any dirt has found its way between journals.
→ Note that severe distortion of the cylinder head on these engines can cause distortion of the integrated camshaft bearings, in which case the entire cylinder head must be renewed.

STEP 3: Refit cylinder head peripherals removed after head removal from the engine. Depending on model, these include:
→ Ignition distributor - align the distributor flange marks made before removal.
→ Ignition coil assembly (petrol engines).
→ Brake vacuum pump (diesel engines).
→ Camshaft sprocket, and camshaft oil spray bar (when fitted)
→ Thermostat housing (XU engine).

Part H: Cylinder Head Refitting

CONTENTS
Page No.

JOB 1: CYLINDER HEAD – *refitting*.   6-46

See *Part B: Which Engine is Which?* for an explanation of the engine types referred to here.

If there are any doubts about the trueness or condition of a cylinder head mating face, have the head skimmed by an engine overhaul specialist. Refitting a head that has not been skimmed may lead to a blowing head gasket. The compression ratio of a Diesel engine will be raised too high if it is skimmed excessively, so machining may only be carried out to a maximum amount of 0.40 mm.

JOB 1: CYLINDER HEAD – *refitting*.

IMPORTANT NOTE: On all engines except the XV/XW/XY series, the cylinder head must only be refitted if the crankshaft and camshaft are locked in their 'safe' positions with locking rods. See *Part C, Job 3* for full details.

FACT FILE
GASKETS AND BOLTS

i) A cylinder head gasket may only be used once, as not only does it compress on first torque-tightening of the cylinder head, but it also 'self-vulcanises' when the engine first reaches operating temperature.

So, if you need to remove the head a second time, even if you have just fitted a new gasket and have torqued the head down, you will need to use yet another new gasket.

ii) Use all new gaskets for all applicable items, such as camshaft/rocker cover, manifolds and so on.

❏ **STEP 1:** Check the cylinder head for cracks, especially around and between valve seats, and for distortion, using a straight edge and feeler gauges.
→ On Diesel engines, do not lay the straight edge across any swirl chambers, as these are often raised.
→ If any cracking or distortion are found and you are not sure whether or not the head can be re-used, have the head checked by a Peugeot dealer or engine specialist.

❏ **STEP 2:** Check that all the cylinder head mating surfaces are thoroughly clean. Ensure that the bolt holes in the block are free of debris and that the threads are free running. Ensure that the pistons are cleaned and that there is no loose debris in the cylinders.

1-3

❏ **STEP 3:** The cylinder head gasket will only fit correctly on to the cylinder block in one direction, as otherwise oil and water holes will not correctly align – a disaster waiting to happen!

DIESEL ENGINES PISTON PROTRUSION

❏ **STEP 4:** Piston protrusion above the block at TDC must be measured. In place of the special tools shown here, you could use a perfectly straight steel bar placed over the piston crown, and use a pair of feeler gauge sets to measure the parallel clearances between the block face and each side of the bar.
→ Set No. 1 piston at TDC and measure protrusion.
→ Measure maximum protrusion of each other piston.
→ Take the highest of the four values.

1-4

TOP TIP!
• If the values differ greatly, discuss the supply of a better matched set of pistons and cylinder liners with your supplier.

❏ **STEP 5A:** Select and fit a Diesel engine gasket as follows:
→ The number of notches at the flywheel end of the gasket indicates gasket thickness. See FACT FILE below.
→ Fit the gasket with its notched end at the flywheel end of the engine.
→ **TUD ENGINE:** There may be a series of notches at this end of the gasket. The notches towards the rear corner (bulkhead side, **A**) only signify the engine type, and can be ignored. The notches at the middle of this end of the gasket (**B**) are also to be ignored. It is the presence of one notch or none at the front of the gasket (radiator side - **C**) that is relevant. No notch signifies a standard, factory gasket, while one notch signifies a gasket 0.1mm thicker, to be used only with a cylinder head that has been re-machined. Usually it is sufficient to replace the gasket with a like-for-like type.

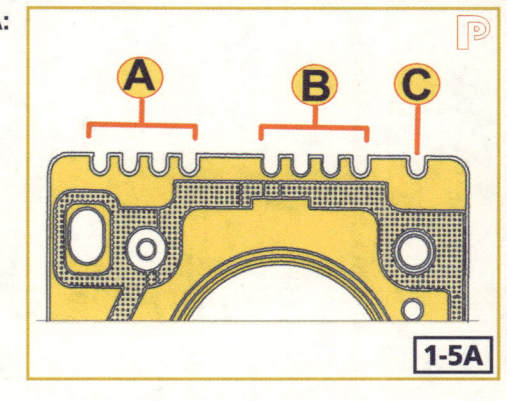

1-5A

❏ **STEP 5B: XUD ENGINE:** There may be a series of notches (or holes) at the end of the gasket. The one or two notches at the centre (**d**) of the gasket end identify either the 1.7-litre engine (one notch) or the turbocharged engine (two notches). The 1-4 notches toward the rear corner (bulkhead side, shown by a, b, c) of the gasket denote gasket thickness.

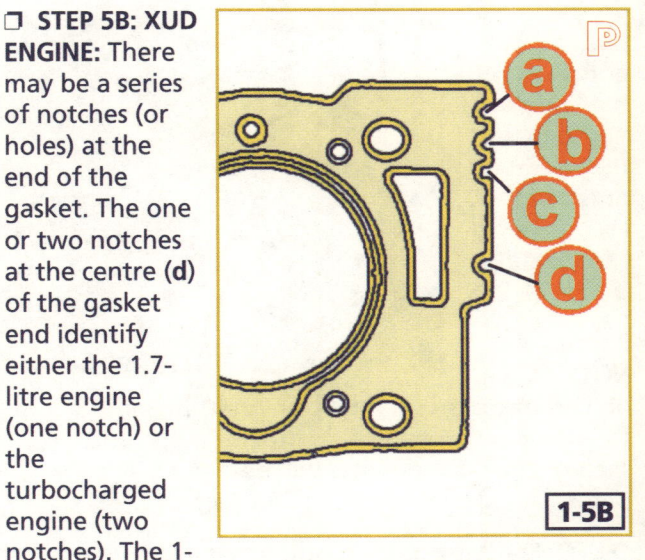

1-5B

FACT FILE

GASKET – XUD DIESEL ENGINE PISTON PROTRUSION (mm)

No. of Notches Protrusion
1 0.54-0.65 mm
2 0.65-0.77 mm
3 0.77-0.82 mm
4 0.84 mm or more

IMPORTANT NOTE: Check with your supplier that the gasket you are buying is the correct one!

PETROL ENGINES – GASKET IDENTIFICATION

☐ **STEP 6:** TU AND XU ENGINE: There is a choice of two different thicknesses of head gasket.
→ The standard gasket is 1.2 mm thick and is identified by punched holes at the left-hand side (flywheel end) of the gasket (gasket laid correctly in place on engine).
→ A non-standard gasket of 1.4 mm thickness is used when the cylinder head is a factory-reconditioned unit which has been machined. This gasket type is identified by two or three holes punched where the standard gasket has just one.

☐ **STEP 7:** Carefully remove the cylinder liner clamps fitted to wet-liner engines, taking care not to disturb the liners, and not to lose the head-bolt nuts from their external channels in the crankcase.

IMPORTANT NOTE: Under no circumstances may the crankshaft be moved once the clamps are removed, as otherwise the bottom seals of the cylinder liners will be broken, necessitating a complete engine overhaul.

☐ **STEP 8:** If the engine is of the aluminium wet-liner type, and the cylinder head was removed because of head gasket problems, or the engine has been completely overhauled (new cylinder liners and/or liner bottom seals have been fitted), you should now check the cylinder liner protrusions, as detailed in *Part K, Engine Rebuild*.

TOP TIP!

☐ **STEP 9:** All these Peugeot engines have one or more locating rings (arrowed) in the cylinder block or head to facilitate engagement of the head gasket and refitting of the head. However, in some cases, such as when refitting the XUD turbodiesel head complete with manifolds, it is much easier to locate the head correctly if pilot (guide) studs are made up, although this advice does not apply to the XV/XW/XY series engines, on which there is limited access for manoeuvring the head. These studs are…
→ Two old cylinder head bolts with the heads cut off.
→ These will act as guides when you lower the cylinder head into position and keep the gasket in the correct place at the same time.

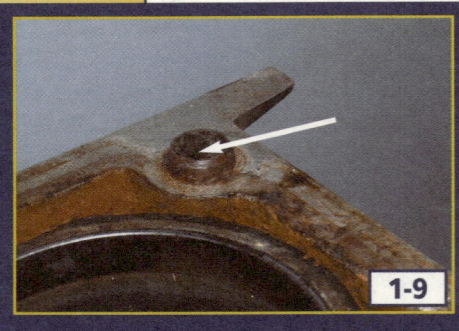

XV/XW/XY ENGINES

☐ **STEP 10:** You must now lift up the cylinder head locating ring at the left-hand front corner of crankcase.
→ It was previously tapped down into the crankcase recess before the head was removed.
→ Lift it sufficiently for it to protrude from the crankcase by approximately the amount shown in illustration *1-9*.

☐ **STEP 11:** Ensure that two locating rings are in place on the crankcase – the one just lifted (**a**), and its opposite at the timing cover end (**b**), along the same front edge of the block.

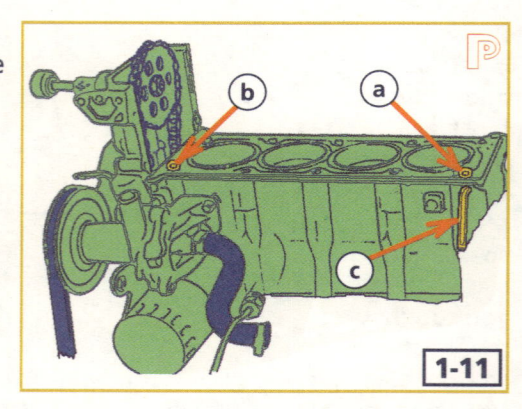

→ Prevent the locating ring from slipping back down by inserting a rod (**c**) or punch in the front crankcase hole just beneath it.

→ This will ensure that the ring is not pushed down by the cylinder head. Make sure the support does not get in the way of the cylinder head bolt.

❏ **STEP 12:** Locate the new cylinder head gasket on the cylinder block, correctly engaged over the locating rings.

❏ **STEP 13:** If camshaft sprocket/timing chain support tool 7.0132 was fitted when removing the head, remove its rear nut and washer and withdraw the threaded rod of the tool.

1-14

❏ **STEP 14:** Run a bead of silicone sealant along the raised mating face of the timing case, then lower the cylinder head into position.
→ Fit the four timing case upper securing bolts (**a**), but do not yet tighten.

❏ **STEP 15A:** You should now use Peugeot Tool No. 7.0132 to lock the camshaft. EITHER, see *Part F* for more information on the tool, OR the following TOP TIP!
→ Push the camshaft to engage it with the tapered end of tool 7.0132.
→ Using the tool key, align the slots in camshaft and pilot body of tool, then screw in the threaded part of the tool: this will push out the key.
→ Slight rotation of the fuel pump eccentric (**a**) may be required in order to line-up the key and camshaft slot.

TOP TIP!

❏ **STEP 15B:**
• You could make up your own tool to lock the camshaft.
• Use the thrust plate and original right-hand bolt (**e**).
• Make up three plates: item (**d**), item (**b**) and the plate situated behind item (**b**).
• Use the slots in plate (**b**) and (**d**) to push the bolts (**a**) against the outer edges of the holes in the sprocket, to prevent it from moving in either direction.
• Tighten the bolts and nuts – DON'T put pressure on the sprocket!

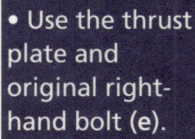

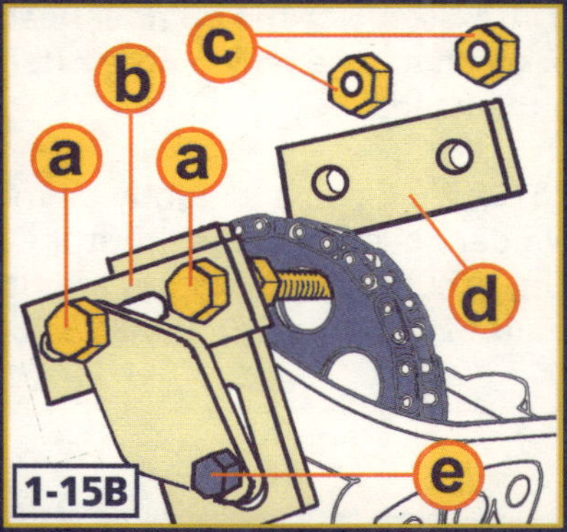

1-15B

❏ **STEP 16:** Re-engage the camshaft thrust plate (illustration *1-14, item b*) with the camshaft, and tighten its securing bolts (**c**) to the recommended torque.

❏ **STEP 17:** Refit the camshaft sprocket central retaining bolt (see illustration *1-15A, item b*), and tighten it to the specified torque.
→ To prevent the camshaft from turning when torque-tightening, pass a suitable rod through an upper hole of the camshaft sprocket (illustration *1-15A, point c*) and wedge it against the top of the cylinder, using suitable protection such as a good thickness of folded rag, between head and rod.

❏ **STEP 18:** Apply sealant to the camshaft sprocket access plate, and refit the plate.

❏ **STEP 19:** Refit the fuel pump pushrod to its hole in the top front of the timing case.

❏ **STEP 20:** Lubricate and refit the rocker shaft, noting that its locating pegs (underside of pedestals) should be towards the front side of the cylinder head.

1-20

IMPORTANT NOTES: • If the valve seats have been recut, it is advisable to slacken off all the rocker

CHAPTER 6   Part H   Job 1

6-49

(valve clearance) adjusters first.

• Depending on working space, it may be beneficial to insert some of the cylinder head bolts into the rocker shaft assembly before offering the assembly to the head.

❏ **STEP 21:** Clean and lightly oil the threads of all cylinder head bolts, then refit the bolts and their nuts, ensuring that washers are fitted beneath the heads of bolts on XY7 and XY8 engines.

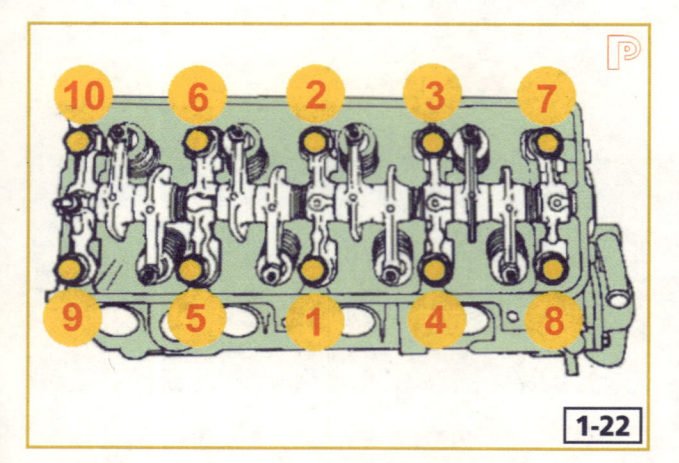

1-22

❏ **STEP 22:** Screw in each bolt in the correct order until it just starts to tighten up.
➔ Now tighten the bolts in two stages with a torque wrench to the figure shown in *Chapter 1, Facts and Figures*.
➔ Torque-tighten the head bolts in the order shown.

❏ **STEP 23:** Tighten the four timing case securing bolts – arrowed, illustration *1-14*.

❏ **STEP 24:** If the valve seats have been recut, or a new camshaft has been fitted, check the valve clearances – see *Part E, Job 1*.

❏ **STEP 25:** Refit the rocker cover, together with a new gasket if required.

❏ **STEP 26:** Refit the fuel pump to the timing case.

❏ **STEP 27:** Remove the wooden support – if used – lower the engine back to its normal position, and re-attach the engine mountings.

❏ **STEP 28:** Re-attach the exhaust system to the manifold, refit the ignition distributor and spark plug leads, reconnect all coolant and fuel hoses, vacuum pipes and electrical wiring, the choke and throttle cables, and all air intake components.

❏ **STEP 29:** Refit the plastic flywheel access plate at the clutch housing opening, reconnect the gear linkage, then refit and reconnect the battery.

❏ **STEP 30:** Refill and bleed the cooling system – see *Chapter 5, Servicing*.

❏ **STEP 31:** Run the engine until it reaches normal operating temperature. Switch off the engine and allow it to cool for at least two hours.

❏ **STEP 32:** Once it is cool, remove the rocker cover and slacken all the cylinder head bolts in the order shown in illustration *1-22*.
➔ Retighten the bolts in this same order to the final tightening torque shown in *Chapter 1, Facts and Figures*.

TU AND TUD ENGINES

FACT FILE
HEAD BOLTS

• Before re-using the head bolts of any of the engines included below, the bolts should be measured, to check for stretching.

TUD ENGINES
• Re-usable bolts should be within the length range 184.5 mm to 185.9 mm, measured from underside of head to end of thread. But if any one bolt is longer than the limit, ALL BOLTS SHOULD BE RENEWED.

❏ **STEP 33:** Check that the cylinder head locating rings are in position on the cylinder block, then position the new cylinder head gasket on block with the maker's name upwards and notched end at flywheel/transmission end of engine - see illustration *1-5A*.

❏ **STEP 34:** Check that the crankshaft, camshaft (and injection pump – diesel engines) are still locked in their correct positions – see *Part C, Job 3*.

❏ **STEP 35:** Lower the cylinder head into position, then, for TU petrol engines, follow *Step 20*.

❏ **STEP 36:** Smear the threads and underside of the bolt heads with Molycote G Rapid Plus grease, which is available from Peugeot dealers.
➔ Insert the head bolts and tighten them finger-tight only.

1-37

☐ **STEP 37: TUD ENGINES ONLY:** Progressively tighten the cylinder head bolts in the order shown to their stage 1 torque setting - see *Chapter 1, Facts and Figures.*
→ Now fully slacken the bolts in the reverse sequence, then retighten in the original order to Stage 2.
→ Complete the tightening procedure given in *Chapter 1, Facts and Figures* for your engine.

☐ **STEP 38: TU ENGINES:** Tighten the head bolts in the correct order - see illustration *1-37* - in the relevant stages given in *Chapter 1, Facts and Figures*.

IMPORTANT NOTE: As different versions of TU and TUD engine have different head tightening procedures, varying from two to four stages, be sure to look up the correct figures for your exact engine. Angle-tightening of the head bolts will require the use of tool such as the Sykes Pickavant Angular Torque Gauge 800700.

☐ **STEP 39:** Refit the camshaft drive (timing) belt, and tension it, as detailed in *Part C, Job 2.*

☐ **STEP 40:** Follow **Steps 24, 25, 28** and **30**. If the engine is a catalyst-equipped, petrol unit, reconnect the wiring to the exhaust system Lambda sensor.

☐ **STEP 41:** Refit the fuel injection system – see *Chapter 9, Ignition, Fuel, Exhaust*. Reattach the bracket that secures the oil dipstick tube to the cylinder head. Reattach the ignition coil (if applicable).

☐ **STEP 42:** On TUD diesel engine, reconnect the waxstat fast idle device cable running between cylinder head and injection pump (if fitted), and prime the fuel system.

☐ **STEP 43:** Reconnect the battery.

XU AND XUD ENGINES

FACT FILE
HEAD BOLTS

Before re-using the head bolts of any of the engines included below, the bolts should be measured, to check for stretching.

1.8 & 2.0-LITRE XU ENGINES
• Re-usable bolts should be no longer than 176.5 mm (1.8-litre engine) or 122mm (2.0-litre engine) measured from underside of head to end of thread.
• If any one bolt is longer than the limit, ALL BOLTS SHOULD BE RENEWED.

☐ **STEP 44: XUD ENGINES ONLY:** Three different types of cylinder head bolt are used on XUD diesel engines.
→ These are the plain, hex-headed bolts used prior to September 1986, the grooved-shank hex-headed bolts used from September 1986, and the Torx-headed bolts introduced during 1989.
→ Note that the tightening procedure is different for each and that the grooved-shank bolt used between 1986 and 1989 MUST NOT BE RE-USED - a replacement bolt set should be obtained.
→ On all XUD engines except the turbocharged 1.9-litre the maximum permissible length of any head bolt is 121.5 mm, measured from underside of head to end of thread.
→ On 1.9-litre turbo, this maximum measurement is 146.5mm.
→ Bolts that have stretched beyond limit can be replaced individually.
→ ALL CYLINDER HEAD WASHERS MUST BE RENEWED.

☐ **STEP 45:** Check that the cylinder head locating rings are in position on the cylinder block.
→ On the XU engine it may be necessary to extract one of the rings from the left-hand side of the cylinder head, and fit it into the cylinder block.
→ Once in the block, it should be supported from beneath with a suitable rod or punch to prevent it from slipping down below the block face.

☐ **STEP 46:** Position the new cylinder head gasket on the block with its notched end at the transmission end of engine.

☐ **STEP 47:** Check that the crankshaft, camshaft (and injection pump – diesel) are still locked in their correct positions – see *Part C, Job 3.*

☐ **STEP 48:** Lower cylinder head into position.

❏ **STEP 49:** Smear the threads and underside of the bolt heads with Molycote G Rapid Plus grease, which is available from Peugeot dealers.
➜ Insert the head bolts (and washers, as applicable), and – on aluminium engines – engage the head-bolt retaining nuts in the crankcase external channels.
➜ Remove the two pilot studs, if used, and insert the last two bolts.
➜ IMPORTANT NOTE: All XU/XUD engines except for the 2.0-litre XU petrol have a thick spacer beneath the head of the cylinder head bolt situated directly above the water pump. If this spacer is omitted, tightening of the bolt will cause damage to the cylinder block.

❏ **STEP 50:** Remove the locating ring support.
➜ For the XU engine, see **Step 43** then tighten the head bolts finger-tight only.

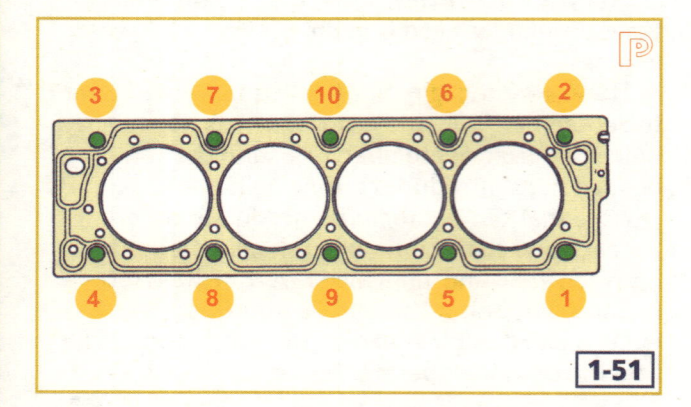

1-51

❏ **STEP 51: NON-2.0-LITRE XU ENGINES ONLY:** Progressively tighten the cylinder head bolts in the order shown to their stage 1 torque setting - see **Chapter 1, Facts and Figures**.
➜ Now fully slacken the bolts in the reverse sequence.
➜ Retighten in the original order to Stage 2.
➜ Complete the tightening procedure given in **Chapter 1, Facts and Figures** for your engine.

❏ **STEP 52: 2.0 LITRE XU ENGINES ONLY:** Tighten the head bolts in the correct order (see illustration **1-51**) in the relevant stages given in **Chapter 1, Facts and Figures**.
➜ IMPORTANT NOTE: As different versions of XU and XUD engine have different head tightening procedures and numbers of stages, be sure to look up the correct figures for your exact engine. Angle-tightening of the head bolts will require the use of a tool such as the Sykes Pickavant Angular Torque Gauge 800700.

❏ **STEP 53:** Pass the timing camshaft drive (timing) belt over the camshaft sprocket, then refit the right-hand engine mounting bracket to the engine - XUD engine shown.
➜ Reconnect and torque-tighten the engine mounting, then remove the trolley jack from beneath the engine.

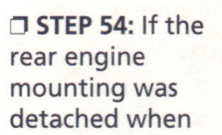

1-53

❏ **STEP 54:** If the rear engine mounting was detached when removing the head, reconnect and torque-tighten it.

❏ **STEP 55:** Refit and tension the camshaft drive (timing) belt as detailed in **Part C, Job 2**.

❏ **STEP 56:** Reconnect/refit the following items (if necessary, refer to the relevant sections of this manual):
➜ The exhaust downpipe to the manifold.
➜ All coolant hoses and any oil lines to the cylinder head and its components.
➜ **PETROL ENGINES:** The ignition distributor and ignition coil unit, the spark plug HT leads and all other connections to the distributor/ignition coil. If the engine is catalyst-equipped, reconnect the wiring to the exhaust system Lambda sensor.
➜ **DIESEL ENGINES:** The glow plugs electrical supply, the injector pipes, the fuel feedback hoses, the turbocharger oil supply and drain pipes (if applicable), and, if the engine is so equipped, the fast idle device cable.
➜ The carburetor or petrol injection system.
➜ The fuel line(s) to/from the engine.
➜ The throttle cable and choke cable, if applicable.
➜ The air filter and housing, air chamber (some diesels are fitted with the chamber over the head) and all associated air and vacuum lines, including warm air ducts, and EGR valve and lines, if applicable.
➜ All remaining wiring to senders etc.

❏ **STEP 57:** Follow **Steps 24, 25** and **30**.

❏ **STEP 58:** Reattach the bracket that secures the oil dipstick tube to the cylinder head or manifold.

❏ **STEP 59:** Reconnect the battery.

Part I: Engine and Transmission Removal, Separation, Refitting

	Page No.
JOB 1: ENGINE AND TRANSMISSION – *removal*.	6-53
JOB 2: ENGINE AND TRANSMISSION – *separation, reconnection*.	6-60
JOB 3: ENGINE – *installation*.	6-62

See *Part B: Which Engine is Which?* for an explanation of the engine types referred to here.

There are two different ways in which engines fitted to the vehicles covered by this manual can be removed.

METHOD 1: LIFT ENGINE UPWARDS

APPLIES TO ALL MODELS: The engine is best removed, complete with the transmission, by lifting it out through the top of the engine bay.

METHOD 2: LOWER ENGINE DOWNWARDS

APPLIES TO MOST MODELS: If you prefer, the engine can be lowered to the floor and the vehicle raised by about 1 metre (3 feet) and the engine pulled from beneath. Those models that have an engine subframe require disconnection and lowering of the subframe, which is a simpler task than it sounds.

JOB 1: ENGINE AND TRANSMISSION – *removal*.

CONTENTS

Section A: 205 with XV/XW/XY engine.
Section B: 205/306 with TU, XU, XUD engine.
Section C: 106 with TU, TUD engine, 206 with TU engine.
Section D: Engine lifting and lowering tips – all models.

TOP TIP!

- Taking stuff off is the easy bit - remembering where it all goes again can be another story - unless you make it easy for yourself!
- Tag each hose, cable, linkage and connection with a piece of masking tape as you take it off.
- Number each tag and write down the place where it connects. If you own a video or digital camera, put it to good use here, taking shots of the engine bay and all the various 'tricky' bits, so producing your instant reference source!
- Alternatively, take photographs.

SAFETY FIRST!

VERSIONS WITH AIR CONDITIONING

- DO NOT open the pressurised pipework on the air conditioning system.

- The air conditioning system contains pressurised gas and specialist equipment is needed to extract it. It is illegal to discharge the gas to the atmosphere.

- The gas used in air conditioning systems is extremely harmful to the environment and may cause injury to the person carrying out the work if released in an uncontrolled manner.

- If air conditioning units are in the way of carrying out other work, whenever possible move units to one side with pipes still attached.

- If this is not possible, or there is a risk of damage to pipes or connections, have an air conditioning specialist de-pressurise the system so that you can dismantle it.

- After it has been re-assembled, the system will have to be tested (usually with inert nitrogen) and recharged by a specialist.

Section A: 205 with XV/XW/XY engine.

IMPORTANT NOTE: After gas has been removed from the air conditioning system by a specialist, seal all open connections to stop any contamination from entering the system.

☐ **STEP A1:** Disconnect the battery negative (-) earth/ground terminal. See *Chapter 10, Electrical, Dash, Instruments, Fact File: Disconnecting the Battery* BEFORE doing so! Remove the battery.

☐ **STEP A2:** Remove the bonnet.

☐ **STEP A3:** Apply the parking brake and raise and support the front of the vehicle.

☐ **STEP A4:** Prepare to drain off the coolant by first removing the radiator filler cap and turning the heater control inside the vehicle to HOT. Drain the coolant into a suitable container through the engine and radiator drain plugs.

☐ **STEP A5:** Drain the engine oil from the sump drain plug, then refit the plug.

☐ **STEP A6:** From beneath the vehicle, disconnect the exhaust downpipe from the manifold, collecting the springs, washers and nuts.

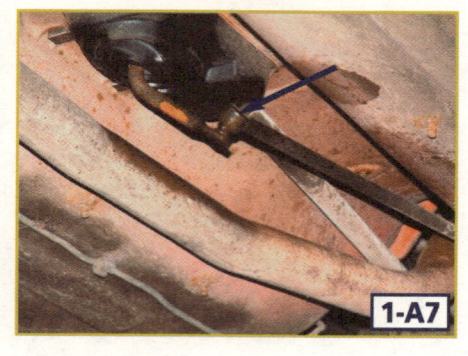

☐ **STEP A7:** Disconnect the ball joint (arrowed) of the gearchange rod (relaying from the gear lever) at the rear of the power unit (from underneath).

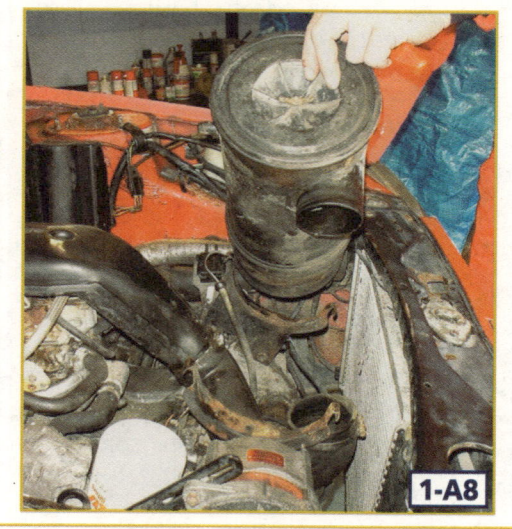

☐ **STEP A8:** Remove the alternator, and the air cleaner body and trunking.

☐ **STEP A9:** Disconnect the following from the power unit:
→ All fuel hoses (seal the ends).
→ All vacuum hoses.
→ All coolant hoses.
→ The accelerator and choke cables.
→ The speedometer cable.

☐ **STEP A10:** Disconnect the following from the power unit:
→ All electrical wiring, including the engine earth lead. Label the connections as you remove them.
→ Don't forget the reversing lights switch wiring, adjacent to the sump pan, beneath the vehicle.

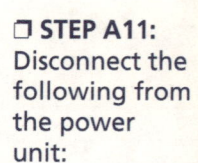

☐ **STEP A11:** Disconnect the following from the power unit:
→ The ignition multi-plug (arrowed).
→ The clutch cable.

☐ **STEP A12:** Connect a hoist to the engine (lifting lugs are provided on the engine).

☐ **STEP A13:** Fit coil spring compressing clamps to one front suspension strut, and compress the suspension spring. Separate the front suspension lower knuckle joint - see *Chapter 11, Steering, Suspension*.

☐ **STEP A14:** Repeat *Step A13* on the opposite side of the front suspension.

1-A15

☐ **STEP A15:** Unscrew and remove the right-hand engine mounting bolts (arrowed).

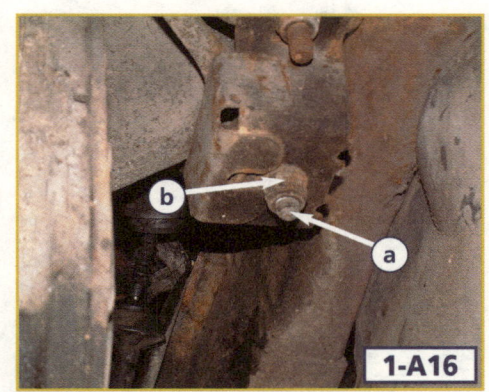

☐ **STEP A16:** Unscrew the left-hand mounting main bolt (**a**) and nut (**b**) - accessible through the battery tray and beneath the vehicle.

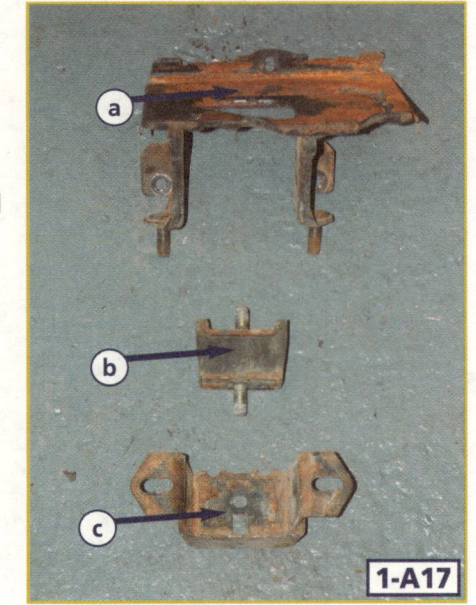

1-A16

☐ **STEP A17:** Unbolt and remove the battery tray (**a**) and the right-hand and left-hand mounting assemblies (**c**) and rubbers (**b**).
→ Note that the battery tray is in two parts. They wrap around the left-hand engine mounting. It also has bolts which pass sideways into the chassis leg, as well as others which pass up from beneath the vehicle.

1-A17

☐ **STEP A18:** Detach both the driveshafts from the transmission unit – see *Chapter 7, Transmission and Clutch* - and let them rest on the subframe.

☐ **STEP A19:** Lift the engine/transmission from the engine bay – see *Section D*.

Section B: 205/306 with TU, XU, XUD engine.

☐ **STEP B1:** Follow *Steps A1 to A5*, then drain the transmission oil.

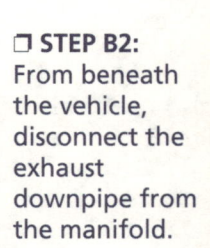

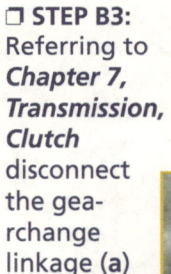

☐ **STEP B2:** From beneath the vehicle, disconnect the exhaust downpipe from the manifold.

1-B2

☐ **STEP B3:** Referring to *Chapter 7, Transmission, Clutch* disconnect the gearchange linkage (**a**) - TU engine linkage shown - from beneath vehicle.
→ On models with automatic transmission, disconnect the selector cable.

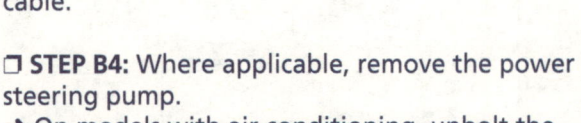

1-B3

☐ **STEP B4:** Where applicable, remove the power steering pump.
→ On models with air conditioning, unbolt the compressor, and position it out of the way of the engine, supporting its weight to prevent damage to pipes - see *Part D*.
→ IMPORTANT NOTE: Do not attempt to disconnect any of the air conditioning pipework – see *Safety First, Versions with air conditioning* at the beginning of *Job 1*.

❏ **STEP B5:** Where applicable, detach the power steering pipe from the underside of the transmission.

❏ **STEP B6: 306 TURBODIESEL MODELS:** Remove the intercooler from the engine.

❏ **STEP B7: DIESEL MODELS:** When relevant, remove the air intake chamber.

TOP TIP!

• If the pre-heater (glow plugs) timer unit is likely to interfere with engine removal, then disconnect, unbolt and remove it.

❏ **STEP B8:** Follow *Steps A8 to A11*, ignoring reference to the reversing lights switch being adjacent to the sump pan – it is on the transmission on these vehicles.

IMPORTANT NOTES:
➔ On petrol fuel injected versions it is vital to depressurise the fuel system before disconnecting any fuel hoses – see *Chapter 9, Ignition, Fuel, Exhaust*.
➔ On 306 models some engine wiring looms conveniently plug in to sockets on the vehicle body. They can be pulled apart after rotating the locking ring on the plug body.
➔ Additionally, on 306, some wires go to a relay box situated in front of the left-hand suspension turret, and these may be disconnected by lifting off the box lid and undoing the nuts of the wires' eyelet terminals.
➔ **HIGHER POWER MODELS:** If applicable, disconnect the oil lines between engine and remote oil cooler.

❏ **STEP B9:** Remove the main (petrol) fuel injection and exhaust gas recirculation components, where fitted - see *Chapter 9, Fuel, Ignition, Exhaust*.

❏ **STEP B10:** Follow *Steps A10 to A14*.

TOP TIP!

• On 306 models the job is simpler because the suspension arm can be separated from the strut by undoing the three nuts and bolts that hold the ball joint to the lower arm.
• These nuts and bolts must not be re-used, but should be renewed - see *Chapter 11, Steering, Suspension*.

❏ **STEP B11:** Pull the left-hand hub outwards, withdrawing the driveshaft from the final drive (see illustration *1-C25*).
➔ **XU/XUD ENGINES:** See *Chapter 7, Transmission, Clutch* for details of how to fit the special tool required for preventing the differential side gear from dropping into the final drive casing.
➔ IMPORTANT NOTE: This does not necessarily apply to all models with XU/XUD engine, see *Chapter 7, Transmission, Clutch* for further details before withdrawing the driveshaft.

❏ **STEP B12A:** Unbolt the rear engine mounting (stabiliser link) – TU engine shown...

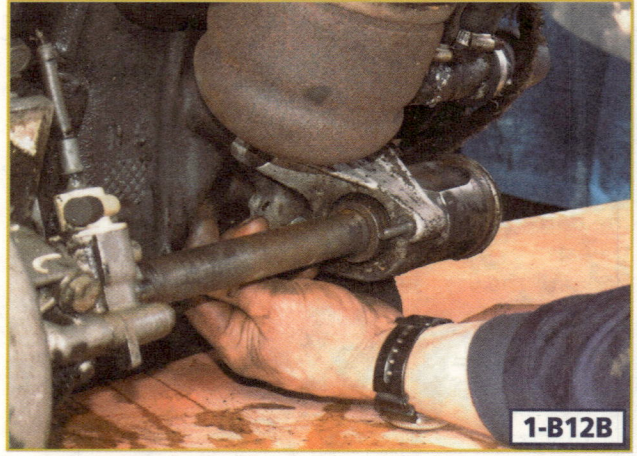

❏ **STEP B12B:** ...and slacken the nuts of the two special 'L-headed' bolts that secure the driveshaft support bearing to its alloy casting (bolted to the back of the block).

❏ **STEP B13:** Turn the special bolt heads through 90 degrees to free the bearing, then pull the right-hand hub carrier outwards, withdrawing the driveshaft from the final drive at the same time.

❏ **STEP B14:** Unbolt the driveshaft support bearing bracket from the cylinder block, and, while in this area, disconnect the wiring to the oil temperature sensor.

❏ **STEP B15:** Remove the radiator.

☐ **STEP B16:** Remove the fuel injection system, if engine is fuel injected - see *Chapter 9, Fuel, Ignition, Exhaust*.

☐ **STEP B17:** Take the weight of the power unit with a hoist.

☐ **STEP B18:** Undo the left-hand engine mounting upper nut (accessed via an aperture in the battery tray – 106/TU engine shown).

1-B18

1-B19

☐ **STEP B19:** Lower the engine a little to unbolt and withdraw the battery tray and bracket.

☐ **STEP B20:** Undo the right-hand engine mounting upper nut (bracket to rubber) then lift the engine/transmission from the engine bay – see *Section D*.

IMPORTANT NOTE: 306 MODELS: When detaching the right-hand engine mounting, undo the two bolts and remove the curved securing plate and rubber damper (if fitted) from the mounting top - see *Part K*.
→ Loosen and remove the mounting bracket nuts and bolts and withdraw the bracket.

Section C: 106 with TU, TUD engine, 206 with TU engine.

206 models are fitted with an engine undershield held by four peripheral bolts and four peripheral screws. The undershield should be removed before carrying out the following job.

☐ **STEP C1:** Follow *Steps A1 to A5* previously, then remove the battery support bracket.

☐ **STEP C2:** Disconnect the Lambda sensor – if fitted - from the exhaust downpipe.

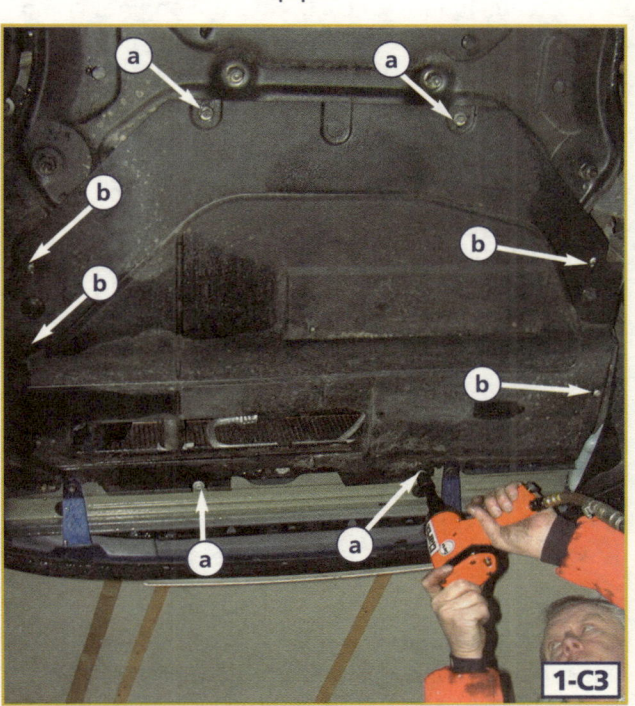

1-C3

☐ **STEP C3: 206 MODELS ONLY:** From beneath the vehicle, remove the engine undershield and the exhaust heat shield.
→ Remove the four bolts (**a**).
→ Loosen the four screws (**b**) – they stay in the tray.

☐ **STEP C4: 106 AND 206:** Disconnect the exhaust downpipe from the manifold - see illustration *1 A6* – 106/TU engine shown.

☐ **STEP C5:** Disconnect the gearchange linkage - see *Chapter 7, Transmission & Clutch*.

☐ **STEP C6: 206 MODELS WITH AUTOMATIC TRANSMISSION:** Disconnect the selector cable and the transmission ECU (arrowed), and place the ECU out of the way - see *Chapter 7,*

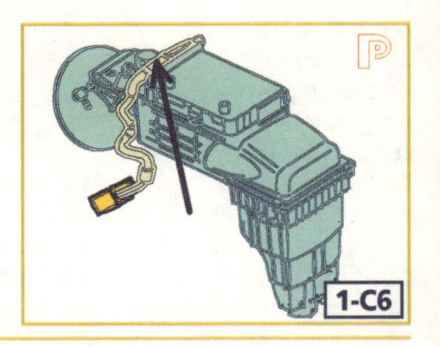

1-C6

CHAPTER 6 Part I Job 1

6-57

Transmission, Clutch.

☐ **STEP C7: 106 PETROL INJECTION:** Remove the complete exhaust system.

☐ **STEP C8: 106 PETROL INJECTION:** Remove the plastic cover from the ECU mounting plate (right-hand side of engine bay), and disconnect the wiring from the ECU and components. Free the wiring loom so that it stays with the engine when it is removed.

☐ **STEP C9: 106 DIESEL:** Disconnect and remove the pre-heating (glow plugs) control unit.

☐ **STEP C10: 106 MODELS:** Locate the engine wiring loom connector in the front left-hand corner of the engine bay, and disconnect it by rotating the plug locking ring and detaching the plug.

☐ **STEP C11: 106 MODELS:** Remove the radiator cooling fan – see *Chapter 8, Cooling System*.

☐ **STEP C12:** Follow **Steps A8 to A9**, ignoring reference to the reversing lights switch being adjacent to the sump pan – it is on the transmission unit on these models – and also ignoring reference to the choke cable if engine is fuel injected.

SAFETY FIRST!

• On fuel injected versions it is vital to depressurise the fuel system before disconnecting any fuel hoses - see *Chapter 9, Ignition, Fuel, Exhaust*.

☐ **STEP C13:** Remove the main (petrol) fuel injection and exhaust gas recirculation components, where fitted - see *Chapter 9, Fuel, Ignition, Exhaust*.

☐ **STEP C14:** Drain the power steering system, where appropriate. See *Chapter 11, Steering, Suspension*.

☐ **STEP C15: 206 MODELS WITH POWER STEERING AND AIR CONDITIONING:** Remove the external drive belt and its tensioner pulley.

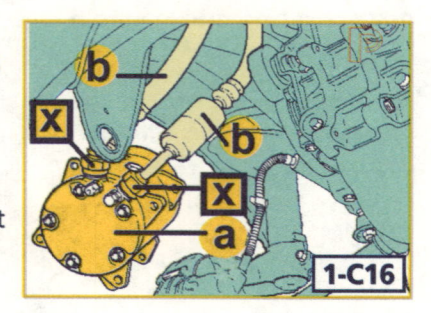

☐ **STEP C16: 106 AND 206 MODELS WITH AIR CONDITIONING:** Unbolt the compressor (a) and position it out of the way of the engine, supporting its weight to prevent damage to pipes (b) - see *Part D*.
→ IMPORTANT NOTE: Do not attempt to disconnect any of the air conditioning pipework, such as at positions (X) – see *Safety First, Versions with air conditioning* at the beginning of *Job 1*.

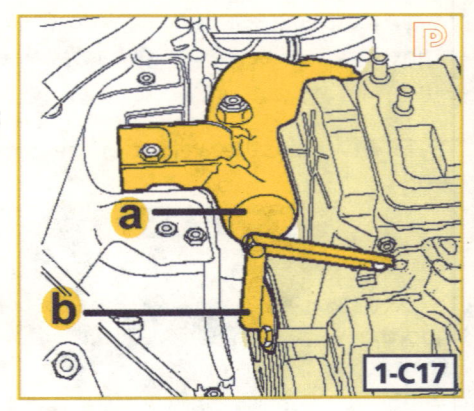

☐ **STEP C17: 206 MODELS:** Remove the engine mounting bracket (**items a** and **b**) from the cylinder head.

☐ **STEP C18: 206 MODELS:** Disconnect the multi-connectors of the engine wiring loom from the fusebox, and if necessary, unclip the loom from the vehicle body.

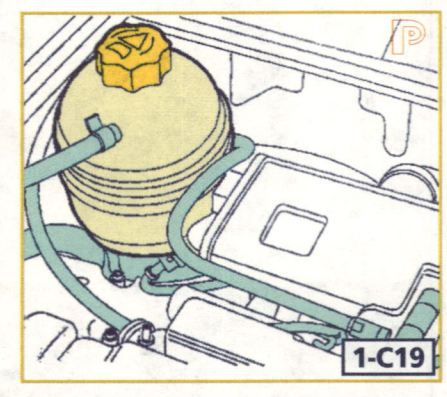

☐ **STEP C19:** Disconnect and remove the coolant expansion bottle and its support – 206-type shown.

☐ **STEP C20: 206 MODELS:** Disconnect the relay connectors situated near the radiator.

☐ **STEP C21:** On models fitted with a remote engine oil cooler, disconnect the oil lines between engine and cooler.

☐ **STEP C22:** Where applicable, detach the power steering pipe from the underside of the transmission.

☐ **STEP C23:** Drain the transmission oil.

☐ **STEP C24:** Follow **Steps A10 to A12** previously.

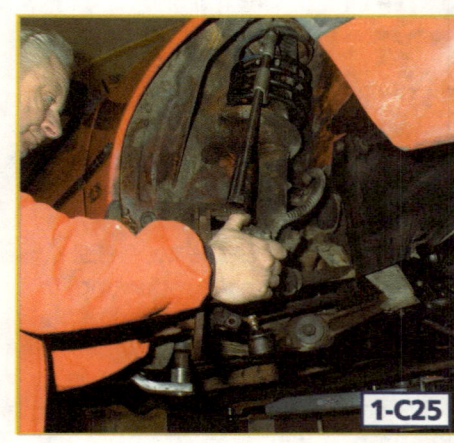

☐ **STEP C25:** Pull the left-hand hub/strut outwards, withdrawing the driveshaft from the final drive.
→ Support the driveshaft then repeat the procedure for the opposite side.

❏ **STEP C26:** Follow *Steps B12 and B13*. Note that not all 106 models have an intermediate support bearing for the right-hand driveshaft.

❏ **STEP C27:** Where fitted, unbolt the driveshaft support bearing bracket from the cylinder block.

❏ **STEP C28:** Take the weight of the power unit with a hoist.

❏ **STEP C29:** Undo the left-hand engine/transmission mounting and bracket - see *Part K*.

❏ **STEP C30:** Undo the right-hand engine mounting and remove the mounting components - see *Part K*.

❏ **STEP C31:** Lift the engine/transmission unit from the engine bay – see *Section D*.

Section D: Engine lifting and lowering tips – all models.

METHOD 1: LIFT ENGINE UPWARDS

❏ **STEP D1:** While an assistant helps with the engine hoist, manoeuvre the engine free of all obstacles, while carrying out the final check that nothing remains connected…

❏ **STEP D2:** …then lift the engine sufficiently high to clear the front of the bodywork.
→ You will probably find that the engine has to be brought out at a pronounced angle end-to-end, and then, in order to clear the body, the transmission-end will have to be lifted manually while an assistant either trolleys the engine hoist or (preferably) pushes the vehicle back until the engine is clear.

TOP TIP!

• Arrange the work area so that there is enough room behind the vehicle before you start work.

METHOD 2: LOWER ENGINE DOWNWARDS

❏ **STEP D3:** When a Peugeot engine is to be lowered to the ground rather than lifted out of the engine bay, you can leave the bonnet/hood in place and there is the added advantage that you are less likely to cause damage to the surrounding bodywork.
→ On 106 models the power unit can be dropped down quite easily, but all other models require separation of the front suspension struts from the hubs (or the hubs from the subframe) and the complete subframe assembly must be lowered to the ground, complete with power unit.
→ This is not as complicated as it sounds, as the subframe is connected to the body by a number of bolts.
→ You will still need a hoist, because the engine and transmission unit will have to be lowered slowly to the ground.

❏ **STEP D4:** You will also need some means of lifting the vehicle's bodywork over the engine. A vehicle lift is ideally used to raise the whole vehicle, but you may be able to connect your engine hoist to a couple of engine mounting brackets inside the engine bay and raise the front of the vehicle with your hoist, provided that its lifting capacity is sufficient.

❐ **STEP D5:** The last technique – of lifting the vehicle from over the engine – needs a minimum lift of around 1 metre (3 ft) and is generally more suitable for the workshop equipped with a hoist.

JOB 2: ENGINE AND TRANSMISSION – separation, reconnection.

Section A: XV/XW/XY engine.

❐ **STEP A1:** Remove all bolts - one (**a**) arrowed - securing the clutch housing and idler geartrain to the engine.

➜ IMPORTANT NOTE: These are the *peripheral* bolts, not those that retain the idler geartrain to the clutch housing.
➜ You will also have to remove the clutch operating arm (one nut (**b**), and washers) to gain access to one of the periphery bolts, and to remove the clutch cable abutment bracket for access to another of the bolts.

TOP TIP!

❐ **STEP A2:** • One peripheral bolt is very well hidden in a recess, and has often been the cause of housing damage due to frustration and brute force!
➜ IMPORTANT NOTE: Take note of the position of the engine lifting lug before removing it – it is secured by one of the periphery bolts.

❐ **STEP A3:** Remove the starter motor and its rear support bracket.

❐ **STEP A4:** Separate the clutch housing/idler geartrain from the engine by cautiously tapping it at the raised bosses provided, with a soft-faced mallet.
➜ Prevent the crankshaft from turning by jamming a large screwdriver in the flywheel teeth, through the starter motor opening.
➜ Undo the six clutch assembly bolts - internal hex-headed type.
➜ Remove the clutch cover off its locating pegs and take off the clutch plate.

❐ **STEP A5:** Keep the crankshaft from rotating using the same system, and undo the flywheel bolts. Lift off the flywheel.

❐ **STEP A6:** Undo the two bolts and one nut securing the transmission to the underside of the engine at the flywheel end face.

❐ **STEP A7:** Remove all the cylinder block/ transmission flange bolts from the front of the power unit.

❐ **STEP A8:** Unbolt the right-hand rear engine mounting from the timing case.

6-60

☐ **STEP A9:** Refit two flywheel bolts to crankshaft flange, then, using a long bar between them, hold the crankshaft from turning while an assistant undoes the crankshaft pulley nut at the opposite end of the crankshaft.

2-A10

☐ **STEP A10:** Withdraw the crankshaft pulley (**a**) - it may be necessary to use opposed screwdrivers or even a legged puller - and collect its front nut (**b**), washer (**c**), and rear collar (**d**).

☐ **STEP A11:** Remove the camshaft cover and the timing case - see *Part C, Job 4*.

☐ **STEP A12:** Remove all the bolts along the rear transmission-to-engine flange. Note that some of the rear bolts are of differing lengths, so be guided by the heights of the bosses they go into when reassembling.

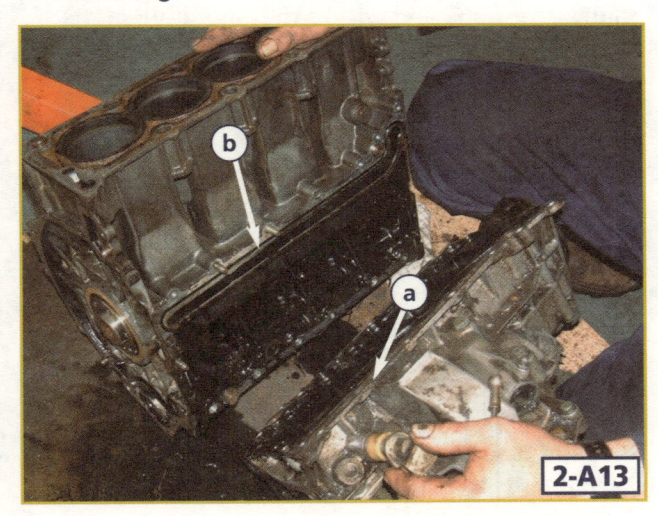

2-A13

☐ **STEP A13:** Lever apart the engine and transmission, using a length of wood positioned between the final drive unit (**a**) and the cylinder block (**b**).

RECONNECTION – XV/XW/XY ENGINE

TOP TIP!

☐ **STEP A14:** • You MUST fit a brand new oil seal ring to the feed stub, shown here, from the oil pump in the transmission, to the crankcase, or oil pressure will suffer. It is located on the transmission mating face edge.

2-A14

☐ **STEP A15:** Installation is carried out in the reverse order to removal. However, you must pay particular attention to the following points:
→ Apply a generous bead of silicone sealant to the engine/crankcase-to-transmission mating faces on the machined surfaces arrowed.
→ Ensuring locating rings for engine-to-transmission location are still in place.
→ Tighten the 13 bolts and 3 nuts securing transmission to engine to the specified torque.
→ Apply thread locking compound to flywheel securing bolts before tightening them.
→ If there is any suggestion that the clutch is approaching the end of its life, renew the clutch assembly now.
→ Make sure the clutch is properly aligned - see **Chapter 7, Transmission, Clutch**.
→ Lubricate the release bearing and input spline shaft before assembling the idler geartrain to the engine and transmission.

Section B: TU, TUD, XU, XUD engines.

☐ **STEP B1:** If not already removed, remove starter motor from transmission (some require a hex adaptor for the bolts), and unbolt and remove the flywheel access plate (underneath engine) on those engines that have it.

☐ **STEP B2:** If a flywheel TDC sensor (arrowed) is fitted, unbolt it from its flange at the rear of the engine/front of

2-B2

6-61

transmission. If wiring runs to the reversing lights switch on the transmission from the engine, disconnect this.

☐ **STEP B3: MANUAL TRANSMISSION:** Undo all the bolts retaining the transmission to the engine, observing the fitted positions of any brackets held by these bolts.

☐ **STEP B4: MANUAL TRANSMISSION:** Withdraw transmission from the engine, ensuring that transmission weight is not allowed to hang on transmission input shaft.

☐ **STEP B5: AUTOMATIC TRANSMISSION:** Turn the driveplate and expose, one at a time, each of the three torque converter mounting bolts and remove each nut (one arrowed).
→ Also undo the nut that retains the transmission fluid dipstick tube to the transmission sump.

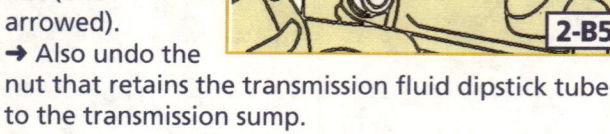

☐ **STEP B6: AUTOMATIC TRANSMISSION:** Carefully withdraw transmission from engine, making sure that the torque converter is held inside the bellhousing to prevent oil spillage and damage.

RECONNECTION – TU, TUD, XU, XUD ENGINES

☐ **STEP B7:** Lubricate the release bearing and input spline shaft before assembling the engine and transmission.

☐ **STEP B8:** Installation is carried out in the reverse order to removal. However, you must pay particular attention to the following points:
→ If there is any suggestion that the clutch is approaching the end of its life, renew the clutch assembly now.
→ Make sure the clutch is properly aligned IF refitting it. See **Chapter 7, Transmission, Clutch**.
→ Ensure transmission-to-engine locating dowels are still in place, and turn transmission as required until its splined input shaft engages with the clutch drive plate.
→ Refit the TDC sensor and its bracket. If it is a new one, it will incorporate three legs that keep the sensor the prescribed 1.0 mm away from the flywheel. If fitting an old sensor, file off any remaining leg lengths, fit sensor until it contacts flywheel, back it off by 1.0 mm, then tighten it in place.

JOB 3: ENGINE – *installation*.

IMPORTANT NOTE: Do not tighten any of the engine mounts until all are in place.

☐ **STEP 1:** Installation is generally carried out in the reverse order to removal. However, you must pay particular attention to the following points:
→ If you lower the engine into position from above, guide it carefully and ensure that the drive shafts are clear.
→ Attach the transmission mounting first, then attach the engine mountings. Align them, then tighten them.
→ Tighten bolts and nuts to prescribed tightening torques, where these are specified.
→ Renew any leaking oil seals (particularly crankshaft and driveshaft oil seals) before the engine/transmission goes back in.
→ Renew the oil filter, and fill the engine and transmission units with the correct grade and quantity of oil.
→ Refill the power steering system, if necessary, and refill and bleed the cooling system.
→ On diesel models, purge the fuel system once reconnected.
→ Align the exhaust system so that no undue force is required to push any part of the system towards a mounting point and so that none of the rubber support loops are loaded more than the others.

Part J: Engine Block Dismantling, Rebuilding

CONTENTS

	Page No.
JOB 1: ENGINES – *identification*.	6-63
JOB 2: CYLINDER BLOCK ASSEMBLY – *layouts*.	6-63
JOB 3: CYLINDER BLOCK, XV/XW/XY ENGINE – *dismantling and reassembly*.	6-66
JOB 4: CYLINDER BLOCK, TU & TUD ENGINES – *dismantling and reassembly*.	6-71
JOB 5: CYLINDER BLOCK, XU & XUD ENGINES – *dismantling and reassembly*.	6-75

See *Part B: Which Engine is Which?* for an explanation of the engine types referred to here.

JOB 1: ENGINES – *identification*.

XV/XW/XY PETROL ENGINES

☐ **TYPE 1:** The smaller, earlier engines from 954cc to 1,360cc, are characterised by near-horizontal installation in the car.

➜ They are all-aluminium in construction, with a hydraulically-tensioned timing chain and gears-in-sump transmission drive, via an external idler geartrain.

➜ See *Part B, illustration 1-1*.

TU PETROL ENGINES

A development of the previous XV type, but conventional in layout.

➜ Capacities are the same as those for XV type, with the addition of a 1587cc.

➜ All but the 1587cc version are aluminium wet-liner engines.

➜ The 1587cc TU engine has a conventional cast iron cylinder block.

➜ Camshaft drive on all is by toothed belt, and these engines have rocker-type screw-adjustable tappets.

➜ See *Part B, illustration 1-2*.

TUD DIESEL ENGINES

Diesel versions of the TU petrol engines, in two capacities – 1360cc and 1527cc.

➜ These engines are of all-aluminium, wet-liner construction and have a camshaft drive by toothed belt, tensioned by spring tensioner.

➜ The tappets are shim-adjustable buckets, acted on directly by the overhead camshaft.

➜ See *Part B, illustration 1-4*.

XU PETROL ENGINES

Generally larger petrol engines of 1580cc, 1761cc, 1905cc and 1998cc, with aluminium block with wet-liner cylinders, and aluminium cylinder head on all but the 1998cc, which uses a conventional cast iron block.

➜ The 1998cc XU engine comes in both 8-valve and 16-valve configurations (the latter not covered by this manual).

➜ All types have a toothed belt type camshaft drive, tensioned by sprung tensioner, and shim-adjustable bucket-type tappets acted on directly by the overhead camshaft.

➜ See *Part B, illustration 1-3*.

XU DIESEL ENGINES

Diesel versions of the XU petrol engines, in two capacities – 1769cc and 1905cc – both available in turbocharged and non-turbocharged guises. These engines are of cast-iron block, aluminium cylinder head construction, with a camshaft drive by toothed belt, tensioned by sprung tensioner.

➜ Bucket-type shim-adjustable tappets are acted on directly by the overhead camshaft.

➜ See *Part B, illustration 1-5*.

JOB 2: CYLINDER BLOCK ASSEMBLY – *layouts*.

TYPES OF ENGINE BLOCK ASSEMBLIES

The following illustrations will help you to familiarise yourself with the layout of the bottom-ends of the engines covered here.

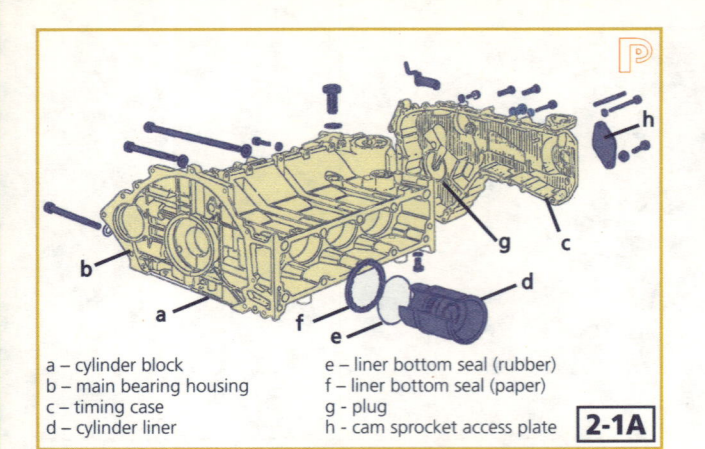

CHAPTER 6 Part J Job 2

Figure 2-1A
- a – cylinder block
- b – main bearing housing
- c – timing case
- d – cylinder liner
- e – liner bottom seal (rubber)
- f – liner bottom seal (paper)
- g – plug
- h – cam sprocket access plate

☐ **STEP 1A:** XV/XW/XY ENGINE: This is the cylinder block and cylinder liners assembly…

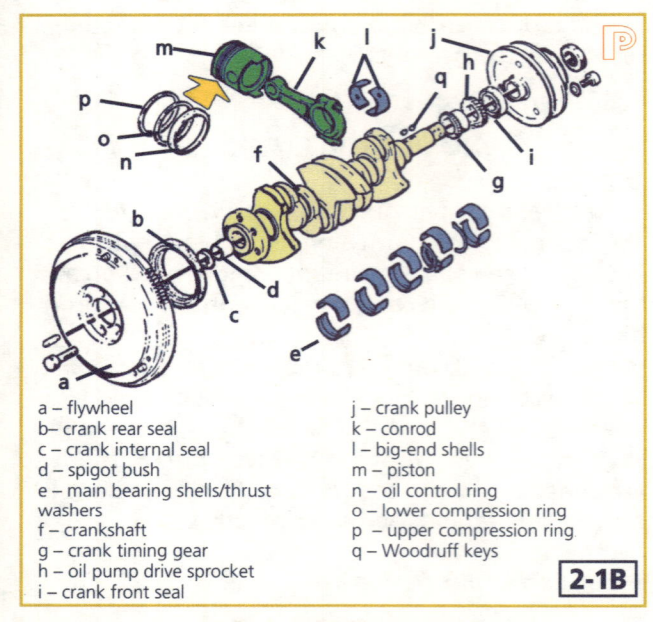

Figure 2-1B
- a – flywheel
- b – crank rear seal
- c – crank internal seal
- d – spigot bush
- e – main bearing shells/thrust washers
- f – crankshaft
- g – crank timing gear
- h – oil pump drive sprocket
- i – crank front seal
- j – crank pulley
- k – conrod
- l – big-end shells
- m – piston
- n – oil control ring
- o – lower compression ring
- p – upper compression ring
- q – Woodruff keys

☐ **STEP 1B:** …and this is the crank and associated parts.

☐ **STEP 2: TU PETROL ENGINES:** These are the engine bottom-end components.
→ The block can be seen to have an upper and a lower part to it.
→ NOT

Figure 2-2

Annotations to Step 2-2
- a – oil pump cover
- b – oil pump
- c – oil pump drive sprocket
- d – oil pump drive chain
- e – pump valve assembly
- f – oil dipstick tube
- g – oil pressure switch
- h – oil filter
- i – main bearing housing
- j – crankshaft
- k – oil pump drive sprocket
- l – crank front seal
- m – crank timing sprocket
- n – crank pulley
- o – crank rear seal
- p – crank thrust washers
- q – main bearing shells
- r – flywheel
- s – flywheel ring gear
- t – conrod
- u – piston
- v – piston rings
- w – big-end bearing shells
- x – gudgeon pin
- y – Woodruff key

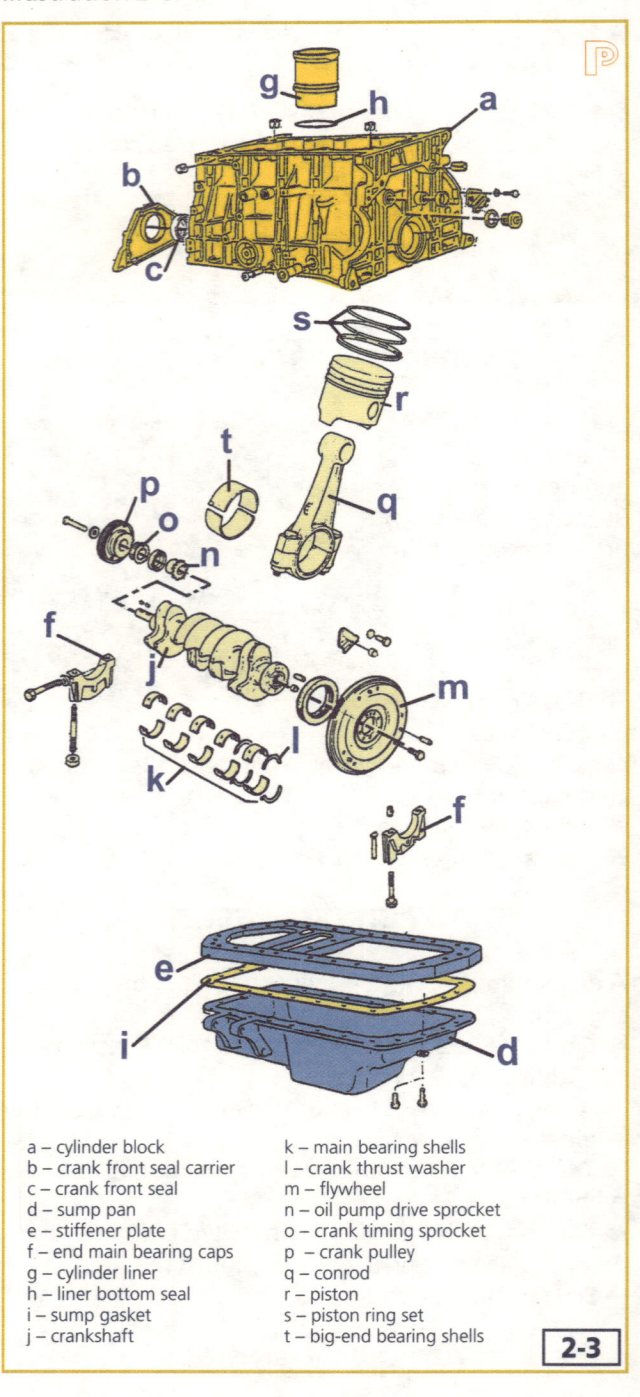

to be confused with the TU 'solid-block' see illustration **2-6**.

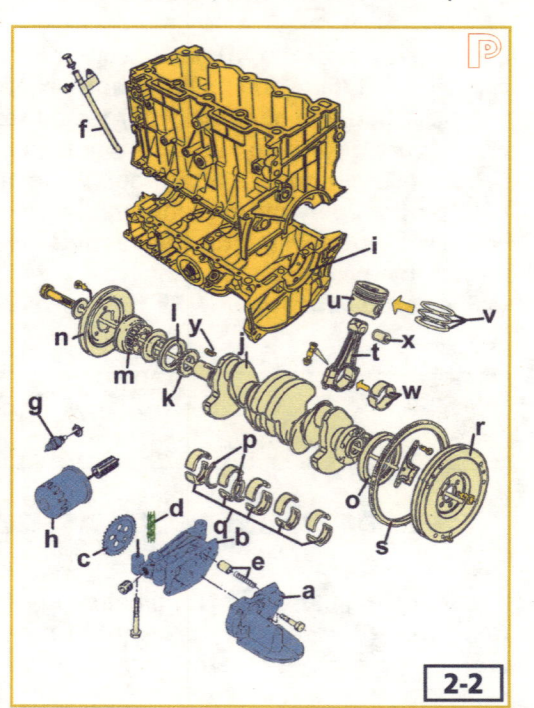

Figure 2-3
- a – cylinder block
- b – crank front seal carrier
- c – crank front seal
- d – sump pan
- e – stiffener plate
- f – end main bearing caps
- g – cylinder liner
- h – liner bottom seal
- i – sump gasket
- j – crankshaft
- k – main bearing shells
- l – crank thrust washer
- m – flywheel
- n – oil pump drive sprocket
- o – crank timing sprocket
- p – crank pulley
- q – conrod
- r – piston
- s – piston ring set
- t – big-end bearing shells

☐ **STEP 3: XU PETROL ENGINES:** These are the bottom-end components of a typical XU engine.

6-64

2-4

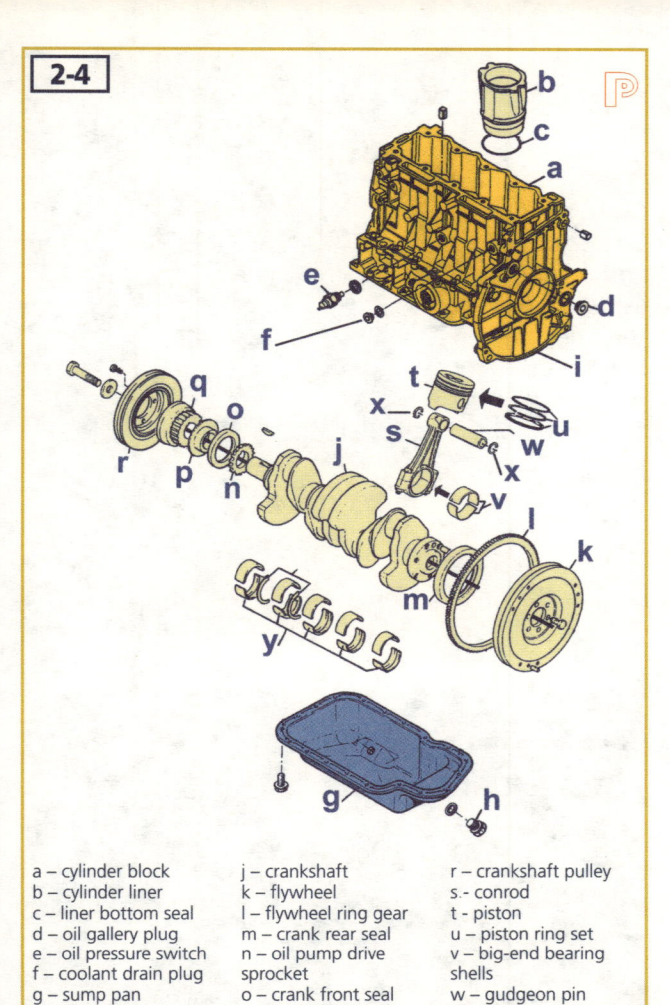

- a – cylinder block
- b – cylinder liner
- c – liner bottom seal
- d – oil gallery plug
- e – oil pressure switch
- f – coolant drain plug
- g – sump pan
- h – sump drain plug
- i – main bearing housing
- j – crankshaft
- k – flywheel
- l – flywheel ring gear
- m – crank rear seal
- n – oil pump drive sprocket
- o – crank front seal
- p – oil deflector plate
- q – crank timing sprocket
- r – crankshaft pulley
- s – conrod
- t – piston
- u – piston ring set
- v – big-end bearing shells
- w – gudgeon pin
- x – gudgeon pin circlips
- y – bearing shells

☐ **STEP 4: TUD DIESEL ENGINE:** The TUD diesel engine components are typically as shown here.

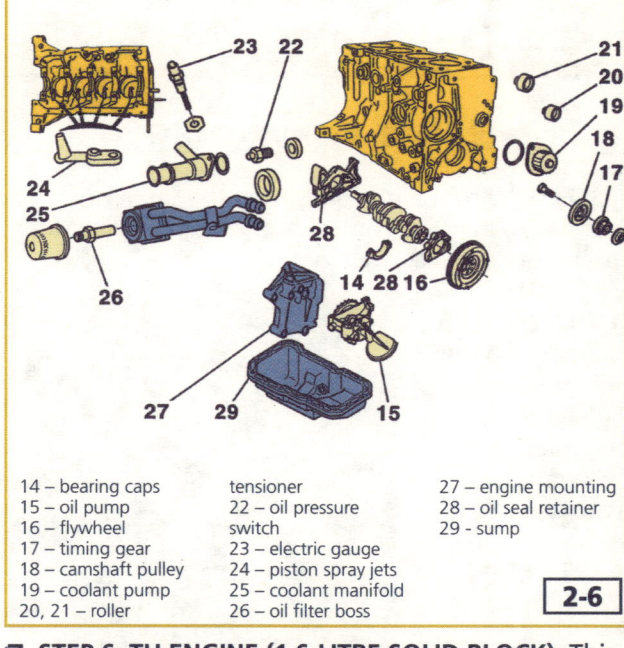

2-5

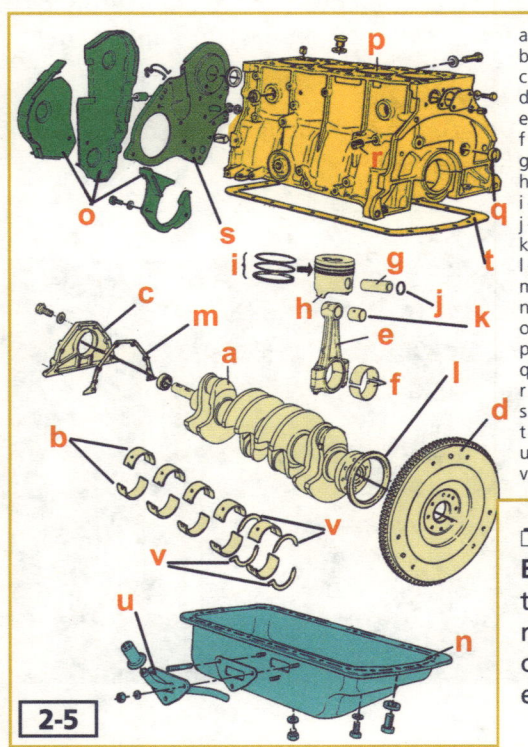

- a – crankshaft
- b – main bearing shells
- c – crank front seal carrier
- d – flywheel
- e – conrod
- f – big-end bearing shells
- g – gudgeon pin
- h – piston
- i – piston ring set
- j – gudgeon pin circlip
- k – small-end bearing
- l – crank rear seal
- m – seal carrier gasket
- n – sump pan
- o – timing cover sections
- p – cylinder block
- q – core plugs
- r – screw plug
- s – engine front plate
- t – sump gasket
- u – breather outlet assembly
- v – thrust washers

☐ **STEP 5: XUD DIESEL ENGINE:** These are typical engine block-related components on this type of engine.

2-6

- 14 – bearing caps
- 15 – oil pump
- 16 – flywheel
- 17 – timing gear
- 18 – camshaft pulley
- 19 – coolant pump
- 20, 21 – roller tensioner
- 22 – oil pressure switch
- 23 – electric gauge
- 24 – piston spray jets
- 25 – coolant manifold
- 26 – oil filter boss
- 27 – engine mounting
- 28 – oil seal retainer
- 29 – sump

☐ **STEP 6: TU ENGINE (1.6-LITRE SOLID BLOCK):** This engine is NOT to be confused with the TU 'split-block' engine – see *Step 1*.

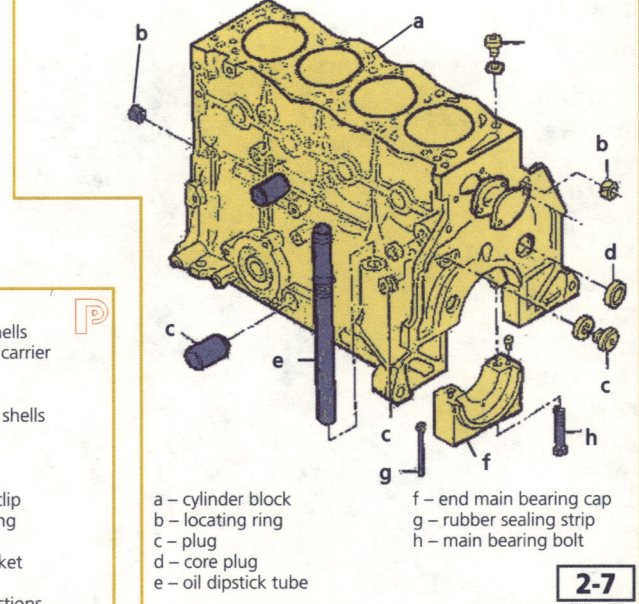

2-7

- a – cylinder block
- b – locating ring
- c – plug
- d – core plug
- e – oil dipstick tube
- f – end main bearing cap
- g – rubber sealing strip
- h – main bearing bolt

☐ **STEP 7: XU ENGINE (2.0-LITRE SOLID BLOCK):**

CHAPTER 6 Part J Job 2

6-65

JOB 3: CYLINDER BLOCK, XV/XW/XY – dismantling and reassembly.

ENGINE DISMANTLING

☐ **STEP 1:** With the power unit on the floor, or preferably, mounted on an engine stand, clean dirt from around all casing joints.

☐ **STEP 2:** Remove all bolts and nuts holding the clutch housing and idler geartrain assembly to the engine.
➔ IMPORTANT NOTE: One bolt is hidden beneath the oil pipe casting.

☐ **STEP 3:** Remove the starter motor and its support bracket.

☐ **STEP 4:** Remove the idler geartrain assembly and clutch housing from the engine.
➔ You may need to tap it carefully with a mallet in order to ease separation.

☐ **STEP 5:** Undo the six bolts that secure the clutch assembly to the flywheel, using an appropriate hex socket adaptor, and withdraw the clutch assembly.

☐ **STEP 6:** Undo the flywheel retaining bolts and remove the flywheel.
➔ Prevent the flywheel/crankshaft from turning by jamming a large screwdriver between the flywheel ring gear teeth and the starter motor opening.

☐ **STEP 7:** Undo the two bolts (**a**) and one nut (**b**) between the cylinder block and the transmission/sump unit.

☐ **STEP 8:** Undo and remove the five bolts securing the cylinder block to the transmission/sump at the front of the power unit.

☐ **STEP 9:** Detach the right-hand engine mounting from the timing case.

TOP TIP!

☐ **STEP 10:**
• Refit two flywheel securing bolts to the end of the crankshaft, and position a long bar between them.
• Have an assistant hold this bar tightly to prevent crankshaft rotation while you undo the crankshaft pulley nut at the other end.
• Remove the pulley.
• If the pulley is very tight it may be necessary to use a two-or three-legged puller to ease removal.

☐ **STEP 11:** Remove the camshaft cover and timing case – see *Part C, Job 4*.

☐ **STEP 12:** Remove the bolts and nuts (some arrowed) retaining the engine to the transmission on the back side of the power unit, then separate the engine and transmission.

☐ **STEP 13:** Remove the timing chain and tensioner – see *Part C, Job 4*.

☐ **STEP 14:** Remove the cylinder head and clamp the cylinder liners – see *Part F, Job 1* previously.

☐ **STEP 15:** Unbolt and remove the oil and water pumps, and remove the oil filter.

☐ **STEP 16:** Invert the engine, then progressively slacken and remove the ten bolts (arrowed) retaining the main bearing housing to the cylinder block.

☐ **STEP 17:** Remove the seven short bolts retaining the main bearing housing to the cylinder block, and lift off the housing, taking care not to lose the positions of the main bearing shells in their housing recesses.

☐ **STEP 18:** Check that all the connecting rods and their big-end bearing caps are marked with matching numbers, starting from the timing cover end.
→ Make sure that the markings tell you which way round they go.
→ Undo all the big-end bearing nuts, then lift off the bearing caps.

☐ **STEP 19:** Lift the crankshaft from the cylinder block, and retrieve the two crankshaft thrust washers.
→ Collect all the main bearing shells; if they are to be reused, number them to ensure they return to their original locations.
→ IMPORTANT NOTE: If you are to refit the same pistons, before removing them, mark them to show their position.

TOP TIP!

☐ **STEP 20:** Assuming you are not disturbing the cylinder liners, piston removal is as usual:
• Use a hammer handle to tap the piston/connecting rod assemblies carefully out of the bores.
• Inspect the top of each cylinder bore - there may be a small ring of carbon build-up which can make it difficult to remove the pistons. If so, scrape it carefully away.

☐ **STEP 21:** Keep the piston assemblies aligned in the correct order out of the engine, and the matching conrods and bearing caps together.

☐ **STEP 22:** If the cylinder liners are to be removed, remove the liner clamps (if previously fitted) and pull the liners out from the top of the block, together with their piston and conrod.

TOP TIP!

☐ **STEP 23:** • If the cylinder liners refuse to budge, invert the cylinder block and tap them out from the bottom, using a wooden drift.

• IMPORTANT NOTE: The pistons of the XV family engines cannot be separated from their conrods without a hydraulic press, and once separated the piston and piston pin are rendered unserviceable.
• The only re-usable item after piston separation is the conrod, and new pistons and piston pins are bought complete with new cylinder liners in kits.

ENGINE REASSEMBLY

IMPORTANT NOTES:
- This Job must be read in conjunction with the general fitting notes given in *Part A: General Procedures*.
- All bearings, shells, piston rings and ALL seals that bear on moving parts MUST be copiously lubricated with fresh engine oil as the engine is being reassembled.
- Work ONLY in clean conditions, with clean components and clean hands.
- Two different types of cylinder liner are used on the XV family engines: 1) selective thickness paper type, 2) non-selective rubber O-ring type, and these necessitate different refitting procedures.

PAPER-SEAL TYPE

☐ **STEP 24:** If refitting original cylinder liners, fit them in their original locations in the block, without any bottom seals.

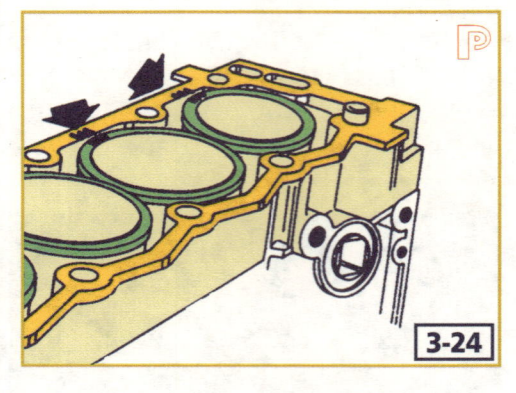

→ Make sure they face in their original, previously marked directions – see arrows.

☐ **STEP 25:** If fitting new, replacement cylinder liners, position them in the block in any order, again without bottom seals.

☐ **STEP 26A:** Press the liners down hard in their seats, then measure their protrusions from the cylinder block upper face.

→ Use a steel rule and feeler gauges…

☐ **STEP 26B:** …or a dial gauge as shown, measuring against both sides of the block.

TOP TIP!
- If any one NEW liner (not re-used ones), shows a higher protrusion on one side of the block than on the other, it is permissible to take it out, turn it through 180 degrees and refit it to redress the balance.

☐ **STEP 27:** With liner bottom seals in place, the protrusion for each liner should be between 0.13 and 0.18mm, and the closer to the higher protrusion, the better.

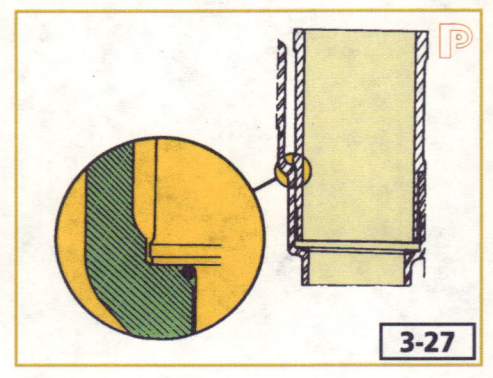

→ Seals are available in thicknesses of 0.087 mm, 0.102 mm, 0.122 mm and 0.147 mm – identified by the colours blue, white, red and yellow respectively.

→ For each cylinder liner, choose the ideal seal thickness so that, when added to the measured protrusion, it brings the liner protrusion as near as possible to 0.18mm, and within the range of acceptable limits given.

→ IMPORTANT NOTES: Protrusion difference between adjacent liners should not exceed 0.04mm, and reduction, if necessary, can be made by varying the selected seal thickness of the relevant liners.

→ With a NEW liner set only, arrange the liners such that the difference in their protrusions reduces progressively from one end of the block to the other.

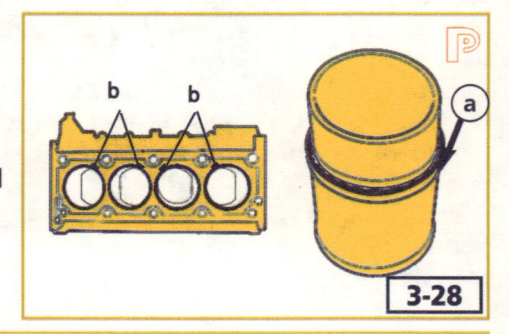

☐ **STEP 28:** Once the correct seals have been chosen, and the ideal liner positions too, mark the liners to this effect, and remove them from the cylinder block, with paper seals (**a**) slipped over the liner bottoms.

→ Position the seals so that their protruding tabs (**b**) will be on the side of the cylinder block opposite to the oil gallery.

→ It is important that the seal inner tabs should tuck neatly into the groove around the cylinder liner, and that the protruding tabs should not overlap.

RUBBER O-RING LINER SEAL TYPE

❑ **STEP 29:** With this type of liner seal, usually fitted to later XV family engines, exacting manufacturing tolerances sees to it that the need for liner protrusion adjustment is eradicated, and that all protrusions should be within tolerance.

❑ **STEP 30:** Proceed as described in **Steps 25** and **26**.

❑ **STEP 31:** With liner bottom seals in place, the protrusion for each liner should be between 0.10 and 0.17 mm.

→ The maximum permissible height difference between adjacent liners is 0.05 mm.

→ When fitting the O-ring seals to the liner bottoms, take great care not to twist them. Roll them up evenly into position under the liner bottom-shoulder.

→ IMPORTANT NOTE: If any liner reveals a protrusion outside the specified limits, swap it for another liner and measure again. Out-of-protrusion is rare, and is invariably due to a defect of either the liner or the cylinder block.

PISTON/CONNECTING ROD ASSEMBLIES

❑ **STEP 32:** If the pistons and conrods were separated, new pistons should be fitted to the conrods. This can only be done by an engineering shop, as the conrods must first be heated, and the piston pins need to be inserted with a hydraulic press.

❑ **STEP 33:** Ensure that any marks previously made on the conrod match those made on the big-end cap, and that they both face in the same direction.

❑ **STEP 34:** Make sure that the bores and pistons are clean.

→ Fit the rings, using a piston ring spreader, if possible.

→ Fit the piston ring gaps at equal intervals round the piston circumference.

→ Align gaps (**a** and **b**) in the thin rings at the top and bottom of the slotted (oil control) ring so that they are offset by between 20 and 50 mm. Lubricate all rings copiously.

→ Make sure the rings are fitted with their Peugeot marking (**c**) facing upwards, or with the word TOP or OBEN upwards.

❑ **STEP 35:** Check NEW piston/liner pairs for correct matching.

→ Where piston crown bears letter A, liner should have one notch on its edge.

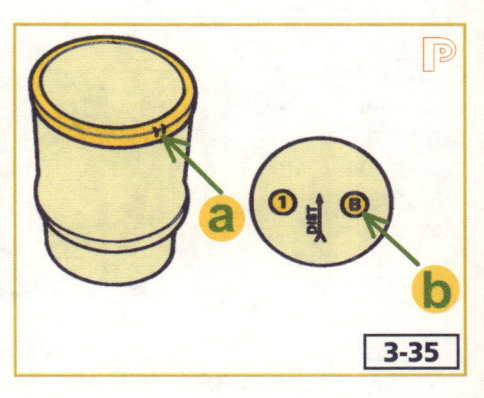

→ Where piston crown bears letter B, liner should have two notches (**a**).

→ Where piston crown has C marking, liner should have three notches.

→ Check also that all four pistons are of the same class – i.e. A, B or C. This is marked on the piston crown in a circle (**b**).

TOP TIP!

• Wrap insulation tape, or a short piece of plastic tube, over each con. rod thread, so that it cannot damage the crank as it goes in.

❑ **STEP 36:** Lubricate the piston rings and compress them with a ring clamp.

❑ **STEP 37:** Fit the piston to each liner, ensuring that it is fitted such that when the liner is reinstalled (with its edge marks matching those on the block edge), its 'DIST' marking and arrow will face the timing chain end of the engine – see illustration **3-35**.

☐ **STEP 38:** With the piston ring clamp touching the cylinder block liner, use a hammer shaft to carefully tap the piston through and into the bore.

→ IMPORTANT NOTE: The conrods are symmetrical, and so have no directional requirement, although the piston position is critical.

☐ **STEP 39:** Install each piston/liner assembly in the block in the correct position, observing alignment of marks – see *Step 37*.

→ Be careful not to damage the paper-type liner seals.

☐ **STEP 40:** Refit liner clamps (one, arrowed) to secure the liners and prevent the bottom seals from being disturbed.

CRANKSHAFT

☐ **STEP 41:** Invert the cylinder block.

→ Here, the conrods are shown with bearing caps fitted to prevent mix-ups. You will have to remove them before fitting the crankshaft.

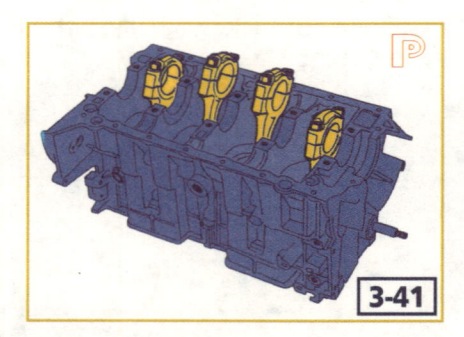

☐ **STEP 42:** Make sure the bearing seats in the caps and block are perfectly clean and locate the shells so that their tabs engage with the slots (arrowed).

☐ **STEP 43:** Note that the two grooved shells (arrowed) belong in the second and third bearing housings.

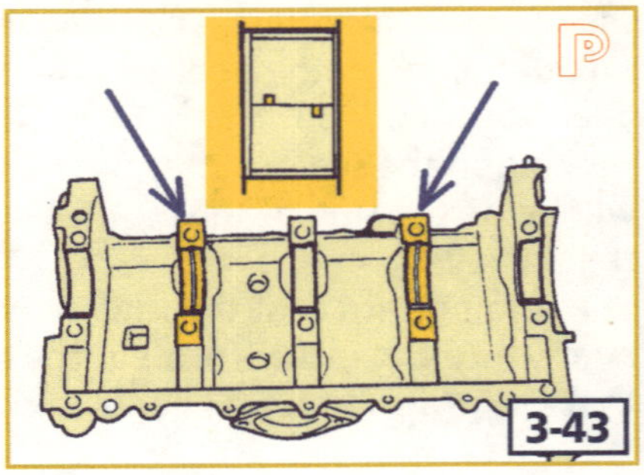

→ Make sure that the two locating indents (inset), in the ends of the bearing shells, are on the same side.

→ Refit the two crankshaft thrust washers at either side of the fourth main bearing, with their grooved side towards the crankshaft.

→ Lubricate the bearing shells liberally with fresh engine oil and lower the crankshaft into position.

→ Measure the crankshaft endfloat, using a feeler gauge between thrust washer and crankshaft web – see illustration *4-35*.

→ If it is outside specified limits (see *Chapter 1, Facts and Figures*) fit new thrust washers of suitable thickness to adjust.

☐ **STEP 44:** Locate the upper half of the big end shell bearing in the conrod, making sure that the mating surfaces are clean.

→ Lubricate the crankpin and the big-end shell and draw the conrod down the bore so that the big end locates with the crankpin.

→ Fit the other half of the big-end shell to the bearing cap and lubricate.

→ Offer the cap to the connecting rod and make sure that the numbers match.

→ Screw in the fixing bolts and tighten progressively to the correct torque.

TOP TIP!

• Turn the crankshaft so that the journal for the conrod you are working on is at bottom dead-centre.

☐ **STEP 45:** Fit the remaining piston/conrod assemblies.

☐ **STEP 46:** Make sure the two locating rings are still in position on the block lower mating face, and fit a new O-ring seal around the oil supply stub on the opposite side of the engine mating face.

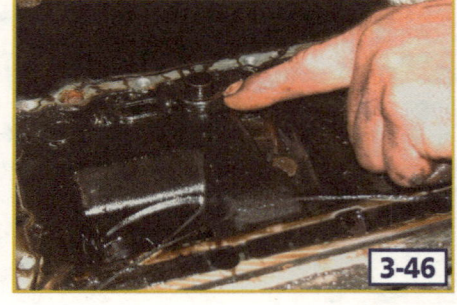

→ IMPORTANT NOTE: This O-ring is crucial to engine survival, as it seals the main oil passageway between engine and transmission, and without it, all oil pressure is lost.

❏ **STEP 47:** Apply a generous bead of silicone sealant to the main bearing housing mating face, then fit it to the underside of the block.
→ Refit and progressively torque-tighten its ten securing bolts in the sequence shown.
→ Check that the crankshaft turns smoothly.

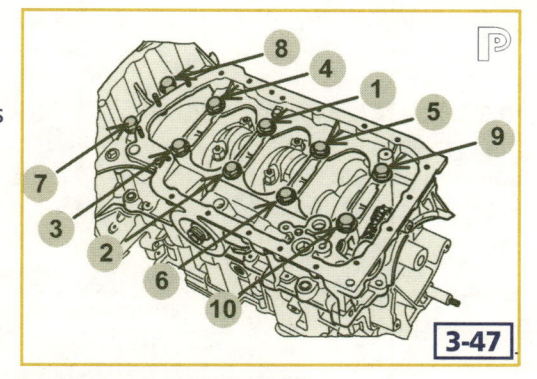

3-47

❏ **STEP 48:** Refit the seven short bolts and washers to the main bearing housing/cylinder block mating flange and torque-tighten them.

❏ **STEP 49:** First lubricate, then drift into position, a new flywheel-end crankshaft oil seal, tapping it in squarely until it is flush with the cylinder block.

❏ **STEP 50:** Carry out the following operations, referring to the relevant sections of this manual:
→ Refit the transmission unit.
→ Refit the flywheel.
→ Refit the cylinder head.
→ Fit the oil pump.
→ Fit the timing chain and tensioner.
→ Fit the right-hand engine mounting.
→ Fit the idler geartrain assembly.
→ Refit the clutch.
→ Refit the water pump.
→ Refit the starter motor.
→ Lubricate the sealing ring and screw on a new oil filter.
→ Refit all remaining auxiliary components using new gaskets as necessary.

❏ **STEP 51:** Start the engine - this might take a few turns more than normal on the initial start up.
→ Allow the engine to warm up on fast idle until it reaches working temperature and then slow it down to its normal speed.
→ Stop the engine and allow it to cool, check the oil and coolant levels and look for any leaks.
→ Avoid over-revving or overloading the engine during its settling down period of 600 miles. We recommend an oil and filter change at this mileage - this will help to extend the life of your new engine.

JOB 4: CYLINDER BLOCK, TU & TUD ENGINES – *dismantling and reassembly*.

ENGINE DISMANTLING

❏ **STEP 1:** With the engine on the floor, or preferably, mounted on an engine stand, clean dirt from around all casing joints.

❏ **STEP 2:** Remove air conditioning pump, if fitted, and alternator and starter motor.

❏ **STEP 3:** Undo the three nuts securing the right-hand engine mounting bracket, and remove the bracket.

❏ **STEP 4:** Lock the crankshaft and the camshaft sprocket – see *Part C, Job 3*.

❏ **STEP 5:** Remove the crankshaft pulley, the timing covers and the timing belt, and remove the belt tensioner.

❏ **STEP 6:** Remove the crankshaft sprocket and the oil seal plate (arrowed) immediately behind it, either by levering with two screwdrivers, or with the aid of a legged puller.

4-6

❏ **STEP 7:** Remove the cylinder head, and, on all but the 1.6-litre TU engine, clamp the cylinder liners to prevent them from being disturbed. See *Part G, Job 1*.

❏ **STEP 8:** Remove the oil filter, unbolt the dipstick tube bracket and withdraw the dipstick tube from the engine.

❏ **STEP 9:** Unbolt and remove the water pump assembly and coolant block from the back of the cylinder block, and, on TUD diesel, remove the fuel injection pump.

4-9

CHAPTER 6   Part J   Job 4

6-71

☐ **STEP 10:** Unbolt the plate from front face of engine, to which the TDC flywheel sensor leads are attached, then remove the TDC sensor.

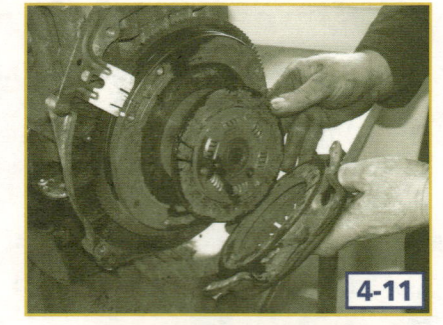

☐ **STEP 11:** Unbolt the clutch assembly and remove it from the flywheel.

☐ **STEP 12:** Prevent the flywheel/crankshaft from turning by jamming a large screwdriver (arrowed) between the flywheel ring gear teeth and a belt screwed into the block.
→ Undo the flywheel retaining bolts and remove the flywheel.

☐ **STEP 13: ALUMINIUM ENGINES** On aluminium engines remove the bolts retaining the lower crankcase to the cylinder block.
→ Note that there are 16 bolts in total, and that two of them, positions shown here, can be found below the crankshaft nose.

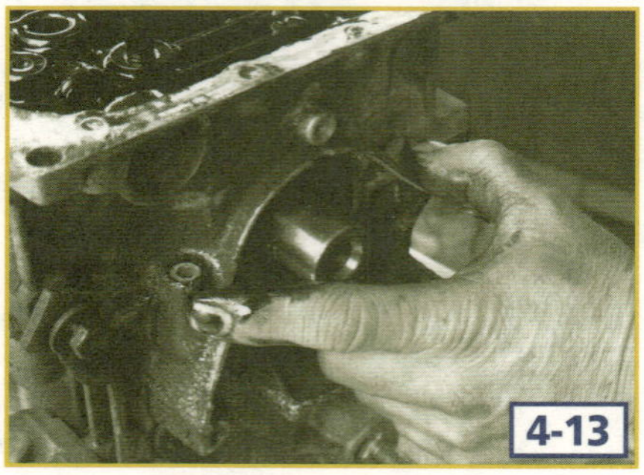

☐ **STEP 14: BOTH ENGINE TYPES:** Turn engine upside down, unbolt and remove sump pan.

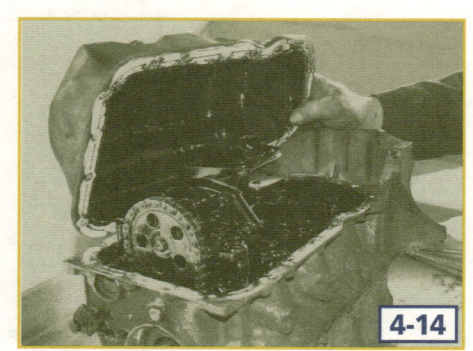

☐ **STEP 15: 1.6-LITRE PETROL ENGINE:** Unbolt and remove the left-hand and right-hand crankshaft oil seal housings. Take care not to lose their locating pegs.

☐ **STEP 16: 1.6-LITRE PETROL ENGINE:** Remove the chain that drives the oil pump sprocket, then slide the sprocket off the crankshaft nose. Be careful not to lose the Woodruff key that locks the sprocket to the crankshaft.

☐ **STEP 17: ALUMINIUM ENGINES:** Using a suitable Torx-headed driver, remove the blanking plug situated at each end of the engine oil gallery (see illustration **2-4, item d**).

☐ **STEP 18: BOTH ENGINE TYPES:** Undo the three bolts retaining the oil pump (arrowed) and pick-up strainer to the underneath of the cylinder block.
→ Detach the drive-chain from the sprocket and withdraw the pump from the engine.

ALUMINIUM ENGINES

☐ **STEP 19:** Undo the ten main bearing bolts and withdraw them. Lift the main bearing crankcase casting from the cylinder block.

☐ **STEP 20:** If the cylinder liners are to be removed, remove the liner clamps (if previously fitted) and pull the liners out from the top of the block, together with their piston and conrod.

> **TOP TIP!**
> • If the cylinder liners refuse to budge, invert the cylinder block and tap them out from the bottom, using a wooden drift.

1.6-LITRE PETROL ENGINE

☐ **STEP 21:** Number the big-end bearing caps, mark them for direction of fitting, then remove them.

☐ **STEP 22:** Follow **Job 3, Steps 18 to 21**.

❐ **STEP 23:** Undo the retaining bolts and remove the individual piston oil spray tubes from inside the cylinder block.

BOTH ENGINE TYPES

❐ **STEP 24:** Remove all oil gallery plug, where fitted (see illustration *2-4, item d*) in preparation for cleaning out the oilways.

FACT FILE
REMOVING PISTONS

❐ **STEP 25:** You may now be able to separate the pistons from the conrods.

TU PETROL ENGINES
• The pistons cannot be separated from their conrods without a hydraulic press, as the piston pin is an interference-fit in the small-end. Once separated, the piston and piston pin are rendered unserviceable. The only re-usable item after piston separation is the conrod, and new pistons and piston pins are bought complete with new cylinder liners in kits.

TUD DIESEL ENGINES
• The pistons CAN be separated from the conrod, as the piston pin is merely retained by circlips, and can be pushed out once these are levered out.

ENGINE REASSEMBLY

IMPORTANT NOTES:
• This Job must be read in conjunction with the general fitting notes given in *Part A: General Procedures*.
• All bearings, shells, piston rings and ALL seals that bear on moving parts MUST be copiously lubricated with fresh engine oil as the engine is being reassembled.
• Work ONLY in clean conditions, with clean components and clean hands.
• A cylinder liner (a rubber O-ring) is used on all TU/TUD aluminium engines, but not on the solid-block 1.6-litre petrol TU. While no adjustment procedure exists for cylinder liner protrusion from the block, it is necessary to measure liner protrusions when new liner-and-piston kits are fitted.

ALUMINIUM ENGINES

❐ **STEP 26:** Proceed as in *Job 3, Steps 25* and *26*.

❐ **STEP 27:** With liner bottom seals in place, the protrusion for each liner should be between 0.03 and 0.10 mm. The maximum permissible height difference between adjacent liners is 0.05 mm.

IMPORTANT NOTES:
• When fitting the O-ring seals to the liner bottoms, take great care not to twist them. Roll them up evenly into position under the liner bottom shoulder.
• If any liner reveals a protrusion outside the specified limits, swap it for another liner and measure again. Out-of-protrusion is rare, and is invariably due to a defect of either the liner or the cylinder block.

PISTON/CONNECTING ROD ASSEMBLIES

❐ **STEP 28A: BOTH ENGINE TYPES:** Follow *Job 3, Steps 32* to *38*.
➔ IMPORTANT NOTE: If working on a TUD diesel engine, ignore reference in *Step 31* to pistons needing to be reassembled to conrods by press, and note that the 'DIST' and arrow marking referred to on the piston crown may be marked 'DT' instead.

❐ **STEP 28B: TUD ENGINE:** Note that it is ESSENTIAL to connect the piston to the conrod so that the combustion recess in the crown (**a**) is on the side opposite to the big-end bearing shell locating tags (**b**).

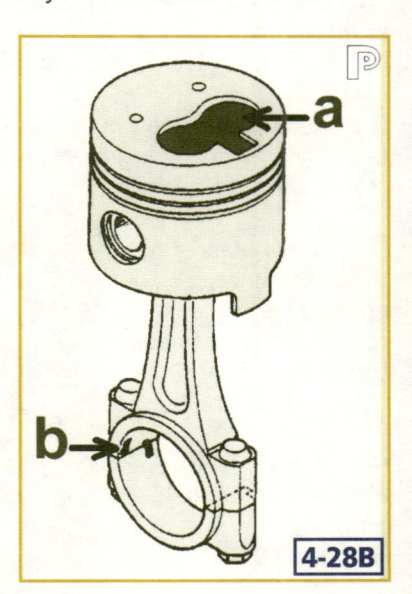

4-28B

❐ **STEP 29: 1.6-LITRE PETROL ENGINE:** Refit the four piston oil spray tubes inside the cylinder block. Apply thread locking compound to the retaining bolt threads and torque-tighten the bolts.

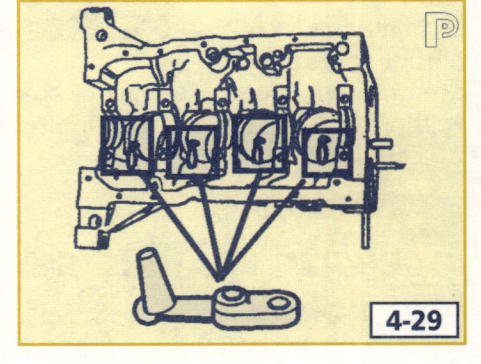

4-29

❐ **STEP 30: ALUMINIUM ENGINES:** Install each piston/liner assembly in the block in the correct position, observing alignment of marks. Refit liner clamps to secure the liners and prevent the bottom seals from being disturbed.

CRANKSHAFT

☐ **STEP 31:** Invert the cylinder block.
→ Make sure that the bearing seats in the caps and block are perfectly clean and locate the shells so that their tabs engage with the slots.
→ Note that the two grooved shells belong in the second and fourth bearing housings, and also that the two locating indents in the end of the bearing shells are on the same side – see **Job 3, Step 43**.

☐ **STEP 32:** Refit the two crankshaft thrust washers at either side of the second main bearing, with their grooved side towards the crankshaft.

☐ **STEP 33:** Lubricate the upper main bearing shells liberally with fresh engine oil and lower the crankshaft into position.

☐ **STEP 34:** Measure the crankshaft endfloat, using a feeler gauge between thrust washer and crankshaft web. These are the limits:
→ **TU1 AND TU3 ENGINES:** 0.052-0.452 mm.
→ **TU5 AND TUD ENGINES:** 0.07-0.27 mm.
→ If endfloat is outside these limits, fit new thrust washers of suitable thickness to adjust.
→ Thrust washers are available in sizes of 2.40, 2.50, 2.55 and 2.60 mm.

☐ **STEP 35:** Refit the oil pump drive sprocket to the crankshaft nose, with its Woodruff key and drive chain.

☐ **STEP 36:** Fit and lubricate the correct main upper and lower bearing shells - grooved shells for bearings 2 and 4.
→ **1.6 LITRE PETROL:** Refit the main bearing caps.
→ **ALUMINIUM ENGINES:** Apply silicone sealant all along the mating face of the crankcase/main bearing housing.
→ Then offer this up to the cylinder block, while holding the oil pump drive chain up – see illustration **4-19**.

☐ **STEP 37: 1.6-LITRE PETROL ENGINE:** Progressively tighten all the main bearing cap nuts to the specified torque, then complete the tightening, using a tool such as the Sykes Pickavant Angular Torque Gauge 800700, to further tighten the nuts by 45 degrees.

☐ **STEP 38: ALUMINIUM ENGINES:** Refit and tighten the ten crankcase/main bearing bolts to the specified torque, then further tighten them by 45 degrees, using an angle-tightening tool such as the Sykes Pickavant Angular Torque Gauge 800700.
→ Refit the short bolts securing the periphery of the crankcase/main bearing housing to the cylinder block flange.
→ Fit and torque-tighten the two bolts underneath the crankshaft nose – see illustration **4-13**.

☐ **STEP 39: BOTH ENGINE TYPES:** Follow **Job 3, Steps 44 and 45**, tightening the big-end nuts to 30 lb ft.

☐ **STEP 40: ALUMINIUM ENGINES:** Check that the crankshaft rotates smoothly.
→ Lubricate the oil pump drive chain and refit the pump and strainer.

☐ **STEP 41: 1.6-LITRE PETROL ENGINE:** Note the correct fitted depth of the crankshaft front oil seal in its carrier.
→ Lever out the seal then squarely drift in a new, lubricated one.
→ Apply silicone sealant to the seal carrier then relocate it to the end of the cylinder block, sliding it

FACT FILE
OVERSIZE BEARING SHELLS

- The upper main bearing shell remains of one fixed thickness, while the lower main bearing shell is available in selected thicknesses, to adjust main bearing operating clearance.
- Three different size classes of lower bearing shell exist, identified by the colours blue, black or green on the shell edge.
- Each in turn is available in standard thickness or oversize thickness, as follows:

	ALUMINIUM ENGINES		1.6-LITRE PETROL ENGINE	
	Standard	Oversize	Standard	Oversize
Blue (A)	1.823	1.973	1.844	1.994
Black (B)	1.835	1.985	1.858	2.008
Green (C)	1.848	1.998	1.869	2.019

over the crankshaft nose, and engaging its locating dowels.
➔ Tighten the carrier securing bolts.

❑ **STEP 42: 1.6-LITRE PETROL ENGINE:** Repeat *Step 41* for the rear oil seal and carrier, then refit the oil pump and strainer, ensuring that the pump chain is oiled and properly engaged on the pump sprocket. Check that the crankshaft turns smoothly.

❑ **STEP 43: ALL ENGINES:** Fit a new sump pan gasket, then refit the sump pan and progressively tighten its bolts.

❑ **STEP 44: ALUMINIUM ENGINES:** Fit a new crankshaft front oil seal.
➔ First lubricate the seal, then drift it into position using a suitable annular drift, such as a socket.
➔ Tap it in squarely until is flush with the cylinder block.
➔ Repeat this for the crankshaft rear oil seal.

❑ **STEP 45:** Refit any oil gallery plugs previously removed.

❑ **STEP 46:** Carry out the following operations, referring to the relevant sections of this manual:
➔ Refit the flywheel (use some locking compound on bolt threads)
➔ Refit the clutch.
➔ Refit the front oil seal plate and crankshaft sprocket.
➔ Refit the cylinder head.
➔ Refit the engine front plate and flywheel TDC sensor.
➔ Refit the injection pump (TUD diesel engine).
➔ Refit the timing belt, tensioner and covers.
➔ Refit the crankshaft pulley.
➔ Fit the right-hand engine mounting bracket.
➔ Refit the water pump.
➔ Refit the starter motor.
➔ Lubricate the sealing ring and screw on a new oil filter.
➔ Refit all remaining auxiliary components using new gaskets as necessary.
➔ Reconnect the engine to the transmission and refit the complete unit to the car.

❑ **STEP 47:** Start the engine - this might take a few turns more than normal on the initial start up.
➔ Allow the engine to warm up on fast idle until it reaches working temperature and then slow it down to its normal speed.
➔ Stop the engine and allow it to cool, check the oil and coolant levels and look for any leaks.
➔ Avoid over-revving or overloading the engine during its settling down period of 600 miles.

JOB 5: CYLINDER BLOCK, XU & XUD ENGINES – *dismantling and reassembly*.

ENGINE DISMANTLING

❑ **STEP 1:** Follow *Job 4 Steps 1 to 5*.

❑ **STEP 2:** Remove the cylinder head, and if cylinder liners are not to be removed, on all but the 2.0-litre petrol cast iron engine, clamp them to prevent their bottom seals from being disturbed – see *Part F, Job 2*.

❑ **STEP 3:** Unbolt and remove the camshaft sprocket and its backplate. Remove the water pump, and, on diesel engines, remove the injection pump, shown here.

❑ **STEP 4:** Unbolt and remove the flywheel TDC sensor (arrowed) from the rear of the engine, complete with its mounting bracket - XUD engine shown.

❑ **STEP 5:** Remove the oil filter from the cylinder block.

❑ **STEP 6:** Remove the sump pan by removing all the bolts securing it to the underside of the engine.

IMPORTANT NOTE: Higher-powered versions of the XU petrol engine have additional bottom-end strengthening in the form of a plate between the sump and the underneath of the cylinder block (illustration *2-3, item e*).
➔ This should be removed after sump removal, by unscrewing the two bolts from its opposite corners, then levering it off carefully, if stuck by gasket compound.

❏ **STEP 7:** Remove the crankshaft sprocket (**a**) and the oil seal carrier (**b**) from the front end of the engine.
➜ XUD carrier shown; XU is similar.

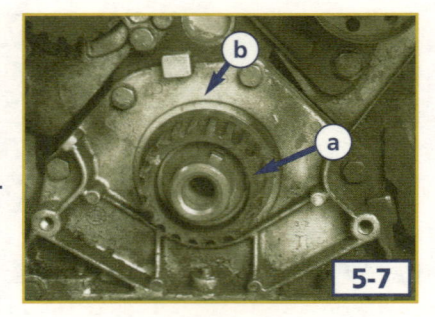

5-7

❏ **STEP 8:** Remove the oil pump drive chain from its sprocket on the crankshaft nose.
➜ Slide the sprocket (**a**) and spacer from the nose.
➜ Collect the Woodruff key (position **b**) that locks the sprocket to the nose.

5-8

❏ **STEP 9:** Unbolt and remove the clutch assembly from the flywheel.

❏ **STEP 10:** Prevent the flywheel/crankshaft from turning by jamming a large screwdriver between the flywheel ring gear teeth and the starter motor opening, undo the flywheel (or driveplate – automatic transmission models) retaining bolts and remove the flywheel/driveplate.

❏ **STEP 11:** Undo the three bolts retaining the oil pump (arrowed) and pick-up strainer to the underneath of the cylinder block.

5-11

➜ XUD pump shown; XU is similar.
➜ Lift the pump from its location while withdrawing the chain and sprocket, from the crankshaft nose.
➜ Collect the Woodruff key (that locks the sprocket to the crankshaft) if it is loose.

❏ **STEP 12:** Follow *Job 3, Steps 18 to 23*.

❏ **STEP 13:** Undo the main bearing bolts and withdraw them.
➜ Note that the centre main bearing of XU petrol engines has

5-13

retaining nuts (**a**) and two side bolts (**b**).
➜ Lift the main bearing caps from the cylinder block, keeping them in order.
➜ Lift out the crankshaft.
➜ Retrieve the two (or four – depending on engine) thrust washer halves from either side of the fourth main bearing (counting from timing belt end).

❏ **STEP 14:** On all XU petrol engines but the 2.0-litre, if the cylinder liners are to be removed, remove the liner clamps (if previously fitted) and pull the liners out from the top of the block, together with their piston and conrod.

TOP TIP!

❏ **STEP 15:** •If the cylinder liners refuse to budge, invert the cylinder block and tap them out from the bottom, using a wooden drift.

❏ **STEP 16:** Remove all oil gallery plugs (where fitted) in preparation for cleaning out the oilways.

REMOVING PISTONS: See *Job 4, Step 26, Fact File*.

ENGINE REASSEMBLY

IMPORTANT NOTES:
• This Job must be read in conjunction with the general fitting notes given in *Part A: General Procedures*.
• All bearings, shells, piston rings and ALL seals that bear on moving parts MUST be copiously lubricated with fresh engine oil as the engine is being reassembled.
• Work ONLY in clean conditions, with clean components and clean hands.
• A non-selective thickness cylinder liner seal (a rubber O-ring) is used on all XU/XUD aluminium engines, but not on the solid-block 2.0-litre petrol XU. While no adjustment procedure exists for cylinder liner protrusion from the block, it is necessary to measure liner protrusions when new liner-and-piston kits are fitted – see illustration *3-26* previously.

☐ **STEP 17: ALUMINIUM ENGINES:** Proceed as in *Job 3, Steps 25* and *26*. With liner bottom seals in place, the protrusion for each liner should be between 0.03 and 0.10 mm. The maximum permissible height difference between adjacent liners is 0.05 mm.

IMPORTANT NOTES:
• When fitting the O-ring seals to the liner bottoms, take great care not to twist them. Roll them up evenly into position under the liner bottom shoulder.
• If any liner reveals a protrusion outside the specified limits, swap it for another liner and measure again. Out-of-protrusion is rare, and is invariably due to a defect of either the liner or the cylinder block.

PISTON/CONNECTING ROD ASSEMBLIES

☐ **STEP 18: BOTH ENGINE TYPES:** Follow *Job 3, Steps 32* to *38*.
→ IMPORTANT NOTE: If working on a XUD diesel engine, ignore reference in *Step 32* to pistons needing to be reassembled to conrods by press, and follow *Job 4, Steps 29A* and *29B*.

☐ **STEP 19: ALUMINIUM ENGINES ONLY:** Follow *Job 4, Step 31*.

CRANKSHAFT

☐ **STEP 20:** Follow *Job 4, Steps 32* to *34*.

☐ **STEP 21:** Measure the crankshaft endfloat, using a feeler gauge between thrust washer and crankshaft web – see illustration *4-35*.
→ If endfloat is outside the limits of 0.07-0.32 mm, fit new thrust washers of suitable thickness to adjust.

5-22

☐ **STEP 22:** Fit the correct, lubricated upper and lower bearing shells to the block recesses (grooved shells) and to the main bearing caps, ensuring the locating tags of upper and lower shells are at same end).

FACT FILE
OVERSIZE BEARING SHELLS

MOST XU ENGINES
• The upper main bearing shell remains of one fixed thickness, while the lower main bearing shell is available in selective thicknesses, to adjust main bearing operating clearance.
• Three different size classes of lower bearing shell exist, identified by the colours blue, black or green on the shell edge.
• Each in turn is available in standard thickness or oversize thickness, as follows:

1.8-LITRE PETROL ENGINE

	Standard	Oversize
Upper bearing (Yellow)	1.856	2.006
Lower bearing		
Blue (A)	1.836	1.986
Black (B)	1.848	1.998
Green (C)	1.859	2.009
Red (D)	1.870	2.020

2.0-LITRE PETROL ENGINE

	Standard
Upper bearing (Black)	1.847
Lower bearing	
Blue (A)	1.844
Black (B)	1.857
Green (C)	1.866
Red (D)	1.877

EARLIER XU ENGINES AND XUD DIESEL
• Both the upper and lower bearing shells are of the same thickness.

☐ **STEP 23:** Fit the thrust washers, grooved side outward, to either side of the fourth main bearing (counting from timing belt end).

☐ **STEP 24:** Fit main bearing caps 2 and 5 the correct way round, and hold them in place with their bolts no more than nipped up.

☐ **STEP 25:** Apply a modest amount of sealant to No. 1 main bearing cap face in the block around the seal-peg holes (the smaller holes, alongside the bolt holes).

❏ **STEP 26:**
Use new No. 1 main cap sealing strips (two of them - one arrowed)
→ Locate the tab of each strip over the pins at the base of the bearing cap.
→ Push the lengths of the strips into the grooves provided at either side of the cap.

TOP TIP!

• You will need to improvise a simple tool for refitting the No.1 main bearing cap without dislodging or damaging its sealing strips.
• You will need to slide two very thin metal plates (no more than a quarter of a millimetre thick) between the sides of the cap and the cylinder block as the cap is refitted.
• Strips cut from an aluminium drinks can should be ideal.

❏ **STEP 27:** Oil the sealing strips and position the cap (with the thin plates) into the cylinder block recess, and when it is seated, withdraw the plates sideways, pulling them with pliers.

❏ **STEP 28:** Fit No. 1 main bearing cap bolts, and refit the remaining main bearing caps and bolts.
→ Progressively tighten all the main bearing cap nuts to the specified torque then complete the tightening, using a tool such as the Sykes Pickavant Angular Torque Gauge 800700, to further tighten them to Stage 2 tightening.

❏ **STEP 29:** Use a sharp blade to slice off the protruding ends of the No. 1 cap sealing strips, leaving just 1 mm of protrusion.

❏ **STEP 30:**
IMPORTANT NOTE: Remember that XU petrol engines have side retaining bolts at the centre main bearing (see illustration *5-13*).
→ These bolts should be tightened last.

❏ **STEP 31:** Follow *Job 3, Steps 44 and 45*.

→ Tighten the big-end nuts to the correct torque.
→ Note that XU and XUD engines have their big-end nuts tightened in three stages, the final being an angle-tightening stage - see *Step 28*.

❏ **STEP 32:** Make sure the Woodruff key is in place, then refit the oil pump drive sprocket to the crankshaft nose, followed by the drive chain.

❏ **STEP 33:** Note the correct fitted depth of the crankshaft front oil seal in its carrier.
→ Lever out the seal then squarely drift in a new, lubricated one.
→ Apply silicone sealant to the seal carrier then relocate it to the end of the cylinder block, sliding it over the crankshaft nose, and engaging its locating dowels. Tighten the carrier securing bolts.

❏ **STEP 34:** Fit a new crankshaft rear oil seal.
→ First lubricate it, then drift it into position using a suitable annular drift, such as a socket.
→ Tap it in squarely until it is flush with the cylinder block.

❏ **STEP 35:** Check that the crankshaft rotates smoothly. Lubricate the oil pump drive chain and refit the pump and strainer.

❏ **STEP 36:** Fit a new sump pan gasket, then refit the sump pan and progressively tighten its bolts.

❏ **STEP 37:** Refit any oil gallery plugs and external brackets previously removed.

❏ **STEP 38:** Carry out the following operations, referring to the relevant sections of this manual:
→ Refit the flywheel (use some locking compound on bolt threads).
→ Refit the clutch.
→ Refit the front oil seal plate and crankshaft sprocket.
→ Refit the cylinder head.
→ Refit the engine front plate and flywheel TDC sensor.
→ Refit the injection pump bracket and pump (diesel engine).
→ Refit the timing belt, tensioner and covers.
→ Refit the crankshaft pulley.
→ Fit the right-hand engine mounting bracket.
→ Refit the water pump.
→ Refit the starter motor.
→ Lubricate the sealing ring and screw on a new oil filter.
→ Refit all remaining ancillary components using new gaskets as necessary.
→ Reconnect the engine to the transmission and refit the complete unit to the car.

❏ **STEP 39:** See *Job 3, Step 51*. Follow the engine start-up procedures described there.

Part K: Engine/Transmission Mountings Replacement

CONTENTS

	Page No.
JOB 1: MOUNTING TYPES – *overview*.	6-79
JOB 2: EXISTING ENGINE MOUNTS – *realigning*.	6-79
JOB 3: ENGINE MOUNTS – *replacing*.	6-80

See *Part B: Which Engine is Which?* for an explanation of the engine types referred to here.

JOB 1: MOUNTING TYPES – *overview*.

All the engine mounting systems used on this Peugeot range of cars, are of the three-point type:
➔ One left-hand mounting supporting the transmission;
➔ One right-hand mounting supporting the right-hand end of the engine at a high level;
➔ One stabiliser/torque reaction mounting connecting the lower rear of the engine to the car subframe.
➔ The XV/XW/XY engine is unique in having one left-hand mounting, and two right-hand mountings affixed to the timing case, with no torque reaction (stabiliser) link.
➔ There are detail differences between the systems used but the basic principles are the same.

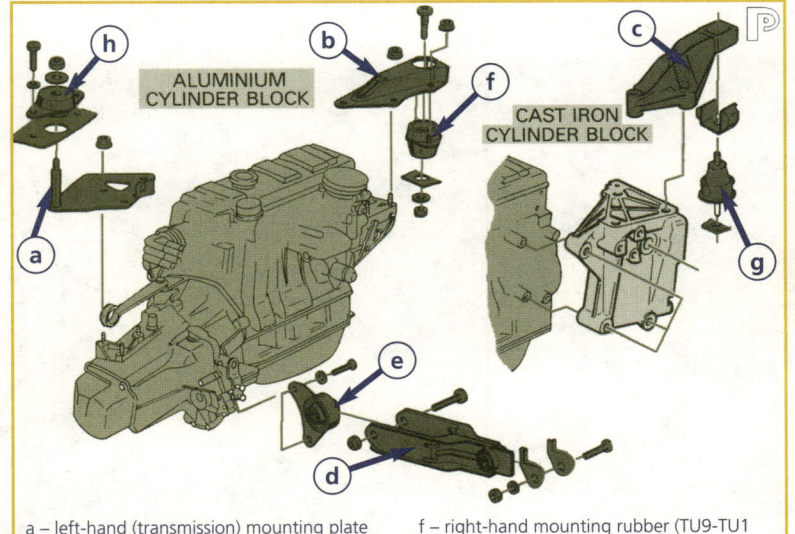

a – left-hand (transmission) mounting plate
b – right-hand mounting bracket (TU9-TU1 engines)
c – right-hand mounting bracket (TU 3.2 engine)
d – rear (stabiliser) mounting
e – rear mounting rubber
f – right-hand mounting rubber (TU9-TU1 engine)
g – right-hand mounting rubber (TU 3.2 engine)
h – left-hand (transmission) mounting rubber

1-1

❏ **ILLUSTRATION 1:** This is a typical mounting system and is the type used on some 106 models.

➔ Detail differences exist between the petrol TU mountings and the diesel TUD.

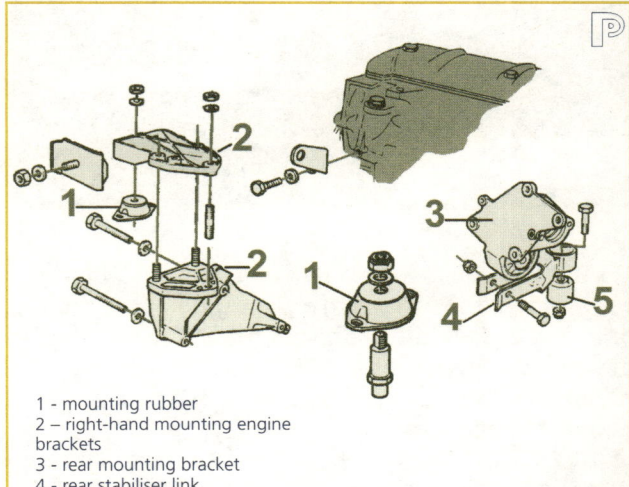

1 - mounting rubber
2 – right-hand mounting engine brackets
3 - rear mounting bracket
4 - rear stabiliser link
5 - stabiliser bush

1-2

❏ **ILLUSTRATION 2:** This is another variation on the same theme – this is a 306 model arrangement.
IMPORTANT NOTE: Some types are fitted with shims.
• Always put the same number of shims back in the same location if disturbing the buffer part of the mounting.

JOB 2: EXISTING ENGINE MOUNTS – *realigning*.

❏ **STEP 1:** Without removing any of them, loosen all the mounting bolts.

❏ **STEP 2:** Shake the whole engine/transmission assembly to settle it into position.

❏ **STEP 3:** Align the mounts and retighten the bolts.

JOB 3: ENGINE MOUNTS – *replacing*.

IMPORTANT NOTE: Only replace one engine mounting at a time.

3-1

□ **STEP 1:** If you are replacing an engine mounting, you will need to introduce extra support from above or below to take the weight of the unit while the old mounting is replaced. This can be achieved either by using a jack from below, as shown, or an engine hoist from above.
➜ IMPORTANT NOTE: If supporting the engine from below, take care not to break any engine castings or dent the sump pan with the head of a jack – use wood in between jack pad and engine.

□ **STEP 2:** With most Peugeot engine installations, access to the left-hand engine mounting necessitates removal of the battery first, and in some cases, the battery tray too.
➜ Disconnect the battery negative (-) earth/ground terminal. See *Chapter 10, Electrical, Dash, Instruments, Fact File: Disconnecting the Battery* BEFORE doing so!

□ **STEP 3: 205 MODELS WITH XV/XW/XY 'GEARS-IN-SUMP' ENGINE:** The rubber block of the front right-hand (lower timing case) mounting can be removed by undoing the two nuts (one at the body bracket and one on the engine) detaching the bracket arm from the timing cased and withdrawing the block. The remaining two mountings must be unbolted and renewed complete with the mounting brackets.

□ **STEP 4: XU/XUD SERIES ENGINE:** If the large rubber bush of the lower stabiliser (rear) mounting needs replacement, a new driveshaft support bracket will have to be fitted, as the bush is integrated with it.

□ **STEP 5:** When fitting new mountings, observe the positions of any washers and spacers when removing, and always observe nut/bolt tightening torques, where these are specified in *Chapter 1, Facts & Figures*.

CHAPTER 7: TRANSMISSION, CLUTCH

Please read **Chapter 2 Safety First** before carrying out any work on your car.

Part A: Clutch Cable and Pedal Box - Repair, Replacement
Part B: Gear Lever and Linkage - Removal, Refitting
Part C: Auto. Gear Selector and Transmission Cooler
Part D: Driveshafts and Joint Gaiters - Removal, Replacement
Part E: Transmission - Removal, Refitting (with engine in car)
Part F: Clutch - Replacement

Part A: Clutch Cable and Pedal Box – Repair, Replacement

CONTENTS

	Page No.
JOB 1: PEDAL BOXES AND CABLES – *types*.	7-1
JOB 2: MANUALLY ADJUSTED CLUTCH CABLE – *adjustment*.	7-3
JOB 3: CLUTCH CABLE – *replacement*.	7-3

JOB 1: PEDAL BOXES AND CABLES – *types*.

Many models covered by this manual have a manually adjusted clutch cable, while the following have an automatically adjusted cable requiring no regular intervention.
➔ All 206 models, and 306 models with 1.8, 1.9 and 2.0-litre engines, and also those with later 1.1, 1.4 and 1.6–litre engines.
➔ There are two other fundamentally different clutch mechanism types:
➔ The first type uses a release bearing that is pushed against the clutch diaphragm to release the clutch, the release arm being operated by the clutch cable INNER cable.
➔ The second type has a release bearing that is integrated with the pressure plate, and lifts away from the friction plate to release the clutch.
➔ The release arm is operated by the clutch OUTER cable and the inner cable is terminated at an abutment bracket.

There are some detailed variations between pedal box and cable components on the vehicles listed in this manual. However, the basic principles can be broken down in to a smaller number of different types.

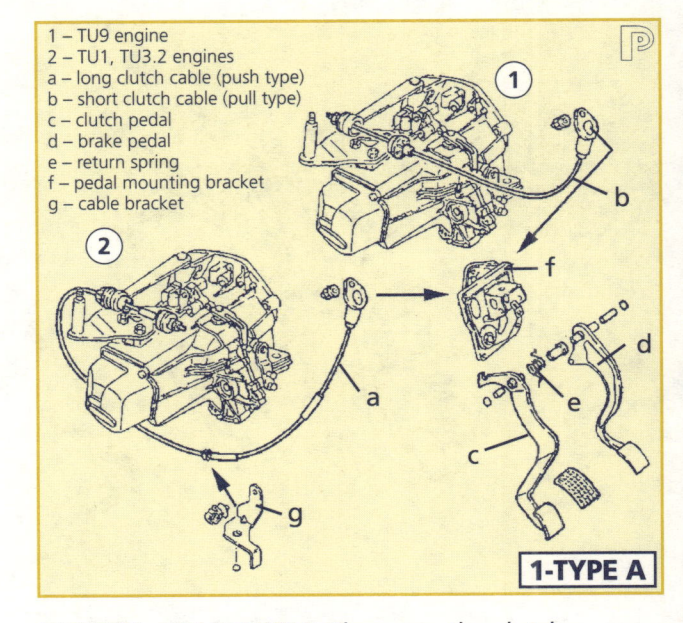

1 – TU9 engine
2 – TU1, TU3.2 engines
a – long clutch cable (push type)
b – short clutch cable (pull type)
c – clutch pedal
d – brake pedal
e – return spring
f – pedal mounting bracket
g – cable bracket

1-TYPE A

❏ **TYPE A: 106 MODELS:** These are the clutch

actuation components for 106 models, both petrol and diesel.

☐ TYPE B: 205 MODELS WITH THE XV/XW/XY ENGINES: This is the clutch assembly and release mechanism of these models.

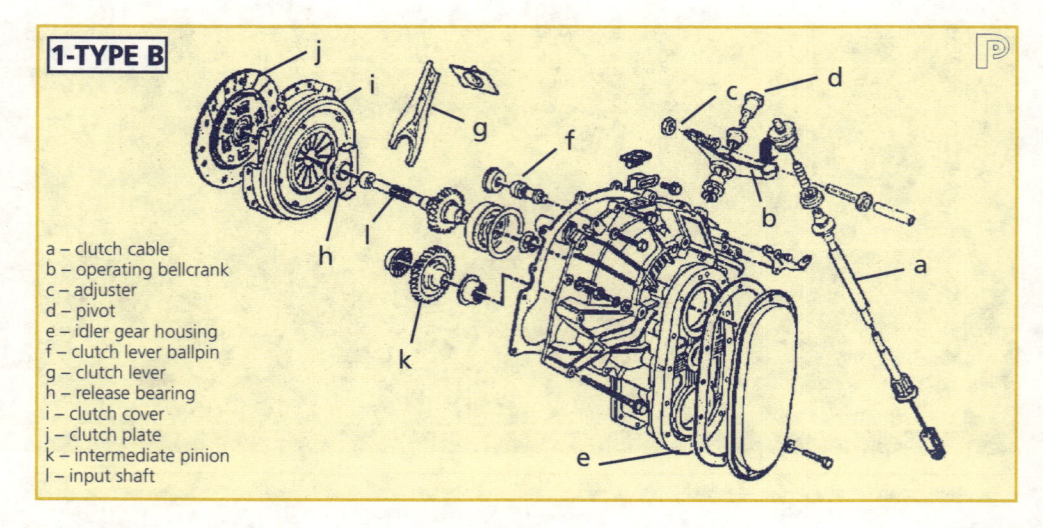

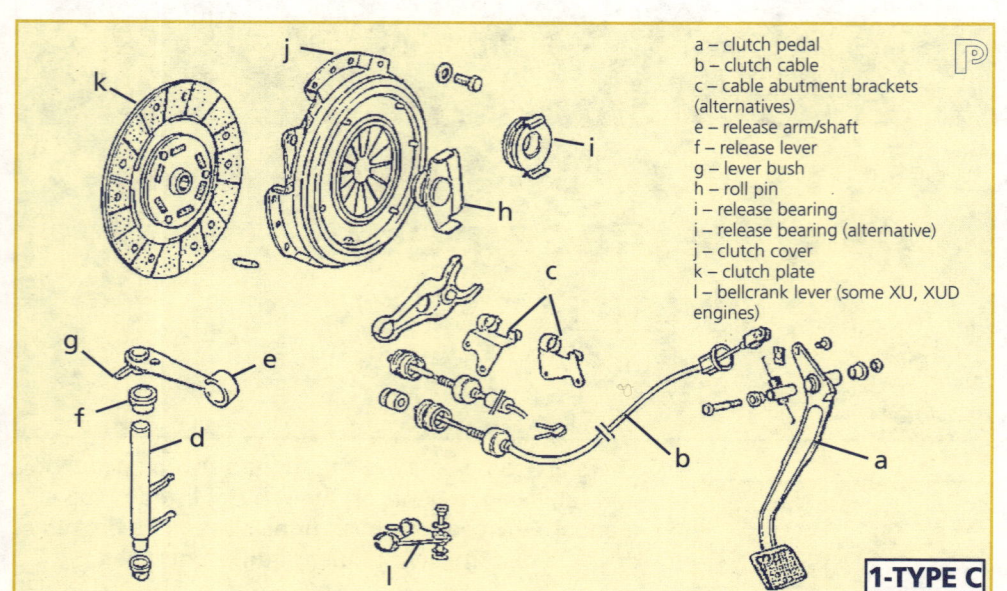

1-TYPE B

a – clutch cable
b – operating bellcrank
c – adjuster
d – pivot
e – idler gear housing
f – clutch lever ballpin
g – clutch lever
h – release bearing
i – clutch cover
j – clutch plate
k – intermediate pinion
l – input shaft

a – clutch pedal
b – clutch cable
c – cable abutment brackets (alternatives)
e – release arm/shaft
f – release lever
g – lever bush
h – roll pin
i – release bearing
i – release bearing (alternative)
j – clutch cover
k – clutch plate
l – bellcrank lever (some XU, XUD engines)

☐ TYPE C: OTHER 205 MODELS: This is the clutch assembly and release mechanism of 205 models EXCEPT those with the XV/XW/XY engines.

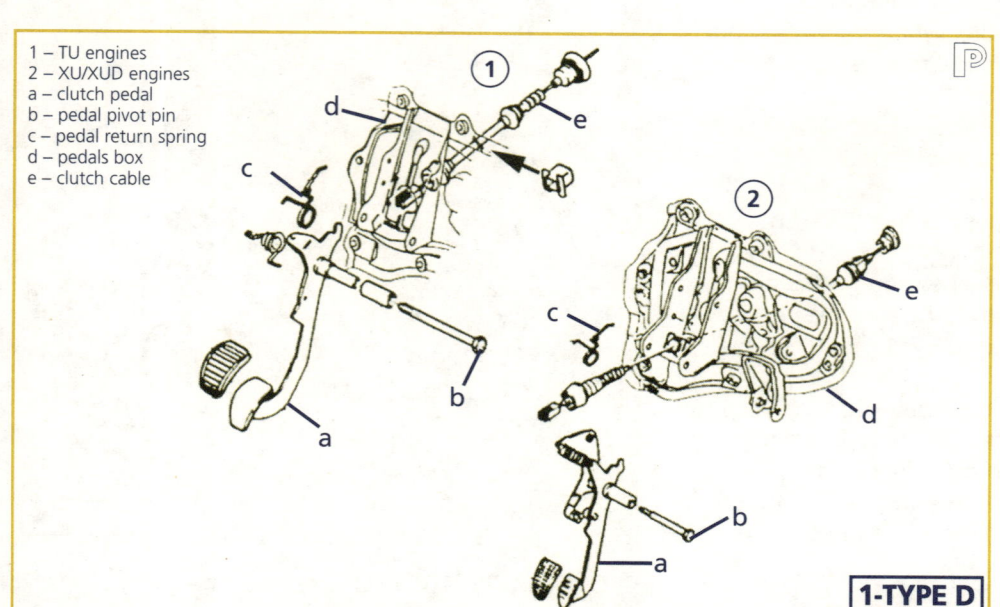

1-TYPE C

1 – TU engines
2 – XU/XUD engines
a – clutch pedal
b – pedal pivot pin
c – pedal return spring
d – pedals box
e – clutch cable

☐ TYPE D: 306 PETROL MODELS: This is the pedals box and clutch cable.

1-TYPE D

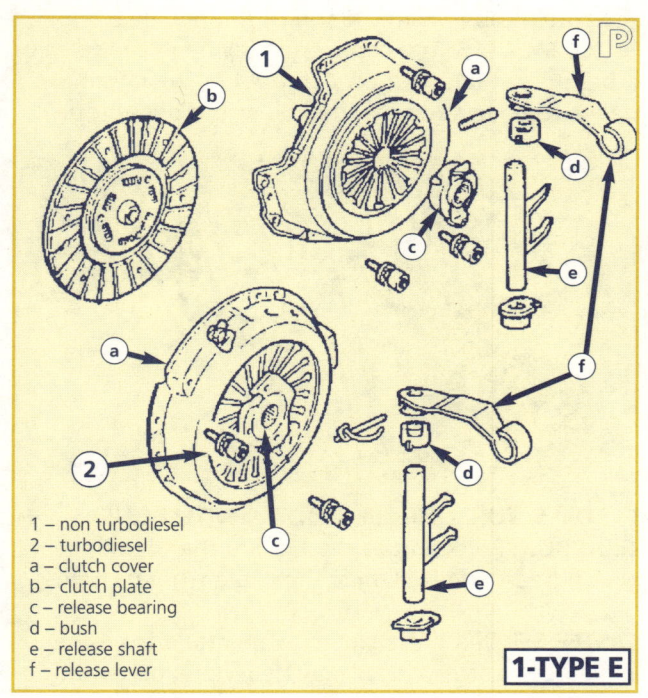

1 – non turbodiesel
2 – turbodiesel
a – clutch cover
b – clutch plate
c – release bearing
d – bush
e – release shaft
f – release lever

1-TYPE E

☐ **TYPE E: 306 DIESEL:** This is the clutch and operating lever assembly for these models.

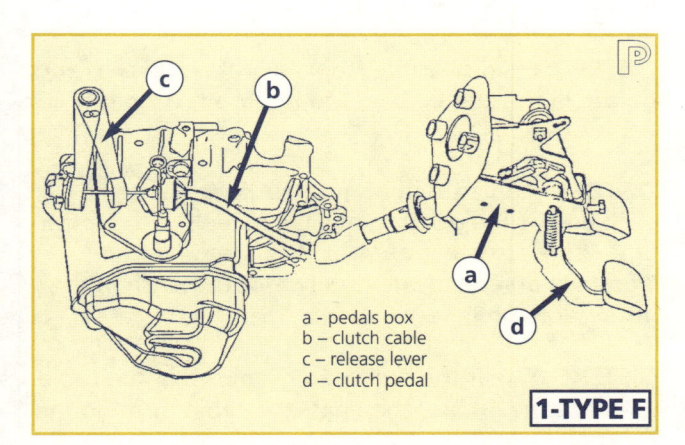

a – pedals box
b – clutch cable
c – release lever
d – clutch pedal

1-TYPE F

☐ **TYPE F: 206:** This shows the pedals box and external clutch release mechanism of 206 models.

JOB 2: MANUALLY ADJUSTED CLUTCH CABLE – *adjustment*.

Many models covered by this manual have a manually adjusted clutch cable, while the following have an automatically adjusted cable requiring no regular intervention: all 206 models, 306 models with 1.8, 1.9 and 2.0-litre engines, and 306 with later 1.1, 1.4 and 1.6–litre engines.

ALL MODELS WITH MANUAL-ADJUST CABLE

☐ **STEP 1:** Check the clutch cable adjustment by measuring the clutch pedal travel.

→ Measure the travel from the at-rest position of the edge of the pedal rubber, to the fully depressed position, near the bulkhead/floor.
→ If this travel is less than 140 mm (5.5 in.) or 131 mm (306 models), adjustment is required.

TOP TIP!

• If the travel is more than the permissible amount specified and cannot be correctly adjusted, this is probably an indication that the clutch is worn and needs replacing.

☐ **STEP 2:** With any floor mats removed, 'work' the clutch pedal a few times throughout its full travel. Check the clutch cable adjustment by…

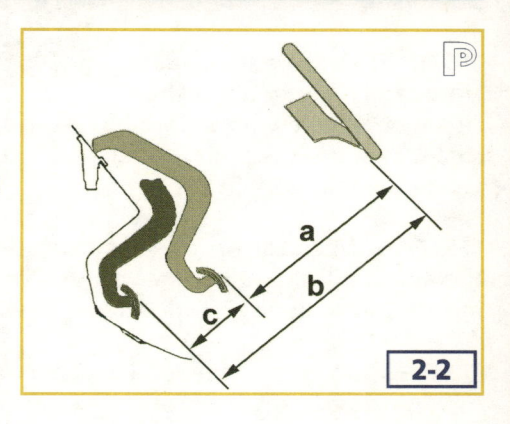

2-2

→ …first measuring the distance from the clutch pedal (at rest) to the bottom of the steering wheel rim – measurement (**a**).
→ Then repeat this with the clutch pedal fully depressed (**b**).
→ Subtract the first measurement (**a**) from the second (**b**), to obtain the clutch pedal travel figure (**c**).
→ If this travel is less than 140 mm (5.5 in.) or 131 mm (306 models), adjustment is required.

☐ **STEP 3: ALL MODELS:** Adjust the clutch cable at the adjuster nut on the gearbox end of the cable, having first undone the locknut which is against it.

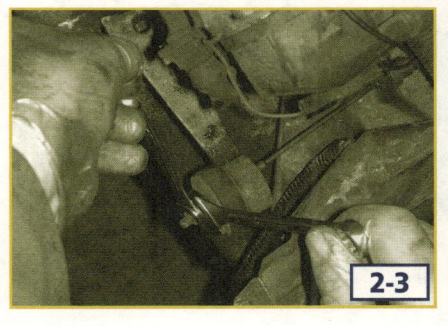

2-3

TOP TIP!

• Access to this nut can be difficult, depending on engine-bay components.
• For instance, on some models it is best to remove the battery and air filter casing and ducting for access.
• With the front of the car raised and supported, it is often possible to gain access to the adjuster from beneath the car, without removing the aforementioned components.

CHAPTER 7 Part A Job 2

7-3

❐ **STEP 4: 205 MODELS WITH THE XV/XW/XY SERIES ENGINE:** The threaded adjuster (**a**) is on the pushrod between the bellcrank lever (**b**) to which the cable is attached, and the clutch operating lever (**c**), which protrudes from the clutch housing.
➜ As with the cable-end adjuster, this type also has a locknut (**d**) that must first be slackened.

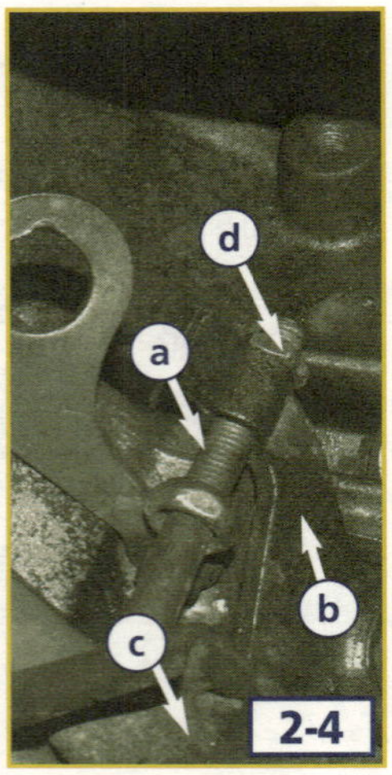

❐ **STEP 5:** Measure the pedal travel again, then 'work' the clutch pedal a few times throughout its full travel. Again measure the pedal travel, and adjust further if still not within permissible limits.

❐ **STEP 6:** When correct travel is achieved, tighten the adjuster locknut, then re-measure the travel, just in case you've inadvertently altered the setting.

❐ **STEP 7:** Smear the threaded adjuster and nuts with multipurpose grease to protect against corrosion and to make it easier to adjust next time around.

JOB 3: CLUTCH CABLE – *replacement*.

206 AND 306 MODELS

❐ **STEP 1:** If required, give yourself better working access by removing one, some or all of the following: the air cleaner housing, air intake ducting, battery and battery tray.

❐ **STEP 2:** Disconnect the inner and outer clutch cable from the clutch operating arm and abutment bracket. This may require the cable-end adjuster nut to be backed off a little.
➜ **206 MODELS:** If it proves difficult to pull the cable free of the clutch operating arm, back off the adjuster screw (**a**) at the front of the pedals box, inside the vehicle.

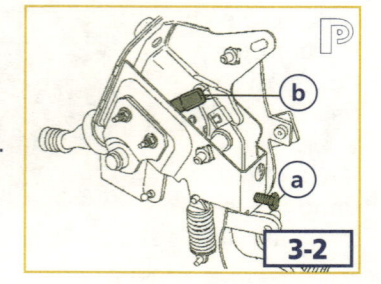

❐ **STEP 3:** From inside the vehicle, remove the fusebox cover from the dashboard, and detach the heater duct from behind it.

❐ **STEP 4:** Detach the dashboard lower cover for access to the pedals box, then unhook the end of the clutch cable from the top of the pedal.
➜ **206 MODELS:** The cable end may be in the form of a ball-socket (illustration **3-2, item b**), which simply needs to be levered off the ball at the pedal top.

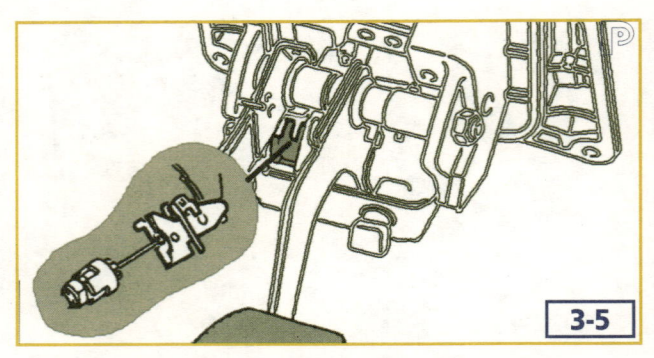

❐ **STEP 5: TURBODIESEL MODELS WITH BE3/5 GEARBOX:** Press on the clip behind the top of the clutch pedal to disconnect the cable from its holder.

❐ **STEP 6:** Release the clutch cable guide from the bulkhead (a screwdriver may help here, depending on fitting type), and pull the cable away from the bulkhead.
➜ On certain models there is a rubber boot to be levered from the bulkhead.

❐ **STEP 7:** Free the cable from any retaining clips and guides in the engine bay, and remove it from the engine bay.

❐ **STEP 8:** Apply a dab of multipurpose grease to each end of the clutch cable. On models with a push-type cable assembly, apply a little grease to the transmission-end of the outer cable rather than the inner cable.

❐ **STEP 9:** Smear the bulkhead grommet of the cable with silicone grease, then pass the cable through the bulkhead from the engine side.

❐ **STEP 10:** From inside the vehicle, hook (or snap – depending on type) the inner cable to the end of the clutch pedal.

❐ **STEP 11:** Clip the dashboard lower cover back into position, reconnect the heater duct and refit the fusebox cover.

❐ **STEP 12:** Fit the cable back into its guides and clips, then reconnect the cable inner and outer ends to the operating arm and abutment bracket, ensuring that the rubber sections and washers are in the correct order.

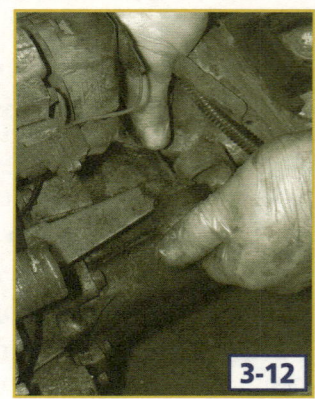

❐ **STEP 13: MANUAL-ADJUST CABLES:** Adjust the clutch pedal travel – see *Job 2*.

206 MODELS

❐ **STEP 14:** Adjust the clutch pedal position.
→ Operate the clutch fully several times.
→ Make sure that the pedal adjuster screw (**a**) at the front of the pedals box is adjusted so that free play (**X**) is just eliminated.

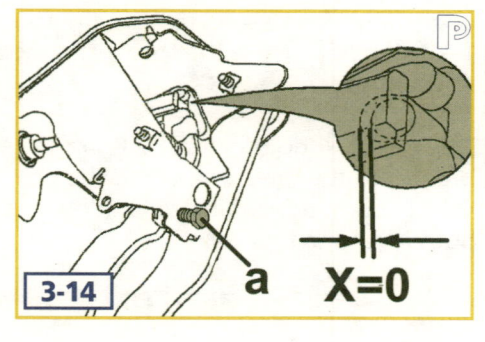

❐ **STEP 15:** Pull the cable at (position **a**).
→ If it moves by about 5 mm, clutch cable adjustment is correct.
→ If there is no movement, or too much, this can only be because of a fault with the cable assembly. 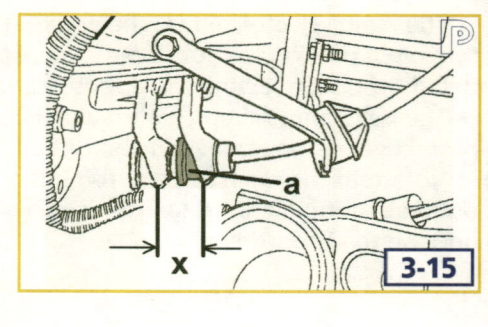
→ Check that the travel 'X' of the clutch operating arm is at least 24 mm. If it is any less than 24 mm, this can only be because of a fault with the cable assembly.

ALL MODELS

❐ **STEP 16:** Refit all previously removed components such as battery and air filter.

Part B: Gear Lever and Linkage Removal, Refitting

CONTENTS

	Page No.
JOB 1. GEAR LEVER AND LINKAGE – *adjustment, removal, refitting*.	7-5
JOB 2. GEAR LEVER – *removal, refitting*.	7-8

See **Chapter 6, Part B: Which Engine is Which?** for an explanation of the engine types referred to here.

JOB 1: GEAR LEVER AND LINKAGE – *adjustment, removal, refitting*.

Section A: XV/XW/XY engines.

ADJUSTMENT

❐ **STEP A1:** The gearchange linkage does not normally require adjustment. When replacing individual gearchange linkages, compare the lengths of the new and old linkages, and if necessary, set the lengths of the new linkages to those of the old, by slackening the locknuts and screwing the end-balljoints either in or out.

❐ **STEP A2:** If the linkage has been disturbed or renewed, set it to initial measurements...
→ For the short cross-link with two adjustable balljoints (illustration *1-1A, item e*) – 73 to 86 mm.
→ For the longer cross-link with one adjustable balljoint (illustration *1-1A, item g*) – 171 to 173 mm.

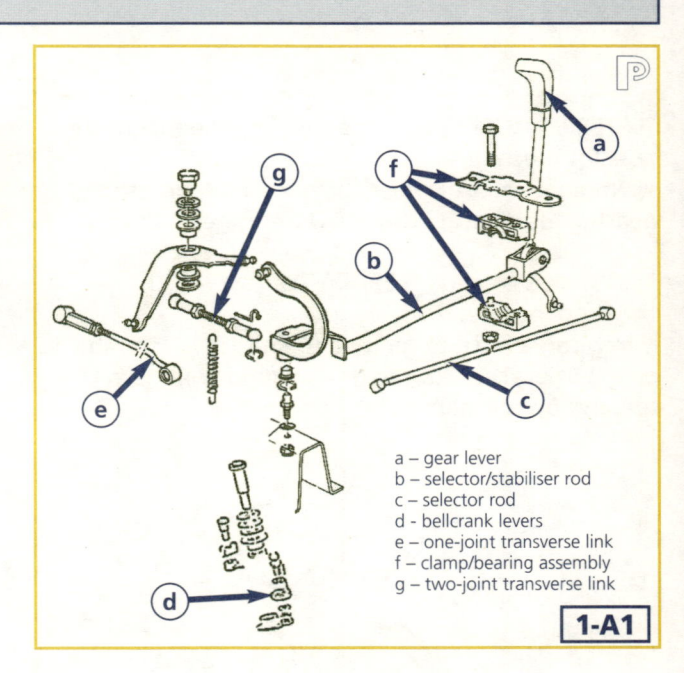

a – gear lever
b – selector/stabiliser rod
c – selector rod
d – bellcrank levers
e – one-joint transverse link
f – clamp/bearing assembly
g – two-joint transverse link

REMOVAL

❐ **STEP A3:** The gearchange linkage comprises four rods and a bellcrank lever - see illustration *1-A1A*.
→ Three of the rods detach by snapping apart their ball joints.

→ The main selector rod, at the engine end, circlips to a pivot post on the subframe - see *Job 2* for details of disconnecting the opposite end of this rod.
→ The bellcrank is simply bolted down, and has a protective plastic cap over its bolt head.
→ Note that the main selector rod has a two-part bolted bearing along its length, which must be undone to allow rod removal.

REFITTING

☐ **STEP A4:** Reassembly is a reversal of the removal procedure, noting that balljoint sockets should first be greased, and noting also that a hook-ended spring acts on one of the transverse selector rods.

Section B. TU and TUD engines.

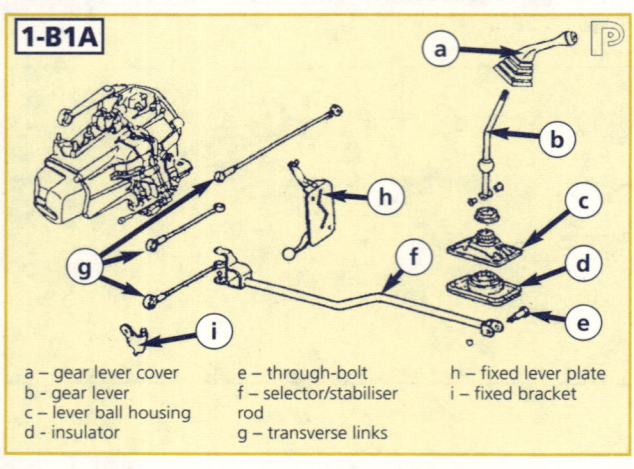

1-B1A

a – gear lever cover
b – gear lever
c – lever ball housing
d – insulator
e – through-bolt
f – selector/stabiliser rod
g – transverse links
h – fixed lever plate
i – fixed bracket

☐ **STEP B1A: 106:** These are the components of the selector mechanism.
→ No adjustment is needed to the linkage of the MA gearbox used with TU and TUD engines.

REMOVAL

It may be helpful to remove the air filter assembly to give better access to the gearchange linkage within the engine compartment.

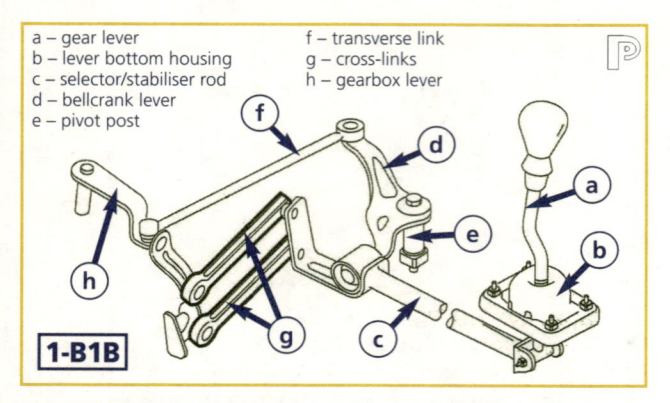

a – gear lever
b – lever bottom housing
c – selector/stabiliser rod
d – bellcrank lever
e – pivot post
f – transverse link
g – cross-links
h – gearbox lever

1-B1B

☐ **STEP B1B: 206:** These are the components of the selector mechanism.

☐ **STEP B2:** From both ends of the main selector rod, undo and remove the pivot bolt and collect the nut and washer.

☐ **STEP B3:** Disconnect the rod from the selector and gearchange levers, and remove the rod from the car. Take care not to lose the spacer that goes on the selector lever.

☐ **STEP B4:** Undo the nuts/bolts which retain the bracket of the selector lever to the gearbox (or vehicle body, depending on model), and withdraw both lever and bracket.

REFITTING

☐ **STEP B5:** Reassembly is a reversal of the removal procedure, noting that balljoint sockets should first be greased, and that linkage bolts should be torque-tightened, where applicable.

Section C: XU and XUD engines.

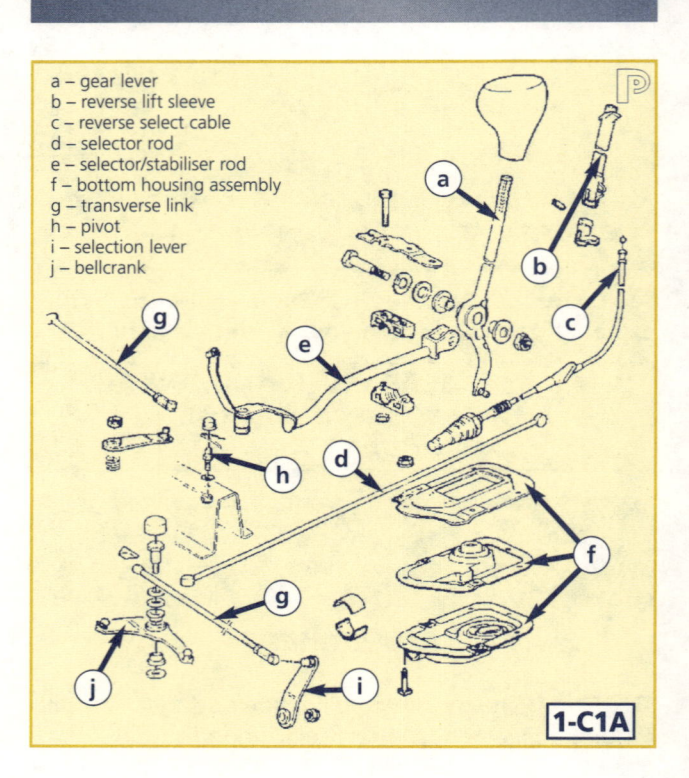

a – gear lever
b – reverse lift sleeve
c – reverse select cable
d – selector rod
e – selector/stabiliser rod
f – bottom housing assembly
g – transverse link
h – pivot
i – selection lever
j – bellcrank

1-C1A

☐ **STEP C1A: 205:** These are the components of the petrol selector mechanism.

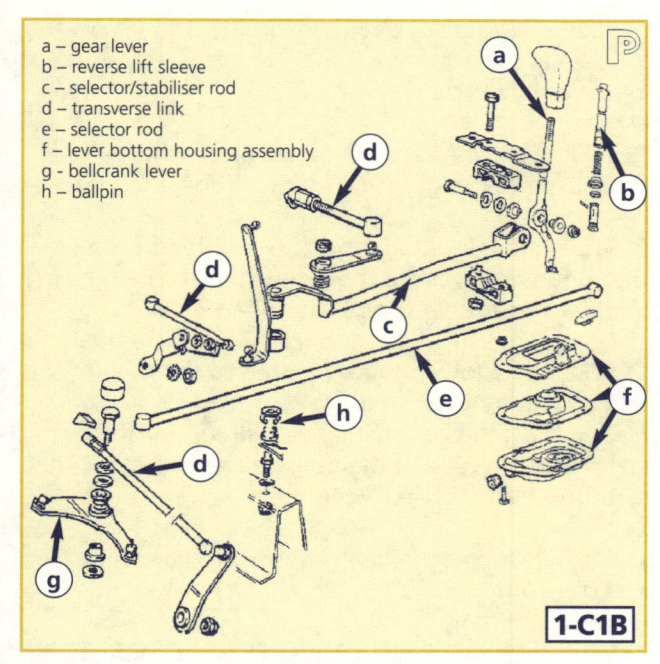

a – gear lever
b – reverse lift sleeve
c – selector/stabiliser rod
d – transverse link
e – selector rod
f – lever bottom housing assembly
g – bellcrank lever
h – ballpin

1-C1B

☐ **STEP C1B: 205 DIESEL:** These are the components of the selector mechanism.

a – gear knob
b – gear lever
c – selector/stabiliser rod
d – cap
e – gear lever ball housing
f – lever bottom housing assembly
g – transverse links
h – bellcrank lever
i – fixed ball plate

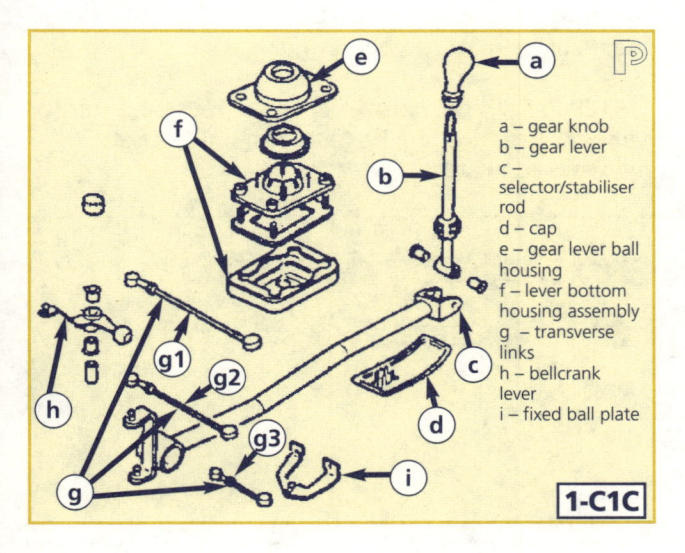

1-C1C

☐ **STEP C1C: 306:** These are the selector mechanism components.

ADJUSTMENT – 205 (PRE-'86)

On models from 1986, equipped with cable operated lift-reverse selection (illustrations *1-C1A* and *1-C1C*), no adjustment is necessary.

☐ **STEP C2:** On models prior to 1986, place the gear lever in neutral, and move it to the left until you feel resistance.
→ Measure the distance the lever has travelled - check it a few times.

☐ **STEP C3:** If this distance is outside the limits of 36 to 40 mm, detach the gear lever gaiter and remove the O-ring and spring clip from the base of the gear lever.

☐ **STEP C4:** Lift the white plastic eccentric off its splines at the bottom of the gear lever, then reposition on the splines to effectively vary the position of the gear lever.

☐ **STEP C5:** Recheck the lever travel as in **Steps B1 and B2**, and when it is correct, refit the spring clip to secure the eccentric. Refit the O-ring and gear lever gaiter.

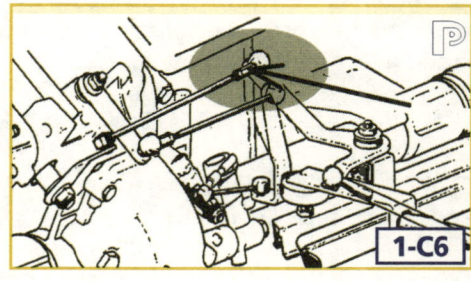

☐ **STEP C6:** If you cannot achieve the correct travel, it will be necessary to adjust the length

1-C6

of the selector rod (arrowed) by 6.0 mm.

306 ADJUSTMENT

☐ **STEP C7:** There should be no need to alter the adjustment of the gearchange linkage of XU and XUD engined models unless someone has interfered with them.

☐ **STEP C8:** Working in the engine bay and/or beneath the car, measure the length of each link rod (between balljoint centres), and compare with the specified lengths. Referring to illustration *1-C1C*, rod **g1** should be from 259.5 to 261.5 mm, rod **g2** 105 to 107 mm, and rod **g3** 105.5 to 107.5 mm.

☐ **STEP C9:** If adjustment is necessary, slacken the locknut(s) of the relevant rod, disconnect one balljoint and screw it in or out to meet the length range allowed. Grease the ball socket, reconnect the joint, and tighten the balljoint locknut.

REMOVAL

☐ **STEP C10:** Remove the nut, and withdraw the pivot bolt securing the selector rod to the bottom of the gearchange lever.

☐ **STEP C11:** Using a screwdriver, lever the link rod ball sockets off their ballpins on the gearbox.

☐ **STEP C12:** Detach the main selector rod from the bellcrank lever, and also from its pivot post on the subframe (retained by circlip). Withdraw it from beneath the vehicle.

☐ **STEP C13:** Lever the plastic cap from the bolt that retains the bellcrank on the subframe, and

1-C13

undo the bolt, washer and bellcrank. Take care not to lose the bushes and spacer from the bellcrank centre.

❏ **STEP C14: MODELS WITH THE BE1/5 GEARBOX (FROM 1986) WITH CABLE-CONNECTED LIFT-UP REVERSE GEAR SELECTION:** See illustrations *1-C1A* and *1-C1B*).
→ Disconnect the reverse cable by unscrewing it from the gearbox top, and at the gear-lever end, freeing its nipple from the lever slide.

REFITTING

❏ **STEP C15:** Check and, if necessary, adjust the link rods as in *Steps C6 and C9*.

❏ **STEP C16:** Reassembly is a reversal of the removal procedure, noting that balljoint sockets should first be greased, and that linkage bolts should be torque-tightened, where applicable.

> **JOB 2: GEAR LEVER** – *removal, refitting*.

Refer to illustrations *1-B1A to 1-C1B*.

❏ **STEP 1:** Unscrew/remove the gear lever knob.

❏ **STEP 2:** Unclip the gear lever gaiter and lift off the gaiter. On some models it may be necessary to remove the centre console.

❏ **STEP 3:** Lift the carpet and unbolt the floor-plate from around the gear lever base; lift off the plate.

❏ **STEP 4:** Raise and support the front end of the car, and undo and remove the exhaust heat shield from the floor near gear lever base, when fitted.

❏ **STEP 5:** If a lower gaiter is fitted to the base of the lever (under the car) remove it.
→ Pop the gearchange linkage ball socket off the ballpin at the base of the gear lever - not later MA gearboxes with TU/TUD engines.

❏ **STEP 6:** Unbolt the gear lever from the main selector rod.

❏ **STEP 7: MODELS WITH REVERSE GEAR SELECTOR CABLE:** See illustrations *1-C1A* and *1-C1B*.
→ Detach the cable end-nipple from the gear lever sleeve and remove the two bolts holding together the main selector rod bearing halves.

❏ **STEP 8:** Refit the gear lever in the reverse order to removal, greasing the ballpins and ball-sockets before reconnection.

Part C: Auto. Gear Selector and Transmission Cooler

CONTENTS

	Page No.
JOB 1: AUTO. GEAR SELECTOR CABLE AND HANDLE – *adjustment, replacement*.	7-8
JOB 2: 205/306 KICKDOWN CABLE – *adjustment, replacement*.	7-10
JOB 3: TRANSMISSION OIL COOLER – *removal, refitting*.	7-11

See *Chapter 6, Part B: Which Engine is Which?* for an explanation of the engine types referred to here.
→ Two general types of automatic shift control have been fitted: both operate on similar principles.

> **JOB 1: AUTO. GEAR SELECTOR CABLE and HANDLE** – *adjustment, replacement*.

Section A: 205 and 306 transmission selector adjustment.

To gain access the cable at the transmission end, it may be necessary to remove the air filter assembly, intake ducting, battery and battery tray.

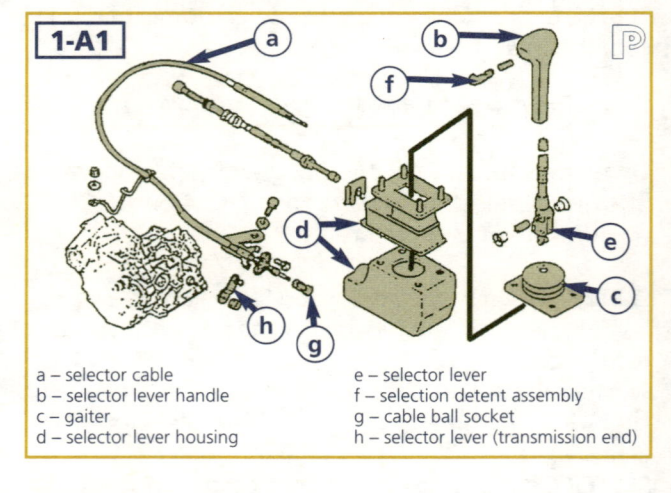

1-A1

a – selector cable
b – selector lever handle
c – gaiter
d – selector lever housing
e – selector lever
f – selection detent assembly
g – cable ball socket
h – selector lever (transmission end)

❏ **STEP A1: 205 MODELS:** These are the components of the selector mechanism. Adjust the cable as follows:

☐ **STEP A2:** Lever the selector cable end-socket off its ballpin (**a**) at the transmission selector lever. 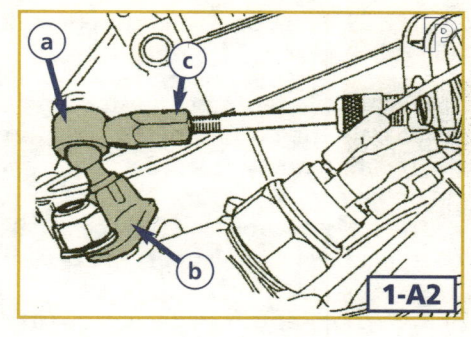
→ Select transmission Park position with the manual selector lever inside the car, and select the same position on the transmission unit selector lever to which the cable is normally attached.
→ Check that the ball socket of the cable aligns perfectly with its ballpin on the selector lever at the transmission unit, such that neither the hand-lever nor the lever (**b**) at the transmission needs to be moved to reconnect the balljoint.
→ If alignment is not perfect, slacken the locknut securing the ball-socket to the threaded end of the cable, and turn the ball-socket (**c**) by one turn (in or out) to suit.
→ Retighten the locknut, lightly grease the ballpin and snap the balljoint back into engagement.
→ Test transmission selection with the engine running.
→ Refit all previously removed components.

☐ **STEP A3: 306 MODELS:** Refer to the components in illustration *1-A1*. Adjust the cable as follows:

☐ **STEP A4:** Select Neutral position with the manual selector. 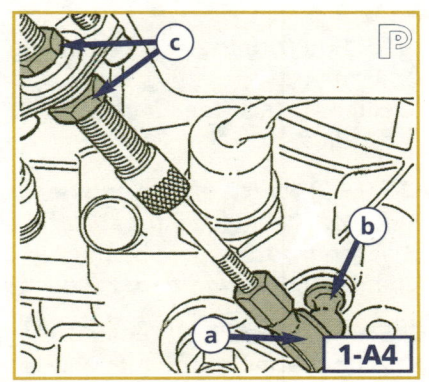
→ Lever the selector cable ball-socket (**a**) off ballpin (**b**) at transmission selector lever, but DO NOT MOVE the lever.
→ Check that the ball socket of the cable is threaded onto the cable by at least 5 mm of cable thread.
→ Check that, with the manual selectors inside car, and at the transmission, still in Neutral position, the cable is just the right length to allow the ball socket to be snapped back onto the lever ballpin without bending the cable or turning the socket.
→ If the cable is not exactly the correct length in this respect, adjust its length by screwing the ball-socket (**a**) further in or out on the threaded end of the cable, but make sure that its minimum engagement on the threads is 5 mm.
→ If it is not possible to effect the correct engagement by this means, further adjustment is possible at the selector OUTER cable abutment, where there is a locknut and an adjuster nut (**c**).
→ Lightly grease the ballpin and snap the balljoint back into engagement. Refit components.

Section B: Selector adjustment, 206 transmission.

TOP TIP!

• To gain proper access to the cable at the transmission end, it may be necessary to remove the air filter assembly, air intake ducting, battery and battery tray.

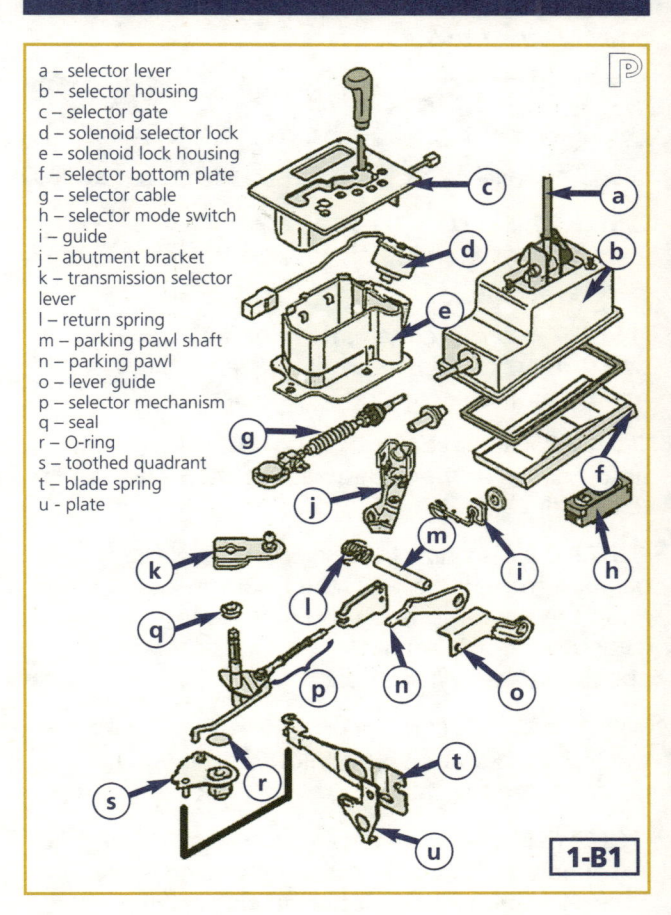

a – selector lever
b – selector housing
c – selector gate
d – solenoid selector lock
e – solenoid lock housing
f – selector bottom plate
g – selector cable
h – selector mode switch
i – guide
j – abutment bracket
k – transmission selector lever
l – return spring
m – parking pawl shaft
n – parking pawl
o – lever guide
p – selector mechanism
q – seal
r – O-ring
s – toothed quadrant
t – blade spring
u – plate

☐ **STEP B1:** These are the selector components referred to here. Place the manual selector lever in the 'P' (park) position.

☐ **STEP B2:** Unlock the manual selector cable from the selector lever at the transmission by pressing down on the black plastic catch of the cable end (**a**).

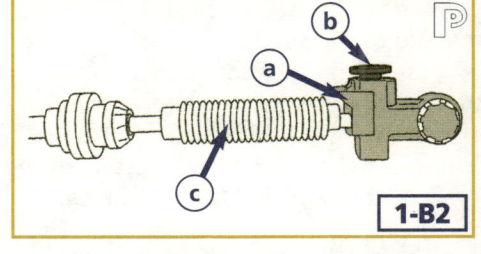

☐ **STEP B3:** Position the selector lever, at the transmission-end, as far towards the rear as possible.

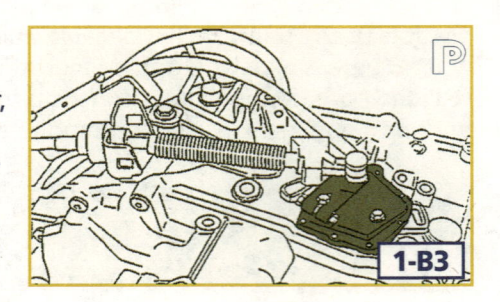

1-B3

☐ **STEP B4:** Lock the selector mechanism adjustment position by pressing down on the plastic catch (illustration *1-B2, item b*) of the selector cable (**c**).

☐ **STEP B5:** From inside the vehicle, check that gear selection is correct – i.e. that each gear function is engaged as marked on the selector gate. If not, repeat *Steps 1* to *5*.

Section C: Selector replacement, 205/306 transmission.

☐ **STEP C1:** Select 'N' (neutral) at the manual selector lever, then raise and safely support the front of the vehicle.

☐ **STEP C2:** Remove the battery, battery tray, and tray support plate. On certain models it may help to remove air intake ducting for the best access.

☐ **STEP C3:** Remove the exhaust heat shield to give better access to the underneath of the transmission selector lever unit.

☐ **STEP C4:** Disconnect the selector cable end balljoint from the lever at the transmission unit, and undo the screws securing the cable outer casing to its abutment bracket at the transmission, where applicable – see *illustration 1-A2*.

IMPORTANT NOTE: Make sure the selector lever at the transmission unit is not moved after you have disconnected the cable.

☐ **STEP C5:** From inside the car, lever the selector lever surround trim from the console, and remove the screws that retain the selector handle to the shaft.

☐ **STEP C6:** From inside the engine compartment, free the cable from all its retaining clips.

☐ **STEP C7:** Referring to *illustration 1-A1*.
→ Remove the screws securing the selector lever handle to the shaft.
→ Push in the selector detent button.
→ Turn the handle a quarter-turn (anti-clockwise), lift it, and turn it back in the reverse direction – this will allow the detent button to be freed.
→ Collect the detent button spring.

☐ **STEP C8:** Remove the nuts retaining the selector lever assembly to the vehicle body.

☐ **STEP C9:** From beneath the vehicle, lower the lever and cable assembly from the vehicle.

☐ **STEP C10:** Referring to illustration *1-A1*, lever the cover from the bottom of the lever assembly, loosen the securing nut of the outer cable, and detach the retaining clip.
→ The selector cable can now be separated from the gear lever by levering apart the balljoint connection.

☐ **STEP C11:** Refitting is carried out in the reverse order to removal. Connect at the transmission end first, and clip the cable run to its guides last.

IMPORTANT NOTE: Before refitting cable, apply molybdenum disulphide grease to selector lever detent assembly, and to the cable end balljoint. Once cable is refitted, check adjustment - see *Step 1*.

Section D: 206 transmission replacement.

At the time of writing, detailed information concerning replacement of the auto selector cable of the 206 is not available. However, procedure is similar for 205 and 306 models, see illustration *1-B1*.

JOB 2: 205/306 KICKDOWN CABLE – *adjustment, replacement*.

ADJUSTMENT

☐ **STEP 1:** With the engine running at normal operating temperature, check that the engine idle speed is correct (see **Chapter 1, Facts and Figures**). If not, adjust it

☐ **STEP 2:** Switch off the engine, disconnect the kickdown cable from the throttle body, and check that the throttle cable is adjusted correctly (see **Chapter 9, Fuel, Ignition, Exhaust, Job 11**).

☐ **STEP 3: CARBURETTOR MODELS ONLY:** Remove the clip that holds the throttle outer cable against its stop, and reposition it to give a small clearance between the clip and the stop. Fully depress the accelerator, and check that the carburettor throttle valve(s) is/are open. Gently pull the end of the kickdown cable until you feel resistance, then hold it in this position.

☐ **STEP 4: FUEL INJECTION MODELS ONLY:** Pull the kickdown cable fully from its outer sleeve.

☐ **STEP 5: ALL TYPES:** Note that a nipple (**a**) is crimped to the inner cable. While still holding the cable out as in *Step 3* or *Step 4*, measure from the nipple to the end of the threaded section (**X**) of the outer cable.

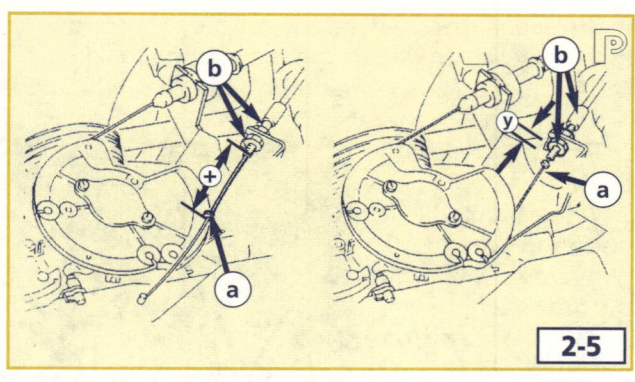

canister to which are connected two coolant hoses, mounted on the top of the automatic transmission. Depending on exact model of vehicle, access to this unit may require removal of the air filter assembly, air intake ducting, and/or battery.

JOB 3: TRANSMISSION OIL COOLER – removal, refitting.

→ The following Steps refer to illustration 2-5.

☐ **STEP 6:** If the measured distance is not 39 mm, adjust to this measurement by moving the outer cable in relation to its abutment bracket (adjust nuts **b**).

☐ **STEP 7:** Reconnect the kickdown cable, and recheck the measurement to the pellet.

☐ **STEP 8:** With the throttle body cable quadrant in the at-rest position (idle), check the distance between the cable pellet and the threaded end of the outer cable (**Y**), using a feeler gauge. The measured gap should be 0.5 to 1.0 mm – if not, readjust the outer cable position to achieve this, then tighten up the outer cable locknuts.

REPLACEMENT

IMPORTANT NOTE: The job of replacing the kickdown cable should be entrusted to a Peugeot dealer or automatic transmission specialist, as it necessitates opening of the transmission hydraulic valve block. The transmission oil cooler is a circular or square

☐ **STEP 1:** Clamp the two coolant hoses to the cooler, and unclip and detach them from the cooler stubs.

☐ **STEP 2:** Undo and remove the centre retaining bolt (**a**) of the cooler unit (**b**), and lift off the unit.

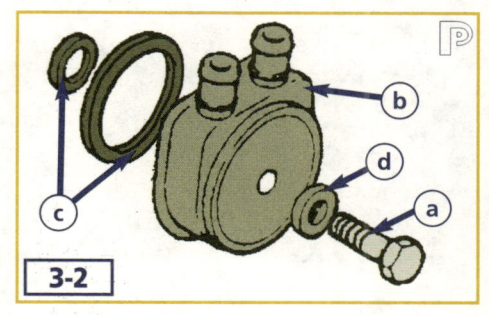

→ Remove and discard the two seals (*item c*) at the base of the cooler, and the single seal (**d**) on its centre bolt.

☐ **STEP 3:** Refit the cooler in the reverse order to removal, using three NEW seals, and tightening the centre bolt to the specified torque.

☐ **STEP 4:** Top-up (and purge, if necessary) the cooling system, and refit previously removed ancillary components.

Part D: Driveshafts and Joint Gaiters
Removal, Replacement

CONTENTS

	Page No.
JOB 1: DRIVESHAFT – removal, refitting.	7-11
JOB 2: DRIVESHAFT JOINT AND GAITERS – removal, replacement.	7-13
JOB 3: INTERMEDIATE SHAFT BEARING	7-14

See **Chapter 6, Part B: Which Engine is Which?** for an explanation of the engine types referred to here.

JOB 1: DRIVESHAFT – removal, refitting.

FACT FILE
AVOIDING DRIVESHAFT DISASTER!

• On models with XU/XUD engine and BE gearbox, manufactured until early 1985, removal of both driveshafts at once will cause alignment of the differential side gears in the final drive to be lost.
• This will make it impossible to reinsert the driveshafts.
• To be safe, on models that you suspect may have been built prior to 1986, only remove one shaft at a time.
• Alternatively it is possible to retain the side-gear alignment using Peugeot tool 80317.

Continued...

FACT FILE

Continued...

☐ **STEP 1:** Prepare to remove the driveshaft as follows:
→ Raise and support the car on axle stands. Remove the road wheel.
→ Remove the inner wheelarch access panel, where fitted.
→ Drain the transmission oil.
→ **MODELS WITH ABS BRAKES:** Trace the wiring back from the wheel sensor, and disconnect it at the first multi-plug.
→ Slacken the centre hub nut – note that, depending on type, there may be a spring clip and retainer cap securing the nut, which must first be removed – see *Step 13*.
→ The hub nut may require a great deal of torque to undo!
→ You may well need an extra-long lever to undo the hub nut.
→ Take care not to pull the car off its stands when undoing this nut.

TOP TIP!

• Undo the hub nut while the car is still on the ground.
• Have an assistant apply the brakes hard while the nut is undone.

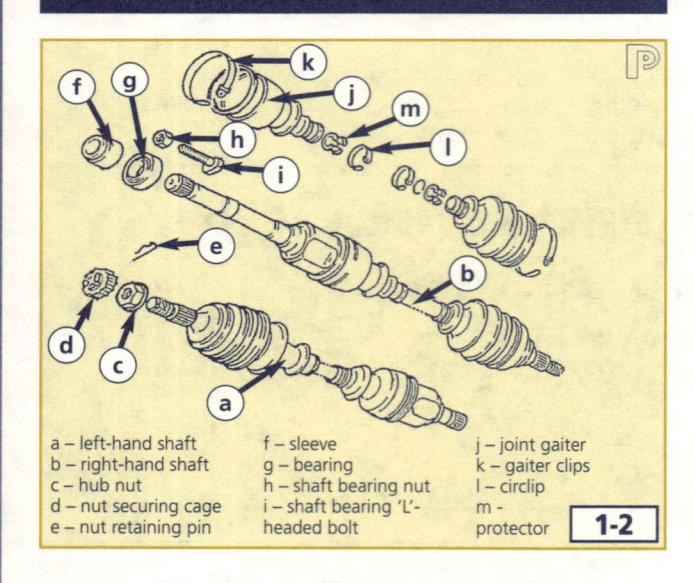

a – left-hand shaft
b – right-hand shaft
c – hub nut
d – nut securing cage
e – nut retaining pin
f – sleeve
g – bearing
h – shaft bearing nut
i – shaft bearing 'L'-headed bolt
j – joint gaiter
k – gaiter clips
l – circlip
m – protector

1-2

☐ **STEP 2:** Take note of the driveshaft and joint components. To remove the driveshaft from the vehicle.

☐ **STEP 3:** Fit coil spring compressing clamps to one front suspension strut, and compress the suspension spring.
→ Separate the front suspension lower balljoint - see *Chapter 11, Steering, Suspension*.

☐ **STEP 4:** Remove the balljoint protective shield, where fitted.

→ On models that have the anti-roll bar connected to the suspension strut, undo the nut securing the drop link to the strut, and move the link away from the strut.

☐ **STEP 5:** If removing the left-hand driveshaft, pull the suspension strut outwards away from the driveshaft, to release the shaft from the hub.

1-6

☐ **STEP 6:** Prepare for transmission oil loss, and withdraw the inboard joint of the driveshaft from the transmission unit.
→ Careful levering can help.

☐ **STEP 7:** If removing the right-hand driveshaft…
→ Use much the same technique as in *Step 5* – in fact, the same technique if you have an XV/XW/XY engine - but be aware that all models with XU/XUD engine and BE gearbox, and most (but not all) models with TU/TUD engine and MA gearbox have an intermediate driveshaft support bearing to complicate matters. See *Job 3*.

☐ **STEP 8: MODELS WITH AN INTERMEDIATE DRIVESHAFT SUPPORT:** Remove the shaft support bearing by slackening the two nuts securing the L-headed bolts (arrowed) that retain the bearing in its aluminium bracket.

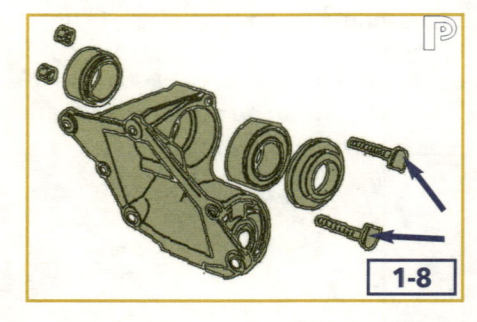

1-8

☐ **STEP 9:** Turn the L-headed bolts so that the heads clear the bearing, then withdraw the driveshaft.

1-9

TOP TIP!

☐ **STEP 10:** •
When refitting, it always pays to renew the final drive driveshaft oil seals (**a**), using tool (**b**), before refitting the driveshafts.

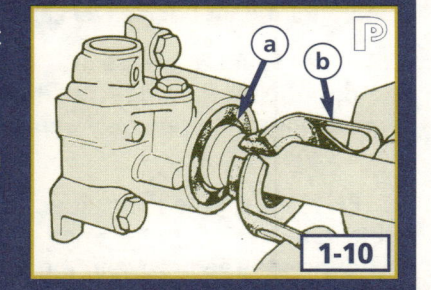

• **BE TRANSMISSIONS (FITTED TO XU/XUD ENGINES) UP TO NOVEMBER 1988:** Take the seals that are supplied together with a seal protector for the right-hand seal – necessary to prevent damage when reinserting the driveshaft.

• If you do not intend to renew the seals, and do not already have such a protector, you must fit new seals and obtain a protector.

• **LATER BE TRANSMISSION:** These units do not need to be fitted with the protector.

• If you purchase a seal set that does not include a protector (**b**) it means the seals are modified and the right-hand seal does not need protection – provided that you have the correct seals!

☐ **STEP 11:** Refitting is carried out in the reverse order to removal, noting the following points…

→ The old seals can be levered out with a flat-ended screwdriver.

→ **XV/XW/XY ENGINE/BH TRANSMISSION:** New seals combination should be drifted in as far as they will go.

• **MA AND BE TRANSMISSION TYPES:** New seals should be drifted in until they protrude from the casing by 1 mm.

→ Lightly grease the final drive oil seal lips, the driveshaft splines and the seal area on the inboard driveshaft joint.

→ Remember to grease the intermediate support bearing seal, where fitted.

☐ **STEP 12:**
Rotate the driveshaft slightly when fitting it back into the final drive, to align and engage the drive splines with those inside the final drive.

→ Make sure the L-headed bolts retaining the intermediate bearing are turned sufficiently to secure it.

→ Only use NEW suspension bottom balljoint nuts on models with a three-bolt retained balljoint.

→ If the hub centre nut is of the stake-nut type (see Chapter 11, Steering, Suspension), use a new nut and stake its collapsible collar into the groove in the driveshaft stub axle.

☐ **STEP 13:** If the hub centre nut is of the spring clip and retainer type, make sure that they are correctly refitted.

→ It is advisable to renew the clip and retainer every time they are removed.

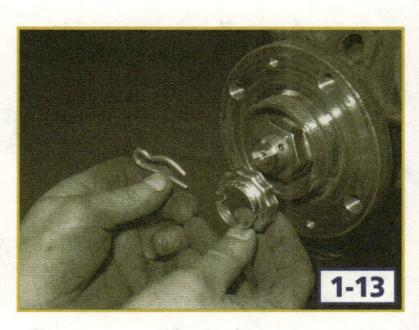

JOB 2: DRIVESHAFT JOINT AND GAITERS – *removal, replacement*.

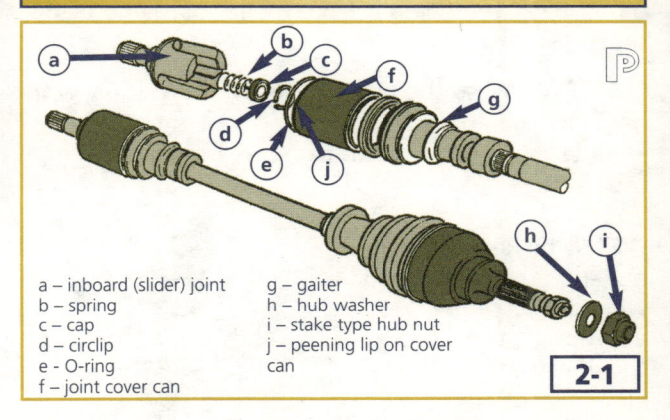

a – inboard (slider) joint
b – spring
c – cap
d – circlip
e – O-ring
f – joint cover can
g – gaiter
h – hub washer
i – stake type hub nut
j – peening lip on cover can

☐ **STEP 1:** The typical driveshaft assembly is detailed here. There is very little difference in detail between driveshafts used across the Peugeot ranges covered by this manual.

☐ **STEP 2:** Remove the driveshaft - see *Job 1*.

☐ **STEP 3:** Hold the driveshaft in a vice, and measure the distance between the clips securing the narrow end of each gaiter. This will be useful when reassembly the driveshaft and gaiters, if there are no location grooves provided.

☐ **STEP 4:** Using pincers or side-cutters, peel back the peened-over edge (illustration *2-1, item j*) of the inboard joint cover can, to free it from the joint slider section (**a**). Remove the joint slider, collecting the spring (**b**) and cap (**c**) from the end of the shaft.

☐ **STEP 5:** Discard the large-diameter rubber O-ring (illustration *2-1, item e*) that seals between joint slider and protective can.

☐ **STEP 6:** Fold back the gaiter, and wipe all grease from the tripod joint.

☐ **STEP 7:** Look at the spherical rollers of the joint to see if they are secured by a circlip. If not, tape all three onto their stubs, so they don't fall off.

☐ **STEP 8:** Mark the angular alignment of the tripod in relation to the splines of the driveshaft, and, using circlip pliers, remove the eyed circlip (illustration *2-1, item d*) securing the spider to the shaft.

☐ **STEP 9:** Withdraw the tripod; if it is tight, tap it from behind using a suitable drift.
→ Make sure you do NOT tap on the spherical rollers.

☐ **STEP 10:** Slide the gaiter/joint cover can (illustration *2-1, item f*) off the shaft.

☐ **STEP 11:** Cut off the two outer joint gaiter securing clips, and slide the gaiter back, removing it from the inboard end of the shaft.

☐ **STEP 12:** Wash the outboard joint thoroughly with paraffin, then dry it.
→ Slide the new gaiter on from the inboard end of the shaft.

☐ **STEP 13:** Replacement gaiter kits come supplied with sachets of the appropriate grease for the driveshaft joints, along with a new inboard joint coil spring, thrust cap and sealing O-ring.
→ With fresh grease applied to the inside of the outboard joint (worked into all contacting parts of the joint) and the excess put in the gaiter, fit the gaiter back on to the joint, ensuring it is correctly lipped over the recess in the joint body, and engaged in the groove on the driveshaft (where there is one) at the narrow end.
→ Secure the new gaiter with new clips.

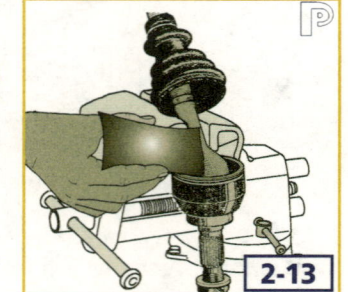

☐ **STEP 14:** Thoroughly clean the end of the driveshaft with paraffin/kerosene, dry it, then fit the new inboard joint gaiter and cover can on to the shaft.

☐ **STEP 15:** Squeeze grease into the gaiter, refit the tripod to the shaft, and secure it with a new circlip. Remove any tape previously applied to retain the tripod spheres.

☐ **STEP 16:** Clean the joint slider, fit a new coil spring inside it, a new cap to the end of the spring, and a new O-ring to the groove in the joint slider body.

☐ **STEP 17:** Feed the joint slider over the tripod, locating the thrust cap against the end of the driveshaft. Before the spring is fully compressed and the slider is fully engaged, squeeze more grease into the joint, then fully close the joint.

☐ **STEP 18:** Secure the joint cover can to the slider section by peening the end of the cover evenly over the chamfered edge of the slider section, using a small ball pein hammer.

☐ **STEP 19:** Lift the narrow end of the inboard joint gaiter with a small screwdriver to relieve air pressure, then secure the end of the gaiter with a clip.

☐ **STEP 20:** Refit the driveshaft to the car - see *Job 1*.

JOB 3: INTERMEDIATE SHAFT BEARING.

☐ **STEP 1:** Check for rough rotation of the intermediate shaft bearing (not XV/XW/XY engines or some, lower-power TU petrol engines); if it's rough it will need to be renewed as follows…

☐ **STEP 2:** Unbolt the bearing casting from the back of the cylinder block – see illustration *1-6*.

☐ **STEP 3:** Drift out the bearing, and seal (and end cover, where fitted), using a suitable size of socket.

☐ **STEP 4:** Drift in a new assembly and refit the casting to the block.
→ Do not forget to refill the transmission with oil!

Part E: Transmission Removal, Refitting (with engine in car).
CONTENTS

	Page No.
JOB 1: GENERAL.	7-15
JOB 2: 4/5-SPEED GEARBOX (XV/XW/XY ENGINES) – removal, installation.	7-15
JOB 3: 4/5-SPEED GEARBOX (ALL OTHER MODELS) – removal, installation.	7-15
JOB 4: AUTO. TRANSMISSION – removal, installation.	7-17

See *Chapter 6, Part B: Which Engine is Which?* for an explanation of the engine types referred to here.

IMPORTANT NOTES: • On all models but the 205 with the XV/XW/XY series 'gears-in-sump' engines transmission removal can be carried out with the engine in the vehicle. The 205 with this series of engine requires complete removal of the power unit, and separation of engine and transmission on the bench or workshop floor.
• If you want to change the clutch on all but the 205 with XV/XW/XY engine, the transmission will have to be removed from the vehicle, although the 205 with this series of engine can have its clutch renewed with the engine in situ.
• For further information on removal of several of the components covered here, such as engine and transmission mountings, refer to *Chapter 6, Engine*.

JOB 1: GENERAL.

➔ *Always start by disconnecting the battery terminals – see Chapter 10, Electrical, Dash, Instruments, Fact File: Disconnecting the Battery BEFORE doing so!*
➔ Follow the detailed instructions given in the relevant parts of this manual for information on detaching gearchange mechanism and engine mountings.
➔ There are many different types of connectors used on Peugeot transmission units for items such as electrical connectors, brackets and covers.
➔ Many modern units have electrically operated speedometers with a dedicated cable plug, which has to be removed after undoing the retaining clips.
➔ Where a separate Automatic Transmission Fluid cooler is fitted, the hoses must be clamped near to where they are removed from the transmission.
➔ On the vast majority of models it is necessary to remove the air filter assembly, air intake ducting and battery to gain access to the transmission.

JOB 2: 4/5-SPEED GEARBOX (XV/XW/XY ENGINES) – *removal, installation.*

The complete power unit (engine and gearbox) must be removed from the vehicle, and then engine, idler geartrain and gearbox must be separated. See *Chapter 6, Part J* for details of removal, separation and refitting.

JOB 3: 4/5-SPEED GEARBOX (ALL OTHER MODELS) – *removal, installation.*

Section A: Gearbox removal.

☐ **STEP A1:** Before starting work, ensure that you can support the car sufficiently high off the ground for the transmission to be removed from beneath.
➔ Make sure that the transmission-end of the engine is supported from above the car, or from beneath.
➔ Disconnect the battery earth/ground (-) terminal (**1**). See *Chapter 10, Electrical, Dash, Instruments, Fact File: Disconnecting the Battery BEFORE doing so!*

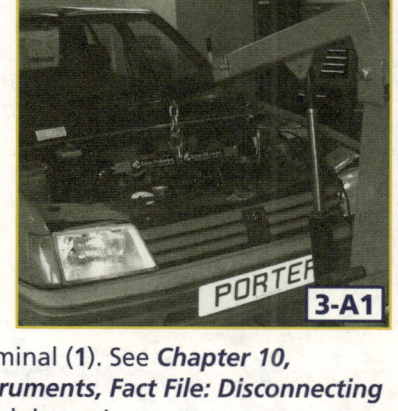

☐ **STEP A2:** Remove the following:
➔ The battery and battery tray.
➔ The air filter and air intake ducting.
➔ The left-hand under-wing access panel (on models so fitted – 205 panel fixing positions shown).
➔ **206 MODELS ONLY:** The engine undershield.
➔ **TURBODIESEL MODELS ONLY:** The intercooler.
➔ The steel flywheel-access plate (larger-engined and TUD models).

Some models with air conditioning may have AC pipes clamped to the flywheel access plate: free these but under no circumstances try to disconnect (open) the pipework.

☐ **STEP A3:** Disconnect the following:
➔ The speedometer cable from the transmission – pull out rubber pin (**a**) and lift out the cable (**b**). (TU engine/MA transmission shown).
➔ The clutch cable at the transmission end (see *Part A*).
➔ The battery negative lead/power unit earth lead from the transmission casing.

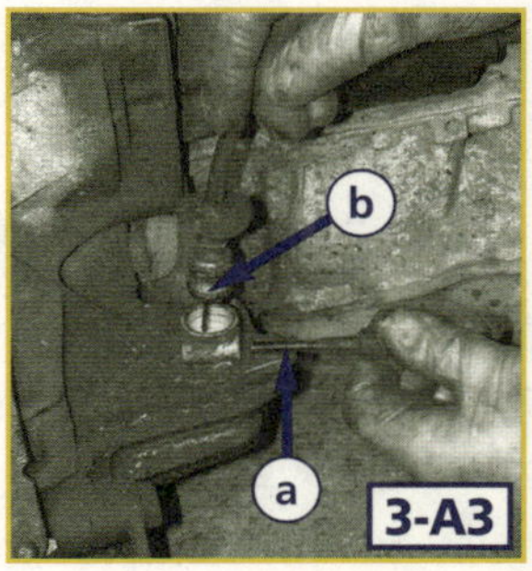

☐ **STEP A4:** Disconnect the following:
➔ The wiring from the reversing lights switch.
➔ The wiring from the flywheel TDC sensor.
➔ Any wiring that is clipped to the transmission unit.

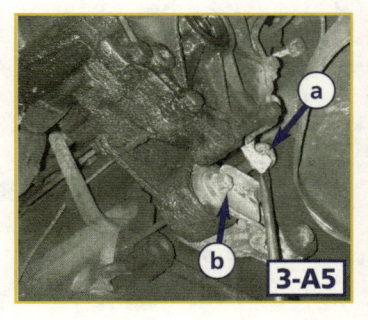

☐ **STEP A5:** Disconnect the following:
➔ The gearchange control rods from the gearbox levers.
➔ The gearchange linkages (**a**) at the back of the engine (TU engine/MA gearbox shown).

→ Detach any coolant and power hoses from their clips/guides on the gearbox.

☐ **STEP A6:** Disconnect the rear engine stabiliser mounting link (between power unit and subframe or body – TU engine/MA transmission link (**b**) shown in illustration *3-A5*).

☐ **STEP A7:** Unbolt the starter motor and – if applicable – the air filter mounting bracket.

TOP TIP!

- The starter motor does not necessarily need to be disconnected from its wiring.
- Tie it safely and securely out of the way.

☐ **STEP A8:** From beneath the vehicle, drain the transmission oil, then refit the drain plug(s) for safekeeping.

☐ **STEP A9:** Raise and safely support the vehicle on axle stands.

☐ **STEP A10:** Remove both driveshafts - see *Part D*.

IMPORTANT NOTE: See especially FACT FILE: AVOIDING DRIVESHAFT DISASTER in *Part D*.

☐ **STEP A11: 206 MODELS:** Undo the three bolts securing the speedometer drive housing to the final drive, and remove the housing from the transmission unit.

☐ **STEP A12:** Unscrew and remove the lower rear bolt securing the transmission unit to the engine. Make a note of the position of any exhaust brackets attached to it.

☐ **STEP A13:** Support the left-hand end of the engine, ideally from above with a hoist, although a trolley jack from below will do the job.

☐ **STEP A14:** Undo the left-hand engine mounting (the transmission mounting) and remove it - see *Chapter 6, Engine*.
→ **TU-ENGINED MODELS:** It is necessary to unbolt a mounting plate from the top of the transmission unit.
→ **CERTAIN MODELS WITH ABS BRAKES:** It may be advantageous to unbolt the ABS modulator and move it carefully out of the way, taking care not to strain the brake hydraulic pipes.

☐ **STEP A15:** Lower the engine/transmission as far as the remaining mountings will allow.
→ On some models, you will need to disconnect the exhaust front downpipe from the manifold to gain further engine downward travel.

☐ **STEP A16: MODELS WITH PULL-TYPE CLUTCH:** Where clutch disengagement is effected by movement of the clutch outer cable rather than the inner - see *Part A*.
→ Mark the relationship of the clutch lever to its shaft (which protrudes from the clutch housing) by scribing a line along the top of the shaft and the lever (arrowed).
→ Now remove the clutch lever from the shaft by either withdrawing its retaining pin (**a**) or unscrewing the retaining bolt, depending on type.
→ Removing the lever will allow the pivot shaft to rotate fully as the transmission is withdrawn from the engine, and the release bearing disengages.

☐ **STEP A17:** Unscrew the remainder of the engine-to-transmission bolts.
→ Note that on some diesels it will be necessary to unbolt the fuel filter assembly for access to some upper bolts.
→ Have two people ready to support the unit as it is removed.

☐ **STEP A18:** Push or lever the transmission off its dowels and remove it downwards.
→ Do not allow the weight of the transmission to bear against the input shaft (arrowed).

SAFETY FIRST!

- The unit is heavy and should not be lowered without the use of suitable jacking or lifting equipment and by two people.

Section B: Transmission installation.

☐ **STEP B1:** When reinstalling the transmission unit to the vehicle, carry out the installation in the reverse of the removal sequence, noting the

following...
➔ It pays to renew the final drive oil seals, and filler/drain plug washers (where fitted) before reinstalling the transmission.
➔ Grease the input shaft splines, clutch release bearing sleeve and release fork contact areas with molybdenum disulphide grease.
➔ Observe any bolt tightening torques given in *Chapter 1, Facts & Figures*.
➔ Refill the transmission with the correct grade of oil.
➔ **MODELS WITH PULL-TYPE CLUTCH:** Refit the clutch lever to its pivot shaft, aligning the scribe mark made on removal.
➔ Adjust the clutch cable.

❏ **STEP B2:** IMPORTANT NOTE: When installed, the engine and transmission mountings should be free of strain. Don't tighten any of them up until all are in place.

| JOB 4: | AUTOMATIC TRANSMISSION – *removal, installation*. |

Section A: Transmission removal.

❏ **STEP A1:** Follow *Job 3, Steps A1* and *A2*, but note that reference to the flywheel access plate only applies to manual transmission types. Instead, for auto. transmission, such references should instead be understood as 'torque converter access plate'.

❏ **STEP A2:** Carry out the following:
➔ Place the transmission selector lever in 'N' (Neutral).
➔ Detach the earth/ground strap and the positive cable from the battery.
➔ Detach the speedo cable from the transmission unit, and free it from any securing clips on the transmission.
➔ Disconnect the starter inhibitor/reversing lights switch (transmission end).
➔ **206 MODELS:** Disconnect and remove the automatic transmission Electronic Control Unit (arrowed), along with its mounting bracket. Also disconnect the wiring harnesses serving the automatic transmission.
➔ Disconnect the power unit earth lead from the transmission casing.
➔ Undo the nut retaining the dipstick tube to the transmission, and the bolt retaining the tube to the transmission housing, then remove the dipstick from the transmission.
➔ Clamp the two coolant hoses to the auto transmission cooler unit on the transmission, and disconnect the hoses from the unit.
➔ **206 MODELS:** Remove the transmission cooler unit - see *Job 3, Part C*.
➔ **206 MODELS:** Detach the exhaust front downpipe support bracket from the transmission.
➔ Disconnect the manual selector cable from the transmission (see *Part C*). Take care not to disturb the position of the selector lever at the transmission while or after disconnection. Free the cable from its clips on the transmission unit.
➔ Disconnect the kickdown cable from the carburettor/fuel injection system – see *Part C*, and free it from any cable clips so that it can be removed together with the transmission.
➔ Detach power steering pipe from clips/guides on the transmission, where applicable.
➔ Disconnect and remove the starter motor.
➔ Drain the transmission fluid from the transmission, and refit the drain plug for safe keeping.

❏ **STEP A3:** Remove the driveshafts - see *Part D*.

❏ **STEP A4:** You can now gain access to the torque convertor from beneath the transmission, where the access plate was previously removed.
➔ Slacken and remove the three torque converter retaining nuts or bolts (arrowed).
➔ You will need to turn the engine via the crankshaft pulley to gain access to all three, one at a time.

❏ **STEP A5:** Take the weight of the transmission unit on a trolley jack or other suitable support and have two people ready to support the unit.

❏ **STEP A6:** Undo the left-hand engine (transmission) mounting - see *Chapter 6, Engine*.

TOP TIP!
❏ **STEP A7:** • Take out the engine-to-transmission bolts – make a note of their different sizes for when you come to reinstall the unit.

❏ **STEP A8:** Withdraw the transmission unit slightly, and secure the torque converter with wire to ensure that it does not fall out.

☐ **STEP A9:** Pull the transmission unit off the mounting dowels and lower it to the ground.
➔ Beware – it is VERY heavy!

Section B: Transmission installation.

☐ **STEP B1:** Installation is carried out in the reverse sequence to removal, noting the following…
➔ Ensure that the spigot bush in the centre of the crankshaft is in good condition.
➔ Sparingly apply some Molykote G1 grease to the torque converter centre pin.
➔ Do not forget to remove the wire used to hold the torque converter to the transmission when refitting the transmission!
➔ To engage splines, turn converter to-and-fro.
➔ Torque-tighten any bolts for which a torque is specified in *Chapter 1, Facts and Figures*.
➔ Refill the transmission with transmission fluid.
➔ Check the adjustment of the manual selector and kickdown cables - see *Part C*.

Part F: Clutch Replacement

CONTENTS

	Page No.
JOB 1: CLUTCH (205 WITH XV/XW/XY ENGINES) – *dismantling, fitting*.	7-18
JOB 2: CLUTCH (ALL OTHER ENGINES) – *dismantling, fitting*.	7-20
JOB 3: CLUTCH (ALL) – *inspecting*.	7-20

FACT FILE
CLUTCH TYPES

• The clutch assemblies of the TU, TUD, XU and XUD engines are conventional in layout, and very similar. They are all accessed by removing the transmission unit from the vehicle. There are two clutch release mechanism types - the conventional push-type clutch and the less common pull-type.

PUSH-TYPE
• This type uses a release bearing pushed against the clutch diaphragm to release the clutch.

PULL-TYPE
• This has a release bearing that is integrated with the pressure plate, and lifts away from the friction plate to release the clutch.
• **XV/XW/XY SERIES ENGINE:** The clutch assembly is conventional, but access to it does not require removal of the gearbox. This is because the gearbox is underneath the engine, and drive is relayed to it from the clutch, down the side of the power unit, by an idler geartrain. Access to the clutch assembly therefore requires removal of the idler geartrain.

JOB 1: CLUTCH (205 WITH XV/XW/XY ENGINES) – *dismantling, fitting*.

Section A: Clutch dismantling.

See *Chapter 6, Part B: Which Engine is Which?* for an explanation of the engine types referred to here.

XV/XW/XY SERIES CLUTCH: An exploded view is shown in *Part A, Job 1, illustration 1-B*.

☐ **STEP A1:** Items **h, i** and **j** (release bearing, clutch cover and clutch plate) are the parts you will need to obtain when you renew the clutch.
➔ See *Job 3* for details of clutch component inspection.

☐ **STEP A2:** Before dismantling, disconnect the battery negative (-) earth/ground terminal. See *Chapter 10, Electrical, Dash, Instruments, Fact File: Disconnecting the Battery* BEFORE doing so!

☐ **STEP A3:** Remove the air filter assembly and air intake ducting.

☐ **STEP A4:** Disconnect and remove the battery and battery tray.
➔ Note that the battery tray is secured by two bolts down into the chassis leg, and two side bolts into the leg (underneath the tray).
➔ Also, loosen the top left-hand engine mounting.

☐ **STEP A5:** Support the weight of the engine – either with a hoist from above (see *Part E, Job 3, illustration 3-A1*, or with a trolley jack from below.
➔ If supporting from below, support under the sump, but use a piece of wood as protection between jack pad and sump pan.

☐ **STEP A6:** Disconnect the clutch cable at its transmission end.

☐ **STEP A7:** Disconnect the gearchange linkage.

☐ **STEP A8:** Drain the engine oil.

☐ **STEP A9:** Lower the power unit until the left-hand-side driveshaft contacts the subframe.

☐ **STEP A10:** Undo all the clutch/idler gear housing bolts.
→ Note that it is necessary to remove the clutch release bellcrank lever and the clutch cable abutment bracket to gain access to some of these bolts.
→ Also, note the position of the left-hand engine lifting lug retained by two of the bolts.

TOP TIP!

☐ **STEP A11:** There is one 'hidden' clutch/idler gear housing that catches out many people!
→ It is hidden up within a recess of the casting and its position shown here.
→ If you cannot find it, follow the circular shape of the clutch housing, along which all the bolts lie – this should lead you to it.

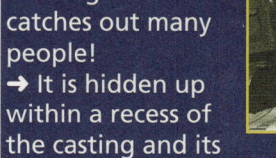

☐ **STEP A12:** A couple of raised casting lugs are provided at the edge of the housing – use them to tap the clutch/idler gear housing off the engine. The housing will bring with it the input shaft to the gearbox.

☐ **STEP A13: Remove the clutch as follows:**
→ If you intend refitting the same clutch, make alignment marks between cover plate and flywheel.
→ Unscrew the clutch cover bolts progressively, half a turn at a time, until the spring pressure is released, then remove the bolts. Note that bolts with an internal-hex head or often used, for which a hex socket adaptor is required.
→ Ease the cover off its dowels and catch the driven plate as it falls.

Section B: Clutch fitting.

☐ **STEP B1:** Clean any oil (or protective wax) from the clutch cover and flywheel faces.

☐ **STEP B2:** Offer the driven plate to the flywheel, with its spring hub facing outwards (toward the clutch pressure plate).

☐ **STEP B3:** Use a clutch aligning tool (a) to centrally align the clutch driven plate (b) otherwise the gearbox will not relocate on the engine and damage can be caused to the centre plate. Re-align any alignment marks.

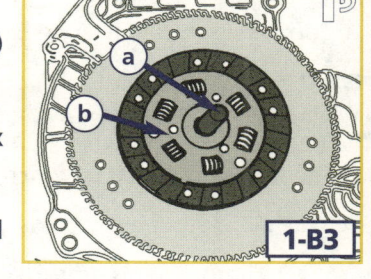

☐ **STEP B4:** Locate the clutch cover on the flywheel dowels and screw in the fixing bolts finger tight.

☐ **STEP B5:** Tighten the cover bolts evenly to the correct torque. See *Chapter 1, Facts and Figures*.
→ The illustration shows a method of locking the engine against rotation which can equally be used when tightening the cover bolts.

☐ **STEP B6:** Pull the clutch release arm off its pivot ball pin (b) in the bell housing - it is held to it by a spring blade.
→ Clean the arm socket and ball pin, and regrease both with copper grease.
→ Refit the release arm.
→ Smear a little copper grease on the release bearing guide (a) and the gearbox input shaft.

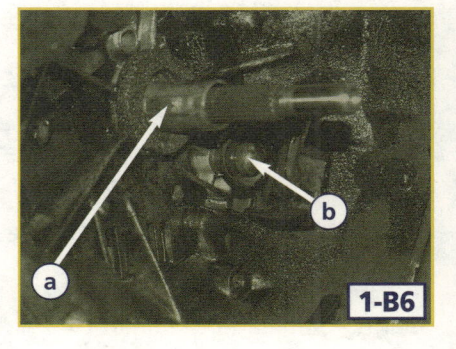

☐ **STEP B7:** Refit the clutch housing/idler geartrain, tighten to the correct torque.

☐ **STEP B8:** Refit/reconnect all components and take care to check and adjust the clutch cable when reconnected – see *Part A, Job 2*.

JOB 2: CLUTCH (ALL OTHER ENGINES) – *dismantling, fitting*.

Section A: Clutch dismantling.

An exploded view of the clutch assembly is shown in *Part A, Job 1, illustration 1-Type C*, and detail differences in release mechanism can be seen in *Part A, Job 1, illustration 1-Type E*.

☐ **STEP A1:** *Part A, Job 1, illustration 1-Type C, item 9, 10 and 11* are the parts you will need to obtain when you renew the clutch.
→ See *Job 3* for details of clutch component inspection.

☐ **STEP A2:** Remove the transmission - see *Part E*.

☐ **STEP A3:** If you intend refitting the same clutch, make alignment marks between cover plate and flywheel.

☐ **STEP A4:** Remove the clutch as follows:
→ Unscrew the clutch cover bolts progressively, half a turn at a time, until the spring pressure is released, then remove the bolts.
→ Ease the cover off its dowels and catch the driven plate from behind it, as it falls.

Section B: Clutch fitting.

☐ **STEP B1:** Clean any oil (or protective wax) from the clutch cover and flywheel faces.

☐ **STEP B2:** Offer the driven plate to the flywheel.

☐ **STEP B3:** Locate the clutch cover on the flywheel dowels and screw in the fixing bolts finger tight.

☐ **STEP B4:** Use an aligning tool – see *Job 1, Section B, 1-B3* - otherwise the gearbox will not relocate on the engine and damage can be caused to the centre plate. Re-align any alignment marks.

☐ **STEP B5:** Tighten the cover bolts evenly to the correct torque. See *Job 1, Step B5*.
→ Smear a little 'copper' grease on the release bearing guide and the gearbox input shaft.
→ Refit the transmission.

JOB 3: CLUTCH (ALL) – inspection.

TOP TIP!

☐ **STEP 1:**
• Check the inside of the transmission bell housing for a leak.
• Replace the transmission seal by removing the clutch release fork arm (arrowed), then levering out the old seal and fitting a new one.
• See *Chapter 6, Part A* for the replacement of the rear crankshaft seal.

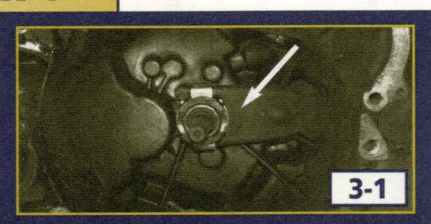

3-1

☐ **STEP 2:** Carry out the following checks:
→ Check the ends of the diaphragm spring - the clutch 'fingers' (a) - for grooves worn by the release bearing.
→ Check the release fork pivots, inside the bellhousing, for wear.
→ Check the release bearing (b) for wear and noise.
→ Check the surface of the flywheel - replace if necessary.

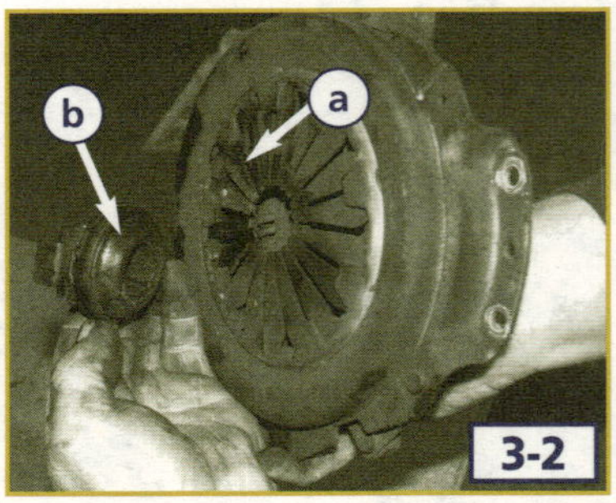

3-2

☐ **STEP 3: RELEASE FORK PIVOT SHAFT:**
→ **MODELS WITH PUSH-TYPE RELEASE:** Unhook the release bearing (a) from the operating arm/fork (b), and slide the release bearing off the input shaft. Drive out the roll pin (c) and slide the release lever off its pivot shaft.

a – release bearing
b – release pivot shaft
c – roll pin
d – lower bush
e – upper bush

3-3

→ **PUSH OR PULL-TYPE RELEASE:** Remove the shaft upper bush (e) by pushing in its retaining tags and sliding it up off the end of the shaft (b). Pull the shaft out of its lower bush (d), and remove the lower bush in the same manner as the upper. New bushes can be clipped into place, and should be lubricated with molybdenum disulphide grease before reinsertion of the pivot shaft.

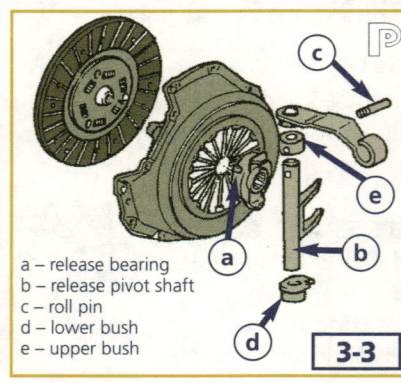

CHAPTER 8: COOLING SYSTEM

Please read **Chapter 2 Safety First** before carrying out any work on your car.

| Part A: System Explained | Page No. 8-1 | Part B: Repair Procedures | Page No. 8-3 |

Part A: System Explained
CONTENTS

	Page No.
JOB 1: SYSTEM EXPLAINED	8-1

JOB 1: SYSTEM EXPLAINED.

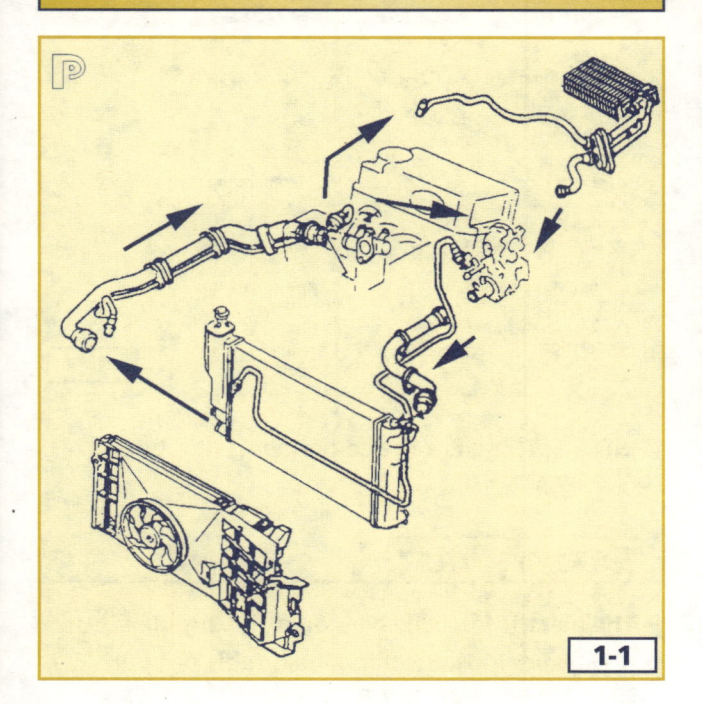

1-1

XV ENGINES

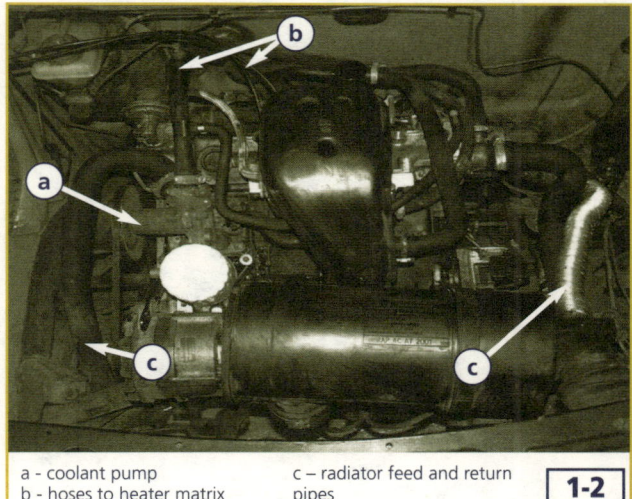

a - coolant pump
b - hoses to heater matrix
c – radiator feed and return pipes

1-2

☐ **STEP 2:** The layout of the XV engine coolant system is similar to the other engine types shown here.

☐ **STEP 1:** All the models covered by this manual have, in principle, the same type of cooling system. This diagram shows a typical coolant flow.

ALL ENGINES EXCEPT XV

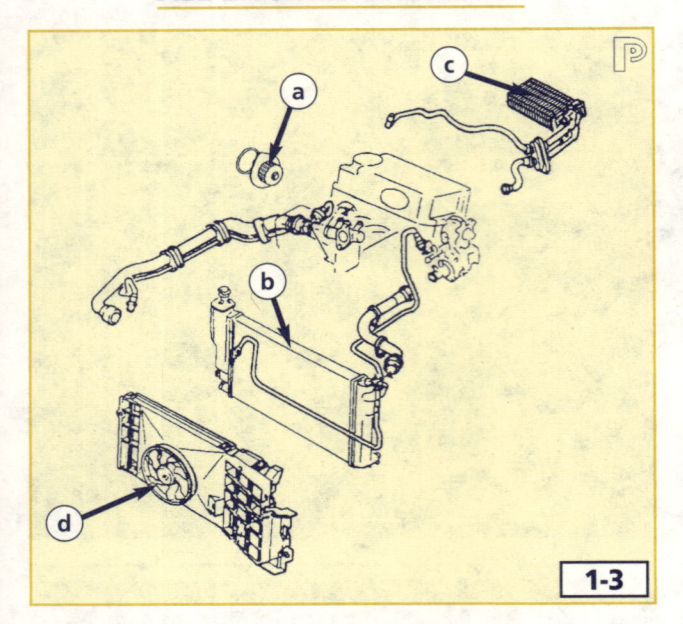

1-3

☐ **STEP 3:** The cooling system is pressurised, powered by a pump (**a**) driven from the timing belt.
➔ This forces coolant round the cylinder block and head and, via hoses through an aluminium radiator (**b**), which cools it.
➔ An electric fan (**d**) increases air flow when necessary.
➔ The coolant can also be directed into the heater matrix (**c**) – a small radiator – and air passing through the matrix is warmed to heat the vehicle interior.

ALL SYSTEMS

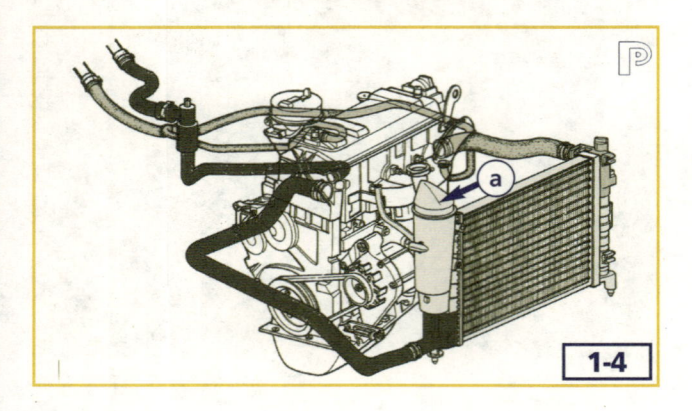

1-4

☐ **STEP 4:** The radiator works by transferring the coolant liquid's heat to air passing through it as the car is on the move.
➔ If the car is stationary, a thermostatic switch will switch on an electric fan to draw air through the radiator when the coolant reaches a certain temperature.
➔ When the car starts up, the engine is cold. In order to get the engine to working temperature as quickly as possible, a thermostatic valve is closed, restricting the water to circulating within the engine block and head.
➔ When the engine's working temperature is reached the thermostat opens, allowing the water to travel through the radiator and be cooled.

TOP TIP!

• Whenever you have drained and disconnected any part of the cooling system, always bleed the system then run the engine to normal working temperature and check for leaks.

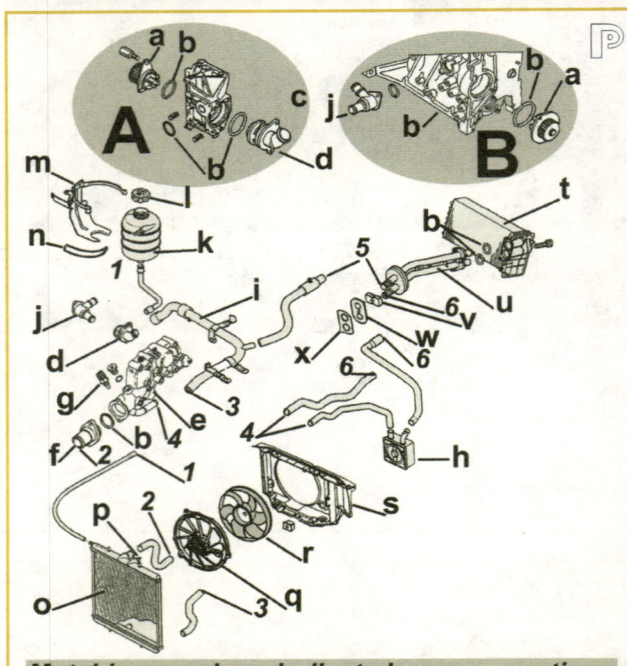

1-5

Matching numbers indicate hose connections

A - Water pump fitted to TU1-TU3 engines
B - Water pump fitted to TU5 engines
a - water pump
b - O-rings
c - pump housing
d - connector
e - thermostat housing
f - connection
g - temperature sender, air conditioning (when fitted)
h - oil/coolant heat exchanger
i - water pipe
j - connector
k - expansion tank
l - cap
m - support
n - clip
o - radiator
p - temperature sender, models without air conditioning
q - fan motor assembly
r - fan
s - housing
t - heater radiator
u - pipes
v - filler
w - joint
x - plate

☐ **STEP 5:** These are the components of a typical cooling system.

SAFETY FIRST!

• The electric fan can come on if the engine is hot.
• Make sure loose clothing, hair, tools or your hands are never near the fan while checking the cooling system.
• Remember that on many vehicles, the fan can turn itself on even if the engine is stopped and the ignition switch turned to OFF.

Part B: Repair Procedures

	Page No.
JOB 1: COOLANT - *change*.	8-3
JOB 2: COOLANT HOSES - *change*.	8-4
JOB 3: COOLING FAN(S) - *remove, refit*.	8-5
JOB 4: RADIATOR - *remove, clean, refit*.	8-8
JOB 5: THERMOSTATIC SWITCH(ES) - *test, replace*.	8-10
JOB 6: THERMOSTAT - *remove, test, replace*.	8-10
JOB 7: COOLANT TEMPERATURE/LEVEL GUAGE SENDERS - *remove, replace*.	8-11
JOB 8: COOLANT PUMP - *remove, replace*.	8-12
JOB 9: SCREEN WASHER PUMP - *remove, replace*.	8-13
JOB 10: WASHER JET - *remove, replace*.	8-13
JOB 11: HEADLIGHT WASHER NOZZLES - *remove, replace*.	8-13
JOB 12: HEATER MATRIX - *remove, replace*.	8-13

JOB 1: COOLANT - *change*.

SAFETY FIRST!

- Anti-freeze is an irritant to your skin, and harmful to car paintwork.
- Wear rubber gloves while dealing with it, and if it gets on any body panels, rinse it off with water.
- DO NOT change coolant while the engine is hot!

☐ **STEP 1:** Raise the front of the vehicle - see *Chapter 2, Safety First!* If you are not using a car hoist, secure it on axle stands.
→ Place a container under the radiator to catch the coolant.

☐ **STEP 2A:** Remove the radiator drain plug (arrowed).

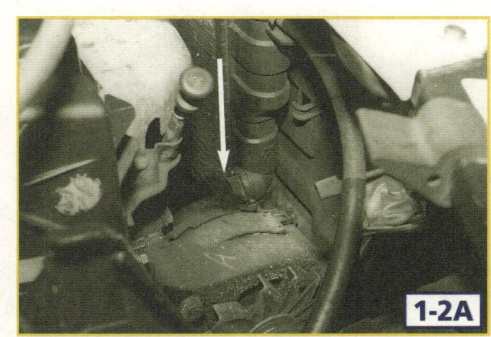

1-2A

1-2B

☐ **STEP 2B:** Where there is a drain plug in the radiator block, remove that as well.

☐ **STEP 3: VEHICLES WITHOUT DRAIN PLUGS:** Undo the clip securing the lower hose to the radiator and slide it down the hose, away from the stub – see *Job 2*.
→ On some versions of the 306, the hose has a bayonet connector. Turn the locking ring and pull the connector away.

☐ **STEP 4:** When all the coolant has run out, check there is no corrosion on the stub. If there is, clean it off with a wire brush, before reattaching the hose and tightening its clip.
→ Remove the expansion tank and tip the contents out to completely empty the system.

☐ **STEP 5:** This is a good opportunity to test the condition of the hoses by squeezing them – if you hear a 'cracking' sound, the hose is going brittle inside and should be renewed. Replace any that have deteriorated – see *Job 2*.
→ Refit the hose/drain plug.

☐ **STEP 6:** Refill the system.
→ Prepare a 50/50 mix of clean water and coolant additive (anti-freeze) ready for filling the system.

1-7

☐ **STEP 7:** Refill the system first through the radiator filler cap.

➜ If the expansion tank is integral with the radiator (see **Part A, illustration 1-4, item a**), go to **Step 13**.

❏ **STEP 8: VEHICLES WITH SEPARATE EXPANSION TANK:** Refill the expansion tank and bleed the system.
➜ Remove the bleed screw or screws **(5)**. They will be on the heater return hose or inlet manifold hose.

1-8

TOP TIP!

❏ **STEP 9:**
• Peugeot recommend releasing and raising the expansion tank for re-filling.
• Slowly pour new coolant into the expansion tank. The more gradually you do this, the less likely it is that air bubbles get trapped in the circuit.
• When coolant comes out of the bleed valve (s), refit the bleed screws.

1-9

❏ **STEP 10:** Continue filling the expansion tank until the water level reaches the 'Full' marker line on the expansion tank.

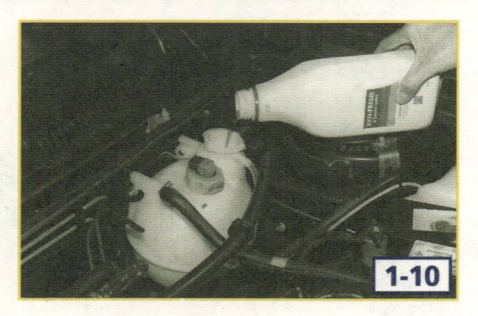

1-10

❏ **STEP 11:** Start the engine. This allows the water pump to circulate the coolant, and expel any trapped air.
➜ The coolant level will probably drop swiftly as you do this. Pour in more coolant as it does so, to make sure no extra air is drawn into the engine.
➜ Continue to fill the system until the coolant is level with the 'Full' mark on the expansion tank, and bubbles have stopped appearing on the surface.
➜ Turn off the engine.

❏ **STEP 12:** Refit the filler cap.

MODELS WITH INTEGRAL EXPANSION TANK

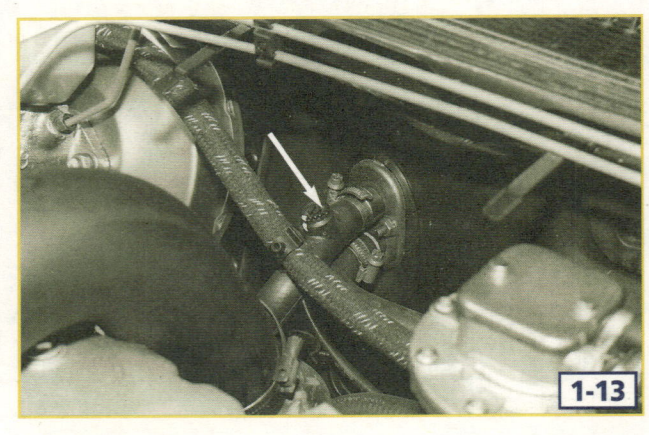

1-13

❏ **STEP 13:** Refill the system through the expansion tank with the radiator cap in position.
➜ Unscrew the bleed valve (arrowed) on the heater hose to release trapped air, closing it when coolant appears.
➜ Run the engine briefly and check again (only when cold).
➜ Run and check thoroughly before the vehicle is used on the road, and after the first short journey.

JOB 2: COOLANT HOSES - *change*.

SAFETY FIRST!

• **DO NOT drain coolant while the engine is hot!**

❏ **STEP 1:** Raise the front of the car – see **Chapter 2, Safety First!**. If you are not using a car hoist, secure it on axle stands.
➜ Drain the cooling system – see **Job 1**.

❏ **STEP 2:** Undo the clips or release the bayonet fixing securing the hose you are replacing.

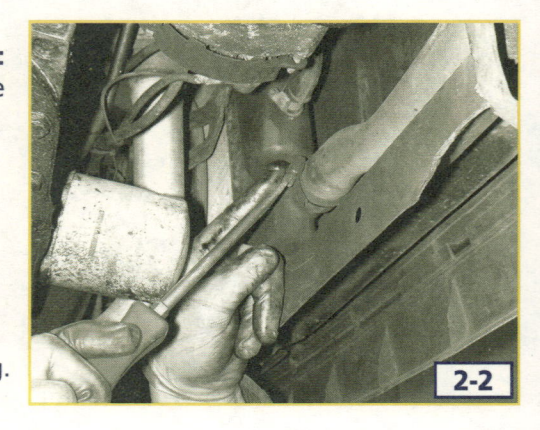

2-2

☐ **STEP 3:** It will help to work the hose up and down, as well as to twist it, so that the chances of pulling it free are increased.

2-3

TOP TIP!

☐ **STEP 4:**
• If the hose is old, it may not come off. Hoses can 'weld' themselves to their stubs.
• Use too much force and you could cause damage! Instead, cut through the hose with a sharp knife and replace it.
• If the stub is a plastic one, take extra care not to cut through the stub as well!

2-4

☐ **STEP 5:** Check that there is no corrosion on the metal stub. If there is, clean it off with a wire brush, before re-attaching the hose and tightening its clip.

☐ **STEP 6:** Refill the system – see *Job 1* – and refit the radiator cap.

JOB 3: COOLING FAN(S) - *remove, refit.*

SAFETY FIRST!

• If the engine is warm, the fan can start, whether or not the ignition is on.

• Before working on the fan, disconnect the earth lead from the battery.

• On some models, this can affect the radio's memory, so instead remove the cooling fan's fuse from the fuse box – see *Chapter 10, Disconnecting the Battery*.

ALL VEHICLES

☐ **STEP 1:** Some vehicles covered by this manual are fitted with single electric cooling fans, others with twin fans.
→ The principles of removal and refitting are the same.

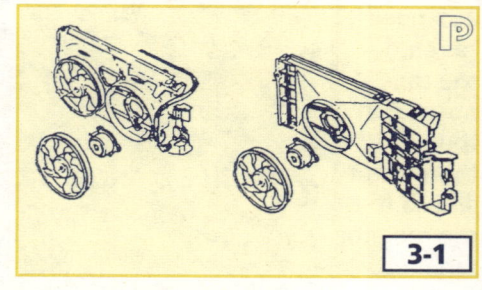

3-1

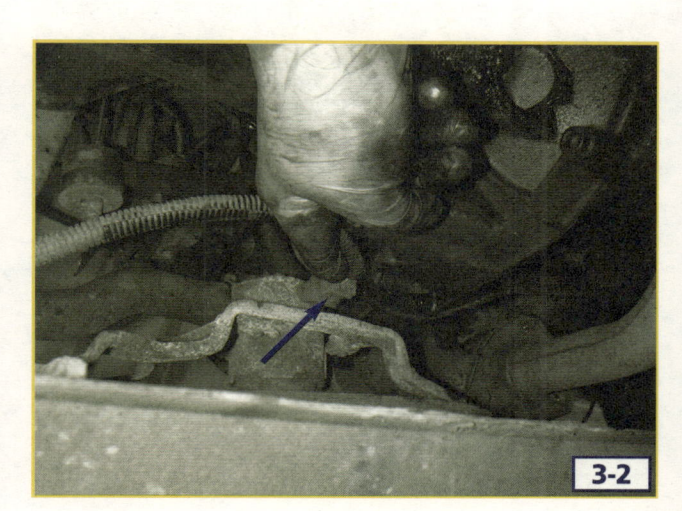

3-2

☐ **STEP 2:** Disconnect the fan's wiring connectors.
→ On early models there will be just one connector.
→ On later models there will be several.

106

We show the fan being removed after the radiator has been taken out, for ease of photography. The fan can be removed with the radiator left in the vehicle.

☐ **STEP 3:** Remove any obstacles from inside the engine bay, such as the manifold shield.

3-3

CHAPTER 8 Part B Job 3

8-5

❑ **STEP 4:** You will also need to remove the top hose (**a**) at the thermostat end so that the radiator fan motor (**b**) can be pulled clear.

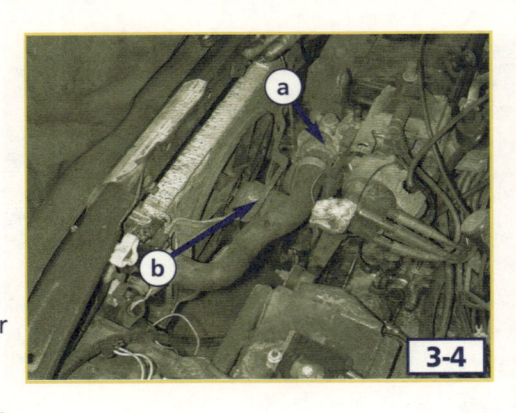

❑ **STEP 5:** The fan is held to the radiator with a single bolt (**a**) and a pair of push-in pegs (**b**).

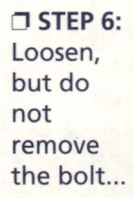

❑ **STEP 6:** Loosen, but do not remove the bolt...

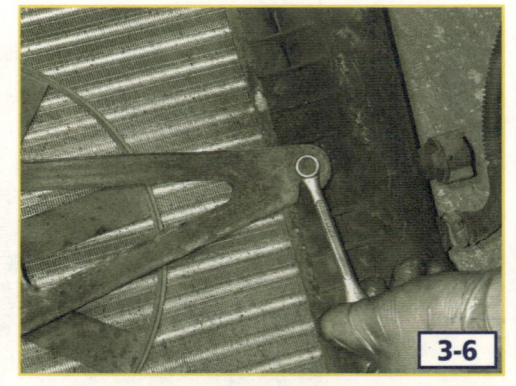

❑ **STEP 7:** ...and you will then be able to slide the frame upwards...

❑ **STEP 8:** ...and out of the collars in the radiator surround.
➜ Lift the fan and frame out of the vehicle or (as in this case) away from the radiator.

❑ **STEP 9:** The fan and motor are held to the frame by rivets which have to be drilled out.
➜ When replacing the fan, it may be simpler to use small nuts and bolts, but be sure to use shake-proof washers or thread lock to prevent threads from coming undone.

❑ **STEP 10A:** The fan assembly may be removed complete with or following removal of the radiator (see *Job 4*) or on its own, after removal of the grille and crossmember.

❑ **STEP 10B:** Unbolt the fan shroud from the radiator.

→ Remove the radiator fastenings (see **Job 4**) and raise the radiator slightly to disengage the studs from the holes in the fan housing.

206

☐ **STEP 11A:** The fan can be removed with the front panel, but it is far easier to remove it on its own as follows:
→ Remove the front bumper assembly – see **Chapter 13, Bodywork**.

☐ **STEP 11B:** The electrical connectors are contained in a waterproof housing.
→ Remove the cover fixing screw.

3-11B

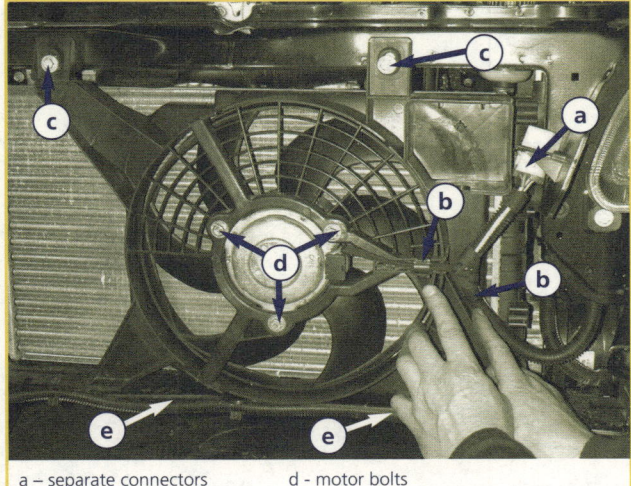

a – separate connectors
b - wiring cables from clips
c - frame bolts
d - motor bolts
e - frame to pegs to body

3-11C

☐ **STEP 11C:** Remove the fan securing bolts (**d**) disconnect the wiring plug and free the wiring from its clips. Manoeuvre the fan clear.

306

☐ **STEP 12:** Remove the fan/radiator assembly complete – see **Job 4**.

ALL VEHICLES

☐ **STEP 13A:** Remove any clips or cable ties holding the fan feed wire, the bolts holding the

3-13A

fan motor to the shroud and pull the fan free. It is a non-serviceable unit, so if there's anything wrong with it, it should be replaced.

☐ **STEP 13B:** On some vehicles the fan is secured by rivets.
→ Drill them out.

3-13B

3-14

☐ **STEP 14:** If applicable, remove the clip or screw securing the fan to the motor shaft as shown, and separate them.

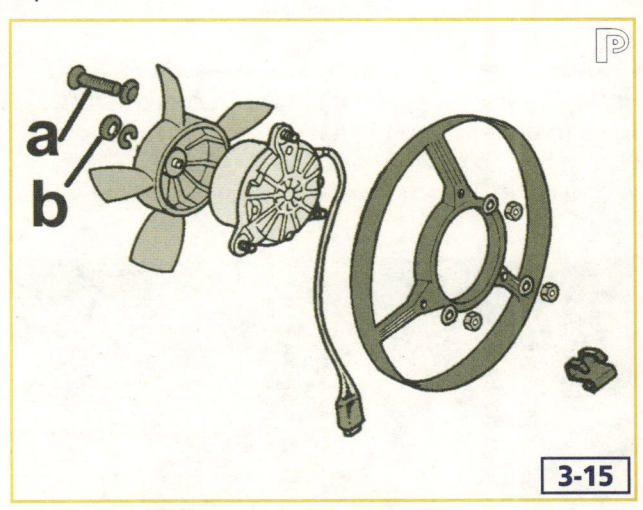

3-15

☐ **STEP 15:** Refitting is the reverse of removal. However, before tightening the screw (**a**) make sure the fan blade locates correctly on the motor shaft key, and that the washers are fitted correctly.
→ Some versions have the fan blades held to a shaft with clips (**b**) instead of a screw.
→ Ensure that the shroud is properly fitted into its clip(s) on the radiator.

JOB 4: RADIATOR - remove, clean, refit.

SAFETY FIRST!

MODELS WITH AIR CONDITIONING.

• DO NOT open the pressurised pipework on the air conditioning system.

• The air conditioning system contains pressurised gas and specialist equipment is needed to extract it. It is illegal to discharge the gas to the atmosphere.

• The gas used in air conditioning systems is extremely harmful to the environment and may cause injury to the person carrying out the work if released in an uncontrolled manner.

• If air conditioning units are in the way of carrying out other work, move units to one side with pipes still attached.

• DO NOT open the cooling system while the engine is hot!

IMPORTANT NOTE: The radiator fins are very fragile and easily damaged. Take care when working in their vicinity and when removing the radiator.
• On models with air conditioning the workspace is cramped. Take care not to damage the radiator matricies.

GENERAL

☐ **STEP 1:** Drain the cooling system - see *Job 1*.
➔ Depending on the model, various components will have to be removed to gain access to the radiator fixings and to provide working clearance.
➔ **106 PETROL:** Remove the left-side headlight.

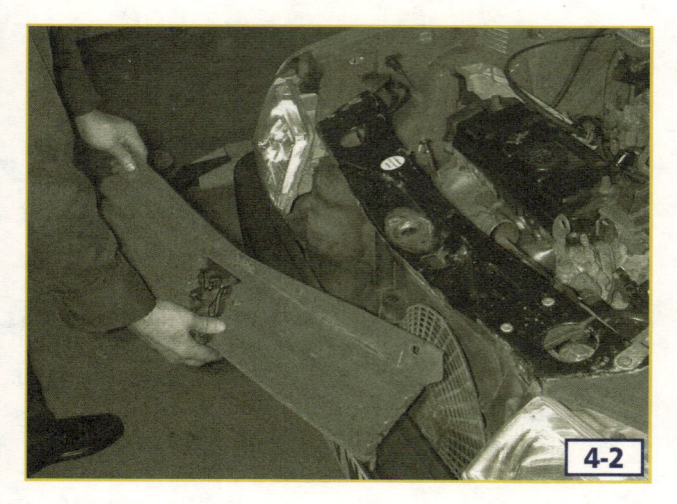

4-2

☐ **STEP 2: 205:** The front grille is secured by bolts.

☐ **STEP 3: 205:** The cross member has to be removed after taking out the fixing bolts.

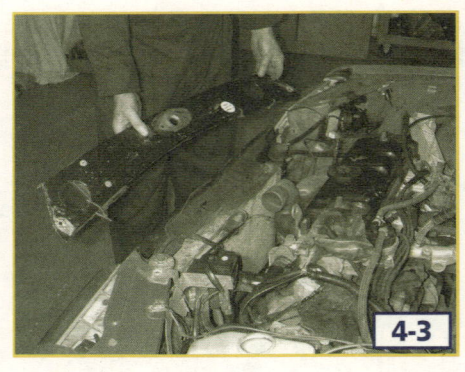

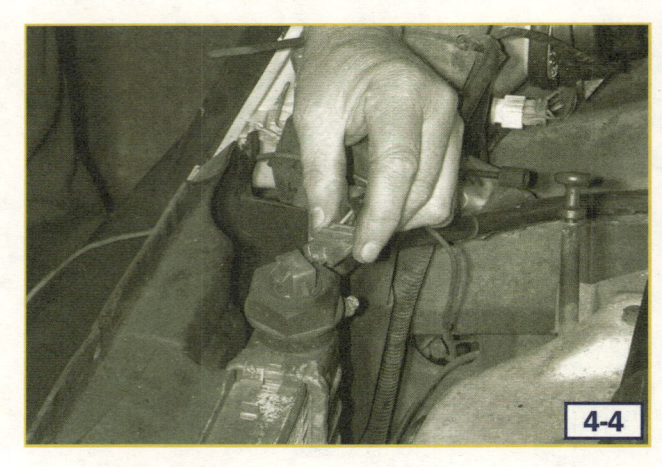

4-3

4-4

☐ **STEP 4: ALL MODELS:** Disconnect the coolant temperature sensor.
➔ Disconnect the cooling fan wiring connector(s) – see *Job 3*.
➔ Disconnect the cooling and expansion tank hoses as applicable from the radiator - see *Job 2*.

TOP TIP!

• If the engine bay is cramped, first disconnect radiator hoses from the opposite end to the radiator.
• You can then remove them with the radiator assembly.

☐ **STEP 5:** Disconnect the coolant thermostatic switch(es) from their wiring connector(s).

106

☐ **STEP 6:** On the 106, the fan is on the engine-side of the radiator.
➔ You will need to remove the bonnet catch so that you can lift the radiator out.
➔ If necessary to improve access, remove the exhaust heat shield.
➔ Remove the air cleaner intake duct.
➔ Remove the radiator fan and shroud with the radiator – see *Job 3*.
➔ On petrol models, remove the left-side headlight, and remove the left-side radiator shield bolt.
➔ Remove the radiator shield right-side bolt.
➔ On diesel versions, remove the radiator shield bolts.

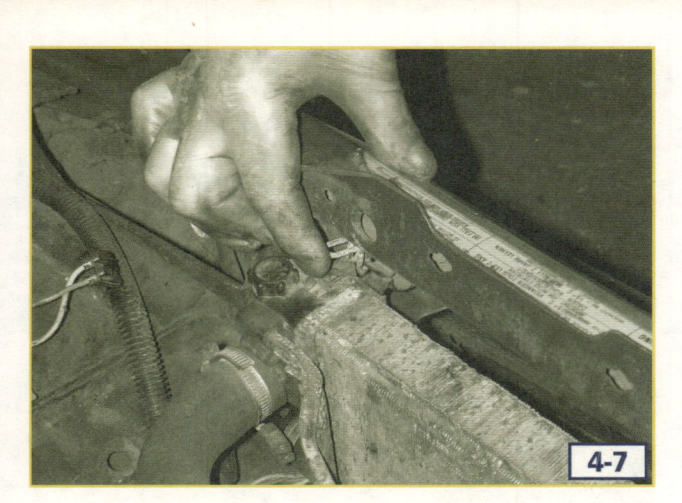

☐ **STEP 7:** Disconnect the radiator upper mounting clips.

☐ **STEP 8:** The radiator has to be eased upward so that the locating pegs on the base are freed from their rubber sockets (positions shown).

☐ **STEP 9:** The radiator may now be lifted from the engine bay or lowered, whichever is easier, depending on variant and access.

205

☐ **STEP 10:** Remove the grille and the crossmember – see **Step 2 and 3**.
➔ Check that all wiring and hoses have been disconnected.
➔ Disconnect the radiator top mountings.
➔ Lift the radiator from the vehicle.

206

☐ **STEP 11:** Remove the radiator upper mounting bracket screws.
➔ Unclip the brackets.
➔ The radiator can now be lifted off its lower mounting bushes and out of the engine bay.
➔ Recover the bushes

306

☐ **STEP 12:** Remove the air intake duct.

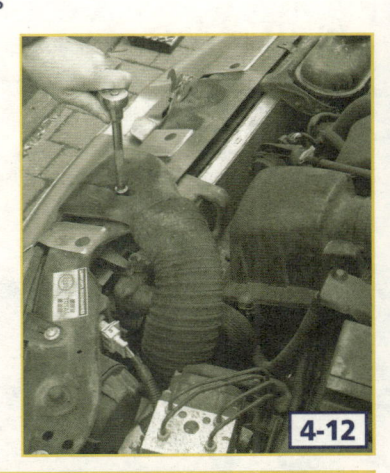

☐ **STEP 13:** The radiator is held by clips.
➔ Remove the clips from the top corners of the radiator – two per side (arrowed).
➔ The radiator can now be lifted out of the engine bay.

CHAPTER 8 Part B Job 4

8-9

ALL MODELS

☐ **STEP 14:** This is a good opportunity to flush the radiator. Use a garden hose to flush it, in the reverse direction to normal flow.

☐ **STEP 15:** Clean dust and road debris from the radiator fins using a soft brush or an air hose, but never a high-pressure water jet. This can easily distort the fins.

TOP TIP!
- If the radiator is leaking, it is possible to repair it.
- However, replacements for Peugeot cars are reasonably priced, so it will probably prove more cost-effective to renew it than to have a specialist repair it.

☐ **STEP 16:** Check that the lower mounting rubbers are in good condition, and replace them if not. Refitting is the reverse of removal.

JOB 5: THERMOSTATIC SWITCH(ES) - *test, replace.*

SAFETY FIRST!
- DO NOT open the cooling system while the engine is hot!

5-1

☐ **STEP 1:** Disconnect the wiring plug(s) from the terminals on the switch(es).

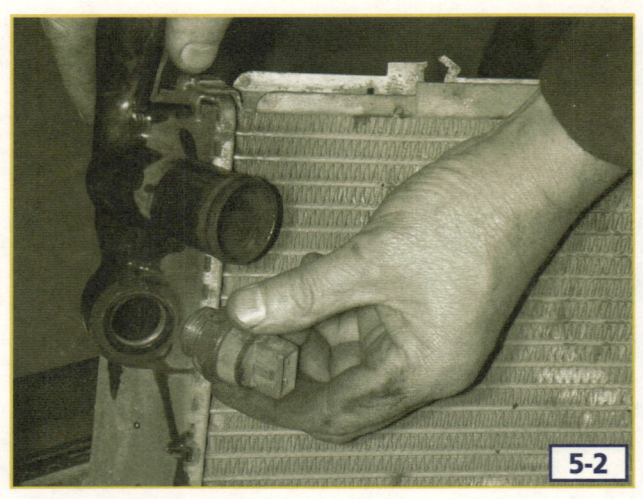

5-2

☐ **STEP 2:** To test a switch, run the engine up to normal working temperature, but (in case the fan is not working) don't run the engine to the point where the coolant boils, or the temperature gauge says the engine is overheating. The fan should come on at this point.
→ First, check to see if the fuse has blown.
→ If not, pull the connector from the switch and bridge the gap between the two plug terminals. This should make the fan start.
→ If it does not, there may be a wiring fault, and the loom should be checked for breakages or corroded connectors.
→ If it does, the switch may not be doing its job, and should be replaced.

☐ **STEP 3:** If a switch requires replacing, undo the expansion tank cap, then unscrew the thermostatic switch from the radiator. Have a container ready to catch the coolant that will run out.

☐ **STEP 4:** When coolant has drained to the level of the switch aperture:
→ Refit as the reverse of removal.
→ Use a new sealing washer.
→ Top up the coolant and bleed the system - see *Job 1*.

JOB 6: THERMOSTAT - *remove, test, replace.*

The thermostat housing varies in design among the models covered by this manual, but it's always in between the coolant top hose and the cylinder head!

SAFETY FIRST!
- DO NOT open the cooling system while the engine is hot!

☐ **STEP 1:** Drain the cooling system – see *Job 1*.

☐ **STEP 2:** Disconnect the radiator top hose from the thermostat housing.

8-10

❏ **STEP 3:** Remove the bolts securing the thermostat housing from the engine.
➔ This is the thermostat housing from the TU engine.

6-3

❏ **STEP 4:** Pull the thermostat from its housing. If it is stuck, waggle it from side to side to free it.
➔ This is the thermostat housing from the XUD engine.

6-4

❏ **STEP 5:** To test the function of the thermostat:
➔ Lower it, on a length of wire, into a pan of boiling water. It should open.
➔ Remove it from the water, and as it cools it should close.
➔ If this does not occur, replace the unit.

❏ **STEP 6:** Refitting is the reverse of removal. However, the thermostat's rubber seal should always be renewed.

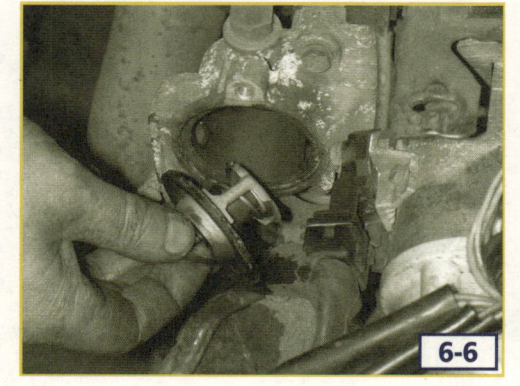

6-6

❏ **STEP 7:** Refill the system with coolant - see *Job 1*.

JOB 7: COOLANT TEMPERATURE /LEVEL GAUGE SENDERS - *remove, replace.*

FACT FILE
TEMPERATURE SENSORS

• Some of the more recent vehicles covered in this manual have several coolant and other temperature sensors.
• Separate coolant temperature sensors may be fitted for the engine management system, coolant temperature gauge, electric cooling fan, air conditioning control system and the fuel injection/pre-heating system.
• Sensors are most commonly fitted on or near the thermostat housing, the coolant outlet housing, on the cylinder head or radiator assembly.

SAFETY FIRST!

• Do not attempt to work on the cooling system while the engine is hot!

❏ **STEP 1:** Drain the cooling system, as described in *Job 1*.

❏ **STEP 2:** Disconnect the wiring connection from the coolant level sender unit. Unscrew and remove the sender unit.

7-2

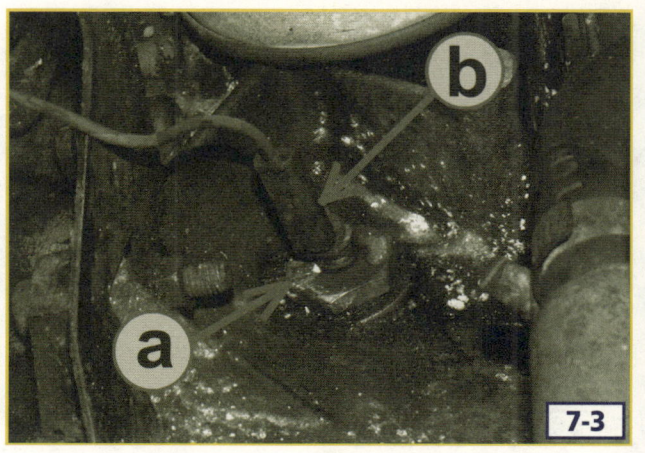

7-3

❏ **STEP 3:** Remove the electrical connector (**b**); unscrew and remove the temperature sender (**a**).

CHAPTER 8 Part B Job 7

8-11

CHAPTER 8 Part B Job 8

☐ **STEP 4:** This shows the engine management system coolant temperature sender and plug (**a**) and the position of the air conditioning coolant temperature sender (**b**) fitted in this case with a blanking plug.

7-4

☐ **STEP 5:** The electric cooling fan thermoswitch (sender) is typically located in the radiator.

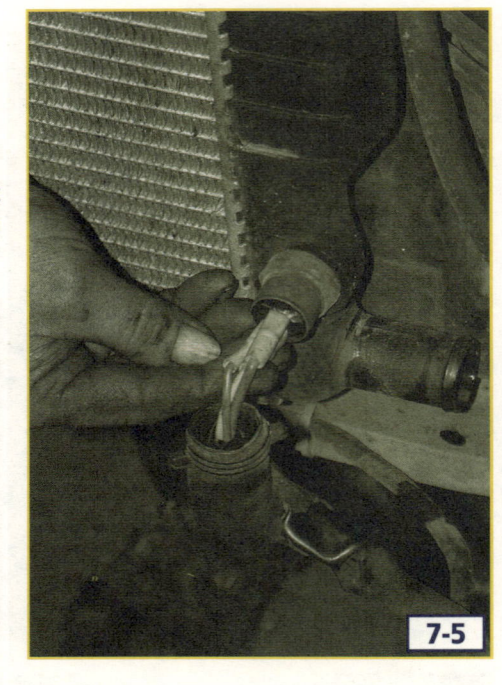

7-5

☐ **STEP 6:** Refit, as the reverse of removal.
→ New sealing washers MUST be fitted.

JOB 8: COOLANT PUMP - remove, replace.

On all models, the coolant pump is a non-serviceable item, and must be replaced if it is worn.

SAFETY FIRST!
• DO NOT open the cooling system while the engine is hot!

☐ **STEP 1:** Drain the cooling system - see *Job 1*.

☐ **STEP 2:** Remove the auxiliary drive belt – see *Chapter 6, Part D, Job 1*.

☐ **STEP 3:** Remove the outer timing belt cover - see *Chapter 6, Part C, Job 1*.

☐ **STEP 4:** Loosen the timing belt - see *Chapter 6, Part C, Job 3*.
→ Remove the timing belt before removing the pump.

☐ **STEP 5:** Remove the coolant pump mounting bolts (positions arrowed).

☐ **STEP 6:** The pump may well be stuck, and require a few light taps with a soft headed mallet before it can be freed.

8-5

TOP TIP!
• This is an ideal opportunity to replace the timing belt, which is a relatively inexpensive part for Peugeot cars - see *Chapter 6, Part C, Job 3*.

☐ **STEP 7:** Remove the coolant pump.
→ This is the coolant pump from the XUD engine.

☐ **STEP 8:** Fitting a new coolant pump.

8-7

→ Ensure that a new O-ring and/or gasket is used, and smeared with a light film of white silicone grease before fitting.
→ Tighten the pump mounting bolts to their specified torque settings.

JOB 9: SCREEN WASHER PUMP - remove, replace.

The screen washer pump can be removed independently of the reservoir.

☐ **STEP 1:** The washer pump is situated within the right-front wheelarch.
→ The one pump and reservoir serve both front and rear washers.
→ Remove the wheelarch liner.

☐ **STEP 2:** Drain the reservoir.

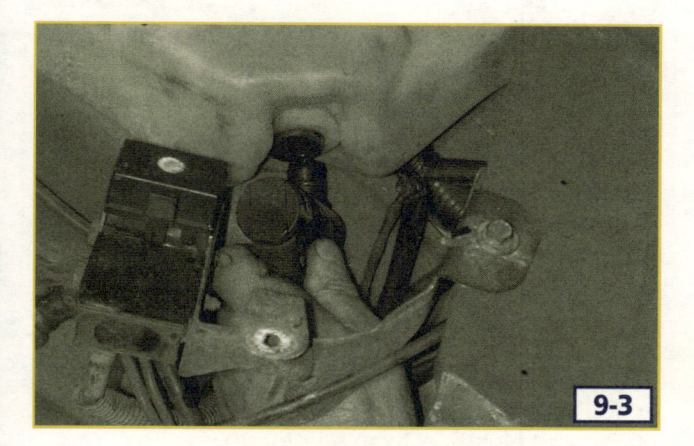

☐ **STEP 3:** Pull the pump away from and out of the reservoir.

☐ **STEP 4:** Disconnect the following:
→ The wiring connectors from the pumps.
→ The fluid hoses from the pump.
→ If the hoses are old, this could be difficult. Cut the pipe as close to the pump nozzle as possible, then slice the remainder carefully off the nozzle when you have removed the pump.

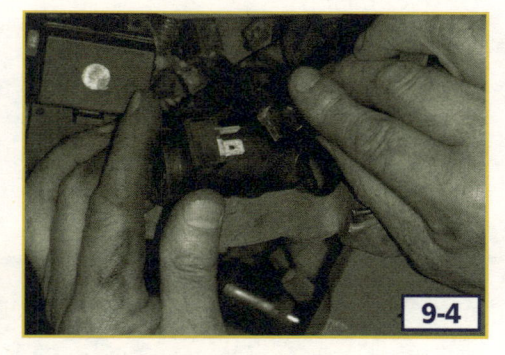

☐ **STEP 5:** Refitting is the reverse of removal. Note that the pump mounting rubber seal can deteriorate and leak. If necessary, renew it.

JOB 10: WASHER JET - remove, replace.

☐ **STEP 1:** The washer jets can be unclipped from their mounting holes in the engine bay lid or tailgate by hand.

☐ **STEP 2:** Open the engine bay lid, unfasten the clips where fitted and push the nozzles through from behind.
→ To gain access to the tailgate nozzle on some vehicles it will be necessary to remove the high level stop light and remove the light holder.

☐ **STEP 3:** Pull the hoses off the nozzle units.
→ Be careful not to let the tailgate hose fall back into the tailgate.
→ It will drip water down inside the unit, and prove hard to retrieve.
→ Secure it outside the hole with tape.

☐ **STEP 4:** Refitting is the reverse of removal.

JOB 11: HEADLIGHT WASHER NOZZLES - remove, replace.

☐ **STEP 1: 106 AND 206:** The headlight washer nozzles are secured by clips or nuts.
→ Remove the bumper.

☐ **STEP 2: 306:** The headlight washer nozzles can be levered out.

☐ **STEP 3:** Disconnect the washer fluid supply pipes from the nozzles by withdrawing the pipe.

☐ **STEP 4:** Refit as the reverse of removal.

JOB 12: HEATER MATRIX - remove, replace.

Whether or not the car you are working on is equipped with air conditioning, it has a heater matrix, which supplies heat from the engine cooling system, on demand into the airstream of the heating system. As it is separate from the closed, pressurised loop of an air conditioning system, which must only be worked on by an air conditioning specialist or Peugeot dealer, it is safe to work on the matrix.

SAFETY FIRST!

• The heater matrix must not be worked on while the engine is hot!

GENERAL

☐ **STEP 1:** Remove the expansion tank cap to allow air to enter the system as coolant flows out.

☐ **STEP 2:** Remove any components necessary to access the hoses, such as air intake trunking.

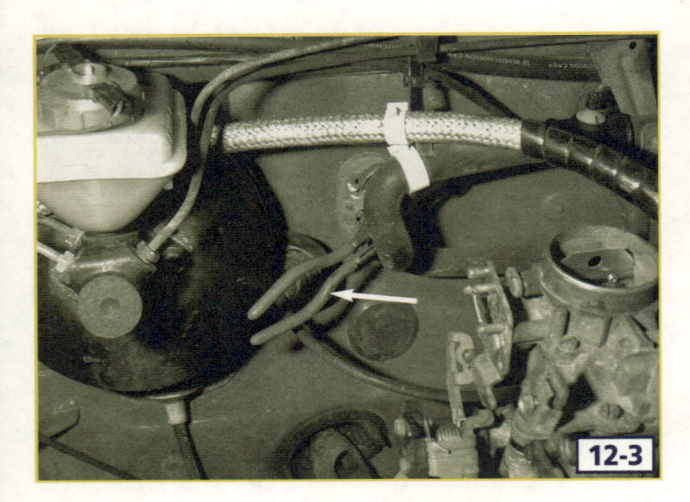

☐ **STEP 3:** Clamp the hoses with hose clamps (arrowed) or self-grip wrenches.
→ There will be some leakage when the pipes are disconnected – place a suitable container underneath.

☐ **STEP 4:** Disconnect the hoses from the matrix.
→ Seal the ends and tie the hoses upwards with cable ties, to stop coolant escaping.

MODEL SPECIFIC

☐ **STEP 5:** Depending on which model you are working on, you may have to remove items of trim, such as the dashboard, to access the matrix - see *Chapter 14* for details. The components are:
→ **106:** Dashboard, air ducts. Remove the heater unit complete.
→ **205:** Dashboard, lower air vents. Remove the heater unit complete.
→ **206:** Battery and tray. Clamp and disconnect the heater pipes at the bulkhead. Dashboard.
→ **306 WITHOUT AIR CONDITIONING:** Dashboard. Clamp and disconnect the heater pipes at the bulkhead. Remove the heater unit complete.
→ **306 WITH AIR CONDITIONING:** As above, plus temperature sensor from heater unit. Remove screws securing heater unit to evaporator/heater blower casing.

TOP TIP!

- It's a good idea to place a large absorbent cloth under the heater as you remove the matrix, to absorb any spilt coolant.
- Take care to protect upholstery, but if coolant splashes any trim, wipe it off immediately with a damp cloth.
- Remember that the matrix is full of coolant!

☐ **STEP 6:** Reassemble as the reverse of removal.

CHAPTER 9: IGNITION, FUEL, EXHAUST

Please read **Chapter 2 Safety First** before carrying out any work on your car.

We have placed both **Ignition** and **Fuel** systems in a single chapter. The two areas could once be treated separately, but that is no longer the case, and with today's electronic devices, ignition and fuel systems are inter-related.

Before carrying out any adjustments, checks or dismantling of the fuel system, note the following:
• It may be illegal in some territories for an unauthorised person to remove tamperproof plugs on carburetors or fuel injection systems. Only carry out any of the following if it is legally permissible to do so.
• Do not connect a capacitor/condenser to the coil terminals.
• The ignition should be turned off when washing the engine or engine bay.
• If electric arc, MIG or spot welding is carried out on the car, BOTH battery terminals must be disconnected.
• Never disconnect the battery with the engine running.
• Do not disconnect the ECU with the ignition in the on position.
• Setting the idle speed and mixture is not just a matter of making the car run smoothly and economically; it's also a question of allowing it to run within the legal hydrocarbon (HC) nitrous oxide (NO) and carbon monoxide (CO) emissions limits for the territory in which the vehicle is used.
• Do NOT touch ignition wires while the engine is running or being turned on the starter.
• Never attempt to adjust any fuel injection system without appropriate CO content measuring equipment.
• NEVER try turning adjustment screws at random: the chances of making things better are remote; the chances of making things much worse are very high!
• Many injection systems cannot be adjusted. Their elements can be tested as described here, or by a fully equipped injection specialist or main dealer.
• The accelerator linkage must be adjusted and lubricated if the fuel injection system is to operate smoothly and correctly.

	Page No.		Page No.
Part A: Petrol/Gasoline Engines	9-2	**Part C:** Both Engine Types	9-41
Part B: Diesel Engines	9-28		

SAFETY FIRST!

IGNITION SYSTEMS
• **Disconnect the battery before carrying out any work on the ignition or fuel systems. See Chapter 10, Electrical, Dash, Instruments, Fact File: Disconnecting the Battery BEFORE doing so!**
• Make sure that you first have the radio code, or use a backup power supply.
• Take very great care when working on a vehicle equipped with electronic ignition.
• ELECTRONIC IGNITION SYSTEMS MAY INVOLVE VERY HIGH VOLTAGES! All manufacturers recommend that only trained personnel should go near the high-tension circuit (coil, distributor and HT wiring) and it is ESSENTIAL that anyone wearing a medical pacemaker device does not go near the ignition system.
• Do NOT touch ignition wires while the engine is running or being turned on the starter.
• Make sure the ignition is switched off before removing any wires from the ignition system.
• If the engine has to be turned over on the starter but without starting, for example when checking compression, disconnect all the cables from the distributor and also remove the HT lead from the coil.

Continued...

SAFETY FIRST!

CRANKING AN ENGINE WITH ELECTRONIC IGNITION: Severe damage can be caused to the ignition system if the engine is cranked with plugs/leads removed – and a severe electric shock can be experienced.
1. With the latest 'distributorless' systems, disconnect the multi-plug from the base of the 'black box'.
2. With earlier systems, disconnect the multi-plug leading to the distributor/control unit from the ignition (early 205 shown).

FUEL SYSTEMS

Where fuel injectors are fitted with electrical plugs, disconnect the plug from each of the four injectors.
- Never work on the fuel system unless the engine is completely cool.
- Some fuel injection systems inject fuel at extremely high pressure.
- Pressure must be released in a controlled fashion to avoid any risk of a pressurised spray of fuel being produced.
- Residual pressure can remain in the fuel system for some considerable time, even if the engine has been switched off.
- IMPORTANT NOTE: Removing pressure from the fuel lines, as described below, will not necessarily remove pressure from each of the components.
- Before working on any part of the injection system it is necessary to remove the pressure from the system.

Part A: Petrol/Gasoline Engines

CONTENTS

	Page No.
JOB 1: SYSTEMS – *explained*.	9-3
JOB 2: DIAGNOSTICS – *carry out checks*.	9-5
JOB 3: IGNITION TIMING – *check/set*.	9-9
JOB 4: IGNITION COIL – *replacement*.	9-12
JOB 5: DISTRIBUTOR – *removal, refitting*.	9-13
JOB 6: LAMBDA SENSOR (engines with cat.) – *testing, replacement*.	9-14
JOB 7: CARBURETOR – *adjustment*.	9-15
JOB 8: CARBURETOR – *removal, replacement*.	9-17
JOB 9: FUEL INJECTION SYSTEMS – *adjustment*.	9-18
JOB 10: FUEL INJECTION UNITS – *removal, replacement*.	9-21
JOB 11: ACCELERATOR CABLE – *adjustment, replacement*.	9-23
JOB 12: CHOKE CABLE – *adjustment, replacement*.	9-25
JOB 13: MECHANICAL FUEL PUMP – *replacement*.	9-25
JOB 14: ELECTRIC FUEL PUMP – *replacement*.	9-26
JOB 15: FUEL EVAPORATIVE SYSTEM.	9-27
JOB 16: FUEL FILTER – *injection engines*.	9-27

SAFETY FIRST!

- When working on engines with electronic ignition systems, note the following, to avoid personal injury or damage to the ignition system.
- Make sure the ignition is switched off before removing any wires from the ignition system.
- If the engine is to be turned on the starter without starting:

EITHER - NON-ELECTRONIC IGNITION: Pull the centre HT lead from the distributor and connect it firmly to earth/ground.

OR - ELECTRONIC IGNITION: Disconnect the multi-pin plug from the distributor or ignition transformer (i.e. whichever one has the HT spark plug leads connected to it.)

IMPORTANT NOTE: Before dismantling any part of the fuel system, disconnect the battery negative (-) earth/ground terminal. See *Chapter 10, Electrical, Dash, Instruments, Fact File: Disconnecting the Battery* BEFORE doing so!

JOB 1: SYSTEMS – explained.

In general, the earlier the vehicle, the easier it is to attend to ignition and fuel systems, while the later the vehicle, the more complex the electronics become. See the relevant PART of this chapter for detailed illustrations and information.

Section A: Ignition.

FACT FILE
IGNITION AND DISTRIBUTOR TYPES

IGNITION
- All models have breakerless electronic ignition.
- Carburetor types and earlier, smaller-engined fuel-injected models retain a distributor.
- Later, larger-engined variants use static systems controlled by the engine management Electronic Control Unit (ECU).

DISTRIBUTOR
☐ **TYPE 1:** Whether carburetor or fuel injection, these vehicles have a single coil mounted in the engine bay, and a distributor using a reluctor to switch the low tension circuit and a transistorised amplifier to generate the high tension current. On fuel-injected models the distributor also has a vacuum-operated ignition retard system controlled by the ECU, that is designed to reduce nitrous oxide emissions.

LATER VEHICLES
☐ **TYPE 2:** In later models ignition timing and fuel injection are controlled directly by the ECU using either Magneti Marelli or Bosch systems, and it is not possible to make any adjustments without accessing the ECU, which should only be done by a properly-equipped specialist using the diagnostic port provided. Any faults, however, could be caused by little more than corroded multiplug contacts, worn spark plugs or blocked air filter.

Section B: Fuel intake/injection.

The evolutionary process passes through:
→ Carburetors (with increasing amounts of sophistication).
→ Single point injection systems, which more or less fit onto inlet manifolds as a replacement for carburetors.
→ The more sophisticated multipoint injection systems. Several different injection types have been fitted.

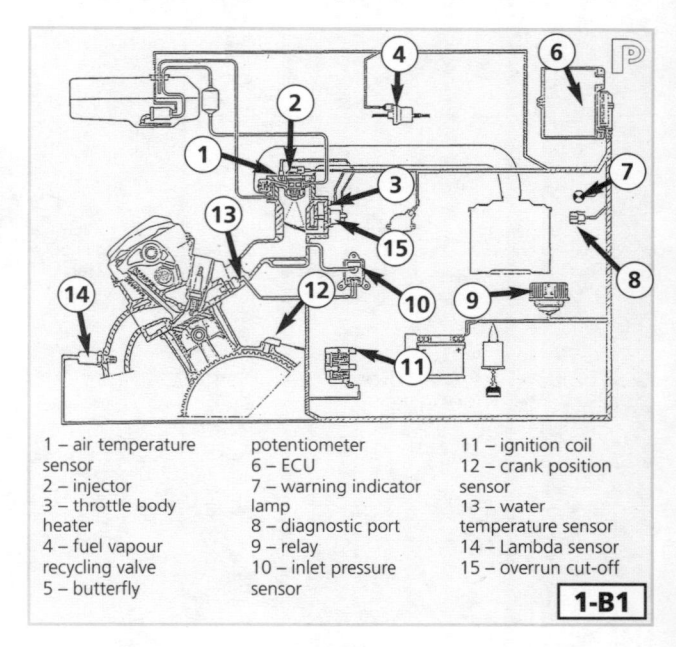

1 – air temperature sensor
2 – injector
3 – throttle body heater
4 – fuel vapour recycling valve
5 – butterfly potentiometer
6 – ECU
7 – warning indicator lamp
8 – diagnostic port
9 – relay
10 – inlet pressure sensor
11 – ignition coil
12 – crank position sensor
13 – water temperature sensor
14 – Lambda sensor
15 – overrun cut-off

1-B1

☐ **STEP B1:** This is the Magneti Marelli G6 singlepoint system.

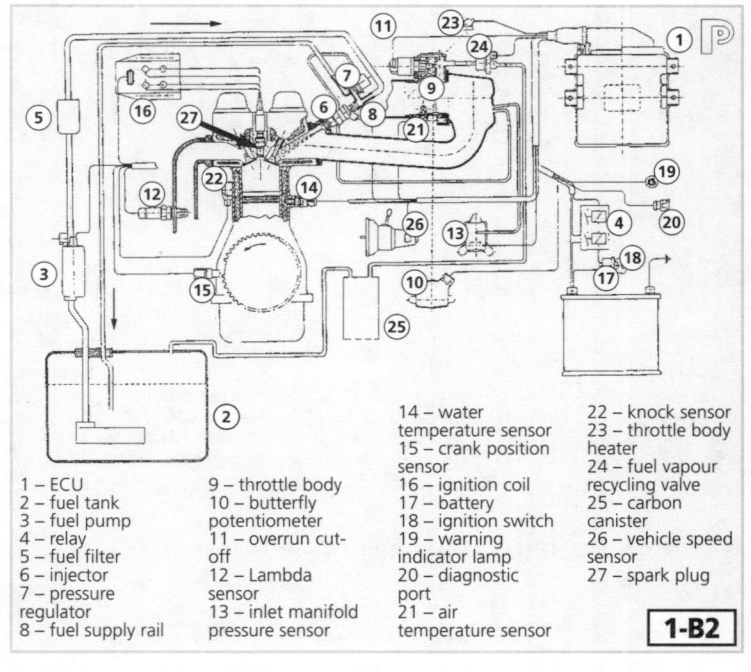

1 – ECU
2 – fuel tank
3 – fuel pump
4 – relay
5 – fuel filter
6 – injector
7 – pressure regulator
8 – fuel supply rail
9 – throttle body
10 – butterfly potentiometer
11 – overrun cut-off
12 – Lambda sensor
13 – inlet manifold pressure sensor
14 – water temperature sensor
15 – crank position sensor
16 – ignition coil
17 – battery
18 – ignition switch
19 – warning indicator lamp
20 – diagnostic port
21 – air temperature sensor
22 – knock sensor
23 – throttle body heater
24 – fuel vapour recycling valve
25 – carbon canister
26 – vehicle speed sensor
27 – spark plug

1-B2

☐ **STEP B2:** This is the Magneti Marelli 8P multipoint system.

CHAPTER 9 Part A Job 1

1 – fuel tank
2 – fuel pump
3 – fuel filter
4 – injector
5 – pressure regulator
6 – throttle body
7 – air filter
8 – overrun cut-off
9 – inlet manifold
10 – ECU
11 – butterfly potentiometer
12 – ignition coil
13 – air temperature sensor
14 – water temperature sensor
15 – Lambda sensor
16 – crank position sensor
17 – diagnostic port
18 – warning indicator lamp
19 – relay
20 – fuel vapour recycling valve
21 – vehicle speed sensor

1-B3

❏ **STEP B3:** This is the Bosch MA3.0 single point system.

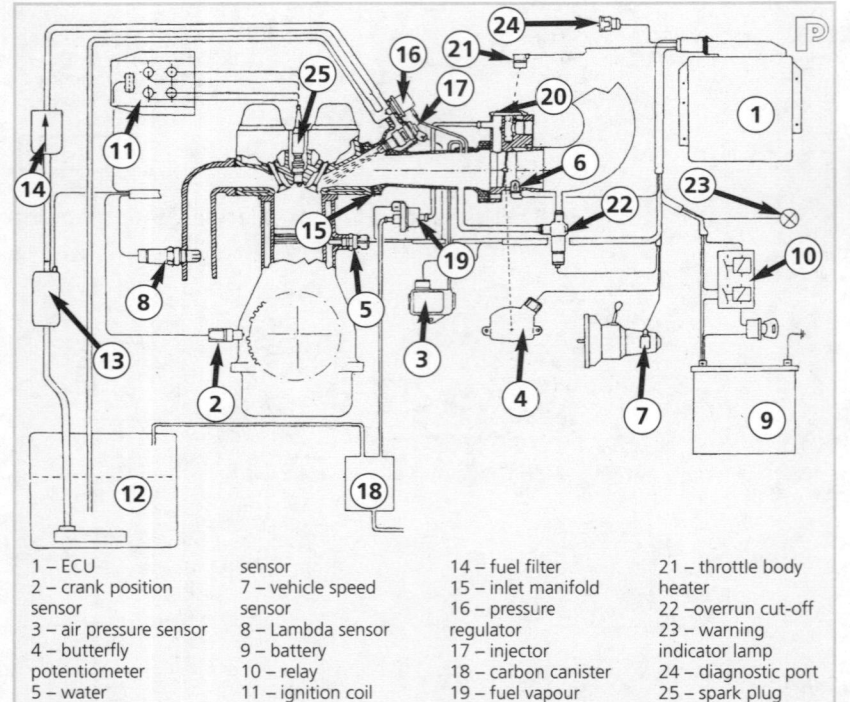

1 – ECU
2 – crank position sensor
3 – air pressure sensor
4 – butterfly potentiometer
5 – water temperature sensor
6 – air temperature sensor
7 – vehicle speed sensor
8 – Lambda sensor
9 – battery
10 – relay
11 – ignition coil
12 – fuel tank
13 – fuel pump
14 – fuel filter
15 – inlet manifold
16 – pressure regulator
17 – injector
18 – carbon canister
19 – fuel vapour recycling valve
20 – throttle body
21 – throttle body heater
22 – overrun cut-off
23 – warning indicator lamp
24 – diagnostic port
25 – spark plug

1-B4

❏ **STEP B4:** This is the Bosch MP5.1 multipoint system.

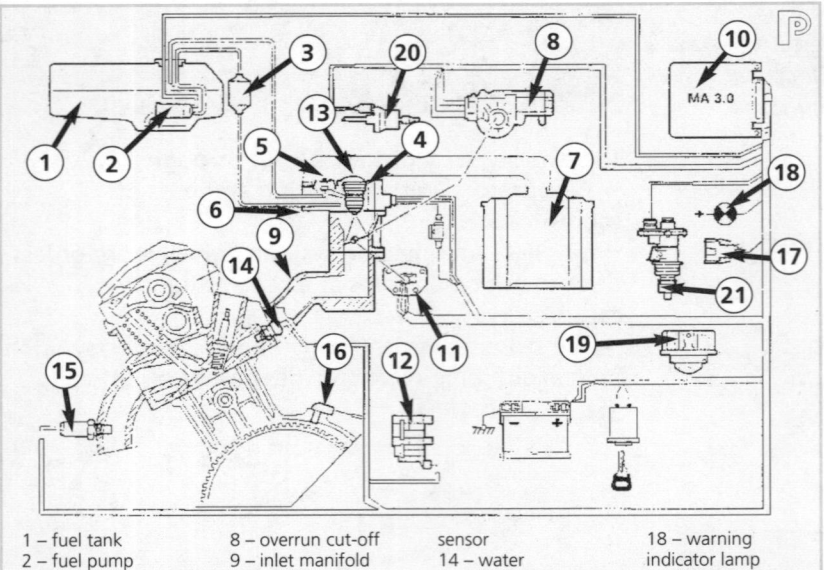

Section C: Fuel supply.

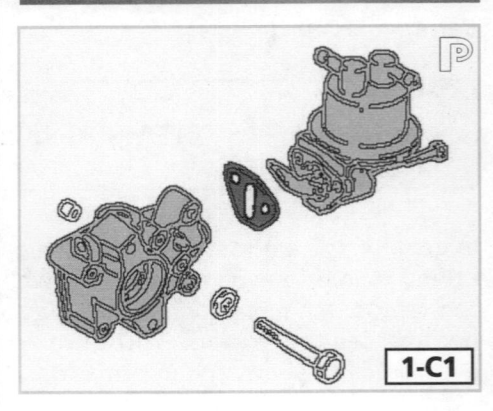

1-C1

❏ **STEP C1:** Carburetor models use a mechanical, camshaft driven pump either on the cylinder head or at the timing case (XV series engines). This draws fuel via an anti-percolation chamber, from where excess fuel is returned to the tank. Fuel-injected models use an electric fuel pump mounted in the tank. All versions draw fuel through a filter mounted under the car. Catalyst-equipped models have a charcoal canister to absorb fuel vapour.

Section D: Exhaust systems.

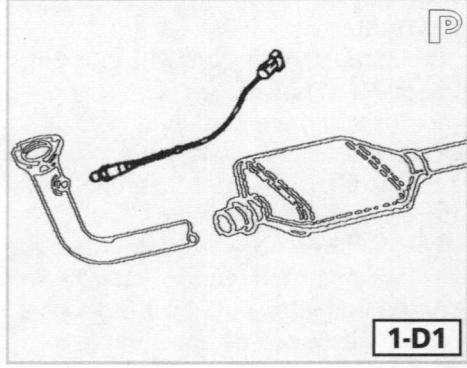

1-D1

❏ **STEP D1:** The largest changes to exhaust systems came about when emission control equipment was fitted, mandatory in the UK from 1992. A catalytic converter is fitted to the front end of the exhaust, and a Lambda sensor is bolted into the exhaust upstream of the 'cat'.

Section E: Engine management.

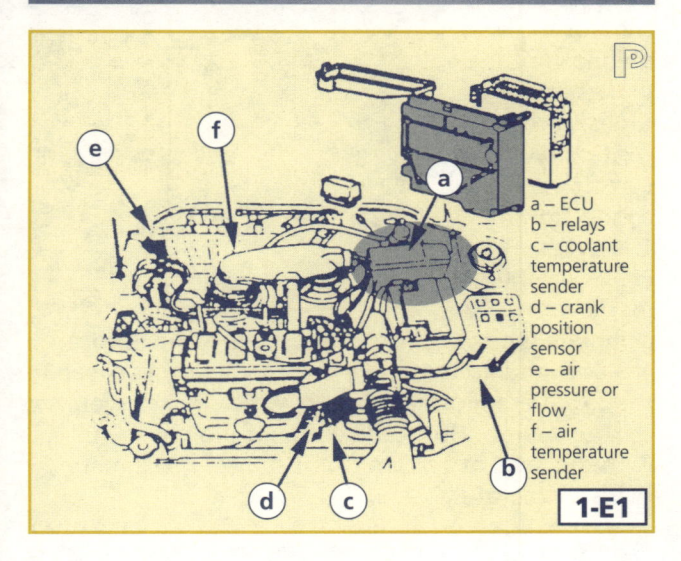

Figure 1-E1:
- a – ECU
- b – relays
- c – coolant temperature sender
- d – crank position sensor
- e – air pressure or flow sensor
- f – air temperature sender

☐ **STEP E1:** To enhance fuel efficiency and clean exhaust emissions, while ensuring good power and response, all modern engines are controlled by a computer-based ECU, or Electronic Control Unit. The ECU uses a wide range of data so that it can control the major ignition and fuel supply components with greater efficiency. Newer engines have a whole range of sensors, including those to measure throttle, and sometimes brake and clutch pedal positions.

JOB 2: DIAGNOSTICS - carry out checks.

Section A: Background.

Vehicles are becoming increasingly dependent on electronics. When things are going well, this has great advantages for the driver, including:
→ Greater efficiency.
→ Better reliability.
→ Less maintenance.

Of course, almost everything has its downside, and vehicle electronics are no exception. Features often seen as 'problems' include:
→ The need for special tools - mainly electronic diagnostic instruments.
→ The need for knowledge and information not found in traditional manuals.
→ The fact that it's impossible to see faults with electronic systems.

However, problems presented by vehicle electronics can be overcome - and indeed, such problems can be turned on their heads. Then, instead of appearing as problems, they can be seen as a set of extra advantages for the mechanic, such as:
→ Rapid fault diagnosis.
→ Less guesswork.
→ Fewer 'grey' areas caused by wear - electronics tend to work or not work, and they don't usually wear out in a mechanical sense.

Turning the minuses into pluses is a matter of knowing where to obtain information and how to use it. It is not possible to fault-find many areas affected by electronics on an old-fashioned common-sense basis. But fortunately, the information is not too difficult to put to use - and it's even easier to find - if you know where to look!

TOP TIP!

• It's a myth that only the manufacturers' own diagnostic gear can do the job! But you will need a plug-in diagnostic tester to interrogate electronic-based systems.
• There are several makes of tester on the market. We feature the pro-oriented Sykes-Pickavant ACR System Tester. It's typical of the best of the testers available.

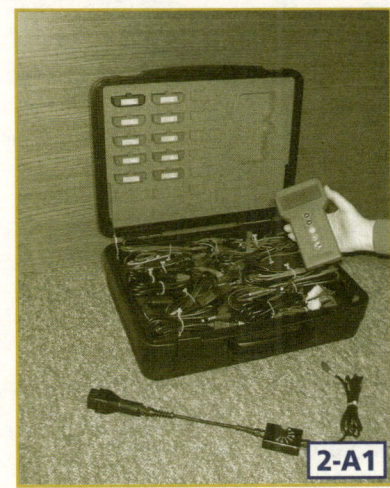

☐ **STEP A1:** It is not possible - even in a manual of this size - to cover diagnostics in specific detail; there's no room, and no need. We will describe how to use diagnostic test equipment and the equipment itself will do the rest. What diagnostic test equipment, such as the Sykes-Pickavant ACR System Tester, is good at is identifying specific fault areas:
→ If a component such as the engine knock sensor, the hall sender unit, or the Lambda sensor is failing to give a reading, the tester can tell you, almost instantly.
→ If you want to fool a component into working without the engine running, an advanced unit such as this one can simulate a signal to the component, so that you listen and feel for a solenoid clicking, a flap opening and closing, or the buzz of an EGR valve working.

What it can't always tell you is the source of the fault. Before fitting an expensive replacement, you will want to know:
→ Is the wiring to or from the component at fault?
→ Is it a corroded plug or socket?
→ Has someone else connected it up incorrectly?

TOP TIP!
- Check the basics before assuming that anything more complex is at fault.
- See *Chapter 4, Workshop Top Tips!*

To analyse the results, you will need to go a step further. You will still need a wiring diagram, to check circuits and connections. And you will need extra diagnostic information to know how to check out potential faults. Most of the information you will need is in this manual - but if all of it had been printed here, the book would have been too thick to carry!

STEP A2: Detailed diagnostic information is available from a number of sources:
→ You can order the manufacturer's own data, although some of it may be restricted information and not widely available. Try your local Peugeot dealer's parts department.
→ There are several companies who specialise in producing detailed data of this sort. The one shown here is produced by CAPS (Computer Aided Problem Solving). It covers, as do all of them, a very wide range of manufacturers and models. All of these data compilations are expensive, typically costing many times the price of this manual!

STEP A3: CAPS lists an immense amount of data on each disk, including:
→ ECU pin settings.
→ Values expected for various test readings using, for instance, a standard test meter.
→ Waveforms for oscilloscope component testing.
→ Virtually everything you may need to carry out extensive diagnostic testing, in conjunction with a fault code reader.

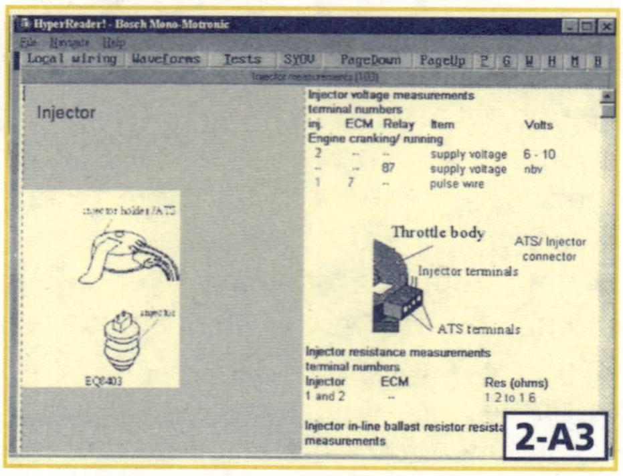

STEP A4: A good quality multi-meter will be an essential tool for the diagnosis of the more basic faults, such as continuity and correct connections. This Sykes-Pickavant multi-meter comes complete with full instructions for use and is both versatile and accurate. We have come across cheaper tools that are most inaccurate, which makes them next to useless. How can you tell if there is a fault with the level of current (for instance) if the meter reads inaccurately?

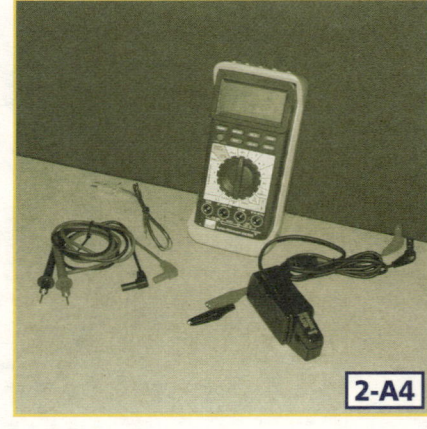

STEP A5: We look later at a more comprehensive and complete diagnostic tool from Sykes-Pickavant, but this sensor simulator and tester is an extremely useful piece of kit in its own right. Although it is not designed to actually drive solenoids and actuators (it will test them both to see if they are receiving a control signal), it will test the following: Camshaft sensor; Crankshaft sensor; Mass Air Flow Meter; Manifold absolute pressure sensors; Oxygen sensor; Power steering pressure switch; Temperature sensors; Throttle position sensor.

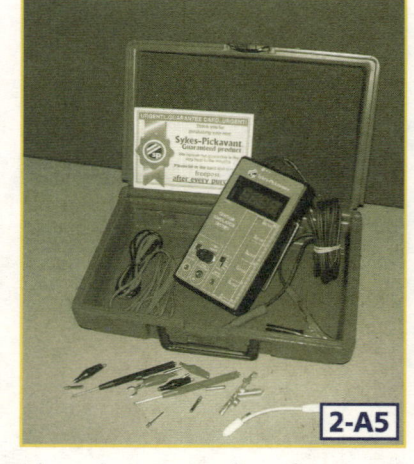

STEP A6: An efficient Lambda sensor is essential for protecting the catalytic converter, allowing the vehicle to run efficiently and enabling the engine to pass the emissions laws. The Sykes-Pickavant tester can be used to check the sensor while it is in situ.

Fact File
DIAGNOSTIC TESTING

BACKGROUND INFORMATION FROM SYKES-PICKAVANT

Electronic fuel injection and ignition systems on modern vehicles have a computer (called an ECU) to provide the proper control of the fuel-air mixture. The ECU works by measuring many different characteristics of the car then, using this information, it calculates the correct quantity of fuel, the time of the fuel injection and the time for the ignition spark.

The ECU is a computer, like any other you could buy from a high street shop, but instead of a keyboard it has SENSORS as inputs, and instead of a TV screen, it has ACTUATORS. These are the output of the computer; for example the ECU controls the fuel injectors by opening and closing them for a few thousandths of a second. During this time fuel is sprayed into the inlet manifold (near the inlet valves) in the exact proportions required for efficient combustion. The ECU also controls the engine's idle speed with the "idle speed control valve".

Sensors are prone to failure, mainly due to being exposed to the harsh engine environment where harness connections can easily deteriorate over a few years. When this kind of fault occurs the ECU can be misled by the information being sent from the sensor, this results in the wrong quantity of fuel or timing for the sparks. Soon, the car allows too much of the wrong exhaust gases to escape, becomes difficult to drive or even does not start at all.

ECUs are able to detect faults in sensor signals by comparing the value with a range of values which are programmed by the designer of the ECU. If a signal is outside the expected range then something is wrong. The ECU does not "know" what exactly is wrong but is can sense that the signal is not in the range it expects to receive. This detected fault is stored as a "fault code" number in the memory of the ECU. ECU designers have built-in limited number of such fault-codes into most modern systems. Each manufacturer has a different coding system and a different way of reading the codes, but they have some basic similarities.

Somewhere on the car's harness is a diagnostic socket which connects directly to the ECU. By connecting a second computer (the ACR Systems Tester, in this instance) to this socket we can send messages back and forth between the two computers and read the stored codes.

A simple code reader will show only the two or three digit code numbers which you then need to look up in a book to find out what they mean. The Sykes-Pickavant ACR Systems Tester does much more, by READING, CLEARING, ACTUATOR TESTS, and COMPONENT TESTS.

READ CODES

The ACR System Tester is able to read codes and display the meaning of each code. For example if the coolant temperature sensor is faulty then on some Bosch ECUs the fault-code stored is "15". The ACR System Tester shows the following on its two line display:

15 COOLANT SENS
VOLTAGE LOW

CLEAR CODES

When this problem has been corrected (perhaps by replacing the sensor) the stored fault code (15) must be removed from the ECU, otherwise the ECU will still think something is wrong. This is what the Clear Codes function is for. After clearing codes, the engine should be started and a final check for any stored fault codes made - just to be certain that nothing else has occurred.

ACTUATOR TEST

This feature is a method of testing the ECU outputs when the engine is turned off. For example to test the injectors involves sending a signal from the ACR System Tester to trigger a special program in the ECU which, in turn, causes the injectors to open and close every second. The injectors can be heard quite clearly "ticking" like a clock every second. With this we have clear proof that a signal is able to reach the injectors, we DO NOT KNOW if the injectors are blocked or gummed, so we do not know if any fuel can get into the engine…there are other ways of testing for that.

The final group of tests are components, (this is another way of saying sensors) where we can show the voltage, time or angle of various sensors which provide input to the ECU.

IMPORTANT NOTES:
• The ECU can only measure what is happening to the car using the sensors it is connected to. If there is no sensor it cannot be measured. This may seem obvious but some people seem to think computers are all-powerful.
• The ECU calculates the value that the ACR System Tester displays; the Tester is NOT connected directly to the sensor. The display you see is what the ECU "thinks" is the correct value. So if you see "Coolant Temperature 79 degrees Celsius" and the engine is stone-cold, you know something is wrong, but the ECU doesn't. This is a vital point to understand about code-readers which connect to the diagnostic socket; they can only display what the ECU is programmed to show and what the ECU calculates from its input.

Section B: The ACR tester – using.

☐ **STEP B1:** The first job is to identify what you will need to use on the car you are testing. Look up the cable number in the handbook entitled "ACR System Tester Applications", supplied with the kit. Out of the Sykes-Pickavant case, you will need to take:
→ The main ACR unit.
→ The correct plug-in pod, containing the ROM of data relevant to the vehicle you are testing.
→ The correct interface cable for connecting the ACR unit to the vehicle.

☐ **STEP B2:** Find the location of the diagnostic sockets.
106 MODELS: Look under the dash on the left-hand side.

☐ **STEP B3: 206 AND 306 MODELS:** Look behind the fuse box cover at the end of the dash.
ALL MODELS: With the ignition OFF, push the plug into the relevant socket/s, following the instructions with the ACR kit.

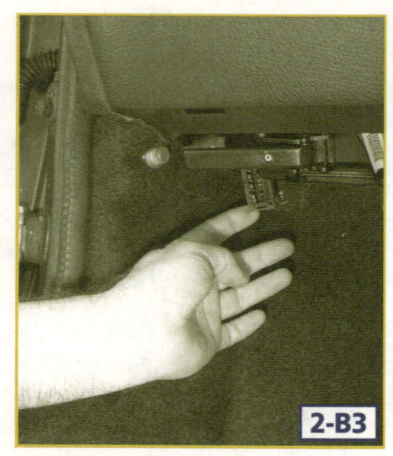

☐ **STEP B4:** Each ROM pod (and there are several - each one covering a range of makes and models) comes with its own small manual that 'walks' you through the setting up and running procedure.
→ When the unit comes to life, you select the type of system (e.g. Motronic or Magneti Marelli) on the menu offered on the read-out. The ACR then communicates with the vehicle's ECU.
→ You then select from the menu which type of test you want to carry out, such as 'Read Errors', 'Clear Errors' or 'Test Actuators'.
→ If you selected 'Test Actuators' for instance, the next menu allows you to choose which one - say, 'Fuel Injector'.
→ The ACR then interrogates the system for errors.
→ If an error is found, the error code number appears AND (unlike many testers) an abbreviated description of the error, such as **"0522: COOLANT TEMP SENSOR"** appears on the screen.
→ Pressing the **'OK'** button on the ACR applications can expand abbreviations. **"INJ P/W"**, for example, becomes **"INJECTOR PULSE WIDTH"** - useful until you are able to memorise the abbreviations.

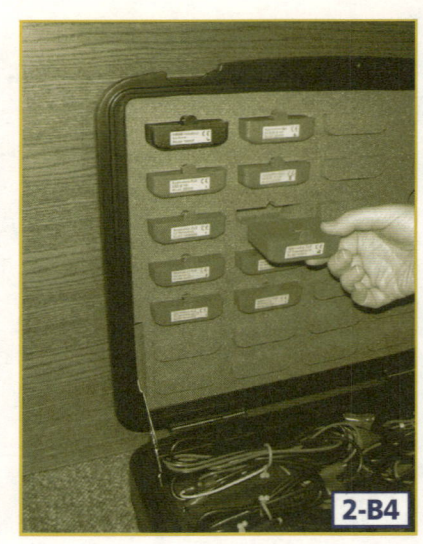

☐ **STEP B5:** A similar approach is followed - a walk-through by the manual, combined with step-by-step on-screen prompts and menus - allowing the user to carry out most of the other functions that would normally only be carried out by the main dealer. Depending on the system, the SP ACR has the following capabilities:
→ Identifies ECU number and type.
→ Reads and clears fault codes.

→ Drives actuators e.g. coil, injectors etc..
→ Shows 'live engine data' e.g. throttle potentiometer, Lambda switching etc.
→ CO timing and base idle adjustment.
→ Service light reset.
→ Instrument panel codes and actuators (gauges, warning lights) on some vehicles.

IMPORTANT NOTES:
• Fault code readers that only display code numbers can be misleading. 'Live engine data' is far more useful.
• A fault code will only be logged by a system if the component has failed open circuit or short to ground. If the component is working but incorrectly, like the hot engine showing a coolant reading of 20 degrees Celsius, this would only be seen using the component 'live data' option.
• Also it is highly recommended that any fault code is read, then deleted. The car should then be driven and re-tested to see if the code has returned, if it does then treat it as real.

TOP TIP!

• Many fault codes are introduced by people simply unplugging components – double-check before assuming a component fault!
• We have dealt in outline with the type of ACR pods and cables used for the vehicles covered by this manual. Other vehicles and other manufacturer's vehicle groups require their own modules and their own specific setting-up approaches. In each case, the set-up is described in the Sykes-Pickavant manual supplied with the relevant ROM pod.

JOB 3: IGNITION TIMING - check/set.

See **Chapter 6, Part B: Which Engine is Which?** for an explanation of the engine types referred to here.

SAFETY FIRST!

• THE IGNITION SYSTEM INVOLVES VERY HIGH VOLTAGES!

• All manufacturers recommend that only trained personnel should go near the high tension circuit (coil, distributor and HT wiring) and it is ESSENTIAL that anyone wearing a medical pacemaker device does not go near the ignition system.

• Also, stroboscopic timing requires the engine to be running – take great care that parts of the timing lights or parts of you don't get caught up in the moving parts! Don't wear loose clothing.

FACT FILE
ENGINES WITH KNOCK SENSORS

• The ignition timing on these engines is constantly monitored and is set automatically as the engine is running. In the majority of cases, no ignition timing adjustments are either necessary or possible.
• It might be possible to set the ignition timing on these engines by traditional means, but we cannot be sure that it will be so for all engines of this type.
• The timing figures quoted by Peugeot are (with vacuum hose disconnected):
→ **XV8, XW7** engines, 6 degrees BTDC at 650 rpm
→ **XY7** engine 8 degrees BTDC at 650 rpm
→ **XY8** engine 0 degrees BDTC (early), 8 degrees BTDC (late) at 950 rpm
→ **XU5** engine 6 degrees BTDC at 700 rpm
→ **TU** engines 8 degrees BTDC at 750 rpm
• During 1985 and 1986 the ignition timing on some GTi and CTi models with XU5J, XU5JA and XU9JA engines was altered.

☐ **STEP A1:** The knock sensor is a device for detecting when the ignition is too far advanced (leading to 'engine knock') and retarding the ignition timing accordingly. Where fitted, this sensor is bolted directly to the rear of the engine block, beneath the intake manifold, between cylinders 2 and 3.

IMPORTANT NOTES: OLDER ENGINES NOT ORIGINALLY SPECIFIED FOR UNLEADED FUEL
• If the ignition timing has been changed to allow an engine to run on unleaded fuel, the timing marks on the flywheel, referred to below, will not apply.
• It will then be necessary to adjust the timing using a relatively sophisticated stroboscopic timing light - one that is capable of being adjusted to give different readings from the TDC mark on the flywheel.
Engines that may be operated on unleaded fuel are:
→ XY7 (after engine No 598051)
→ XU5S
→ XU5J
→ XU5JA
→ TU1
→ TU3S
→ TU9A

The ignition timing of the XY7 engine should be retarded by 3 degrees for unleaded operation. XU engines should be retarded 2 degrees. The TU3S engine should be retarded by 4 degrees, but TU1 and TU9A require no retardation.

ALL ENGINE TYPES

• There are several different ignition and associated carburation/injection systems fitted to the vehicles covered here.

CHAPTER 9 Part A Job 3

ENGINE SAFETY FIRST!

- We believe, after exhaustive research, that the following data is correct. However, it has not been possible to confirm that this is so in every specific case, especially since much of the published data is contradictory or appears to be incomplete.
- If in doubt, consult your local Peugeot dealership.

FACT FILE

DISTRIBUTOR TYPES

❏ **STEP A2:** The distributor will either be by Ducellier or Bosch. Procedures for checking, adjusting and replacing them are similar, but note that the Bosch unit has a one-piece body. During 1986 Ducellier distributor caps were mounted using two screws rather than spring clips.

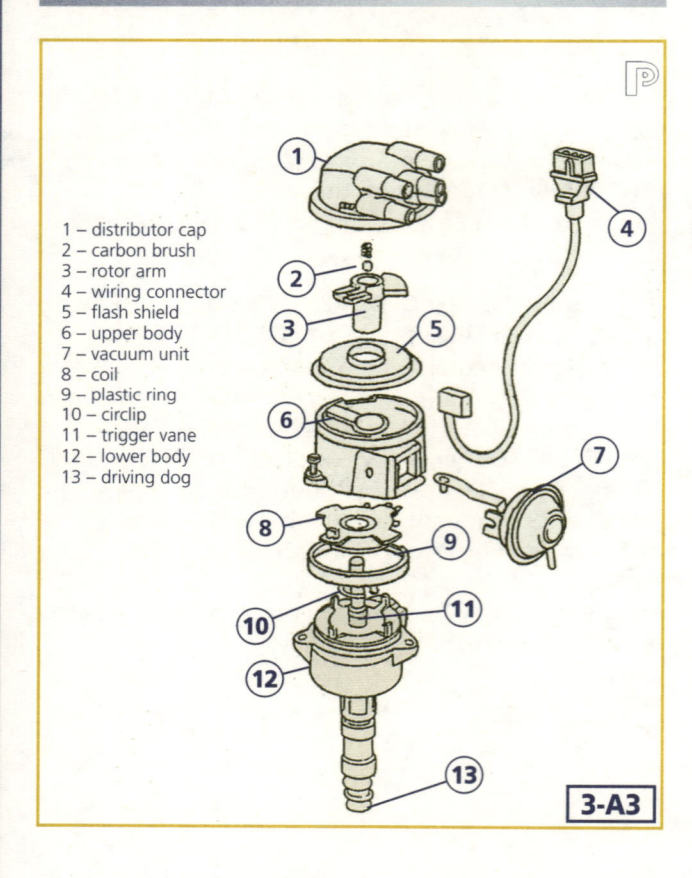

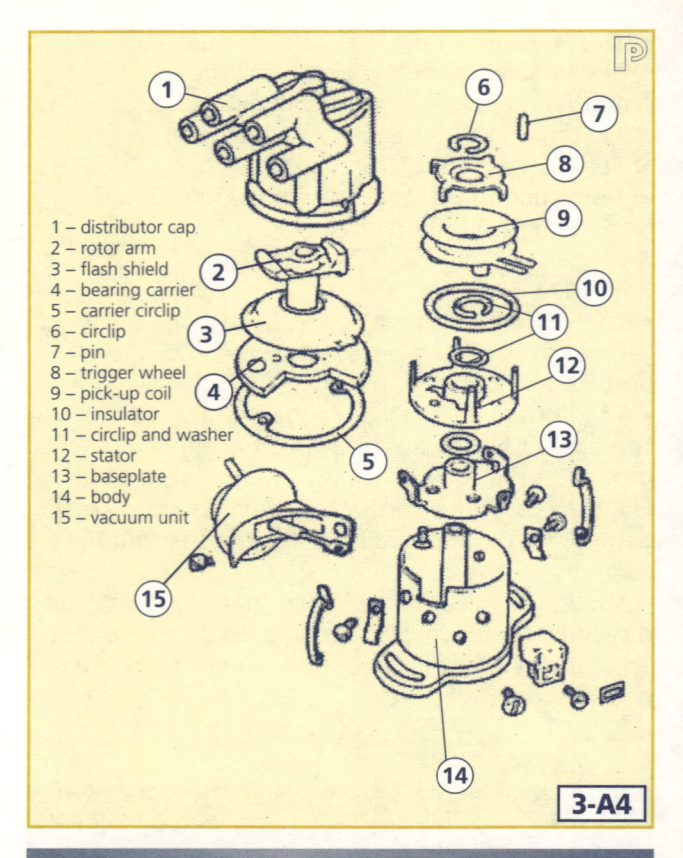

1 – distributor cap
2 – rotor arm
3 – flash shield
4 – bearing carrier
5 – carrier circlip
6 – circlip
7 – pin
8 – trigger wheel
9 – pick-up coil
10 – insulator
11 – circlip and washer
12 – stator
13 – baseplate
14 – body
15 – vacuum unit

3-A4

1 – distributor cap
2 – carbon brush
3 – rotor arm
4 – wiring connector
5 – flash shield
6 – upper body
7 – vacuum unit
8 – coil
9 – plastic ring
10 – circlip
11 – trigger vane
12 – lower body
13 – driving dog

3-A3

❏ **STEP A3:** This is a Ducellier distributor...

❏ **STEP A4:** ...and this is a Bosch distributor.

❏ **STEP A5:** Before checking the ignition timing:
➔ The engine must be at its normal operating temperature.
➔ The idle speed adjustment must be correct - see **Jobs 7** and **9**.

Section B: Timing marks – locating.

❏ **STEP B1:** An aperture (arrowed) at the top of the flywheel housing allows the TDC notches on the flywheel to be viewed after removal of the plastic cover or plug.

3-B1

❏ **STEP B2:** Turn the engine slowly using a spanner on the crankshaft pulley securing bolt until the timing mark appears.

❏ **STEP B3:** This shows the position on XV, XW, XY engines.

3-B3

❐ **STEP B4:** This is the set-up on XU engines...

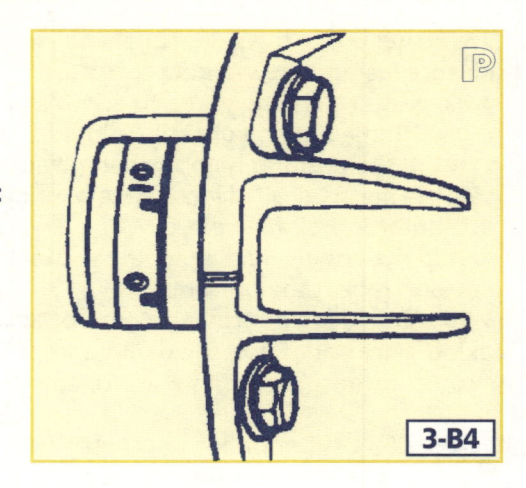

3-B4

❐ **STEP B5:** ...and this on TU engines.

3-B5

FACT FILE
TOP-DEAD-CENTRE MARKS IN TRANSMISSION OPENING

• There are two marks on diametrically opposite sides of the flywheel, one indicating TDC on cylinders 1 and 4, the other on cylinders 2 and 3.
• Most models have a TDC sensor, but this need not be adjusted when setting the timing.
• In some cases the air cleaner inlet duct will have to be removed to allow access to the timing aperture.

3-B6

❐ **STEP B6:** The TDC sensor of any engine needs not be adjusted when setting the timing but the electrical leads must be in good condition and the sensor path clear of dirt, grease or obstructions.

Section C: Timing - checking and adjusting.

FACT FILE
ENGINES WITH ELECTRONIC IGNITION

• Connecting a tachometer (rev counter) to some engines with electronic ignition can damage the ignition system. Check with the equipment instructions that the tachometer you will be using will be suitable for your engine.
• Never use a test bulb instead of a stroboscopic timing light. It might damage the ignition system.
• The ignition timing cannot be checked on models with static distributorless ignition other than by ECU diagnostic equipment.

❐ **STEP C1:** With the engine at operating temperature, connect a stroboscopic lamp with integral rev counter, in accordance with the manufacturer's instructions.

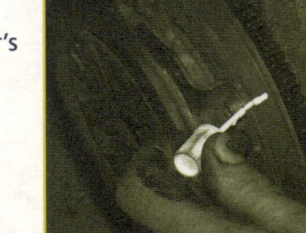

3-C1

❐ **STEP C2:** Painting a white line on the flywheel timing mark helps it show up better under the strobe light.

3-C2

→ Timing checks are made with the rubber vacuum pipe disconnected at the distributor end.
→ Plug the pipe with a suitable instrument, such as a small Phillips-type screwdriver.

❐ **STEP C3:** Start the engine and run it at the specified speed - see page 9-9 **Fact File: Engines with Knock Sensors.**

❐ **STEP C4:** Point the flashing beam of light at the timing marks and ensure that the relevant marks line

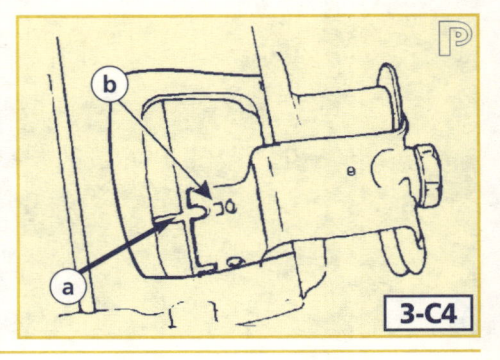

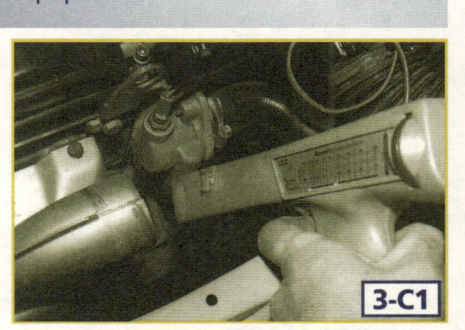

3-C4

CHAPTER 9 Part A Job 3

9-11

up on the flywheel or crankshaft pulley.
→ The strobe effect of the flashing light 'freezes' the moving mark (a) on the flywheel or pulley. If the timing is set correctly the mark should appear stationary adjacent to the static mark on the timing plate (b). The timing marks of XV series engines are shown here.

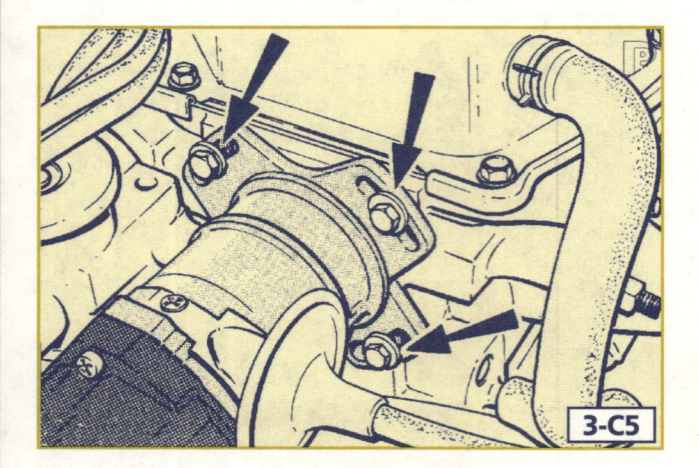

3-C5

☐ **STEP C5:** If the reading is 'out' stop the engine and slacken the clamp bolts (arrowed) on the distributor so that the distributor can just be turned with firm hand pressure. A typical distributor clamp nut is shown here for the TU engine.
→ Turn the distributor a very small amount, restart the engine and check again.
→ Repeat the procedure until, with the engine running, the relevant timing marks line up.

☐ **STEP C6:** Retighten the bolts (arrowed) securing the distributor to the engine block.
→ The stroboscopic timing light is usually triggered from the No 1 spark plug lead, in which case only one of the flywheel timing marks will be visible, and should be lined up with the BTDC mark on the timing plate.

TOP TIP!

☐ **STEP C7:** If the timing light is triggered from the main HT lead to the coil, any discrepancy between the firing of cylinders 1 and 4 and cylinder 2 and 3 will be revealed by a slight spacing between the two timing marks. If this occurs the timing should be adjusted so the two marks straddle the BTDC indication.
→ In this case, instead of a single timing mark (a) lined up with the timing mark on the plate (b), if using No. 1 plug lead there will be two timing marks visible.

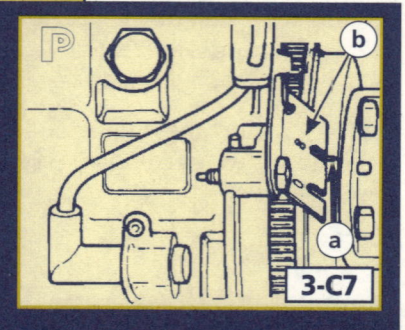

3-C7

☐ **STEP C8:** Check the centrifugal and vacuum advance systems are working correctly.
→ Increase the engine speed to approximately 2,000 rpm, with the timing light still pointed at the timing marks. If the position is no further advanced than it was, the mechanical advance system inside the distributor is probably seized.
→ Stop the engine, reconnect the vacuum advance pipe and repeat the procedure.
→ You should see a further amount of advance taking place and if not, the diaphragm inside the vacuum advance mechanism is probably punctured.

☐ **STEP C9:** If either or both of these faults have occurred, the engine will run uneconomically and inefficiently and it will pay you to fit a new or exchange distributor.

JOB 4: IGNITION COIL - replacement.

☐ **STEP 1:** Locate the ignition coil; the type and location varies from model to model and with the age of the car.

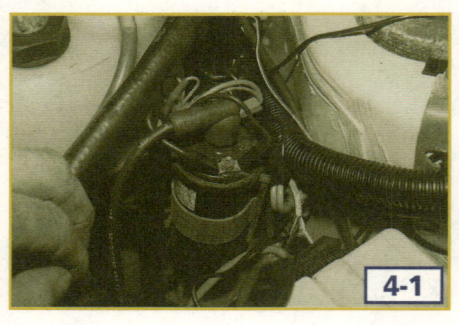

4-1

→ On XV/XW/XY engines the coil and ignition module are mounted in the engine bay by the left hand suspension turret.

☐ **STEP 2:** On TU and XU engines it is usually on the cylinder head near the distributor.
→ On some models it may be necessary to remove the hot-air intake hose to allow access.

4-2

☐ **STEP 3:** Make sure the ignition is switched off.
→ **XV/XW/XY engines:** Disconnect the wiring harness from the module.
→ **OTHER CARBURETOR MODELS:** Remove the capacitor wiring connector, the HT lead and the TDC sensor connector, and finally the multi-plug wiring connector.
→ **ENGINES WITH A DISTRIBUTORLESS SYSTEM:** There is only one multi-plug connector.

❑ **STEP 4:** Undo the mountings and remove the coil (XU/TU coil installation shown).

❑ **STEP 5:** Mount the new coil, remake all connections correctly and firmly.

4-4

JOB 5:	DISTRIBUTOR – *removal, refitting*.

FACT FILE
Breakerless electronic distributors are usually very reliable. Ignition faults are more likely to be caused by bad connections or short circuits through dirt or where insulation has split or cracked, so check the wiring carefully before assuming a distributor fault.

❑ **STEP 1:** If necessary remove the air cleaner and inlet ducting and HT coil to allow access to the distributor.

❑ **STEP 2:** Take off the waterproof cover and remove the distributor cap, which on earlier models is held in place by two clips, on later models by two screws.

❑ **STEP 3:** Disconnect the wiring multi-plug, which is held in place by a retaining clip.

❑ **STEP 4:** Remove the vacuum hose from the vacuum advance unit.

❑ **STEP 5:** Mark the position (illustration **5-6**, arrowed) of the distributor body in relation to its mounting on the cylinder head or thermostat housing.

❑ **STEP 6:** Undo the two mounting nuts and withdraw the distributor.

5-6

❑ **STEP 7:** Check the condition of the distributor cap.
→ Cracks or carbon deposits could indicate tracking and the cap should be replaced.
→ Contacts should be clean and the sprung carbon contact should move easily.

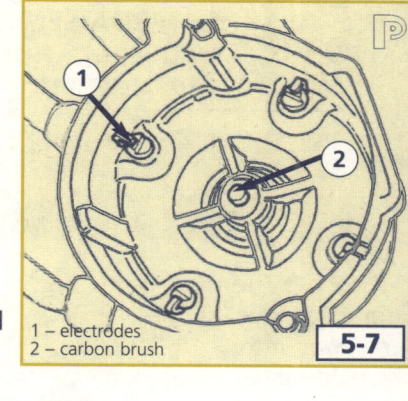

1 – electrodes
2 – carbon brush

5-7

❑ **STEP 8:** Check and if necessary replace the O-ring seal at the back of the distributor, and the distributor cap seal (if fitted).

❑ **STEP 9:** Refit the distributor, aligning the shaft to fit the offset slots (arrowed) in the end of the camshaft.

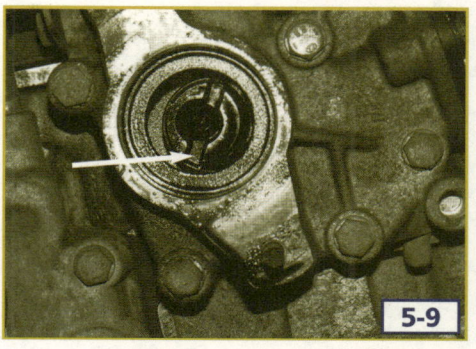

5-9

Also align the marks on the distributor body and the cylinder head.

TOP TIP!
• If fitting a new distributor you can approximately replicate the alignment mark you made before removing the old one.
• Put a length of masking tape around the body of the old distributor and mark the position of a definable point, such as a casting mark or the TDC alignment indicator.
• Then mark the position of your original alignment mark on the tape.
• Peel the tape off and stick it in the same position on the new distributor.
• Transfer the alignment mark on the tape to the distributor casting.

❑ **STEP 10:** Refit the securing nuts and tighten them. Refit the vacuum hose and wiring connections.

JOB 6: LAMBDA SENSOR (engines with cat.) - *testing, replacement*.

Section A: Removing, replacing.

☐ **STEP A1:** The Lambda sensor (a) is screwed into the exhaust manifold or into the top of the exhaust pipe immediately below the manifold sensor.
→ Trace the wiring back from the sensor to the connector on the transmission case and disconnect the plug (b).

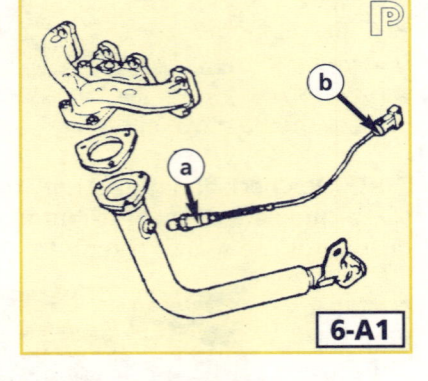

☐ **STEP A2:** Unscrew the sensor and remove it – carefully – taking care not to lose the sealing washer.

FACT FILE
LAMBDA SENSOR CARE
• The Lambda sensor is very fragile and should not be knocked or dropped.
• No cleaners should be used on the sensor.

☐ **STEP A3:** Before refitting, check that the sensor sealing ring is in good condition, and lubricate the thread of the sensor with a high-temperature anti-seize compound.

Section B: Testing.

SAFETY FIRST!
• Beware of hot exhaust components, which can burn badly - wear suitable industrial gloves.
• Work only with the vehicle passing its exhaust gases directly to outdoors, never in an enclosed space.

☐ **STEP B1:** You will need a Lambda sensor tester, such as this Sykes-Pickavant unit that is simply connected up to the sensor wiring as described in the tester manual.

☐ **STEP B2:** Prepare for the test as follows:
→ Run engine to normal full running temperature (fan turns on and off twice).
→ If engine already hot, run for 30 seconds at 3,000 rpm to heat Lambda sensor and ensure exhaust gas at correct temperature.
→ Allow engine to slow to normal tick-over. If testing is prolonged, run engine up to 3,000 rpm for 30 seconds at intervals.

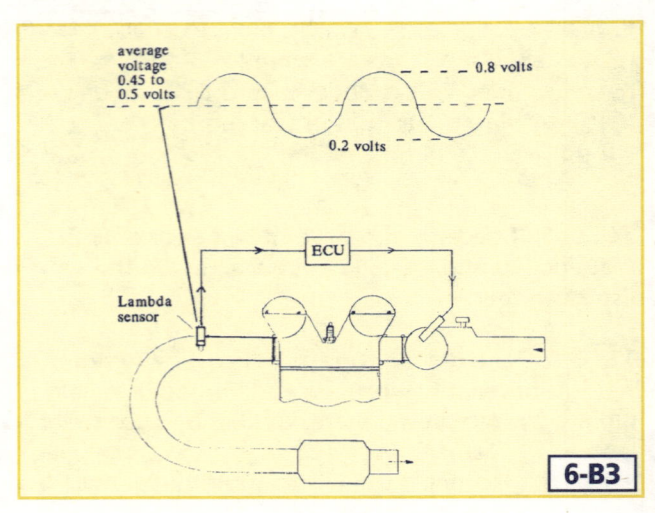

☐ **STEP B3:** Check the voltage at the sensor. The average should be about 0.45 to 0.5 volts but it's okay if it fluctuates between 0.2 and 0.8 volts. (Illustration, courtesy Sykes-Pickavant.)

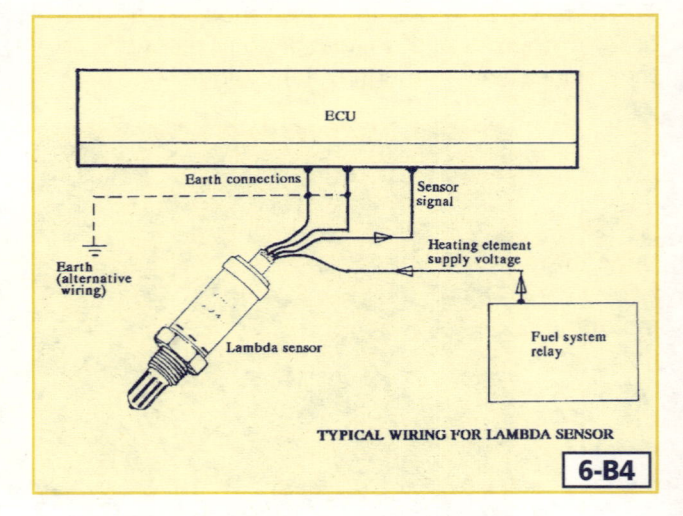

TYPICAL WIRING FOR LAMBDA SENSOR

☐ **STEP B4:** If readings are outside these limits:
→ If the reading is consistently too high (mixture too

strong), snap the throttle open several times and see if the level readjusts itself to within the acceptable range.
→ If the reading is too low (mixture too weak), weaken the mixture - try running without air cleaner - and see if the level readjusts itself to within the acceptable range.
→ If not, the Lambda sensor is probably faulty. (Illustration, courtesy Sykes-Pickavant.)

☐ **STEP B5:** Some Lambda sensors also have a heating element. Typically, the supply is from the fuel system relay - check wiring diagrams - and the earth/ground will be via a separate cable, either to the ECU, or direct to an earth/ground point. To check the heating element, disconnect the plug and check the resistance across the heating element wires. A typical resistance is 5 to 10 ohms. A faulty element usually gives very high resistance (short circuit) or very low resistance (open circuit).

JOB 7: CARBURETOR - adjustment.

All modern Peugeot cars use fuel injection, but many early 106, 205 and 306 variants covered by this manual have a carburetor. Most were single or twin-choke Solex types, but some variants used Weber alternatives. The main types used were:

> Section A: Solex 32 PBISA - 954 and 1124cc engines.
> Section B: Solex 34 PBISA and 35 PBISA - 1360cc engines.
> Section C: Solex 32-34 Z2 and CISAC - 1360cc engines.
> Section D: Weber 35 IBSH - 1360cc engines.
> Section E: Weber 36 TLC - 1580cc engines with automatic transmission.

FACT FILE
TAMPER PROOFING

• Many carburetors originally had a tamper-proof seal placed over the mixture adjustment screw.
• These seals are to prevent anyone unauthorised from altering the mixture and affecting exhaust emissions.
• In certain countries these seals must be retained by law.
• If the seal is a plastic cap placed over the adjuster screw, it can be broken off with pliers.
• If it is a plug within the screw recess, force it out with a sharp object.

USA MODELS AND THOSE IN SOME OTHER STATES
• It may be illegal for an unauthorised person to remove tamperproof plugs on carburetors or fuel injection systems

GENERAL

Setting the idle speed and mixture is not just a matter of making the car run smoothly and economically; it's also a question of allowing it to run within the legal hydrocarbon (HC), Nitrous Oxide (NO) and carbon monoxide (CO) emission limits for the territory in which you live. However, a worn engine will fail even if the carburetor or injection system is set up correctly.

FACT FILE
ESSENTIAL PREPARATIONS

• When tuning the engine you should adjust the carburetor (when fitted) last of all, as its settings will be affected by the state of tune of the rest of the engine.
• Ignition dwell angle and timing must be correct, the air filter should be clean, there should be no air leaks on the induction system, and all electrical consumers and the air conditioning (if fitted) should be switched off (unless stated otherwise in the instructions given below.)
• Run the engine up to full operating temperature before checking and adjusting.
• If you warm the engine on tick-over (instead of on a journey), it won't be hot enough until you have heard the electric cooling fan cut in at least twice.
• Make sure there are no holes or leaks in the exhaust system.

SAFETY FIRST!

• The exhaust gases contain toxic compounds. Run the engine only out of doors.
• Beware of hot exhaust components, which can burn badly – wear suitable industrial gloves.
• Watch out for the rotating cooling fan. Do not wear loose clothing or jewellery, and tie back long hair.
• Apply a strict No Smoking! rule whenever you are servicing your fuel system. Remember that the vapour is most dangerous of all!

IDLE SPEED ADJUSTMENT

Connect a rev-counter according to the maker's instructions, and check the idle speed. Turning the screw clockwise increases the idle speed, anti-clockwise reduces it. Set the idle speed in accordance with **Chapter 1, Facts and Figures** or the figures given in the following sequences.

ROUGH GUIDE: Turn the screw until the engine is running at the slowest speed at which it runs smoothly and evenly.

CO ADJUSTMENT

Check that the idle speed is correct and make sure that the engine is at full operating temperature. Connect an exhaust gas analyser as instructed by the maker. If the CO reading is outside the range shown in the following sequence, or the legal limits for your territory, adjustment is required.

Use a narrow-blade screwdriver and turn the adjuster screw clockwise to weaken (reduce) or anti-clockwise to enrich (increase) the reading.

ROUGH GUIDE: As you turn the mixture screw inwards (clockwise), the tick-over speed will increase, until the point comes where the engine starts to run 'lumpily'. Back off the screw until the engine runs smoothly again, and then some more until the speed just starts to drop. At this point, screw the adjuster back in by a quarter-turn and you'll be somewhere near the optimum setting for smooth running.

IMPORTANT NOTE: After setting the mixture adjustment, re-check and, if necessary, re-adjust the idle speed.

Section A: Solex 32 and 34 PBISA.

☐ **STEP A1:** To achieve correct settings the air filter must be fitted and the engine at operating temperature.

☐ **STEP A2:** Adjust the throttle stop screw until the idle speed is 650rpm.

☐ **STEP A3:** Turn the mixture screw until you get the highest idling speed.

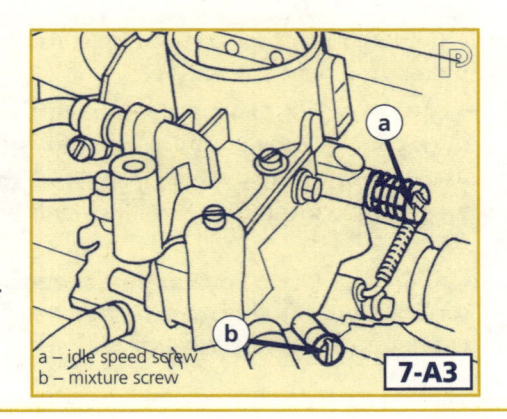

a – idle speed screw
b – mixture screw

7-A3

☐ **STEP A4:** Repeat these adjustments until idle speed settles at 650rpm.

☐ **STEP A5:** Turn the mixture screw slightly clockwise until idle speed reduces or until the gas analyser shows that the CO reading is correct.

Section B: Solex 35 PBISA/Weber 35 IBSH.

☐ **STEP B1:** To achieve correct settings the air filter must be removed and the engine at operating temperature. There are two carburetors.

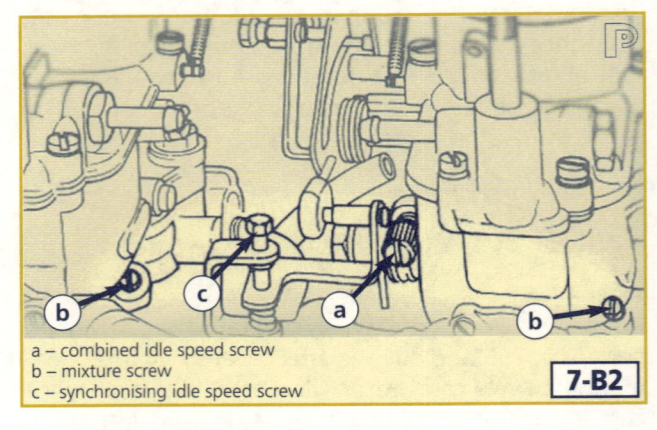

a – combined idle speed screw
b – mixture screw
c – synchronising idle speed screw

7-B2

☐ **STEP B2:** The carburetors must be synchronised using the combined idle speed screw (master carburetor side) and the synchronising idle screw (slave carburetor side.)

☐ **STEP B3:** Screw the mixture screws fully in, then unscrew them both by four complete turns.

☐ **STEP B4:** Using the combined idle screw set the idle speed to 1000rpm.

☐ **STEP B5:** Remove the vacuum pipes from the carburetors and attach a vacuum gauge to the master carburetor. Adjust the combined idle speed screw until the gauge shows 150mbar.

☐ **STEP B6:** Attach the vacuum gauge to the slave carburetor and if necessary adjust the synchronising idle screw to give the same vacuum reading.

☐ **STEP B7:** To adjust the mixture use the combined idle screw to set the idle speed to 950rpm.

☐ **STEP B8:** Adjust the mixture screws on the two carburetors by equal amounts until the correct CO level is achieved.

☐ **STEP B9:** Adjust the idle speed to the correct level using the combined idle screw.

Section C: Solex 32-34 Z2 and CISAC.

❏ **STEP C1:** The air filter must be correctly positioned and the engine at normal operating temperature.

❏ **STEP C2:** Adjust the idle speed to 750 rpm.

❏ **STEP C3:** The mixture adjustment screw can then be turned to give the correct CO level.

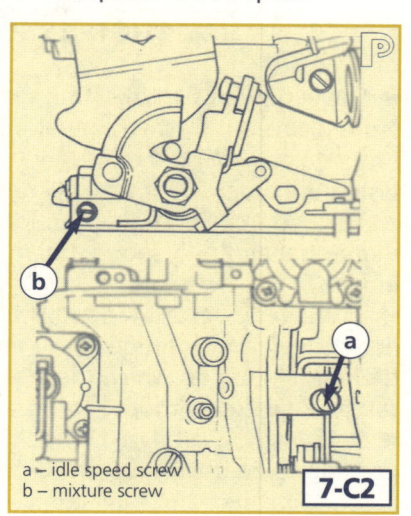

a – idle speed screw
b – mixture screw

7-C2

❏ **STEP C4:** If necessary readjust the idle speed.

Section D: Weber 32 IBSH.

❏ **STEP D1:** To achieve correct settings the air filter must be fitted and the engine at operating temperature.

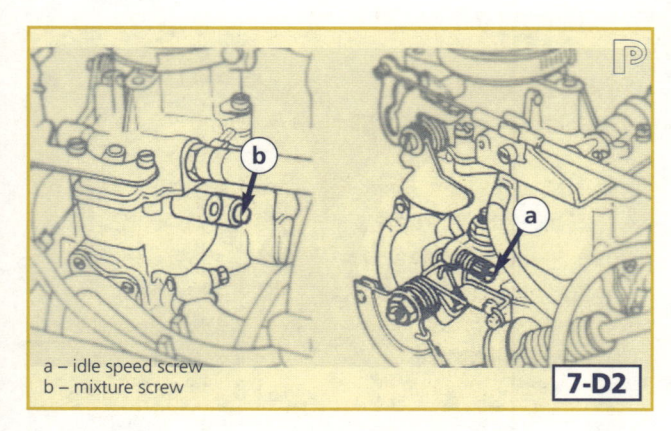

a – idle speed screw
b – mixture screw

7-D2

❏ **STEP D2:** Adjust the throttle stop screw until the idle speed is 650 rpm.

❏ **STEP D3:** Turn the mixture screw to get the highest idling speed.

❏ **STEP D4:** Repeat these adjustments until idle speed settles at 650 rpm.

❏ **STEP D5:** Turn the mixture screw slightly clockwise until idle speed reduces or until the gas analyser shows that the CO reading is correct.

Section E: Weber 36 TLC.

❏ **STEP E1:** The air filter must be correctly positioned and the engine at normal operating temperature.

❏ **STEP E2:** The automatic transmission should be set to Park.

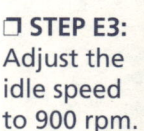

❏ **STEP E3:** Adjust the idle speed to 900 rpm.

1 - idle speed screw
2 – mixture screw

7-E3

❏ **STEP E4:** The mixture adjustment screw can then be turned to give the correct CO level.

❏ **STEP E5:** Readjust the idle speed and if necessary repeat the procedure until the CO level is correct at 900rpm.

| JOB 8: | CARBURETOR - *removal, replacement.* |

❏ **STEP 1:** Disconnect the battery negative (-) terminal See **Chapter 10, Electrical, Dash, Instruments, Fact File: Disconnecting the Battery** BEFORE doing so, and remove the air cleaner (XV engine in 205 shown)…

❏ **STEP 2:** …or air cleaner-to-carburetor duct (TU engine shown in 106).

8-2

CHAPTER 9 Part A Job 9

TOP TIP!

- Check for any vacuum or breather hoses fitted in 'odd' places, such as the underside of the air filter housing.

☐ **STEP 3:** If a plastic cover is fitted this should be removed after levering out the retaining clip.

☐ **STEP 4:** Disconnect any vacuum hoses and solenoid valve or heater element wiring attached to the carburetor.

☐ **STEP 5:** Disconnect any coolant hoses from the carburetor body, and plug them.

☐ **STEP 6:** Disconnect the throttle and choke controls. This is a typical installation on the XV/XW/XY series engine in the 205.

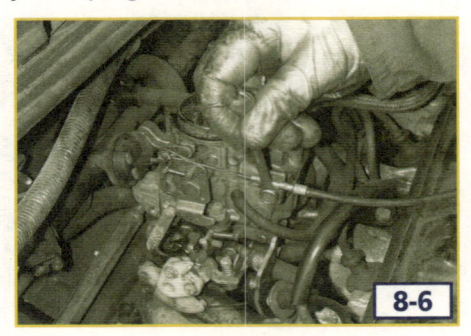

8-6

→ The throttle cable end nipple can be freed from its recess once the cable outer has been slackened by removal of its retaining spring clip.
→ The choke cable is usually fastened to the choke lever by a screw in a cable clamp.

☐ **STEP 7:** Disconnect the fuel lines from the carburetor and plug the ends.
→ If the fuel hose is secured by the original factory-fitted crimped clip, cut it off and replace it with a normal worm-drive type clip.

TOP TIP!

- Ensure that, when two fuel lines are fitted, fuel delivery and return lines are identified for refitting in their correct positions.

☐ **STEP 8:** Unscrew the carburetor mounting nuts (there will be two or four of them – arrowed in illustration) and remove the unit from the intake manifold.

8-8

☐ **STEP 9:** Clean the carburetor and manifold mating flanges, fit a new carburetor base gasket and refit/reconnect in the reverse order.

JOB 9: FUEL INJECTION SYSTEMS - *adjustment*.

INJECTION SYSTEMS

→ The variety of fuel injection systems used on the models covered by this manual follows a logical progression, with the relatively simple Bosch Jetronic system on older 205 models, single-point systems on earlier and smaller engines, to multipoint with semi-sequential and fully sequential injection on later models.
→ In the early Bosch Monopoint A2.2 system the ECU does not control ignition as well as injection. This is the only system on which the idle speed and mixture can be adjusted without reprogramming the ECU.
→ On early non-catalyst 1360cc 106 models it is possible to adjust the CO emissions directly on the Bosch Motronic MP3.1 injection system. On all other versions it is not possible to adjust the idle speed or mixture. (See **Job 2: Diagnostics**).
→ Fuel injection faults, particularly on any 206 or fuel-injected 106 or 306 models, could be caused by poor electrical connections, clogged air filter or worn-out spark plugs. Check also that breather hoses are not clogged. For more detailed diagnosis the ECU should be interrogated via the diagnostic port provided in most later models.

SYSTEM APPLICATIONS

Bosch LE2-Jetronic	1580 & 1905cc engines.
Bosch Monopoint MA3.0/3.1	954, 1124 & 1360cc engines.
Bosch Monopoint A2.2	1124cc & 1360cc engines.
Bosch Motronic MP7.2/7.3	1360 & 1587cc engines.
Bosch Monopoint MA3.0/3.1	1124 & 1360cc engines.
Bosch Motronic MP5.1/5.2	1587 & 1998cc engines.
Magneti Marelli G6	1124 & 1360cc engines.
Magneti Marelli 1 AP	1124 & 1360cc engines.
Magneti Marelli 8P	1761 & 1998cc engines.

FACT FILE
LEGAL RESTRICTIONS

- It may be illegal in some territories for an unauthorised person to remove tamperproof plugs on carburetors or fuel injection systems.

SAFETY FIRST!

- Never work on the fuel system unless the engine is completely cool.
- Some fuel injection systems inject fuel at extremely high pressure.
- Pressure must be released in a controlled fashion to avoid any risk of a pressurised spray of fuel being produced.
- Residual pressure can remain in the fuel system for some considerable time, even if the engine has been switched off.
- IMPORTANT NOTE: Removing pressure from the fuel lines, as described below, will not necessarily remove pressure from each of the components - they may still be pressurised.
- Before working on any part of the system it is necessary to relieve the pressure, as follows:

1. Disconnect the battery negative terminal. See *Chapter 10, Electrical, Dash, Instruments, Fact File: Disconnecting the Battery* BEFORE doing so!
2. Work out of doors and away from any sources of flame or ignition. Wear rubber or plastic gloves and goggles. Have a large rag ready.
3. Place a container beneath the filter to catch the fuel that is likely to be spilt.
4. Place your spanner on the first connection to be undone. Before undoing it, wrap the rag, folded to give several thicknesses, over the joint.
5. Undo the connection very slowly and carefully, allowing the pressure within the pipework to be let out without causing a dangerous jet of fuel.
6. Release the pressure from each of the pipes in the same way.
7. Mop up all traces of fuel and allow to dry thoroughly before reconnecting the battery, starting the car or taking it back indoors.

- Do NOT touch ignition wires while engine is running or being turned on the starter.
- Switch the ignition OFF before disconnecting any components or wires.
- If the engine is to be turned on the starter without starting, disconnect the centre HT lead from the distributor and fix it securely to a good earth/ground connection on the car.

IMPORTANT NOTES:
- Never attempt to adjust any fuel injection system without appropriate CO content measuring equipment.
- NEVER try turning adjustment screws at random: the chances of making things better are remote; the chances of making things much worse are very high!
- In every case, you will need to use a small screwdriver to lever off the anti-tamper cap from the CO adjuster screw, if adjustments need to be carried out. Replace with a new cap when you have finished making adjustments.
- If you use a starting booster, use it at a maximum of 16.5 volts, for no more than 60 seconds.

TYPE A: BOSCH LE2-JETRONIC.

FACT FILE
PEUGEOT RECOMMENDED SETTINGS

- Idle speed: 850 to 900 rpm.
- CO% at idle: 1 to 2.
- CO2% at idle: 10.

☐ **STEP A1:** This, for reference, is the layout of a typical Bosch LE2-Jetronic equipped engine bay.

ADJUSTING IDLE AND CO SETTINGS

☐ **STEP A2:** You will need a suitable exhaust gas analyser to measure the CO level.

☐ **STEP A3:** The engine should be at normal operating temperature with the ignition timing correctly adjusted.

☐ **STEP A4:** Check that the throttle position is correct.

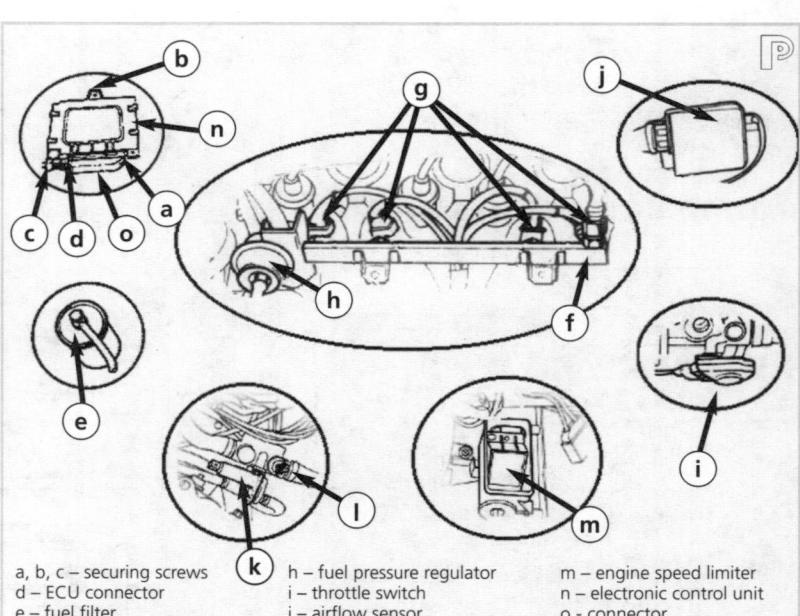

a, b, c – securing screws
d – ECU connector
e – fuel filter
f – distribution pipe
g - injectors
h – fuel pressure regulator
i – throttle switch
j – airflow sensor
k – supplementary air device
l – temperature cover
m – engine speed limiter
n – electronic control unit
o - connector

9-A1

➜ The throttle stop and air volume adjustment screws are located in the front of the engine bay on the inlet tubing between the airflow sensor and the inlet manifold.

☐ **STEP A5:** Turn the air volume adjuster until the engine idles at 850-900rpm.
➜ The CO reading should be between 1 and 2 per cent and the CO_2 reading over 10 per cent.

☐ **STEP A6:** The mixture can be adjusted if necessary by turning the mixture screw on the airflow sensor, after removing the tamperproof cover.
➜ Adjustment is by means of an Allen key – turning it clockwise enriches the mixture, while anti-clockwise weakens it.

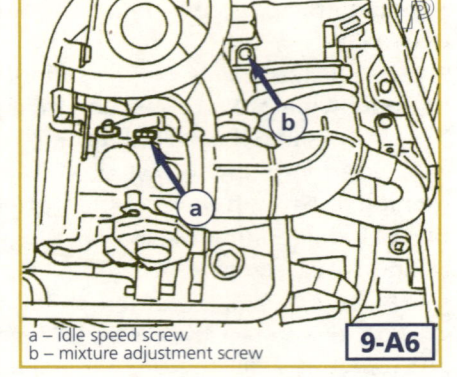

a – idle speed screw
b – mixture adjustment screw

9-A6

TYPE B: BOSCH MONOPOINT/MAGNETI MARELLI G6.

FACT FILE

PEUGEOT RECOMMENDED SETTINGS

- Idle speed: 850 rpm (±50rpm).
- CO% at idle: Below 1%.

It is not possible to adjust the idle speed or mixture other than by accessing the ECU via the diagnostic port see *Job 2: Diagnostics*.

TYPE C: BOSCH MOTRONIC/MAGNETI MARELLI 1AP/8P.

FACT FILE

PEUGEOT RECOMMENDED SETTINGS

- Idle speed: 106: 900 rpm (±50rpm).
              306: 850 rpm (±50rpm).
- CO% at idle: 1360cc (K6B engines): 1-2%
               Others: Below 1%

IMPORTANT NOTE: Only on early 1360cc 106 models not fitted with catalytic converter is it possible to adjust the CO emissions directly.

ADJUSTING CO SETTINGS

☐ **STEP C1:** The engine should be at normal operating temperature with the ignition timing correctly adjusted.

☐ **STEP C2:** Attach an exhaust gas analyser to measure the CO level.

☐ **STEP C3:** Mixture is controlled by a potentiometer sited under the ECU mounting bracket. Adjust the screw until the CO reading is correct.

1 – control unit
2 – inlet manifold pressure sensor
3 – throttle potentiometer
4 – oxygen sensor (KFZ engine)
5 – catalytic converter (KFZ engine)
6 – injection-ignition test warning lamp
7 – injection-ignition test connector
8 – tank
9 – fuel pump
10 – filter
11 – mixture regulation potentiometer (K6B engine)
12 – distribution pipe
13 – pressure regulator
14 – injector
15 – inlet air thermistor
16 – coolant thermistor
17 – engine speed sensor
18 – ignition coil
19 – spark plug
20 – injection multi-function double relay
21 – ignition module
22 – canister*
23 – canister purge solenoid valve*
24 – canister purge cut-off solenoid valve*
25 – idle regulation valve
* according to destination

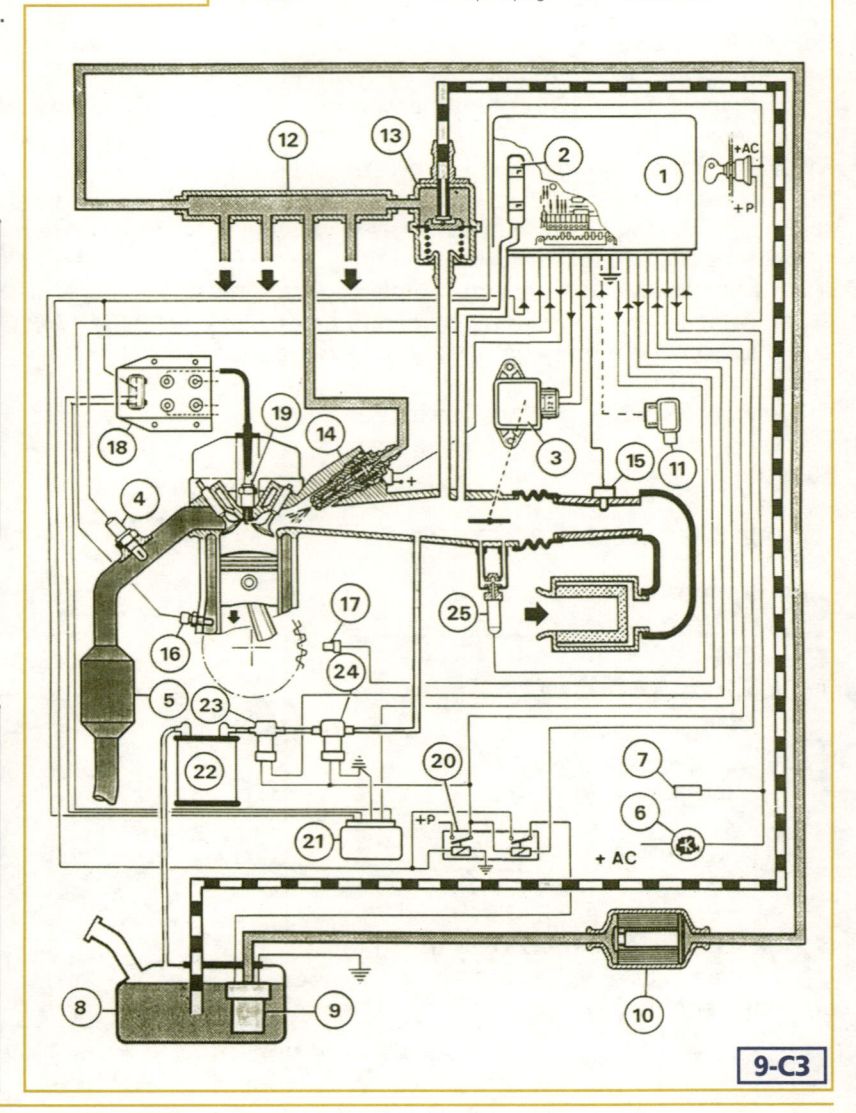

9-C3

JOB 10: FUEL INJECTION UNITS - removal, replacement.

SAFETY FIRST!

• Read and act upon the *Safety First!* notes at the start of *Job 9*.

IMPORTANT NOTES: • There should be no major problem in working on fuel injection systems, provided that you follow the correct *Safety First!* procedures, and use a methodical, informed approach.
• No adjustment or fault diagnosis of the fuel injection system is possible without the correct diagnostic equipment. You may wish to replace components yourself, but we *strongly recommend* that you do not change components at random and without proper diagnosis of faults.
• There are two broad types of fuel injection unit: singlepoint, which injects fuel into the inlet manifold in place of the carburetor, and multipoint, which injects fuel (more efficiently) directly towards each inlet valve.

Section A: Singlepoint injection.

REMOVE/REPLACE THROTTLE BODY

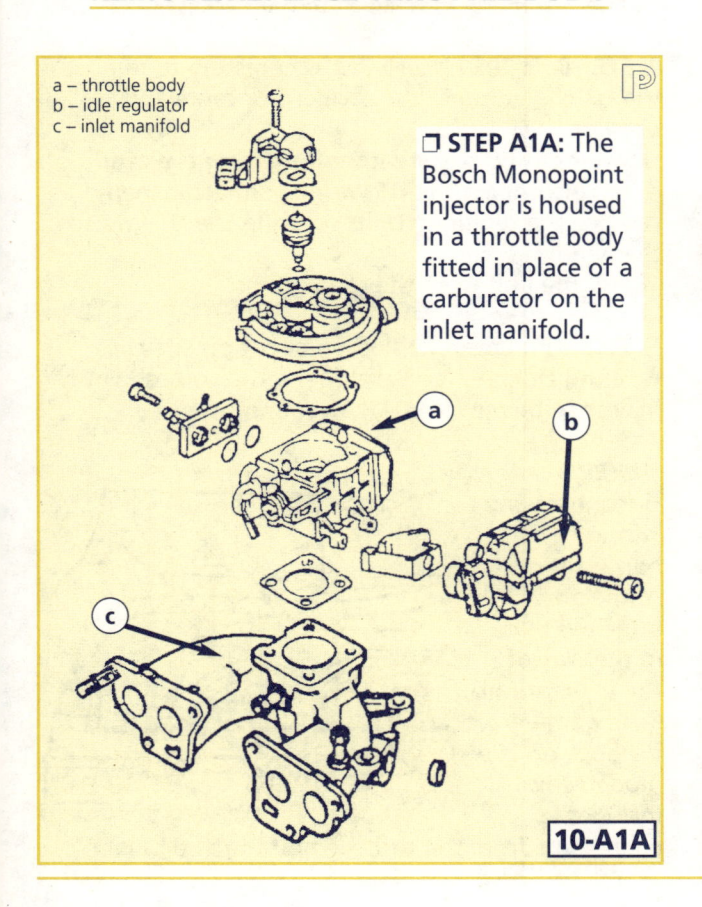

a – throttle body
b – idle regulator
c – inlet manifold

☐ **STEP A1A:** The Bosch Monopoint injector is housed in a throttle body fitted in place of a carburetor on the inlet manifold.

10-A1A

☐ **STEP A1B:** The alternative Magnetti Marelli unit is located in the same position.

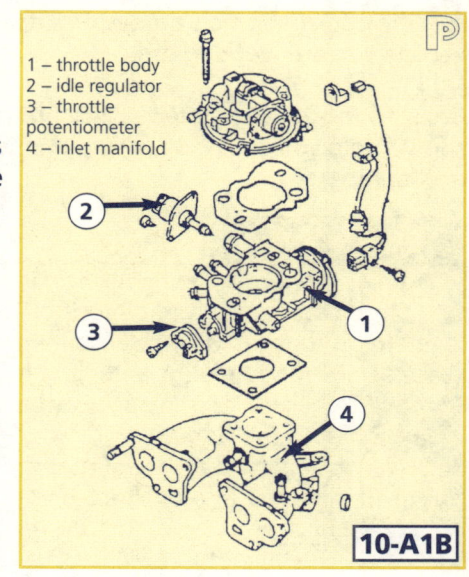

1 – throttle body
2 – idle regulator
3 – throttle potentiometer
4 – inlet manifold

10-A1B

☐ **STEP A2:** Disconnect the battery negative (-) terminal. See *Chapter 10, Electrical, Dash, Instruments, Fact File: Disconnecting the Battery* BEFORE doing so!

☐ **STEP A3:** Remove the air cleaner duct and disconnect all electrical connections from the throttle body, making a written note of their positions.

☐ **STEP A4:** Release the clips and disconnect the fuel supply and return hoses from the throttle body. If retaining clips need to be cut away they may be replaced with normal screw-on clamps.

☐ **STEP A5:** Remove the accelerator cable and, where necessary, any vacuum or air valve hoses, again noting their position for reconnection.

☐ **STEP A6:** Release the Allen-type through-bolts in the top of the injection unit, then lift the unit and its base gasket from the manifold.

☐ **STEP A7:** Refit in the reverse order, making sure mating faces are clean and the base gasket is new.

Section B: Multipoint systems.

☐ **STEP B1:** This illustration shows the typical multipoint injection installation on an XU engine.
➔ Refer also to the illustrations and instructions in *Job 9* for

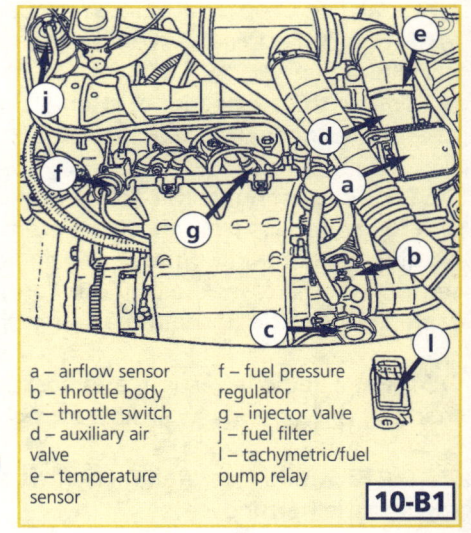

a – airflow sensor
b – throttle body
c – throttle switch
d – auxiliary air valve
e – temperature sensor
f – fuel pressure regulator
g – injector valve
j – fuel filter
l – tachymetric/fuel pump relay

10-B1

CHAPTER 9 Part A Job 10

9-21

specific information on the system fitted to the vehicle you are working on.

Refer to *Job 2: Diagnostics - carry out checks.* This should help you to decide which, if any, components are faulty.

FACT FILE

- There is more complexity to the various multipoint systems. The diagnosis of faults is something that can only be carried out with the necessary test equipment and data. Injectors can be removed, checked and replaced, after first depressurising the system.
- On all systems, it is *essential* that the control unit is only unplugged or reconnected with the ignition turned OFF.

TOP TIP!

- Tag both parts of each connection with a piece of masking tape and write a number on it to identify its location.
- Check all connection plugs for bent or corroded connectors inside the plugs and sockets.
- ALWAYS pull on the connectors themselves NEVER on the cable, when pulling them undone.
- Many electrical connectors have some kind of 'latch' to hold them in place. Disconnect any such latch before attempting to separate connectors.
- Check vacuum pipes and connectors for deterioration, splits and air-tight connections.
- VERY MANY PROBLEMS ARE CAUSED BY POOR ELECTRICAL OR HOSE CONNECTIONS - don't assume straight away that expensive electronic components are at fault!

REMOVE/REPLACE THROTTLE HOUSING

❏ **STEP B2:** Disconnect the battery negative (-) terminal. See *Chapter 10, Electrical, Dash, Instruments, Fact File: Disconnecting the Battery* BEFORE doing so!
➔ Remove the air cleaner duct or entire air cleaner assembly as needed to gain access.

❏ **STEP B3:** Disconnect the accelerator cable and any wiring connectors from throttle potentiometer, air heating element, idle control and air temperature sensor. In some cases the brackets for the accelerator cable and throttle housing may need to be released.

❏ **STEP B4:** Remove vacuum and breather hoses, marking them clearly to ensure correct refitting.

❏ **STEP B5:** Undo the retaining screws and remove the throttle housing.

❏ **STEP B6:** Refit in the reverse order, making sure mating faces are clean, new O-ring or base gasket are fitted and that all vacuum and electrical connections are properly made.

❏ **STEP B7:** Adjust the accelerator cable if necessary.

REMOVE/REPLACE FUEL RAIL AND INJECTORS

The injectors are pressed into place between the fuel rail and the inlet manifold.

TOP TIP!

- Remember that fuel injection systems work under high pressure. When disconnecting any fuel-feed union undo the connectors slowly to prevent any sudden outburst of fuel, keeping a rag handy to soak up any spray or leakage. Petrol – especially in fine spray form – is very flammable, so avoid any possible sources of accidental ignition such as smoking, hot inspection lamps, or carelessly positioned tools that could short-circuit a battery terminal.

❏ **STEP B8:** Disconnect the battery negative (-) terminal. See *Chapter 10, Electrical, Dash, Instruments, Fact File: Disconnecting the Battery* BEFORE doing so!

❏ **STEP B9:** Remove the air cleaner duct or entire air cleaner assembly as needed to gain access.

❏ **STEP B10: 206 ENGINES:** It is necessary to remove the HT coil unit and the accelerator cable and bracket.
➔ After easing the breather hose from the cam cover, disconnect the HT wiring connector then remove the retaining bolts securing the HT unit to the head.
➔ Pull the unit from the spark plugs.

❏ **STEP B11:** Carefully slacken or cut off the clips securing the fuel feed and fuel return hoses, which may then be removed – with caution.

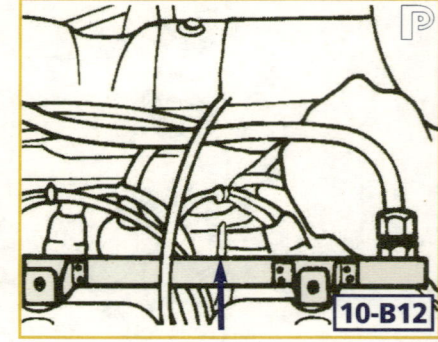

❏ **STEP B12:** Disconnect any wiring harnesses or connectors attached to or in the way of the injector rail (arrowed) – for instance on 206 models this includes connectors from the throttle housing and power steering switch. Connectors to the injectors should also be released, after depressing the retaining tags.

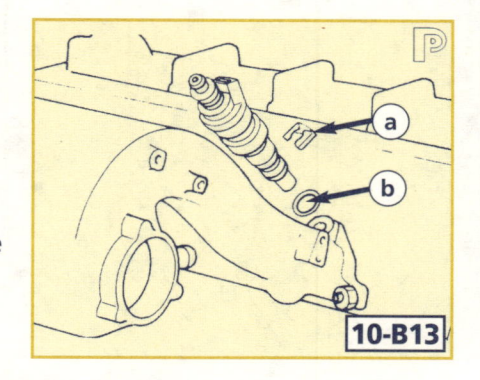

☐ **STEP B13:** Injectors are sandwiched between the inlet manifold and the fuel rail.
→ Injectors are pressed into the manifold and can be removed after extracting the clip (**a**) securing the injectors to the fuel rail.
→ The rubber seals (**b**) must be replaced.

☐ **STEP B14:** Undo the securing bolts and retaining nut or nuts from the fuel rail, which can then be withdrawn with the injectors attached.

☐ **STEP B15:** The injectors are held to the rail by retaining clips that can be extracted to release the injectors.

☐ **STEP B16:** To reinstall the fuel rail reverse the procedure, using new O-rings to seal the injectors against manifold and rail.

JOB 11: ACCELERATOR CABLE – *adjustment, replacement.*

PEDAL REPLACEMENT: See *Part C, Job 4*.

FACT FILE
CABLE CONNECTIONS

• On earlier 205 models the throttle cable is secured at the carburetor end by clamping it in a ferrule.
• Adjustment is simply a matter of repositioning the cable correctly in the ferrule.
• On other carburetor models the cable is adjusted in the same way as on fuel-injected models, by altering the position of the end of the cable sheath in its mounting bracket.

Section A: Early 205 carburetor engines.

☐ **STEP A1:** Disconnect the battery negative (-) terminal. See *Chapter 10, Electrical, Dash, Instruments, Fact File: Disconnecting the Battery* BEFORE doing so!

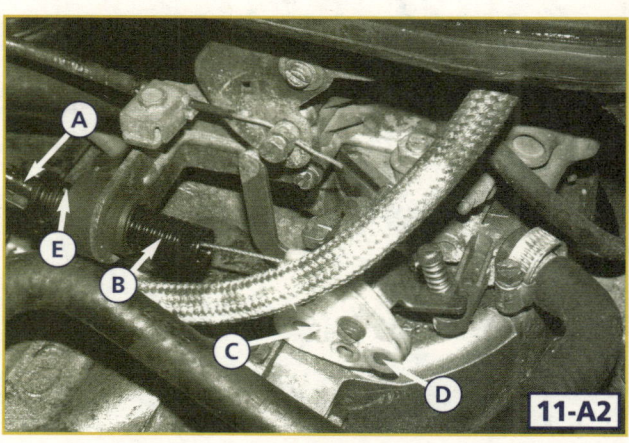

☐ **STEP A2:** The accelerator cable sheath (**A**) terminates in an adjustable ferrule (**B**).
→ The cable's position is set by a spring clip (**E**) in the ferrule.
→ It feeds over the throttle quadrant (**C**) and terminates in a press-fit boss (**D**).
→ Remove the spring clip from the ferrule on the cylinder head bracket.

☐ **STEP A3:** Adjust the cable to allow minimal free play, but ensuring that the throttle can be opened fully when the pedal is depressed.
→ See illustration **11-B3** for a very similar adjustment type.

☐ **STEP A4:** To remove the cable, release the cable from the ferrule at the carburetor end.

☐ **STEP A5:** Slide the other end of the cable from its mounting at the top of the accelerator pedal lever.

☐ **STEP A6:** Free the cable from the support bracket on the air intake cover and pull the cable out through the grommet in the bulkhead.

☐ **STEP A7:** Reverse the procedure to replace the cable.

TOP TIP!
• There are different cable types, so it is advisable to take the old cable as a pattern when buying a replacement to make sure the new one is exactly the same.

Section B: Other engines.

❏ **STEP B1:** Disconnect the battery negative (-) terminal. See *Chapter 10, Electrical, Dash, Instruments, Fact File: Disconnecting the Battery* BEFORE doing so!

❏ **STEP B2:** Some carburetors are protected by a plastic cover which has to be removed to access the cable mechanism.
→ To adjust the cable, remove the spring clip from the cable sheath and pull the cable out of its grommet in the mounting bracket until there is no free play in the inner cable with the throttle cam hard against its stop.

❏ **STEP B3:** Remove the securing clip from the serrated ferrule…

11-B3

❏ **STEP B4:** …and then detach the cable end from the quadrant.

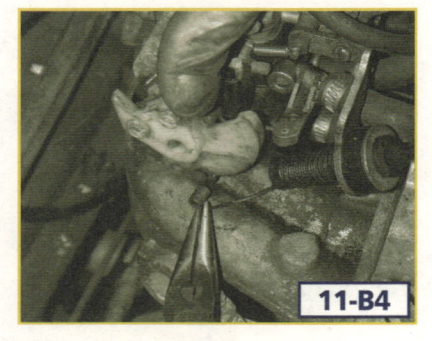

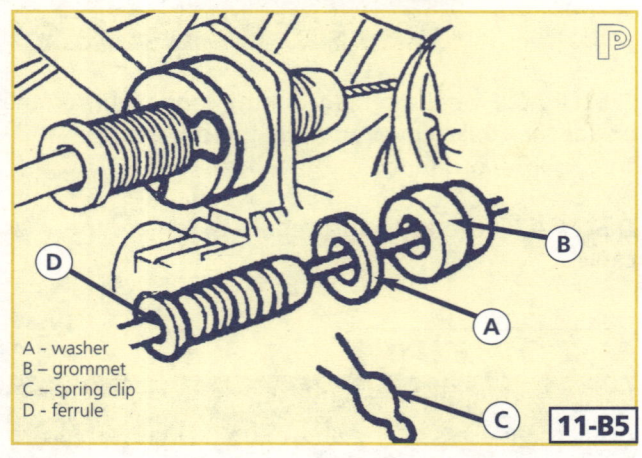

11-B4

A - washer
B - grommet
C - spring clip
D - ferrule

11-B5

❏ **STEP B5:** Press the washer (**A**) hard against the grommet (**B**) and refit the spring clip (**C**) to the groove on the ferrule (**D**) closest to the washer.

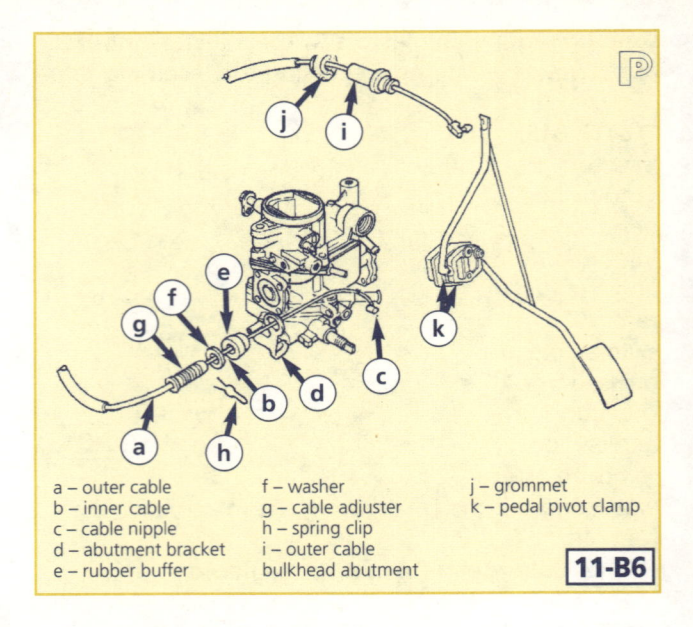

a – outer cable
b – inner cable
c – cable nipple
d – abutment bracket
e – rubber buffer
f – washer
g – cable adjuster
h – spring clip
i – outer cable bulkhead abutment
j – grommet
k – pedal pivot clamp

11-B6

❏ **STEP B6:** Ensure that the throttle cam opens fully when the pedal is depressed.

❏ **STEP B7:** To remove the cable, free the end from the throttle cam, remove the spring clip from the cable sheath and slide off the washer. Release the cable from any securing clips along its length.

❏ **STEP B8:** Release the cable from the top of the accelerator pedal lever.
→ To gain access on some models (106 and 306 in particular) it may be necessary or convenient to remove undercover panels beneath the fascia.

❏ **STEP B9:** Remove the retaining clip (where fitted) from the cable sheath where it terminates against the bulkhead or accelerator pedal bracket.

❏ **STEP B10:** Withdraw the cable from inside the engine compartment.

❏ **STEP B11:** Reverse the procedure to replace the cable.

TOP TIP!

• Attach a length of wire or cord to the cockpit end of the cable before withdrawing it. The cord will then act as a guide to draw the replacement cable back to the bulkhead grommet and mounting point.

AUTOMATIC TRANSMISSION

❏ **STEP B12:** Throttle cables fitted to automatic transmission cars are similar but may include a kick-down actuating cable. See *Chapter 7, Transmission, Clutch* for adjustment details.

JOB 12: CHOKE CABLE – *adjustment, replacement.*

☐ **STEP 1:** Disconnect the battery negative (-) terminal. See *Chapter 10, Electrical, Dash, Instruments, Fact File: Disconnecting the Battery* BEFORE doing so!
→ Remove the air cleaner ducting or entire air cleaner assembly if necessary.

☐ **STEP 2: 205 MODELS:** The cable and its sheath are held in position by a pinch bolt.
→ To adjust the cable, release the pinch bolt (arrowed) holding the cable and reposition the cable so that the choke butterfly is fully open when the choke control is closed.

☐ **STEP 3: OTHER MODELS:** The cable is simply looped on to the actuator and the sheath secured by a clamp holding the terminal rubber collar. Adjustment requires the clamp holding the rubber collar to the sheath to be cut away. Then, with the choke lever on the fascia fully closed and the choke butterfly fully open, adjust the position of the sheath within the rubber collar until there is minimal play in the cable. Using a normal screw-in clamp retighten the rubber collar to the cable sheath.

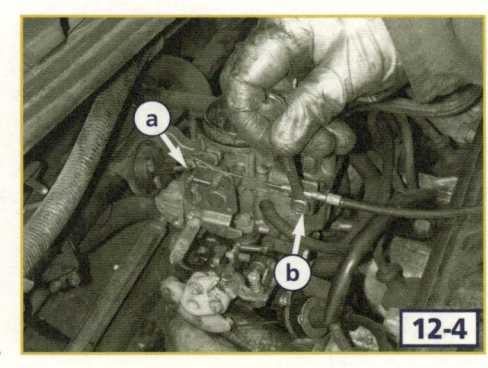

☐ **STEP 4:** To remove the cable on 205 models, slacken the pinch bolts holding the cable (**a**) and its sheath (**b**)...

☐ **STEP 5:** ...and release and withdraw the cable.

☐ **STEP 6:** From inside the vehicle, pull the choke cable out at the dash after disconnecting the warning lamp wiring and releasing the cable from its support bracket.

☐ **STEP 7:** To remove the cable on other models, unhitch the cable from the carburetor linkage and undo the bolt securing the rubber collar to its bracket. Cut away or unscrew the clamp holding the rubber collar to the cable sheath.

☐ **STEP 8:** From inside the vehicle, pull the choke lever out and unclip it from its mounting in the fascia. The cable can then be withdrawn, removing the warning lamp wiring when it appears.

☐ **STEP 9:** Fit the new cable in reverse order.

TOP TIP!
- Attach a length of wire or cord to the underbonnet end of the cable before withdrawing it. The cord will then act as a guide to draw the replacement cable back through the bulkhead.

JOB 13: MECHANICAL FUEL PUMP - *replacement.*

☐ **STEP 1:** Disconnect the battery negative (-) terminal. See *Chapter 10, Electrical, Dash, Instruments, Fact File: Disconnecting the Battery* BEFORE doing so!

☐ **STEP 2:** Locate the fuel pump.
→ On XV/XW/XY engines it is bolted to the top front side of the timing chain case (bolts arrowed).

☐ **STEP 3:** On TU engines, the pump is mounted at the rear of the cylinder head near the ignition distributor (bolts arrowed).

CHAPTER 9 Part A Job 14

☐ STEP 4: BOTH ENGINE TYPES:
Disconnect the two fuel lines, if necessary cutting away the clamps (if of the original crimped type).

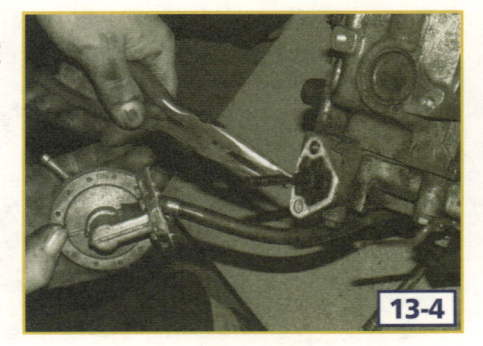

13-4

→ Label the pipes for correct refitting, and plug the ends.
→ Undo the mounting bolts and remove the pump, gasket and insulation block (where fitted).
→ **XV/XW/XY ENGINES:** Take care to extract the pump operating rod - shown held by pliers.
→ **TU ENGINE:** The pump has an integrated operating lever.

☐ **STEP 5:** Clean off any old gasket and refit in reverse order using a new gasket and, where necessary, a new insulation block. Secure the fuel lines using normal screw-in clamps.

TOP TIP!
• Plugging the ends of the fuel lines not only minimises the loss of fuel but prevents the ingress of dirt.
• A wad of rags under the fuel pump will absorb spilt fuel.

JOB 14: ELECTRIC FUEL PUMP - *replacement*.

The electric fuel pump assembly is inside the tank and in some cases is combined with the fuel gauge sender unit.
→ **EARLIER MODELS:** The fuel pump and sender unit are separate units, with the pump installed to the right of the sender unit.
→ **LATER MODELS:** The fuel pump and sender unit are in a single module.

SAFETY FIRST!
• **Depressurise the fuel system before starting work - this is important because fuel can remain under pressure in the system long after the engine has been switched off.**

• **Depressurise the fuel system by unplugging the electrical leads to the fuel pump (or remove the fuse) and run the engine until it stops.**

• **Switch off the ignition and disconnect the battery leads, starting with the negative (-) terminal.**

TOP TIP!
• Before starting work, find a screwdriver or bolt which you can push into the flexible hose from the tank and retighten the clamp.
• This will plug the hose and prevent the tank from draining dangerous and harmful fuel.

☐ STEP 1:
On all models, a plastic cover plate has first to be removed - raise the rear seat base first.
→ Early models will have two

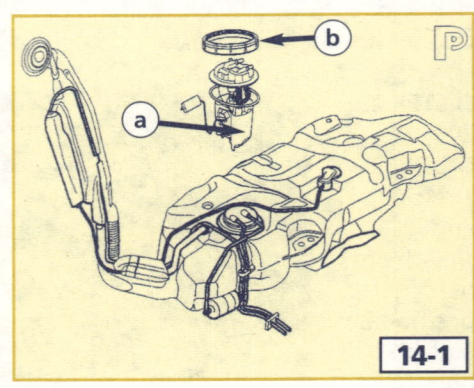

14-1

cover plates, the right-hand one for the fuel pump, the other for the fuel gauge sender unit.
→ During 1996 and 1997 the fuel gauge sender unit was incorporated into the fuel pump housing.

TOP TIP!
• Take care when pulling off the electrical connector!
• The terminals inside the connector are very small and may pull right through if you tug on the cable.

☐ STEP 2:
Pull off the electrical connector (**a**).
→ The original-type pipe connectors, if still fitted, have to be cut off with side-cutters

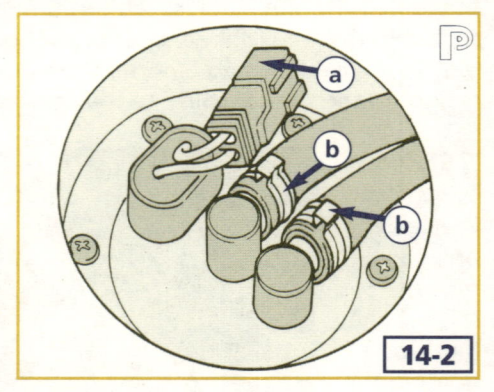

14-2

(positions **b**) and disposed of.
→ Mark the hoses so that they will be refitted to the correct outlet stubs.

TOP TIP!
☐ **STEP 3:** • There isn't room to pull the pipes off, but you can push them off their stubs with the end of a drift or screwdriver.

9-26

☐ **STEP 4: 205 MODELS:** Release the ring of six securing screws.
→ **OTHER MODELS:** Use a drift to push the sealing ring (illustration **14-1, item b**) in an anti-clockwise direction, releasing it from the tank top.
→ **IMPORTANT NOTE:** Undo the plastic sealing ring with extreme care - if you hammer the drift, the lugs will almost certainly break off.

☐ **STEP 5:** Lift the pump out of the top of the tank - quite a fiddly operation!

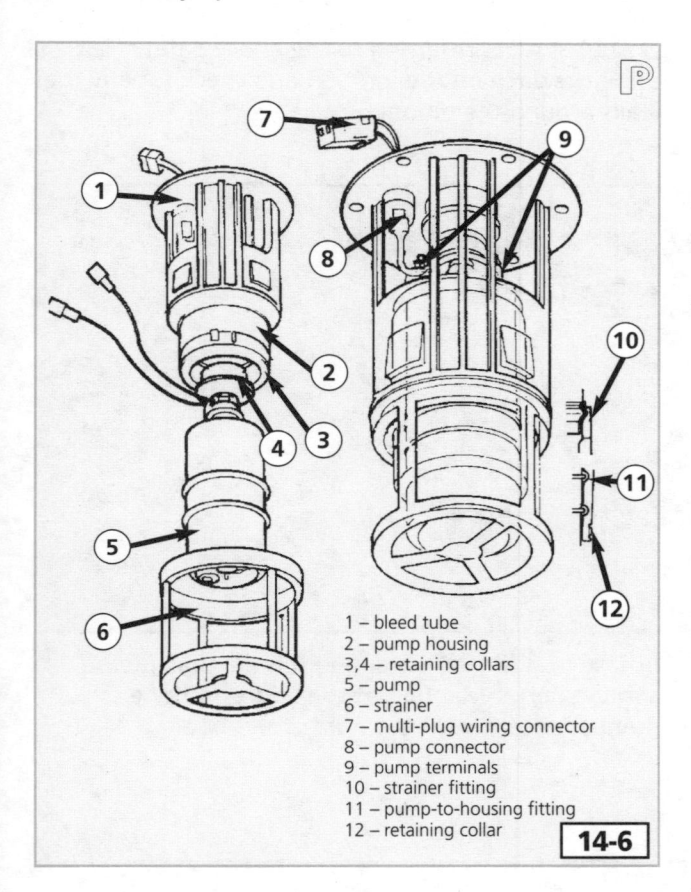

1 – bleed tube
2 – pump housing
3,4 – retaining collars
5 – pump
6 – strainer
7 – multi-plug wiring connector
8 – pump connector
9 – pump terminals
10 – strainer fitting
11 – pump-to-housing fitting
12 – retaining collar

14-6

☐ **STEP 6:** When refitting the pump use new collars (205) and sealing rings (all models).
→ Use new clips - screw-type clips are fine - to secure the flexible fuel pipes in place.

JOB 15: FUEL EVAPORATIVE SYSTEM.

☐ **STEP 1:** A complex control system exists to control fuel tank pressure under different temperature conditions...

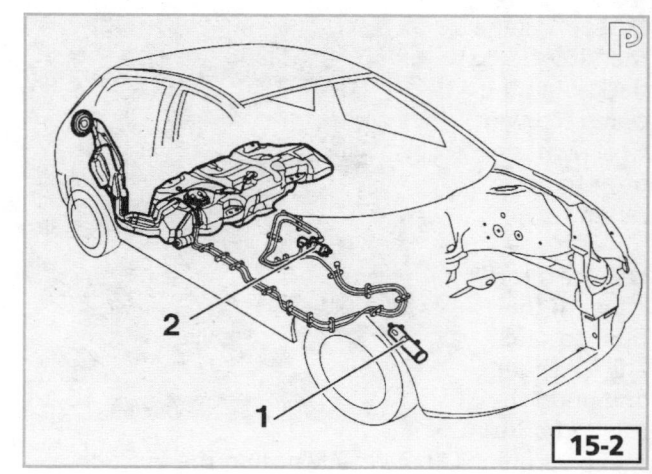

15-2

☐ **STEP 2:** ... and to prevent evaporative loss of fuel vapour to the atmosphere. The system comprises a charcoal canister (**1** - different fitting types also shown) which absorbs fuel vapour from the fuel tank at the filler neck, mostly while the vehicle is standing, then re-injects it when the engine is running.

☐ **STEP 3:** Other than occasional replacement of the charcoal canister, no component maintenance is needed. However, a fault with the system can lead to running problems. See **Job 2: Diagnostics - carry out checks**.

☐ **STEP 4:** Obvious points to check are the network of pipes and especially those at the filler neck, inside the bodywork.

JOB 16: FUEL FILTER – *injection engines*.

SAFETY FIRST!

• Before dismantling, disconnect the battery negative (-) earth/ground terminal. See Chapter 10, Electrical, Dash, Instruments, Fact File: Disconnecting the Battery BEFORE doing so!

• Only reconnect the battery after mopping-up any spilt fuel and clearing away any petrol-soaked materials (rags, paper towels etc.)

• DON'T SMOKE and keep any hot or spark-inducing tools and equipment away from the working area.

On some models, the fuel filter is of the replaceable canister type, located in the left-hand rear corner of the engine bay, adjacent to the brake master cylinder.

☐ **STEP 1:** Renew the filter by first slackening the clamp screw (**A**) to allow the filter to be raised.

→ Place a rag beneath the filter to catch any spilt fuel, and undo the top and bottom fuel-pipe unions (**B**) carefully noting the position of any washers or seals between union and filter.

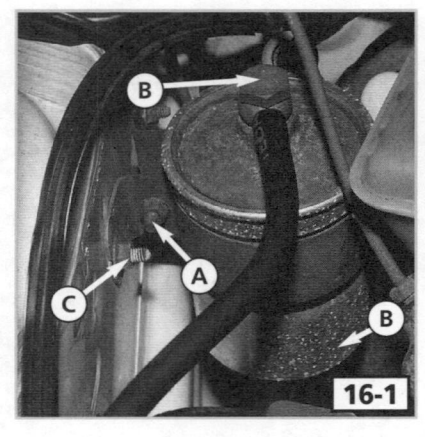

TOP TIP!

- It may be necessary to slacken the clamp-mounting nut (illustration 16-1, item C) in those cases where slackening screw (illustration 16-1, item A) is insufficient to free the canister.

☐ **STEP 2:** After lifting out the canister, connect a new one to the two unions, position it in the clamp and tighten.

☐ **STEP 3:** After referring to the above Safety First section, switch on the ignition and check for any fuel leaks around the unions.

Part B: Diesel Engines
CONTENTS

	Page No.
JOB 1: SYSTEMS – *explained*.	9-29
JOB 2: DIAGNOSTIC – *carry out checks*.	9-29
JOB 3: DIESEL INJECTION PUMP – *removal, refitting, timing*.	9-29
JOB 4: FUEL INJECTORS AND PIPES – *checking, replacement*.	9-33
JOB 5: PREHEAT SYSTEM – *checking, replacement*.	9-35
JOB 6: TURBOCHARGER – *replacement*.	9-36
JOB 7: ACCELERATOR, COLD START CABLE – *adjustment, replacement*.	9-37
JOB 8: FUEL SYSTEM AND FILTERS – *bleeding, changing filters*.	9-38

FURTHER INFORMATION
DIESEL ENGINE FAULT FINDER MANUAL, produced in association with **Perkins Engines**, is the definitive guide to Diesel engine diagnostics, fault-finding, tune-up and overhaul. All Diesel engine types are covered.

In case of difficulty obtaining this manual, please contact **Porter Manuals** at the address/phone number shown near the start of this book.

SAFETY FIRST!

RELIEVING THE FUEL PRESSURE.
- Never work on the fuel system unless the engine is completely cold.
- All diesel fuel injection systems inject fuel at extremely high pressure.
- Pressure must be released in a controlled fashion to avoid any risk of a pressurised spray of fuel being produced.
- If spray from injectors or partly detached pipes penetrates the skin or hits the eyes, severe injury can result.
- Residual pressure can remain in the fuel system for some considerable time, even if the engine has been switched off.
- IMPORTANT NOTE: Removing pressure from the fuel lines, as described below, will not necessarily remove pressure from each of the components - they may still be pressurised.
- Before working on any part of the system it is necessary to relieve the pressure, as follows:

1. Disconnect the battery negative terminal. See *Chapter 10, Electrical, Dash, Instruments, Fact File: Disconnecting the Battery* BEFORE doing so!
2. Work out of doors and away from any sources of flame or ignition. Wear rubber or plastic gloves and goggles. Have a large cloth ready.
3. Place a container beneath the filter to catch the fuel that is likely to be spilt.
4. Place your spanner on the first connection to be undone. Before undoing it, wrap the cloth, folded to give several thicknesses, over the joint.
5. Undo the connection very slowly and carefully, allowing the pressure within the pipework to be let out without causing a dangerous jet of fuel.
6. Release the pressure from each of the pipes in the same way.
7. Mop up all traces of fuel and allow to dry thoroughly before reconnecting the battery, starting the car or taking it back indoors.

JOB 1: SYSTEMS - *explained*.

IMPORTANT INFORMATION
• When working on the diesel fuel delivery system, cleanliness is vital. Clean all fuel connections before disconnecting them.

JOB 2: DIAGNOSTIC - *carry out checks*.

The process of carrying out diagnostic tests on diesel versions of these cars is exactly the same as for petrol versions - see *Part A, Job 2: Diagnostic - carry out checks* - where the test module includes interrogation software for the Lucas or Bosch systems involved.

JOB 3: DIESEL INJECTION PUMP - *removal, refitting, timing*.

SAFETY FIRST!

• Read and follow the *Safety First!* information at the start of this chapter, as well as *Chapter 2, Safety First!*.

Section A: Pump removal, refitting.

☐ **STEP A1:** Read this Job in connection with *Chapter 6, Part C: Timing Belt*. Be sure to set and retain all the TDC settings mentioned there.

IMPORTANT NOTES:
• Injection pumps may be Lucas or Bosch types.
➔ Details of removal procedure vary depending on whether the engine is an older XUD or more modern TUD type but general principles are the same.
➔ Gaining access to the injection pump may require the removal of the intercooler on turbocharged models, air distribution housing or breather hoses on others.
➔ **106 MODELS:** Remove the right-hand headlamp.
• When working on the injection system:
➔ Go to great lengths to ensure that not even the smallest particles of dirt can get in.
➔ Wipe pipe unions clean before dismantling.

☐ **STEP A2:** Disconnect and remove the fuel feed and return lines (plug the ends), the accelerator cable and the fast idle control cable (where fitted).

☐ **STEP A3:** Undo the fuel supply pipes from the injectors (see *Part B, Job 4* later) and from the pump. Remove them from the vehicle, as a unit.
➔ On some models a vacuum hose also needs to be removed, and on some turbo models with Bosch type pump there are coolant hoses that should be removed and plugged to minimise coolant loss.

☐ **STEP A4:** Unplug the cable from the engine shut-off solenoid terminal (arrowed) or plug.

3-A4

☐ **STEP A5:** Undo the bolts or clips and remove the timing cover.
➔ **205 AND 106 MODELS:** Use the timing holes in the

3-A5

camshaft sprocket, injection pump sprocket and flywheel to lock the crankshaft and valve train in place – see *Chapter 6, Engine, Part C*. Remove the timing belt. Undo the injection pump sprocket retaining nut and remove the sprocket, using a two- or three-legged puller if necessary.
➔ **XUD ENGINE:** Two holes are provided in the injection pump sprocket and the engine block so that two bolts (arrowed) can be passed through and lightly tightened to hold the sprocket in place - see *Chapter 6, Engine, Part C* for details. This allows the sprocket to be released from the injection pump shaft by slackening the retaining nut and withdrawing it (slightly) with a puller, but allows the sprocket to remain in place so the timing belt need not be removed or disturbed.
➔ In some cases a small steel Woodruff key is used to locate the sprocket to the injection pump shaft. Take care that you do not lose the key during the extraction process.

9-29

☐ **STEP A6:** BEFORE starting to remove the pump:
➜ Make a precise mark to indicate the position of the pump on its mounting bracket.
➜ The mounting holes are slotted and the pump swivels when the mounting bolts are loose, allowing the injection timing to be altered.
➜ Remove the bolts securing the pump, one at the rear and three at the front, and remove the pump.

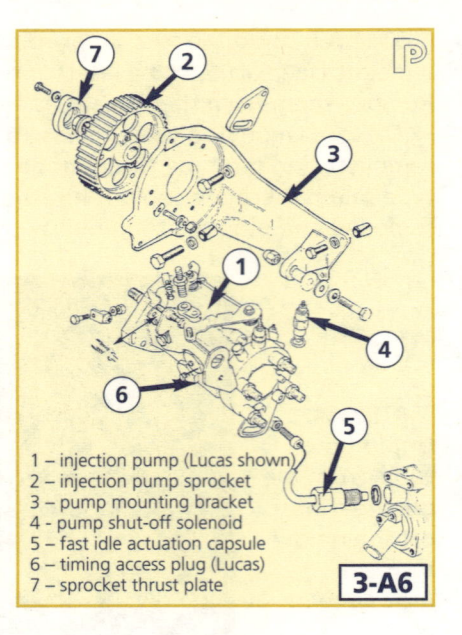

1 – injection pump (Lucas shown)
2 – injection pump sprocket
3 – pump mounting bracket
4 – pump shut-off solenoid
5 – fast idle actuation capsule
6 – timing access plug (Lucas)
7 – sprocket thrust plate

3-A6

TOP TIP!

• The thrust plate (illustration *3-A6, item 7*) of the XUD injection pump sprocket can be fitted on the outside of the sprocket centre nut, and tighten, using its two retaining bolts, to make a sprocket extracting tool.

☐ **STEP A7:** To install the pump, align the marks on the pump body and the mounting plate before tightening the fixing bolts.
➜ Tighten the front mounting bolts first, then the rear mounting bolt.

☐ **STEP A8:** Refit the pump sprocket:
➜ **205, 106 AND 206 MODELS:** Ensure the timing hole in the sprocket is correctly aligned before refitting the timing belt.
➜ **306 MODELS:** Where the sprocket and timing belt have been retained in place ease the pump back into position taking care to align the shaft with the sprocket.
➜ Ensure that the steel Woodruff key, when fitted, is properly positioned to locate the sprocket to the injection pump shaft.

TOP TIP!

• The timing belt should be replaced as a matter of course.
• This applies equally to XUD engines where the belt can be left in place during pump replacement. Leaving the belt in place ensures that the pump is refitted correctly; once the pump is in position the belt should be replaced.
• The cost of a new belt compared to the cost of a damaged engine makes it a false economy not to do so.

☐ **STEP A9:** Reconnect the fixtures and fittings taken off as the pump was removed:
➜ Where banjo unions are used on fuel and fuel return hoses, use new sealing washers.
➜ Push a piece of clear plastic tube over the injection pump bleed screw (where fitted) and bleed fuel from the bleed screw, into a suitable container, until you see fuel, free of air bubbles coming from the tube. If there is no bleed screw, bleed air from the pump's fuel return union.
➜ See *Job 8* for further information.

Section B: Check injection timing – Lucas pumps.

☐ **STEP B1:** The injection timing is checked with a dial gauge (range 0 to 3.0 mm) and special

3-B1

adapter or other means of supporting the dial gauge on the rear of the pump. These tools are available in the form of a diesel injection timing kit from Sykes Pickavant (as shown here).

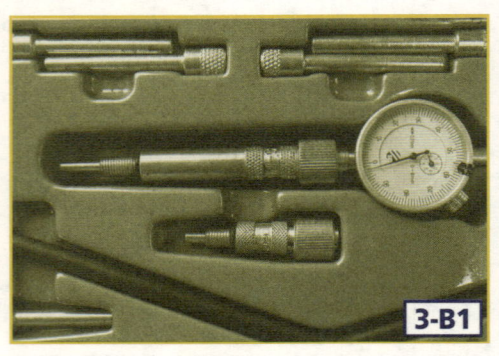

☐ **STEP B2:** Disconnect the battery negative (-) terminal - see *Chapter 10, Electrical, Dash, Instruments, Fact File: Disconnecting the Battery* BEFORE doing so - and remove the injector feed pipes.

☐ **STEP B3:** Remove the access cover from the side of the injection pump and install the dial gauge – position (**a**).

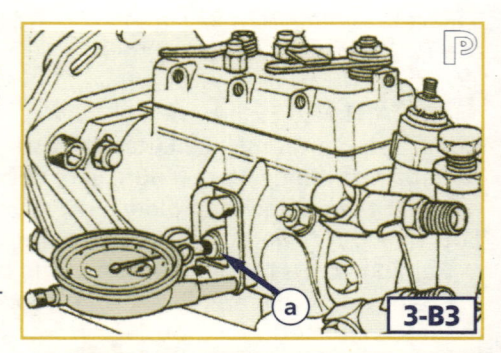

3-B3

☐ **STEP B4:** Begin with the timing holes on flywheel, camshaft sprocket and injection pump sprocket

3-B4

properly aligned at TDC (No. 1 cylinder).
→ Rotate the crankshaft slowly in the opposite direction of normal engine rotation until the dial gauge needle no longer moves.
→ 'Zero' the dial gauge.
→ Rotate crankshaft in normal direction of engine rotation until the TDC position is reached – the timing hole on the crankshaft will be in position for the locking tool (a) to be inserted into the end of the block and flywheel – position (b). See *Chapter 6, Part C: Timing Belt*.

❑ **STEP B5:** On earlier engines an access hole is provided in the cylinder head so that a dial gauge can be used to measure TDC directly, using the piston.
→ Here, the bolt has been removed and dial gauge inserted in its place.

❑ **STEP B6: TEST VALUE:** The required value is stamped on a tag attached to the pump or to the accelerator control lever.
→ If the amount of stroke shown on the pump is within +/- 0.04 mm, no adjustment is necessary.
→ The pump timing can be altered by slackening the bolts holding the pump to its mounting bracket and turning the pump until the correct value is shown on the dial gauge.

Section C: Check injection timing – Bosch pumps.

IMPORTANT NOTE: From 1997 some TUD 5 engines had a Bosch injection pump fitted. Timing values for these pumps are not available. Values given in the table below refer to Bosch pumps fitted to XUD engines.

❑ **STEP C1:** The timing is checked with a dial gauge (range 0 to 3.0 mm) and special adapter or other means of supporting the dial gauge on the rear of the pump. These tools are available in the form of a diesel injection timing kit from Sykes Pickavant (see illustration *3-B1*).

❑ **STEP C2:** Disconnect the battery negative (-) terminal - see *Chapter 10, Electrical, Dash, Instruments, Fact File: Disconnecting the Battery* BEFORE doing so - and remove the injector feed pipes.
→ Slacken the fast idle cable to ensure that the lever is fully against its stop.

→ If a cold start device is fitted (on some turbo engines) this should also be disconnected.

❑ **STEP C3:** Remove the access plug from the rear of the injection pump (position **a**) and install the dial gauge.

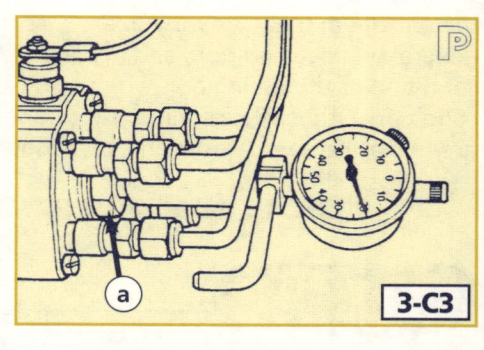

→ Begin with the timing holes on flywheel, camshaft sprocket and injection pump sprocket properly aligned for TDC at No. 1 cylinder.
→ Rotate the crankshaft slowly in each direction until the dial gauge shows that the pump piston has reached the lowest point of its travel.
→ 'Zero' the dial gauge.
→ Rotate crankshaft in normal direction of engine rotation until the TDC position is reached – the timing hole on the crankshaft will be in position for the locking tool to be inserted. See *Chapter 6, Part C: Timing Belt*.
→ **TEST VALUE:** The value on the gauge should be as shown in this table:

1.8-litre engine	0.90 ± 0.02 mm
1.9-litre non-turbo engines	
D9B	1.07 ± 0.02 mm
DJZ	0.77 ± 0.02 mm
DJY	0.90 ± 0.02 mm
1.9-litre turbo engines	
D8A	0.66 ± 0.02 mm
DHY	0.63 ± 0.02 mm

→ The pump timing can be altered by slackening the bolts holding the pump to its mounting bracket and turning the pump until the correct value is shown on the dial gauge.

❑ **STEP C4:** On earlier engines an access hole is provided in the cylinder head so that a dial gauge can be used to measure TDC directly, using the piston - see *illustration 3-B5*.

Section D: Speed adjustments.

To accurately check and adjust the diesel's idle speed you need a diesel-specific rev-counter. If you're happy with the idle speed, leave well alone. But if you wish to adjust the speed:
→ Run the engine to normal operating temperature.
→ Check that there is some free play in the accelerator cable before proceeding.
→ Turn OFF all electrical components.

➜ Ensure knob of cold-start (when fitted) is not pulled.
➜ **MAXIMUM SPEED SETTINGS:** Do not attempt to set the maximum speed unless you are sure that the general engine condition, and in particular the condition of the timing belt, are in sufficiently good condition. Otherwise, running the engine at maximum speed may cause a catastrophic breakdown!

LUCAS INJECTION PUMP

> **FACT FILE**
> **ANTI-STALL DEVICE**
> • Lucas/CAV/Rotodiesel/Condiesel injection pumps feature an adjustable anti-stall function.
> • It is integrated with the idle speed adjustment.

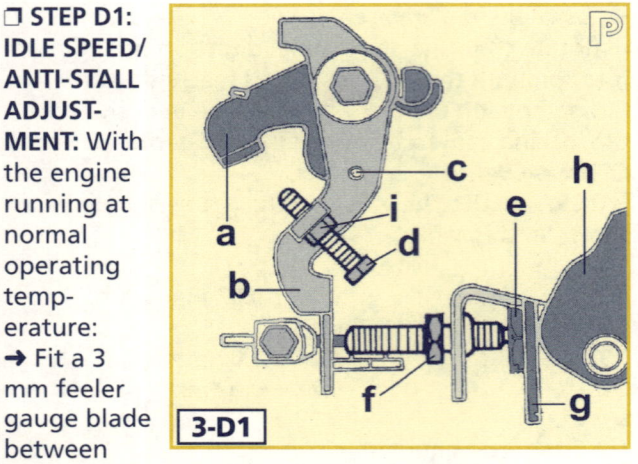

☐ **STEP D1: IDLE SPEED/ANTI-STALL ADJUSTMENT:** With the engine running at normal operating temperature:
➜ Fit a 3 mm feeler gauge blade between lever (**g**) and screw head (**e**).
➜ Move lever (**a**) until a drill bit of 3 mm diameter can be pushed through hole (**c**).
➜ Loosen nut (**f**), turn screw (**e**) until idle speed is 900 rpm, and retighten nut (**f**).
➜ Take the drill bit out of hole (**c**), and remove feeler gauge from between lever (**g**) and screw head (**e**).
➜ Loosen nut (**i**), adjust screw (**d**) to achieve the correct idle speed for the engine you are working on (see *Chapter 1, Facts and Figures*), and retighten nut.
➜ Lift lever (**a**) off its stop by 0.75 mm - use a feeler gauge to measure the gap - and listen for a lowering of engine speed. If speed does not lower, carry out the entire adjustment procedure a second time.
➜ Finally, check that the correct fast idle is being achieved (approximately 400 rpm higher than normal idle) by holding lever (**b**) against its stop.

BOSCH INJECTION PUMP

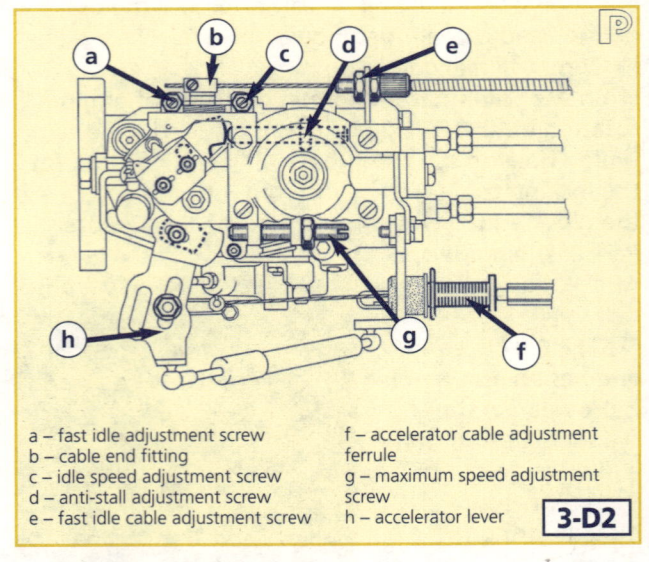

a – fast idle adjustment screw
b – cable end fitting
c – idle speed adjustment screw
d – anti-stall adjustment screw
e – fast idle cable adjustment screw
f – accelerator cable adjustment ferrule
g – maximum speed adjustment screw
h – accelerator lever

☐ **STEP D2:** These are the components of a typical Bosch injection pump.
➜ Although this is top view of a turbodiesel pump, the essential adjusting screws and cable fittings are the same for all Bosch pumps fitted to these vehicles.
➜ There are many detail differences.

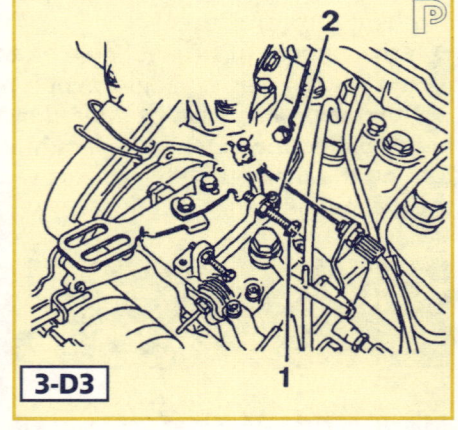

☐ **STEP D3: IDLE SPEED:** Slacken the locknut (**2**) of the adjuster screw (**1**), then turn the screw inwards to increase the speed - or outwards to decrease. Retighten the locknut when the speed is correct – 800rpm (850rpm for models with air conditioning).
➜ The screw is not covered by any other components on this particular version.
➜ **MAXIMUM SPEED:** Slacken the locknut of the adjuster screw (illustration *3-D3, item g*), then turn the screw inwards to increase the speed - or outwards to decrease. Retighten the locknut when the speed is correct.

> **FACT FILE**
> **MAXIMUM ENGINE SPEEDS**
> XUD
> 1.8-litre and 1.9-litre non-turbo: 5,200 rpm
> 1.9-litre turbo engines: 5,100 rpm
> TUD 5,500 rpm

LIMITING SCREW ADJUSTMENT: If there is a limiting screw to prevent the idle speed adjusting screw from lowering the revs below 900 rpm:
➡ Slacken the locknut of the limiting screw and turn screw well back.
➡ Set idling speed as described above.
➡ Turn the limiting screw until it is just touching the minimum idle speed stop and tighten the locknut.

COLD START SPEED ADJUSTMENT: Fast idle is controlled by a thermostatic valve. To check for correct operation:
➡ Begin with the engine cold. Hold the fast idle lever on the pump at the end of its travel.
➡ The cable end stop should just be in contact with the lever; if not loosen the clamping nut and reposition the stop.
➡ Release the fast idle lever and start the engine.
➡ Ensure that the fast idle lever returns to its stop as the engine warms up.
➡ When the engine had reached normal operating temperature there should be a gap of 0.5 mm to 1 mm between the fast idle level and the cable end stop. If necessary readjust the position of the end stop, where applicable by using the thumb-turn adjuster on the mounting bracket.

ANTI-STALL ADJUSTMENT: Bring the engine to normal operating temperature, switch off.
➡ Insert a 1 mm feeler gauge between the accelerator lever (*3-D2, item h*) and anti-stall adjustment screw (*3-D2, item d*).
➡ Start the engine. If the idle speed is not 50 rpm above normal, adjust by loosening the locknut and adjusting the anti-stall adjustment screw.
➡ Re-tighten the locknut.

JOB 4: FUEL INJECTORS AND PIPES – *checking, replacement.*

SAFETY FIRST!

• Read and follow the information given in *Job 1: Systems - explained*, as well as in *Chapter 2, Safety First!*.

Section A: Injector faults.

The following are some of the symptoms of defective injectors:
➡ Misfiring.
➡ Knocking on one or more cylinders (difficult to discern!).
➡ Engine overheating, loss of power, higher fuel consumption.
➡ Excessive blue smoke, starting from cold.
➡ Excessive black smoke when running.

TOP TIP!

The following procedure can be used to check for defective injectors, with the engine running at a fast idle:
• Loosen (then retighten) the high-pressure pipe union on each injector in turn. Follow the *Safety First!* approach at the start of *Job 1: Systems - explained*, to avoid the very harmful effects of high pressure spray penetrating skin or eyes.
• If, after loosening a union, the engine speed and/or note remains unchanged, you have probably identified a faulty injector.

Section B: Injector removal.

☐ **STEP B1:** Disconnect the battery negative (-) terminal. See *Chapter 10, Electrical, Dash, Instruments, Fact File: Disconnecting the Battery* BEFORE doing so!
➡ To gain access to the injectors it may be necessary to remove the intercooler from turbocharged engines, and air intake ducting.

☐ **STEP B2:** First, depressurising the system see *Job 1*.
➡ Clean thoroughly around each injector to prevent dirt from entering the cylinders when removing the injectors.

☐ **STEP B3:** Unscrew each fuel pipe union at the injectors (arrowed), using a 17 mm open-ended spanner.

4-B3

☐ **STEP B4:** Loosen each union at the injection pump end of each injector pipe, again ensuring the adaptor joints are not disturbed.

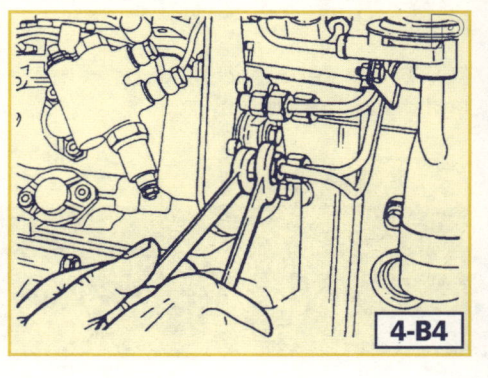

4-B4

➡ Disconnect the fuel-return unions at each injector.

➡ **IMPORTANT NOTE:** If the pump is electronically controlled the No 1 injector may have a needle-lift sensor. The wiring from this sensor should be disconnected where it joins the main harness.
➡ Remove the injector feed pipes, taking care not to distort the shape of the pipes.

☐ **STEP B5:** Unscrew the injector (**a**) using a deep 27 mm A/F socket (**b**), or, preferably, a purpose-made injector socket.
➡ Collect the injector and its base washer and seals (**c**). All seals should be renewed every time the injector is replaced.

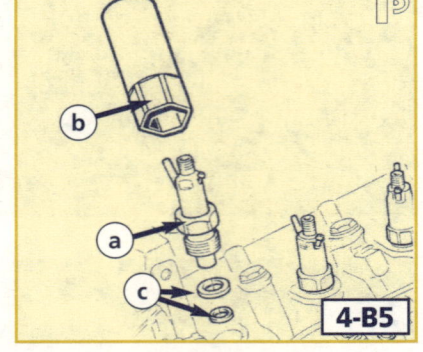

☐ **STEP B6:** Thoroughly clean the injector body before refitting, as dirt here can cause cylinder leakage, as can the re-use of a sealing washer - always use new.

TOP TIP!

• Injector efficiency and spray pattern can only be checked with specialist test equipment.
• This is an inexpensive check to have carried out by a specialist, while the injectors are out.

☐ **STEP B7:** Refit the injector, tightening it to the specified tightening torque. See **Chapter 1, Facts and Figures**. Always fit new seals between cylinder head and injectors.

☐ **STEP B8:** Reconnect all parts in the reverse order and bleed the system.

TOP TIP!

• Run the engine at a fast idle initially to clear air from the high-pressure side of the fuel system.

Section C: Injector servicing.

☐ **STEP C1:** It is possible to dismantle the injectors by clamping the upper part of the injector in the vice and loosening the screw connection. Loosen, but do not yet dismantle.

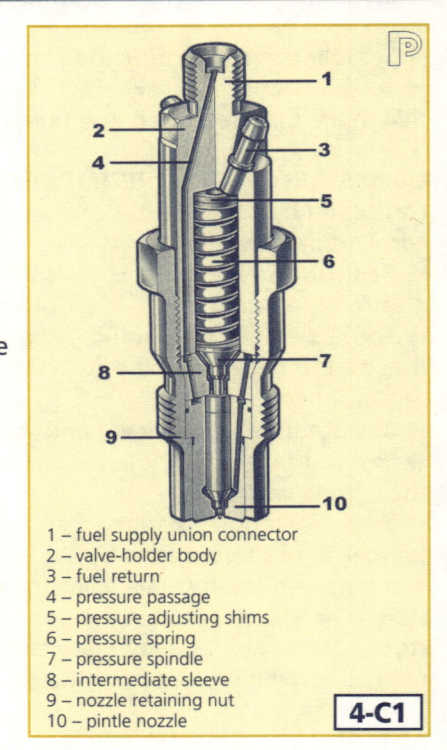

1 – fuel supply union connector
2 – valve-holder body
3 – fuel return
4 – pressure passage
5 – pressure adjusting shims
6 – pressure spring
7 – pressure spindle
8 – intermediate sleeve
9 – nozzle retaining nut
10 – pintle nozzle

TOP TIP!

• Injector dismantling is best left to an injection specialist who can guarantee the requisite cleanliness and will have the know-how and equipment with which to calibrate the injector upon reassembly.

☐ **STEP C2:** Turn the injector over and clamp the lower part in the vice to prevent the components falling out while you dismantle the injector. The items most prone to wear are the nozzle needle and nozzle body. However, it will not be possible to test the injector for leakage, sealing or correct opening pressure without specialist equipment.

☐ **STEP C3:** Replacement shims are available in graduations of 0.05 mm from a specialist or Peugeot dealership.
➡ A thinner shim reduces the opening pressure and a thicker increases the opening pressure.
➡ Increasing the pre-load by 0.05 mm increases the opening pressure by approximately 5 bar.
➡ When pressure testing equipment is available, note that new injectors should start to operate with an opening pressure of 130 to 138 bar and the wear limit is 120 bar.

Section D: Injector pipe removal, replacement.

☐ **STEP D1:** De-pressurise the system as already described in *Job 1*.

☐ **STEP D2:** Slacken the end fittings at the injectors and the pump (see illustrations *4-B3* and *4-B4*).

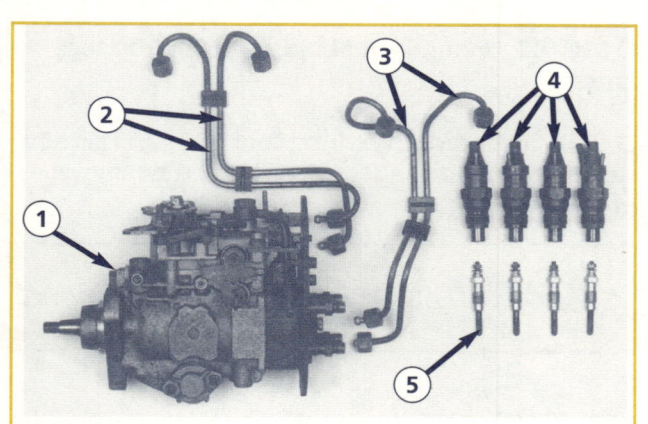

4-D3
1 – injection pump
2 – high-pressure injector pipes 1 & 2
3 – high-pressure injector pipes 3 & 4
4 – injectors
5 – glow plugs

☐ **STEP D3:** Lift the pipes as one item - they are clamped together, either as a bunch of four, or in two pairs of two, usually mid-way along their longest run.

TOP TIP!

• Take care not to bend any of the pipes or they may become extremely difficult to realign.

☐ **STEP D4:** Refit as the opposite of removal.

JOB 5: PREHEAT SYSTEM – *checking, replacement.*

SAFETY FIRST!

• Read and follow the information given in *Job 1: Systems - explained*, as well as in *Chapter 2, Safety First!*.

Section A: Preheating faults.

The preheating system consists of a glow plug inserted into each cylinder or cylinder swirl chamber, which heats the combustion chamber to aid cold starting. Failure of the system results in poor starting and possibly rough running, accompanied by smoking from the exhaust.
Failure could be due to:
→ Corroded contacts.
→ Broken current feed wire or loose connection.
→ Defective relay.
→ Defective glow plugs.

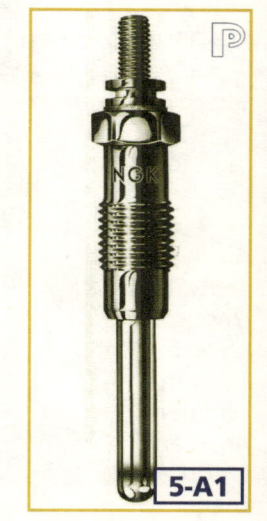

☐ **STEP A1:** The typical glow plug has a threaded contact to take current supply (top), insulated from the threaded main body that screws into the cylinder head, to the heating element inside the long protruding sheath of the plug.

5-A1

☐ **STEP A2:** The following procedure can be used to check for defective glow plugs:
→ Disconnect the current supply to the glow plug. Use a continuity tester to check that a circuit exists between the glow plug terminal and earth.
→ Alternatively, using an ammeter, check that the glow plug draws the correct current of around 12 Amps, after an initial surge of up to 20 Amps.
→ If no circuit is detected or current draw is too low, the glow plug is probably faulty.

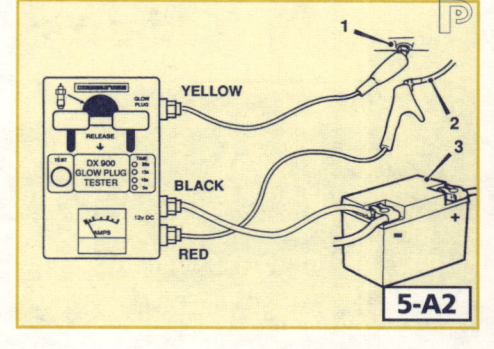

5-A2

Section B: Glow plug removal.

☐ **STEP B1:** Disconnect the battery negative (-) terminal. See *Chapter 10, Electrical, Dash, Instruments, Fact File: Disconnecting the Battery* BEFORE doing so!
→ To gain access to the glow plugs it may be necessary to remove the intercooler from turbocharged engines, and the air intake ducting.

☐ **STEP B2:** Release the nuts holding the current supply cable…

5-B2

CHAPTER 9 Part B Job 5

9-35

☐ **STEP B3:** ...and remove the connections from the glow plug terminals.

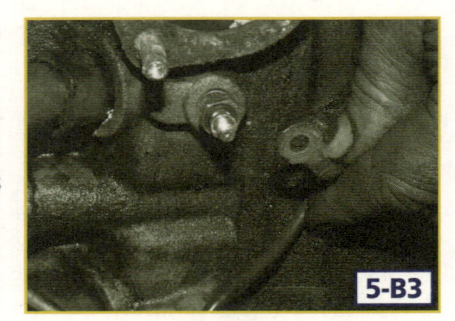

☐ **STEP B4:** Unscrew the glow plugs from the cylinder head and withdraw them.

TOP TIP!

• Check a glow plug's condition by clamping it in a vice and applying a 12-volt power supply.
• Note that the glow plug resistance is very low so ensure that the test equipment is fused to protect against short circuits. Do not attempt to check the plug by connecting it directly to a car battery as the plug's low resistance will cause a dramatic short circuit.
• The tip of the glow plug should glow red hot after about 5 seconds. If the glow begins in the middle of the element or takes much longer to occur the plug is probably faulty.

☐ **STEP B5:** Refitting is a reversal of the removal procedure, but do not overtighten the plug as this could damage the heating element.

Section C: Preheater control unit.

☐ **STEP C1:** Some models have a post-heating function that keeps the glow plugs heating for 30 seconds or more after start- up to ensure clean combustion. This has a microswitch (arrowed) fitted to the pump accelerator lever, which turns off the glow plug when the accelerator is activated.

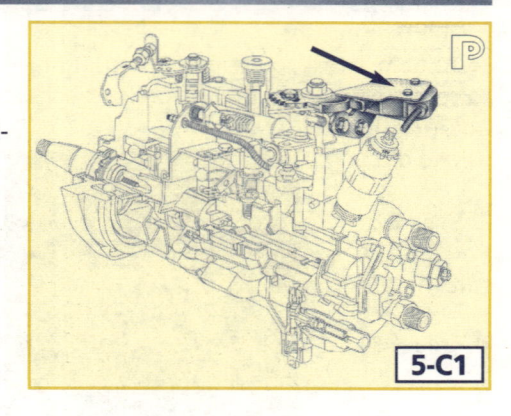

☐ **STEP C2:** The relay and timer unit is usually mounted on the rear of the battery box. Begin by disconnecting the battery negative terminal. See *Chapter 10, Electrical, Dash, Instruments, Fact File: Disconnecting the Battery* BEFORE doing so!

☐ **STEP C3:** Undo the nut holding the unit to the battery box.

☐ **STEP C4:** Detach the wiring connector and current supply leads. Refitting is a reversal of the removal procedure.

JOB 6: TURBOCHARGER - *replacement*.

IMPORTANT NOTE: Always start by disconnecting the battery negative (-) terminal. See *Chapter 10, Electrical, Dash, Instruments, Fact File: Disconnecting the Battery* BEFORE doing so!

☐ **STEP 1:** To gain access to the turbocharger it is necessary to remove the intercooler and inlet manifold.
→ Disconnect hoses from front, left and right-hand sides of the intercooler. Remove the surround from the intercooler top, revealing the securing bolts, three at the rear, two in front. Undo these bolts and lift the intercooler away.
→ Remove accelerator cable, brake servo and exhaust gas recirculation hoses. Unbolt and remove the EGR valves.
→ Remove the inlet and intercooler hoses (**b**) from the turbocharger.
→ Undo the inlet manifold securing bolts. The central hexagon bolt should be slackened but need not be removed as the manifold is slotted at this location to ease reassembly. Remove the manifold.
→ The illustration shows the turbocharger bolted to the exhaust manifold.
→ Take care with turbo oil feed pipes - these are small steel pipes crossing behind the exhaust downpipe (**a**).

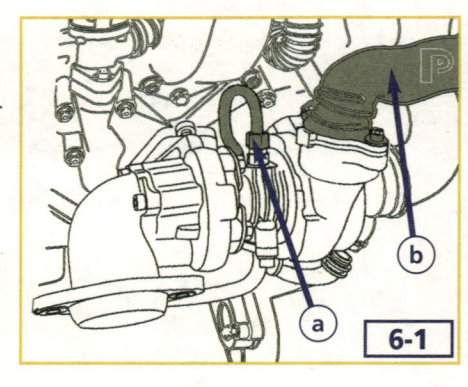

❐ **STEP 2:** Disconnect the oil feed pipe from the top of the turbocharger.

❐ **STEP 3:** With the vehicle raised, free the exhaust downpipe from the turbocharger, then disconnect and remove the oil feed and return pipes between turbocharger and engine block.

❐ **STEP 4:** Undo the two lower securing bolts, then with the turbocharger held carefully in position, remove the upper securing bolt. The turbocharger can now be withdrawn.

❐ **STEP 5:** Replace the turbocharger reversing the above procedures.
➜ The turbocharger oil feed pipe includes a filter element which should be renewed. It is also advisable to renew the engine oil and filter at the same time to reduce the chance of suspended contaminants entering the turbo lubrication system.
➜ Before running the engine, prime the turbocharger lubrication system. Remove the lead from the fuel pump's stop solenoid, then turn the engine over on the starter motor for about 10 seconds. Repeat two or three times.
➜ Replace the stop solenoid lead.

JOB 7:	ACCELERATOR, COLD START CABLE – *adjustment, replacement*.

PEDAL REPLACEMENT: See *Part C, Job 4*.

Section A: Accelerator cable.

REMOVAL AND REPLACEMENT

❐ **STEP A1:** Disconnect the battery negative (-) terminal. See *Chapter 10, Electrical, Dash, Instruments, Fact File: Disconnecting the Battery* BEFORE doing so!

A - typical fast idle cable and adjustment
B - accelerator cable and adjustment
7-A1

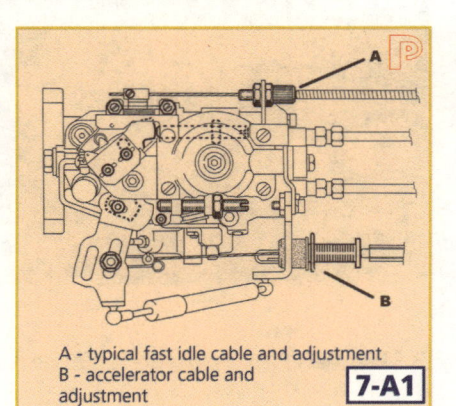

➜ **206 MODELS:** Remove the engine cover, which is held in place by a screw-in type fastener on the right hand side and a clip-on type on top.
➜ Inside the engine bay, slacken the accelerator cable by moving the accelerator lever, then free the cable end.
➜ The cable and its sheath can then be extracted from the bracket.

❐ **STEP A2:** Release any securing clips holding the cable in position around the engine bay.

❐ **STEP A3:** Access to the pedal end of the cable may require the removal of the fuse box cover and protective panels under the fascia.
➜ Release the securing clip and remove the cable end from the pedal, then slide the cable sheath grommet away from the pedal bracket.
➜ Withdraw the cable by pulling it through into the interior of the car, taking care not to damage or disturb the bulkhead grommet.

TOP TIP!

• There are several different cables, so take the old cable as a pattern when buying a replacement to make sure the new one is exactly the same.
• Fix a length of wire or cord to the engine end of the cable before extracting it. The cord can then be used to help draw the replacement cable through the bulk head grommet and makes it easier to follow the correct cable routing around the engine bay.

❐ **STEP A4:** Refit in the reverse order – taking care not to dislodge the grommet in the bulkhead.

ADJUSTMENT

❐ **STEP A5:** The accelerator cable outer sheath is held in position by a spring clip. With the clip removed, and with the accelerator lever on the pump held firmly against its stop, pull on the sheath until all slack is removed from the cable. Ensuring that the metal washer is pressed firmly against the grommet, replace the clip in the groove closest to the grommet.

Section B: Cold start cable and thermostatic sensor.

CABLE REMOVAL

❐ **STEP B1:** The cold start mechanism is controlled by a thermostatic sensor located in the thermostat housing (XUD engines) or cylinder head (TUD engines). Because the sensor is removed as an integral part of the cable system, it is necessary first

to drain the cooling system. For ease of access it may be necessary to remove intercooler or intake air ducting, where fitted. See illustration 3-A6, item 5.
→ Undo the clamp screw or nut on the cable end stop at the fast idle lever on the injection pump.
→ Pull the cable out through the adjustment screw on the positioning bracket.

❏ **STEP B2:** Unscrew the thermostatic sensor from the cylinder head or thermostat housing, and remove it along with the cable.

❏ **STEP B3:** Refit in the reverse order, using fresh sealing compound or new sealing washer at the sensor mounting face. Replace but do not tighten the cable end stop after feeding the cable end through the fast idle lever. Adjust the cable as follows:

CABLE ADJUSTMENT

IMPORTANT NOTE: The adjustment process begins with the engine cold and requires it to be run up to normal operating temperature to ensure that the fast idle mechanism works properly. Remember to reposition air ducting, breather hoses, intercooler and any other items removed for access to the injection pump! Remember also to refill the cooling system if it has been drained to allow the fast idle cable to be removed and replaced.

❏ **STEP B4:** After slackening the locking screw, this is a three-stage process:
→ With the engine cold push the fast idle lever fully towards the rear of the engine. With the cable taut, fix the end stop at a point where it is just touching the lever.
→ After repositioning ducting, hoses, intercooler etc. and refilling the cooling system, run the engine to normal operating temperature.
→ The fast idle lever should be fully against its forward stop and the cable should be slack. On Lucas injection pumps there should be between 0.5 mm and 1.0 mm of play between the cable end stop and the fast idle lever. On Bosch pumps the free play should be between 5 mm and 6 mm.

JOB 8: FUEL SYSTEM AND FILTERS - bleeding, changing filters.

SAFETY FIRST!

• Read and follow the information given in *Safety First!* at the start of this chapter, as well as *Chapter 2, Safety First!*.

• Do not allow diesel fuel onto your skin. Wear impermeable gloves.

IMPORTANT NOTES:
• NEVER slacken a high-pressure connection unless great care is taken to first wrap several layers of cloth around the connection so that no jet of fuel under high pressure can be produced. Fuel under high pressure is capable of penetrating the skin with, potentially, extremely dangerous consequences.
• If the engine stalls because of lack of fuel or if fuel low-pressure lines have been disconnected or the fuel filter has been changed, bleed the pump as shown below.
• Many later systems are self-bleeding and will purge themselves of air as the starter motor is turned over.
• If you need to 'spill' Diesel fuel, make sure that you have plenty of rags and/or containers to catch fuel and keep it from polluting the ground or drains.
• Do not let Diesel fuel get onto rubber components, such as hoses or mountings. If you do, wipe it off.

Section A: Bleeding the system.

❏ **STEP A1:** All models are fitted with a hand-operated priming device.
→ On all models prior to 1992 this is integrated with the fuel filter, and is either in the form of a plunger (B) on the top of the filter head…

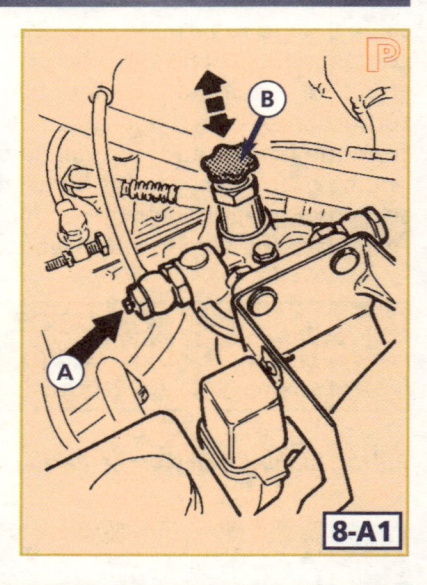

❏ **STEP A2:** …or a button (arrowed).

☐ **STEP A3:** On models from 1992 a rubber bulb (arrowed) is fitted into the fuel line to the right-hand side of the engine.

☐ **STEP A4:** Begin bleeding by loosening the bleed screw at the injection pump inlet union (illustration *8-A1, item A*), or if there is no bleed screw here, simply loosen the union.

→ Pump the rubber bulb until bubble-free fuel drains from the bleed screw, then tighten the bleed screw.

→ Switch on the ignition to open the solenoid-operated stop valve, then continue pumping the bulb until firm resistance is felt.

→ If necessary loosen the union on the pump's fuel return line and continue pumping until bubble-free fuel drains from the union. Tighten the union.

→ If necessary, loosen the unions on the fuel lines at the injectors. Operate the starter motor until fuel drains from the unions.

SAFETY FIRST!

- **It is possible that the engine may fire when turning the engine on the starter motor to bleed fuel at the injector unions.**
- **Don't allow any one near the engine.**
- **Turn off the ignition immediately if it starts up, to avoid hazardous fuel spray under the bonnet!**

☐ **STEP A5:** Tighten the unions.

→ Start the engine. Depressing the accelerator pedal fully will ensure a strong flow that will drive any remaining air through the injectors, but it may still take a while before the system is completely bled.

Section B: Drain water from diesel fuel filter.

Water carried in the fuel accumulates in the bottom of the fuel filter, and should not be allowed to build up.

→ Every type of fuel filter used on these engines has a drain tap either at the very bottom of the filter, or on the side, near the bottom.

→ Usually a length of plastic drain hose is fitted to this drain tap, to allow escaping fuel/water to be guided into a container.

→ Where none is fitted, avoid fuel spills by pushing a piece of plastic tube on to the stub on the base of the drain tap.

IMPORTANT NOTES:
- Place a container under the fuel filter housing to catch spilt fuel.
- Do not let diesel fuel get onto rubber components, such as hoses or mountings. If it does, wipe it off.
- Do not allow diesel fuel onto your skin. Wear impermeable gloves.

☐ **STEP B1:** Slacken the drain screw (arrowed) – pre-1992 filter with heating jacket...

☐ **STEP B2:** ...or the bleed screw (A) on later models.

→ The fitted drain tube (B) is located here.

→ Allow fuel and water to drain until pure fuel appears or until the filter housing empties.

→ It may be necessary to slacken a fuel pipe union at the top of the filter to ease the flow of contaminated fuel – see *Section A, illustration 8-A1, item A*.

→ Tighten the bleed screw and refit any disconnected fuel hoses.

IMPORTANT NOTE: **POST-1992 NON-106 MODELS:** Take care not to confuse valve with drain tap – see illustration *8-C6*.

☐ **STEP B2:** Check for leaks. Start and run the engine before replacing the engine cover (where applicable) in case the system needs to be bled.

→ Accelerate the engine several times, then check that the fuel flowing through the transparent hose is free of bubbles with the engine idling.

→ If necessary, bleed the system as described in *Section A*.

Section C: Change diesel fuel filter.

MODELS PRE-1992, NOT 106

A number of different filter types and mounting methods are used, and the basic principles of filter changing remain the same for all of them.
→ Like the conventional cartridge-type engine oil filter, most diesel fuel filters are disposable and screw hand-tight to a filter head, sealing by means of a rubber ring.
→ Some, such as certain Lucas filters, are of a two-part design in which the filter base/water bowl or canister has a threaded centre tube running up through the filter element and bolting through the filter head.

8-C1

☐ **STEP C1:** If the filter is of the one-piece cartridge type, it is removed by unscrewing by hand, or if too tight, with the aid of an oil filter wrench.

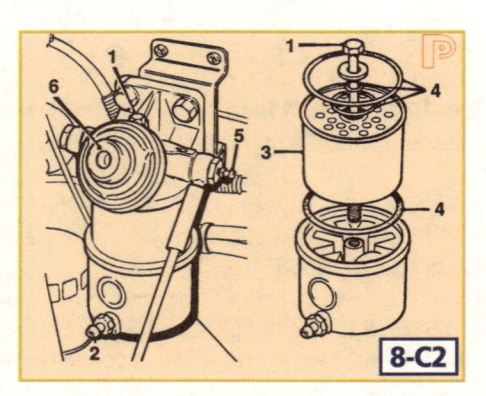

☐ **STEP C2:** Alternatively, removal is a question of undoing the centre nut/bolt (1).
→ Note the sealing rings (4) - ensure that the small one is in the filter box when you buy the replacement cartridge (3)!

8-C2

TOP TIP!

☐ **STEP C3:** • The rubber sealing ring at the top of the filter element or cartridge should be smeared with diesel fuel prior to fitting so that it doesn't buckle and cause leaks.

106 MODELS

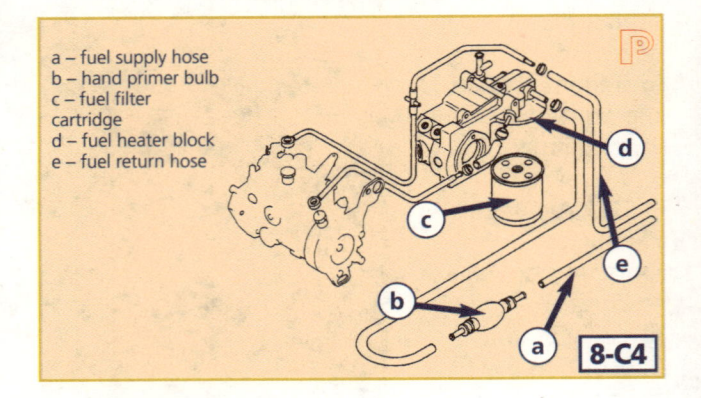

a – fuel supply hose
b – hand primer bulb
c – fuel filter cartridge
d – fuel heater block
e – fuel return hose

8-C4

☐ **STEP C4:** Remove the battery - See *Chapter 10, Electrical, Dash, Instruments, Fact File: Disconnecting the Battery* BEFORE doing so! - to allow access to the fuel filter housing.
→ Unscrew the fuel filter housing using a chain wrench or a special tool shaped to fit the base of the canister.
→ Remove the filter element.
→ Refit in reverse order, using a new sealing ring.
→ Screw the canister into place finger-tight, then tighten it another three quarters of a turn.

TOP TIP!

• On some fuel systems, particularly those which are not provided with a hand priming pump, it is a good idea to fill the fuel filter assembly with diesel fuel before reassembling it.
• This will reduce the amount of air-bleeding required, and will make for quicker, easier engine starting.

POST-1992 (NOT 106)

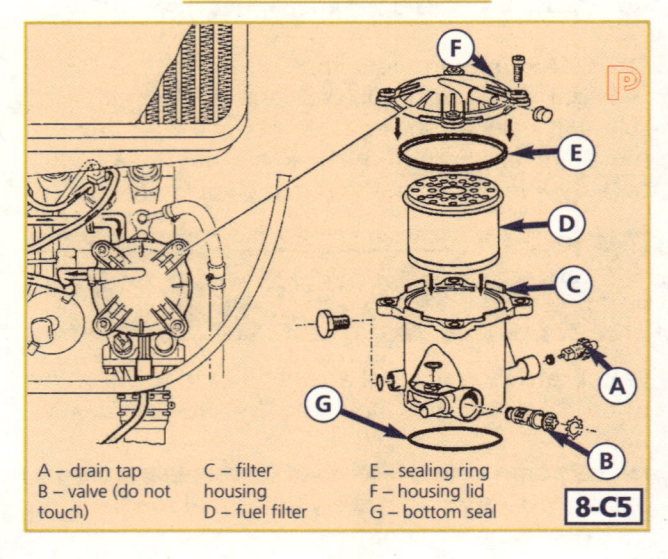

A – drain tap
B – valve (do not touch)
C – filter housing
D – fuel filter
E – sealing ring
F – housing lid
G – bottom seal

8-C5

☐ **STEP C5:** Begin as described in *Section B* by draining the filter housing, then closing the drain

CHAPTER 9   Part B   Job 8

9-40

screw afterwards.
→ Undo the four retaining screws and lift off the housing lid.
→ Remove the filter element.
→ Refit in reverse order, adding some diesel fuel to the housing before refitting the lid and using a new sealing ring.

❏ **STEP C6:** In all cases refill and bleed the fuel system as described in *Section B*.

Part C: Both Engine Types
CONTENTS
	Page No.
JOB 1: FUEL TANK – removal, refitting.	9-41
JOB 2: FUEL GAUGE SENDER UNIT - *replacement*.	9-43
JOB 3: EXHAUST SYSTEM - *replacement*.	9-43
JOB 4: PEDAL REMOVAL	9-44

JOB 1: FUEL TANK – *removal, refitting*.

SAFETY FIRST!

• We strongly recommend that you carry out all of this work out of doors.
• Read *Chapter 2, Safety First!* before carrying out this work!
• Always work away from all sources of heat or ignition.
• Do not smoke.
• Make sure that you have a container large enough to take all of the fuel in the tank.
• Store the drained fuel in an approved, safe container or containers.
• Wear gloves and goggles – petrol and diesel fuel can be harmful to the skin and is always harmful to the eyes.
• On diesel and injection models remember that the fuel feed lines might be pressurised. Disconnect any fuel lines with great care.

IMPORTANT NOTE:
• The tanks do not have a drain plug, so any fuel must be siphoned out before removal.
• In all cases the exhaust system, or at least part of it, must be removed or, where possible, lowered out of the way.
• Also remove any heat shields that may be fitted.

❏ **STEP 1:** Disconnect the battery negative (-) earth/ground terminal. See *Chapter 10, Electrical, Dash, Instruments, Fact File: Disconnecting the Battery* BEFORE doing so!.

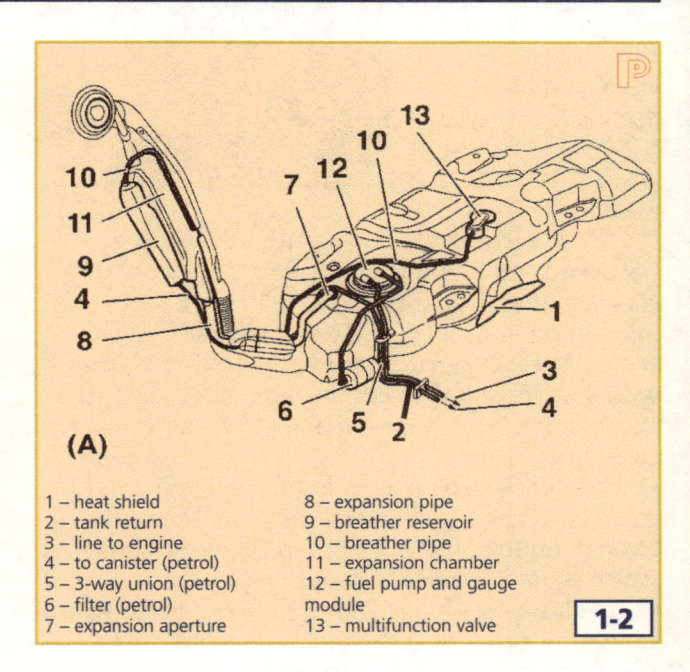

(A)
1 – heat shield
2 – tank return
3 – line to engine
4 – to canister (petrol)
5 – 3-way union (petrol)
6 – filter (petrol)
7 – expansion aperture
8 – expansion pipe
9 – breather reservoir
10 – breather pipe
11 – expansion chamber
12 – fuel pump and gauge module
13 – multifunction valve

1-2

❏ **STEP 2:** The tank installation is similar in all models, with only minor differences in the removal and refitting procedure. The tank installation of the 206 is shown in this illustration.

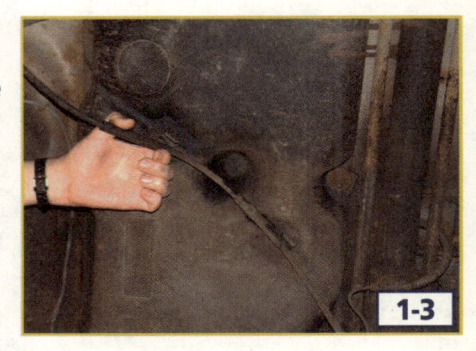

❏ **STEP 3: 205 MODELS:** The parking brake cables should be unclipped from clamps holding them to the fuel tank, but the cables can be left attached to the parking brake lever.

1-3

→ **OTHER MODELS:** Remove the cables from the handbrake lever as well.

☐ **STEP 4:** Unplug the wiring connector from the fuel gauge sender unit and, in diesel and injection models, the connector from the fuel pump.
➔ **205, 306 AND 106:** They are accessed through the floor of the car after raising the rear seat cushion.
➔ **206 MODELS:** Any wiring connections to the tank become accessible as the tank is lowered.

☐ **STEP 5:** Remove the filler neck hose, plus any vent pipes and breather hoses.
➔ The 205 filler pipe is shown under the rear wheel arch, with worm-drive clips on the connecting hose arrowed.

☐ **STEP 6:** Because the tank is located in such a hostile environment, you may find that some of the clips are unwilling to shift. DO NOT use heat or anything that could create a spark while undoing them. If necessary, cut through the rubber pipework with a knife, and then cut through metal clips after the tank has been removed and all fumes have been cleaned out of it.
➔ Note that on some models quick-release connections are used. To free them pull the cover back along the hose and push in the centre ring, which should release the pipe.
➔ **206:** It is necessary to remove the right rear wheel so the front part of the wheel arch lining can be removed to access the fuel filler neck. After taking off the filler cap undo the screws holding the filler neck to the bodywork.
➔ **106 MODELS:** A fuel filter assembly may also be attached to the left-hand side of the tank. Unclip the support strap and remove it.
➔ Disconnect the fuel feed and return hoses where they join the fuel pipes.

☐ **STEP 7:** The fuel tank securing nuts and/or bolts can now be removed. Support the fuel tank on a trolley jack, using a piece of wood to prevent damage to the tank surface.

☐ **STEP 8:** Undo the securing fasteners, then lower the tank, removing support straps and rods where applicable.

☐ **STEP 9:** Remove any other vent pipes or wiring connectors attached to the tank as it is lowered out of position.
➔ Take great care that there are no pockets of fuel to spill out onto your clothes or into your face.
➔ Lower the tank a very small amount at a time, enough to check whether any hoses remain attached, then lower it fully to the ground.

SAFETY FIRST!

• You must NEVER simply leave the fuel tank at this stage!

• If you are only planning to store it for a very short time, all of the apertures must be thoroughly sealed off.

• The biggest danger in a fuel tank comes from the fumes within it. Petrol/gasoline fumes are highly flammable and a tank full of fumes is a bomb waiting to go off if any sparks or cigarette ends should get near it.

• If the tank is to be stored for more than a couple of days, it should be steam cleaned internally to remove all traces of fuel.

◻ **STEP 10:** Refit in reverse order.
→ Remember to adjust the handbrake if the cables were removed.
→ Ensure that pipes and hoses are securely fastened, using new clips or screw-type connectors where necessary, and that pipes are not trapped between tank and bodywork.
→ Check for leaks.
→ Reconnect the battery last of all.

JOB 2:	**FUEL GAUGE SENDER UNIT -** *replacement.*

See *Part A, Job 14. Electric Fuel Pump - replacement.* This shows how to remove and replace the type of unit where the pump and sender unit are combined. The process for the type without an integral fuel pump is exactly the same, except that there are no fuel hoses to disconnect.

JOB 3:	**EXHAUST SYSTEM -** *replacement.*

→ All the sections are connected by clamped flanged joints and the entire system is supported on rubber hangers.
→ As this fitting method is very straightforward, in most cases it is considered easier to remove the entire system after unbolting the downpipe from the manifold, even if only one section is being replaced.
→ See *Chapter 6, Part I: Engine and Transmission Removal, Separation, Refitting* for information on fitting the exhaust.
→ Use all new gaskets.

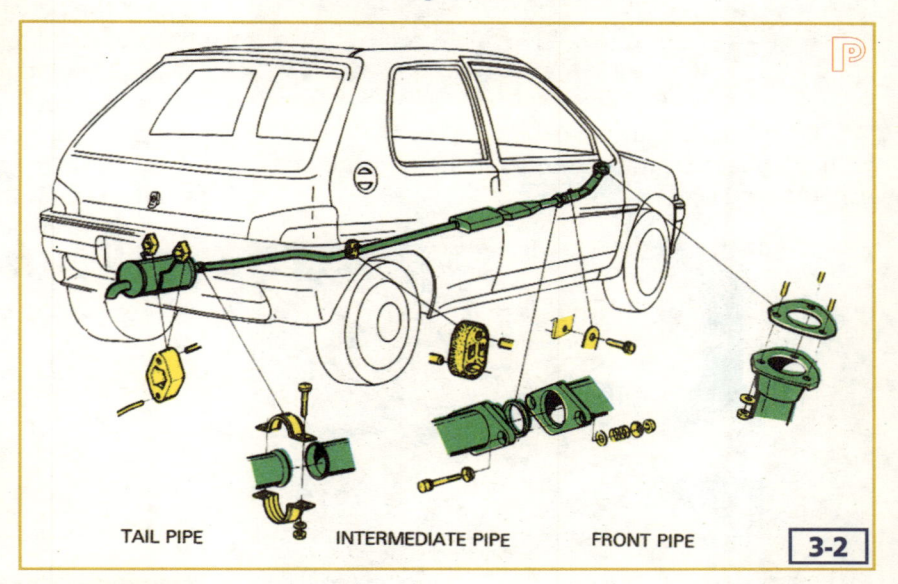

TAIL PIPE   INTERMEDIATE PIPE   FRONT PIPE   3-2

◻ **STEP 1:** Exhaust systems are similar in principle - and mostly in appearance, except that:
→ Some have a Lambda sensor and a catalytic converter. Lambda sensor wiring should be disconnected at its coupling in the engine bay, so the sensor can be removed with the exhaust downpipe. Catalytic converters are fragile and should be handled with great care.
→ The downpipe is bolted to the exhaust manifold, but in some cases a spring-loaded joint is used to allow for engine movement. In some models the downpipe joint is fixed but the intermediate pipe or catalytic converter housing spring-loaded.
→ On spring-loaded joints measure the length of the spring before removal to ensure that the securing nuts are tightened to the same extent on refitting.

◻ **STEP 2:** This is a typical exhaust layout – this one for a petrol 106 model.

◻ **STEP 3:** Fit the exhaust system components into place starting at the manifold end by attaching the downpipe, ensuring that the seal is correctly positioned, and tightening the two or three downpipe bolts/nuts evenly and progressively.

◻ **STEP 4:** Apply exhaust jointing paste, assemble the components and fit the pipe clamps loosely.

JOB 4: PEDAL REMOVAL.

☐ **STEP 1:** There are several different pedal mounting methods. In each case disconnect the accelerator cable from the pedal as described above:
→ On 106 models the pedal bracket is held in place against the bulkhead by two nuts. Removing them allows the pedal and inner and outer sections of the bracket to be removed.
→ On 206 models the pedal pivots on a pin held in place by a retaining clip. Remove the clip, slide out the pivot shaft and remove the pedal.
→ On other models the pivot shaft is held in place by a nut. Flats on the shaft allow it to be held while the nut is unscrewed, after which the shaft can be slid out and the pedal removed.

☐ **STEP 2:** Refit in the reverse order.

☐ **STEP 5:** Ensure that the exhaust is mounted evenly, with adequate clearances and only then tighten the exhaust pipe clamps.

☐ **STEP 6:** Fit new rubber hangers. Ensure no hangers are under more tension than others by realigning the pipe joints as necessary. Only then should the pipe clamps be tightened.

CHAPTER 10: ELECTRICAL, INSTRUMENTS

*Please read **Chapter 2 Safety First** before carrying out any work on your car.*

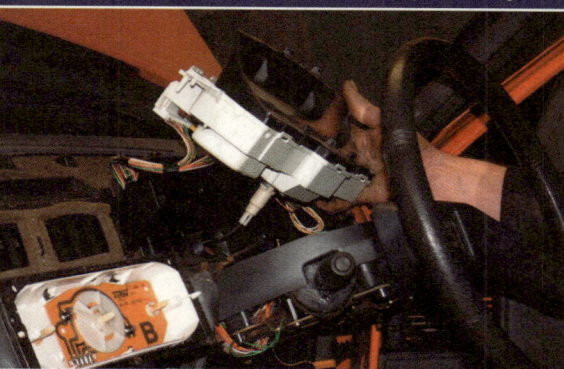

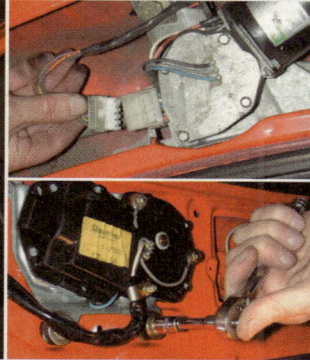

CONTENTS

	Page No.		Page No.
JOB 1: ALTERNATOR - *remove, refit*.	10-2	**JOB 6:** TAILGATE WIPER MOTOR - *remove, refit*.	10-6
JOB 2: STARTER MOTOR - *remove, refit*.	10-3	**JOB 7:** RADIO AERIAL/ANTENNA - *remove, refit*.	10-8
JOB 3: INSTRUMENT PANEL - *remove, refit*.	10-4	**JOB 8:** LIGHTS AND FUSES - *replace*.	10-9
JOB 4: SPEEDOMETER CABLE- *remove, refit*.	10-5	**JOB 9:** CENTRAL LOCKING - *replace components*.	10-14
JOB 5: FRONT SCREEN WIPER MOTOR - *remove, refit*.	10-5	**JOB 10:** DIESEL GLOW PLUGS - *check, replace*.	10-14
		JOB 11: AIR CONDITIONING EQUIPMENT.	10-14

Safety First!

- Never smoke, use a naked flame or allow a spark near the battery.
- Never disconnect the battery with battery caps removed – or with engine running, which will damage electronic components.
- If battery acid comes into contact with skin or eyes, flood with cold water and seek medical advice.
- Don't top up the battery within half an hour of charging it – electrolyte may flood out.

Fact File
DISCONNECTING THE BATTERY

- When disconnecting a battery, always disconnect the earth/ground terminal FIRST, and when reconnecting a battery, connect the earth/ground terminal LAST.
- If you disconnect the battery, you might find the alarm goes off, the ECU loses its 'memory', or the radio needs its security code.
- You can ensure a constant electrical supply with a separate battery, protected with a 1 amp fuse.
- In some cases, you might need to disconnect the battery completely. For instance, if you need to disable the air bags.
- When the battery DOES need to be disconnected, you MUST make sure that you've got the radio security code before disconnecting it.
- Some models are fitted with original equipment alarm systems which have to be disabled before the battery is disconnected. To disable the alarm, switch on the ignition and press the alarm switch for two seconds – the switch light should flash rapidly for around three seconds. Switch off the ignition and disconnect the battery.

FACT FILE
ALTERNATOR TYPES

A number of different alternators have been fitted to the vehicles covered by this manual.

☐ **STEP FF1:** This is an early type with a simple tensioning bracket, fitted to the XV engine.

FF1

☐ **STEP FF2:** This type is fitted to the TU engine and has an auxiliary drive belt tensioner (arrowed).

FF1

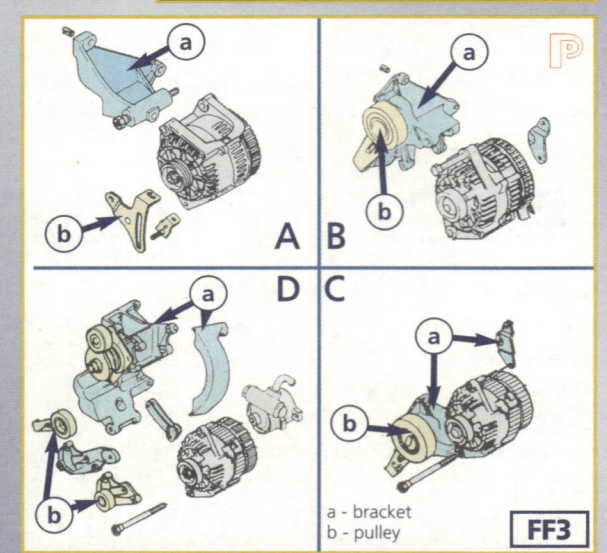

a - bracket
b - pulley

FF3

☐ **STEP FF3:** The alternators and their support brackets fitted to later vehicles varied. These support brackets are typical of:
→ Vehicles (**A**) without power steering or air conditioning retained auxiliary drive belt adjustment via a bracket.
→ Vehicles (**B**) with power steering but without air conditioning used a tension pulley.
→ Vehicles (**C**) without power steering but with air conditioning used a tension pulley.
→ Vehicles (**D**) with power steering and air conditioning used this arrangement, the lower tension pulley being fitted after 1994.

JOB 1: ALTERNATOR - *remove, refit*.

☐ **STEP 1:** Before dismantling, disconnect the battery negative (-) earth/ground terminal. See *Fact File: Disconnecting the Battery* BEFORE doing so!

☐ **STEP 2:** Remove ancillary components as necessary to gain access to the alternator.
→ **205:** Remove the air filter housing.
→ **206 MODELS WITH POWER STEERING:** Unbolt the power steering pump and support it out of the way.
→ **206 DIESEL:** Remove the engine cover.

☐ **STEP 3:** Undo the wiring connectors (arrowed) from the alternator.

1-3

☐ **STEP 4:** Remove the auxiliary drive belt from the alternator pulley – see **Chapter 6, Engine**.

☐ **STEP 5:** On early vehicles, undo the upper mount bolt a little, then slacken the lower mount bolt or bolts, depending on version.
→ Remove the upper mount bolt.
→ If necessary, remove the upper mounting bracket completely.
→ Undo the lower mount bolt.
→ On some models it is not necessary to remove the long lower bolt completely to disengage the alternator.
→ On some models the drivebelt tension pulley must be removed to gain access to the alternator bolts.

1-5

☐ **STEP 6:** On brackets with built-in adjustment, unscrew the adjuster bolt.

1-6

☐ **STEP 7:** On vehicles with auxiliary drive belt adjustment pulleys, slacken the pulley nut (**a**) and turn the centre bolt (**b**) to adjust the tension.

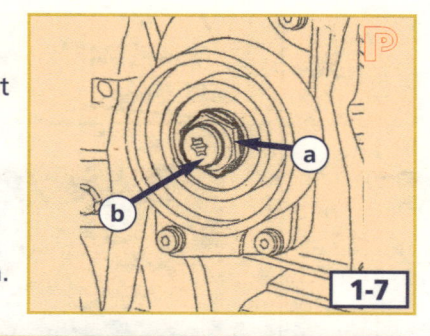

☐ **STEP 8:** This is the tensioning bracket on the VX engine.

☐ **STEP 9:** Remove the alternator fixings (arrowed).
→ The placement of alternator fixings varies according to the vehicle and specification.

☐ **STEP 10:** Take the alternator from the engine and recover the mounting bracket bushes from the bracket.

☐ **STEP 11:** Refit as the reverse of removal, using new mounting bushes if necessary.
→ It is essential that auxiliary drive belts are tensioned correctly. On basic vehicles this can be achieved by pressing the belt and noting its deflection, but on models with power steering and air conditioning Peugeot recommend that a special belt tension measuring tool is used.
→ In the absence of the belt tension measuring tool or to get the car mobile so that it can be driven to a Peugeot dealer to have the tension checked, the belt should deflect by no more than 5 mm half way along the longest run under firm thumb pressure.

JOB 2: STARTER MOTOR - *remove, refit*.

☐ **STEP 1:** Raise the front of the vehicle, and support it off the ground.

☐ **STEP 2:** Before dismantling, disconnect the battery negative (-) earth/ground terminal. See *Fact File: Disconnecting the Battery* BEFORE doing so!

☐ **STEP 3:** With the exception of the VX engine, access to the starter motor is never easy! This is the TU engine.
Remove any ancillary components that prevent access to the starter motor.
→ **205:** Remove the air cleaner.
→ **205 GTI:** Remove the inlet manifold.
→ **106 DIESEL:** Access is easier with the exhaust downpipe removed.
→ **206 Diesel:** Remove the engine cover.

☐ **STEP 4:** This is the XUD engine, showing the location of the starter motor (arrowed) as this engine is being removed from the vehicle, for ease of photography.

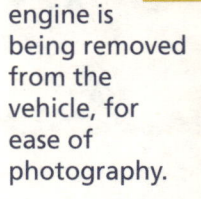

☐ **STEP 5:** Disconnect the electrical connections from the

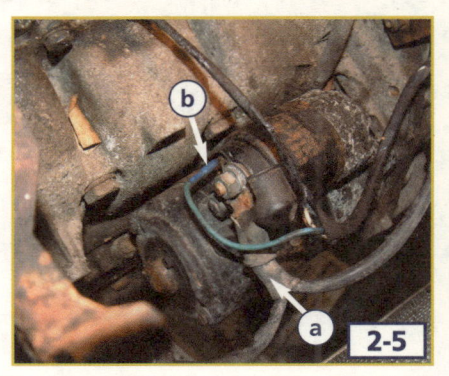

starter motor solenoid.
→ The thicker cable (**a**) carries the heavy starter motor current.
→ The thinner one (**b**) operates the starter solenoid.

☐ **STEP 6:** Remove the starter motor mounting bolts.
→ Some models have bolts at both the flywheel and brush ends.
→ This is the starter motor fitted to XUD diesel engines. The mounting bolts screw into threads (positions arrowed) in the starter assembly after passing through the engine bellhousing.

2-6

☐ **STEP 7:** This is the starter motor fitted to TU engines.
→ The mounting bolts (arrowed) screw into threads in the transmission casing.

2-7

2-8

☐ **STEP 8:** Support the starter motor as you undo its mounting bolts.
→ Remove the starter motor.
→ Recover locating dowels where fitted.

☐ **STEP 9:** Refit as the reverse of removal.

JOB 3: INSTRUMENT PANEL - *remove, refit.*

☐ **STEP 1:** Disconnect the battery negative (-) earth/ ground terminal. See *Fact File: Disconnecting the Battery* BEFORE doing so!
→ Remove the screws (one arrowed) securing the instrument panel surround or shroud.
→ Access can be improved by lowering adjustable steering columns.

3-1

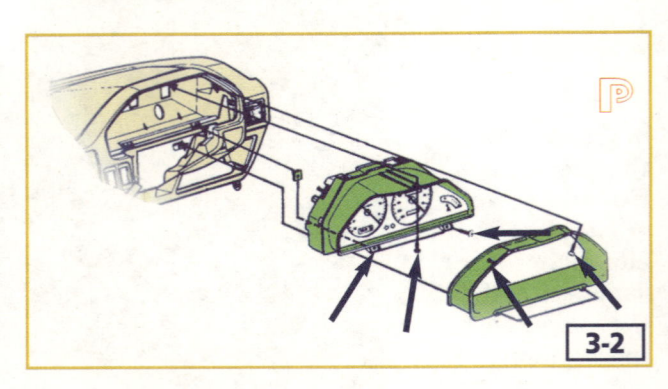

3-2

☐ **STEP 2:** These are typical positions of instrument panel surround securing screws (106 shown).

☐ **STEP 3:** You can now remove the surround.

☐ **STEP 4:** Take out the instrument panel securing screws (one, arrowed).
→ The number and positioning of the screws vary according to the model.

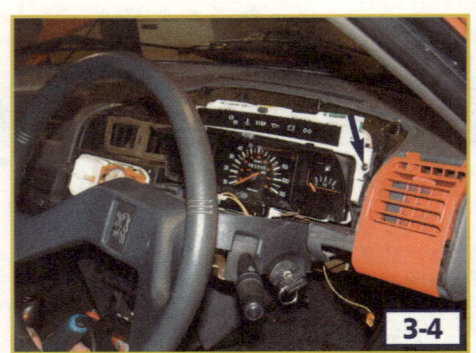

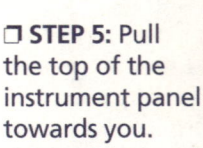

3-4

☐ **STEP 5:** Pull the top of the instrument panel towards you.
→ Reach around the back of it,

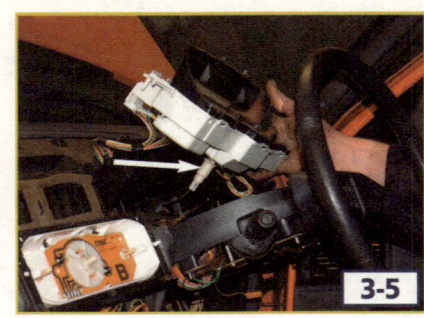

3-5

and release the speedometer cable (arrowed) by pressing the clips and pulling the cable backwards.
➔ Disconnect the wiring plugs.

❐ STEP 6: Remove the panel.

JOB 4: SPEEDOMETER CABLE - *remove, refit.*

❐ STEP 1: Remove the instrument panel and disconnect the cable clips (arrowed) so that you can remove the speedometer cable from the back of the speedometer – see also, *Job 3*.
➔ 106: Remove the glovebox, and tie a fish wire to the speedometer cable to aid re-routing it during refitting.

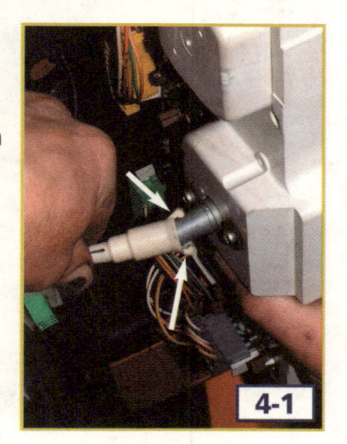

❐ STEP 2: Working from the engine bay, lever the speedometer cable grommet out and pull the cable through the bulkhead/firewall.
➔ On the 306 there is a ball on the cable that fits inside the firewall grommet – pull the cable sharply to remove the ball from the grommet.

❐ STEP 3: Remove the cable from its connection on the transmission casing.
➔ This can be a pin, bolt or collar depending on the model.

❐ STEP 4: Replace as the reverse of removal.
➔ Make sure the rubber grommet is seated correctly in the firewall.

JOB 5: FRONT SCREEN WIPER MOTOR - *remove, refit.*

❐ STEP 1: Before dismantling, disconnect the battery negative (-) earth/ground terminal. See *Fact File: Disconnecting the Battery* BEFORE doing so!

❐ STEP 2: Mark the position of the wiper blades on the screen, or mark the spindles and wiper arm ends.
➔ 106 LHD: Operate the wiper blades and switch off the ignition when they are vertical.

TOP TIP!
• Stick masking tape to the screen, indicating where the wiper blades lie when parked.

❐ STEP 3: Lift the covers, remove the retaining nuts and lift the wiper arms off their spindles.

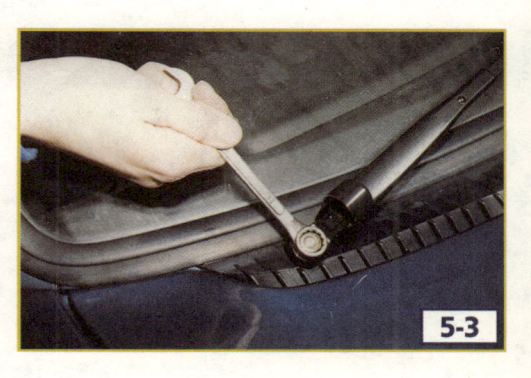

❐ STEP 4: Remove the plastic scuttle cover panel.
➔ The panel and fixings vary between models.
➔ 106: The panel is held by clips and nuts. On some models there is also a plastic wiper motor cover – remove this.
➔ 205: The panel is held by screws.
➔ 206: Remove the firewall sealing strip then the left side water deflector panel, held by clips.
➔ 306: Remove the front door aperture weather strips enough to expose the scuttle cover panel nuts, then remove the screws.

CHAPTER 10 Electrical, Instruments Job 6

☐ **STEP 5:** Disconnect the electrical plug from the motor.
→ You can now remove the motor either alone or with the linkage as follows:

☐ **STEP 6: 106:** Remove the rubber buffer if fitted, remove the wiper motor securing bolts and remove the motor and linkage assembly complete.

☐ **STEP 7A: 205:** Unbolt the spindles…

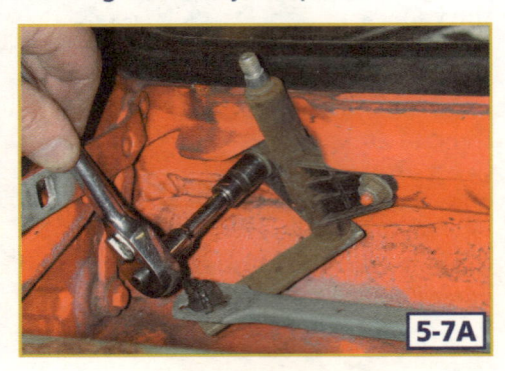

☐ **STEP 7B:** …and remove the single mounting bolt…

☐ **STEP 7C:** …and remove the motor and linkage together.

☐ **STEP 8: 206:** Remove the wiper spindle nuts and washers, remove the wiper motor mounting bolt then remove the motor and linkage complete.

☐ **STEP 9: 306:** Undo the mounting bolts shown here and remove the motor and linkage complete.

REPLACEMENT

☐ **STEP 10:** Refit as the reverse of removal.
→ Replace the wiper arms in the correct positions, according to the masking tape marks you put on the screen.
→ Operate the wipers (with screen wet), to make sure the sweep of the wiper blades is correct.

JOB 6: TAILGATE WIPER MOTOR - *remove, refit*.

IMPORTANT NOTE: The tailgate wiper motor bracket is riveted to the tailgate on some 206 models. A pop-rivet tool and pop rivets are needed for replacement.

☐ **STEP 1:** Before dismantling, disconnect the battery negative (-) earth/ground terminal. See *Fact File: Disconnecting the Battery* BEFORE doing so!

☐ **STEP 2:** Mark the position of the wiper blade on the rear screen.

TOP TIP!
• Stick masking tape to the screen, indicating where the wiper blade lies when parked.

☐ **STEP 3:** Lift the end cap, remove the retaining nut and lift the wiper arm off its spindle.
→ Remove the rubber or plastic grommet from the wiper spindle.

❏ **STEP 4:** Remove the spindle securing nut...

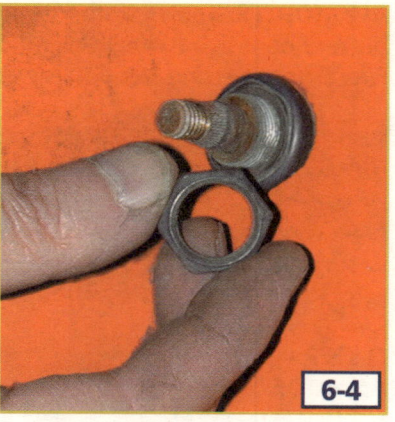

❏ **STEP 5:** ...and the sealing washer.

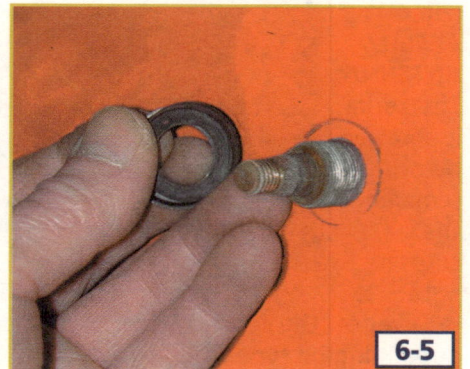

❏ **STEP 6:** Lift the tailgate, and remove the inner trim panel – see *Chapter 14, Interior, Trim*.

TOP TIP!

- The best tool to use here is a trim clip removal tool.
- A screwdriver often snaps or distorts clips.

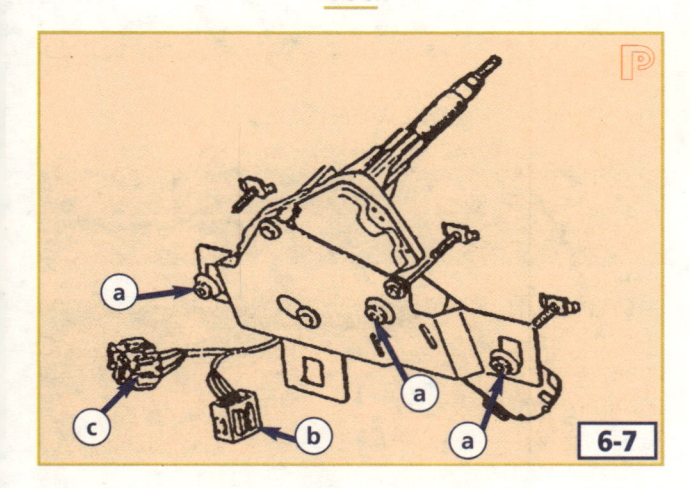

❏ **STEP 7:** Undo the wiring connector on the motor or at the separate plug (**c**), depending on model, and at the relay (**b**).
➔ Unclip the motor wiring wherever it is secured to the tailgate.
➔ Undo the motor mounting bolts (**a**).

➔ On some models the motor relay (**b**) fits into a clip, on others it is bolted.
➔ Lift the motor from the tailgate.

❏ **STEP 8:** Disconnect the wiring plug.

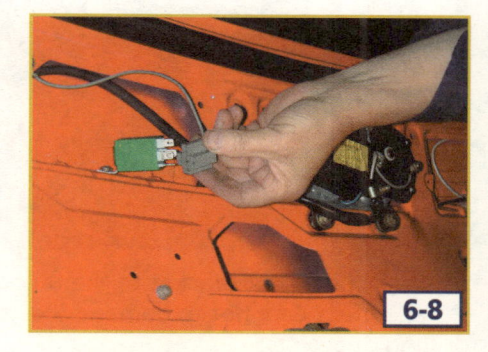

❏ **STEP 9:** Remove the earth/ground cable screw.

❏ **STEP 10:**

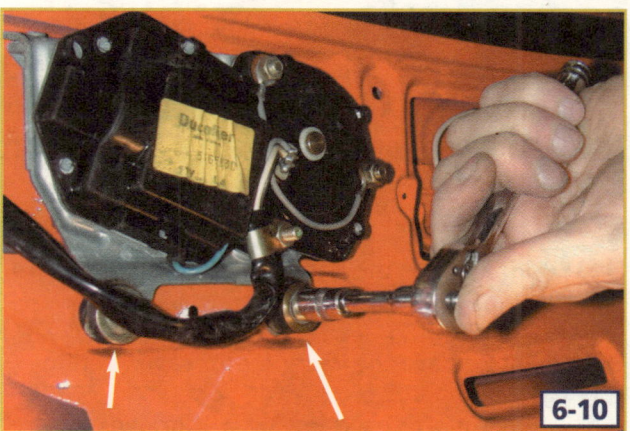

The tailgate wiper motor is secured by two 'bayonet' fixings – positions arrowed.
➔ Turn them approximately 90 degrees to release them.

❏ **STEP 11:** The motor may now be removed.

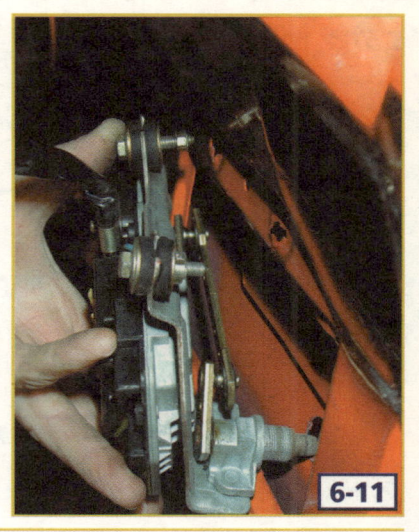

CHAPTER 10 Electrical, Instruments Job 6

10-7

CHAPTER 10 Electrical, Instruments Job 7

206

☐ **STEP 12:** Disconnect the wiring connectors.

☐ **STEP 13:** Take out the bolts or drill out the pop rivets (arrowed) – according to which type of fixing has been used – securing the motor bracket to the tailgate.
→ Take great care not to damage the tailgate when drilling out rivets!
→ Remove the wiper motor.

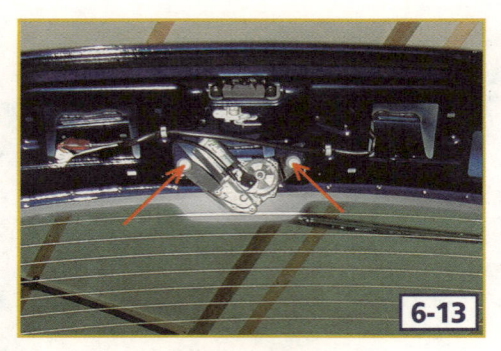

6-13

306 HATCHBACK

☐ **STEP 14:** Disconnect the washer hose and unclip it from the wiper motor.
→ Disconnect the motor wiring connectors.
→ Remove the mounting bolts and slide the motor to the right to disconnect it from the lug underneath.

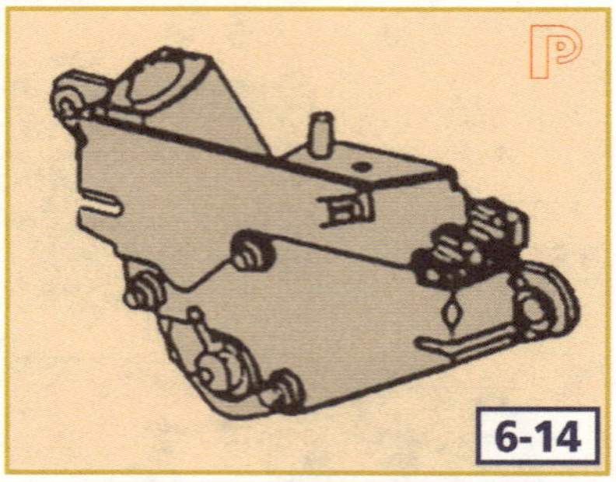

6-14

306 SALOON

☐ **STEP 15:** Remove the parcel shelf – see *Chapter 14, Interior, Trim*.

☐ **STEP 16:** Remove the wiper motor cover, wiring connector and bolts.
→ The wiper motor may now be withdrawn.

☐ **STEP 17:** Replace as the reverse of removal.

> **JOB 7:** RADIO AERIAL/ANTENNA - *remove, refit.*

> **FACT FILE**
> **RADIO AERIAL/ANTENNA**
> • Factory fitted aerials are mounted at the front or rear of the roof.
> • Early vehicles may be fitted with after-market aerials located on the roof or front or rear wing.
> • We describe procedures for both factory and after-market types.

ALL MODELS: Before dismantling, disconnect the battery negative (-) earth/ground terminal. See *Fact File: Disconnecting the Battery* BEFORE doing so!

Section A: Factory fit aerial/antenna.

106, 205, 206

☐ **STEP A1: ROOF MOUNTED (FRONT) AERIAL/ANTENNA:** The aerial is accessed by removing the courtesy light.
→ Lever off the courtesy light or roof console, depending on type fitted to vehicle.

7-A1

306

☐ **STEP A2:** The fixing nut is accessed by removing the roof console.

7-A2

ALL VEHICLES

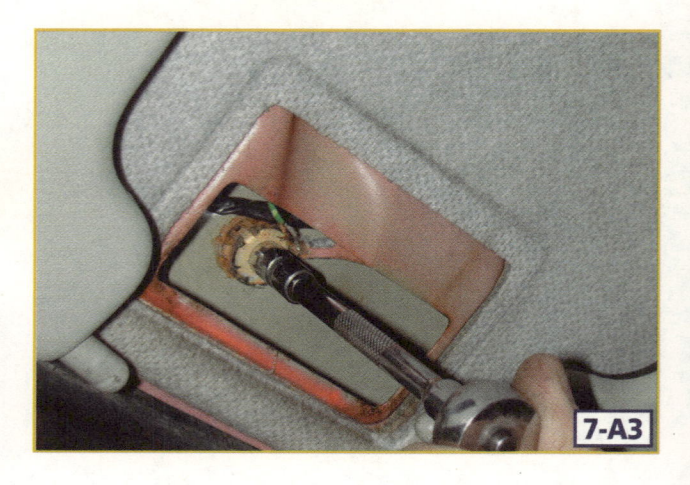

7-A3

☐ **STEP A3:** Remove the fixing nut, detach the lead…

10-8

☐ **STEP A4:** ...and remove the aerial from the roof, from outside the vehicle.

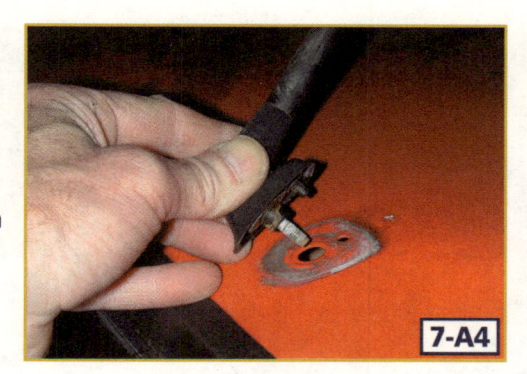

7-A4

ROOF MOUNTED (REAR) AERIAL/ANTENNA: The aerial is accessed by unclipping the tailgate seal, carefully unclipping the roof trim panel and pulling down the headlining.
→ The aerial is held by a base nut. Remove the nut, detach the lead and remove the aerial.

Section B: After-market aerial/antenna.

☐ **STEP B1: FRONT MOUNTED AERIAL/ ANTENNA:** Remove the relevant wheel and remove the inner wheelarch liner.
→ If the aerial is being renewed, cut through the cable near to the aerial.
→ Securely fix the radio-end of the new cable to the aerial-end of the old one.
→ As the old cable is withdrawn, the new one can be carefully fed into place.

☐ **STEP B2:** Inside the engine bay pull the aerial cable through its rubber grommet in the bulkhead. Unclip it along its run through the engine bay.

IMPORTANT NOTE: Depending on which model you are working on, you may have to remove the plastic scuttle trim.

☐ **STEP B3:** Remove the aerial mounting nut(s).
→ If the aerial is an electric-powered model, there will be more fixings behind the wheelarch liner.
→ There may also be a clamp bracket around the aerial stem. If so, undo the bolt to release the aerial.

☐ **STEP B4:** Draw the aerial down from the wheelarch cavity, and pull the aerial/antenna lead through the inner panel.

☐ **STEP B5:** Replace as the reverse of removal.

JOB 8: LIGHTS AND FUSES - *replace*.

CONTENTS
Section A: Headlight and sidelight bulbs - replacement.
Section B: Front indicator bulbs – replacement.
Section C: Indicator side repeater - replacement.
Section D: Headlight and front indicator units - replacement.
Section E: Front foglight or driving light bulbs - replacement.
Section F: Rear light bulbs and units - replacement
Section G: Number plate light.
Section H: 205 rear fog and separate reversing light.
Section I: Interior lights.
Section J: Dashboard bulbs.
Section K: Fuses and relays.

TOP TIP!
• Whenever a light fails to work, check its fuse before replacing the bulb.
• A blown bulb often causes a fuse to blow at the same time.
• See *Section K.: Fuses and relays*.
• If the fuse is okay, check the light earth connection.

There are detail differences between the light units fitted to the various models and variants covered by this manual, but the principles of removing and replacing them are the same in all instances.

IMPORTANT NOTE: After removing and replacing any headlight components, have the headlights aligned with a beam adjuster before using the vehicle at night.

SAFETY FIRST!
• Before dismantling, disconnect the battery negative (-) earth/ground terminal. See *Fact File: Disconnecting the Battery* BEFORE doing so!

• Beware! A bulb that has recently been ON may be extremely hot and cause a burn.

Section A: Headlight and sidelight bulbs - replacement.

TOP TIP!
• If you touch a halogen headlight bulb with bare fingers you will shorten its life, so handle it with a piece of tissue paper.
• If the bulb is accidentally touched, wipe it carefully with methylated (mineralised) spirit.

☐ **STEP A1:** Work inside the engine bay.

☐ **STEP A2: 106, 205:** Remove the headlight cover (2) and the connector (1).
➜ Release the retaining clip or spring (3) and remove the bulb (4).

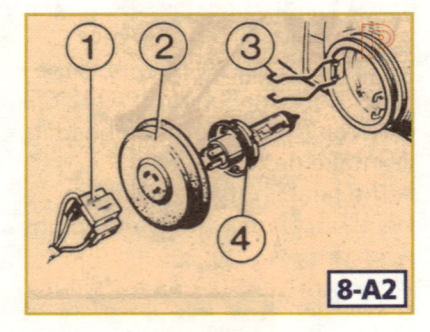

☐ **STEP A3:** Hold the bulb by its contacts and do not touch the glass.

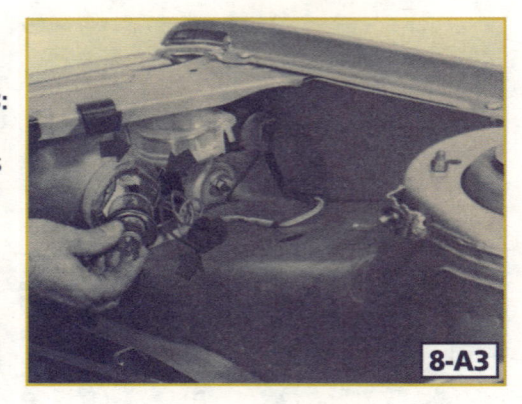

☐ **STEP A4: 206:** Unclip the filler from the radiator if replacing the right-side bulb.
➜ Remove the headlight rear cover (separate main beam/dipped bulbs) or the rubber dust cover (combined bulbs).
➜ Release the retaining clip or spring and remove the bulb.

☐ **STEP A5: 306:** Remove the headlight rear cover - turn the cover and pull.

☐ **STEP A6:** Release the retaining clip or spring and remove the bulb.

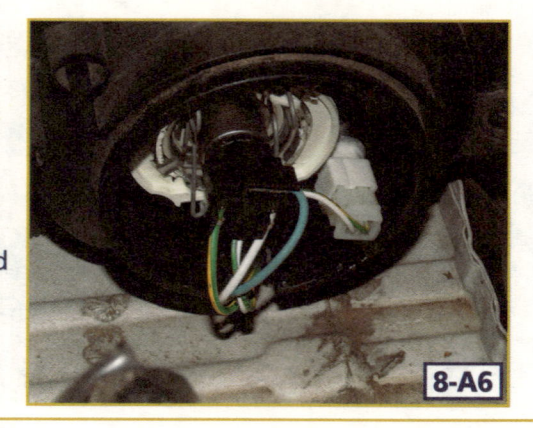

☐ **STEP A:7 ALL VEHICLES:** When refitting the bulb, ensure that the tabs and cutaways on the bulb seat and reflector housing are properly aligned.

Section B: Front indicator bulbs – replacement.

☐ **STEP B1:** Work inside the engine bay.

☐ **STEP B2: 106 – EARLY MODELS:** The indicator unit is held by a spring.
➜ Detach the spring from the body panel.
➜ Pull the light unit forward.
➜ Twist the bulb holder to remove it.
➜ The bulb is a bayonet fit.

☐ **STEP B3: 106 – LATER MODELS:** The indicator bulb is behind a flap, under the wheelarch.
➜ Open the flap, turn the socket 90 degrees and replace the bulb.

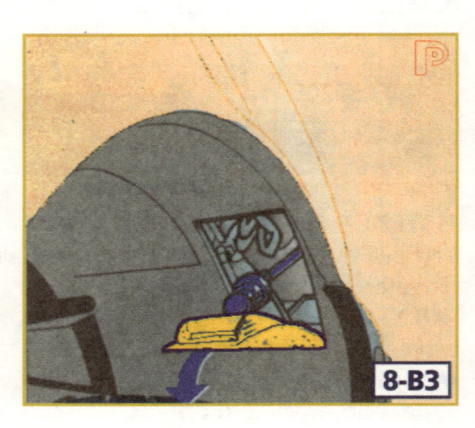

☐ **STEP B4: 205, 206:** Disconnect the indicator bulb plug (arrowed).
➜ Twist the bulb holder 90 degrees anticlockwise, and withdraw it.
➜ The bulb is a bayonet fit.

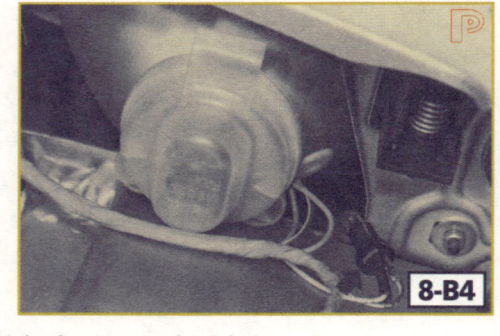

☐ **STEP B5: 306:** There is a retaining lever for the indicator light unit, situated above the headlight.
➜ Push the lever down and pull the indicator light forward.
➜ Twist the bulb holder to remove it.
➜ The bulb is a push fit.

Section C: Indicator side repeater – replacement.

☐ **STEP C1: 106, 306:** Push the unit toward the rear of the car to free it.
→ Pull the bulb holder from the lens unit.

☐ **STEP C2: 206:** Push the unit sideways to disengage one of its clips and then pull it from the wing.
→ Twist the bulb holder to remove it from the lens.

☐ **STEP C3: 205:** There are two types of side repeater.
→ The early type is removed by reaching up behind the wing and squeezing the two plastic lugs on the rear of the holder, when it can be pushed forwards and out. Separate the bulbholder from the lens by twisting anti-clockwise.
→ On later types – shown here – the lens is simple turned a quarter-turn to the left and pulled through the aperture in the wing.
→ On both types the bulb is a simple push-fit in the holder.

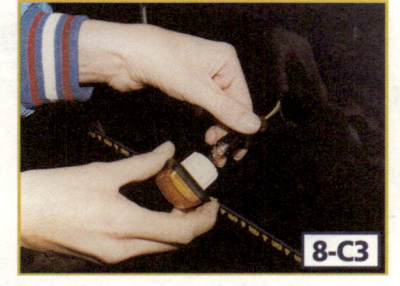

Section D: Headlight and front indicator units - replacement.

☐ **STEP D1: 106:** Remove the front indicator unit – see *Section B*.
→ The headlight is secured from behind by a clip. Release the clip, detach the wiring plugs and remove the headlight.

☐ **STEP D2: 205:** Remove the headlight and front indicator bulbs – see *Section A*.
→ Remove the front grille – see *Chapter 13, Job 7*.
→ The headlight is held by spring clips, accessible from the front. Release the spring clips and disconnect the load level arm.
→ The headlight can now be removed.

☐ **STEP D3: 206, 306:** Remove the front grille and the front trim panel under it – see *Chapter 13, Job 7*.
→ To remove the left side headlight, first unclip the air intake deflector.
→ The headlights are held by three bolts. Remove them, disconnect the wiring plugs and remove the headlight.

☐ **STEP D4: 306:** This is the top headlight fixing bolt.

Section E: Front foglight or driving light bulbs - replacement.

☐ **STEP E1: ALL MODELS EXCEPT 106 AND 206:** Remove the fog light securing screws (arrowed) and pull the glass, surround and reflector from the bumper.
→ Remove the bulb holder.

☐ **STEP E2: 206:** The bulb-holder is accessed through a flap in the front wheel-arch cover. Turn the steering to full lock and press the flap to open it.
→ Turn the cover to remove it, then disconnect the

wiring connector.
→ The bulb is secured by a clip. Press the two ends of the clip and remove the bulb.

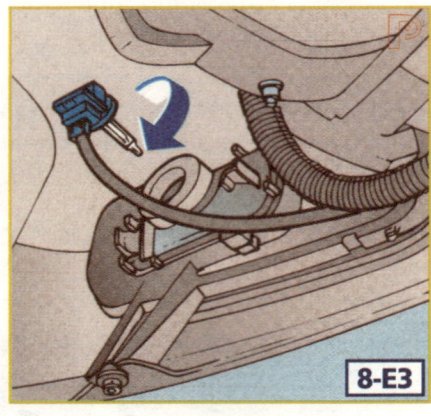

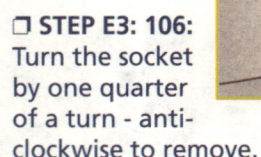

☐ **STEP E3: 106:** Turn the socket by one quarter of a turn - anti-clockwise to remove.

Section F: Rear light bulbs and units - replacement.

106

☐ **STEP F1:** To change a rear bulb, first remove the cluster.
→ Open the tailgate or luggage bay lid.
→ Lever off the cluster inner cover (1) and the air extractor grille (2).
→ Disconnect the wiring plugs and remove the cluster securing nuts (3).
→ The cluster (5) can be lifted away.
→ 106: The lens (4) is held by two screws and clips. Remove the screws and unclip the lens.
→ The bulbs are a bayonet fitting.

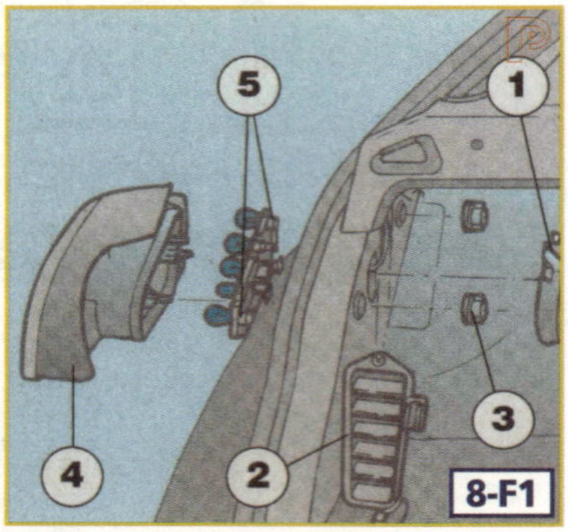

205

☐ **STEP F2:** To change a rear bulb undo the lens screws (a) and disconnect the lens from the lower tabs (b).
→ Remove the lens.

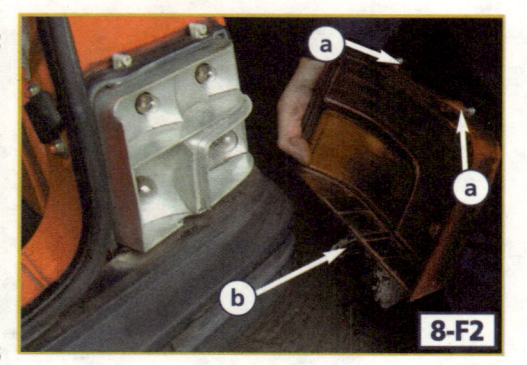

☐ **STEP F3:** The bulbs are a bayonet fitting.

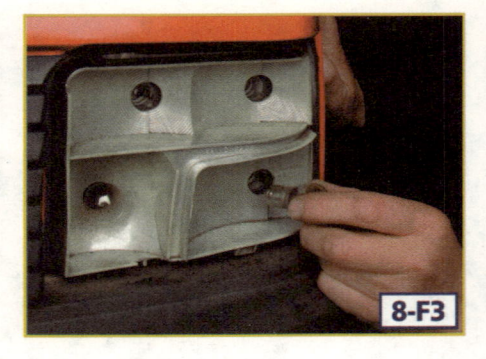

206

☐ **STEP F4:** To access the rear light cluster remove the luggage compartment side panel – see **Chapter 14, Interior, Trim**.
→ Disconnect the wiring connector.
→ To change a light bulb, use the tool (a) clipped to the light unit to unscrew the bulbholder nut (c).
→ The bulbs are bayonet fitting.
→ Tool (a) can be stowed on support (b).

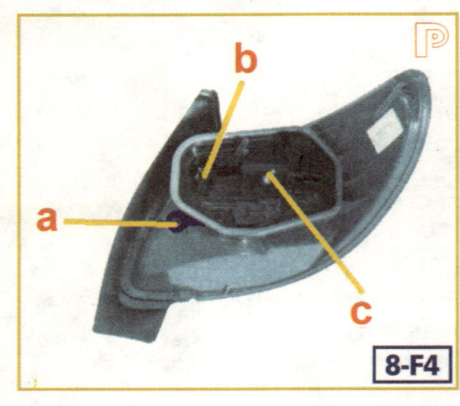

306

☐ **STEP F5:** The rear light cluster is secured by two nuts accessible from within the luggage area.
→ Remove the nuts.

☐ **STEP F6:** Pull the rear cover from the cluster and disconnect the wiring plugs.
→ The bulb holders have a retaining tab – press on the tab and lift the bulb holder away.
→ The bulbs are bayonet fitting.

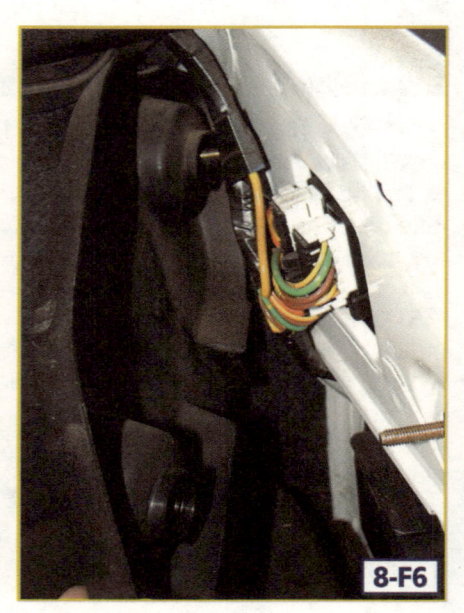

Section G: Number plate light.

❏ **STEP G1: 106, 306:** Use a small flat blade screwdriver to lever off the light lens.
➔ The bulb is a push fit.

❏ **STEP G2: 205:** Twist and pull the lens to remove it.
➔ The bulb is a bayonet fit.

❏ **STEP G3: 206:** Open the tailgate and remove the inner trim panel.
➔ Push the light unit out while depressing the retaining tabs.
➔ Disconnect the wiring connector.

Section H: 205 rear fog and separate reversing light.

❏ **STEP H1:** The rear fog light and/or reversing light lens is secured by two screws, one at each end.
➔ With the screws undone the bulb can be removed by pushing-in slightly and turning anti-clockwise.

Section I: Interior lights.

There are two basic types of interior light. Some have the bulb fitted from the outside, and some have the bulb fitted from behind.

❏ **STEP I1:** Carefully lever off the lens.

❏ **STEP I2:** Carefully lever out the light unit.

➔ Disconnect the wiring connectors.
➔ Remove the bulb holder.

Section J: Dashboard lights.

❏ **STEP J1:** Remove the instrument binnacle - see *Job 3*.

❏ **STEP J2:** The bulb holders are either a push fit or a bayonet fit.

Section K: Fuses and relays.

See also **Chapter 15.**

❏ **STEP K1:** The fuses are colour coded, orange for 7.5 amp, red for 10 amp, blue for 15 amp, yellow for 20 amp, neutral or clear for 25 amp and green for 30 amp.
➔ A 'blown' or defective fuse is indicated by a break in the wire which may appear melted.

TOP TIP!

• If a complete 'set' of bulbs fails to operate (and especially if other electrical components fail at the same time) check the fuses before suspecting any other fault.
• If a replacement fuse blows, you probably have a circuit fault.
• If the fuse protecting the circuit has not blown, it may be that a relay had failed.
• If the 'wrong' bulb illuminates (i.e. indicator instead of brake light) check the earth connections.

SAFETY FIRST!

• Make sure that all electrical circuits are switched off before removing or replacing a fuse.
• Never try to 'cure' a fault by fitting a fuse with a higher amperage rating than the one specified.

❏ **STEP K2:** The location of the main fuse box varies between models, but on older vehicles it is most usually at the left side of the dashboard behind the glovebox (LHD) or under a trim panel on the driver's side (RHD), and on recent models (206, 306) on the right side of the dashboard.

CHAPTER 10 Electrical, Instruments Jobs 9-11

☐ **STEP K3:** Fuses with higher ratings to carry higher currents are usually situated within the engine bay fuse/relay box.

☐ **STEP K4:** Relays are either placed adjacent to the fuses, or on the bulkhead/firewall, in the engine bay.

8-K3

JOB 9: CENTRAL LOCKING - *replace components*.

See *Chapter 13, Job 16*.

JOB 10: DIESEL GLOW PLUGS - *check, replace*.

IMPORTANT NOTE: Unless you are experiencing trouble starting the engine, the glow plugs should demand no more attention than a clean-up when the injectors are checked.

10-1

☐ **STEP 1:** Disconnect the battery negative (-) terminal. Undo the retaining nuts (arrowed) at the top of each glow plug.
➔ Remove the connecting rail/bus – sometimes with a flexible section, as here.

☐ **STEP 2:** Clean away any dirt from around the plugs, then fully unscrew and remove them.
➔ Examine the condition of each plug by wiping soot away and examining for erosion of the element sheath.
➔ Check the internal resistance of each glow plug with an ohmeter. The reading should, if the plug is healthy, be 0.4 ohms.

JOB 11: AIR CONDITIONING EQUIPMENT.

IMPORTANT NOTE: After gas has been removed from the air conditioning system by a specialist, seal all open connections to stop any contamination from entering the system.

SAFETY FIRST!

• DO NOT open the pressurised pipework on the air conditioning system.
• The air conditioning system contains pressurised gas and specialist equipment is needed to extract it. It is illegal to discharge the gas to the atmosphere.
• The gas used in air conditioning systems is extremely harmful to the environment and may cause injury to the person carrying out the work if released in an uncontrolled manner.
• If air conditioning units are in the way of carrying out other work, whenever possible move units to one side with pipes still attached.
• If this is not possible, or there is a risk of damage to pipes or connections, have an air conditioning specialist de-pressurise the system so that you can dismantle it.

☐ **STEP 1:** • If the system needs to be drained for any reason, or if you suspect a leak, take the vehicle to a Peugeot dealer or an air-conditioning specialist such as AutoClimate (see back of book).
• After it has been re-assembled, the system will have to be tested (usually with inert nitrogen) and recharged by a specialist.

11-1

☐ **STEP 2:** Neither the condensor, the compressor, the receiver nor the evaporator should be detached from their pipes.
➔ If the condensor should have to be moved to change the coolant radiator, support it carefully out of the way while the work is being carried out, taking care not to damage the tubes or fins.

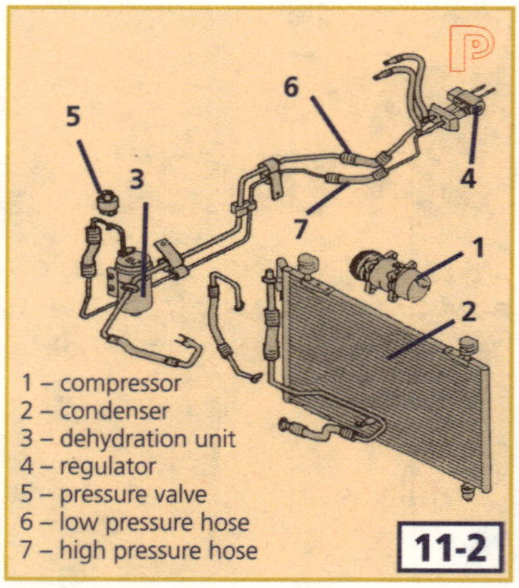

☐ **STEP 3:** If the compressor has to be taken from its bracket, do not disconnect any of the pipes. there are several different types of compressor and bracket.
➔ Make a careful note of the way in which the compressor is mounted and take equally careful note of the system of bushes, shims and bolts which are used in the mounting and adjusting system.

1 – compressor
2 – condenser
3 – dehydration unit
4 – regulator
5 – pressure valve
6 – low pressure hose
7 – high pressure hose

11-2

10-14

CHAPTER 11: STEERING, SUSPENSION

Please read **Chapter 2 Safety First** before carrying out any work on your car.

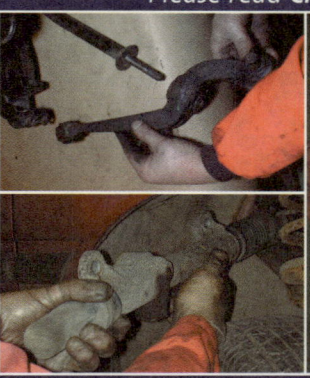

CONTENTS

	Page No.		Page No.
JOB 1: SYSTEMS EXPLAINED.	11-1	JOB 13: FRONT WHEEL BEARINGS - *replace*.	11-17
STEERING		JOB 14: FRONT ANTI-ROLL BAR AND BUSHES - *replace*.	11-19
JOB 2: STEERING WHEEL – *remove, refit*.	11-4		
JOB 3: TRACK ROD END – *replace*.	11-4	JOB 15: FRONT SUBFRAME – *remove, refit*.	11-20
JOB 4: STEERING RACK GAITER - *replace*.	11-6	**REAR SUSPENSION**	
JOB 5: STEERING RACK – *remove, replace*.	11-6	JOB 16: REAR DAMPERS - *replace*.	11-21
JOB 6: POWER STEERING PUMP – *remove, refit*.	11-8	JOB 17: REAR SUSPENSION ASSEMBLY – *remove, refit*.	11-21
JOB 7: POWER STEERING SYSTEM – *filling, bleeding*.	11-9	JOB 18: REAR SUSPENSION MOUNTING BUSHES – *replace*.	11-22
FRONT SUSPENSION			
JOB 8: FRONT LOWER ARM AND BALLJOINT - *replace*.	11-9	JOB 19: REAR SUSPENSION ASSEMBLY – *dismantle, rebuild*.	11-23
JOB 9: FRONT LOWER ARM BUSHES - *replace*.	11-12	JOB 20: REAR HUB, BRAKE DRUM AND WHEEL BEARINGS – *remove, replace, refit*.	11-27
JOB 10: FRONT STRUT - *remove, refit*.	11-12		
JOB 11: FRONT STRUT - *overhaul*.	11-14		
JOB 12: FRONT HUB CARRIER - *replace*.	11-16		

JOB 1: SYSTEMS EXPLAINED.

FRONT SUSPENSION

The models covered by this manual all have independent front suspension of the MacPherson strut type. There are, however, differences between variants.

These annotations apply to all diagrams:

- a – nut
- b – washer
- c – cup
- d – top mounting plate nut
- e – top mounting plate
- f – rubber insulator
- g – cap
- h – stop ring
- i – coil spring
- j1 – suspension strut assembly
- j2 – top strut/damper
- k – spring seat
- l – lower strut
- m – shroud
- n – bush
- o – bolt
- p – hub/bearing carrier
- q – subframe
- r1 – lower suspension arm/wishbone
- r2 – ball joint
- r3 – heat shield
- s – bearing
- t – circlip
- u – clamp plate
- v – anti-roll bar
- w – link arm
- x – driveshaft
- y1 – steering arm/track rod
- y2 – track rod end
- z1 – steering rack
- z2 – steering column assembly
- z3 – steering universal joint

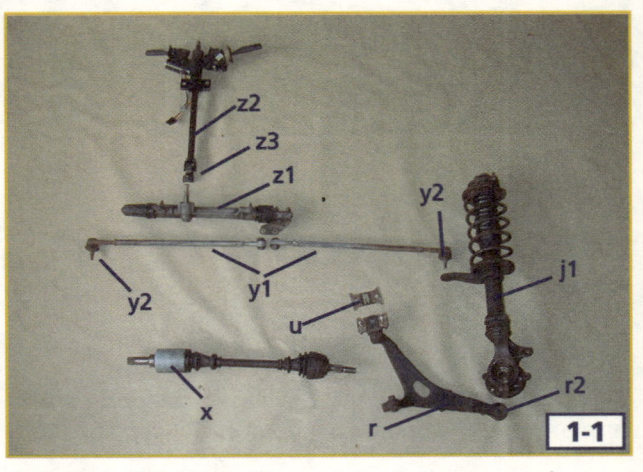

☐ **STEP 1: 106-TYPE:** Shown here is the general layout of the 106 front suspension and steering systems.

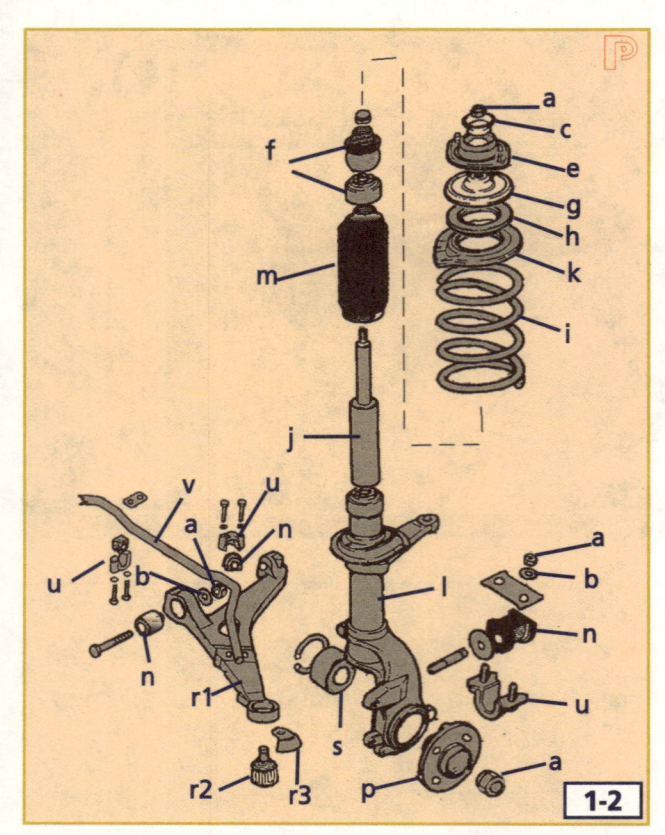

CHAPTER 11 Steering, Suspension Job 1

☐ **STEP 2: 106-TYPE:** These are the individual components of the front suspension. The components are bolted direct to the body shell, unlike all the other types shown here, which have a separate subframe.

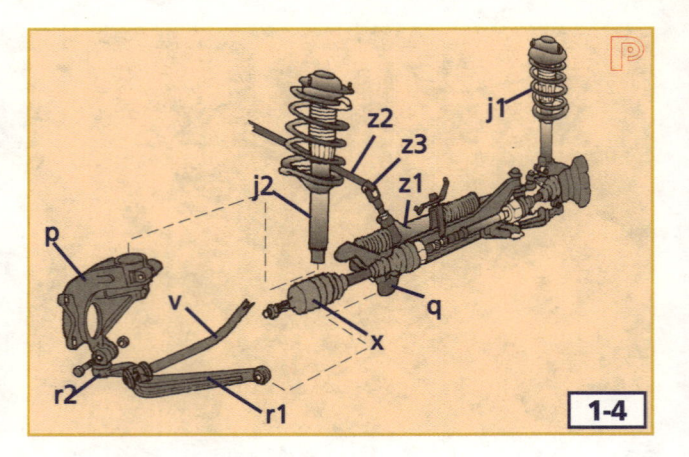

☐ **STEP 3: 205 NON-GTI:** These are the steering and suspension components of the non-GTI-type of 205.

☐ **STEP 4: 205 NON-GTI:** The lower suspension arm on these models has a single inboard mounting, with the anti-roll bar holding the arm in position.

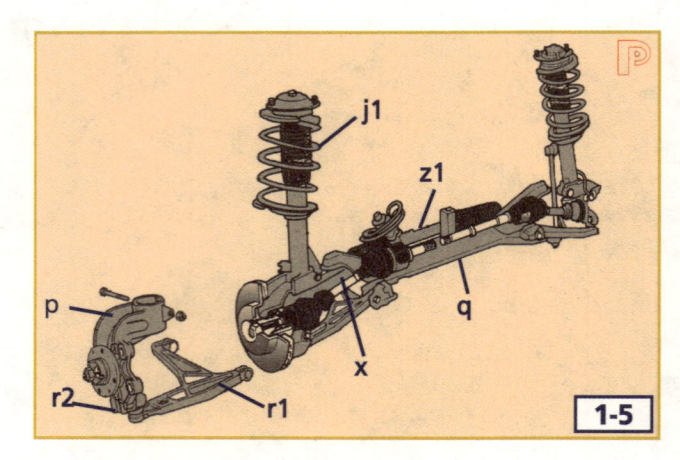

☐ **STEP 5: 205 GTI-TYPE:** This is similar to the non-GTI system, except that the lower arm has two inboard mounting points.

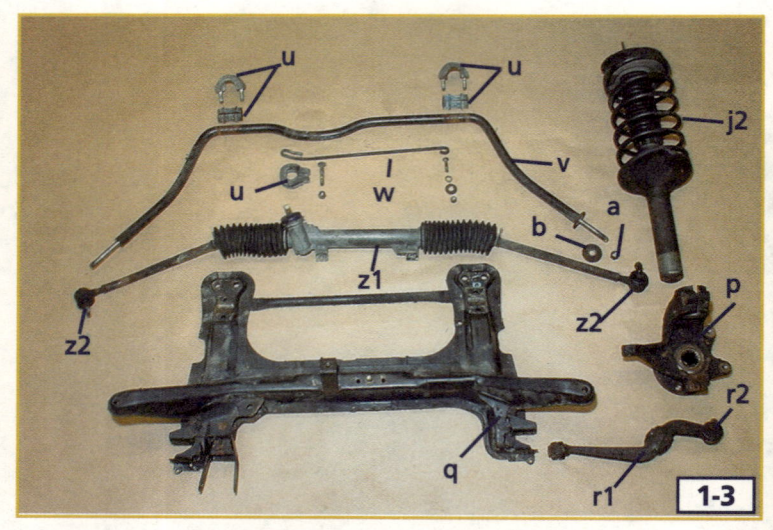

☐ **STEP 6: 206-TYPE:** Although the principle is very similar, the fittings at the inboard-end of the lower arm are very different.

11-2

REAR SUSPENSION

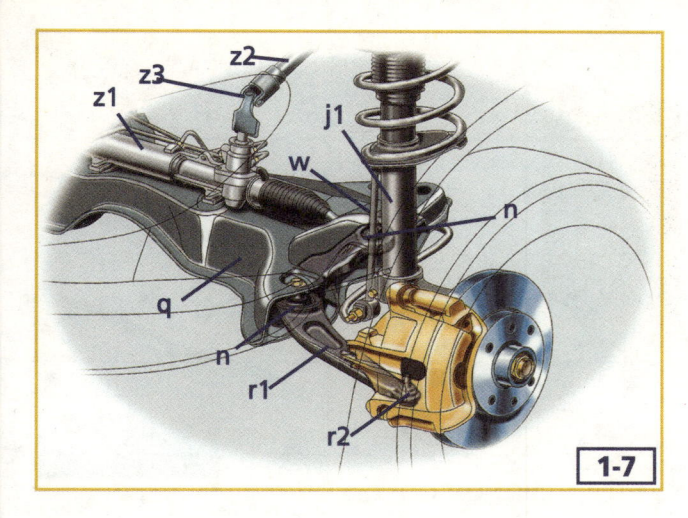

1-7

☐ **STEP 7: 206-TYPE:** There are two vertical bolts holding the inboard-end to the subframe via flexible bushes.

☐ **STEP 8: 306-TYPE:** Once again, there are great similarities – as well as detail differences - between this and the other types shown here.

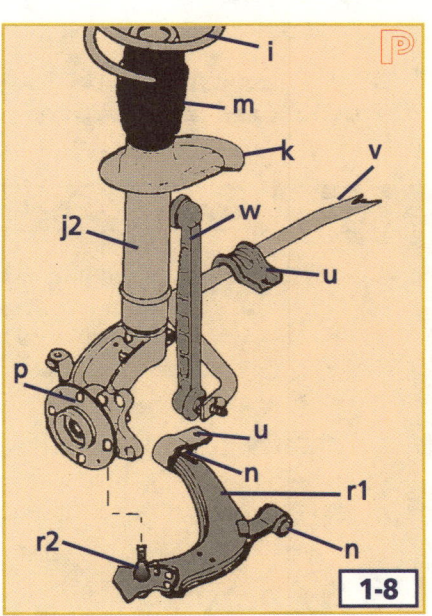

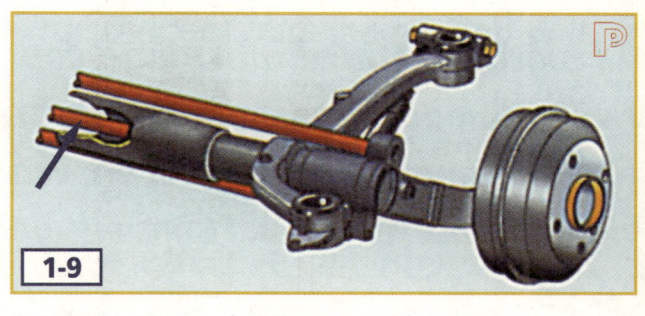

1-8

1-9

☐ **STEP 9:** All the models covered by this manual share a similar - and unusual - torsion bar rear suspension layout.
→ The rear springs are torsion bars.
→ Each rear spring is attached to a trailing arm, and is also attached at its opposite end to a fixed part of the suspension structure.
→ As the trailing arm moves, it twists against the springing in the torsion bar.
→ Note that many models have an anti-roll bar inside the main axle tube (arrowed).

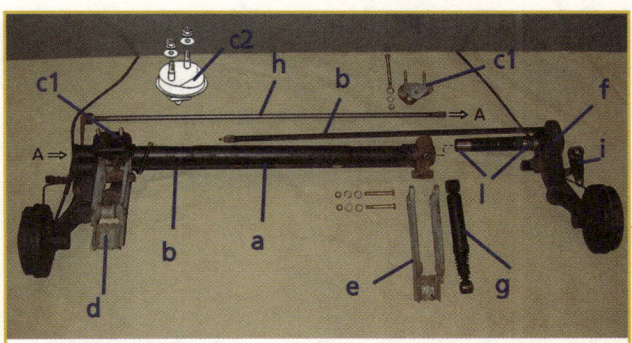

a – cross-tube/'axle'-tube
b – torsion bar
c1 – front suspension mounting
c2 – front suspension mounting - 306-type
d – rear suspension mounting
e – suspension mounting frame
f – trailing arm
g – telescopic damper
h – anti-roll bar
i – anti-roll bar locating lever
j – cap
k – bearing
l – bearing seat
m – torsion bar fixing

1-10

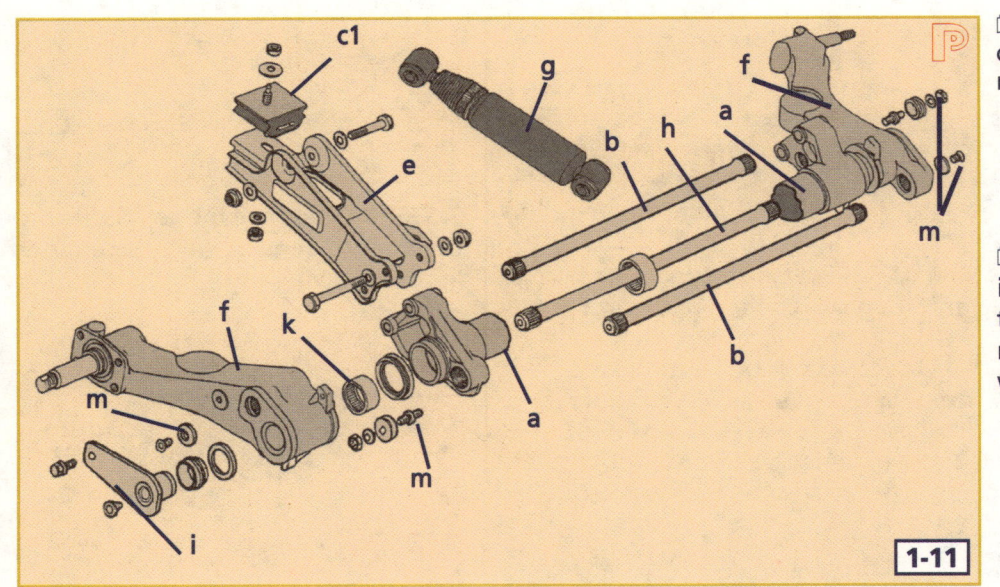

☐ **STEP 10:** These are the components of a typical rear suspension set-up.

☐ **STEP 11:** This illustration shows the torsion bar fixings of a rear suspension system with anti-roll bar.

1-11

CHAPTER 11 Steering, Suspension Job 1

11-3

Chapter 11 Steering, Suspension Jobs 2-3

1-12

☐ **STEP 12: 206 MODELS:** 206 models are fitted with an evolved version of the same system.
→ Note the very different body mounting points and trailing arms.
→ The principle of the transverse torsion bars is the same as on other models.

STEERING

FACT FILE

FACT FILE: STEERING TYPES

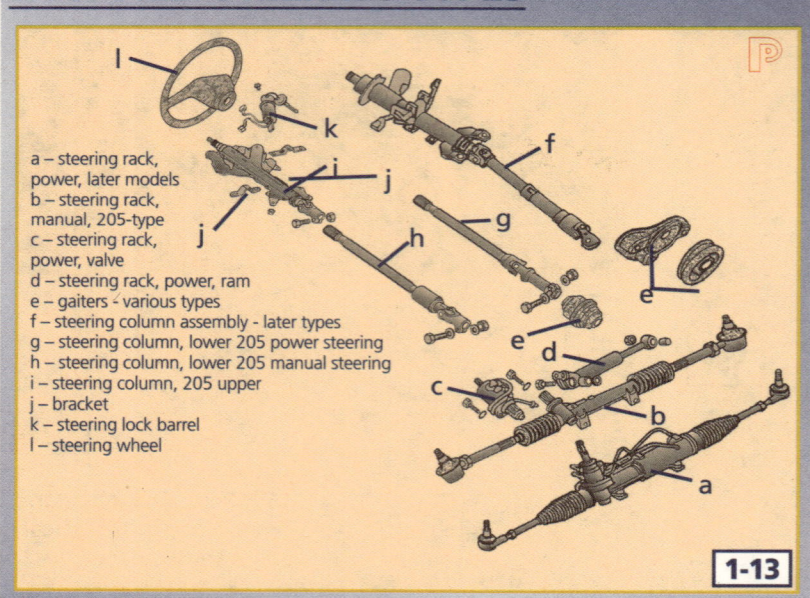

a – steering rack, power, later models
b – steering rack, manual, 205-type
c – steering rack, power, valve
d – steering rack, power, ram
e – gaiters - various types
f – steering column assembly - later types
g – steering column, lower 205 power steering
h – steering column, lower 205 manual steering
i – steering column, 205 upper
j – bracket
k – steering lock barrel
l – steering wheel

1-13

☐ **STEP 13:** Two different types of steering rack have been fitted to the vehicles covered by this manual:
→ **106-TYPE:** See illustration *1-1*. The rack is bolted to the vehicle's bodywork.
→ **ALL OTHER TYPES:** All other models have a steering system similar to the ones shown here. The rack is bolted to the front subframe.
→ On all non-106 models, the manual rack is similar to *item b*.
→ Some models with power steering have a fully-integrated rack (*item a*) while 205 and 306 models with power steering have the version with a separate ram (*item d*) and valve (*item c*) fitted to a rack that is similar in appearance to the standard manual rack.

JOB 2: STEERING WHEEL – *remove, refit.*

See **Chapter 14, Job 6**.

JOB 3: TRACK ROD END - *replace.*

SAFETY FIRST!

• It is important to have the tracking (wheel alignment) checked after disturbing the steering joints.

• This is to ensure the handling of the vehicle remains safe and also to avoid uneven tyre wear.

• When re-assembling, use all new locknuts, stretch bolts and split pins, as originally fitted.

SAFETY FIRST!

• The nut holding the track rod end to the steering arm should be renewed every time it has to be removed.

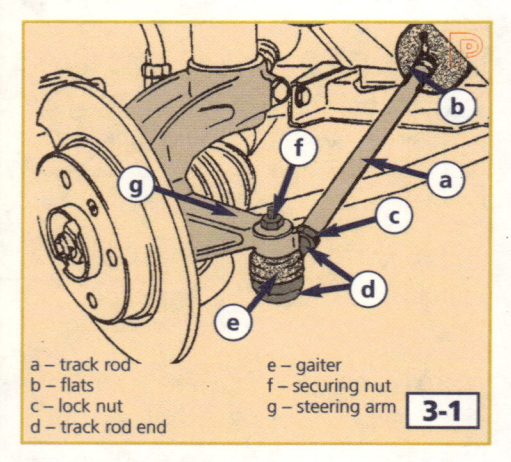

a – track rod
b – flats
c – lock nut
d – track rod end
e – gaiter
f – securing nut
g – steering arm

3-1

☐ **STEP 1:** These are the components of the track rod end assembly referred to in the following text.

11-4

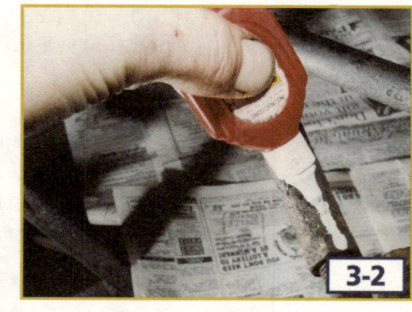

❒ **STEP 2:** After wire brushing off the components so that the threads are clean, use typists' correction fluid to mark the position of the lock nut on the track rod.

3-2

→ The lock nut can now be backed off by a fraction of a turn.
→ The function of the mark is to ensure that the lock nut and thus the replacement track rod end, can be fitted in the same position as previously so that the tracking is as close to being in adjustment as possible.
→ It is unlikely that the new track rod end will be exactly the same size as the old one and so this location will only be approximate.

TOP TIP!

• If the locknut has to be removed to allow a steering gaiter to be fitted, mark its position by applying a dab of paint, or wrap a piece of tape around the steering arm so that the nut, when replaced, will return to its original position.
• Alternatively, count the number of turns when removing the track rod end.

❒ **STEP 3:** Remove the nut securing the track rod end balljoint to the steering arm.
→ This is the 106-type of steering where the balljoint thread faces downwards.

3-3

❒ **STEP 4:** The taper on the balljoint means that the TRE will almost always be seized in position.
→ One way of freeing it is to use a pair of hammers, as shown. Hold the larger of the two against the eye on the steering arm and use the other hammer to shock the end of the steering arm. This temporarily distorts it and frees the TRE.

3-4

TOP TIP!

If the nut seizes on the thread:
• Try releasing fluid.
• It may be necessary to cut the nut from the pin using a hacksaw or nut-splitter.
• Alternatively, it is sometimes possible to use a ball joint removal tool in reverse, so it compresses rather than opens the joint. This can create enough friction in the joint to enable you to remove it.

❒ **STEP 5:** Alternatively, you could use a TRE splitter such as the one shown here.
→ If you need to reuse the track rod end, refit the nut to the thread so that the splitter doesn't damage the thread.

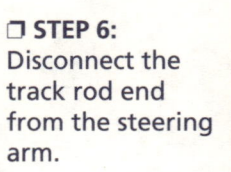

3-5

❒ **STEP 6:** Disconnect the track rod end from the steering arm.

3-6

❒ **STEP 7:** Remove the TRE from the steering arm.
→ Grip the inboard end of the steering arm (also see illustration *3-1*, *item b*) to prevent the steering arm from turning.
→ If the TRE is tight, use a self-grip wrench to unscrew it from the steering arm.
→ Don't disturb the lock nut. Use it to position the replacement TRE – see *Step 2*.

3-7

CHAPTER 11 Steering, Suspension Job 3

11-5

JOB 4: STEERING RACK GAITER - replace.

SAFETY FIRST!

• When re-assembling, use all new locknuts, stretch bolts and split pins, as appropraite.

The gaiters on the steering rack are vulnerable to wear. If they fail, road dirt and water will quickly enter and cause expensive, wear to the rack.

The two different forms of steering rack covered by this manual require different approaches to replacing the rubber gaiters.

Section A: 106.

☐ **STEP A1:** Each track rod bolts to the steering rack, at a sliding collar:
➔ Remove the nut (**a**) and bolt (**b**) securing the track rod to the steering rack.
➔ Remove the locknut (**c**) and take off the inner track rod end (**d**).
➔ Release the clips securing the rubber gaiter.

☐ **STEP A2:** Remove the securing clip(s) and replace the damaged rubber gaiter(s).

☐ **STEP A3:** Refitting is the reverse of removal.

Section B: All other models.

☐ **STEP B1:** If one or both of the gaiters are defective, replace them as follows:
➔ Remove the track-rod-end - see **Job 3**.

☐ **STEP B2:** The clips securing each end of the gaiter can now be removed, the small outer clip of the type shown can be released with pliers and passed over the gaiter.

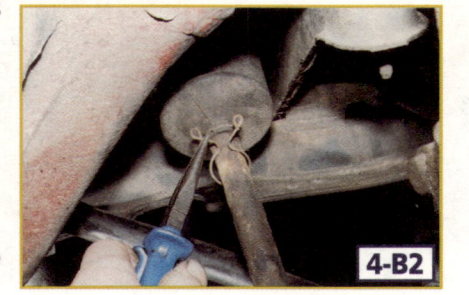

☐ **STEP B3:** The larger tensioned metal-band type can be undone by levering the free-end of the clip upwards with a screwdriver, while the 'cable tie' type can simply be cut off with wire cutters.

☐ **STEP B4:** The gaiter can now be slid-off along the steering arm, and a new one slipped into place.

TOP TIP!

• Some types of rack contain oil. If any oil is lost as the gaiter is removed, or if oil has been lost through a split gaiter, it will have to be replaced.
• Raise the side of the vehicle from which the gaiter has been removed, fit the clip to only the inner end of the gaiter and inject oil through the outer end of the gaiter before fitting the clip.
• Don't over-fill or damage can be caused.

☐ **STEP B5:** Fit new clips, which should have been supplied with the new gaiter:
➔ Replace the track-rod-end.

SAFETY FIRST!

• It is important to have the tracking (wheel alignment) checked after disturbing the steering joints.
• This is to ensure the handling of the vehicle remains safe and also to avoid uneven tyre wear.

JOB 5: STEERING RACK – remove, replace.

SAFETY FIRST!

• When re-assembling, use all new locknuts, stretch bolts and split pins, as appropriate.

☐ **STEP 1:** Before dismantling, disconnect the battery negative (-) earth/ground terminal. See **Chapter 10, Electrical, Dash, Instruments, Fact File: Disconnecting the Battery** BEFORE doing so!

❏ **STEP 2:** Remove items that prevent easy access to the steering rack.
→ Depending on model, these can include: air filter assembly, air box, intake piping and air mass meter housing, radiator expansion tank.
→ Secure pipework and wiring out of the way.

❏ **STEP 3:** If the vehicle has power steering, remove the fluid pipes from the steering rack assembly.
→ Seal the ends of the pipes to keep contamination out, and tie them out of the way, facing upwards to minimise fluid loss.

❏ **STEP 4A: 106 MODELS:** Disconnect the inner ends of the track rods from the steering rack. Remove both nuts and bolts.

❏ **STEP 4B: ALL OTHER MODELS:** Disconnect the outer ends of the track rods (the TREs) from the steering arms - see *Job 3*.

❏ **STEP 5A: 106 MODELS:** Unbolt the steering rack from the body - two locations (arrowed).

❏ **STEP 5B: 205 and 306 MODELS WITH MANUAL STEERING:** These are the positions of the rack mountings (arrowed) on the front face of the subframe.

❏ **STEP 5C: 205 and 306 MODELS:** There are spacers inside the subframe. If they come loose, they can be removed from inside the subframe through access holes (arrowed) in the base of the subframe.

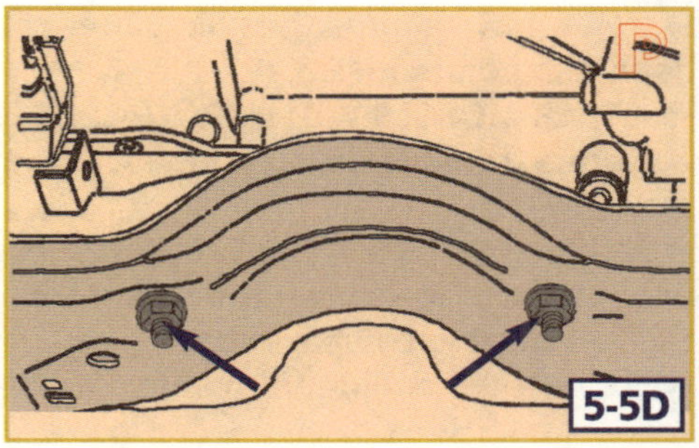

❏ **STEP 5D: 206 MODELS:** These are the locations of the rack mounting bolts (arrowed), on the base of the subframe

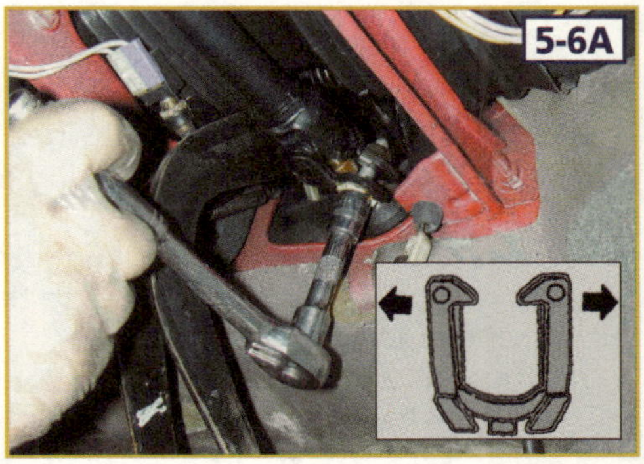

❏ **STEP 6A: 106 and 205 MODELS:** Inside the vehicles, adjacent to the foot pedals, remove the pinch bolt holding the universal joint (UJ) at the base of the steering column to the steering rack pinion shaft.
→ On some 206 versions, there is a safety clip that has to be removed - see inset.

❏ **STEP 6B: 205 and 306 MODELS:** The UJ is found in the engine bay, adjacent to the rack.
→ Remove the pinch bolt holding the universal joint, at the base of the steering column, to the steering rack pinion shaft.

CHAPTER 11 Steering, Suspension Job 5

11-7

CHAPTER 11 Steering, Suspension Job 6

☐ **STEP 7:** Remove the rack from the vehicle.
➔ **106 MODELS:** Remove the steering rack from the engine bay through the aperture in the right-hand side of the engine bay.
➔ It may have a large, flexible gaiter on it, depending on model.
➔ **OTHER MODELS WITH MANUAL STEERING:** There is room to remove the steering rack from one side of the vehicle
➔ **MODELS WITH POWER STEERING:** If there is not enough room to remove the rack from one side of the vehicle, you will have to:
➔ Support the engine from above with an engine support bar - see *Chapter 6, Engine*.
➔ Remove the rear engine mounting.
➔ Remove the bolts holding the subframe to the body and lower the subframe, so that the rack can be removed.

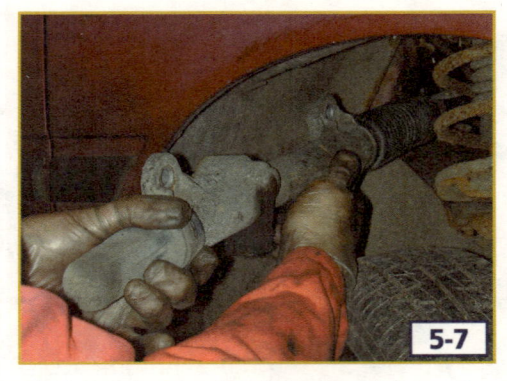

☐ **STEP 8:** Replacement is the reverse of removal.
➔ Set the steering wheel and road wheels to the straight-ahead position before refitting the steering column to the rack pinion shaft.
➔ Use new location nuts/bolts holding the steering rack to the vehicle, tightening them to the recommended torque.
➔ Use threadlock on all threads.
➔ The front wheel track must be correctly set.
➔ **POWER STEERING:** Refit the power steering pipes and renew power steering pipe 'O'-rings.
➔ Top up the power steering fluid reservoir and bleed the system if fluid was lost during removing.

Job 6: POWER STEERING PUMP – *remove, refit*.

FACT FILE
POWER STEERING PUMP
• The power steering pump cannot be serviced. If necessary it must be replaced, or exchanged for a reconditioned item.
• On 206 models, the pump, with integral reservoir, is fitted at the top of the engine.
• On some 205 and 306 models, the pump is fitted beneath the alternator and is more easily reached from underneath the vehicle.

☐ **STEP 1:** Before dismantling, disconnect the battery negative (-) earth/ground terminal. See *Chapter 10, Electrical, Dash, Instruments, Fact File: Disconnecting the Battery* BEFORE doing so!

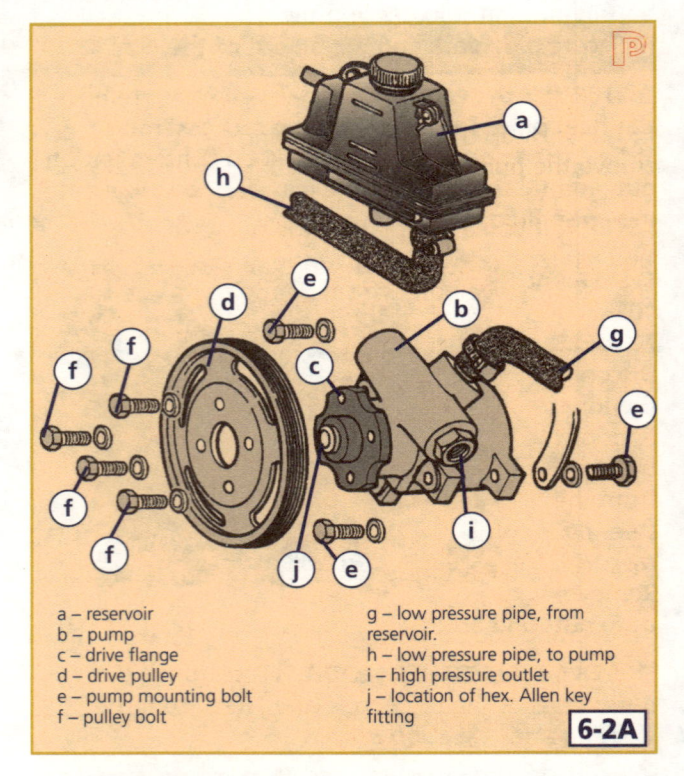

a – reservoir
b – pump
c – drive flange
d – drive pulley
e – pump mounting bolt
f – pulley bolt
g – low pressure pipe, from reservoir.
h – low pressure pipe, to pump
i – high pressure outlet
j – location of hex. Allen key fitting

6-2A

☐ **STEP 2A:** These are the components of a typical power steering system fitted to 205 and 306 models.

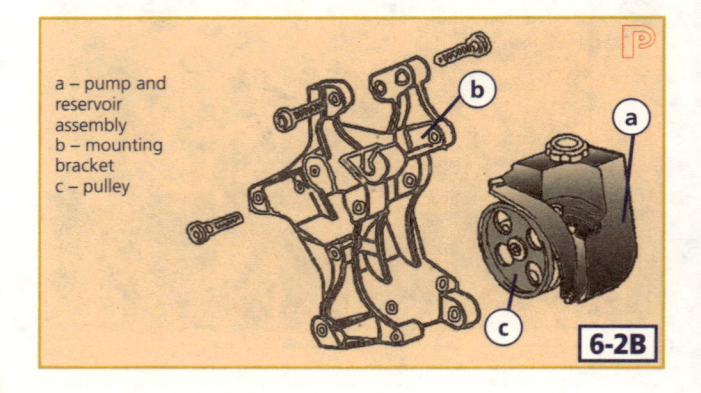

a – pump and reservoir assembly
b – mounting bracket
c – pulley

6-2B

☐ **STEP 2B:** This is a 206 power steering pump.

☐ **STEP 3:** Remove the auxiliary drive belt which drives the power steering pump.

☐ **STEP 4:** Clamp the low-pressure fluid supply hose at its furthest end from the reservoir, to minimise the amount of fluid lost from the system.
➔ On 206 models, the reservoir is integral with, and removed with, the pump

☐ **STEP 5:** Disconnect the fluid supply and feed hoses from the pump.
➔ Seal them to keep contamination out and tie out of the way.

TOP TIP!

- It is inevitable that some fluid will escape from the pipework, no matter how careful you are.
- Have a suitable receptacle at hand to catch spillage.

❑ **STEP 6:** Undo the pump mounting bolts and remove the pump.

❑ **STEP 7:** If you are replacing the pump, you will need to transfer the pulley to the new one. To remove the drive pulley from the power steering pump:
→ Prevent the pulley from turning with an Allen key in the centre of the end of the shaft, when fitted.
→ Alternatively, grip the pulley with a chain wrench, or tightly gripped drive belt, as you undo the mounting bolts.

❑ **STEP 8:** Refitting is the reverse of removal.
→ Replace all 'O'-ring seals on pipe unions before re-attaching them.
→ Bleed and top up the power steering fluid – see *Job 7*.

| JOB 7: | POWER STEERING SYSTEM – *filling, bleeding.* |

❑ **STEP 1:** Check the level of fluid in the power steering fluid reservoir. With the engine cold, it should be at the 'MIN' marking.
→ At full working temperature, it should be at the 'MAX' marking.

TOP TIP!

- If the level is low, because of a leak or work on the system, it should be topped up, and bled at the same time. It's useful to have someone to help you do this.

❑ **STEP 2:** Get the person helping you to start the engine. The fluid level will drop quickly, so you will have to pour in enough to keep the 'MIN' mark covered.
→ If the level drops below this, the pump will draw air into the system, taking it longer to bleed!

❑ **STEP 3:** Once the system has stopped drawing in fluid, turn the wheel slowly several times from lock to lock and return to the centre.
→ Do so several times, until air no longer bubbles into the fluid reservoir.

❑ **STEP 4:** When there is no air left in the system, stop the engine. Make sure the fluid level is correct.

| JOB 8: | FRONT LOWER ARM AND BALLJOINT - *replace.* |

SAFETY FIRST!

- When re-assembling, use all new locknuts, stretch bolts and split pins, as appropriate.

All the models covered by this manual have similar front suspension layouts, in principal.
→ MacPherson struts join a lower arm at a ball joint.
→ The lower arm inner pivot point has its mounting either on the bodyshell (106 models) or on a subframe (all other models).

a – subframe
b – lower arm inner mountings
c – hub carrier
d – balljoint pinch bolt
e – nut
f – lower arm with integral balljoint – 106, 205 and 206 models
g – heat shield
h – removal balljoint – 306 models

8-1

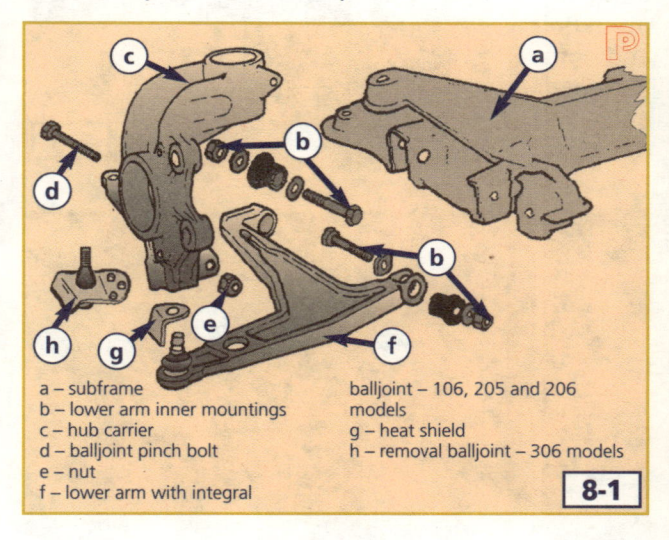

❑ **STEP 1:** The main part of this illustration shows a 205 GTI front suspension lower arm. The principles are similar to those for other types – see later illustrations for differences.
→ The inset (**item h**) shows the removal balljoint which is only fitted to 306 models.
→ On all other models, the complete lower arm has to be changed if the balljoint is worn.

11-9

CHAPTER 11 Steering, Suspension Job 8

☐ **STEP 2:** These are the components of the 206 lower arm and balljoint (**a**), the pinch bolt and nut (**b**) holding the balljoint to the hub carrier (**c**) and the heat shield (**d**).

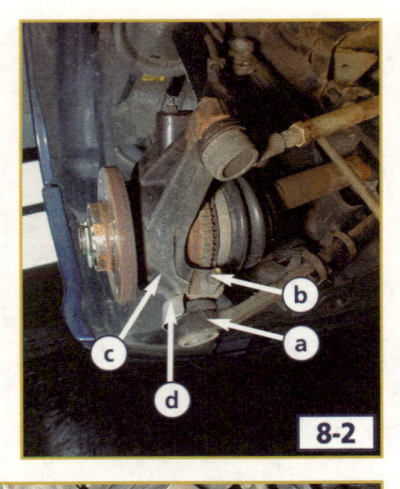

8-2

☐ **STEP 3:** When an air deflector is fitted to the lower arm it must first be removed after undoing the clips (arrows).

8-3

☐ **STEP 4:** On all models, the pinch bolt and nut are loosened and removed.

8-4

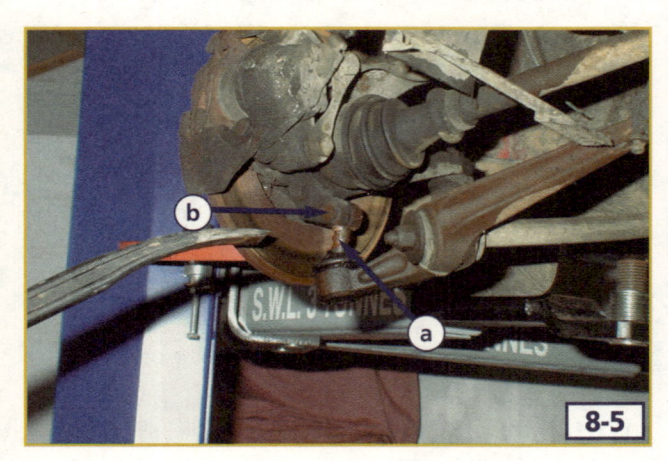

8-5

☐ **STEP 5:** It may now be possible to lever the lower arm balljoint (**a**) out of the bottom of the hub carrier (**b**).

☐ **STEP 6:** When a heat shield is fitted, it should now be removed for re-use later.
➜ If it's rusted away, you'll need to obtain a new one from a Peugeot dealer.

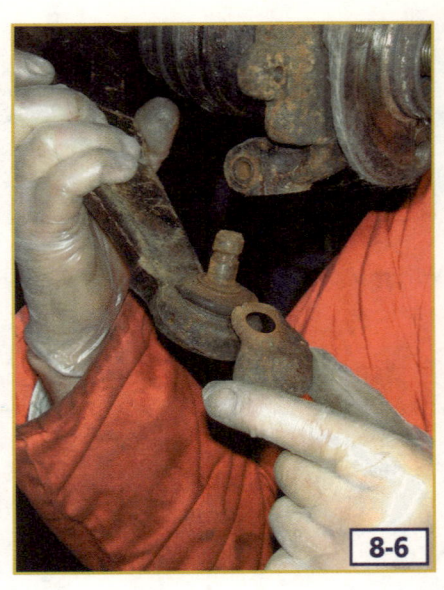

8-6

TOP TIP!

☐ **STEP 7:** It is frequently very difficult to separate the balljoint from the bottom of the hub carrier. Here are two ways of overcoming the difficulty.
• Carefully drive a chisel into the clamp at the bottom of the hub carrier so that the pin on the balljoint becomes free.

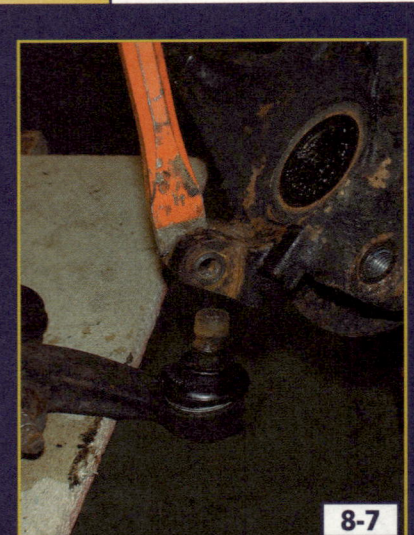

8-7

☐ **STEP 8:** •
This method will require a little more care so as not to cause damage to the vehicle and also so that the vehicle cannot be pulled off its supports:
• A very long, strong lever, braced against the subframe or some other strong part of the underside of the vehicle may be used to lever the lower arm balljoint out of the hub carrier.

8-8

11-10

☐ **STEP 9:** This is the more common type of 205 front suspension, shown off the vehicle for clarity. 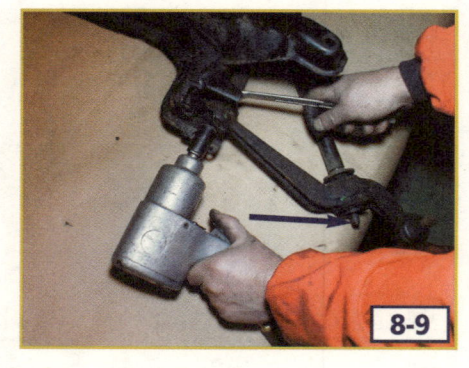
→ Undo and remove the inner lower arm pivot bolts and nuts. (In this case, there is only one).
→ Remove the anti-roll bar mounting nut (position arrowed) – see *Job 14* for other models – and disconnect the anti-roll bar.

106 MODELS

☐ **STEP 10:** Because there is no subframe, the rear lower arm mounting is bolted to the floorpan. 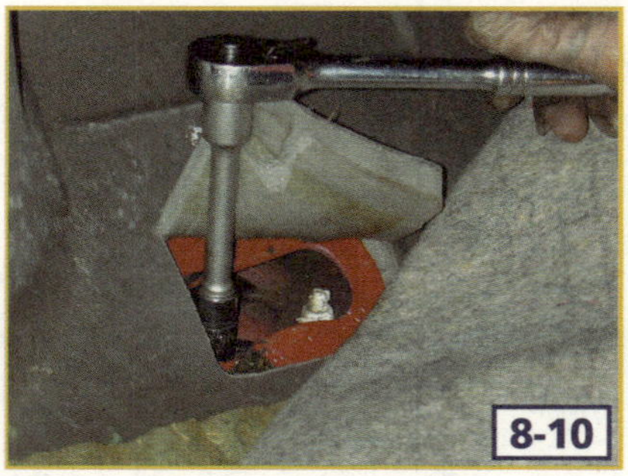
→ Lift the front of the carpet, lift the flap in the sound proofing and pull off the waterproof membrane, if fitted.
→ The two mounting bolts protrude through the floor and the nuts can be removed as shown.

☐ **STEP 11:** This is the 106 lower arm being removed showing the front mounting (a) which is similar to most other types and its unique rear mounting (b).

ALL OTHER TYPES

☐ **STEP 12:** The inner mounting or mountings will need to be levered out of the attachment points.

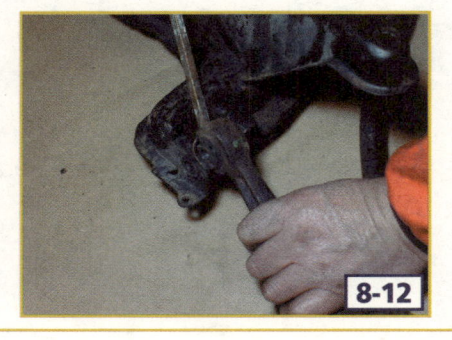

☐ **STEP 13:** This is the lower arm being removed complete with the integral balljoint, fitted to all 106, 205 and 206 models.

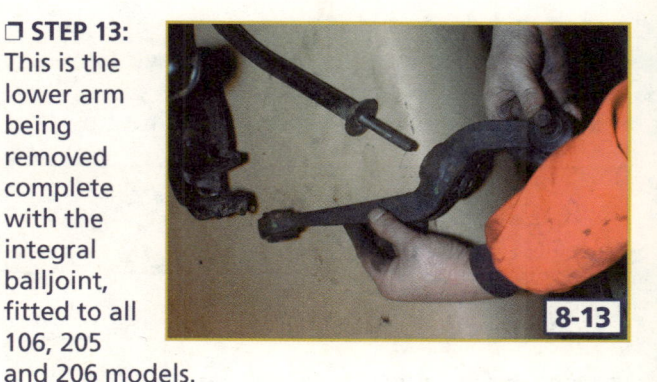

206 MODELS

See *Job 1* for detailed drawings of these models.

☐ **STEP 14:** Each of the two inner mountings is held with a vertical bolt, accessed from beneath the subframe.

☐ **STEP 15:** The bolt has a Torx-head at the top and can just be reached from inside the subframe and there is a regular hexagonal nut at the bottom of the bolt. 
→ If you don't have the equipment for gripping the Torx bolt heads through the limited space available above the subframe, it may be necessary to lower the subframe in order to remove the lower arm.

☐ **STEP 16:** Clean the lower arm and its mounting(s).
→ Check for damage, corrosion and distortion.
→ Check the pivot bolt/s for wear and renew if necessary.
→ If the inner bushes are soft or damaged, renew them. See *Job 9*.

❑ **STEP 17:** Loosely refit the arm assembly.
➔ Tighten the bolts to their recommended torques, but ONLY when the whole assembly is in place.
➔ Start at the outboard end, and work inwards.

JOB 9: FRONT LOWER ARM BUSHES - *replace*.

SAFETY FIRST!

• When re-assembling, use all new locknuts, stretch bolts and split pins, as originally fitted.

Depending on the model, the lower arm has either one or two pressed-in bushes. See *Job 1* for the various types used.
➔ Some pressed-in bushes may be easy to remove, but can be stuck in their mounts so hard that a press is needed to get them out.
➔ See the instructions below on cleaning and lubrication as new bushes are fitted.

❑ **STEP 1:** Remove the front lower arm - see *Job 8*.

❑ **STEP 2A:** Press the bush(es) out of their mountings.
➔ A combination of differently sized sockets and a strong vice is often effective. It helps to trim the lip away, as shown.
➔ Use soapy water to i) help the craft knife cut the rubber and ii) help slide the bush out.

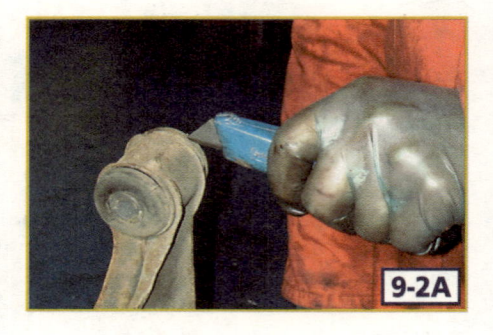

❑ **STEP 2B:** The vertically mounted bush on some versions should be pressed out as shown, using a press or large vice.

❑ **STEP 3:** Clean off any traces of corrosion or rubber clinging to the inner arm and mounting points.

❑ **STEP 4:** Lubricate the new bushes.
➔ They may come supplied with a suitable lubricant. If not, use soapy water or silicone lube.
➔ DO NOT use oil or grease they 'rot' rubber.

❑ **STEP 5:** Press in the new bushes.

❑ **STEP 6:** Refit the lower arm - see *Job 8*.

JOB 10: FRONT STRUT - *remove, refit*.

SAFETY FIRST!

• Do NOT remove the centre nut at the top of the strut, inside the engine bay.

• Follow the instructions carefully and only remove the nuts holding strut to bodywork.

• When re-assembling, use all new locknuts, stretch bolts and split pins, as originally fitted.

See *Job 1* for an overview of the components covered here.

TOP TIP!

• The hub nut has to be undone – and it is extremely tight!
• Always loosen it while the vehicle is still on the ground.
• Apply the parking brake, and loosen the nut with an extension bar, having removed the split pin from it first. See **Chapter 7, Transmission, Clutch**.

FACT FILE
PEUGEOT MAKE IT EASY!

On all of the models covered here, Peugeot have made it easy to replace the top spring and/or damper.
• The top of the strut can be disconnected from the lower part.
• You don't have to remove the whole of the assembly if you don't need to.
• See *Section B* of this Job for details of removing the whole strut assembly.

Section A: Remove upper strut components.

❑ **STEP A1:** If the model you are working on has ABS (anti-lock brakes), unclip the electrical cable for the wheel sensor from the strut.

❐ **STEP A2:** These components are shown off the vehicle so that they can be seen more clearly.
→ Remove the clamp bolt and nut position (**a**).
→ Carefully drive the chisel into the clamp so that it is no longer tight on the upper strut.

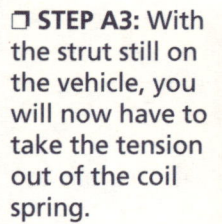

❐ **STEP A3:** With the strut still on the vehicle, you will now have to take the tension out of the coil spring.
→ You will need the type of coil spring compressors that can be safely located beneath the wheel arch.
→ Make sure that the compressors are opposite each other, are securely located on the coils and compress as many coils of the spring as possible. Tighten them (and later undo them) evenly.

❐ **STEP A4:** Inside the engine bay remove any earth/ground clips that may be fitted to the strut top.

❐ **STEP A5:** On all of the vehicles covered here the top of the strut is held to the strut mounting with a number of studs and nuts.
→ This 106 has two studs and nuts but other vehicles have different numbers and different positions for the studs.
→ Take careful note of the positions of the mounting studs and make sure that all of the nuts are fitted in the correct places when the strut is later replaced.
→ DO NOT loosen the central strut nut (arrowed).

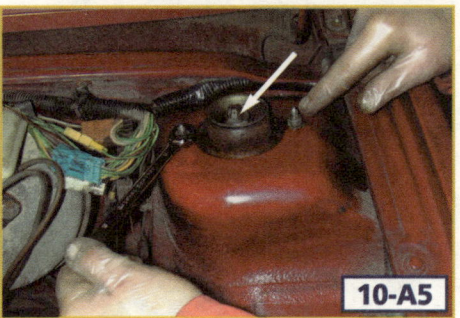

❐ **STEP A6: 306 MODELS:** There are three important features with regard to the 306 suspension tops:
→ The strut top may be held in position with two or three bolts (**a**). Use typists' correction fluid or a felt pen to mark the holes from which the bolts are taken so that they can be replaced correctly on reassembly.
→ There is a locating pin or pins (**b**) and this must be located correctly when the strut is refitted.
→ On some versions, the strut top has an eccentric shape (**c**) in the top plate. This eccentric must be fitted towards the front on vehicles with power assisted steering and towards the rear on vehicles with manual steering.

❐ **STEP A7:** With the strut loose at the top, it can now be lifted out of the clamp on the hub carrier.

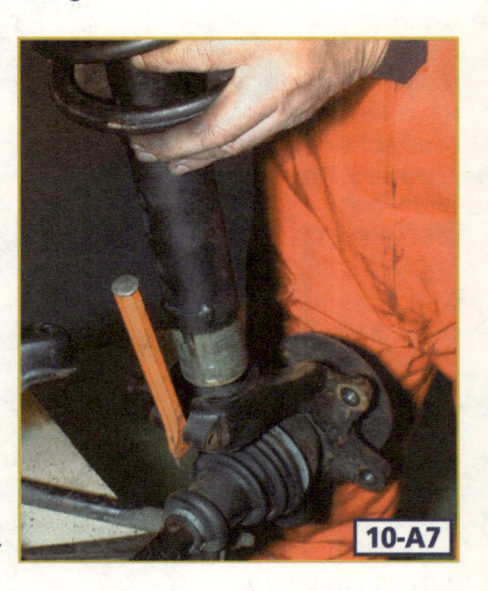

❐ **STEP A8:** When refitting the strut top to the clamp at the top of the hub carrier:
→ Put a smear of copper grease on the bottom of the strut, where it fits into the clamp, to reduce the risk of corrosion.
→ Make sure that the lug on the upper strut is correctly located in the slot in the clamp.

CHAPTER 11 Steering, Suspension Job 10

11-13

→ Make sure that the top part of the strut is inserted right down onto the stops or flange (depending on model).

Section B: Remove complete strut assembly.

❏ **STEP B1:** Loosen the hub nut while the vehicle is on the ground. See *Chapter 7, Transmission, Clutch*.

❏ **STEP B2:** If the model you are working on has ABS, unclip the electrical cable for the wheel sensor from the strut.

❏ **STEP B3:** Remove the brake caliper from the hub carrier - see *Chapter 12, Brakes*. Tie the caliper out of the way with wire or a strong cable tie.

❏ **STEP B4:** Disconnect the track rod end balljoint from the steering arm. See *Job 3*.

❏ **STEP B5:** Remove the hub nut and washer. See *Job 12*.

❏ **STEP B6:** Disconnect the bottom balljoint. See *Job 8*.

❏ **STEP B7:** Remove the outboard end of the driveshaft from the hub.
→ Use a soft-faced hammer, and don't hit it too hard, or the driveshaft constant velocity (CV) joint may be damaged. See *Chapter 7, Transmission, Clutch*.

10-B7

❏ **STEP B8:** Tie the driveshaft up, using wire or a strong cable tie.
→ If you let the driveshaft hang free the CV joint might be damaged.

❏ **STEP B9:** Inside the engine bay, undo the nuts holding the strut to the suspension turret. See *Steps A4* and *A5*.
→ Hold the strut as

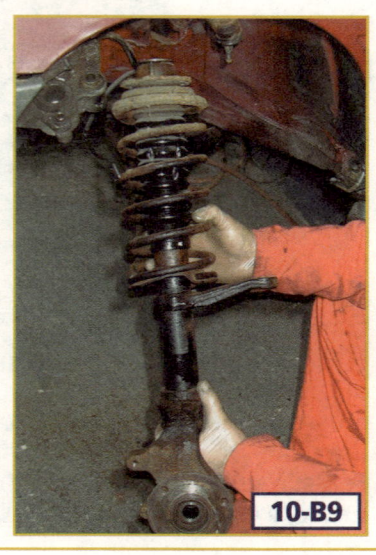

10-B9

you do so to prevent it from falling.
→ Remove the strut from beneath the wheelarch.

❏ **STEP B10:** To refit:
→ Have a helper offer the strut up into the suspension turret.
→ Locate it properly, then fit new nuts to secure it.

❏ **STEP B11:** Grease the splines of the driveshaft, and refit the end into the hub.
→ Fit a new washer and nut, and tighten the nut.

❏ **STEP B12:** Refit the lower arm balljoint to the hub carrier and tighten the nut to its specified torque settings.

❏ **STEP B13:** Refit the track rod end balljoint to the hub carrier, using a new self-locking or a new split pin with a castellated nut, as applicable.

❏ **STEP B14:** Refit the brake caliper - see *Chapter 12, Brakes*.

❏ **STEP B15:** If the vehicle has ABS brakes, refit the sensor to the hub carrier, and clip its wiring loom back onto the strut.

❏ **STEP B16:** Fit the wheel, and lower the vehicle.

❏ **STEP B17:** Tighten the hub nut to its specified torque setting, and fit a new split pin. See *Chapter 7, Transmission, Clutch*.

SAFETY FIRST!

• It is essential to have the tracking checked and adjusted with tracking equipment, to avoid dangerous handling and uneven tyre wear.

JOB 11: FRONT STRUT - *overhaul*.

SAFETY FIRST!

• Leaking dampers guarantee MoT failure. Moreover, tired suspension components can have a marked effect on a vehicle's handling and compromise its safety.

• Dampers and springs MUST be replaced in pairs, front and rear. If only one side is renewed, it will have a significant effect on the vehicle's handling, and make it extremely dangerous to drive!

• When re-assembling, use all new locknuts, stretch bolts and split pins, as originally fitted.

Fact File

INSPECT AND PREPARE DAMPERS

• Push the damper rod up and down a few times. If you feel any jerkiness in its movement, or hear bubbling, or it leaks fluid, it must be renewed.
• New damper units should be 'primed' before fitting. Depress the damper rod and pull it back out about five times. This draws oil into the reservoir and seals, ready to do its job.

Safety First!

• If used incorrectly, spring compressors can cause serious injury.
• Place the compressor on opposite sides of the spring and covering as many coils as possible.
• Tighten and release spring compressors evenly on both sides, a couple of turns at a time.
• Stop when the spring comes clear of the top mount.

a – upper strut top mounting plate
b – lower strut top mounting plate
c – bearing ring
d – upper spring seat
e – coil spring
f – strut top nut
g – threaded cap for holding insert into strut
h – strut insert
i – bump stop
j – gaiter
k – remainder of strut assembly

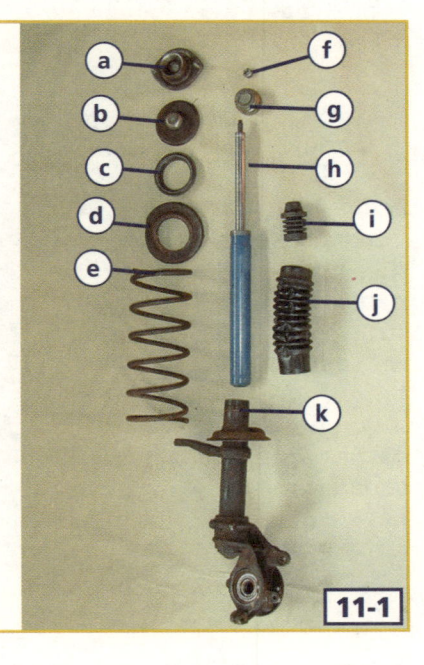

STEP 1: These are the components of a typical front strut assembly. Note that they include a strut insert that can be replaced separately. On some models, the strut insert cannot be removed from the strut and the entire strut upper section will have to be replaced as a unit.

STEP 2: Holding the spring/damper assembly firmly in a vice, compress the spring using coil spring compressors, such as the Sykes-Pickavant tool shown here.

STEP 3: Use a small ring spanner or Allen key, as appropriate to prevent the damper shaft (a) from turning. Loosen and remove the piston rod nut (b).

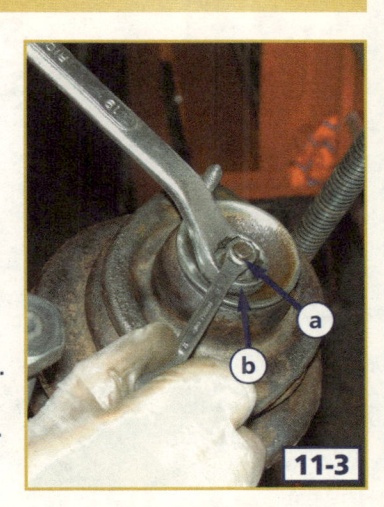

STEP 4: Remove the top plates and the upper spring seat and their associated components.

STEP 5: You can now remove the spring, the gaiter and the bump stop (arrowed).

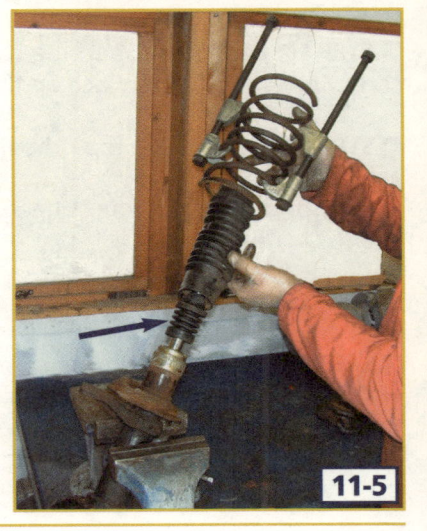

TOP TIP!

• If the spring is not to be renewed, it can stay in the compressors until it is replaced but ONLY if it is to be immediately refitted.
• However, store the compressed spring extremely carefully and out of the way, as it is effectively a 'loaded weapon'.

☐ **STEP 6:** If you don't have the correct C-ring spanner to remove the cap from the top of the strut, you could use a large Stillsons wrench as shown, taking great care not to damage the cap.

☐ **STEP 7:** With the cap (a) removed the strut insert (b) can be pulled out of the strut and a new one fitted in its place.

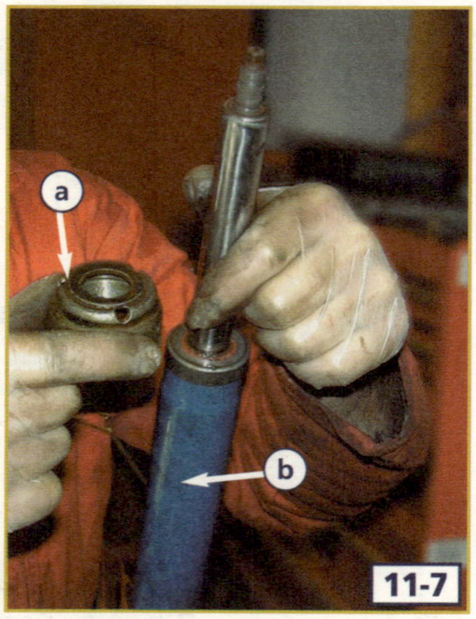

☐ **STEP 8:** Renew the struts, springs, bump stops, dust shields or top mount assemblies as necessary.

☐ **STEP 9:** Replace the bump stop and dust shield. Fully extend the damper rod.

☐ **STEP 10:** Compress the spring if necessary, and carefully put it back in place on the damper unit.

☐ **STEP 11:** Replace the top rubbers and top mount assembly.
➔ The spring top plate must line up correctly with the coil spring end.

☐ **STEP 12:** Always fit a new damper rod locknut.

☐ **STEP 13:** Release the spring compressors.
➔ Check again that the spring is seated correctly in the contours of the spring top and bottom plates.
➔ Locate the end of the spring against the stop on the lower spring plate.

☐ **STEP 14:** Refit the spring/damper/strut assembly – see *Job 10*.

JOB 12: FRONT HUB CARRIER - *replace*.

SAFETY FIRST!

• When re-assembling, use all new locknuts, stretch bolts and split pins, as originally fitted.

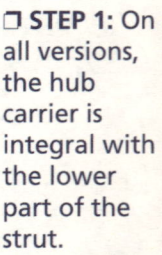

☐ **STEP 1:** On all versions, the hub carrier is integral with the lower part of the strut.
➔ See *Job 1* for illustrations of the variations between different types of hub carrier.

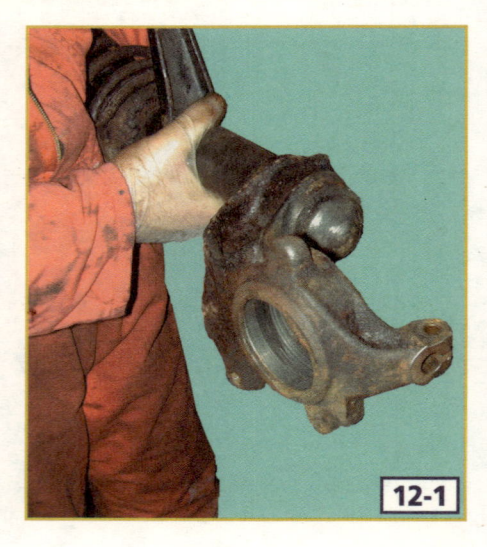

☐ **STEP 2:** The hub nut will need to be removed, but it is extremely tight, so loosen it while the vehicle is still on the ground.
➔ Apply the parking brake, and loosen the nut with an extension bar, having first removed the split pin, if fitted. See **Chapter 7, Transmission, Clutch**.
➔ Raise the vehicle, remove the wheel and remove the hub nut and its washer.

☐ **STEP 3:** If the vehicle you are working on has ABS, disconnect the sensor, and unclip its wiring loom from the strut. Tie it out of the way.

☐ **STEP 4:** Remove the brake caliper from the hub carrier - see **Chapter 12, Brakes**.
➔ Tie the caliper out of the way with wire or a strong cable tie.

☐ **STEP 5:** Remove the brake disc - see **Chapter 12, Brakes**.

☐ **STEP 6:** Undo the pinch bolt holding the bottom balljoint to the hub carrier.
➔ Remove the bolt and lever the lower arm down, to remove the balljoint spindle. See *Job 8*.

☐ **STEP 7:** Disconnect the track rod end at the steering arm on the hub carrier. See *Job 3*.

☐ **STEP 8:** Fit spring compressors to the coil spring and release the hub carrier from the lower part of the strut top section. See *Job 10, Part A*.

☐ **STEP 9:** Pull the hub outwards, off the driveshaft.
➔ If it is unwilling to leave the driveshaft splines, tap the end of it gently with a soft-headed hammer.

☐ **STEP 10:** Tie the driveshaft up, using wire or a strong cable tie. If you let it dangle, its CV joint may be damaged.

☐ **STEP 11:** Before reassembly, grease the splines of the driveshaft, and refit the end into the hub.

☐ **STEP 12:** Re-assemble as the reverse of dismantling.
➔ Fit all new stretch bolts (to brake caliper mountings), locknuts and split pins, as appropriate when refitting suspension and brake components.

JOB 13: FRONT WHEEL BEARINGS - *replace*.

SAFETY FIRST!

• When re-assembling, use all new locknuts, stretch bolts and split pins, as originally fitted.

☐ **STEP 1:** Remove the brake disc from the hub - see *Chapter 12, Brakes*.

☐ **STEP 2:** Remove the hub carrier – see *Job 12*.

☐ **STEP 3:** To remove the hub from the hub carrier:
➔ **EITHER:** Place the end of the carrier over a strong support and drift the hub out.
➔ **OR:** Place the hub carrier in a vice or press, with wooden blocks supporting the hub.
➔ Position a drift, such as a suitably sized socket against the inboard rim of the hub.
➔ Close the vice, to press the hub out of the hub carrier.

☐ **STEP 4:** The inner bearing race outer half will come away with the hub.

☐ **STEP 5:** Remove the inner bearing race outer half with a bearing puller...

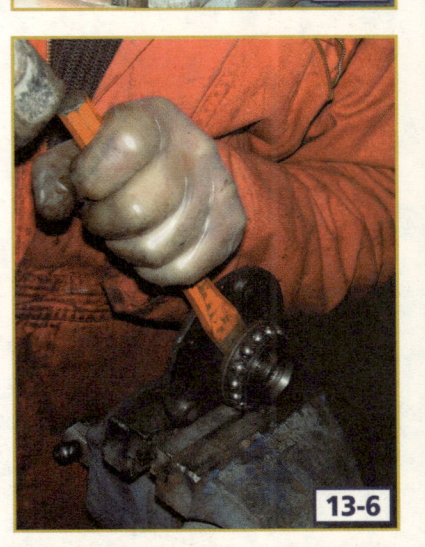

☐ **STEP 6:** ...or carefully hammer it off with a suitable drift or chisel.

☐ **STEP 7:** The inner race is now taken off the hub. It can be extremely tight!

CHAPTER 11 — Steering, Suspension — Job 13

☐ **STEP 8:** Using strong circlip pliers...

☐ **STEP 9:** ...remove the circlip holding the bearing in the hub carrier.

☐ **STEP 10:** Remove the bearing outer race from the hub carrier with a hydraulic press, or a large vice, using a suitably sized tube to push the bearing race out of the hub.

☐ **STEP 11:** Clean both the hub and hub carrier. Check them for wear.
→ If either are worn or damaged, replace.
→ Use very fine abrasive paper to clean up any burrs or 'pick-ups' that might be on the hub flange bearing mounting.

☐ **STEP 12A:** Prepare to push the new bearing, complete, into the hub carrier.

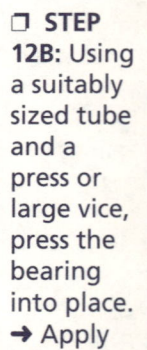

☐ **STEP 12B:** Using a suitably sized tube and a press or large vice, press the bearing into place.
→ Apply copper grease to the outside of the bearing, to make it easier to fit.
→ ONLY press on the outer race of the bearing.
→ Be very careful that the bearing goes in level!
→ Push the bearing right up against the shoulder in the hub.

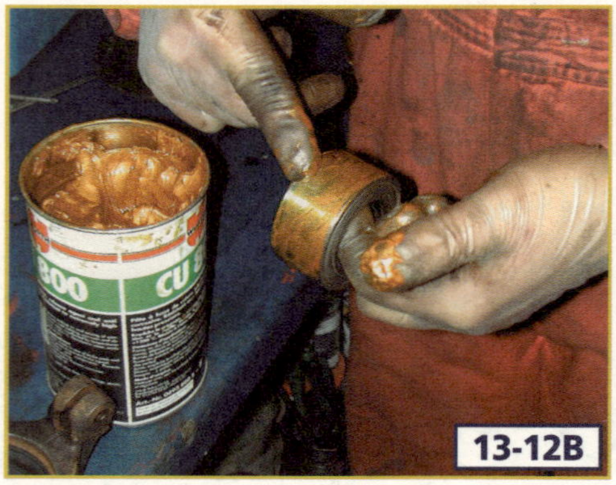

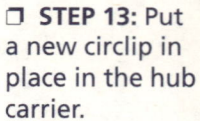

☐ **STEP 13:** Put a new circlip in place in the hub carrier.
→ Also see *1-2, items l, p, s and t*.

☐ **STEP 14:** Press the hub into the bearing in the hub carrier.
→ Place a suitably sized socket or tube over the outer track of the bearing - against the circlip, in fact.
→ Place the assembly in a vice and press the hub carrier (**a**) on to the hub (**b**).

11-18

☐ **STEP 15:** Refit the hub carrier or front strut assembly, as described in *Job 10*.

JOB 14: FRONT ANTI-ROLL BAR AND BUSHES – *replace*.

SAFETY FIRST!

• When refitting, use all new locknuts, stretch bolts and split pins, as originally fitted.

Not all the models covered in this manual have a front anti-roll bar.
➔ There are several different detail types of anti-roll bar.
➔ See *Job 1* for illustrations of the types fitted.

205 MODELS

a – anti-roll bar
b – vertical link
c – anti-roll bar tie rod
d – lower suspension arm
e – strut
f – clamp
g – subframe
h – anti-roll bar mounting plates – one of two types fitted
i – anti-roll bar locating nut

14-6

ALL TYPES

☐ **STEP 1:** There is a number of components that may have to be removed before the anti-roll bar can be reached or extracted. There is wide variation between models and equipment levels, so it will be necessary to carry out a little common-sense detective work first. For example:
➔ If you are working on a later model, there may be a plastic engine undertray to be removed.
➔ Some models with power steering will have to have the power steering fluid hoses disconnected at the pump. Clamp the hoses as close to the pump as possible. See *Job 7* when refitting.
➔ On some models, the clutch cable will have to be disconnected.
➔ It may also be necessary on some models, to remove the front section of the exhaust pipe - see *Chapter 9, Ignition, Fuel, Exhaust*.

☐ **STEP 2:** Mark the positions of the tie bar clamps, so that they can be replaced accurately.

☐ **STEP 3:** Undo the clamp nuts holding the anti-roll bar to the subframe, releasing that part of the anti-roll bar.
➔ Make sure you don't lose washers and any rubber components.
➔ Observe how they are to be refitted.

☐ **STEP 4:** When re-assembling, renew the clamp bushes if they appear at all soft, damaged or spread-out.

106 MODELS

☐ **STEP 5:** Undo the links between the anti-roll bar and the lower arms. See *1-2, items r1, n, u and v*.

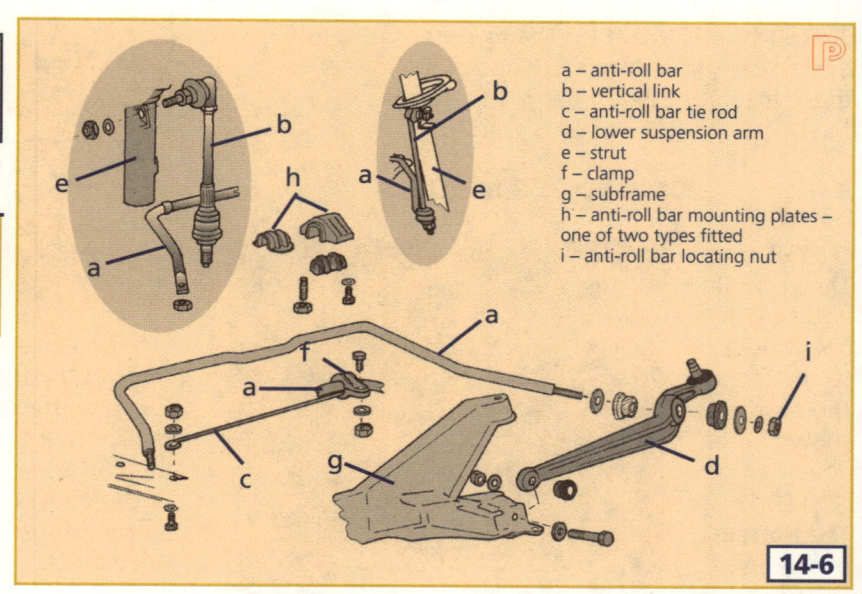

☐ **STEP 6:** These are the components of the two types of anti-roll bar fitted to 205 models.

☐ **STEP 7: NON GTI MODELS:** Before the anti-roll bar can be removed, the lower suspension arm (illustration *14-6, item d*) must be removed from one side of the vehicle. See *Job 8*.
➔ From the other side of the vehicle, the nut (*14-6, item i*) and washers are removed allowing the anti-roll bar to be pulled back out of the lower arm on that side.

☐ **STEP 8:** This is the view of a front subframe removed from the vehicle for reference purposes.
➔ Remove the nuts and bolts holding the clamp plate (*14-6, item f*) to the subframe and also the outer end of the tie rod (*item c*) to the subframe.

14-8

☐ **STEP 9:** Again removed from the vehicle for reference purposes, you can see how, with the lower arm

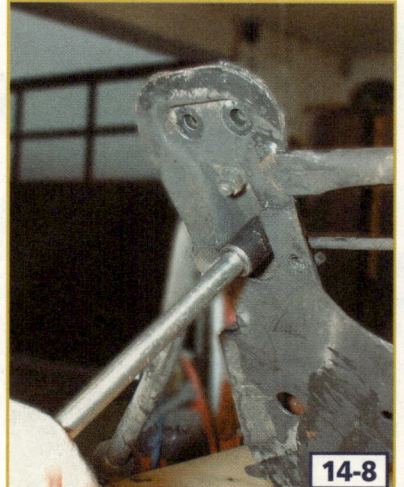

14-9

CHAPTER 11 Steering, Suspension Job 14

11-19

removed from one side of the subframe, the anti-roll bar, complete with the tie rod can be pulled free.

☐ **STEP 10: GTI MODELS:** The link arm fitted to GTI models (see **14-6, items a, b and e**) are similar to those fitted to other models. See below.

206 AND 306 MODELS

☐ **STEP 11:** The vertical anti-roll bar link is bolted to the strut at the position shown here.

☐ **STEP 12:** The bottom of the link (arrowed) is held to the outer end of the anti-roll bar with a stud and nut.
→ This is an instance where the Halfords ratchet ring spanner is an extremely useful tool. The nut is quite difficult to undo and so the full force of the spanner can be applied to the axis of the nut, while the ratchet speeds things up considerably.

ALL MODELS

☐ **STEP 13:** When refitting an anti-roll bar, make sure that:
→ The flats on the insides of the rubber bushes (**b**) are fitted to the flats (**c**) on the anti-roll bar.
→ The shape of the brackets (**a**) is correctly fitted to the recesses on the outsides of the bushes.

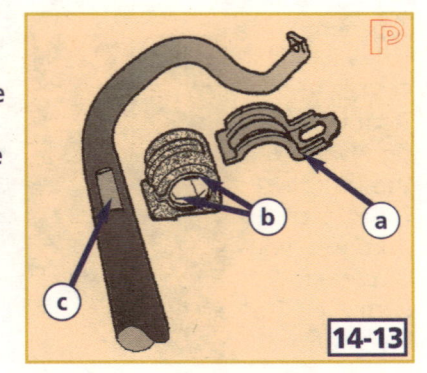

JOB 15: FRONT SUBFRAME - *remove, refit.*

SAFETY FIRST!

• When re-assembling, use all new locknuts, stretch bolts and split pins, as originally fitted.

☐ **STEP 1:** There is normally no need to completely remove the front subframe. Sometimes, it has to be lowered, for example:
→ When removing the power steering rack on some models.
→ Disconnecting the suspension lower arms on 206 models if there is otherwise no access to the Torx-head bolts.

☐ **STEP 2:** If the subframe has to be lowered, the engine is supported from above. See **Job 5**.

☐ **STEP 3:** These are typical of the subframe-to-body lower mounting bolts (one, arrowed) on all 205, 206 and 306 models.
→ 106 models do not have a subframe.

☐ **STEP 4:** All versions also have an upper mounting on each side, similar to this one (arrowed).
→ It is possible to remove the entire front suspension, brakes, engine/transmission and steering rack complete with the subframe. The only reasons we can think of for doing so would be to remove parts from a scrap vehicle or for crash-damage repair, in which case you will have to:
→ Detach the steering at the bottom of the steering

column.
→ Detach the suspension struts at the tops of the suspension turrets.
→ Disconnect the gear linkage and clutch connections.
→ Detach brake hoses, fuel lines and electrical connections.

JOB 16: REAR DAMPERS - *replace*.

See *Job 1* for illustration relating to the components referred to here.

SAFETY FIRST!

- Leaking dampers guarantee an annual-test failure!
- Worn suspension will have a detrimental effect on a vehicle's handling and will compromise its safety.
- Dampers and springs MUST be replaced in pairs, front and rear. If only one side is renewed, the vehicle could be unsafe to drive!
- When re-assembling, use all new locknuts, stretch bolts and split pins, as originally fitted.

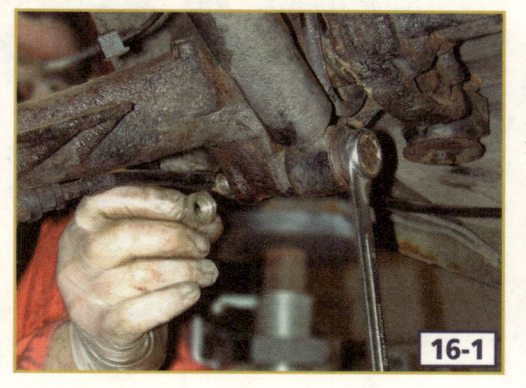

☐ **STEP 1:** On all versions, the rear dampers are held by two sets of nuts, bolts and washers.
- Prevent the bolt from turning while removing the nut.
- Hose clips are attached to the damper mounts in some locations. Remove and replace them (when re-assembling) with care.

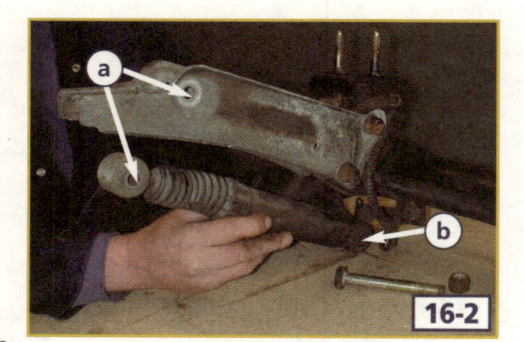

☐ **STEP 2: 205 AND 306 MODELS:** The top fixings (**a**) bolt the damper to the suspension frame, with the lower fixings (**b**) attach to the trailing arm.

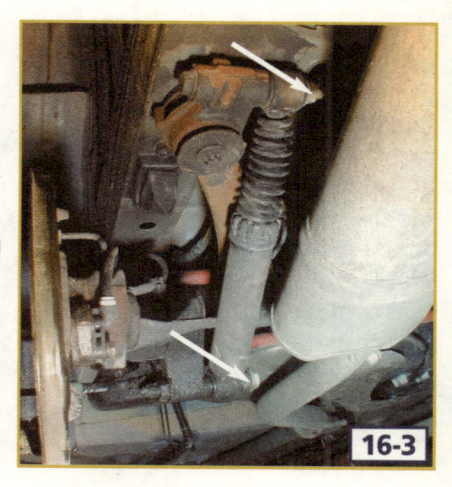

☐ **STEP 3: 106 AND 206 MODELS:** The upper and lower mounting points (arrowed) are very similar to those described in *Step 2*.

JOB 17: REAR SUSPENSION ASSEMBLY – *remove, refit*.

For detailed illustrations of the components described in this job, see *Job 1*.

SAFETY FIRST!

- When refitting, use all new locknuts, stretch bolts and split pins, as appropriate.

☐ **STEP 1:** Before the rear suspension assembly can be removed, various other components will have to be taken off the vehicle:
→ Spare wheel, when fitted beneath the vehicle.
→ The rear of the exhaust system.
→ The parking brake cables, either at the brake drums or the parking brake lever – see *Chapter 12, Brakes*.
→ The brake hydraulic hoses – see *Chapter 12, Brakes*.
→ Two of the rear suspension mounting nuts are reached from beneath the vehicle – see arrows.

11-21

CHAPTER 11 Steering, Suspension Job 18

☐ **STEP 2:** When the mounting nuts are removed, the rear part of the rear suspension assembly will slide off the studs fitted to the mounting plate on the bodywork.
➜ Alternatively, you could undo the mounting plate from inside the luggage bay.

17-2

☐ **STEP 3: 205 AND 306 MODELS:** There are two more mounting bolts on each side of the vehicle and these can only be accessed from inside the luggage bay, just behind the rear seats.

17-3

☐ **STEP 4: 106 MODELS:** There are two mounting bolts on each side of the vehicle and both are accessed from beneath.

17-4

☐ **STEP 5:** The fittings on 206 models are similar except that they are mounted via rubber bushes and the bolts (arrowed) have Torx-heads.

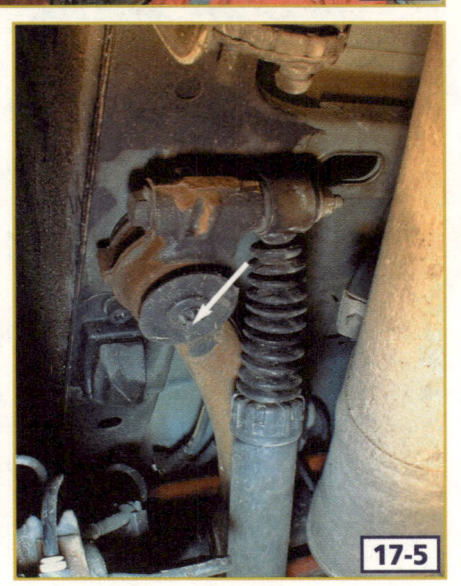

17-5

☐ **STEP 6:** The front mountings on 206 models are similar to those on the rear.

17-6

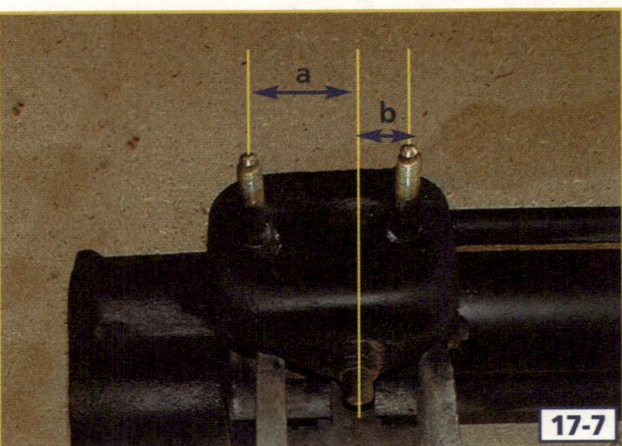

17-7

☐ **STEP 7:** When refitting the suspension top mountings, make sure the wider part of the offset (a) is to the outside of the suspension.

JOB 18: REAR SUSPENSION MOUNTING BUSHES – *replace*.

For detailed illustrations of the components described in this job, see **Job 1**.

SAFETY FIRST!

• When refitting, use all new locknuts, stretch bolts and split pins, as appropriate.

☐ **STEP 1:** Rear suspension bushes do not often wear or become soft, but if they do need replacing, start by removing the rear suspension unit complete - see **Job 17**.

☐ **STEP 2:** To remove the old bushes:
➜ **205 AND 306 TYPES:** Cut one end off the old bush then force the bush out of its housing.

11-22

➔ **106 AND 206 TYPES:** Each bush has a shoulder only on one side, so can more easily be pushed out.
➔ Clean all the stuck-on residues of rubber and rust that will probably be left behind in each housing.

☐ **STEP 3: 205 AND 306 TYPES:** The cut-out in the bushes (arrowed) must be fitted in the vertical plane.

18-3

☐ **STEP 4:** To fit the new bushes, apply soapy water or silicone lubricant to help them slip into position.
➔ DO NOT use oil or grease - they both 'rot' rubber.

JOB 19: REAR SUSPENSION ASSEMBLY – dismantle, rebuild.

Before working on the rear suspension components, it helps to understand how the system works - and it is quite unusual!
➔ See *Job 1, Step 11-on* for detailed drawings and explanations.
➔ It is possible (theoretically) to replace a torsion bar with the suspension in place on the vehicle and without dismantling other components. However, if the vehicle is new, there is almost certainly no reason for doing so. If the vehicle is old, the torsion bar may be somewhere from difficult to impossible to shift.
➔ We describe torsion bar removal the 'proper' way, but the way we show it is more likely work!
➔ The jobs shown here are described in sequence. You can sometimes carry out each part of the work in isolation - it all depends on whether parts have rusted together or not.

IMPORTANT NOTE: While it is certainly possible to dismantle and reassemble the rear suspension assembly it is a job that would only rarely need to be carried out. The only reasons for dismantling the rear suspension assembly might be:
➔ Because the trailing arm bearings are worn. However, you would need specialised equipment to be able to extract the bearings from the axle tube and, in any case it is very unusual for these bearings to wear out.
➔ You may wish to readjust the rear ride height (we strongly recommend that you do not deviate from the manufacturer's recommended ride height at the rear of the vehicle). Be warned that setting the rear ride height can be difficult and can take some little time to get right.
➔ You may wish to replace damaged components. However, if damage is so severe as to require replacement of rear suspension components, we strongly suggest that you fit new, main-dealer overhauled or good second-hand units to the vehicle.
➔ The following information is therefore given for reference.

FACT FILE
IDENTIFICATION MARKS

You will need to refer to at least some of the identification marks shown here:

☐ **STEP 1:** The anti-roll bar (when fitted) is held in position by a pair of locating plates.

19-1

➔ Each end of the anti-roll bar has a notch (see inset) which must align with the centre-line of the locating plate.
➔ Both ends must be properly aligned and the bar must not be under torsion when the rear suspension is level.

☐ **STEP 2:** Anti-roll bar locating plates are handed. The right-hand plate has three notches on the end face of the splined socket (arrowed); the left-hand plate has one.

19-2

☐ **STEP 3:** The anti-roll bar also has a shoulder (arrowed) at its left-hand end.

19-3

Continued...

FACT FILE

Continued...

☐ **STEP 4:** Torsion bars are also handed and are marked accordingly.
→ The right-hand torsion bar has two bands in the metal and the left-hand bar has one. The bands are not all that easy to see.
→ On some versions, the bands are painted on.

ANTI-ROLL BAR

IMPORTANT NOTE: This part of the work relates to disconnecting the anti-roll bar which runs down the centre of the rear axle tube. If no anti-roll bar is fitted, there is a cap in this location and the following Steps are not relevant. Go straight to **Step 10**.

☐ **STEP 5:** There is a plastic plug - use a splined socket - in the end of the anti-roll bar fitting.

☐ **STEP 6:** Remove the plug.
→ If the plug cannot be easily removed, it may have to be destroyed.
→ Always refit - or fit a new plug - when re-assembling.

☐ **STEP 7:** A screw (position arrowed) holds the end of the locating plate to the trailing arm. Remove it before pulling the plate off the trailing arm.
→ The locating plate is a tight fit on the spline on the end of the anti-roll bar.
→ Use a well-lubricated bolt, screwed in to the locating plate and pushing against the end of the anti-roll bar.

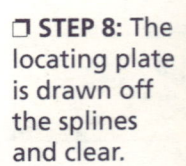

☐ **STEP 8:** The locating plate is drawn off the splines and clear.

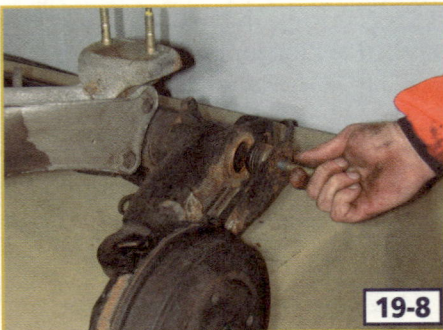

☐ **STEP 9:** From the other side of the vehicle, the anti-roll bar and locating arm can be withdrawn together.
→ Draw the plate off the anti-roll bar using the same bolt as was used for the other side.

TORSION BAR

IMPORTANT NOTE: Before removing a torsion bar, the suspension must be 'set' so that it cannot lose its correct position. See **Steps 15** and **16** for information on how to do so.

☐ **STEP 10:** Remove the nut and washer from the end of the torsion bar attached to the fixed part of the suspension.

☐ **STEP 11:** At the trailing-arm end, remove the countersunk-head screw.
➔ The screw - and all-important retaining washer beneath it - will almost certainly be gripped and may be surrounded by rust and dirt. Clean them off thoroughly.
➔ Use the end of a scriber to chase dirt out of the grooves (arrowed) into which the eccentric washer is located.
➔ Use a punch to drift the washer in the direction of the arrow, taking care not to damage the thread in the end of the torsion bar.

☐ **STEP 12:** Use the scriber to work the retaining washer out of the recess in the trailing arm.

☐ **STEP 13:** Make centre punch marks on the end of the torsion bar, and on the area surrounding the torsion bar, in the recess in the trailing arm, so that it can be refitted - if necessary - in precisely the same position.

☐ **STEP 14:** When the vehicle is new, you will be able to use a slide-hammer, screwed into the end of the torsion bar, to drive the torsion bar out of the suspension assembly.
➔ The torsion bar will be VERY difficult to shift after it has been in place for a while. You might need to remove the trailing arm - see following section.

TRAILING ARM

☐ **STEP 15:** Settle the ride height of the vehicle.
➔ Place it on level ground.
➔ Bounce the rear several times to settle it.

CHAPTER 11 Steering, Suspension Job 19

11-25

CHAPTER 11 Steering, Suspension Job 19

→ Measure the ride height.
→ Bounce and measure again twice.
→ Take an average of the three readings.
→ With the rear height at the average you have established, measure precisely, the length of the damper on that side of the vehicle.

☐ **STEP 16:** Make up a dummy but rigid 'damper' (arrowed) the same length as the measurement of the damper you made earlier and fit it to the vehicle.

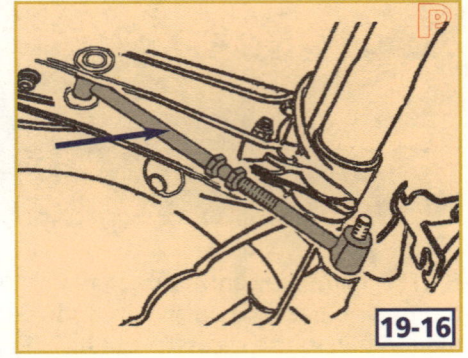

→ You could, in theory, use the measurement to set the suspension to the correct height as the torsion bar is refitted, but this would need to be done with very great precision.
→ If the suspension height is not set correctly when the suspension is re-assembled, the vehicle's handling could be dangerous.

☐ **STEP 17:** Remove the shock absorber from the relevant side. See **Job 16**.

☐ **STEP 18:** Remove and/or dismantle the following:
→ Remove the anti-roll bar location plate. See **Steps 5 to 8**.
→ Prepare to remove the torsion bar, but do not remove it. See **Steps 10 to 13**.
→ Remove the nut and washer holding the other torsion bar to the fixed part of the suspension on the side you are working on. See **Step 10**.
→ Disconnect the parking brake and hydraulic brake lines.

☐ **STEP 19:** The 'correct' way to remove the trailing arm is to use a puller, but you cab use a drift and hammer if you work carefully.

☐ **STEP 20:** The trailing arm assembly can now be withdrawn, complete with one of the torsion bars.

☐ **STEP 21: 205 AND 306 MODELS:** Deep in the recesses of the axle tube lie the two bearings. If they need replacing:
→ You could extract them with a suitable puller.
→ You may be able to drift them out, from the other end of the tube.
→ You may wish to have a Peugeot dealer carry out the work - they should have a special puller made for the job.

RE-ASSEMBLY

☐ **STEP 22:** Make sure that all splines and threads are clean, undamaged and well greased. Be sure to grease all seals before refitting them.

☐ **STEP 23:** Fit the location plate to one end of the anti-roll bar (when fitted) and tighten it to the bar. Fit the screw holding the end of the plate in position.
→ Insert into the anti-roll bar into axle tube with the suspension level.

☐ **STEP 24:** Fit the other location plate, using the thread you used for extracting it, with a nut running over the thread, to push the plate onto the splines.
→ Tighten the

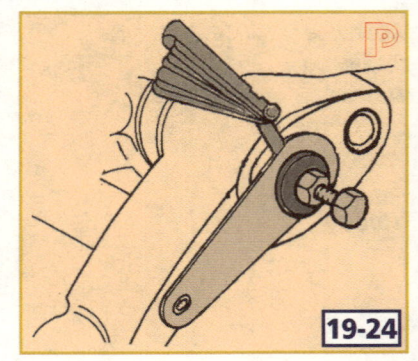

11-26

plate until the distance between the anti-roll bar location plate and the trailing arm is 1 mm. Check with a feeler gauge.

☐ **STEP 25: 206 MODELS:** The distance (**a**) between the trailing arm and fixed section of suspension arm is 4.5 mm.

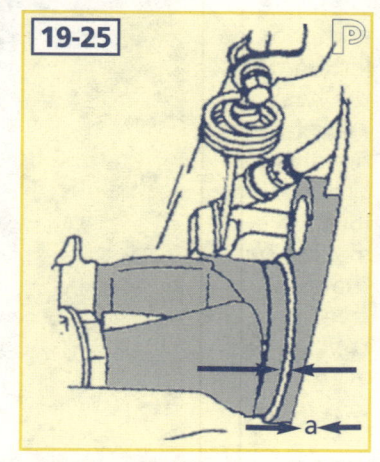

JOB 20: **REAR HUB, BRAKE DRUM AND WHEEL BEARING -** *remove, replace, refit.*

You may find *Chapter 12, Brakes* useful in connection with this Job.

Section A: Rear brake drum models.

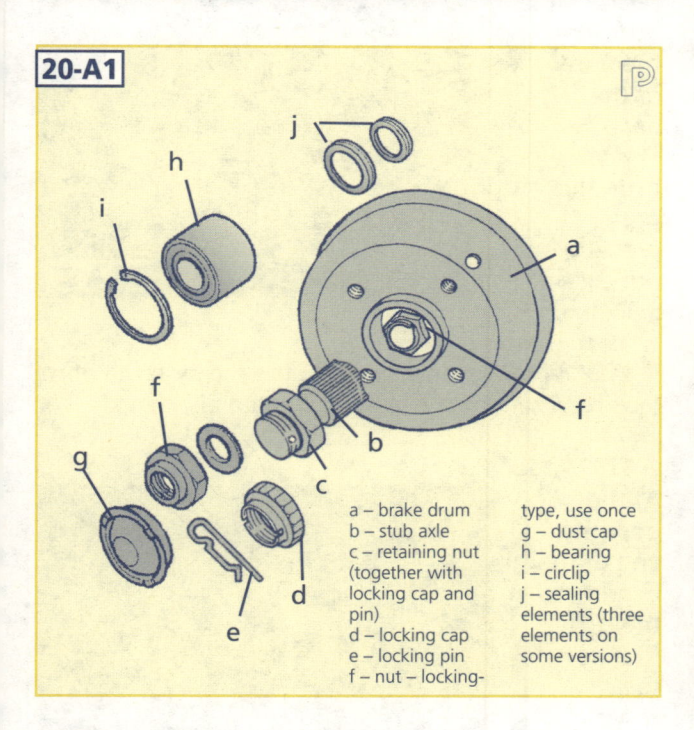

☐ **STEP A1:** These are the components of the rear brake drum and bearings.

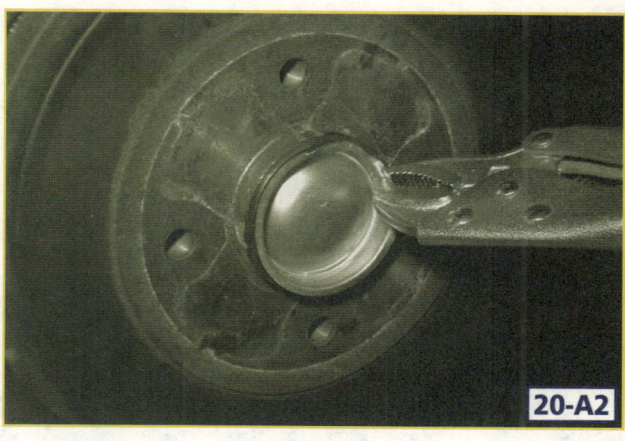

a – brake drum
b – stub axle
c – retaining nut (together with locking cap and pin)
d – locking cap
e – locking pin
f – nut – locking-type, use once
g – dust cap
h – bearing
i – circlip
j – sealing elements (three elements on some versions)

☐ **STEP A2:** Remove the dust cap.

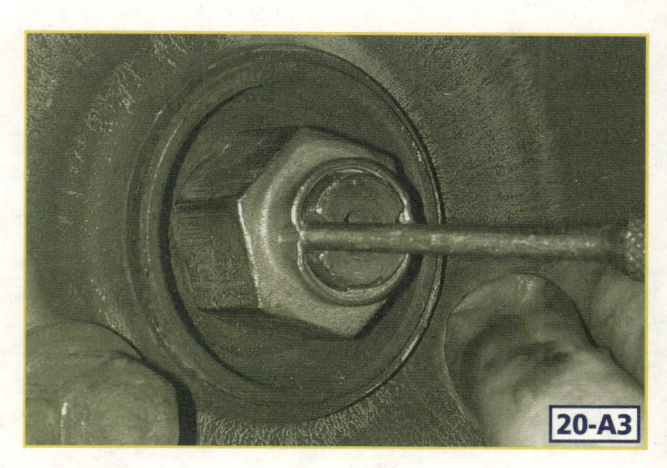

☐ **STEP A3:** If the hub nut is of the locking type, open up the locking collar to make it easier to undo the nut.
➔ If the nut is of the retaining pin and plate type, remove the pin and plate and unscrew the nut.

☐ **STEP A4:** Remove the nut and thrust washer from behind it.

☐ **STEP A5:** Remove the brake drum. See *Chapter 12, Brakes.*

CHAPTER 11 Steering, Suspension Job 20

□ **STEP A6:** Use a pair of circlip pliers to remove the circlip from the drum.

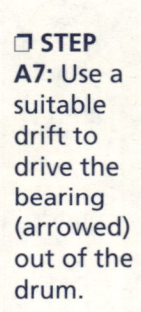

□ **STEP A7:** Use a suitable drift to drive the bearing (arrowed) out of the drum.

□ **STEP A8:** The bore of the bearing housing must be scrupulously cleaned. Look out for small burrs or 'pick-ups' which must be cleaned off with emery cloth.
→ Put a wipe of copper grease onto the bore.

TOP TIP!
• Before fitting the bearing to the hub, wipe suitable grease into the bearing from both sides.
• Before fitting the dust cap – see *Step A16* – wipe more grease around the bearing recess, but there is no need to pack the area with grease.

□ **STEP A9:** Fit the new bearing – with the lettering on the bearing edge facing towards the circlip location – making sure that it is started completely evenly all the way round.

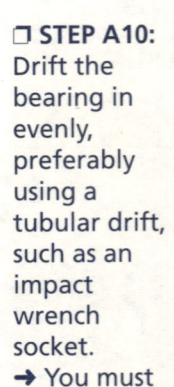

□ **STEP A10:** Drift the bearing in evenly, preferably using a tubular drift, such as an impact wrench socket.
→ You must bear (only) on the outer race of the bearing.
→ If you use a hydraulic press, pressure must not exceed 5,000 kg.

□ **STEP A11:** Fit a new circlip to the recess in the bore, making sure that it is properly seated all round.

□ **STEP A12:** At the opposite end of the bearing to the circlip, fit a new seal.
→ Make sure that the seal is fitted evenly.
→ Grease the seal, both inside and out.

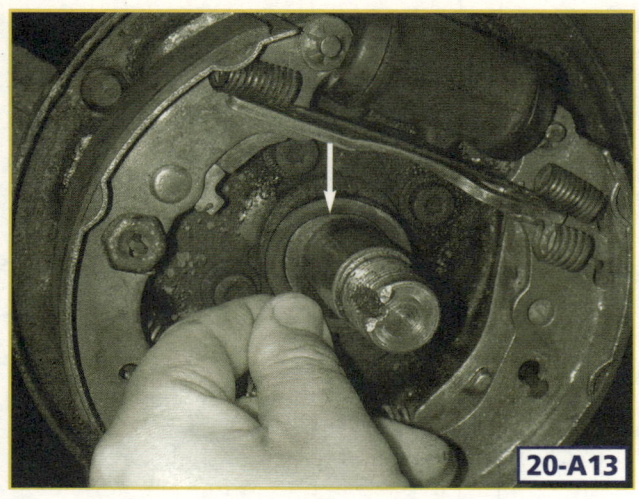

□ **STEP A13:** The old oil seal (arrowed) should also be taken from the stub axle and a new one fitted in its place.

□ **STEP A14:** To refit the hub and hub nut:
→ Fit the thrust washer and nut and tighten the nut until the hub is properly seated on the stub axle.
→ Back off the nut and retighten to the correct torque.

□ **STEP A15:** Fit the locking plate and pin or drive the locking collar into the keyways in the stub axle shaft to prevent it from turning.

□ **STEP A16:** Fit a new dust seal.

Section B: Rear disk brake models.

□ **STEP B1:** These are the components of the rear disk brake hub.
→ All of the illustration references in the rest of this Section refer to the items in this illustration.

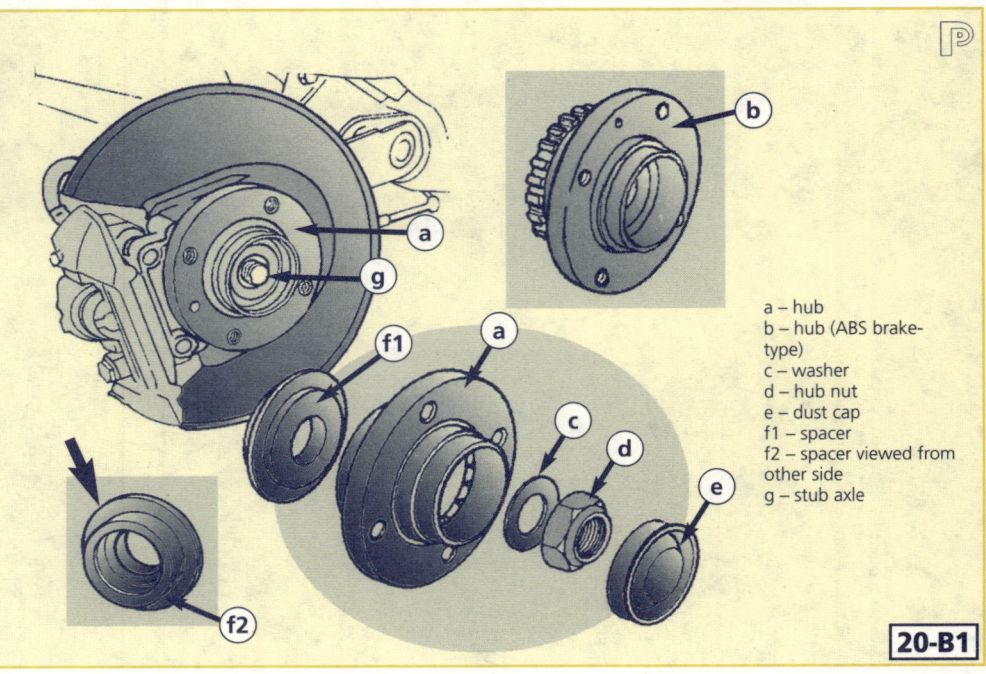

a – hub
b – hub (ABS brake-type)
c – washer
d – hub nut
e – dust cap
f1 – spacer
f2 – spacer viewed from other side
g – stub axle

❑ **STEP B2:** Lever off the dust cap and undo the hub nut – see *Section A: Step 3*.

❑ **STEP B3:** Use a two-or-three-legged pulled to pull the hub off the stub axle.

❑ **STEP B4:** The inner bearing track will probably be left on the stub axle. If so:
➜ Use a knife-edge pulled to draw it off the stub axle, or…
➜ …start the inner track moving with a chisel as shown in *Job 13*.

❑ **STEP B5:** Remove the spacer from the stub axle.
➜ If the spacer was damaged as the inner bearing was pulled off the stub axle, it will need to be renewed. Obtain one from a Peugeot dealership.

❑ **STEP B6:** Place the spacer (*item f2*) on to the stub axle with the shoulder (arrowed) facing the suspension trailing arm.

TOP TIP!

• Before fitting the bearing to the hub, wipe suitable grease into the bearing from both sides.
• Before fitting the dust cap – see *Step A16* – wipe more grease around the bearing recess, but there is no need to pack the area with grease.

❑ **STEP B7:** Place the new inner bearing track on the spacer shoulder and push it on as far as it will go using a new hub nut. Remove the hub nut.

❑ **STEP B8:** Use a suitable impact socket as a drift and drive the bearing inner race fully on to the spacer shoulder.

❑ **STEP B9:** Fit the bearing outer race to the hub using the techniques described in *Section A*.

❑ **STEP B10:** Fit the hub assembly on to the stub axle and tighten the hub nut until the hub and bearing are properly located.
➜ Back off the hub nut, make sure that the thrust washer is fitted in place and retighten the hub nut to the correct torque.
➜ Stake the locknut into the keyway on the stub axle – see *Section A, Step 15*.

❑ **STEP B11:** Fit a new dust cap.

CHAPTER 12: BRAKES

Please read **Chapter 2 Safety First** before carrying out any work on your car.

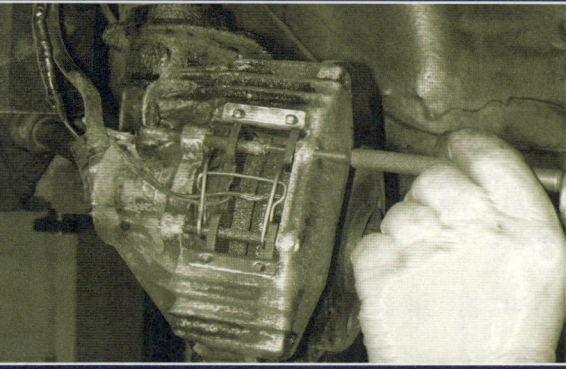

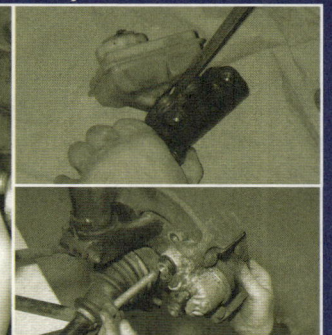

Part A: General Procedures	12-1	Part C: Rear Brakes	12-12
Part B: Front Brakes	12-2	Part D: Hydraulics, Servo, ABS	12-21

Part A: General Procedures

CONTENTS

	Page No.
JOB 1: SYSTEMS EXPLAINED.	12-1
JOB 2: ABS SYSTEM - *service operations*.	12-1

JOB 1: SYSTEMS EXPLAINED.

GENERAL

→ The foot brake system is hydraulic and is in two, separate, split circuits. This ensures that, in the event of a leaking hydraulic pipe, the vehicle retains some braking ability.
→ Some models are equipped with ABS anti-lock braking. This uses wheel speed sensors to tell a central control unit whether a wheel is starting to lock under heavy braking manoeuvres. The control unit then pulses the braking pressure being supplied to that wheel.
→ Most non-ABS equipped vehicles are fitted with a pressure regulating system to help prevent the rear wheels from locking under heavy braking.
→ Directly connected to the brake pedal mechanism is the servo, which is powered by inlet manifold vacuum on petrol models, or by an engine-driven pump on diesel models. This loads the whole system via the master cylinder.

FRONT BRAKES

→ All the models covered in this manual have front disc brakes - several types have been fitted - see *Part B*.

REAR BRAKES

→ Some models have drum brakes at the rear, while others have disc brakes. All of them are self adjusting.
→ The parking brake operates, via a cable or cables, on the rear wheels, operating the drum brakes if present, or on the rear discs, if fitted.
→ On some, there is a pressure regulation valve built into each rear brake pipe.
→ On others, pressure is variable, regulated by a single valve, which changes the pressure according to the weight over the rear wheels.
→ The most common system is a pressure-operated regulator which serves both rear brake pipes.

JOB 2: ABS SYSTEM - *service operations*.

ABS systems use advanced electronics. Work on this system should be referred to a Vauxhall dealer or specialist. The only exception to this is the removal, cleaning and replacement of the ABS sensors - see *Part D, Job 7*.

Part B: Front Brakes

CONTENTS

	Page No.
JOB 1: UNDERSTANDING FRONT BRAKE TYPES.	12-2
JOB 2: BRAKE PADS - READ THIS FIRST! - *applies to all types.*	12-3
JOB 3: BRAKE PADS - SPECIFIC TYPES - *remove replace.*	12-4
JOB 4: FRONT BRAKE CALIPER – *removal, replacement.*	12-10
JOB 5: FRONT BRAKE DISC - *replacement.*	12-11

JOB 1: UNDERSTANDING FRONT BRAKE TYPES.

Several different types of front brake have been fitted to the models covered by this manual.
➔ Use the illustrations below to see which brakes are fitted to the vehicle you are working on.
➔ Not all brakes are exactly as shown here. Manufacturers sometimes make changes during the production life of components.
➔ It is important that you note the correct positions of springs and other components as the brakes are dismantled so that they can be put back together correctly and safely.

TOP TIP!
- Only dismantle the brakes on one side of the vehicle at a time.
- If you need to, you can then refer to the other side to see how it should go together.

☐ **TYPE A: ATE TEEVES:** This was fitted to some 106 models.

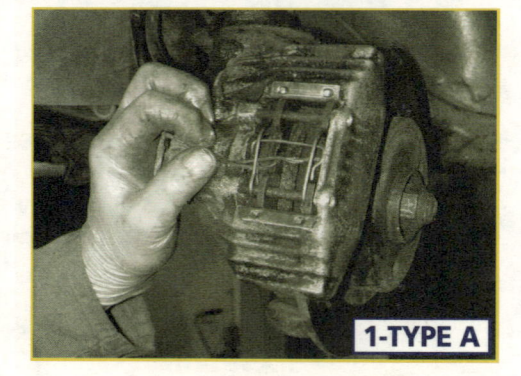

1-TYPE A

☐ **TYPE B: BENDIX:** This was fitted to some 106, 205, 306 models.

1-TYPE B

☐ **TYPE C: GIRLING TYPE J48:** This was fitted to some 205, 306 models.

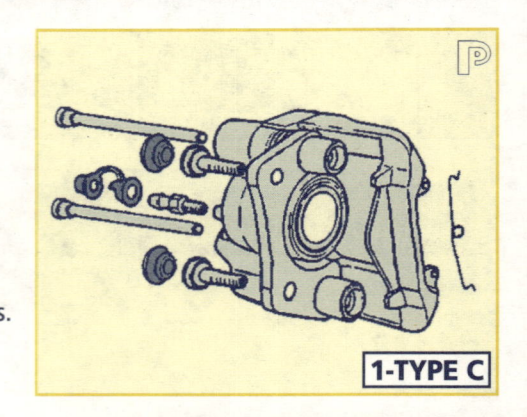

1-TYPE C

☐ **TYPE D: GIRLING TYPE CJPE:** Fitted to some 205 models, and **BOSCH S5 Z0** fitted to 206 models. These two types of caliper and pad arrangement are quite similar to work on.

1-TYPE D

☐ **TYPE E: ATE TEEVES (with screw-in guide pins):** This was fitted to some 306 models. See also *Job 3, Section E, illustration 3-E3*.

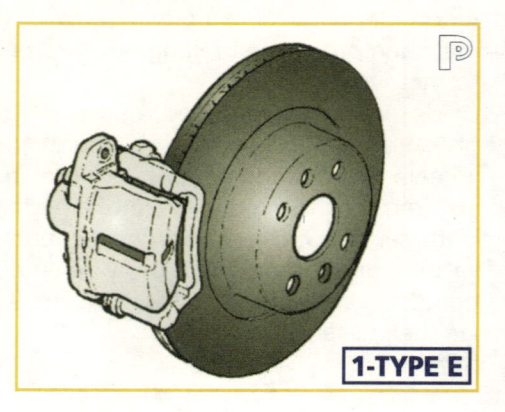

1-TYPE E

IMPORTANT NOTE: The work described in *Job 3* for each Type must be read in conjunction with *Job 2*.

JOB 2: BRAKE PADS - READ THIS FIRST! - *applies to all types.*

This Job applies to all brake types fitted to the vehicles covered here.
➜ It is ESSENTIAL that you read the information shown here AND the relevant Section of *Job 4*.
➜ See *Job 1* to identify the brakes fitted to the vehicle you are working on.

With the front of the vehicle raised and supported safely off the ground and the front wheel removed:

SAFETY FIRST!

• **STEP 1:** Before starting work, always wash brake dust off brake components – using a proprietary brand of brake cleaner such as the Wurth brake cleaner shown here.

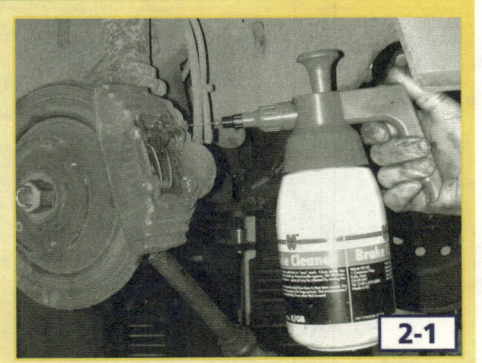

• Always renew brake pads on BOTH front wheels or the vehicle could suffer from dangerous, uneven braking.

• Read the detailed notes in *Chapter 2, Safety First!* before starting work.

• ALWAYS use new caliper retaining bolts when refitting calipers.

☐ **STEP 2:** The pad wear indicator cables, sheathed in heat-resistant material, can be disconnected
➜ On some models, you disconnect the bullet connectors fitted near the strut.
➜ On others, the cable is disconnected at the pad.

FACT FILE
BRAKE PAD WEAR

• If any one of the brake pads is worn below the minimum recommended thickness, all pads, on both wheels (front or rear, as applicable), must be renewed.
• If a single pad is worn more than the others, this suggests that the caliper may be seized. The problem needs to be resolved before the vehicle is used on the road.
• It is wise to replace brake pads before they are at their minimum recommended level. You should bear in mind the likely interval between inspecting the brake pads and the next service.

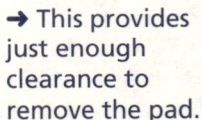

☐ **STEP 3:** Use a self-grip wrench on the pad backing plate (arrowed) and the caliper to push the pad and piston just a small distance away from the brake disc.
➜ This provides just enough clearance to remove the pad.
➜ If you push the pad too far back, you will probably find brake fluid spilling over the top of the master cylinder. To be avoided!

TOP TIP!

☐ **STEP 4:** • You should always take this opportunity to check the condition of the caliper and piston:
• This dust seal is severely damaged but small splits are more prevalent.
• Look out for any traces of fluid which indicates a leaking caliper.
• Look out for rust on the outsides of the piston skirt.
• If a brake caliper is faulty, we strongly recommend replacing with a new or factory-exchange unit.

STEP 5: Before fitting new pads, the piston will need to be pushed back into its bore to make room for the extra thickness of the new pad friction material.
→ Temporarily refit the outer pad, as shown.
→ Use a lever – taking very great care not to cause damage to the seal on the piston – to push the piston back into its bore.
→ Keep a close eye on the brake fluid level in the master cylinder and, if necessary, drain out some of the fluid to prevent it from overflowing as the piston is pushed back into its bore.
→ IMPORTANT NOTE: Not all piston types can be pushed back in. See *Job 3* for specific information.

SAFETY FIRST!

• When you push a brake caliper piston back into its bore, do so slowly and smoothly.
• If you force the piston back too vigorously, you risk 'flipping' back the lips on the seals in the master cylinder, which then stops the master cylinder from operating the brakes.
• The safest way is to fit a brake bleeding pipe to the brake bleed nipple, (see *Part D, Job 5*) and slacken the bleed nipple. As the piston is pushed back, fluid will be ejected through the bleed nipple. Retighten the bleed nipple.

STEP 6: The back face, and the top and bottom edges of each pad (arrowed), where they touch the sides of the caliper, should receive a thin smear of copper grease before fitting. This helps to keep the brakes quieter when in use and prevents pads from seizing so that they can be more easily replaced next time.

SAFETY FIRST!

• It may sound obvious, but it *has* been done wrongly!...
• ALWAYS fit pads with the friction material - not the steel backing plates - facing the brake disc.
• When you have had to remove caliper fixing bolts, always replace them with new, and use fresh threadlock when fitting the new bolts.

STEP 7: After fitting new pads, pump the brake pedal several times to correctly locate the pads - and to make sure that there is firm pedal pressure - before the vehicle is used on the road.

JOB 3: BRAKE PADS - SPECIFIC TYPES – *remove, replace*.

Section A: ATE Teeves - fitted to some 106 models.

The work described here should be read in conjunction with *Job 2*.

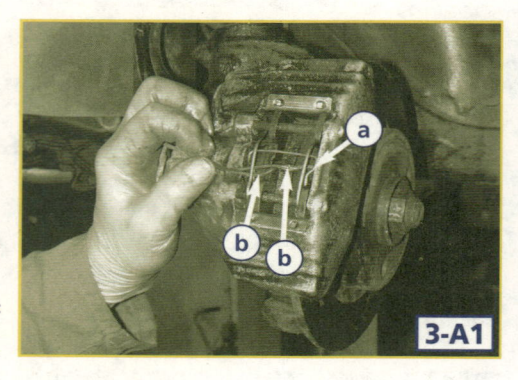

STEP A1: Note the correct fitting of the pad anti-rattle spring (a). It goes inboard of both pads.
→ Also, note the correct routing of the brake pad wear sensor cables (b).

STEP A2: Use a suitable punch to drift each of the pad locating pins (arrowed), drifting them towards the centre of the vehicle.

❒ **STEP A3:** With both pins drifted clear, the anti-rattle spring can now be removed.

❒ **STEP A4:** Work the inner pad out of the caliper using pliers – or a lever in the holes in the pad backing plates – and then repeat the process on the outer pad.
→ The caliper is now free to slide from side-to-side. Before removing the outer pad, lever it towards the outside of the vehicle to free the outer pad.

❒ **STEP A5:** Before refitting the pads to the caliper, make sure that each retaining pin slides easily into position – they can become corroded or bent – and put a coating of copper grease on each pin.

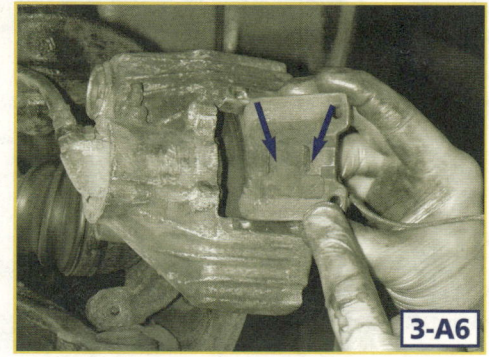

❒ **STEP A6:** Note that the inboard pad has a locating clip (arrowed) which must be seated inside the piston when the pad is fitted.

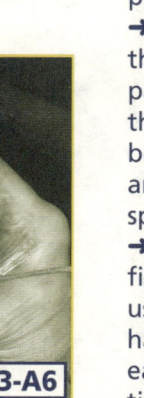

❒ **STEP A7:** With the pads pushed fully home, prepare to fit the anti-rattle spring.
→ Note that both brake pad wear cables pass through the inner loop of each spring.

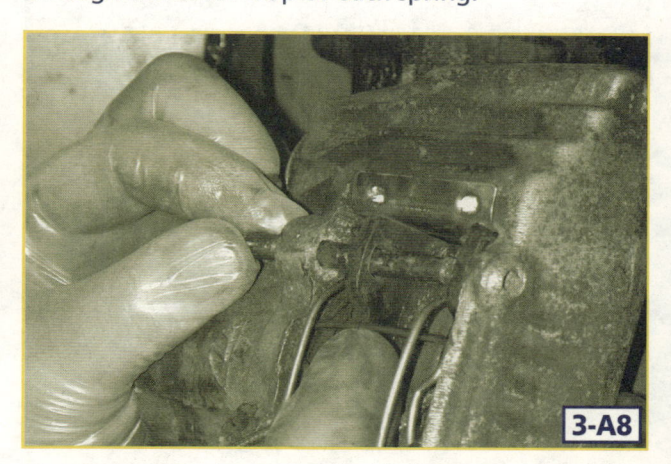

❒ **STEP A8:** Push in the top retaining pin, narrowest end first, through the holes in the lugs on the caliper and the brake pad backing plates.
→ Each pin goes **FROM** the inside of the vehicle, **TO** the outside.
→ Remember the correct location of the anti-rattle spring and cables – see *Step 1*.

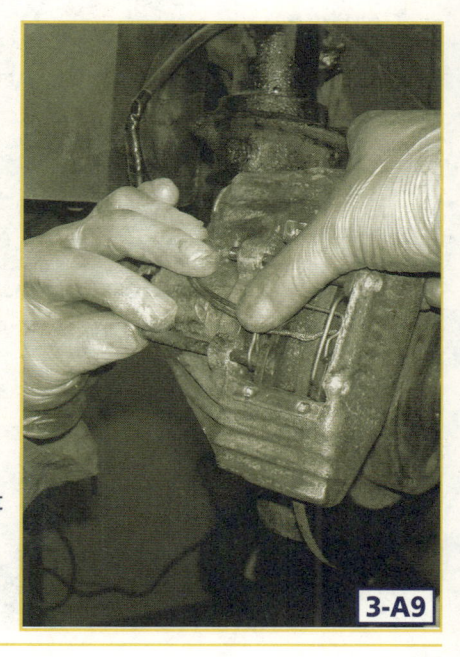

❒ **STEP A9:** Now the bottom pin can be pushed into place.
→ Make sure that the pin passes through the loop at the bottom of each anti-rattle spring.
→ Tap each pin firmly home using a hammer so that each one is tightly located in the caliper.

CHAPTER 12 Part B Job 3

12-5

Section B: Bendix DBA Series IV - fitted to some 106, 205 and 306 models.

The work described here should be read in conjunction with **Job 2**.

Check the pads' thicknesses. The maker's recommend minimum thickness for the friction material is 2 mm but you should usually renew earlier than this.
→ It is normal for one pad to wear slightly more than the other but, if it appears that only one pad is doing all the work while the other has hardly worn at all, it is a sure sign that the caliper is sticking.

TOP TIP!
• Wear gloves, brake dust gets in cut and skin cracks and pores and can take ages to 'wear out!

ALL MODELS EXCEPT GTI AND CTI

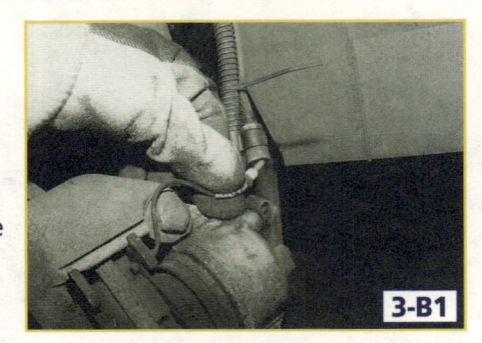

☐ **STEP B1:** First disconnect the pad wear indicator wire at its connector.

☐ **STEP B2:** The pads are retained by a sliding key, which in turn is retained by this small spring clip – easily removed with pliers.

☐ **STEP B3:** The sliding key can then be pulled or drifted sideways from between the caliper and the pad ends – towards the outside of the vehicle.

☐ **STEP B4:** Using a stout screwdriver, carefully lever the caliper away from the outer pad slightly to allow the pad some clearance...

☐ **STEP B5:** ...so that the pad can be lifted away.
→ Slide the caliper towards the suspension leg so that the inner pad can also be removed.

☐ **STEP B6:** If new pads are being fitted, transfer the anti-rattle clips from the old pads to the new, ensuring they are located properly. Note their orientation before removing.
→ Fit the inner pad first, then slide the caliper outwards and fit the outer pad.
→ Ensure the lower and upper locating lips of the pads are seated correctly.
→ Position the sliding key between pads and caliper and tap it carefully home with a hammer.
→ Fit the key retaining clip and re-connect the wear indicator cable electrical connections.

☐ **STEP B7:** The anti-rattle springs (**c**) should be fitted, one to each pad, as shown.
➔ The large arrow indicates the outside of the vehicle.
➔ Some DBA Bendix Mark IV brakes have offset brake pads, the outer pad (**a**) being fitted lower than the inner pad (**b**).

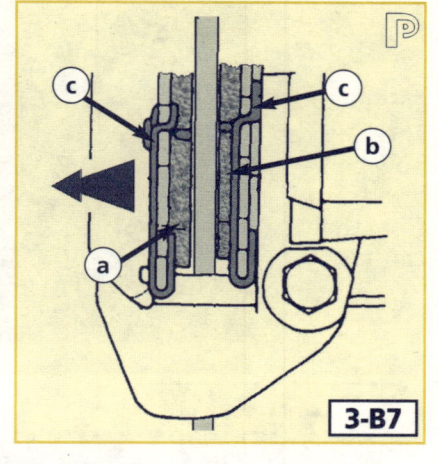

3-B7

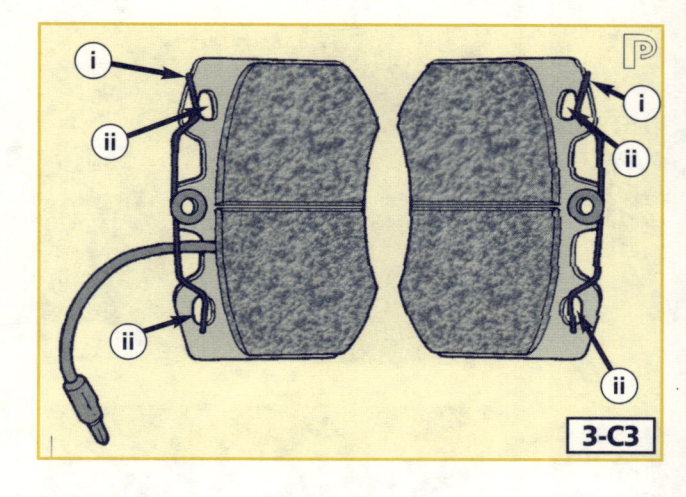

3-C3

☐ **STEP C3:** When fitting new pads, the anti-squeal shims (*3-C2, item b*) must be fitted with the direction arrow (*3-C2, item c*) facing down.
➔ If they don't come ready-fitted, transfer the anti-rattle springs from the old pads to the new.
➔ As the pins are pushed back in to the caliper, they must pass through the holes (**ii**) in the pad backing plates.
➔ Make sure that the springs (**i**) are pushed beneath the pins so that the springs are bearing on the pins.
➔ Tap each pin into position with a hammer until it is firmly located in the caliper.
➔ Refit the spring clip (*3-C1, item a*).

Section C: Girling Type J48 - fitted to some 205 and 306 models.

The work described here should be read in conjunction with *Job 2*.

☐ **STEP C1:** To remove the brake pads:
➔ Disconnect the wear sensor cable (**d**).
➔ Remove the spring clip (**a**) but leave the anti-rattle springs (**e**) in place.
➔ The pins (**c**) will appear through the holes (**b**) as they are drifted out.

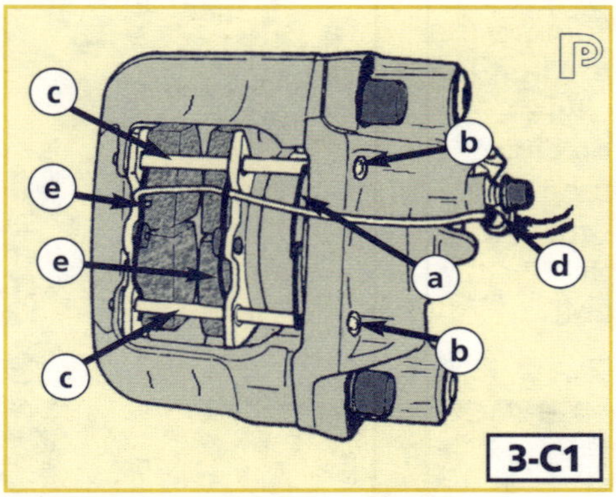

3-C1

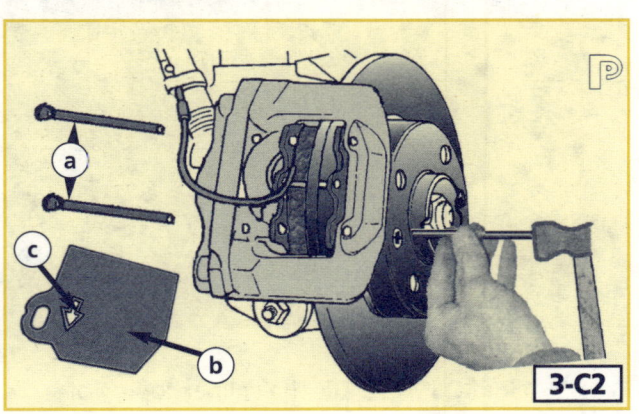

Section D: Girling Type CJPE - fitted to some 205 and 306 models, and Bosch S5 Z0 fitted to 206 models.

The work described here should be read in conjunction with *Job 2*.

IMPORTANT NOTE: These two types of caliper and pad arrangement are quite similar to work on. Take note of any detail differences when dismantling the caliper and pad of the type you are working on.

BOSCH S5 Z0

☐ **STEP D1A:** Start by removing the bottom caliper retaining bolt...

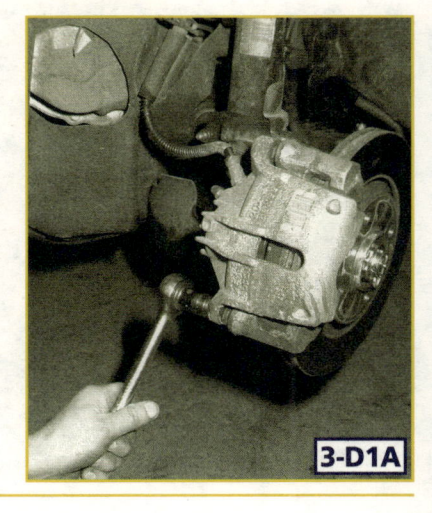

3-D1A

☐ **STEP C2:** Use a thin punch to drift the pins (**a**) towards the inside of the vehicle.

3-C2

CHAPTER 12 Part B Job 3

12-7

☐ **STEP D1B:** ...and take out the bolt and lock plate.

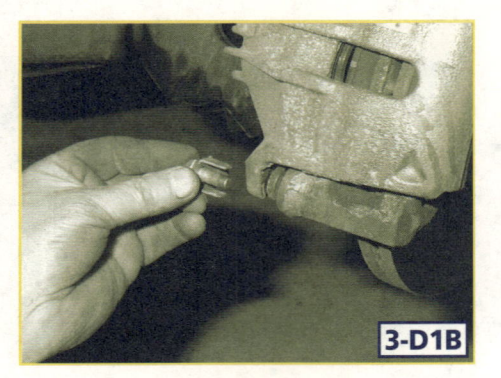

☐ **STEP D1C:** Push the inner pad towards the piston to provide a little clearance for when the caliper is removed.

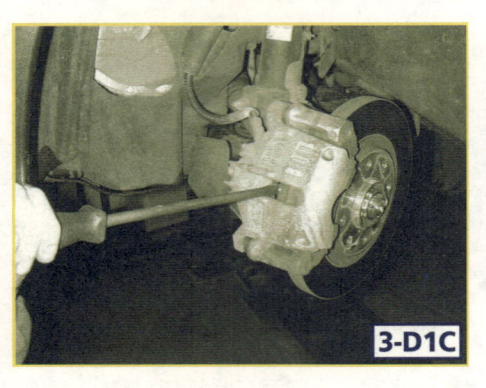

GIRLING CJPE

☐ **STEP D2:** Remove the front-most bolt:
→ Prevent the sleeve from turning with a 17mm spanner (**a**).
→ Remove the bolt with a socket wrench (**b**), as for the Bosch-type, but without the lock plate.

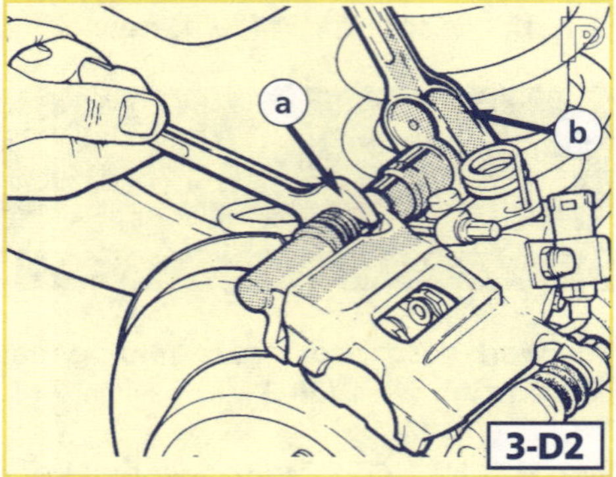

BOTH TYPES

☐ **STEP D3:** Lift the caliper, pivoting it as shown.

☐ **STEP D4:** The pads can now be lifted away from their carriers.

TOP TIP!

- It's strongly recommended that you completely remove the caliper and clean off all accumulated rust and brake dust from the insides of the calipers.
- This helps to prevent pads from jamming and cuts down on the risk of brake squeal.

☐ **STEP D5A: GIRLING CJPE:** Remove the top bolt (**a**) while holding the tube (**b**) as shown for the bottom bolt.

☐ **STEP D5B: BOSCH S5 Z0:** The caliper top pivot slides off the carrier.

3-D6

☐ **STEP D6:** The piston now has to be retracted into the caliper before new pads can be fitted.
➔ **GIRLING CJPE:** This type of piston (arrowed) must NOT be pushed; it has to be screwed back in. See *Step D7*.
➔ **BOSCH S5 Z0:** See *Job 2*.

GIRLING CJPE

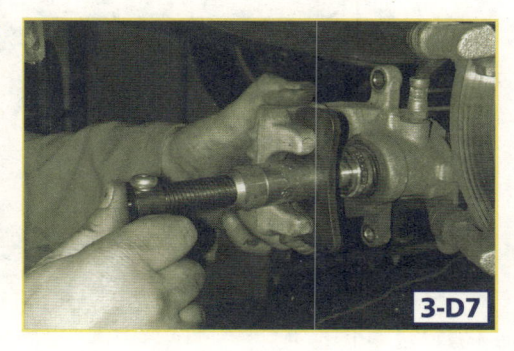

☐ **STEP D7:** You will need to use a piston retraction tool, such as the Sykes-Pickavant type shown here, to screw the piston back into the caliper.
➔ Don't allow the master cylinder to overflow. See *Job 2*.

3-D7

3-D8

☐ **STEP D8:** When fitting the new pads, make sure that the pegs on the pad backing plates fit into the slots on the insides of the pistons (arrowed).

BOTH TYPES

☐ **STEP D9:** Apply brake grease and fit new pads - see *Job 2*.

Section E: ATE Teeves (with screw-in guide pins) - fitted to some 306 models.

The work described here should be read in conjunction with *Job 2*.

☐ **STEP E1:** Start by noting the correct fitting of the pad retaining spring.
➔ Remove one end of the spring with pliers, or by levering with a screwdriver, and remove the spring.

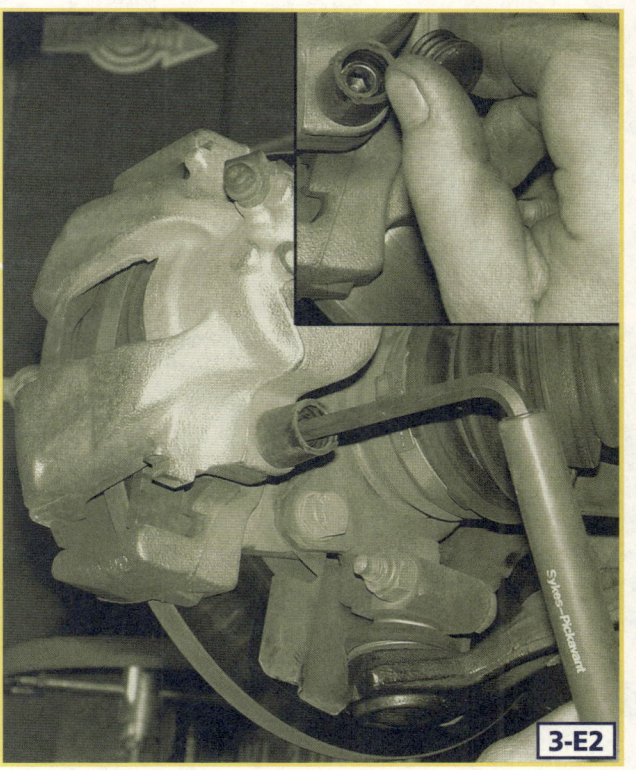

3-E1

3-E2

☐ **STEP E2:** To remove the caliper:
➔ Lever out the dust cap (**inset**) from the end of each of the two caliper guide pins.
➔ Loosen then remove the pins.

CHAPTER 12 Part B Job 3

12-9

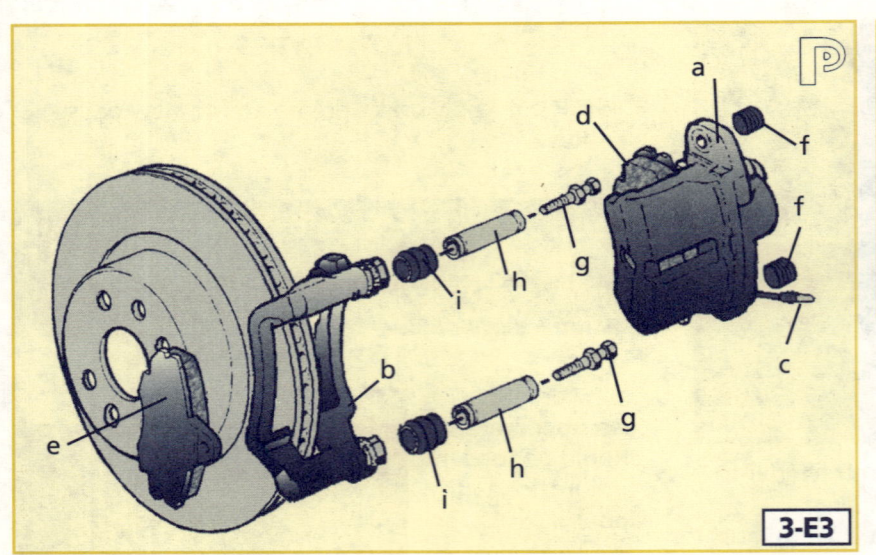

STEP E3: When removing the caliper (**a**) from the carrier (**b**), which stays in place:
→ Be sure to disconnect the brake pad warning cable (**c**), because the inner pad (**d**), to which the cable is attached, is removed with the caliper.
→ As the caliper is lifted away, the outer pad (**e**) becomes free and can be lifted away.
→ For reference, other components shown here are: dust cap (**f**); guide pin (**g**); slider tube (**h**); bellows (**i**).

STEP E4: Remove the inner pad (illustration *3-E3, item d*) from the piston in the caliper by levering it away. It is held into the piston with a spring clip.

STEP E5: When refitting:
→ Refer to *Job 2*.
→ Make sure that the inner pad is properly clipped into the piston.
→ Fit new caliper guide pins to the correct torque and refit the dust caps.
→ Refit the pad retaining spring. Make sure that the spring is in exactly the correct position (compare it with the brake on the other side) and that the spring ends are properly located in the caliper.

JOB 4: FRONT BRAKE CALIPER - *removal, replacement.*

In many cases, the caliper is removed as part of the process of removing the pads. See the relevant Section of *Job 3*.
→ If the caliper is being removed so that you can carry out other work on the vehicle, but the brake hose is not to be disconnected, see *Step 5*.

STEP 1: In all cases, start by loosening (but do not attempt to remove) the flexible hose at the caliper.
→ Clamp the flexible hose near to the caliper to minimise brake fluid loss.
→ Have a rag handy for mopping up spills.

STEP 2: In those cases where the caliper stays in place when the pads are removed:
→ Remove the pads - see *Job 3*.
→ Slacken and remove both caliper retaining bolts.

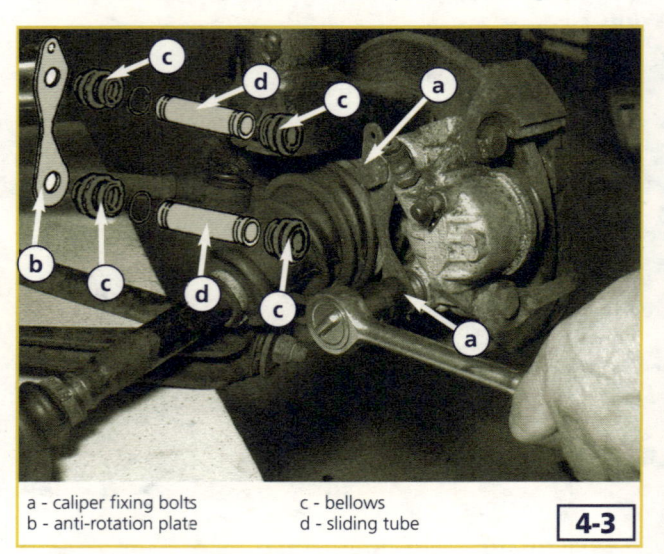

a - caliper fixing bolts   c - bellows
b - anti-rotation plate   d - sliding tube

STEP 3: Remove the bolts (**a**) and (when fitted) the anti-rotation plate (**b**).
→ The caliper can now be lifted away from the disc.
→ When clear, turn the caliper to unscrew the already loosened flexible hose.

→ If you do it this way, you won't have to disconnect the flexible hose from the adjacent rigid hose.

☐ **STEP 4:** When re-assembling use new bolts and tighten them to the correct torque.
→ Use fresh threadlock when fitting the new bolts.

☐ **STEP 5:** If the caliper is being removed so that you can carry out other work on the vehicle, it may not be necessary to disconnect the brake hose.
→ If so, use a piece of stiff wire to hang the caliper somewhere suitable inside the wheel arch, taking great care not to strain the flexible brake hose.
→ Do not leave the caliper to hang on the brake hose - severe risk of damage to the hose.

JOB 5: FRONT BRAKE DISC - *replacement*.

☐ **STEP 1:** Remove the caliper. See *Job 4*.

☐ **STEP 2:** If necessary, unbolt and remove the caliper carrier.
→ This is usually not necessary; you can usually remove the disk with the carrier still in place.
→ If you do remove the carrier, you will have to obtain new bolts for when it is refitted.
→ Use fresh threadlock when fitting the new bolts.

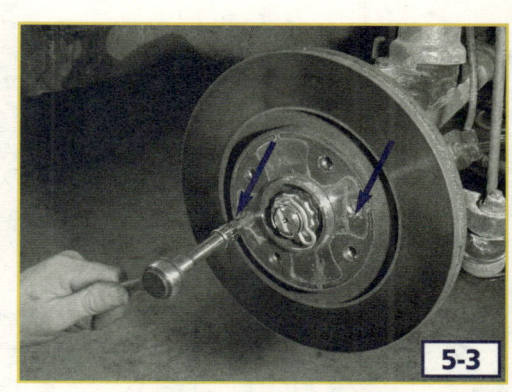

☐ **STEP 3:** Remove the two (usually Torx-head) screws (arrowed) holding the disc in place.

☐ **STEP 4:** The disc is more often than not rusted into place. Tap it free with a soft-faced hammer - NEVER with a steel hammer.

☐ **STEP 5:** Check the disc for the amount of wear on its surface and, if there is obvious wear and/or grooving, fit new replacements.
→ Always fit new disc as 'axle' pairs - never renew a single disc.

☐ **STEP 6:** Before fitting a replacement (or refitting the old) disc, clean off the mating surfaces so that the disc can sit true - as it must - on the hub.

Part C: Rear Brakes

CONTENTS

	Page No.
JOB 1: UNDERSTANDING REAR BRAKE TYPES.	12-12
JOB 2: REAR BRAKE SHOES – *check, replace*.	12-15
JOB 3: REAR WHEEL CYLINDER - *replace*.	12-18
JOB 4: PARKING BRAKE CABLE – *adjust, replace*.	12-18
JOB 5: REAR BRAKE DISC PADS - *replacement*.	12-19
JOB 6: REAR BRAKE CALIPER - *replacement*.	12-20
JOB 7: REAR BRAKE DISC - *replacement*.	12-20
JOB 8: PRESSURE REGULATING VALVES – *replace, adjust*.	12-20

JOB 1: UNDERSTANDING REAR BRAKE TYPES.

Several different types of rear brake have been fitted to the models covered by this manual.
→ Use the illustrations below to see which brakes are fitted to the vehicle you are working on.
→ Not all brakes are exactly as shown here. Manufacturers sometimes make changes during the production life of components.
→ It is important that you note the correct positions of springs and other components as the brakes are dismantled so that they can be put back together correctly and safely.

TOP TIP!

• Only dismantle the brakes on one side of the vehicle at a time.
• If you need to, you can then refer to the other side to see how it should go together.

IMPORTANT NOTE:
• **REAR DRUM BRAKES:** The work described in *Job 2* must be read in conjunction with *Job 1: Rear Brakes: Read This First!*.
• **REAR DISC BRAKES:** The work described in *Job 2* must be read in conjunction with *Part B: Job 2: Brake Pads: Read This First!*.

These annotations apply to all of the illustrations in Types A to F:

a - wheel cylinder	lever	cable and return
b - brake shoe	h - auto. adjuster	spring
c - steady	return spring	o - lower anchorage
pin/spring/cap	i - parking brake lever	point
d - upper brake shoe	j - parking brake lever	p - backplate
return spring	return spring	grommet
e - lower brake shoe	k - auxiliary return	
return spring	spring	
f - auto. adjuster	l - clip	
mechanism	m - connecting rod	
g - auto. adjuster	n - parking brake	

TYPE A: DBA BENDIX DRUM BRAKES

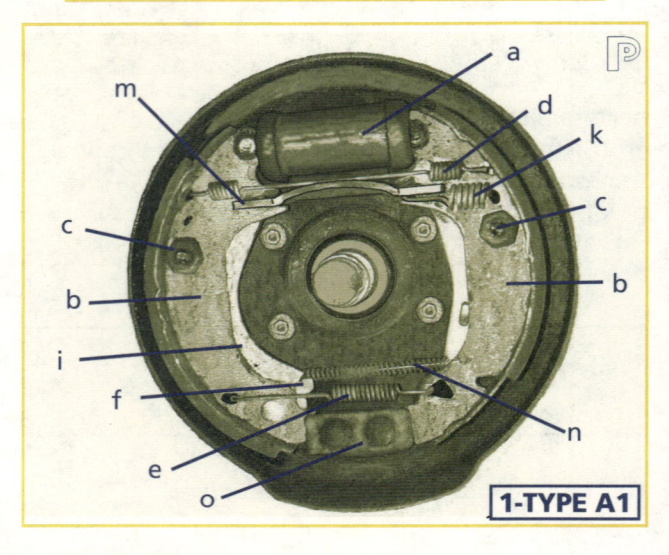

1-TYPE A1

❏ **TYPE A1:** This is one type of system, fitted to 205s.

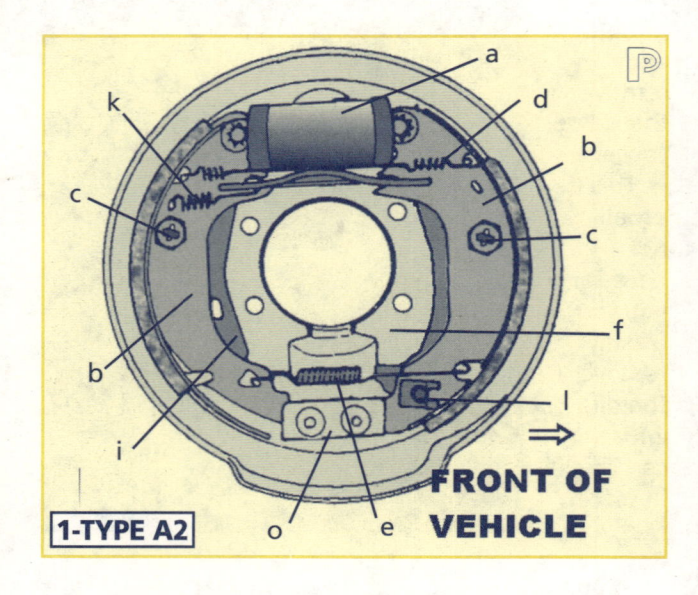

1-TYPE A2 FRONT OF VEHICLE →

❏ **TYPE A2:** This type has a different auto-adjuster fixing. There is a removable spring clip.

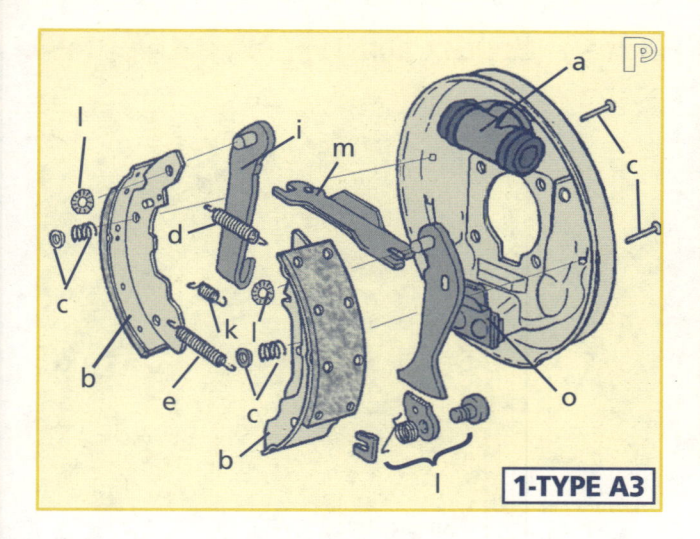

1-TYPE A3

❑ **TYPE A3:** These are the same components in exploded form.

TYPE B: 106-TYPE BENDIX DRUM BRAKES

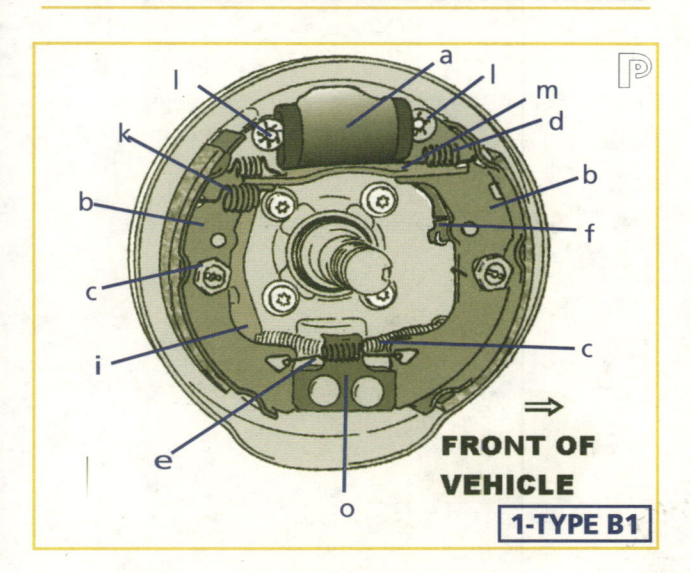

1-TYPE B1

❑ **TYPE B1:** These 106-type Bendix brakes are similar, but not the same as the DBA type.
➔ The auto-adjuster is fitted to the top of the leading brake shoe.
➔ On this version, a plate on the lower anchorage point (o) has the parking brake spring passing behind it, and the lower return spring over the top of it.

1-TYPE B2

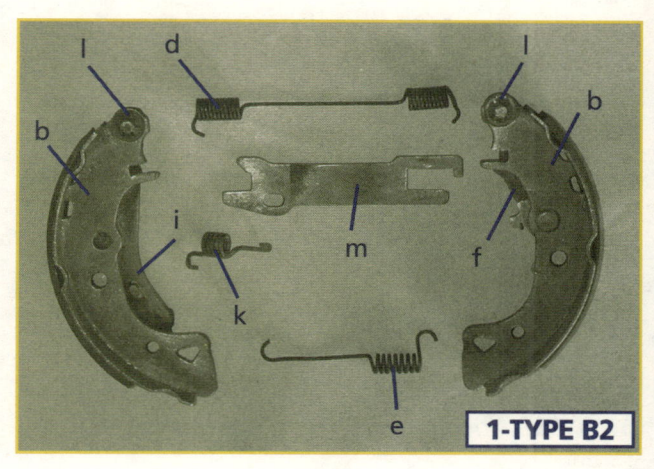

❑ **TYPE B2:** These are the same components in exploded form.

TYPE C: GIRLING DRUM BRAKES

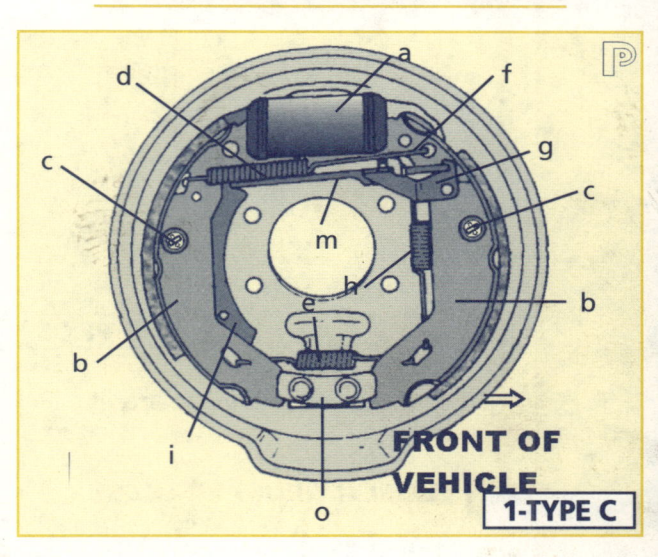

1-TYPE C

❑ **TYPE C:** These are the components of the Girling system. It is quite similar to the Lucas system, but note the spring anchorage points shown here.

TYPE D: LUCAS DRUM BRAKES

❑ **TYPE D1:** This is the Lucas system - similar in some ways to the earlier Girling system - assembled on the vehicle.

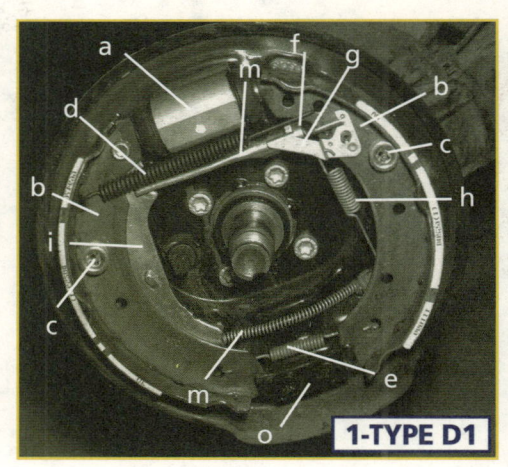

1-TYPE D1

CHAPTER 12 Part C Job 1

12-13

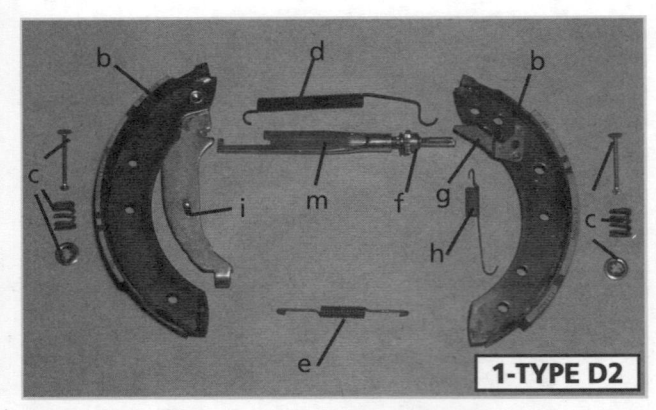

❏ **TYPE D2:** These are the components of the Lucas system.

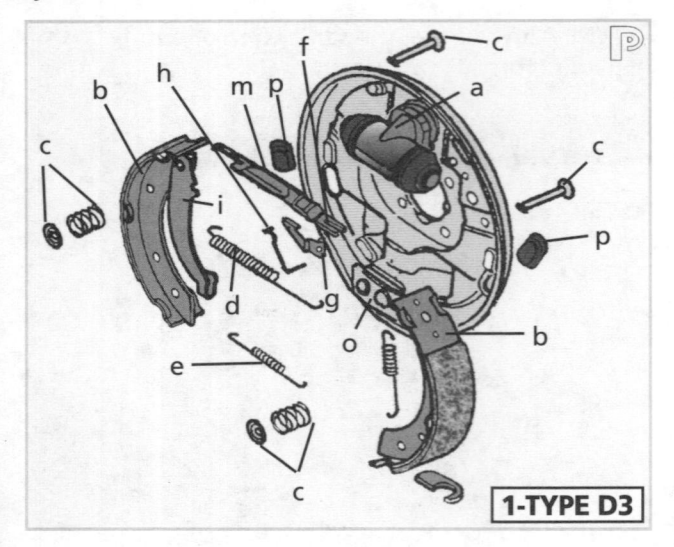

❏ **TYPE D3:** These are the same components in exploded diagram form.

TYPE E: BOSCH DRUM BRAKES

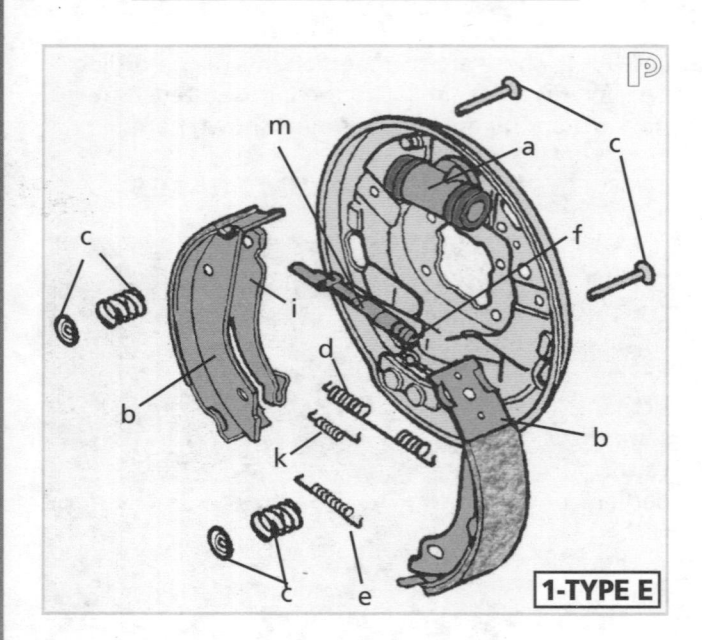

❏ **TYPE E:** This is the Bosch type without ABS (anti-lock) brakes.

TYPE F: BENDIX 306-TYPE DRUM BRAKES

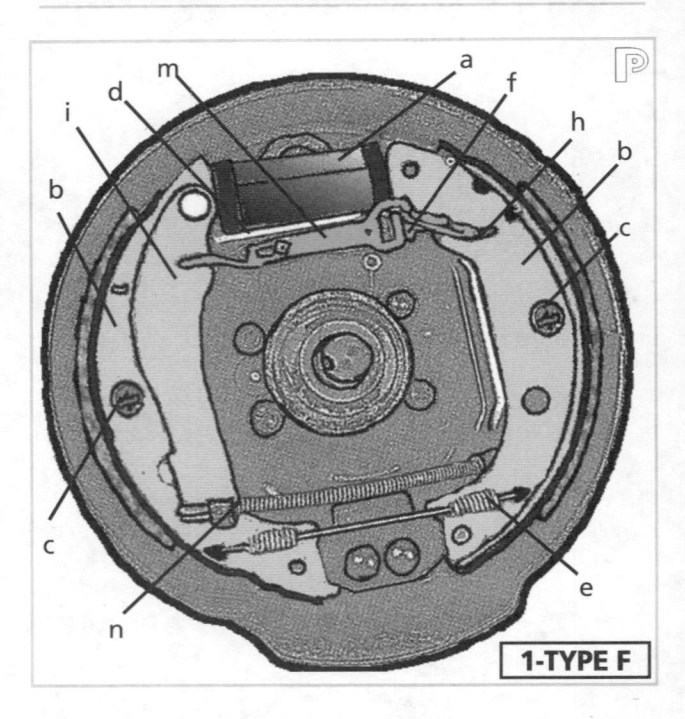

❏ **TYPE F:** Note that the parking brake lever is on the outside of the shoe assembly on this version.

TYPE G: BENDIX DISC BRAKES

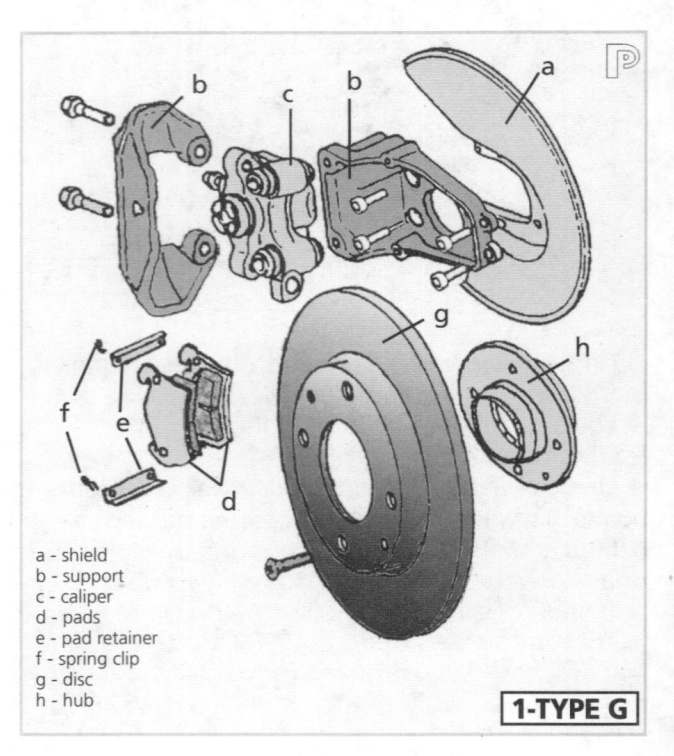

a - shield
b - support
c - caliper
d - pads
e - pad retainer
f - spring clip
g - disc
h - hub

❏ **TYPE G1:** This is the arrangement of the rear disc brake assembly.

JOB 2: REAR BRAKE SHOES – *check, replace*.

Make sure that wheels remaining on the ground are chocked in both directions and that the parking brake is off.

CHECKING BRAKE SHOES

☐ **STEP 1:** On brakes **Type A, B and C** (see *Job 1*) you may be able to release the parking brake at the drum:
→ Turn the brake drum so that one of the holes in the drum lines up with the parking brake operating lever.
→ Push the operating lever through the aperture so that the auto. adjuster releases itself and the shoes are moved away from the drum.
→ If this doesn't work, see the following *TOP TIP!*.

> **TOP TIP!**
> If the drum sticks, try:
> • Slackening the parking brake cable at the adjuster - see *Job 4*.
> • Tap carefully around the drum with a soft-faced mallet to help loosen it.

☐ **STEP 2:** Remove the brake drum.
→ Clean the inside of the drum and the brake with aerosol brake cleaner.
→ If the drum is badly scored or cracked, replace it.
→ Examine the brake shoes for wear or oil contamination.
→ If the latter, the wheel cylinder is probably leaking and the shoes will have to be scrapped, as well as the wheel cylinder renewed.

> **TOP TIP!**
> • Most manufacturers recommend a **minimum** 1.5 mm shoe lining thickness, but it's advisable to replace shoes well before they're this thin.

☐ **STEP 3:** Fold back each of the two rubbers on the wheel cylinder.
→ Any fluid found inside requires a new cylinder.
→ Note that newish cylinders will have a little brake grease still in there.

REPLACING BRAKE SHOES

> **TOP TIP!**
> • Before removing the shoes, mark them F(ront) and R(ear) respectively, so that you can compare old and new shoes and ensure refitting in the correct positions.
> • Complete work on one side at a time so that you have always got the other side as a visual guide.
> • Study the illustrations in *Job 1* when refitting the springs as a double check that they are fitted in precisely the correct positions.

☐ **STEP 4:** Carry out *Steps 1 to 3*.

☐ **STEP 5:** Take the spring caps off the shoe retaining pins.
→ Use a pair of pliers to push in and twist a quarter-turn.
→ Recover the caps and springs and withdraw the pins from the backplate.

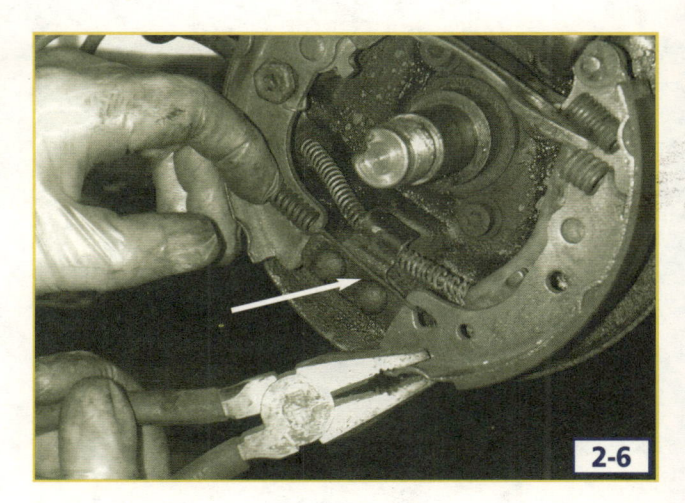

☐ **STEP 6:** Take the pressure off the lower spring before you try to remove it.
→ Lever the shoe away from its lower anchorage (arrowed), pull it a little way forwards, so that it slides over the front of the anchorage and carefully release the tension.

☐ **STEP 7:** Unhook and remove the lower return spring, remove the brake shoes and retrieve the return springs.

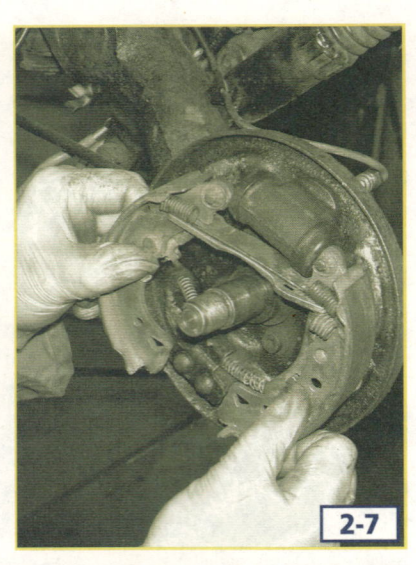

2-7

☐ **STEP 8:** Place a cable tie around the wheel cylinder. If you don't, the wheel cylinder pistons might pop out.

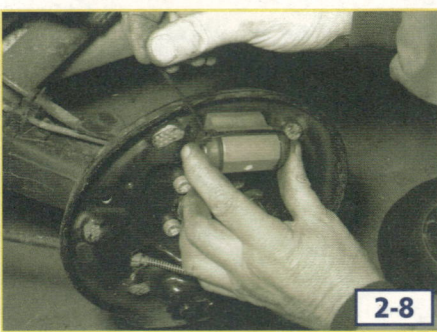

2-8

☐ **STEP 9:** Smear a little brake grease or copper grease (NOT ordinary grease) very sparingly on all the shoe contact points on the backplate and the springs, then continue to re-assemble in reverse order.

2-9

☐ **STEP 10A:** Back off the self adjuster.
➔ On this Lucas-type, turn the wheel so that the expander retracts inside the connecting rod.

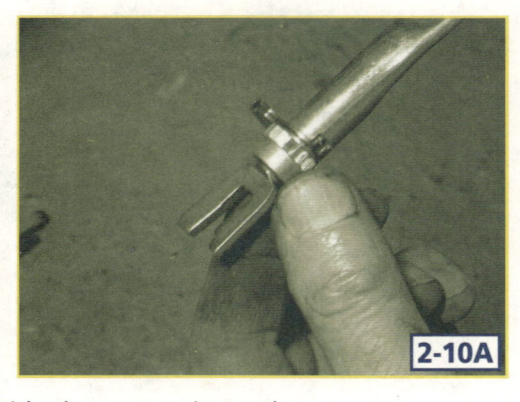

2-10A

☐ **STEP 10B:** This is the earlier Bendix auto-adjuster mechanism, viewed from INSIDE the brake shoe. To allow the adjuster lever to return to its original position:
➔ Work from the other side of the brake shoe.
➔ Push the ratchet arm (**a**) down - in the direction of the arrow.

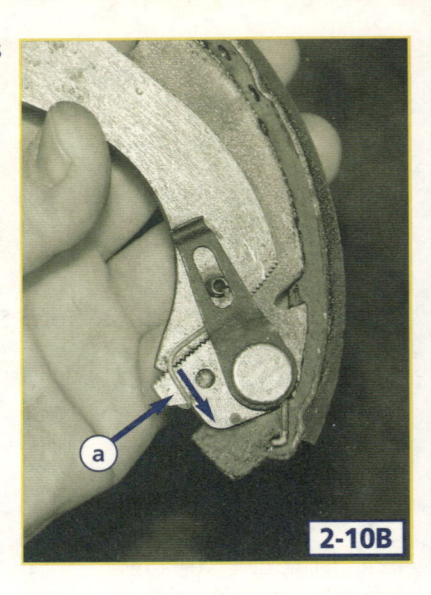

2-10B

☐ **STEP 11:** On this Girling version, it is best to fit the auto. adjuster return spring to the inside of the brake shoe before refitting the shoes.

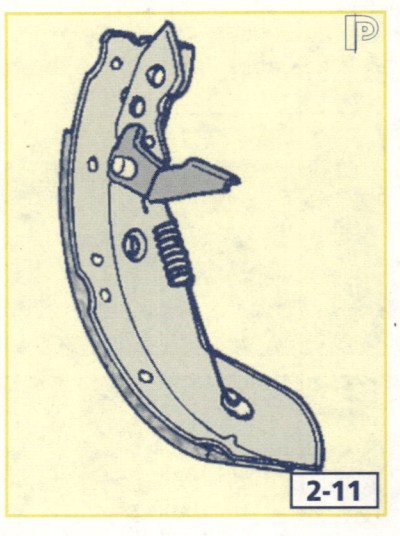

2-11

☐ **STEP 12: ALL TYPES:** Clean the adjuster assembly and lubricate sparingly with copper grease.

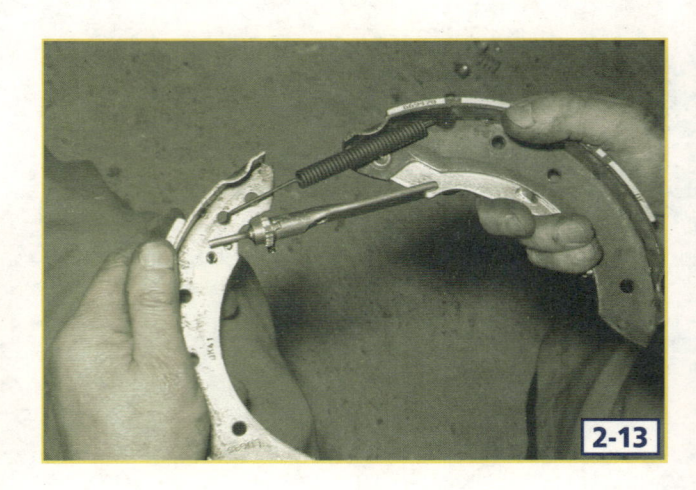

2-13

☐ **STEP 13:** Make absolutely certain that all of the springs are in good condition (replace any with stretched coils or straightened ends) and are fitted in their correct locations.

☐ **STEP 14:** Re-assemble the brake shoes while off the vehicle:
➜ Fit the top return spring.
➜ Fit the connecting rod assembly.
➜ Fit the lower return spring.

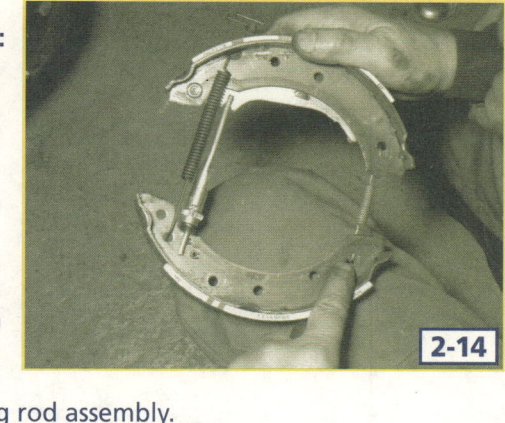

☐ **STEP 15:** This is the Bendix 106-type of shoe with the auto. adjuster near the top of the left-hand shoe and the top of the shoes assembled, ready for refitting.

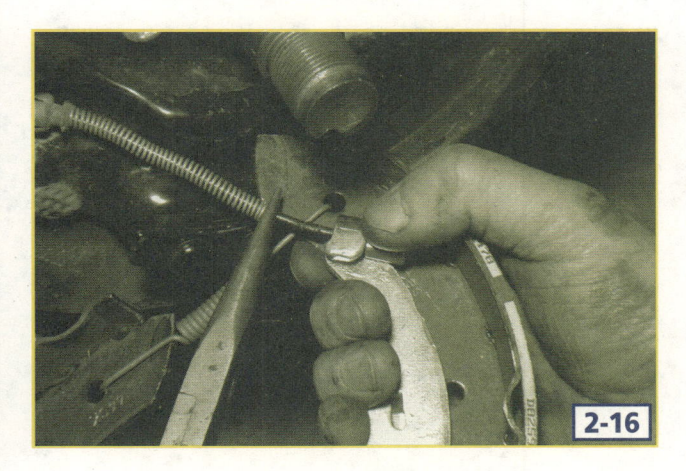

☐ **STEP 16:** In all cases, the parking brake cable now has to be refitted to the relevant brake shoe lever.
➜ Use long-nosed pliers and push the return spring back along the cable.
➜ Leave as much cable bare as you can, and slot the cable and cable-end nipple into place on the parking brake lever.

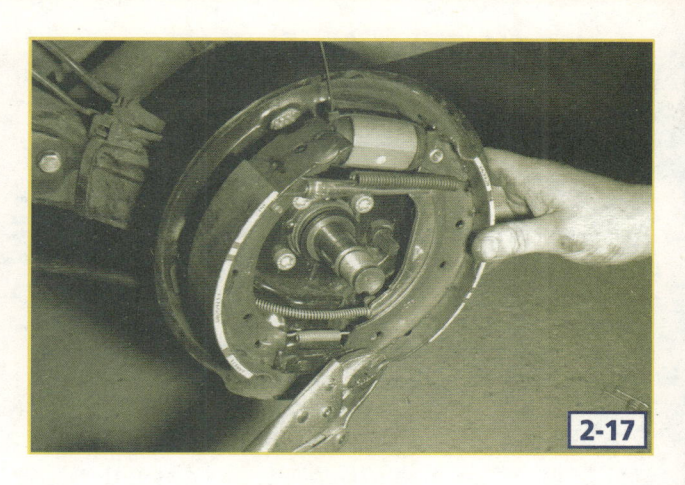

☐ **STEP 17:** Fit the tops of the shoes first, levering the lower-ends over the anchor point with a self-grip wrench to grip the metal backing (NOT the friction material) of the shoe.

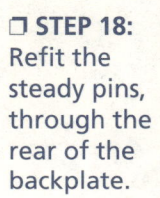

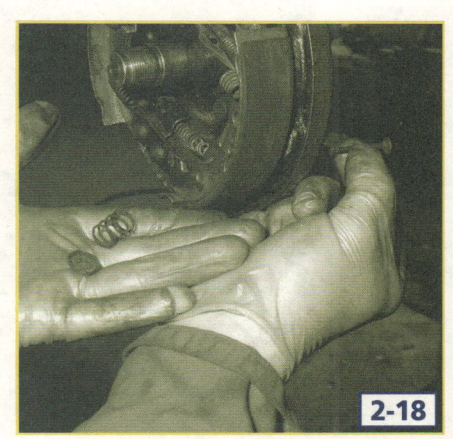

☐ **STEP 18:** Refit the steady pins, through the rear of the backplate.

☐ **STEP 19:** Hold the pin from behind while refitting the spring and cap from the front, using pliers.

☐ **STEP 20:** On this Lucas-type of brake, the auto. adjuster return spring can be fitted with the shoes in place. The lower end of the spring hooks into the shoe from behind the shoe, as shown.

CHAPTER 12 Part C Job 2

12-17

☐ **STEP 21:** When an auto. adjuster works on the ratchet principle, it is essential to ensure that the operating lever is correctly located in the adjuster wheel.

☐ **STEP 22: DON'T FORGET!** Remove the cable tie from around the wheel cylinder, or the brakes won't work!
→ Cut through it and pull it out.

☐ **STEP 23:** After refitting the brake drums, pump the brake pedal vigorously, several times to bring the linings into contact with the drums. Refit the road wheels and lower the vehicle to the ground. Check the wheel bolts for tightness.

JOB 3: REAR WHEEL CYLINDER - replace.

☐ **STEP 1:** Remove the brake shoes - see *Job 2*.

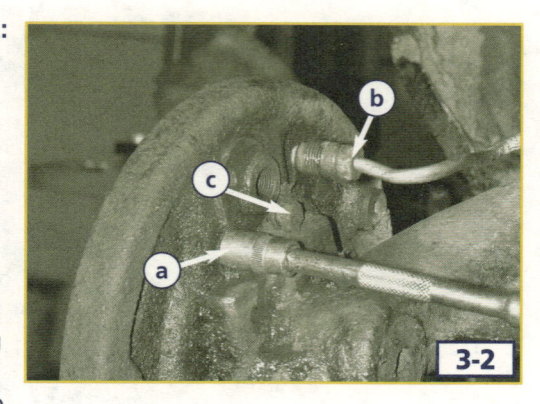

☐ **STEP 2:** To remove the wheel cylinder.
→ Take out the bleed screw (**a**) first. You can then undo the other screws much more easily.

→ Undo the brake pipe union (**b**) at the back of the wheel cylinder and plug the end.
→ Unscrew the fixing bolt (**c**) and withdraw the cylinder.

☐ **STEP 3:** Do not attempt to overhaul a seized, leaking or damaged wheel cylinder.
→ Replace it with a new unit.
→ Refit in the reverse order of removal.
→ Bleed the brakes - see *Part D, Job 5*.

JOB 4: PARKING BRAKE CABLE – adjust, replace.

SAFETY FIRST!

Raise the rear of the vehicle to adjust or replace the parking brake cable.

• It is ESSENTIAL to ensure the front wheels are securely chocked in both directions.

Section A: Parking brake cable adjust.

You don't normally need to adjust the parking brake cables, although they can stretch after a long period of time.
→ Make sure that the rear brakes are not worn, are working properly and the auto-adjusters are not seized.

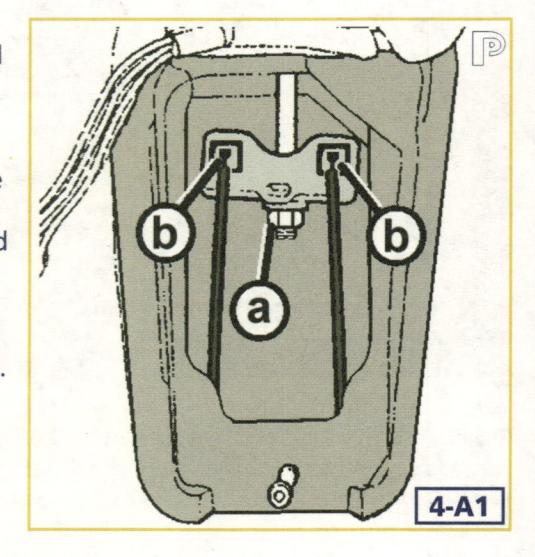

☐ **STEP A1:** On all models, two separate cables are both connected to an equaliser bar (**points b**). The equaliser is attached to an adjuster nut (**a**) at the parking brake lever.

❑ **STEP A2:** Release the parking brake lever to its lowest position. To adjust the parking brake cable:
➔ Remove the screws holding the trim from around the base of the parking brake lever.

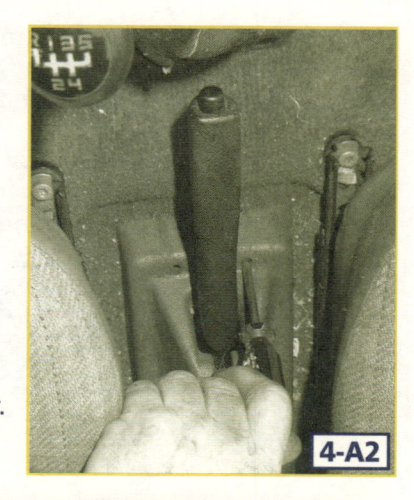

4-A2

❑ **STEP A3:** Apply the parking brake lever by one 'click' of the ratchet.
➔ From inside the vehicle, turn the adjusting nut (**a**) until the cables (**b**) start to be pulled tight.
➔ Pull the parking brake lever up two more 'clicks' and check that both rear wheels are now 'locked'. Check also that both rear wheels are completely free when the parking brake is fully OFF.
➔ When everything works properly, lower the vehicle to the ground, and check again that moving the parking brake lever through about three notches is sufficient to hold the vehicle stationary.
➔ A proper check of parking brake efficiency can only be carried out by a garage with a 'rolling road' brake tester.

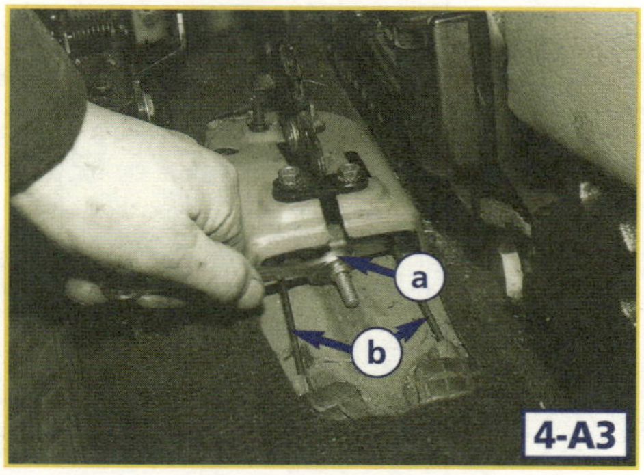

4-A3

Section B: Parking brake cable replacement.

❑ **STEP B1:** See illustration *Job 4, A3*.
➔ Turn the adjusting screw until the cable is freed from the adjuster.

❑ **STEP B2:** Remove the cables from the bodywork clips.
➔ Remove the exhaust heat shield, when fitted, from around the cables.

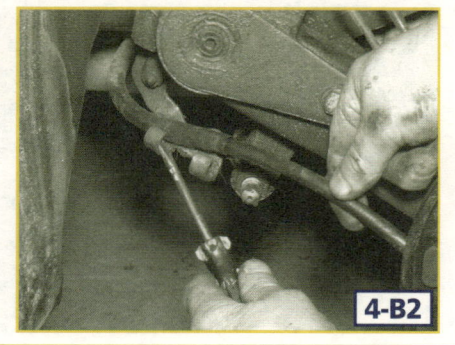

4-B2

REAR DRUM BRAKES

❑ **STEP B3:** Working at each brake backplate in turn, free the parking brake cables from the brake operating mechanism. See *Job 2. Rear brake shoes - replacement*.

❑ **STEP B4:** Compress the clip at the backplate...

4-B4

❑ **STEP B5:** ...and ease the cable free.

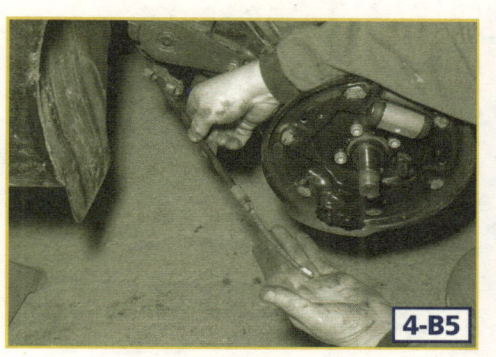

4-B5

REAR DISC BRAKES

❑ **STEP B6:** Detach the cable from the operating lever (**a**) at the brake caliper.

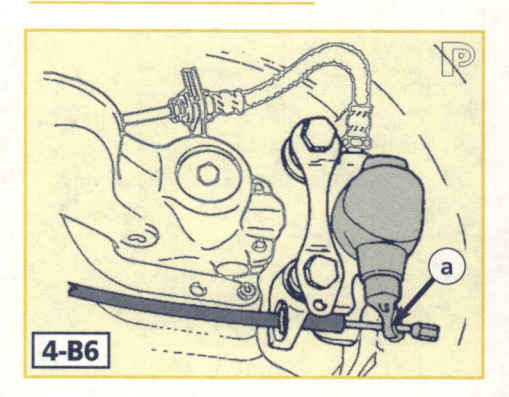

4-B6

Section C: Parking brake lever replacement.

❑ **STEP C1:** Remove the parking brake lever trim. See *Step A2*.

JOB 5: REAR BRAKE DISC PADS - *replacement*.

See *Part B: Front Brakes, Jobs 2 and 3* for information on the DBA Bendix caliper-type.

CHAPTER 12 Part C Job 4

12-19

JOB 6: REAR BRAKE CALIPER - replacement.

☐ **STEP 1:** This job is carried out and completed in the same way as for front brakes of the DBA Bendix caliper-type (see *Part B: Front Brakes, Job 4*) with reference to the following:
➜ Disconnect and detach the parking brake cable.
➜ Slacken the brake hose at the caliper end.
➜ Undo the caliper fixing bolts, remove the caliper.
➜ Unscrew the caliper and flexible hose from the end of the previously slackened rigid hose.
➜ Plug the hose ends.

☐ **STEP 2:** Refit the caliper using NEW self locking bolts.

JOB 7: REAR BRAKE DISC - replacement.

This job is carried out and completed in the same way as for front brakes of the DBA Bendix caliper-type - see *Part B, Job 5*.

JOB 8: PRESSURE REGULATING VALVE - replace, adjust.

TOP TIP!

• A pressure regulator (or regulators) is (or are) fitted in the pipes connecting the master cylinder to the rear wheel cylinders.
• A regulator/s prevent/s the rear wheels from locking during emergency stops when the vehicle's weight shifts to the front wheels.
• If the valve does not work properly, it cannot be repaired but must be replaced.

TYPE A: BRAKE LINE REGULATORS.

☐ **STEP A1:** Find the positions of the valves by tracing each metal brake pipe.
➜ On very early 205 models, without split-circuit braking, there is just one regulator in the front part of the rear circuit.
➜ On all other models, there are two valves, one in each rear pipe. In most cases, they are just ahead of the rear axle.

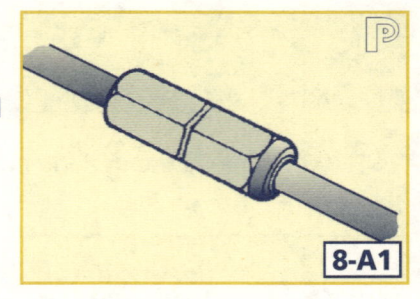

➜ The regulator valves are unscrewed, removed and replaced as for other brake components.
➜ Do not allow any dirt to get into the system.

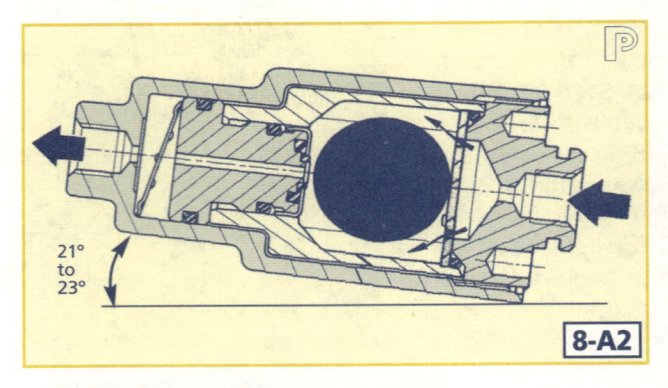

☐ **STEP A2: 205 GTI:** The regulator must be fitted at an angle of between 21 and 23 degrees to the horizontal, as shown, and bearing in mind the direction of flow of the brake fluid.

☐ **STEP A3:** Fit the new unit/s and remake all hydraulic connections.
➜ Bleed the brakes - see *Part D, Job 5*.

TYPE B: LOAD-SENSING REGULATOR.

This type is affected by the amount of weight on the rear of the vehicle.

☐ **STEP B1:** To remove the valve:
➜ Undo the brake pipe unions (**a**) using (preferably) a split ring spanner and plug the ends of the pipes.
➜ Pull off the actuating spring from the lever.
➜ Remove the securing bolts (**b**).

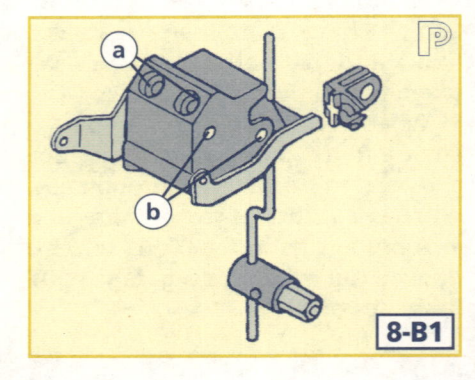

☐ **STEP B2:** Install the new valve, connect the brake pipes and bleed the brakes.

☐ **STEP B3: 205 WITH ABS:** The type shown here was fitted to 205s with ABS. It can be adjusted as follows:

→ Make sure that the rear of the vehicle is on level ground and sitting evenly on all four wheels - not jacked or raised off the ground, other than on a four-post hoist.

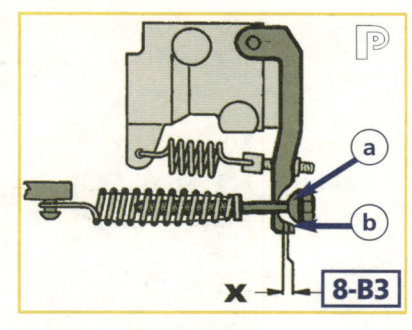

→ Make sure the rear ride height is 210mm, measured from the rear jacking cut-out point to the ground. Add weight if necessary.

→ Adjust the bolt (**a**) so that the clearance (**X**) between the end face of the bolt (**a**) and the lever (**b**) is between 0.5 mm and 1.5 mm.

☐ **STEP B4: ALL OTHER MODELS:** The valve will now need to be correctly adjusted by a Peugeot dealer, who will have the specialised equipment necessary to carry out the work.

→ Drive carefully and slowly to the Peugeot dealer who will be carrying out the work.

→ Do not otherwise use the vehicle on the road until the regulator has been adjusted.

Part D: Hydraulics, Servo, ABS

CONTENTS

	Page No.
JOB 1: MASTER CYLINDER - *replace*.	12-21
JOB 2: SERVO – *check, remove, refit*.	12-22
JOB 3: FLEXIBLE HOSES – *replacement*.	12-24
JOB 4: METAL PIPES – *replacement*.	12-24
JOB 5: BRAKE BLEEDING.	12-25
JOB 6: SERVO VACUUM PUMP, (Diesel engines) – *replacement*.	12-25
JOB 7: ABS BRAKE, WHEEL SENSORS – *check*.	12-25

JOB 1: MASTER CYLINDER - *replace*.

IMPORTANT NOTE: Protect all paint surfaces from possible brake fluid spillage before starting work. Brake fluid makes a slow but effective paint stripper!

☐ **STEP 1:** Empty as much fluid as you can out of the master cylinder.

→ Siphon off as much brake fluid as possible or bleed it out through one of the front brakes until the master cylinder makes 'sucking' noises.

☐ **STEP 2:** Use (preferably) a purpose-made split ring wrench to undo all the pipe unions from the master cylinder.

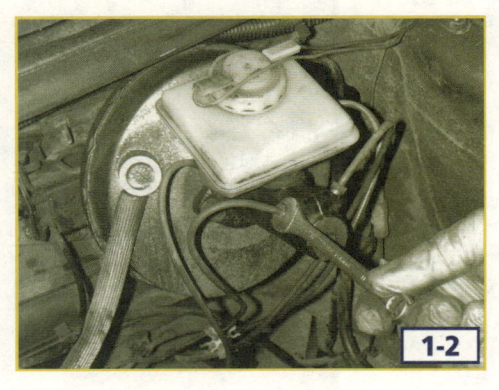

☐ **STEP 3:** Undo the nuts securing the master cylinder to the servo bolts. Take off the reservoir cap and remove the master cylinder from the servo.

→ Retrieve the O-ring – see illustration **1-4, item c**.

> **TOP TIP!**
> • Don't take the reservoir off the master cylinder until both are off the vehicle.
> • That way, you won't spill fluid in the engine bay.

CHAPTER 12 Part D Job 2

☐ **STEP 4:** Remove the reservoir from the master cylinder:
→ Some types have a retaining pin (**b**) and clip (**a**) – remove if necessary.

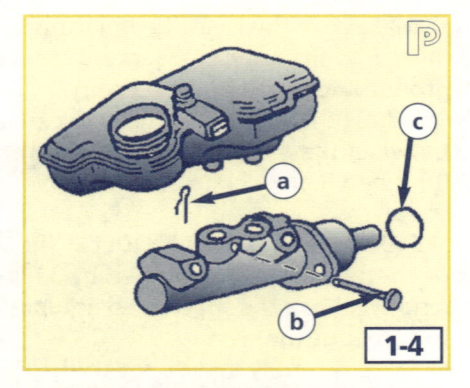

1-4

☐ **STEP 5:** It is usually necessary to carefully lever the reservoir stubs out of their tight fixings in rubber seals in the master cylinder.

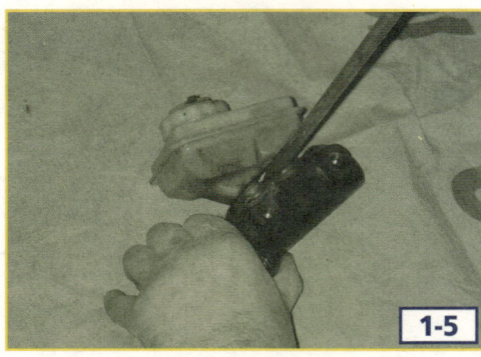

1-5

☐ **STEP 6:** Refit in the reverse order and bleed the brakes - see *Job 5*.

JOB 2: SERVO - check, remove, refit.

FACT FILE
SERVO CHECKS

• Before condemning the servo for lack of efficiency, check the condition of the one-way valve and vacuum pipe connecting it to the inlet manifold.
• Ease the valve out of the front of the servo and disconnect the pipe from the inlet manifold.
• Check that you can only blow one way through the valve - from the servo end towards the inlet manifold.
• Check for loose connections - and the vacuum pipe can suffer failure in many ways. Age can harden it until it cracks, causing an air leak which sometimes results in a whistling noise and rough slow-running.
• The other type of vacuum hose failure is a hose collapse - where the hose - or the inner lining - is sucked flat by the vacuum - often because oil has softened the hose.
• This is not so easily detected, as it rarely upsets engine performance - check with engine running.

☐ **STEP 1:** Remove the master cylinder. See *Job 1*.
→ Pull the vacuum hose out of the servo body, as shown.

2-1

VEHICLES WITH SERVO ON LEFT AND CROSS-SHAFT TO BRAKE PEDAL

☐ **STEP 2:** Slacken the cross-shaft fixing at the right-hand side, furthest away from the servo.

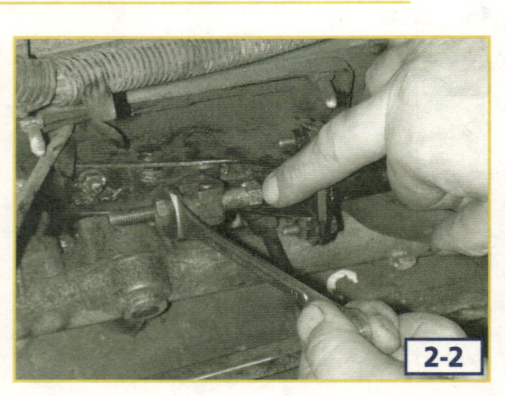

2-2

TOP TIP!
• There is no need to lose the adjustment setting when you detach the cross-shaft.
• Undo the lock nut shown, NOT the adjuster nut being pointed to.

☐ **STEP 3:** Slacken the two bolts (arrowed) - there is no need to remove them - and retrieve the spacers found there. Keep them for use when refitting.

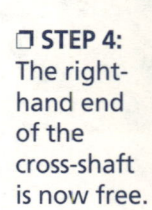

2-3

☐ **STEP 4:** The right-hand end of the cross-shaft is now free.

2-4

12-22

❑ **STEP 5:** Remove the four nuts holding the servo support bracket to the vehicle's body.

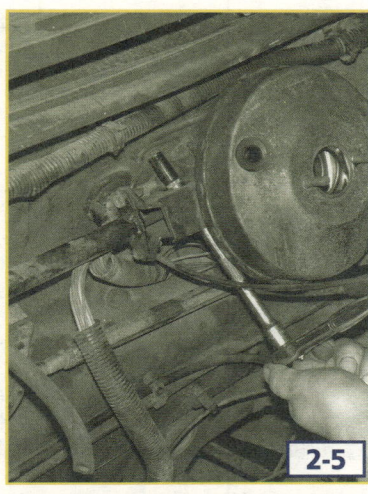

2-5

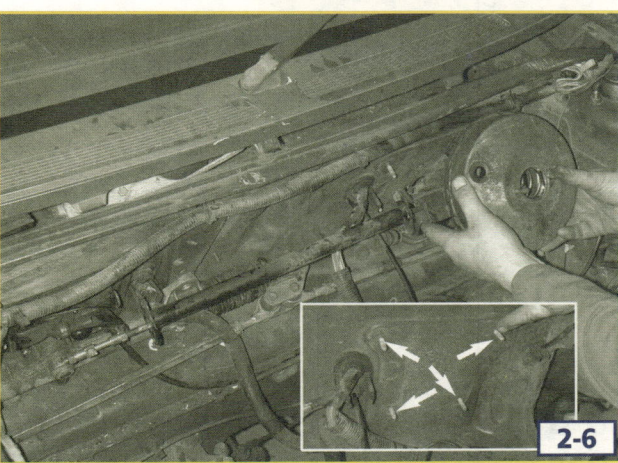

2-6

❑ **STEP 6:** Lift the whole servo and cross-shaft assembly out of the engine bay.
→ Note the positions of the four studs on which the servo bracket is fitted (inset).

ALL VEHICLES

TOP TIP!

- Some later models have very little room in the engine bay for removal of the servo unit.
- If there is a problem with clearance, try removing (as appropriate): air intake trunking; camshaft cover; inlet manifold.
- It may even be necessary to disconnect the engine mounting and push the engine forwards, in some cases.

❑ **STEP 7:** Disconnect the servo pushrod (a) from the pedal or cross-shaft relay (b) by removing the split pin or spring

2-7

clip (c) then pushing out the pivot pin (d).
→ **VEHICLES WITH SERVO ADJACENT TO BRAKE PEDAL:** Work inside the vehicle, in the driver's-side footwell.

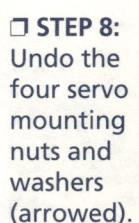

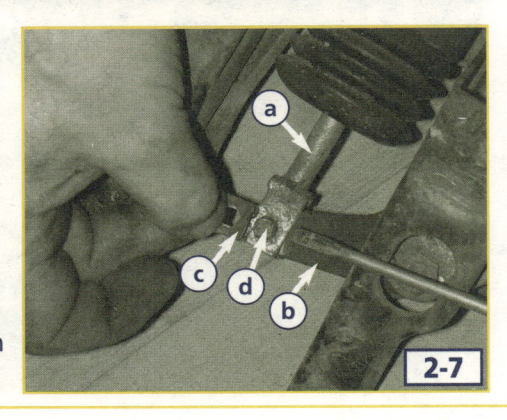

❑ **STEP 8:** Undo the four servo mounting nuts and washers (arrowed).

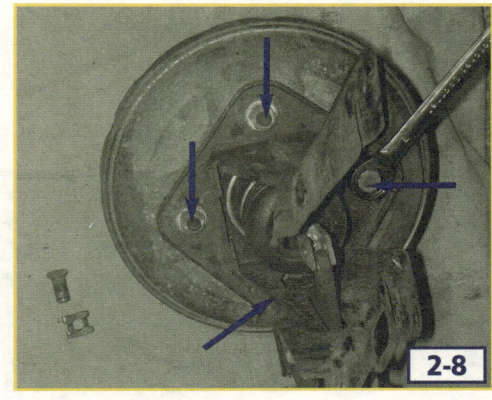

2-8

❑ **STEP 9: VEHICLES WITH SERVO ADJACENT TO BRAKE PEDAL:**
→ Lever off the two clips (a).
→ Remove the bolt (b) holding the support in place.
→ The pivot pin (d) and four nuts (c) are removed - see **Step 7**.

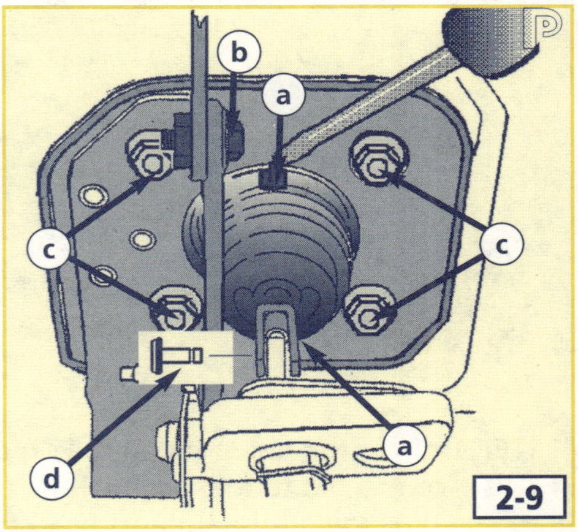

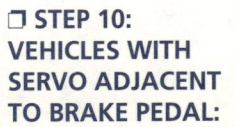

2-9

❑ **STEP 10: VEHICLES WITH SERVO ADJACENT TO BRAKE PEDAL:**
→ Lever off the clips (arrowed).
→ Remove the servo from the vehicle.

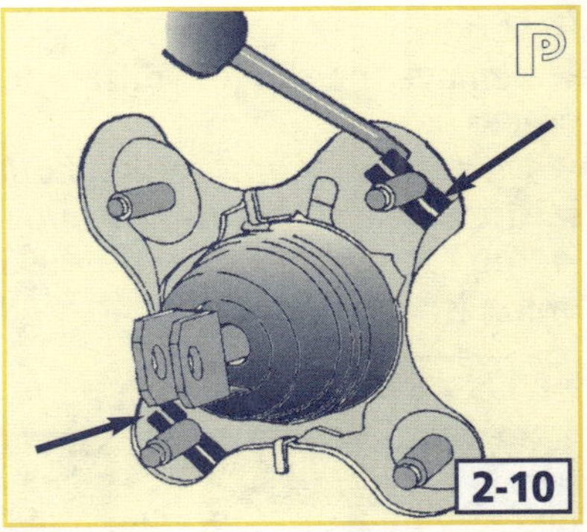

2-10

❑ **STEP 11:** When refitting the servo to the bulkhead:
→ Always fit a new gasket.
→ With the pushrod connected to the brake pedal...
→ ...the gap 'X' should be between 22.2 and 22.4 mm.

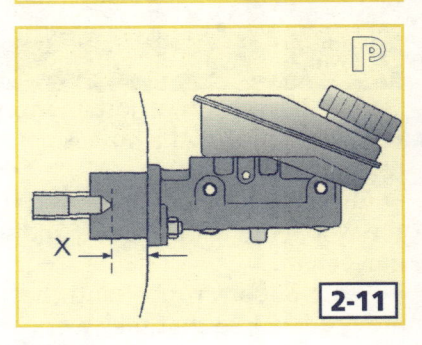

2-11

CHAPTER 12 Part D Job 2

12-23

❏ **STEP 12:** Reassemble in the reverse order and bleed the brake hydraulics. See *Job 5*.

JOB 3: FLEXIBLE HOSES - *replacement.*

TOP TIP!

When disconnecting brake pipes or hoses, minimise brake fluid loss:
• Unscrew the master cylinder reservoir cap, lay a sheet of kitchen cling film across the opening, and refit the cap.
• This will help to minimise the amount of fluid that runs out of opened brake lines.

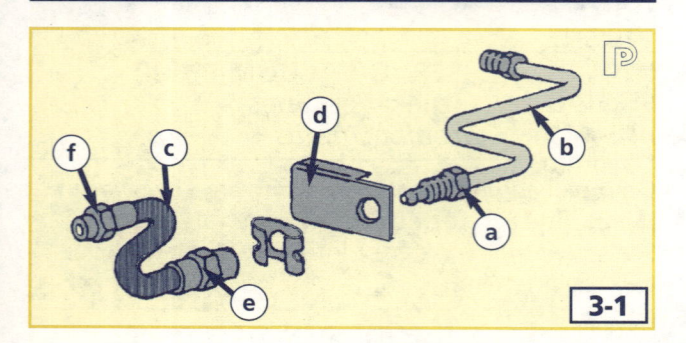

3-1

❏ **STEP 1:** Undo the union (**a**) on the rigid pipe (**b**).
➔ This is connected to the flexible hose (**c**) where hose and pipe join at the support bracket (**d**).
➔ Hold the hexagon (**e**) to prevent the flexible hose from turning.
➔ Take care not to damage the bracket or tear it off the body.
➔ Remove the clip (**e**) - different shapes and types used.
➔ On some versions, you pull out the clip, which secures the hose to the bracket, with pliers.
➔ You can now unscrew the flexible hose from its union (**f**) at its other end.

TOP TIP!

• If the pipe starts to twist with the union, grip the pipe as lightly as possible with pliers or self-grip wrench - try to stop it from turning.
• If you can't, cut through the pipe and replace it.

❏ **STEP 2:** Fit the new hose in reverse order:
➔ Make sure that the hose is not twisted when refitting the rigid pipe.
➔ Check that the hose cannot chafe anywhere over the whole range of steering and suspension movement.
➔ Space out any rubber anti-chaff washers, if they are not fixed, so that they work as well as possible.
➔ Bleed the brake hydraulics. See *Job 5*.

JOB 4: METAL PIPES - *replacement.*

TOP TIP!

When disconnecting brake pipes or hoses, minimise brake fluid loss:
• Unscrew the master cylinder reservoir cap, lay a sheet of plastic across the opening, and refit the cap.
• This will prevent atmospheric pressure from pushing the fluid out of opened lines.

❏ **STEP 1:** Undo the unions at each end of a pipe length.
➔ See *TOP TIP!* after *Job 3, Step 1*.
➔ Use penetrating oil to help free seized unions, and use a split-ring spanner rather than an open-ended one, to reduce the risk of rounding off the union nuts.

❏ **STEP 2:** Detach the pipe length from its securing clips and remove it.

TOP TIP!

❏ **STEP 3:** • Where possible, use the old pipe as a pattern to shape the new one before fitting it.
• Follow the original route and secure the pipe in the body clips.
• Connect the unions and bleed the brake hydraulics.

JOB 5: BRAKE BLEEDING.

FACT FILE
BRAKE BLEEDING SEQUENCE
When you need to bleed the complete system, follow either:
• a clockwise route, starting from the bleed nipple behind the right front wheel, or
• anti-clockwise starting from the left front bleed nipple.
• Go round the sequence at least twice. The two sequences are:
• EITHER - CLOCKWISE: right front; right rear; left rear; left front
• OR - ANTI-CLOCKWISE: left front; left rear; right rear; right front.
• The engine needs to be running while bleeding the brakes to operate the vacuum brake servo unit.

SAFETY FIRST!
• Work out of doors, to avoid breathing dangerous exhaust fumes.
• You will need to work with an assistant. Make sure he/she does not put the vehicle in gear while the engine is running.
• Chock a pair of wheels, both in front and behind each wheel.

❑ **STEP 1:** Start the engine running and leave it ticking over in neutral (or 'N').

❑ **STEP 2:** To bleed the brakes:
➔ Push a tight fitting length of plastic or rubber tubing (**a**) with a non-return valve onto the first bleed screw (**b**) and immerse the other end in a small quantity of brake fluid in a glass jar (**c**) so that no air can possibly be pulled up the tube.
➔ Undo the bleed screw with a ring spanner by half a turn.
➔ Have your assistant pump the brake pedal several times.
➔ After several 'pumps', hold the pedal to the floor while you lock up the bleed screw, then release the pedal slowly.
➔ Repeat until no air bubbles - only fluid - are pushed out of the pipe.
➔ Take great care not to let the master cylinder run out of brake fluid, or you will introduce fresh air into the system and have to start again.
➔ Use ONLY fresh brake fluid from a previously unopened container.

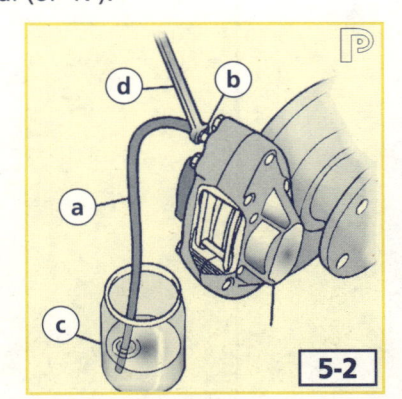

❑ **STEP 3:** Bleed each remaining brake in the same way, going round the sequence at least twice.

SAFETY FIRST!
• After completing the bleeding operation, and with your helper's foot firmly on the brake pedal, check all connections for leaks.
• Remember to top up the fluid, replace the master cylinder cap and reconnect the wires to it.

JOB 6: SERVO VACUUM PUMP, (Diesel engines) - *replacement*.

On diesel engines, the servo is powered by a vacuum pump, fitted to the end of the camshaft housing. See **Chapter 6, Engine** for information on removal and replacement.

JOB 7: ABS BRAKES, WHEEL SENSORS - *check*.

FACT FILE
ABS WHEEL SENSORS:
• When ABS (anti-lock) brakes are fitted, there is very little that can be replaced or even checked without specialised equipment.
• The gaps between the wheel speed sensors and the toothed rotor wheels can be checked to see if they fall within the limits shown here.
• The gap cannot be adjusted. If the gap is 'out', check to see if components are correct or damaged.
• If the ABS warning light shows on the dash, check the sensor and rotor for cleanliness and contamination.

STEP 1: Check the gap between front sensor and rotor to make sure that the wheel is not damaged and that the gap is not contaminated with dirt or brake dust - common causes of ABS malfunction.
→ This is the toothed rotor seen with caliper and disc removed.

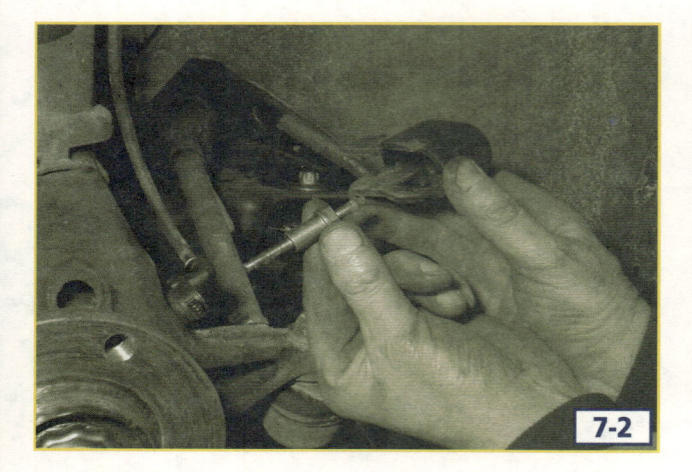

STEP 2: The front sensor can be removed, if necessary, after taking off the protective cover. Make sure that it is watertight!

STEP 3: The toothed rotor is found on the inside of the brake drum on vehicles with ABS and rear drum brakes.
→ Check rotor and sensor (arrowed) for contamination with brake dust.

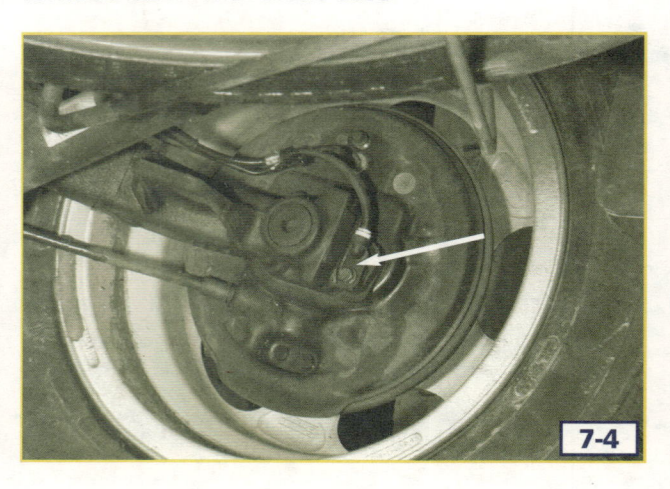

STEP 4: The sensor (arrowed) is removed from the rear of the backplate.

CHAPTER 13: BODYWORK

Please read **Chapter 2 Safety First** before carrying out any work on your car.

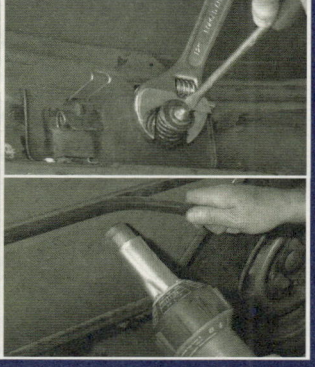

CONTENTS

	Page No.		Page No.
JOB 1: ENGINE BAY LID - removal, refitting, adjusting.	13-1	**JOB 8:** FRONT WING (typical) - replacement.	13-10
JOB 2: ENGINE BAY LID RELEASE - adjustment, removal.	13-2	**JOB 9:** EXTERNAL TRIM (typical) - removal, refitting.	13-11
JOB 3: TAILGATE AND STRUTS - removal, refitting, adjustment.	13-3	**JOB 10:** DOOR - removal, refitting, adjustment.	13-11
JOB 4: LUGGAGE BAY LID 306 ONLY - removal, refitting.	13-5	**JOB 11:** WINDOW INDER MECHANISM, WINDOW GLASS - removal, refitting.	13-12
JOB 5: TAILGATE/LUGGAGE BAY LID, LOCK ASSEMBLY - removal, refitting.	13-5	**JOB 12:** DOOR LOCK/HANDLE - removal, refitting.	13-14
JOB 6: WHEEL ARCH LINERS AND UNDERTRAYS (typical) - removal, refitting.	13-7	**JOB 13:** DOOR MIRROR - replacement.	13-16
JOB 7: BUMPERS (TYPICAL) - removal, refitting.	13-7	**JOB 14:** SUN ROOF.	13-16
		JOB 15: SCREEN GLASS - replacement.	13-17
		JOB 16: CENTRAL LOCKING.	13-20

JOB 1: ENGINE BAY LID – removal, refitting, adjusting.

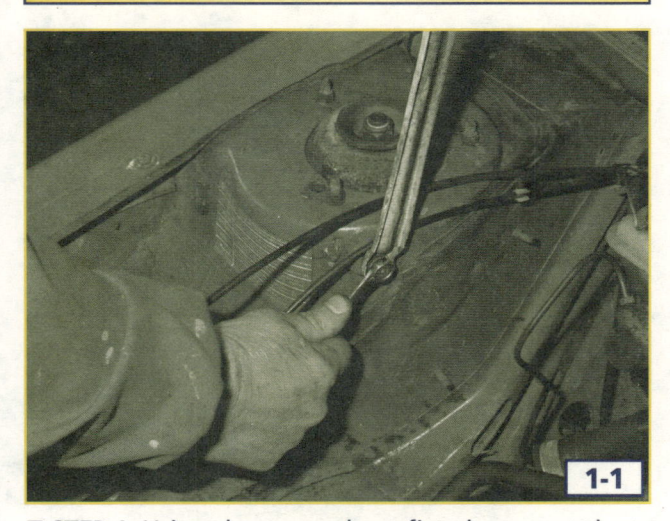

☐ **STEP 1:** Using the prop where fitted, support the engine bay lid in the open position.
➔ If there is a fixed engine bay lid stay, remove it and insert a temporary prop.

☐ **STEP 2:** Detach the windscreen washer tube from the lid.

☐ **STEP 3:** Use a felt pen or masking tape to mark out the hinge positions then get a helper to support the engine bay lid while you undo the four hinge bolts (two at each side).

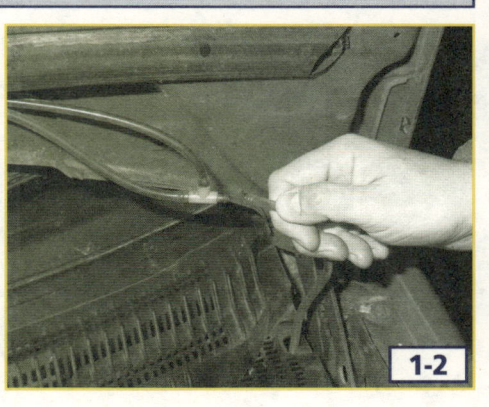

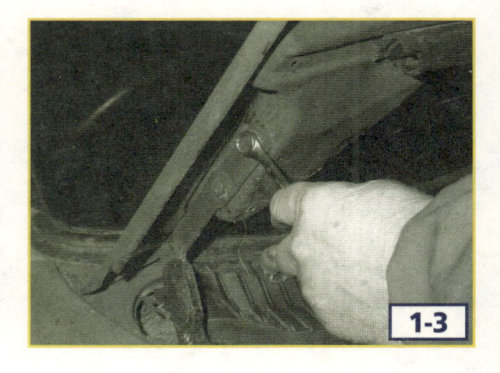

STEP 4: Lift the bonnet up off the hinges.

STEP 5: Refit in the reverse order but tighten the bolts just enough to hold the lid firmly in position, then lower it carefully and check for an equal gap between wings and lid, and for proper alignment of its leading edge.
→ Make any minor adjustments and when you are satisfied, tighten the hinge bolts.

TOP TIP!

STEP 6: • When you and your assistant replace the engine bay lid, place a piece of cloth under each back corner so that it doesn't damage your car's bodywork.

IMPORTANT NOTE: Removing and replacing the engine bay lid might affect the adjustment of the release mechanism. See *Job 2*.

JOB 2: ENGINE BAY LID RELEASE – *adjustment - removal*.

Section A: Removal.

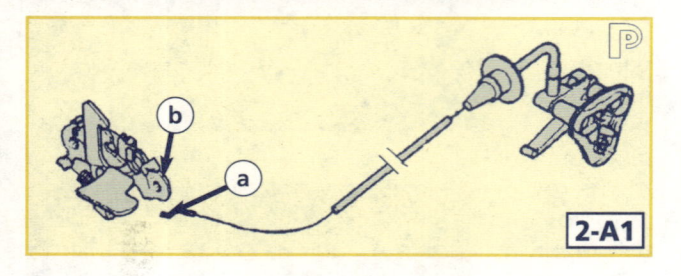

STEP A1: To remove the lock, disconnect the end of the operating cable (**a**) from the lever (**b**) on the lock and remove the lock fixing bolts.

STEP A2: Trace the operating cable through the engine bay, and disconnect any fasteners.

STEP A3: There is a connecting plate between the two sections of the engine bay lid release cable, held in a plastic frame (arrowed).

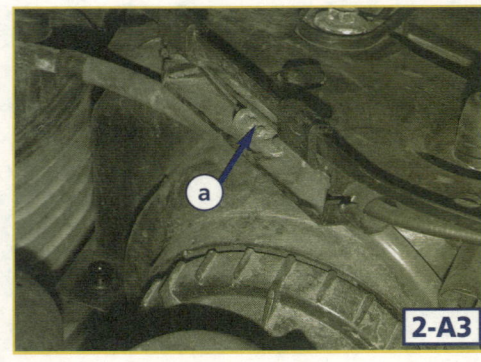

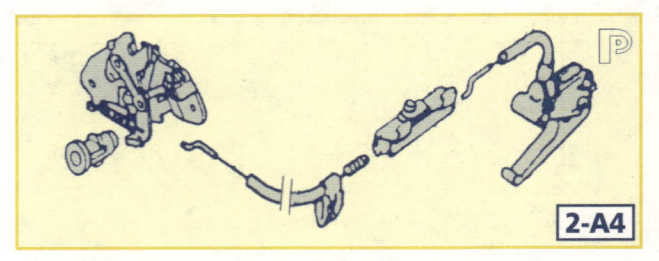

STEP A4: Uncouple the rear cable from the connecting plate.
→ The front section of cable can now be removed.
→ To remove the rear section, tie a fish wire to the end and draw the cable back into the vehicle.

ALL OTHER MODELS

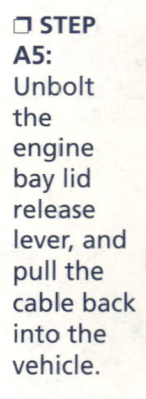

STEP A5: Unbolt the engine bay lid release lever, and pull the cable back into the vehicle.

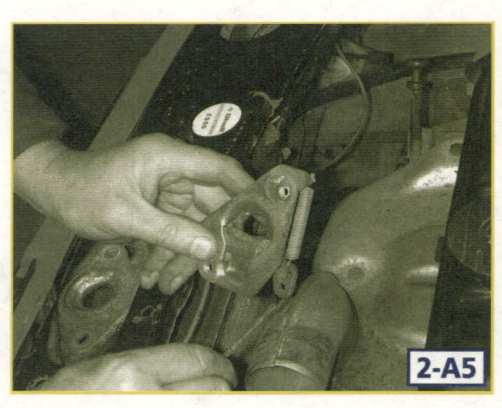

STEP A6: The release handle, inside the vehicle, is usually held by a single bolt (arrowed).

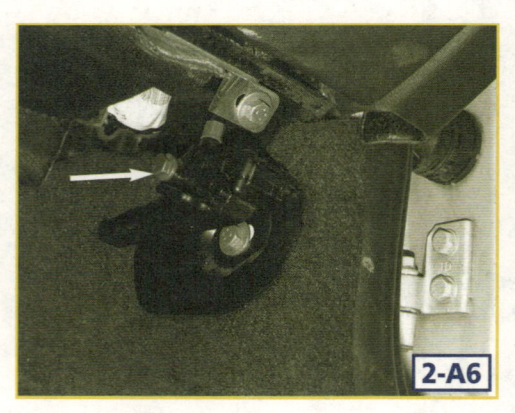

STEP A7: Reassemble as the reverse of removal.

Section B: Adjustment.

☐ **STEP B1: EARLY VEHICLES:** Early vehicles have a horizontally mounted lock. Check that the striker pin passes through the centre of the lock.
➜ If not, slacken the lock plate bolts (arrowed) and adjust as necessary.

☐ **STEP B2:** The height of the engine bay lid leading edge is adjusted via the striker pin.
➜ To adjust the height, slacken the lock nut (**a**), turn the pin (**b**) and retighten the nut.

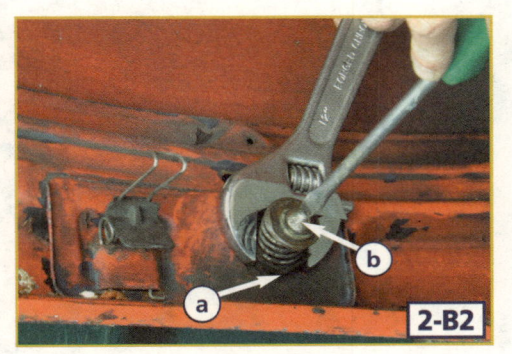

☐ **STEP B3: LATER VEHICLES:** Later vehicles have a vertically mounted lock.
➜ Check that the striker engages with the centre of the latch (arrowed).
➜ To adjust the bonnet leading edge height, slacken the lock fixing nuts and adjust.

☐ **STEP B4:** If, in either corner, the leading edge of the engine bay lid sits too high or low on one side, adjust the height of the buffers found there.

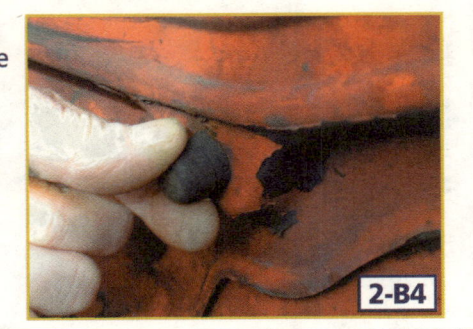

☐ **STEP B5:** If the trailing edge in the engine bay lid is too high or low at one side, adjust the hinges.

JOB 3: TAILGATE AND STRUTS - *removal, refitting, adjustment.*

The tailgate is fitted to the bodywork via a pair of top-mounted hinges and is held aloft with hydraulic struts.

☐ **STEP 1:** Disconnect the battery negative (-) earth/ground terminal. See **Chapter 10, Electrical, Dash, Instruments, Fact File: Disconnecting the Battery** BEFORE doing so!

STRUT REMOVAL AND REPLACEMENT

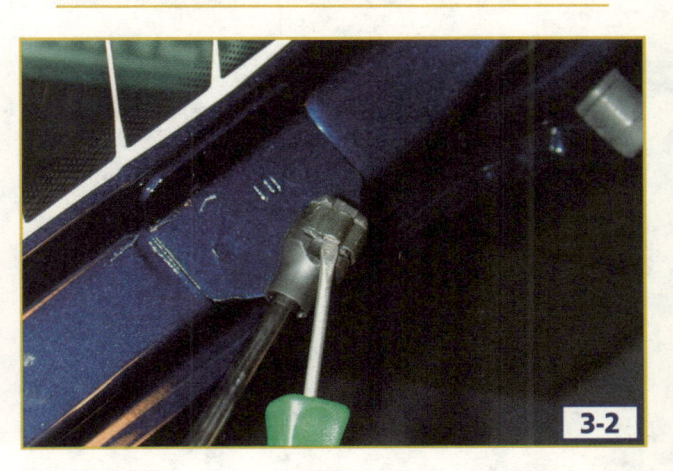

☐ **STEP 2:** The struts are held by ball and socket joints at either end, secured by a plastic clip. To remove them, lever off the clip using a small screwdriver and pull the strut end from the ball.
➜ Replace as the reverse of removal.

☐ **STEP 3:** Remove the high level braking lights where fitted.

☐ **STEP 4:** Remove the trim from the inside of the tailgate - see **Chapter 14, Interior, Trim.**

CHAPTER 13 Bodywork Job 3

13-3

☐ **STEP 5:** Disconnect the screen washer pipes and electrical connections.
➔ On some models, the wiring from the body shell into the tailgate is continuous. In this case, disconnect the ends of the leads and attach fish wires to them before pulling the wires from the tailgate, then part the wires and fish wires.

☐ **STEP 6:** Disconnect the rear screen heater element feed wire.

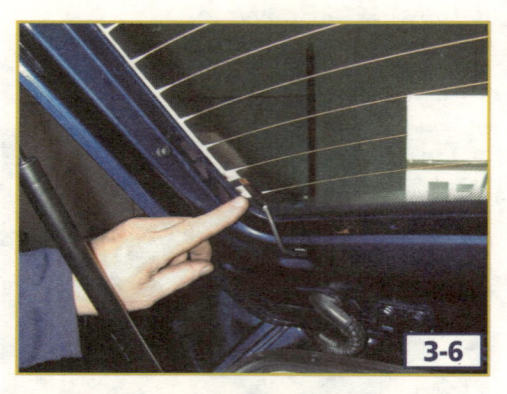

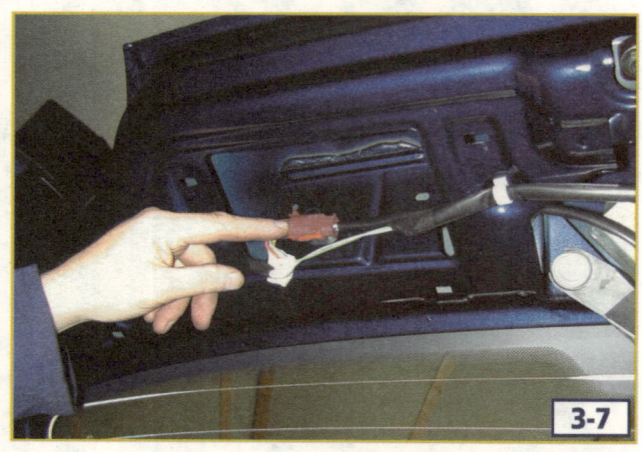

☐ **STEP 7:** Disconnect the wiring to the rear screen wiper and central lock motor where fitted.

☐ **STEP 8:** Raise the tailgate and ask an assistant (preferably two – it's heavy) to support its weight.
➔ If you're working alone, use a prop.

☐ **STEP 9:** Lever out the plastic clips and disconnect the struts – see **Step 2**.

☐ **STEP 10:** Mark the positions of the hinges.

☐ **STEP 11:** Remove the hinge nuts or bolts.
➔ Hinge nuts are hidden under either blanking plates or the trailing edge of the headlining. Lever off the plates OR pull away the weatherseal and headlining to expose them.

☐ **STEP 12:** Remove the tailgate.

TOP TIP!
• When you and your assistant replace the tailgate, place a piece of cloth under each top corner so that it doesn't damage the bodywork.

☐ **STEP 13:** Refit all components in the reverse order, making sure that the tailgate sits correctly and that its release latch works correctly.

☐ **STEP 14:** If the tailgate needs to be adjusted:
➔ If necessary, adjust the hinges first to align the tailgate top edge.
➔ Further adjustment is via the striker.

JOB 4: LUGGAGE BAY LID 306 ONLY – *removal, refitting.*

☐ **STEP 1:** Disconnect the battery negative (-) earth/ground terminal. See *Chapter 10, Electrical, Dash, Instruments, Fact File: Disconnecting the Battery* BEFORE doing so!

☐ **STEP 2:** The luggage bay lid is fitted to the bodywork via a pair of hinges and is held aloft with hydraulic struts.
➔ Open the luggage bay lid and remove the inner trim panel, which is secured with self-tapping screws.

☐ **STEP 3:** Disconnect the wires from the luggage bay lid electrical components, attach fish wires or string to the tailgate wires and pull the tailgate wires from the luggage area.
➔ Disconnect the fish wires and leave them in the tailgate to simplify refitting.

☐ **STEP 4:** With an assistant taking the weight of the luggage bay lid, lever out the strut clips and disconnect the top ends of the struts – see *Job 3, Step 2*.

☐ **STEP 5:** Put some protective cloth on the body, under the sharp corners of the lid.
➔ Use masking tape to outline the hinge positions on the lid and assist in re-alignment.

☐ **STEP 6:** Undo the hinge screws;
➔ Disconnect each hinge assembly.
➔ Remove the lid.

☐ **STEP 7:** Refit in reverse order.

☐ **STEP 8:** If adjustment of the luggage bay lid is needed, the front end is adjusted via the hinges, the rear by the striker and the two buffers.

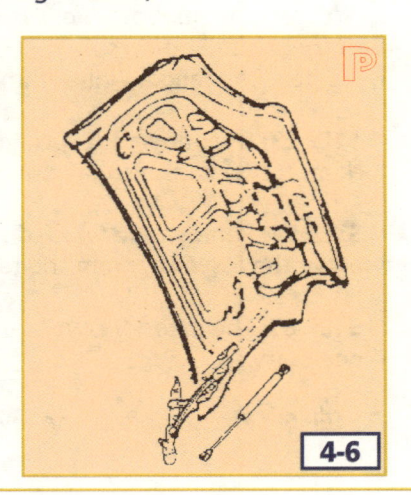

JOB 5: TAILGATE / LUGGAGE BAY LID LOCK ASSEMBLY – *removal, refitting.*

TOP TIP!
• Don't loosen or remove both the striker and latch at the same time!
• Do them one at a time, leaving the other one tightly fixed in place.

Section A: Locks.

☐ **STEP A1:** If the vehicle has central locking, disconnect the battery negative (-) earth/ground terminal. See *Chapter 10, Electrical, Dash, Instruments, Fact File: Disconnecting the Battery* BEFORE doing so!

☐ **STEP A2:** Remove the tailgate or luggage bay lid interior trim panel.

☐ **STEP A3:** The lock is secured by two bolts and is attached to an operating lever.
➔ Detach the operating lever, remove the bolts and remove the lock.
➔ On the 106, detach the lever as the lock is withdrawn.

☐ **STEP A4:** Refitting is the reverse of removal.

Section B: Striker.

☐ **STEP B1:** On hatchbacks, the striker is held by two bolts.
➔ Mark the position of the striker on the body panel.

☐ **STEP B2:** Remove the bolts.

CHAPTER 13 Bodywork Jobs 4-5

13-5

❏ **STEP B3:** On saloons, remove the rear bumper – see *Job 7* – lever out the plastic covers and remove the bolts and striker.

❏ **STEP B4:** Reassemble as the reverse of removal.

Section C: Lock motor.

❏ **STEP C1:** Disconnect the battery negative (-) earth/ground terminal. See *Chapter 10, Electrical, Dash, Instruments, Fact File: Disconnecting the Battery* BEFORE doing so!

❏ **STEP C2:** Remove the tailgate or luggage bay lid interior trim panel.

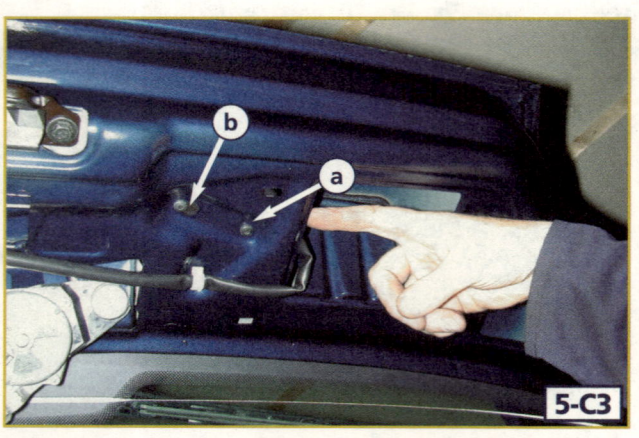

❏ **STEP C3:** The lock motor is secured by screws (except 306).
→ **306:** Only the right-hand screw (**a**) should be removed completely – slacken the left-hand screw (**b**) sufficiently to slide the motor clear.

❏ **STEP C4:** As the motor is withdrawn, disconnect the lock operating rod and the lock motor wiring plug.

❏ **STEP C5:** Refit as the reverse of removal.

Section D: Lock cylinder – 106.

❏ **STEP D1:** Remove the tailgate inner trim panel – see *Step A2*.

❏ **STEP D2:** Remove the tailgate wiper motor if fitted – see *Chapter 10, Job 6*.

❏ **STEP D3:** Remove the lock cylinder securing screw and lever of the securing clip.

❏ **STEP D4:** Unhook the lock lever as the lock cylinder is withdrawn.

❏ **STEP D5:** Reassemble as the reverse of removal.

Section E: Lock cylinder and handle - 206.

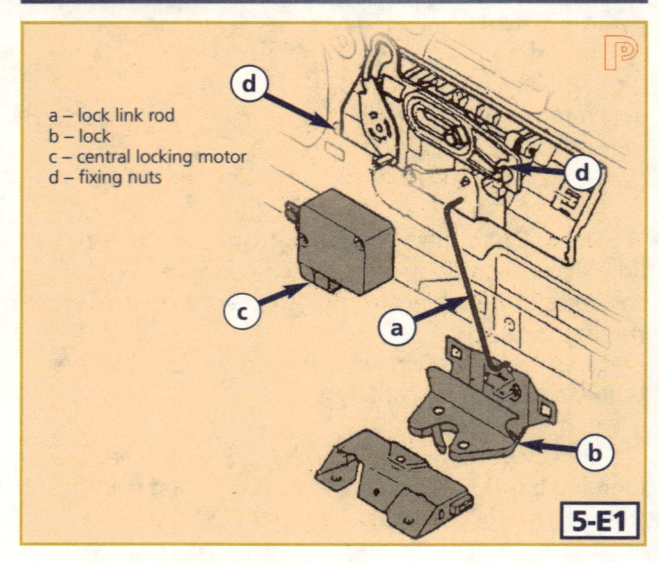

a – lock link rod
b – lock
c – central locking motor
d – fixing nuts

❏ **STEP E1:** On the 206, the lock cylinder, lock motor and handle can be removed as an assembly.
→ The following Steps refer to illustration **5-E1**.

❏ **STEP E2:** Disconnect the battery negative (-) earth/ground terminal. See *Chapter 10, Electrical, Dash, Instruments, Fact File: Disconnecting the Battery* BEFORE doing so!
→ Remove the tailgate inner trim panel – see *Step A2*.

❏ **STEP E3:** Disconnect the lock link rod (**a**) and the lock motor (**c**) wiring connector.

❏ **STEP E4:** Remove the two fixing nuts (**d**) and remove the assembly from the tailgate.

❏ **STEP E5:** The exterior cover can now be unclipped if necessary.

❏ **STEP E6:** Reassemble as the reverse of removal.

Section F: Lock cylinder – 306.

❏ **STEP F1:** Remove the lock motor – see **Section C**.

❏ **STEP F2:** Disconnect the lock operating rod from the lock.

❏ **STEP F3:** Remove the two lock securing screws.

❏ **STEP F4:** The lock can be removed from outside the panel.

❏ **STEP F5:** Remove the inner lock section from inside the panel.

❏ **STEP F6:** Reassemble as the reverse of removal.

JOB 6:	WHEEL ARCH LINERS AND UNDERTRAYS *(typical)* – *removal, refitting*.

❏ **STEP 1:** Plastic underbody protection mouldings are secured by screws, bolts, rivets and clips.
➔ There are no 'hidden' fastenings as used for interior trim.

❏ **STEP 2:** The clips used vary, but the most common comprise a head with two legs attached and a central pin that pushes the legs part when pressed in.
➔ To remove these clips, lever up the pin and the clip will then pull out – see **Chapter 14, Job 1**.

❏ **STEP 3:** Work your way around the moulding, removing fasteners as you go.

❏ **STEP 4: UNDERTRAY:** Unfasten the turnbuckles **(a)**.
➔ Slacken the front mounting bolts **(b)**.
➔ There is no need to remove them completely if the undertray is slotted.

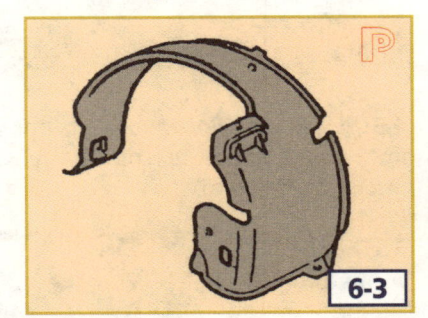

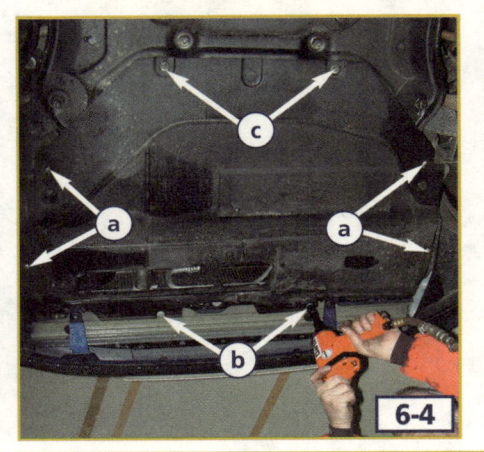

❏ **STEP 5:** Remove the rear bolts (*6-4, items c*) last and slide the undertray from the front mounting bolts.

❏ **STEP 6:** Refit as the reverse of removal.

JOB 7:	BUMPERS *(typical)* – *removal, refitting*.

Note that there are numerous different fixing locations for bumpers, but the method of holding them in place is similar across most models.

Section A: Grille.

IMPORTANT NOTE: **106:** This model does not have an air intake grille.

❏ **STEP A1:** On most models the grille is secured by fasteners at the top and lugs or clips at the bottom.

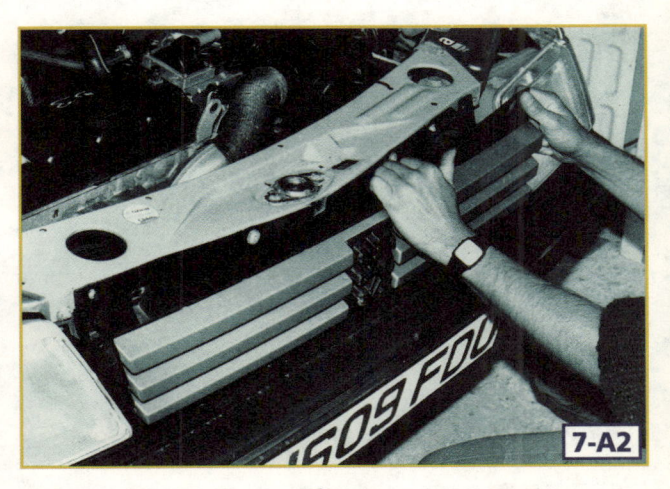

❏ **STEP A2: 205:** The top fasteners are screws. Remove them and lift the grille from the lug holes.

CHAPTER 13 Bodywork Job 7

☐ **STEP A3:**
206: The top fasteners are four expanding clips (**a**) with central pins.
➜ Pull the pins partially out of the expanding clips and then remove the expanding clips.
➜ The lower edge of the grille is held by clips (**b**). Release them then pull the grille upwards.

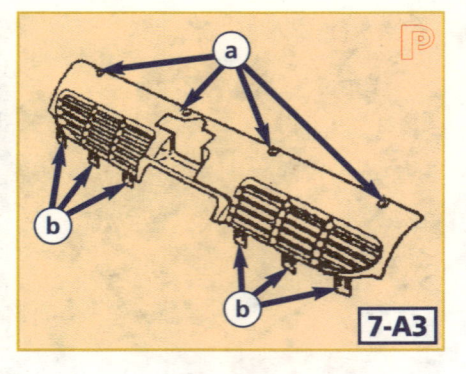

7-A3

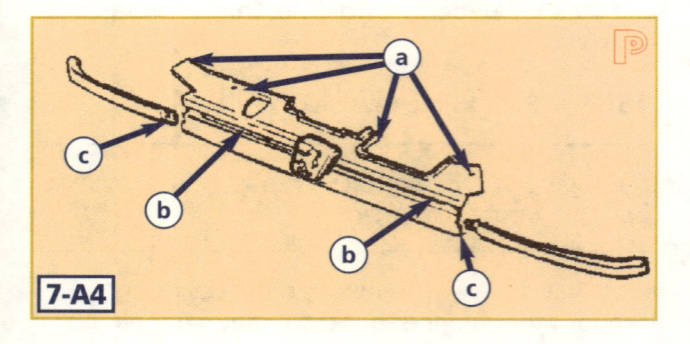

7-A4

☐ **STEP A4: 306:** The grille is secured by four bolts at the top, two Torx fittings and two clips at the lower outer edges.
➜ Remove the top fasting bolts (**a**).
➜ Remove the Torx fittings, accessible through the grille aperture (**b**).
➜ Release the lower mounting clips (**c**).
➜ Pull the grille forward and away.

Section B: Front bumper.

☐ **STEP B1:** Disconnect the battery negative (-) earth/ground terminal. See *Chapter 10, Electrical, Dash, Instruments, Fact File: Disconnecting the Battery* BEFORE doing so!
➜ Raise the front of the vehicle to improve access.

☐ **STEP B2:** Remove the front wheelarch liners – see *Job 6*.

☐ **STEP B3:** Disconnect wires attached to bumper-mounted electrical equipment as applicable.

☐ **STEP B4:** On most models it is necessary to remove the grille – see *Section A*.

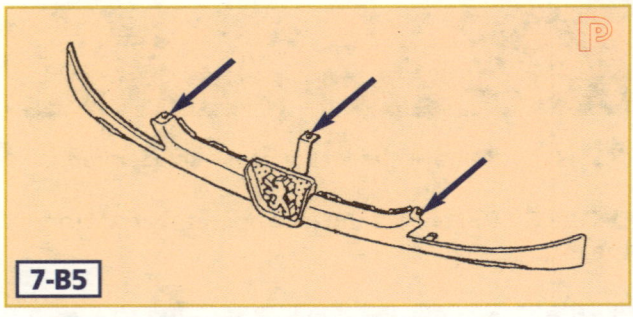

7-B5

☐ **STEP B5:** Depending on the model and year, some of the bumper fixings may be obscured by various components, which have to be removed, most notably.
➜ **206:** The front trim panel. Remove the retaining screws (arrowed) and unclip the ends from the wings.
➜ **EARLY 106:** The headlights, washer fluid reservoir or washer fluid reservoir neck – see *Chapter 10*.
➜ **LATER 106:** The horn.
➜ **EARLY 205 GTi:** the driving lights.
➜ **306:** The washer fluid reservoir.

7-B6

☐ **STEP B6: 205:** Remove the bumper chrome trim and remove the nuts from the two front mounting brackets (arrowed).

☐ **STEP B7:** Depending on the model and year, the position of the lower and side bumper mountings differs.
➜ Some are secured to brackets, others are also bolted to the underside of the front wing.
➜ Working down each rear

7-B7

13-8

edge and along the lower front edge, remove the fastenings.
→ Remove bumper to wing bolts if applicable.

☐ **STEP B8:** Remove the smaller fastenings first and leave the main bolts until last.

7-B8

☐ **STEP B9:** Remove the bumper upper bolts and withdraw the bumper.
→ Disconnect the headlight washer feed tubes if applicable.

7-B9

☐ **STEP B10:** Reassemble as the reverse of removal.
→ Fit the larger bolts in the brackets loosely first, then the smaller fixings.
→ This allows you to correctly align the bumper.

Section C: Rear bumper.

☐ **STEP C1:** Disconnect the battery negative (-) earth/ground terminal. See *Chapter 10, Electrical, Dash, Instruments, Fact File: Disconnecting the Battery* BEFORE doing so!
→ Raise the tailgate or luggage bay lid and raise the rear of the vehicle.

☐ **STEP C2:** On some models the wheelarch liners cover the rear bumper side bolts and have to be removed. On other models the rear bumper side bolts are accessible with the wheelarch liner in situ.
→ Remove the bumper side fastening bolts.

☐ **STEP C3:** On some models, the rear bumper is attached to the wheelarch liners with screws or clips.
→ Remove them as applicable.

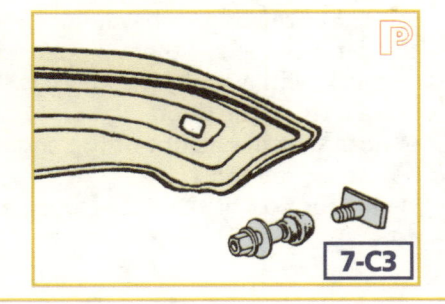

7-C3

☐ **STEP C4:** If the rear bumper has integral electric equipment, the wire connectors will have to be disconnected.
→ The connectors will usually be found behind a rear light inner cover.
→ 106: The number plate light wiring connector is behind the air extraction grille on the side of the luggage bay area.
→ 306: The connector is plugged into the light unit and covered by a trim panel inside the luggage bay area.

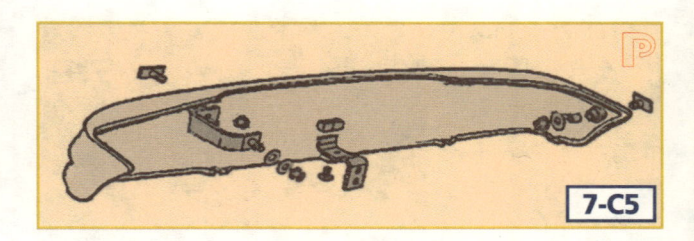

7-C4

7-C5

☐ **STEP C5:** Remove the lower bumper mounting bolts.
→ On all models except the 106 they are under the vehicle.
→ 106: They are inside the luggage bay area.

7-C6

☐ **STEP C6:** The upper bumper mountings, inside the luggage bay area, may have covers. Carefully lever them off, if fitted.

☐ **STEP C7:** Working inside the luggage bay area, remove the upper mounting bolts.

7-C7

CHAPTER 13   Bodywork   Job 7

13-9

CHAPTER 13 Bodywork Job 8

☐ **STEP C8:** The bumper may now be lifted away.
➔ On some models wires attached to bumper mounted electric equipment pass through a grommet in the rear panel – ease the grommet out as the bumper is withdrawn.

☐ **STEP C9:** Reassemble as the reverse of removal.

| **JOB 8:** | **FRONT WING - *(typical)* - *replacement*.** |

☐ **STEP 1:** If any light units or an electric aerial are situated on the wing, disconnect the battery negative (-) earth/ground terminal. See *Chapter 10, Electrical, Dash, Instruments, Fact File: Disconnecting the Battery* BEFORE doing so!
➔ Disconnect the wires from the light or aerial.

☐ **STEP 2:** Remove the wheelarch liner.

☐ **STEP 3:** Remove the front bumper – see *Job 7*.

☐ **STEP 4:** Remove the single wing mounting bolt in the wheelarch.

8-4

☐ **STEP 5:** Remove the footwell side trim panel and remove the rearmost wing bolt.
➔ On some vehicles there may be two bolts, the second higher up.

8-5

☐ **STEP 6:** The front wing fastening bolts are located under the bumper ends.

8-6

☐ **STEP 7:** Remove the bolts in the engine bay guttering.

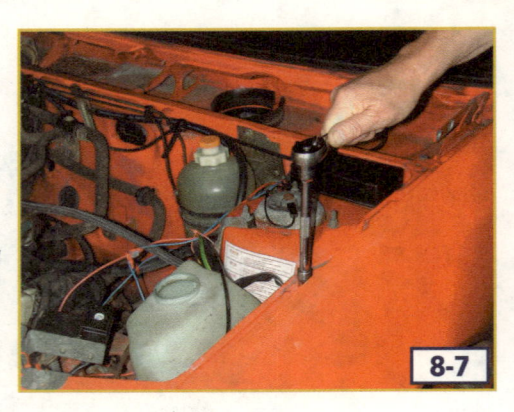

8-7

TOP TIP!

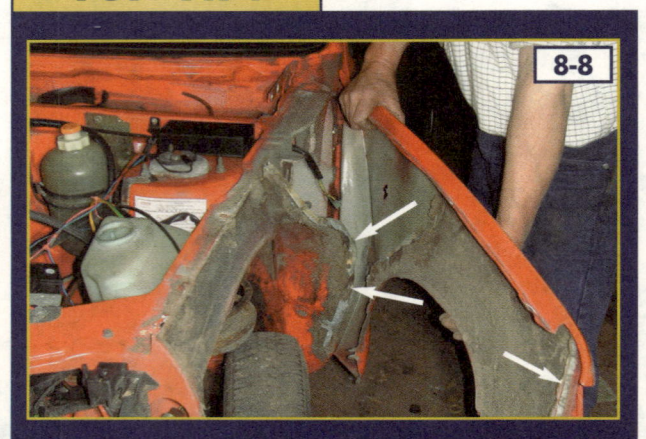

8-8

☐ **STEP 8:** • The wings are bedded into sealant (arrowed) and are usually stuck firmly in place.
• If you intend to re-use the wing, don't wrestle it off because this will usually cause it to fold!
• Gentle heat from a heat gun around the outer edge of the splash panel inside the wheelarch can soften the sealant and make removal of the wing easier.

☐ **STEP 9:** Before fitting the new wing:
➔ Clean all of the old sealant from the body shell.
➔ Apply fresh Wurth sealant, available from your Peugeot dealer or automotive body parts specialist.

☐ **STEP 10:** IMPORTANT NOTE: Fit the new wing but before tightening the screws and before the sealant becomes hard, check the gaps against the position of the closed engine bay lid and the door and ensure that:
➔ gaps are constant and even all the way along.
➔ neither the engine bay lid nor the door rubs on the wing as each of them is opened.
➔ check with a straight edge that the wing is on the same level as the door.
➔ note that the height of the engine bay lid can be adjusted - see *Job 1*.
➔ the position of the door can be adjusted - see *Job 10*.

13-10

JOB 9: EXTERNAL TRIM (typical).

☐ **STEP 1:** External trim is fixed using adhesive materials.
➔ To remove trim it is necessary to heat it sufficient to soften the adhesive.
➔ The heating process carries a high risk of damage to the underlying paintwork, unless heat is applied with extreme care and at not too high a temperature.

☐ **STEP 2:** External trim items can be refitted using double-sided adhesive body tape.
➔ Before fitting the tape, thoroughly clean and degrease the trim and the contact area of the adhesive on the bodywork.

JOB 10: DOOR – *removal, refitting, adjustment*.

TOP TIP!

• Doors with all their 'furniture' can be surprisingly heavy, so you should try to arrange for a helper to be present if a door is to be removed.

☐ **STEP 1:** Disconnect the battery negative (-) earth/ground terminal. See *Chapter 10, Electrical, Dash, Instruments, Fact File: Disconnecting the Battery* BEFORE doing so!

☐ **STEP 2:** Disconnect the door wiring plug by unscewing until free, then pulling.
➔ On some early vehicles there is no plug, so remove the door trim and disconnect the speaker and any other wires and pull them from the door.

☐ **STEP 3:** Drift out the checkstrap roll pin – position shown here.

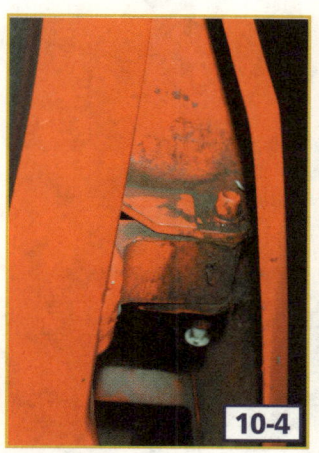

☐ **STEP 4:** The hinge pins are a friction fit in some earlier vehicles.
➔ Remove the plastic cap and drift them out.

☐ **STEP 5:** Later models have hinge bolts with Torx heads.

☐ **STEP 6:** As an assistant takes the weight of the door, drift out or unscrew the hinge pins.
➔ The rear door hinge pins can be accessed with the door closed and the front door open. This is the recommended way to work if no assistant is available.

☐ **STEP 7:** Refit as the reverse of removal.

ADJUSTMENT

During simple removal and refitting of the doors, the hinges need not be disturbed and so adjustments should not be necessary.

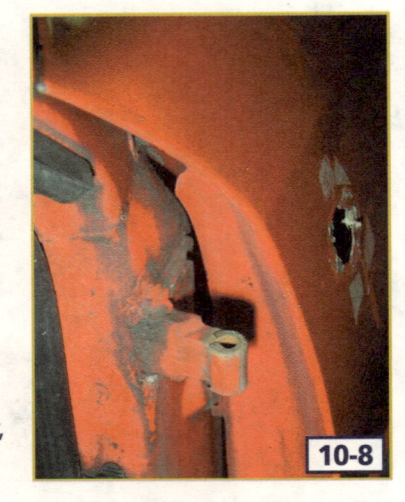

☐ **STEP 8:** Not all doors fitted to the vehicles covered by this manual can be adjusted.
➔ Some have the door hinges welded to the body shell, like this 205.
➔ Some have the bolted-on door hinges located by fixed pins on the bodywork and door, and adjustment is only possible by removing the hinges and elongating the holes in which the pins locate.

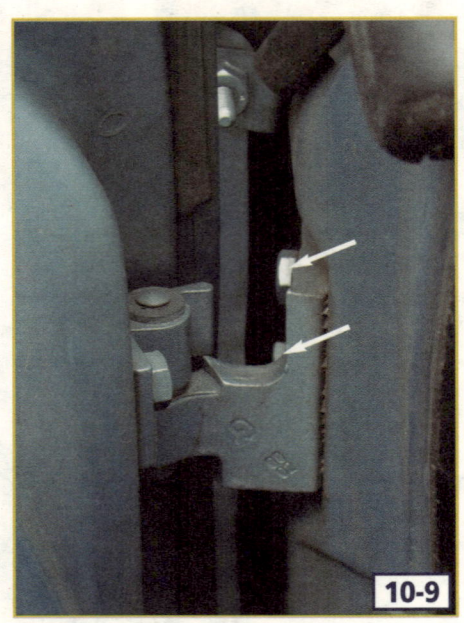

☐ **STEP 9:** On some models, such as the 306, the hinges can be adjusted.
➔ Slacken the door hinge bolts (arrowed) to make adjustments.
➔ The latch position will also have to be moved.
➔ To gain access to the hinge bolts on some models, remove the front wheelarch liner.

JOB 11: WINDOW WINDER MECHANISM, WINDOW GLASS – removal, refitting.

☐ **STEP 1:** Lower the door glass to the half-way position, then disconnect the battery negative (earth/ground) lead. See *Chapter 10, Electrical, Dash, Instruments, Fact File: Disconnecting the Battery* BEFORE doing so!

☐ **STEP 2:** Remove the door inner trim panel – see *Chapter 14, Job 2*.

WINDOW WINDER MECHANISM REMOVAL

☐ **STEP 3:** Remove the door trim and waterproof inner membrane.

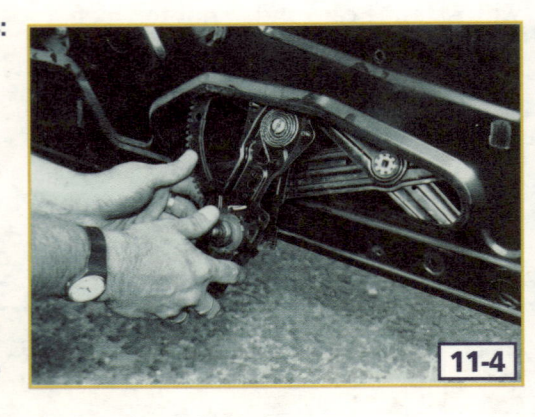

☐ **STEP 4: 205:** Secure the window in the closed position using masking or other adhesive tape.
➔ Remove the regulator fixing nuts.
➔ Slide the lifting arms from the channels.
➔ Remove the regulator from the access panel.

☐ **STEP 5: OTHER MODELS:** Remove the glass – see *Steps 10 to 12*.

☐ **STEP 6:** If the windows are operated by electric motors, disconnect the battery negative (-) earth/ground terminal. See *Chapter 10, Electrical, Dash, Instruments, Fact File: Disconnecting the Battery* BEFORE doing so!
➔ Disconnect the wires from the window operating motor.

☐ **STEP 7:** The later electric window regulator mechanism is secured to the door frame with rivets and nuts.
➔ Drill out the rivets using a 6 mm bit.

➜ Remove the nuts securing the regulator.
➜ Tilt the regulator and remove it from the door.

☐ **STEP 14:** Remove the winding window aperture rear weather strip.

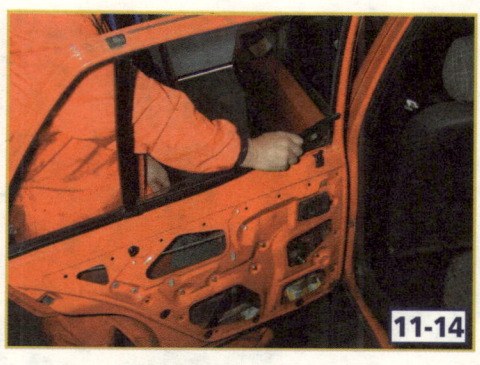

☐ **STEP 8:** Earlier electric (lower) and manual winder (top) mechanisms are simply bolted (arrowed) into position.

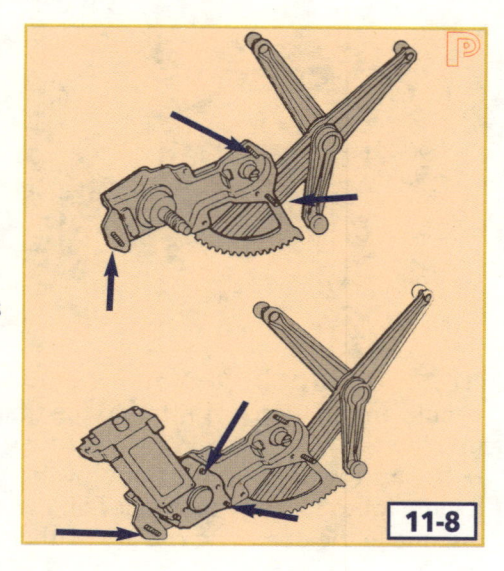

11-8

☐ **STEP 9:** Reassemble as the reverse of removal.

☐ **STEP 15:** Unbolt the rear window channel top fixing from the door.

DOOR GLASS REMOVAL

☐ **STEP 10:** Remove the inner lower weather strip from the window aperture of the door top.
➜ On some models it may be necessary to pull the weather strip from the sides of the window aperture.

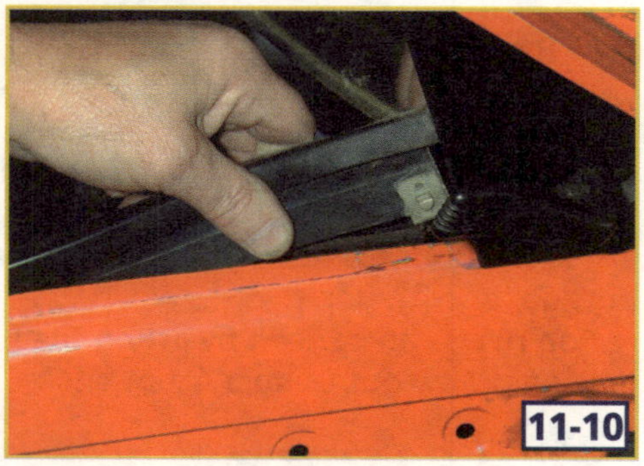

☐ **STEP 11:** Release the regulator to glass securing clips, then lift the window out if its aperture in the door top.

☐ **STEP 12:** Reassemble as the reverse of removal.

☐ **STEP 16:** Unbolt the rear window channel lower fixing.

REAR DOORS

Removing the rear door regulator is essentially the same as working on the front doors. Removing the glass is also similar, though the rear window channel should be removed first.

☐ **STEP 17:** Unbolt the bottom rear window channel fixing from the door and remove the channel.

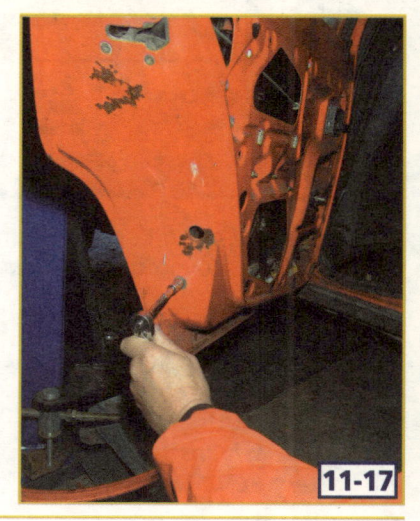

☐ **STEP 13:** To remove the rear door fixed glass, lower the winding window fully down.

CHAPTER 13 Bodywork Job 11

13-13

❏ **STEP 18:** Remove the rear window channel.

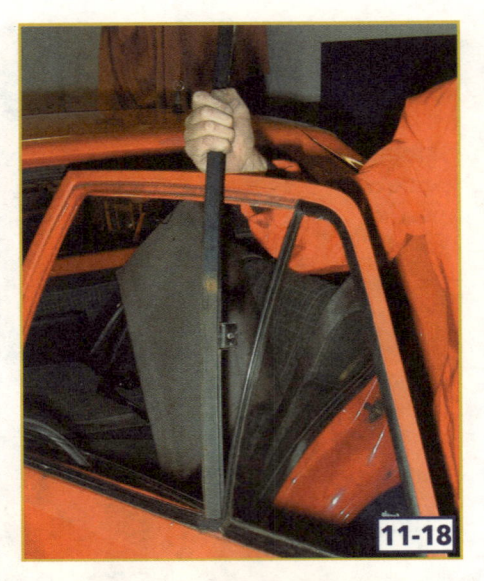

❏ **STEP 19:** The fixed glass can now be angled forward and removed if required.

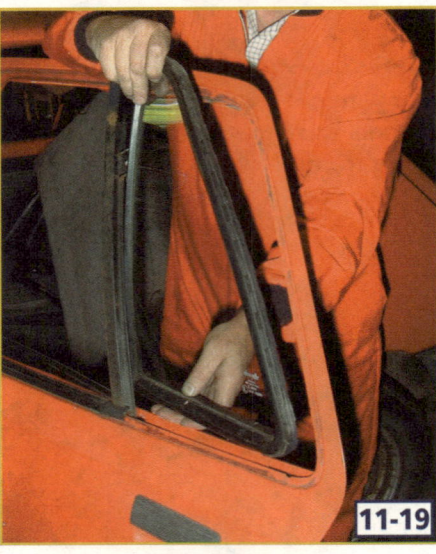

❏ **STEP 20:** Removing the rear door winding glass is now the same as dealing with the front door glass.

❏ **STEP 21:** Reassemble as the reverse of removal.

JOB 12: DOOR LOCK/HANDLE – removal, refitting.

Section A: Door handles.

A variety of lock and handle assemblies were used on the vehicles covered by this manual.

❏ **STEP A1:** Make sure that the window glass is at its highest position and remove the door trim panel and protective covering. Disconnect the battery negative (-) earth/ground terminal. See *Chapter 10, Electrical, Dash, Instruments, Fact File: Disconnecting the Battery* BEFORE doing so!

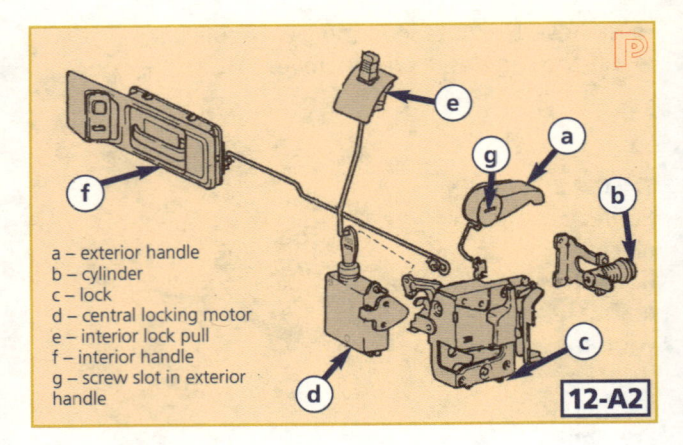

a – exterior handle
b – cylinder
c – lock
d – central locking motor
e – interior lock pull
f – interior handle
g – screw slot in exterior handle

❏ **STEP A2: 3 DOOR EARLY 106 ONLY:** The exterior handle on this vehicle is fitted to the trailing edge of the door.
→ Use a screwdriver in the slot provided in the handle (**g**) to turn the central locking section, then disengage the operating rod and withdraw the handle.

❏ **STEP A3: OTHER VEHICLES INCLUDING ALL 5-DOOR 106:** The exterior handle may be secured with nuts inside the door frame, a nut inside plus a screw outside, or with pop rivets.
→ Pop rivets can be seen by lifting the handle, and may be drilled out using a 4 mm bit.

❏ **STEP A4:** Remove the fixings, then disengage the operating rod from the handle assembly and withdraw the handle.

❏ **STEP A5:** The interior handles vary in design, but most are dealt with in the same manner.

➜ Remove the door interior trim panel.
➜ Slide the interior handle to unclip it from the door, then remove the operating rod.

☐ **STEP A6:** Reassemble as the reverse of removal.

Section B: Door lock cylinder.

TOP TIP!
LOCK CYLINDER CLIP
• The door lock cylinder is secured by a clip which can be disengaged without removing the interior trim panel.
• Weld a self-tapping screw to a length of thin rod, lever the small cover from the door rear edge, insert the rod and turn it so that the screw engages with a hole in the lock clip.
• Pull the tool and the clip is disengaged from the lock barrel.
• When refitting the lock cylinder, use the rod to push the clip into position, then unscrew the rod.

☐ **STEP B1:** Make sure that the window glass is at its highest position and remove the door trim panel and protective covering.
➜ Before dismantling, disconnect the battery negative (-) earth/ground terminal. See *Chapter 10, Electrical, Dash, Instruments, Fact File: Disconnecting the Battery* BEFORE doing so!

☐ **STEP B2:** Remove the lock cylinder clip (arrowed), either as described in TOP TIP!, LOCK CYLINDER CLIP, or by reaching inside the door frame.
➜ The lock cylinder can then the withdrawn from the door and the operating rod disengaged.

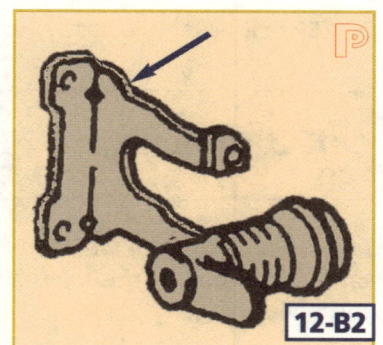

Section C: Door lock assembly.

☐ **STEP C1:** The door lock is secured with Torx-headed screws. Remove them.

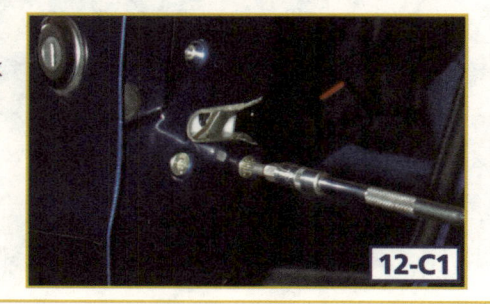

☐ **STEP C2:** Make sure that the window glass is at its highest position and remove the door trim panel and protective covering. Disconnect the battery negative (-) earth/ground terminal. See *Chapter 10, Electrical, Dash, Instruments, Fact File: Disconnecting the Battery* BEFORE doing so!

☐ **STEP C3:** If fitted, remove the plastic shield from behind the door lock.
➜ Disconnect the operating rods from the door lock.
➜ They are held with clips and guides.

☐ **STEP C4:** Remove the interior handle. Disconnect the link rod (arrowed).

☐ **STEP C5:** If fitted, disconnect the wiring from the central locking.

☐ **STEP C6:** Free the lock button rod from its foam guide and angle it forward.

☐ **STEP C7:** The lock may now be withdrawn.

☐ **STEP C8:** Reassemble as the reverse of removal.

Section D: Central locking motor.

The central locking system is described in *Job 16*.

☐ **STEP D1: 106:** To remove the central locking motor, remove it and the lock together – see *Section C* – then separate the two.

☐ **STEP D2: 206 AND 306:** The central locking motor is integral with the lock assembly. If an integral lock unit is faulty, the entire lock assembly should be removed and renewed.

☐ **STEP D3: 205:** To remove the central locking motor, remove the door lock components.
➜ The motor is secured by two bolts.

JOB 13: DOOR MIRROR - *replacement*.

❏ **STEP 1:** If the mirrors are electrically operated, disconnect the battery negative (-) earth/ground terminal. See **Chapter 10, Electrical, Dash, Instruments, Fact File: Disconnecting the Battery** BEFORE doing so!

❏ **STEP 2:** Remove the adjuster stalk securing screw if applicable.
➔ Unclip the triangular trim panel from the side of the door.

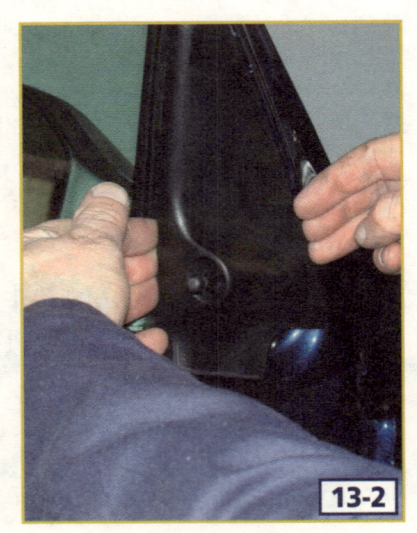

MODELS WITH ELECTRICALLY OPERATED MIRRORS

❏ **STEP 3:** If the trim panel is to be removed, remove the mirror control switch securing screw and pull the switch from the panel.

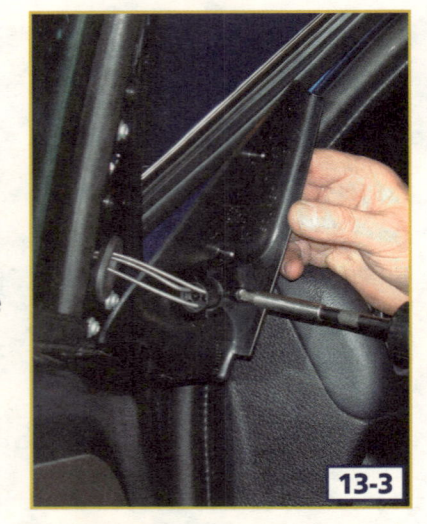

❏ **STEP 4:** Remove the mirror fastening screws.
➔ Disconnect the wiring connector if applicable.
➔ The mirror can now be removed.

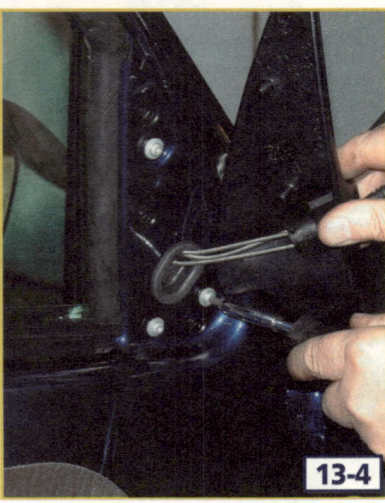

❏ **STEP 5:** If the glass is to be renewed:
➔ **205:** Lever off the outer rim and lift the glass out.
➔ **ALL OTHER MODELS:** Locate the small retaining clip.
➔ This is generally at the lower centre of the glass, or the outer edge in the case of the 206.
➔ Push the clip open and carefully remove the glass.

❏ **STEP 6:** Reassemble as the reverse of removal.

JOB 14: SUN ROOF.

Two types of sunroof were fitted to the vehicles covered by this manual: one tilting and one sliding.

TILTING-TYPE

❏ **STEP 1:** The glass in tilting sunroofs can be removed easily, by disc- onnecting the rear handle, tilting the sunroof fully up and lifting it out.

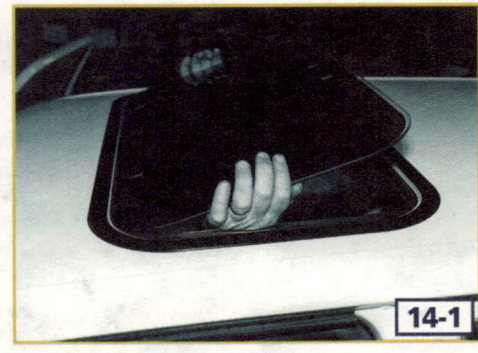

☐ **STEP 2:** Removal of the sunroof surround necessitates removal of the headlining, and is a job best left to authorised dealers or specialist sunroof fitting companies

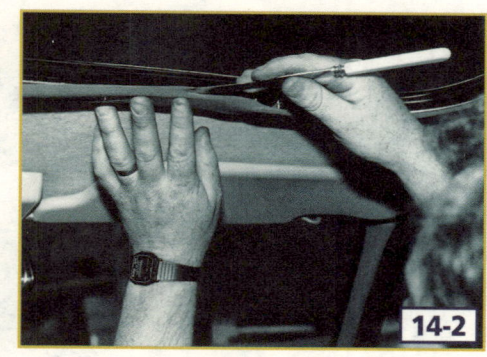

SLIDING-TYPE

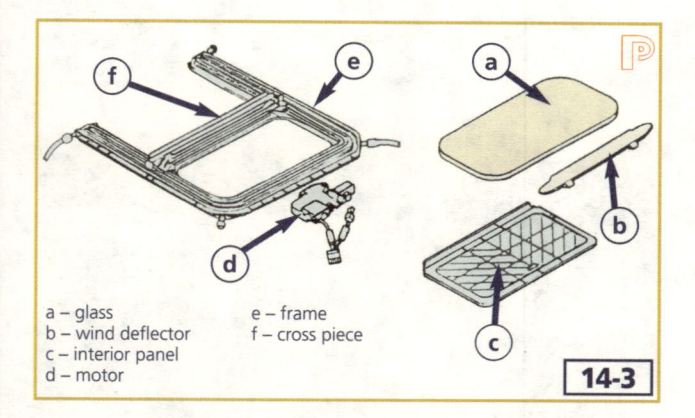

a – glass
b – wind deflector
c – interior panel
d – motor
e – frame
f – cross piece

☐ **STEP 3:** The sliding sunroof – electrically operated or manual – is generally too complex for DIY removal and refitting, which involves removal of the headlining. Such work should be left to authorised dealers of specialist sunroof companies.

☐ **STEP 4:** For removal of the sliding type sunroof or the surround of the tilting sunroof, these are the steps.
→ Remove the headlining.
→ Disconnect the motor if fitted.
→ Disconnect the drainage pipes.
→ Remove the six sunroof fixings.

JOB 15: SCREEN GLASS – *replacement*.

Section A: Screen held in with rubbers.

It is possible to fit a new windscreen yourself where an early vehicle has its screen held in place with windscreen rubbers. However, we don't recommend it! A company such as Autoglass will be able to supply and fit a screen for little more than the cost of buying one. The risk of breaking a screen when you fit it yourself is quite high.

☐ **STEP A1:** Mel from Autoglass removed the old screen from the vehicle and cleaned off any adhesive from the aperture.
→ Allow time for de-rusting and painting any affected areas.
→ The new rubber has been fitted to the glass.
→ Fitting string into the groove on the rubber which will fit over the lip in the windscreen aperture.
→ The loose ends seen here have simply been tucked in to the upper edge of the rubber so that they are out of the way as the glass is being fitted.
→ Soapy lubricant is applied to the rubber to help it slip in to place.

☐ **STEP A2:** If you are doing this yourself, it's best to have two people offer up the new glass with rubber. The rubber must be seated evenly in to the aperture all the way around.

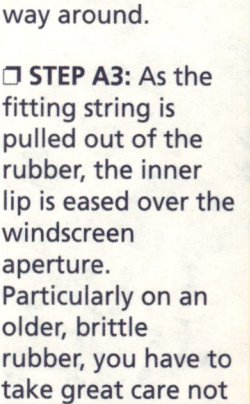

☐ **STEP A3:** As the fitting string is pulled out of the rubber, the inner lip is eased over the windscreen aperture. Particularly on an older, brittle rubber, you have to take great care not to pull the string through the rubber.

☐ **STEP A4:** There is always a little tidying up of rubber flanges to carry out, to make

CHAPTER 13   Bodywork   Job 15

13-17

sure that they are all sitting evenly. If the screen is pushed in too far, the rubbers will start to recess in to the seating around the windscreen aperture. The outer lip should lie more or less flush with the bodywork.

Section B: Bonded glass.

It is best to have a windscreen specialist replace a bonded windscreen because of the equipment required. Once again, Autoglass demonstrated how they replaced a typical type of bonded windscreen.

TOP TIP!

STEP B1: • Mel from Autoglass recommends putting masking tape over the screen vent outlets to prevent debris from falling into the vents.
• If debris – or worse still, shards of broken glass – fall into the vent, it could be thrown into the eyes of the car's occupants next time the screen vent fan is turned on.

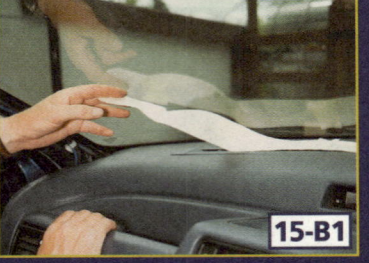

STEP B2: There will inevitably be interior trim to remove from around the screen. In this case, the trim is partly screwed and partly clipped into place.
→ Use an upholstery lever for freeing the trim clips.
→ Take special care where, as in this case, an alarm sensor is fitted on the trim. Be sure not to disturb the wiring.

STEP B3: In cases where a trim cover is fitted at the base of the screen, remove the wipers and unscrew or clip off the trim cover.

STEP B4: Mel wears protective goggles and gloves for this stage of the work.
→ The bonded glass has to be cut from the screen aperture.
→ This special tool has a blade which reaches behind the glass and cuts through the sealant as Mel pulls it around the perimeter of the screen.

STEP B5: The old glass can now be lifted away.

STEP B6: Mel spends quite a considerable amount of time cleaning up the screen aperture before applying the adhesive hardener to the aperture frame.
→ On anything more than a few years old, there will almost inevitably be rust found behind the glass or glass trim.
→ In worst cases, some welding may be necessary; in almost all cases it will be necessary to clean off the rust, apply a product such as Wurth Rust Killer and then prime and paint the metal.

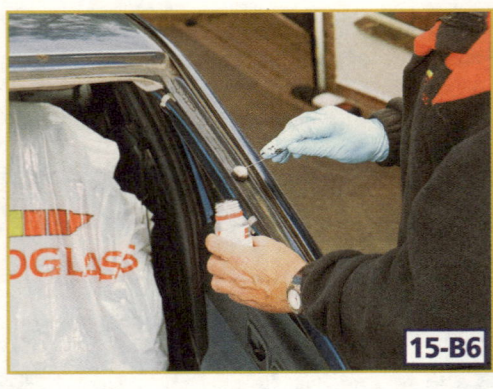

❏ **STEP B7:** As with the screen frame, Mel uses a panel wipe to clean all traces off the surface of the glass (where it will touch the screen frame) before wiping hardener on to the surface of the glass.

15-B7

❏ **STEP B8:** The glass seals are now fitted in place around the edge of the glass – only applicable to certain types of screen.

15-B8

15-B9

❏ **STEP B9:** A very thick bead of bonding filler is now applied by Mel all the way around the screen frame.

❏ **STEP B10:** Note the special suction lifting pads that Mel uses to grip the glass so that he can lower it accurately in to position on the screen frame. Note also the tabs of masking tape fitted ready in place on top of the screen…

15-B10

❏ **STEP B11:** …so that they can be used to hold the screen at the correct height while the bonding filler goes off.

15-B11

15-B12

❏ **STEP B12:** Where the rear view mirror is fitted to the glass, use special double-sided mirror fixing tape but be sure to clean both the mounting pad on the mirror and the area of the glass to which it is fitted with panel wipe so that there are no traces of grease on either.

TOP TIP!

• The screen that Mel took from this vehicle was cracked right down the middle, starting from the rear view mirror mounting position.
• The crack was caused by someone having previously fitted the mirror using Superglue or epoxy resin.
• Either of them will cause differential expansion to take place in the glass and will, in every case, cause it to crack.

❏ **STEP B13:** A properly fitted screen will be free from leaks and also free from crack-inducing stresses.

15-B13

CHAPTER 13   Bodywork   Job 15

13-19

TOP TIP!
- Be sure to clean the windscreen wiper blades and, if necessary, replace them so that the new screen is not instantly marked with disfiguring scratches.

JOB 16: CENTRAL LOCKING.

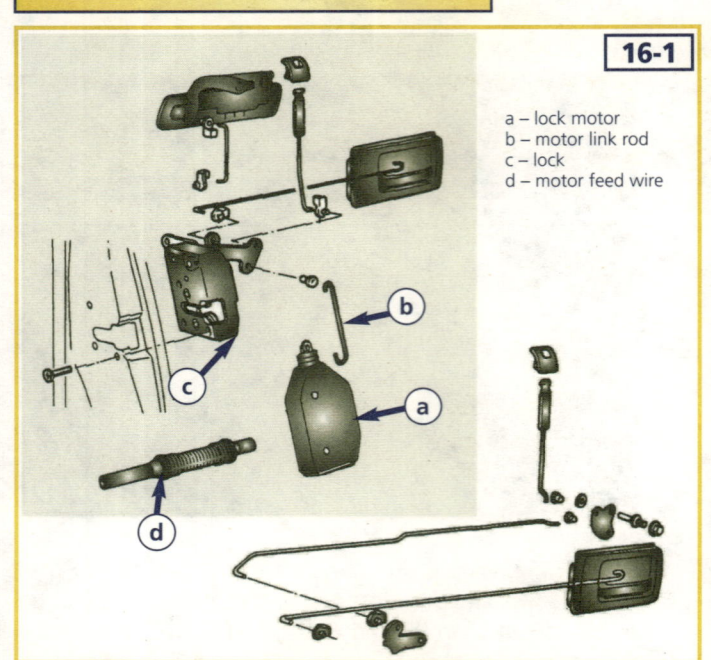

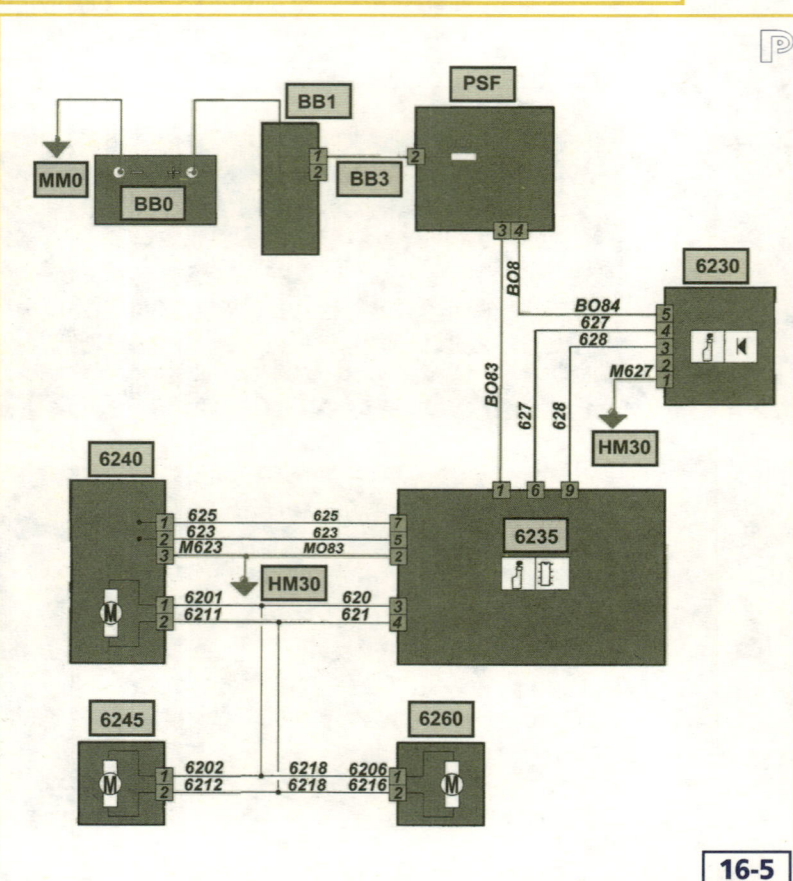

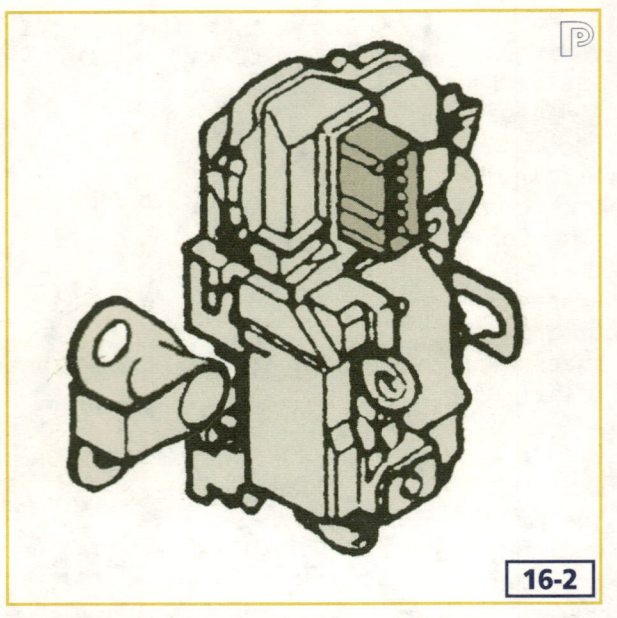

16-1

a – lock motor
b – motor link rod
c – lock
d – motor feed wire

16-2

☐ **STEP 1: 205:** These are the components of the door central locking system.
→ The assembly bottom right is the interior handle linkage for the rear doors.

☐ **STEP 2: 206:** This is the integral lock/motor.

☐ **STEP 3:** There are two types of control unit for the central locking system.
→ Earlier cars have a dedicated control unit situated at the base of the B-post.
→ This can be accessed for replacement by disconnecting the battery, removing the right hand front seat, the B-post trim panel and the lower seat belt mounting.
→ Lift the carpet to expose the control unit.

☐ **STEP 4:** The more recent control unit for the central locking system is part of the *Built-in Systems Interface* (BSI), situated under the fascia. This device controls a range of electrical equipment and is NOT user serviceable beyond replacing any of the six surface mounted fuses if they fail.

☐ **STEP 5:** This is the central locking wiring diagram for the 106 – see *Chapter 15, Wiring Diagrams* for the keys to the component parts and wire colours and connections.

16-5

CHAPTER 14: INTERIOR, TRIM

Please read Chapter 2 Safety First before carrying out any work on your car.

CONTENTS

	Page No.		Page No.
JOB 1: TRIM FIXINGS.	14-2	**JOB 9:** DASHBOARD – *removal, replacement.*	14-13
JOB 2: SIDE DOOR TRIM PANEL – *remove, refit.*	14-3	**JOB 10:** HEADLINING.	14-16
JOB 3: FRONT SEATS – *removal, replacement.*	14-5	**JOB 11:** RADIO – *remove and refit.*	14-16
JOB 4: REAR SEATS – *removal, replacement.*	14-6	**JOB 12:** AIRBAGS AND PRE-TENSIONERS	
JOB 5: SEAT BELTS – *remove, replace.*	14-7	*- essential Safety First!*	14-16
JOB 6: STEERING WHEEL – *removal, refitting.*	14-10	**JOB 13:** AIRBAG SYSTEM	
JOB 7: INTERIOR MIRROR – *removal, refitting.*	14-11	*- deactivating, reactivating.*	14-19
JOB 8: CENTRE CONSOLE		**JOB 14:** AIR BAGS – *replacement.*	14-19
– removal, replacement.	14-12		

SAFETY FIRST!

AIRBAGS

• Some of the vehicles covered by this book are fitted with driver's, passenger and side airbags. They contain a pyrotechnic (explosive) charge and it is highly recommended that they must only be worked on by a qualified technician.

• Do not dismantle any body or trim components in the region of an airbag.

• Read and follow the instructions in *Jobs 12 and 13* first.

• Note the location of all airbags before starting work.

SEATBELT PRE-TENSIONERS

• Some of the models covered by this book are fitted with seat belt pre-tensioners. They contain a pyrotechnic (explosive) charge and it is highly recommended that they must only be worked on by a qualified technician.

• No belt tensioner should be removed from a vehicle or handled unless made safe as described in *Job3, Section B*.

• Belt tensioner components have no time-expiring or wearing parts and must never be opened or repaired.

• If the tensioner device needs to be replaced, take the old unit to your Peugeot dealer and have them dispose of it - there will probably be a cost involved.

• DO NOT leave an old tensioner lying around, or dispose of negligently. You could cause an accident with the possibility of criminal liability!

• A belt tensioner which has been dropped on the floor, or dented or damaged in any way must not be used.

• A new belt tensioner must be kept in its packaging at all times until fitted to the vehicle.

• Keep belt tensioners away from grease, cleaning solvents and temperatures of over 100 degrees Celsius (212 degrees Fahrenheit) at all times.

• A seat belt on which the tensioner has been 'fired' is not safe to use. The seat belt cannot be checked for locking under these circumstances.

• Do not dismantle any body or trim components in the region of an airbag.

• Read and follow the instructions in *Jobs 12 and 13* first.

• Note the location of all airbags before starting work.

CHAPTER 14 — Interior, Trim, Job 1

The information given in this chapter is applicable to all of the vehicles covered in this manual.
→ There are many detail variations both between different models and between different versions and ages of the same models - too many to cover here in detail.
→ The details given here may well need to be related to the specific fixtures that you may find on a vehicle, but are designed to be applied to the variations you are likely to come across when working on these vehicles.

JOB 1: TRIM FIXINGS.

INTERIOR STRIPOUT

At first sight, it may look as though interior trim was never designed to be removed! But with a little thought and the certain knowledge that all the fixings *can* be found once you know where to start looking for clues, you'll find yourself able to work through the whole proceedings, step-by-step.
→ Start with the outer fixings first. Work patiently and methodically.
→ Pull carefully on plastic trim - you'll be able to see where it flexes and this often tells you where fixings are located and whether panels are separate, with a concealed join, or all-in-one.
→ If you are certain that there are no fixings that can be unscrewed, try pulling carefully - the trim may be held with concealed clips.

☐ **STEP 1:** In some cases, self-tapping screws are used to hold trim in place. Whenever you see a cap or other type of finisher, you can assume that it's there to cover something up. In this case, the cap is levered off, exposing the screw head beneath.

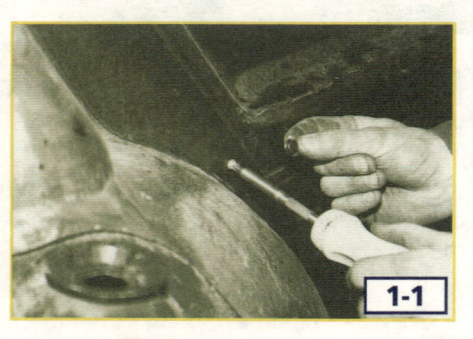

☐ **STEP 2:** Similar at first sight, but in fact much flatter, is this type of plastic clip. To remove it, all you need to do is carefully lever under the head of the clip.

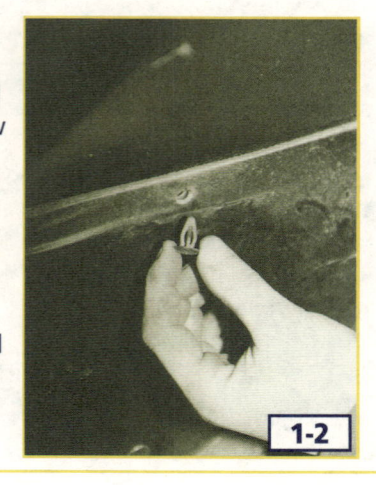

☐ **STEP 3:** Some similar looking clips (1) have a peg under the head, rather like a plastic nail, which pushes into a plastic socket mounted in the bodywork. The peg is pulled out first and then the socket (sometimes still attached to the peg; sometimes not) pulls out after it. On these door aperture trims (2), the cover is also clipped down to spring clips (3) on the body.

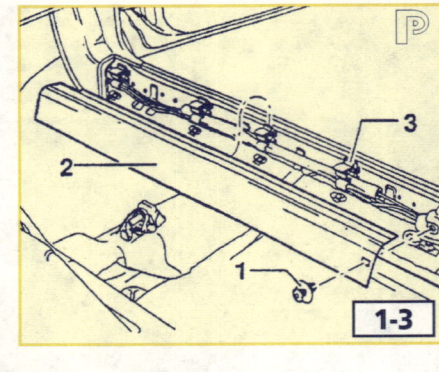

☐ **STEP 4:** Door seals are simply pushed on to the edge of the door and tread plates are either clipped or screwed down. Replacement door seals are remarkably expensive so, if yours are in good condition, do your best to save them.

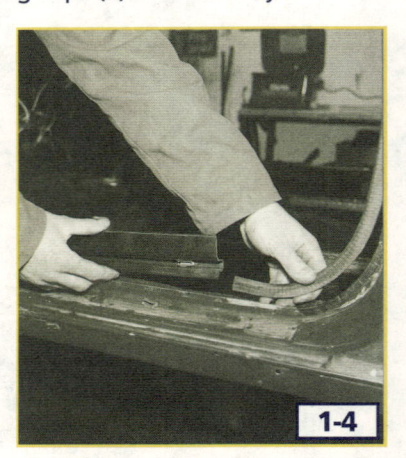

☐ **STEP 5:** On some models, the tread plates may be held in place with metal clips which stayed on the body seam after the trim has been removed and need to be levered off separately.

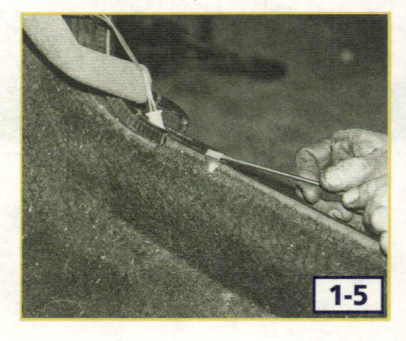

☐ **STEP 6:** Two fixing types shown here:
→ Another version of the hidden clip (3) may pull out of the trim panel, or might stay in the body. Whichever - before refitting, make sure it's first properly clipped into the trim panel.
→ The threaded screw (1) is covered by a cap (2) which has to be carefully levered out with a flat-bladed screwdriver. The screw goes into an expanding plastic plug (4) which is pushed into a square hole in the body. On some versions, the cap is a softer material and is flush-fitting to the trim.

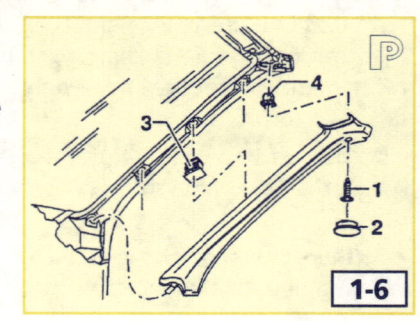

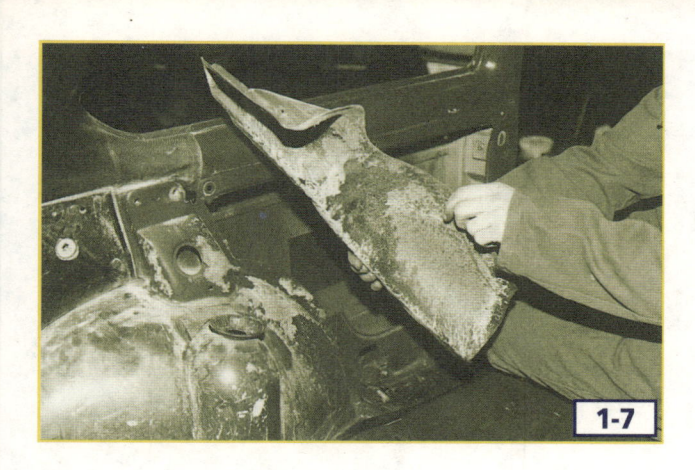

STEP 7: Some sections of plastic trim and, more often, carpet are glued down. Take the very greatest care when pulling them off because the carpet is shaped and will be impossible to replicate from a flat piece.

| JOB 2: | SIDE DOOR TRIM PANEL - *remove, refit*. |

Refer to **Job 1: Trim fixings** for general information on releasing trim parts.

NOTE: Not every one of the jobs listed below will be relevant to every vehicle.

STEP 1: Disconnect the battery negative (-) earth/ground terminal. See *Chapter 10, Electrical, Dash, Instruments, Fact File: Disconnecting the Battery* BEFORE doing so!

STEP 2: Remove the door mirror interior trim panel – see *Chapter 13, Job 13*.

STEP 3: On some models there will be a door trim fixing underneath the mirror interior panel.

STEP 4: 306: Push a thin rod into the hole (arrowed) in the interior lock button to release the clip, and remove the button.

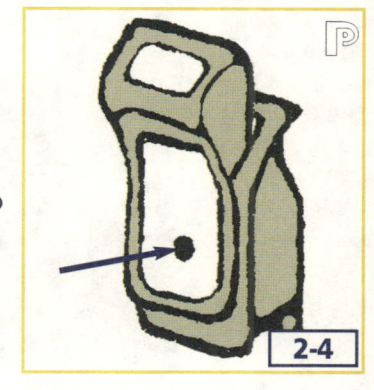

STEP 5: Unclip or lever away the door inner handle surround trim.

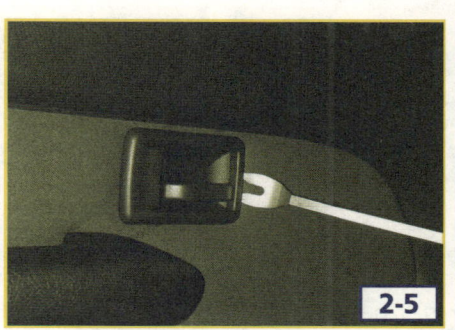

STEP 6: If fitted, unscrew or lever away the speaker cover, remove the speaker screws, extract the speaker and disconnect the wires.

STEP 7: If fitted, pull the window winder handle off its spindle, and remove the trim plate from underneath.

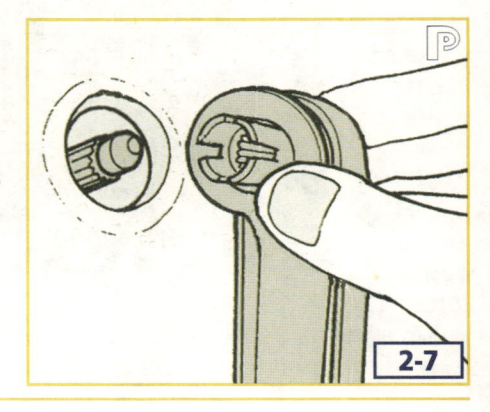

CHAPTER 14 Interior, Trim Job 2

14-3

CHAPTER 14 Interior, Trim Job 2

☐ **STEP 8:** If there are switches on the door trim panel, they can carefully be levered out and their wires disconnected.

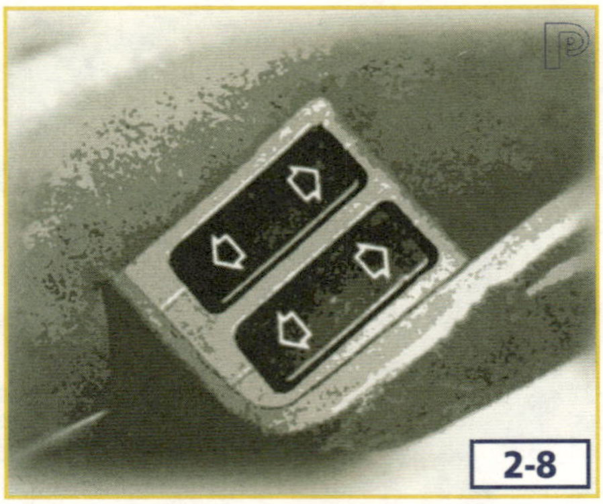

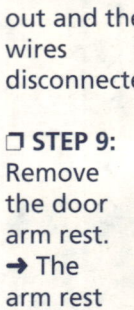

2-8

☐ **STEP 9:** Remove the door arm rest.
→ The arm rest can be fixed with screws and/or nuts. They may be covered by small fill panels or plugs, which must carefully be levered off first.

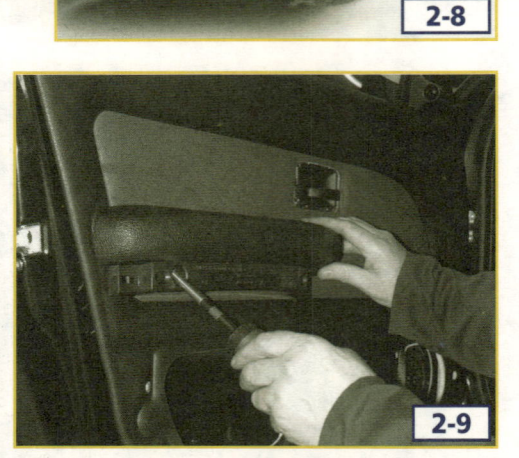

2-9

☐ **STEP 10:** If there is a small door trim panel pocket, remove the screw.

2-10

☐ **STEP 11:** Depending on the model, the edges of the trim panel can be held with screws and/or push-in clips.
→ Where the panel is held by clips, the edges can be levered off using the proper tool.

2-11

→ Place cardboard or cloth under the tool to protect the door paint work.

☐ **STEP 12:** If screws are fitted, remove them.
→ Some fixings are easily found.

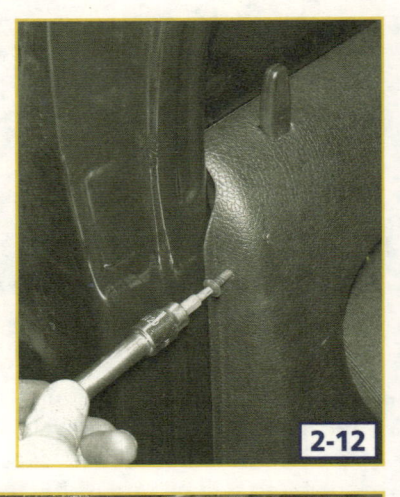

2-12

☐ **STEP 13:** ...others are partially hidden.

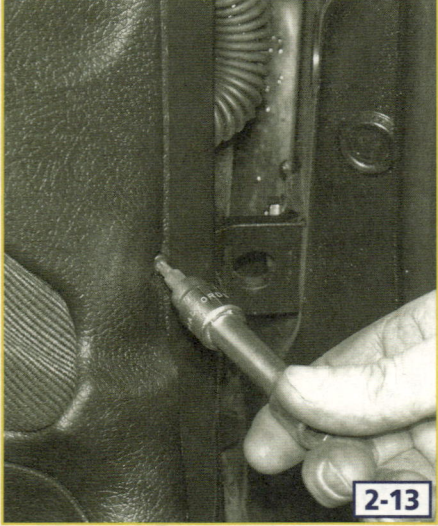

2-13

TOP TIP!
- If the door interior trim panel doesn't lift away with only slight resistance, you've missed a fixing, so look again!
- DON'T keep applying more pressure because trim panels will distort and clips break quite easily.

☐ **STEP 14:** Lift the door trim away.
→ If any electrical switch gear has been left on the door panel, disconnect the wiring plugs - DON'T put any strain on the loom!

☐ **STEP 15:** Refit as the reverse of removal.

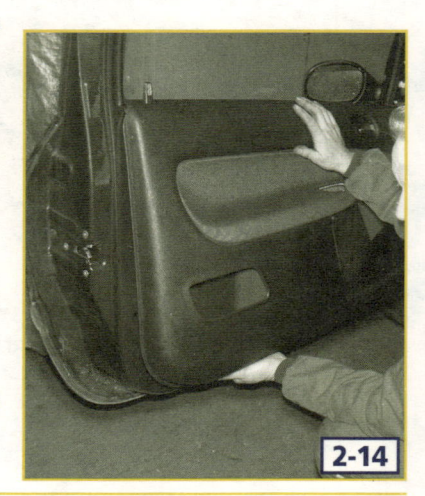

2-14

14-4

JOB 3: FRONT SEATS - *removal, replacement*.

SAFETY FIRST!

• Side airbags are either standard equipment or optional extras on recent examples of the 106, 206 and 306.
• Side airbags are fitted in the front seats, and there is a warning label on the seat trim.
• Side airbags are activated individually by side impact, but can also be activated by impact and electrical current.
• Before working on or in the vicinity of airbags or control units, before using any electric welding equipment on the vehicle, disconnect the battery and wait at least thirty minutes for the system capacitors to discharge, then remove the centre console and disconnect the airbag control unit wiring harness plug.

SPECIAL NOTE:
• Recent vehicles are fitted with seatbelt pre-tensioners, which are part of the inertia reel mechanism or the seatbelt stalk. If the seat belt pre-tensioner activates while the seatbelt is buckled, the seatbelt assembly must be replaced.

Section A: All vehicles except those with seatbelt pre-tensioners.

☐ **STEP A1:** If the seats are fitted with airbags, disconnect the battery negative (-) earth/ground terminal. See *Chapter 10, Electrical, Dash, Instruments, Fact File: Disconnecting the Battery* BEFORE doing so!
➔ Wait at least thirty minutes before proceeding.

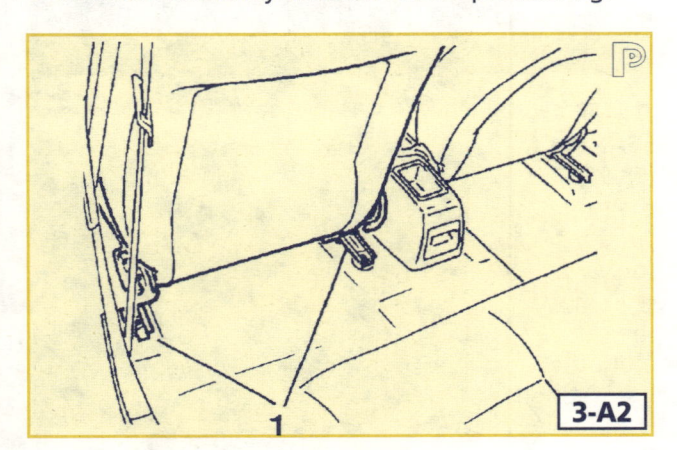

☐ **STEP A2:** Slide the seat fully forward, tilt the back and remove the rear seat runner bolts (**1**).

☐ **STEP A3:** Slide the seat fully backwards and remove the seat runner front bolts.

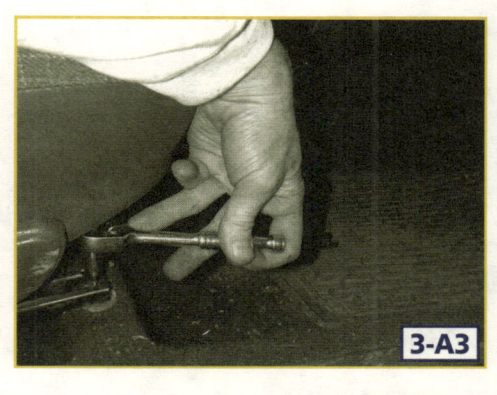

☐ **STEP A4:** The seat may now be lifted out.

☐ **STEP A5:** Refit as the reverse of removal.

Section B: 106 and 306 with seatbelt pre-tensioners.

SPECIAL NOTE:
• Read *Section B* and *Job 12: Airbags and Pre-Tensioners - essential Safety First!* BEFORE starting work on or near airbags or pre-tensioners.
• The 106 and 306 seatbelt pre-tensioners are part of the seatbelt stalk.
• The seat belt stalk is attached to the seat frame. DO NOT attempt to separate them – if the seatbelt pre-tensioner has to be removed, take the seat assembly to a Peugeot specialist.
• In a collision, seatbelt pre-tensioners are activated whether the belt is buckled or not. They cannot be reset and must be replaced!

CHAPTER 14 Interior, Trim Job 3

14-5

SAFETY FIRST!

• Handle pre-tensioners with extreme care – don't drop.
• Never cause impact to the tensioning device - which could set off the pre-loaded spring.
• The pre-tensioner will activate if it receives any voltage – even from a test meter.
• Never attempt to service or dismantle the unit.
• Never grasp the buckle or the power unit.

☐ **STEP B1:** Disconnect the battery negative (-) earth/ground terminal. See *Chapter 10, Electrical, Dash, Instruments, Fact File: Disconnecting the Battery* BEFORE doing so!
➜ Wait at least ten minutes before proceeding.
➜ If the vehicle is also fitted with side airbags, wait at least thirty minutes before proceeding.
➜ Unless the seat unit is to be refitted immediately, there are legal and safety issues concerned with the handling, storage and transport - see *Job 12: Airbags and Pre-tensioners – essential Safety First!*

☐ **STEP B2:** Disconnect the wiring harness plug from the pre-tensioner – see *Job 5*.

☐ **STEP B3:** Slide the seat fully forward, tilt the back forward and remove the seat runner Torx rear bolts.

☐ **STEP B4:** Slide the seat fully backward and remove the seat runner Torx front bolts.

☐ **STEP B5:** Keeping clear of the seatbelt stalk and pre-tensioner mechanism, carefully lift the seat out.
➜ DO NOT jar the seatbelt pre-tensioner mechanism.
➜ Seatbelt stalk pre-tensioner mechanisms are pyrotechnic devices and in addition to important safety issues there are legal constraints on their handling, storage and transport – see *Job 12: Airbags and Pre-tensioners – essential Safety First!*
➜ Unless the seat is to be re-fitted imminently, retrieve and store the four seat runner washers.

☐ **STEP B6:** Refit as the reverse of removal.
➜ There is always a small chance that electrically triggered safety devices could deploy when the battery is reconnected – see *Job 13, Reconnecting the Battery*.

JOB 4: REAR SEATS - *removal, replacement.*

SEAT BASE

☐ **STEP 1: HATCHBACK MODELS:** The rear seat base hinges are secured with screws or bolts on some models and simply pull apart on others.
➜ Swing the seat base up and fully forward.
➜ The hinges will be visible.
➜ Lift the base up and out of the hinges…
➜ OR: …remove the hinge fixings, as applicable.

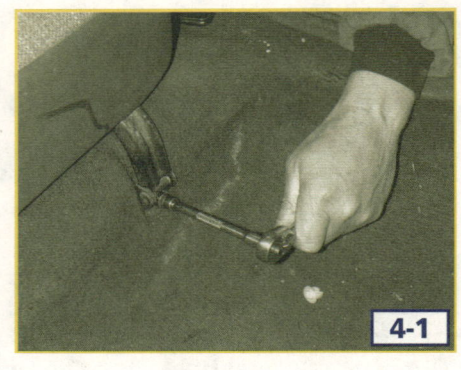

☐ **STEP 2: SALOON/SEDAN MODELS:** Remove the rear seat base hinge covers from their position under the front edge of the seat base.
➜ Remove the hinge screws.
➜ Pull the rear of the seat base up to release it from the locking catch (where fitted).
➜ The seat base may now be removed.

SEAT BACK

☐ **STEP 3: SEAT BACK:** Tilt the seat cushion forward.
➜ Tilt the seat back forward.
➜ Remove the hinge bolts.

☐ **STEP 4: SEAT BACK (SPLIT):** Tilt the seat cushions forward.
➜ Remove the centre mounting bracket bolts.
➜ Remove the outer bracket bolt from the smaller seat back, release the top mount mechanism and remove the seat back.

→ Remove the centre seatbelt anchor (if fitted).
→ Remove the other seat back outer bracket bolt, release the top mount mechanism and remove the seat back.

JOB 5: SEAT BELTS - *remove, replace.*

FACT FILE
SEAT BELT PRE-TENSIONERS
• All later vehicles have front seat belts with pre-tensioners.
• Pre-tensioners are, in effect, devices which contain an explosive charge. In the event of a crash the charge is triggered and pulls the seat belt tight, reducing harmful body movement.

SAFETY FIRST!
• See *Section C: Seat Belt Pre-tensioners* BEFORE attempting to remove the seat belt from a 206.

• If you are not sure whether or not a vehicle is fitted with pre-tensioners, or which type you are dealing with, or you are not fully competent to carry out this work, consult with, or take the vehicle to your chosen Peugeot dealership.

Section A: Three door vehicles.

☐ **STEP A1: VEHICLES FITTED WITH SEATBELT PRE-TENSIONERS:** Disconnect the battery negative (-) earth/ground terminal. See *Chapter 10, Electrical, Dash, Instruments, Fact File: Disconnecting the Battery* BEFORE doing so!
→ Wait at least ten minutes then disconnect the wiring harness plug from the seatbelt tensioner unit.
→ On the 206, the tensioner unit is built into the inertia mechanism.
→ On the 106 and 306, the tensioner unit is built into the seatbelt stalk – an integral part of the seat.

☐ **STEP A2: ALL THREE DOOR VEHICLES:** The seatbelt assembly includes:
→ The inertia reel.
→ The upper anchorage

point (adjustable for height on some models).
→ The lower anchorage point (a rail on some models – as illustrated).
→ The stalk.
→ Each is fitted by a bolt with a washer and spacer, which MUST be refitted in the original order.

☐ **STEP A3:** Access is improved if the relevant front seat is removed, though this is not vital.
→ Wait at least thirty minutes after disconnecting the battery before attempting to move a seat with a side airbag - see *Job 3*.

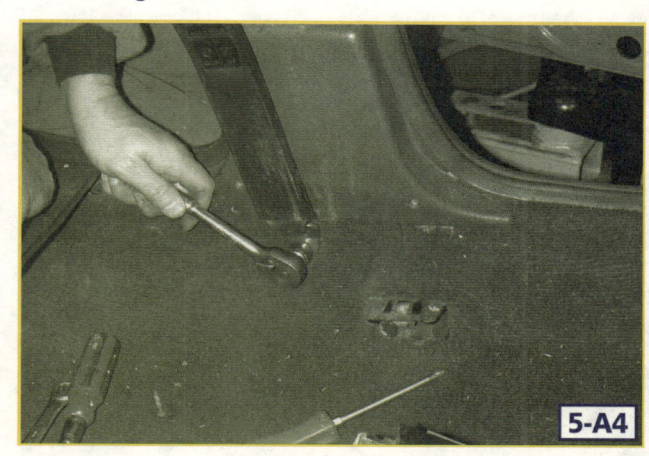

☐ **STEP A4:** Remove the lower seatbelt anchorage bolt.
→ This may be covered by a trim cap that simply levers off.
→ On models with a lower rail or bar, it can be removed, along with its washer.

☐ **STEP A5: NON-ADJUSTABLE UPPER ANCHORAGE:** Remove the upper anchorage point cap and bolt.

☐ **STEP A6: ADJUSTABLE UPPER ANCHORAGE:** Remove the height adjuster button, its fixing screw, the trim cover, then remove the anchorage bolt.
→ Unclip the upper B-post trim panel and free it from the seat belt webbing.

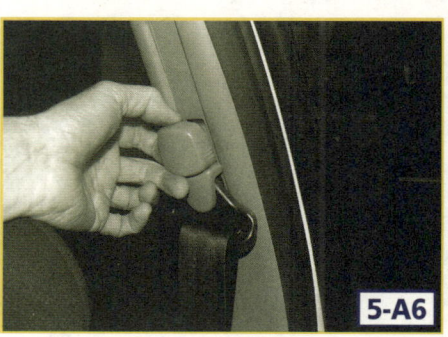

☐ **STEP A7:** The inertia reel is under the lower B-post trim panel. Remove the two trim panel screws and remove the panel.
→ If not already done and if fitted, disconnect the pre-tensioner wiring plug.
→ Free the belt from the slot in the panel.

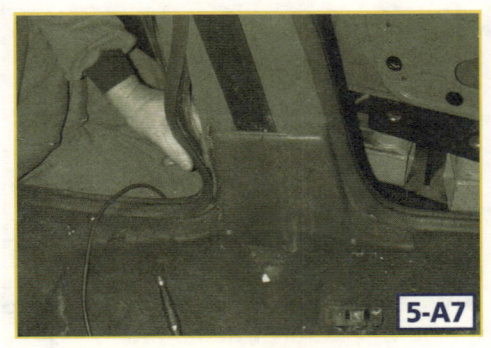

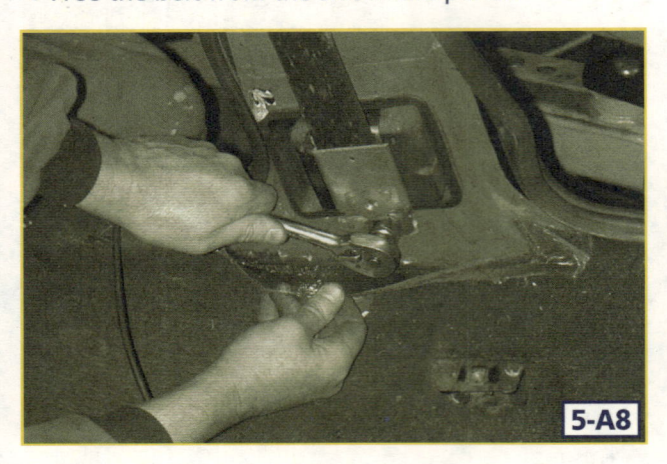

☐ **STEP A8:** Remove the inertia reel bolt, spacer and washer.
→ 206: See *Section C: Seat Belt Pre-tensioners* for important information on the handling and storage of pre-tensioners.

306 ONLY

☐ **STEP A9:** The inertia reel is under the rear side trim panel.
→ Remove the trim panel from the rear roof pillar.
→ Unclip the lower side window seal.
→ Unclip the side trim panel and free the seat belt webbing.
→ If not already done and if fitted, disconnect the pre-tensioner wiring plug (1).
→ Remove the inertia reel mounting bolt (2), spacer and washer.

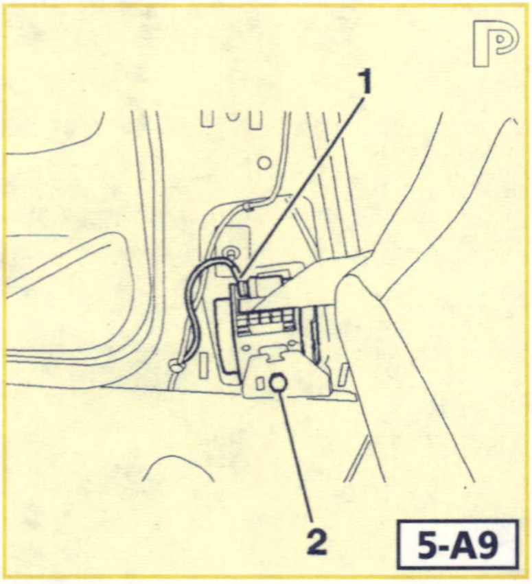

☐ **STEP A10:** Refit as the reverse of removal. Tighten all mounting bolts to the recommended torque.

Section B: Rear seat belts.

☐ **STEP B1:** The inertia reel is under the parcel shelf support panel.
→ Lever the weather strip from the relevant section of the tailgate aperture.
→ Lever the roof rear interior trim panel away.
→ Angle the rear seat back forward.
→ Remove the parcel shelf support panel screws.
→ Lever out the luggage bay light and switch (and/or speakers) and disconnect the wiring.
→ Remove the wheel arch interior trim panel screws to allow the panel to move.
→ Pull the parcel shelf support panel free, unhook it from the inner wheel arch trim panel and pull the seat belt webbing out.

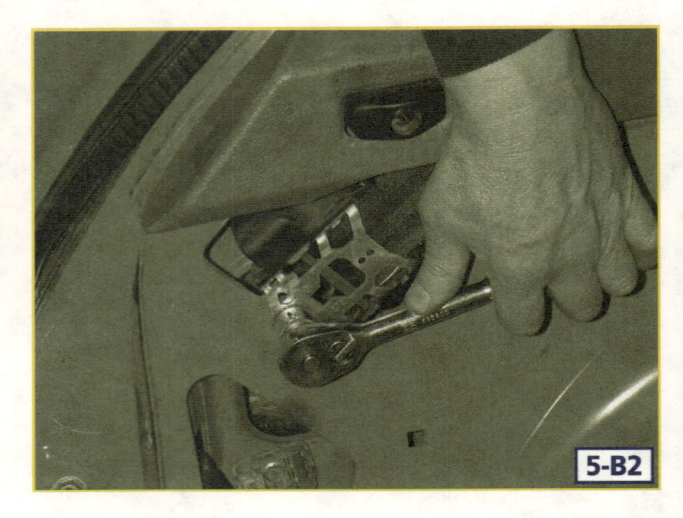

☐ **STEP B2:** Remove the upper seat belt anchor bolt assembly and inertia reel bolt assembly.
→ Remove the lower seat belt anchor bolt assembly and remove the seat belt from the vehicle.

☐ **STEP B3:** To remove the centre seatbelt, lift the seat base and undo the anchorage bolt assemblies.

Section C: Seat belt pre-tensioners.

SAFETY FIRST!

☐ **STEP C1:**
- If you are not sure whether or not a vehicle is fitted with pre-tensioners, or which type you are dealing with, or you are not fully competent to carry out this work, consult with, or take the vehicle to your chosen Peugeot dealership.
- A seat belt pre-tensioner is a pyrotechnic (explosive) device which is designed to pull the seat belt tight in the event of a frontal crash.
- Because pre-tensioners contain pyrotechnic materials, their handling and storage must be carried out correctly in order to prevent damage or injury.
- IF FOR ANY REASON, YOU ARE UNABLE TO COMPLY EXACTLY WITH THE INSTRUCTIONS AND WARNINGS GIVEN BELOW, DO NOT HANDLE OR WORK ON THE SEAT BELT PRE-TENSIONERS - leave it to a Peugeot dealership.
- The following instructions MUST be observed for the safety of operators, the security of the seat belt assembly with pre-tensioners and in accordance with the laws concerning explosives (category V group A).

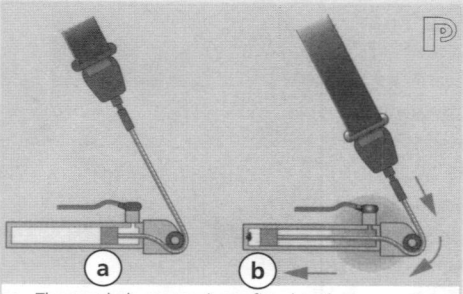

a - The seat belt pre-tensioner fitted to the 106 and 306 before deployment.
b - The seat belt tensioner deployed.

5-C1

HANDLING A PRE-TENSIONER

☐ **STEP C2:** Follow these precautions:
→ When carrying a pre-tensioner, keep it upright.
→ Do not tamper with the pre-tensioner or carry out any repairs on it. All defective pre-tensioners should be taken safely to a Peugeot dealership.
→ Do not subject pre-tensioners to blows, drilling, mechanical working, heating or to any electrical current, either directly or caused by electric welding.
→ NEVER use an electrical test meter on a circuit including seatbelt pre-tensioners, because even the tiny current generated will trigger the devices.
→ DO NOT drop pre-tensioners or subject them to impacts. If one is accidentally dropped from a height of more than 1 meter, it should not be used but returned to a Peugeot dealership.
→ When operations on the vehicle require the temporary removal of the pre-tensioner, it should be stored in a locked metal cupboard suitable for pyrotechnic charges which meets the laws in force on the subject.
→ Do not place naked flames, liquids, solvents or lubricants near this cupboard and do not expose it to temperatures above 110 degrees C. At temperatures in excess of 180 degrees C, the gas generator may self-ignite.
→ If the device has been activated, ALWAYS wait for at least 30 minutes after the activation before carrying out any operations to it.
→ If a pre-tensioner which has been activated has to be handled, use protective gloves and goggles.
→ Wash your hands with soap and water after handling a pre-tensioner.

☐ **STEP C3:** When working on the vehicle:
→ Do not subject an area surrounding the pre-tensioner (60-70 cm radius) to strong impacts. When, during bodywork repairs, for example, the use of a hammer is necessary, remove the complete pre-tensioner unit.
→ If it is necessary to heat the area surrounding the pre-tensioner or to carry out welding or brazing, then the complete pre-tensioner reel assembly MUST be removed.
→ If a vehicle with one or more pre-tensioners removed has to be moved, the tensioner/s should be placed in the luggage compartment and EMPHATICALLY NOT in the passenger compartment.

IMPORTANT GENERAL NOTES

If flood water or mud reaches the height of a pre-tensioner, it must be replaced.
- Pre-tensioners are maintenance-free and should definitely not be lubricated or modified in any way.
- A locked belt is an indication that the pre-tensioner has been activated, or of a malfunction of the reel. In both cases, the device must be replaced.
- A pre-tensioner which has not been activated in the case of an accident should be considered still active.
- A pre-tensioner that has not activated because of a defect or which has reached the end of its warranty, or for any other reasons, should be replaced. The old unit should be taken to a Peugeot dealership or special center capable of dealing with such pyrotechnic devices.
- Pre-tensioners have been designed to be fitted only on the type and model of vehicle for which they are intended. They cannot be adapted, reused or fitted on other vehicles, but only on those for which they were designed and produced. Any attempts to reuse, adapt or fit pre-tensioners on different types of vehicles could cause serious or fatal injuries to the occupants of the vehicle, either in the case of an accident or in normal usage.
- After being fitted the pre-tensioner can be activated if it receives any impact of sufficient force.

PRE-TENSIONER REMOVAL

☐ **STEP C4: 206:** Before removing the pre-tensioner and before handling it, disconnect the battery, wait at least ten minutes then disconnect the pre-tensioner wiring plug.

☐ **STEP C5:** The pre-tensioner/seatbelt stalk of the 106 and 306 should NOT be separated from the seat. The assembly should be taken to a Peugeot dealer complete and the work carried out there – see *Job 3, Section B*.

PRE-TENSIONER REFITTING

☐ **STEP C6:** After refitting a pre-tensioner, reconnect the battery and switch on the ignition from OUTSIDE the car. Do not allow anyone inside the car until the pre-tensioners have been 'tested' in this way.

JOB 6: STEERING WHEEL – *removal, refitting*.

Section A: Steering wheel with air bag.

> **SAFETY FIRST!**
>
> • Read *Jobs 12, 13 and 14* BEFORE removing a steering wheel fitted with an airbag.

☐ **STEP A1:** Disable the airbag mechanism as described in *Job 13*.
→ Even though the airbag is 'disabled' do not sit in the driver's seat whilst removing the air bag.
→ Never place any part of your body or any tool in the inflation zone of the airbag when working on it.

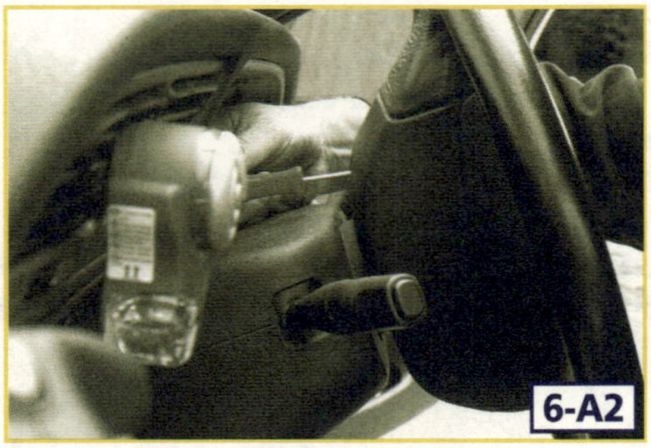

☐ **STEP A2:** Remove the steering column shrouds – see *Job 9 Step 3*.
→ The airbag is secured by two screws at the back of the steering wheel.
→ Remove the screws.
→ To access the screw heads, turn the steering wheel.

→ It will be necessary to re-insert the ignition key to release the steering lock.
→ Remove the ignition key afterwards.

☐ **STEP A3:** Keeping yourself out of the inflation zone of the airbag, carefully lift it away from the steering wheel, and disconnect the wiring plug (arrowed)
→ Inside the airbag half of the plug, a spring plate contacts both terminals as the plug halves are pulled apart. This shorts out the airbag terminals and prevents the airbag from deploying.
→ The airbag unit must still be treated with caution.

☐ **STEP A4:** Store the airbag with the inflation side uppermost.

☐ **STEP A5:** Remove the steering wheel nut and its washer.

☐ **STEP A6:** Disconnect the airbag control unit wiring connector.

☐ **STEP A7:** Lift away the steering wheel. If the steering wheel is tight, light blows to the reverse side with the heels of your hands usually frees it.

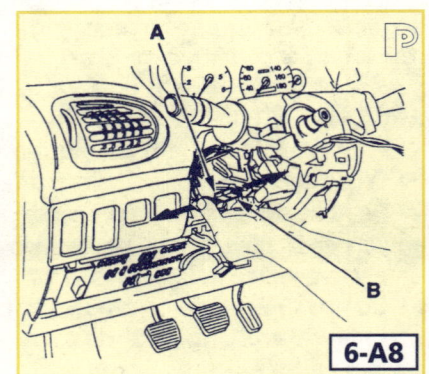

☐ **STEP A8:** Lever the rotary connector wiring plug from its mounting, and disconnect it by pulling parts **A** and **B** apart.

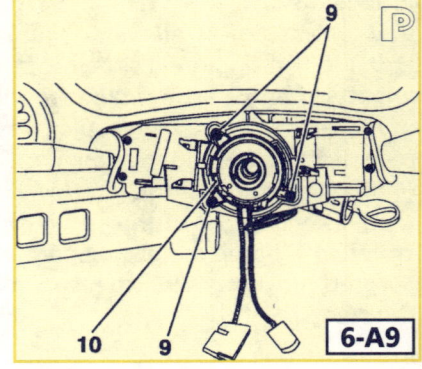

☐ **STEP A9:** To remove the rotary connector, remove the fasteners (**9**), then pull the harness (**10**) through the stalk mounting.

☐ **STEP A10:** Reverse order of removal operations to refit.
→ NEVER RECONNECT THE BATTERY UNTIL AIR BAG FITTING HAS BEEN COMPLETED CORRECTLY.
→ There must be no-one in the vehicle when the battery is reconnected.
→ There must be no-one in the vehicle when the ignition is first switched on.
→ After refitting, have the system checked by a main dealer using Peugeot test equipment.

Section B: Steering wheel without air bag.

☐ **STEP B1:** Lever out the steering wheel boss trim plate.

☐ **STEP B2:** Lock the front wheels in the dead ahead position.

☐ **STEP B3:** Remove the steering wheel nut, and remove its washer.

☐ **STEP B4:** Lift away the steering wheel. If the steering wheel is tight, light blows to the reverse side with the heels of your hands usually frees it.

TOP TIP!
• Leave the nut on the end of its thread.
• Pull or, if necessary, bang the steering wheel towards you with your hands to get it off the splines.
• Remove the nut and the wheel when it is loose on the splines.
• You won't risk bashing yourself in the face as the wheel comes free!

☐ **STEP B5:** Refit as the reverse of removal.

JOB 7: INTERIOR MIRROR – *removal, refitting*.

☐ **STEP 1:** The interior mirrors of nearly all modern vehicles are bonded to the screen glass.

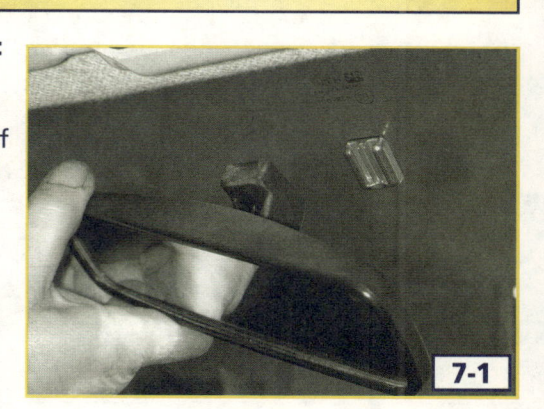

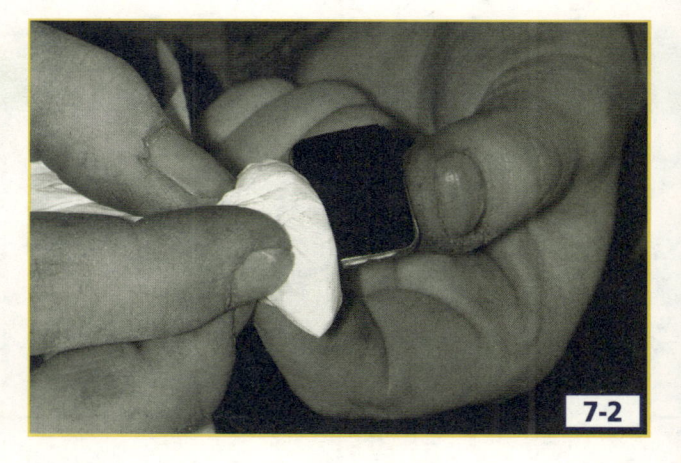

☐ **STEP 2:** If the base comes adrift from the screen:
→ Mark the outside of the screen with a felt pen to show where the mirror is to be relocated.
→ Use ONLY a proprietary mirror base adhesive for relocating the base.
→ Other types of adhesive may 'work', but will probably cause the screen to crack.
→ Clean off all traces of old adhesive from screen and base with a sharp blade.
→ Wipe the base and screen with degreaser and allow to dry.

CHAPTER 14 Interior, Trim Job 7

14-11

CHAPTER 14 Interior, Trim Job 8

☐ **STEP 3:** The Wurth mirror adhesive we used comes in two parts:
→ Break the phial of green adhesive and use the integral applicator to wipe adhesive onto the base pad.
→ Some types of mirror adhesive involve special double-sided tape - the principles are the same. Follow instructions on the pack.

☐ **STEP 4:** Use the markings on the outside of the screen. Apply hardener to the area of the screen where the base is to be fixed.

☐ **STEP 5:** Hold the base into position. It will stick into place very quickly, but will need to be allowed to cure before re-attaching the mirror - see instructions on the pack.

JOB 8: CENTRE CONSOLE - *removal, replacement.*

IMPORTANT NOTE: There are minor differences in the interior trim of the vehicles covered by this manual.
→ The following instructions offer generally applicable instructions.
→ There is no alternative, when carrying out this sort of job, to having to carry out some detective work to discover all of the fixings among the trim.
→ See *Job 1* for further advice.
→ Also, see **Chapter 10, Job 4: Instrument Panel** for further information.

SAFETY FIRST!

• Disconnect the battery negative (-) earth/ground terminal. See *Chapter 10, Electrical, Dash, Instruments, Fact File: Disconnecting the Battery* BEFORE doing so!
• DO NOT open any of the hoses or connections on an air conditioning system.

VEHICLES WITH SEPARATE PARKING BRAKE LEVER AND GEARSHIFT LEVER CONSOLES

☐ **STEP 1:** Unclip the gear lever gaiter (arrowed).

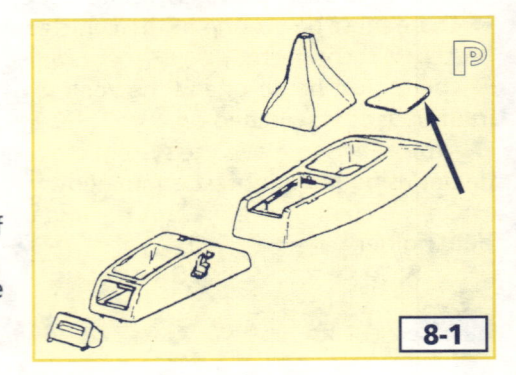

☐ **STEP 2:** If fitted, remove the radio – see *Job 11*.

☐ **STEP 3A:** Remove the gear lever console fixing screws, which are;

☐ **STEP 3B: 106:** One either side of the console.

☐ **STEP 3C: 205 to 1988:** One at the rear plus one either side.

☐ **STEP 3D: 205 – 1988-ON:** Two screws at the gear lever surround plus bolt at rear plus either nuts and bolts or screws and clips inside oddments compartment – the air vent must be levered out.

☐ **STEP 3E: 306:** Two screws in the oddments tray, two nuts accessible through the gear lever aperture.

☐ **STEP 4:** The console can now be lifted away.

☐ **STEP 5:** The rear (parking brake lever) console is secured by two screws under the ashtray and two in the oddments bin.
→ The parking brake lever handle can be very difficult to remove from the lever – using gentle heat helps free it.

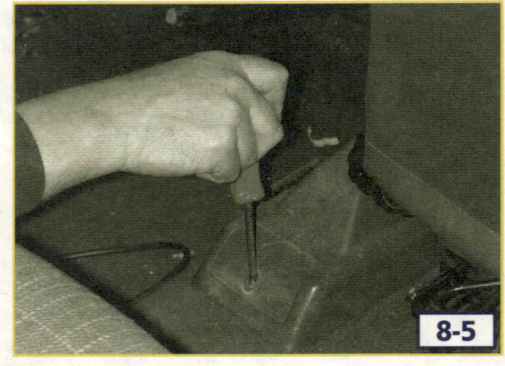

VEHICLES WITH FULL LENGTH CONSOLES

☐ **STEP 6:** Disconnect the battery negative (-) earth/ground terminal. See *Chapter 10, Electrical, Dash, Instruments, Fact File: Disconnecting the Battery* BEFORE doing so!

❏ **STEP 7:** Unclip the gear lever gaiter or, on automatics, unclip the lever surround.

❏ **STEP 8:** Remove the parking brake lever handle.
➡ The handle can be very difficult to remove from the lever – using gentle heat helps free it.

❏ **STEP 9:** Some models have switches mounted on the console.
➡ Lever them out and disconnect the wiring.
➡ On the 206 remove the ashtray and unclip the bulb holder.

306

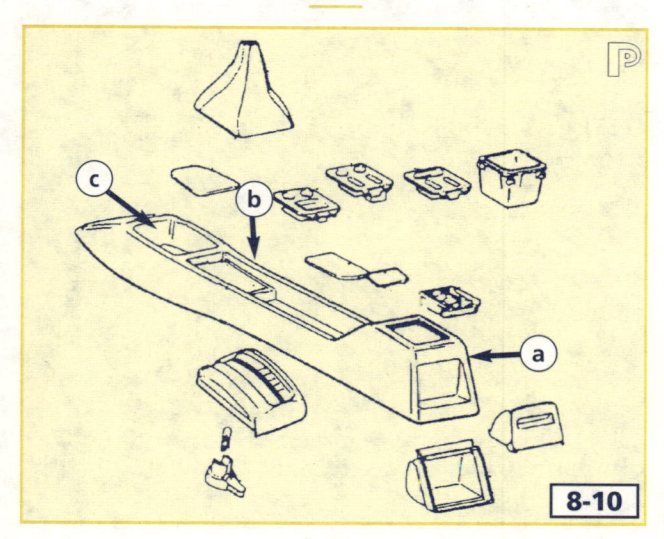

[Figure 8-10]

❏ **STEP 10: 306:** The console is secured by the following fixings, which must all be removed.
➡ Two screws inside the ashtray aperture (**a**) at the rear of the console.
➡ One screw in the oddments tray (**b**).
➡ Two centre console nuts accessible though the gear lever aperture (**c**).
➡ Go to *Step 13*.

206

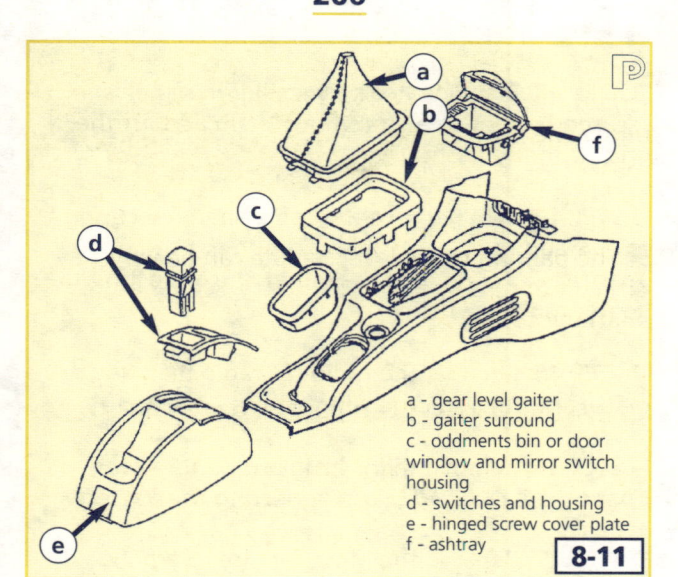

[Figure 8-11]

a - gear level gaiter
b - gaiter surround
c - oddments bin or door window and mirror switch housing
d - switches and housing
e - hinged screw cover plate
f - ashtray

❏ **STEP 11:** The console has a separate rear section,

secured by a screw under a hinged flap (**e**).
➡ Lever out the switches and their housing (**d**) and disconnect the wiring.
➡ Remove the fixing screw and lift away the rear section of the console.
➡ Lever out either the door glass winder/mirror control switch housing (**c**) and disconnect the wiring, or the oddments tray, as applicable.
➡ Lever out the ashtray (**f**) and unclip the bulb holder.

❏ **STEP 12:** The 206 console is secured by the following fixings, which must be removed.
➡ Two screws under the hinged flap at the front of the center console.
➡ One nut at the rear.

❏ **STEP 13:** Lift the rear of the console and withdraw it, disconnecting the cigarette lighter socket wiring if fitted.
➡ Check that no wires are still connected to console-mounted equipment.

❏ **STEP 14:** Replace as the reverse of removal.

JOB 9: DASHBOARD - *removal, replacement*

SAFETY FIRST!

• **Many recent vehicles are fitted with passenger airbags in the dashboard.**
• **If fitted, the area of the dashboard covering the airbag will be embossed 'AIRBAG'.**
• **Before carrying out any work on a dashboard containing an airbag, or working on or near the airbag, disconnect the battery, wait at least thirty minutes and then disconnect the airbag control unit wiring.**
• **Read *Job 12* and *13* IN FULL before working on a dashboard fitted with airbags.**

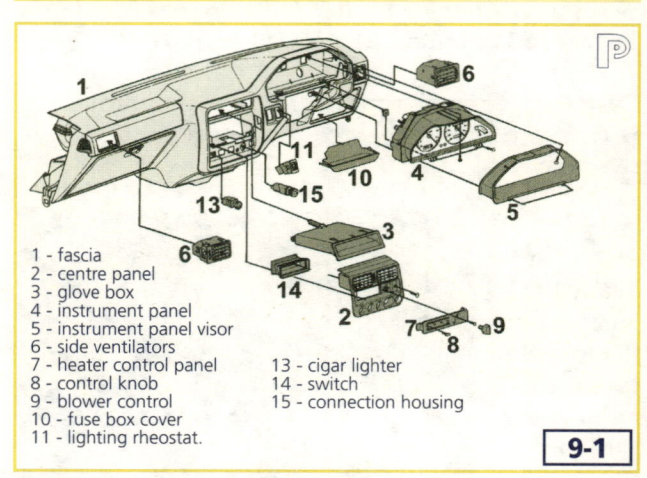

[Figure 9-1]

1 - fascia
2 - centre panel
3 - glove box
4 - instrument panel
5 - instrument panel visor
6 - side ventilators
7 - heater control panel
8 - control knob
9 - blower control
10 - fuse box cover
11 - lighting rheostat
13 - cigar lighter
14 - switch
15 - connection housing

❏ **STEP 1:** A typical dashboard layout – this is the 106.

→ Disconnect the battery negative (-) earth/ground terminal. See **Chapter 10, Electrical, Dash, Instruments, Fact File: Disconnecting the Battery** BEFORE doing so!
→ If the vehicle is fitted with airbags, wait at least thirty minutes before proceeding, then disconnect the airbag control unit – see **Job 13**.

GLOVEBOX

❏ **STEP 2:** To remove the glove box:

❏ **STEP 3: 106:** Open the glove box and remove the two fixing screws.

❏ **STEP 4A: 205 (EARLY):** Remove the hinge screws.

❏ **STEP 4B: 205 (LATE):** Remove the lower fascia cover panel and the two screws underneath, the support bracket screws and nut, then remove the glove box and support bracket together.

❏ **STEP 5: 206:** Unclip the lid then remove the six fixing screws and lower the glove box out from under the fascia.

❏ **STEP 6: 306:** Open the lid, remove the six screws and withdraw the glove box and lid together.

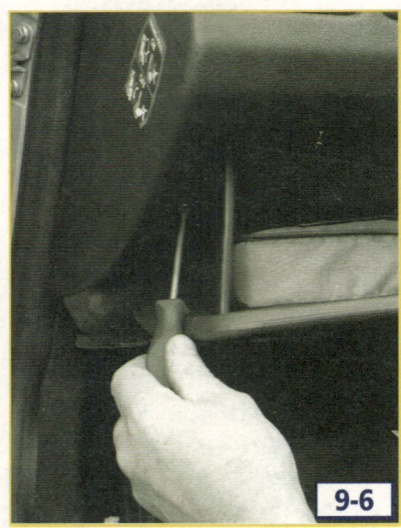

STEERING COLUMN SHROUD

❏ **STEP 7:** To remove the steering column shroud.
→ On some models the steering wheel must be removed – see **Job 6**.

❏ **STEP 8: 106 AND 205:** Remove the four nuts holding the shroud in position.

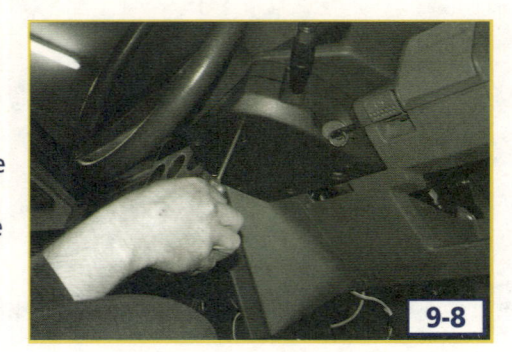

❏ **STEP 9: 206:** Remove the driver's side lower fascia cover, remove the lower shroud (4 screws), unclip wiring from the shroud and unclip the upper shroud.

❏ **STEP 10: 306:** Remove the lower shroud screws and the lower shroud, unclip wiring from the shroud and unclip the upper shroud.

DASHBOARD - REMOVAL

TOP TIP!

• The dashboard assembly has become increasingly sophisticated, and more recent models contain more electric, electronic and other components and their wiring and switches.
• Attach labels to wiring and control cables as you remove it, to remind you where it goes during the rebuild!
• Store fixing screws, bolts, nut and clips with the component they are associated with to make re-assembly easier.
• It is also worth labelling some components such as heater ducts, to remind you where they fit.
• Working on individual dashboard components in situ can be very awkward due to the poor access, but this is nearly always preferable to removing the entire dashboard.

❏ **STEP 11:** Remove the centre panel.
→ Pull the heater controls off (early models) or lever off the switch/clock trim panel.
→ (Early models). Remove the fixing screw, pull the heater control panel off and disconnect the bulb feed wire.

❏ **STEP 12: 206:** The centre vent panel is secured by screws at the top; remove them then unclip the panel.

❏ **STEP 13: 206:** The heater/ventilation panel is secured by four screws; remove them and lift the unit from the dashboard.

❏ **STEP 14: 306:** Remove the center panel securing screws and nuts (accessible through the radio aperture), and remove the panel, disconnecting the heater motor switch.

❏ **STEP 15:** Remove the radio (or radio blanking plate) and the radio housing screws – see **Job 11**.

❏ **STEP 16:** Remove the instrument panel – see **Chapter 10, FACT FILE: Disconnecting the Battery**.

❏ **STEP 17:** Remove the glove box (see **Step 2**).

☐ **STEP 18:** Remove the steering column shroud (see *Steps 7 to 10*).

☐ **STEP 19:** Remove the centre console (see *Job 8*).
➔ Remove the ashtray.

☐ **STEP 20:** Disconnect the heater ducts from the heater assembly and, where possible, remove their mountings and remove them.
➔ DO NOT disconnect air conditioning hoses.

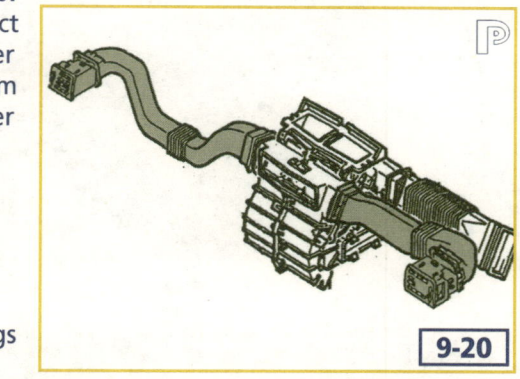

9-20

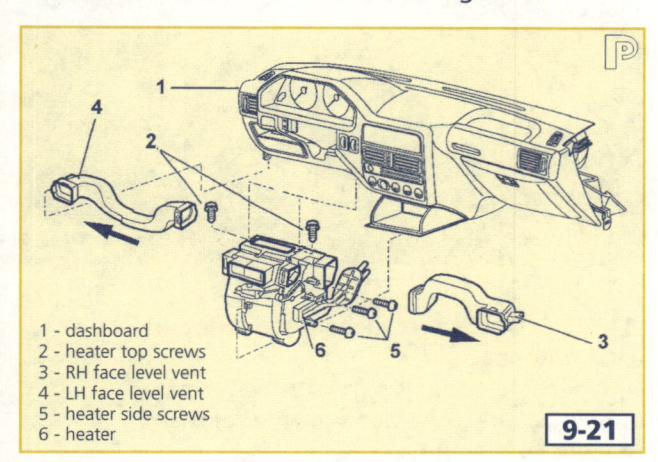

9-21
1 - dashboard
2 - heater top screws
3 - RH face level vent
4 - LH face level vent
5 - heater side screws
6 - heater

☐ **STEP 21:** Remove the heater unit securing screws.

☐ **STEP 22:** Disconnect the dashboard earth lead.

☐ **STEP 23:** On recent models there is a main dashboard wiring harness connector in the engine bay.
➔ Remove the plastic cover, disconnect the plug.
➔ Remove the two nuts holding the wiring connector to the body shell.

☐ **STEP 24:** Disconnect the speedometer cable and choke cable.

9-24

☐ **STEP 25:** The type and placement of dashboard securing screws and nuts varies between models.

☐ **STEP 26: 206:** The end bolts (and the aerial coaxial lead plug) are accessible through end covers (arrowed) that can be unclipped.
➔ On other models, the end fixings are accessed from under the dashboard.

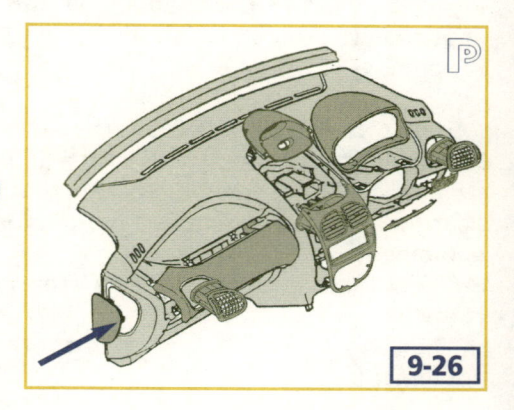

9-26

☐ **STEP 27:** At this point, any remaining dashboard fixings accessible from inside the vehicle should be visible and may be removed.

☐ **STEP 28: 206:** There is a mounting bolt situated in the instrument panel aperture.
➔ With the exception of the 206, the dashboard will still be firmly anchored in place, because the main mountings are situated on the engine bay side of the front panel.

☐ **STEP 29:** Disconnect all other dashboard switch wires, and the aerial lead.

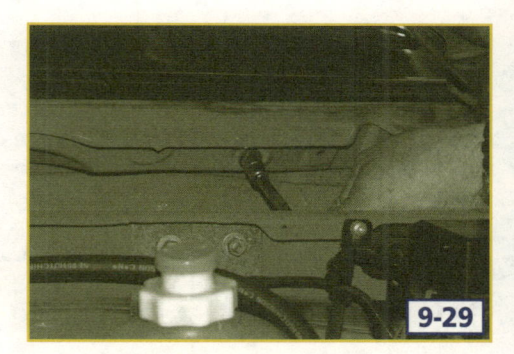

9-29

ALL MODELS EXCEPT 206

☐ **STEP 30:** Remove the windscreen wiper arms, the scuttle panel, and undo the main dashboard securing nuts.

☐ **STEP 31:** Disconnect any remaining wiring, and pull the dashboard from the vehicle.

9-31

CHAPTER 14 Interior, Trim Job 9

14-15

CHAPTER 14 Interior, Trim Jobs 10-12

☐ **STEP 32:** Reassemble as the reverse of removal.
➔ Offer the dashboard into position then manoeuvre wiring, cables and hoses into their approximate position before fitting any dashboard fastenings.

IMPORTANT NOTE: VEHICLES WITH AIRBAGS
➔ Reconnect the battery and switch on the ignition from OUTSIDE the vehicle, ensuring that no-one is near the airbags and seat belt pre-tensioning equipment.
➔ Check that the airbag warning light operates correctly.
➔ Then check for correct function of other electrical equipment.

JOB 10: HEADLINING.

☐ **STEP 1:** The majority of the roof liners are held in place with clips, and replacement first entails removing all of the trim panels and weather strips that overlap them.
➔ This is not only a time consuming job, but also one that demands experience.
➔ It is recommended that headlining replacement is carried out by a professional vehicle upholsterer or a Peugeot dealer.

☐ **STEP 2:** The head lining of the 206 is bonded into place. In addition to the amount of work involved in removing all overlapping trim, its replacement entails even greater experience than the clipped-in headlining, and should be left to a professional trimmer.

JOB 11: RADIO - *remove/refit*

The removal of the radio is a standard procedure in most cars using DIN removal tools. The chief variations include:
➔ Differing wiring plugs.
➔ Other switches or lights integral to the radio panel.
➔ Some vehicles may require partial dismantling of the dash or removal of masking covers to access retaining screws or nuts.
➔ Older radios may require the removal of the control knobs to access the nuts beneath.

☐ **STEP 1:** Disconnect the battery negative (-) earth/ground terminal. See **Chapter 10, Electrical, Dash, Instruments, Fact File: Disconnecting the Battery** BEFORE doing so! On radios with a radio code, make sure you have the radio code before disconnecting.

☐ **STEP 2:** Insert the DIN removal tools into the holes on each side until they click into place releasing the spring 'locks'.

☐ **STEP 3:** Having released the locks, gently pull the radio from the fascia.

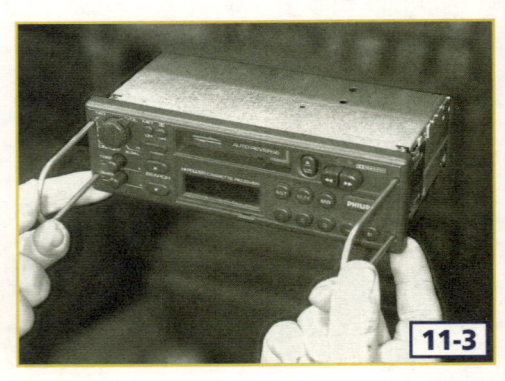

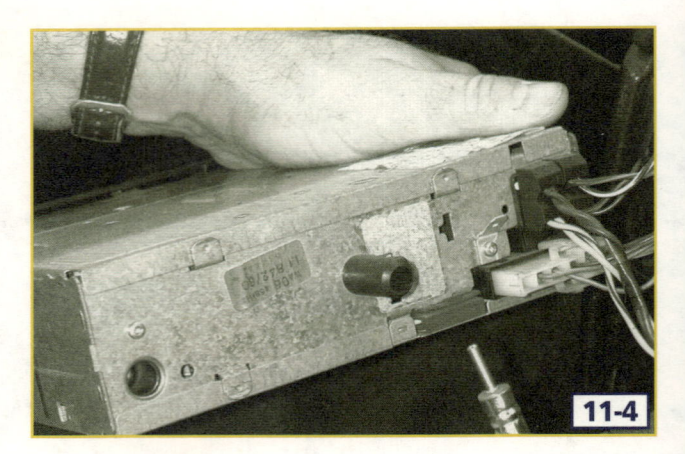

11-3

11-4

☐ **STEP 4:** Disconnect the wiring plugs and aeria/antenna lead.
➔ Where the radio is part of a bigger panel disconnect any other leads and label them.
➔ Remove the unit.

☐ **STEP 5:** Refitting is the reversal of removal.
➔ Ensure the securing clips engage when the unit is pushed home.
➔ Reconnect the battery and enter the security code if applicable.

JOB 12: AIRBAGS AND PRE-TENSIONERS - *essential Safety First!*

SAFETY FIRST!

• **THE WHOLE OF THIS JOB IS *SAFETY FIRST!***

• Read ALL of the information in this Job before working ON OR NEAR air bags and seat belt pre-tensioners.

14-16

Section A: Essential safety notes

A seat belt pre-tensioner is a device which is designed to pull the seat belt tight in the event of a frontal crash.
➜ Air bags and seat belt pre-tensioners all normally contain a pyrotechnic (explosive) charge.
➜ It is MOST IMPORTANT that the whole of this Job is read and understood before you consider how to deal with air bags and seat belt pre-tensioners and the components surrounding them.
➜ The risks of harm from these items are not extreme, but they are real and must be acted upon in an appropriate way.

❐ **STEP A1:** Note the location of all airbags and seat belt pre-tensioners before starting work.
➜ **AIR BAGS:** Air bags may be fitted, for example, in the steering wheel, in front of the passenger seat, in the door or in the side of the seat. There is normally an embossed label at the position of an air bag.
➜ **SEAT BELT PRE-TENSIONERS:** Pre-tensioners may not easily be visible until the seat is partly dismantled. See the vehicle's handbook and also see *Job 3: Front Seats* and *Job 5: Seat belts* in this Chapter.
➜ If you are not sure whether or not a vehicle is fitted with air bags or pre-tensioners, or which type you are dealing with, or you are not fully competent to carry out any of the work described here, consult with, or take the vehicle to the vehicle manufacturer's dealership.

❐ **STEP A2:** All manufacturers recommend that air bags and seat belt pre-tensioners are worked on only by their own, trained personnel.
➜ IF FOR ANY REASON, YOU ARE UNABLE TO COMPLY EXACTLY WITH THE INSTRUCTIONS AND WARNINGS GIVEN HERE, DO NOT HANDLE OR WORK ON THE AIR BAG OR SEAT BELT PRE-TENSIONER COMPONENTS - leave it to the vehicle manufacturer's dealership.

❐ **STEP A3:** You may choose to have a dealer carry out the removal and replacement of air bag and/or pre-tensioner components so that you can carry out other work on the vehicle.
➜ If you choose to drive the vehicle to or from a main dealer with any of the pyrotechnic safety devices removed or disarmed, you will be taking a risk. In the event of a crash, you and/or your passengers will not be able to benefit from the normal function of the safety devices.
➜ Take care not to commit an offence or illegal act. For instance, in the UK, the seat belts must be functional and used by those in the vehicle. Do not contravene any laws or regulations by using the vehicle with safety devices disabled.

❐ **STEP A4:** If a tensioner device or airbag needs to be renewed:
➜ Remember that levering an airbag can cause it to be triggered.
➜ If an airbag or seatbelt tensioner receives a voltage across its terminals it can deploy. Almost any voltage is enough, even the very low current from a test meter or one inducted from an electric welder. Disconnect the battery and the airbags and controller – see *Job 13* - before welding the body shell. Never use a test meter on any airbag circuit.
➜ Make sure the new unit is supplied in its correct safety packaging. It must be kept in its packaging at all times until fitted to the vehicle.
➜ Place the old unit in the safety packaging after removing and fitting the new one.
➜ Immediately take the old unit to the vehicle's main dealer and have them dispose of it
➜ Make sure that you carry out the work when you have access to the main dealer's premises - do not store new or old pyrotechnic safety devices.
➜ If air bags or pre-tensioners have to be moved in a motor vehicle, the tensioner/s should be placed in the (closed) luggage compartment and EMPHATICALLY NOT in the passenger compartment.

❐ **STEP A5:** It must not be assumed that a replaced air bag or seat belt pre-tensioner will work properly.
➜ Take the vehicle to the vehicle's main dealer to have the unit checked and, if necessary, re-programmed.
➜ Take note of the warning in *Step A3*.

❐ **STEP A6: IMPORTANT GENERAL NOTES:** The following notes apply to all seat belt pre-tensioners and air bags, where relevant.
➜ Both air bags and pre-tensioners are referred to as 'safety devices' in the following notes.
➜ Where a safety device has a safety locking mechanism, the safety device should not be removed from a vehicle or handled unless the locking mechanism is used, activated or fitted, as described in the relevant part of this manual.
➜ A belt tensioner which has been dropped on the floor, or dented or damaged in any way must not be used.
➜ On some vehicles, a seat belt on which the tensioner has been 'fired' is not safe to use. On those vehicles, the seat belt cannot be checked for locking once 'fired'.
➜ Do not subject safety devices to blows, drilling, mechanical working or heating.
➜ DO NOT drop safety devices or subject them to impacts. If one is accidentally dropped, it should not be used but returned to the main dealership.
➜ If the safety device has been activated, ALWAYS wait for at least 30 minutes after the activation before carrying out any operations to it - it may be hot enough to burn skin.
➜ If a safety device which has been activated has to

be handled, use protective gloves and goggles.
➔ Wash your hands with soap and water after handling a safety device.

❑ **STEP A7: WHEN WORKING ON THE VEHICLE:** Both air bags and pre-tensioners are referred to as 'safety devices' in the following notes.
➔ Do not subject an area surrounding the safety device to strong impacts. When, during bodywork repairs, for example, the use of a hammer; is necessary, remove the complete unit.
➔ If it is necessary to heat the area surrounding any of the safety devices or to carry out welding or brazing, then the complete safety devices in that area MUST be removed.
➔ Safety devices have been designed to be fitted only on the type and model of vehicle for which they are intended. They cannot be adapted, reused or fitted on other vehicles, but only on those for which they were designed and produced. Any attempts to reuse, adapt or fit safety devices on different types of vehicles could cause serious or fatal injuries to the occupants of the vehicle, either in the case of an accident or in normal usage.

❑ **STEP A8:** IN THE DEPLOYMENT AREA OF THE AIRBAG...: NEVER fit accessories or store objects.
➔ Use ONLY seat covers approved by the vehicle's main dealer.

Section B: Airbags and Seat Belt Pre-tensioners - handling and storage.

This Section is taken from general information on how to handle and store airbags and seat belt pre-tensioners aimed originally at garages and workshops which handle and store only limited numbers, i.e. up to three or four, at any one time.
➔ *Anyone working in domestic premises is strongly advised to follow the guidelines laid down here.*
➔ This information is reproduced from the leaflet INDG280 10/98 C400 produced by the British Health & Safety Executive (HSE), and contains notes on good practice which are not at the time of publication compulsory in the UK but which you may find helpful in considering what you need to do.
➔ Users in other territories must consider laws and regulations which may apply to them.
➔ This information is current at August 1998 and is reproduced with thanks to HSE.

**More and more vehicles are being fitted with a range of airbags and seat belt pre-tensioners. There is therefore an increasing likelihood that you will come across these devices at work.
Even though these devices are designed to save lives, there is the possibility of:**
• **physical injury; and poisoning;**

if they are not handled correctly. While the likelihood of an accident involving an airbag or seat belt pre-tensioner is low, a few simple precautions can be taken to reduce the risks further.

❑ **STEP B1: WHAT TO DO:** Find out from your supplier the UN hazard classification of the airbags and seatbelt pre-tensioners that you may handle.
➔ **If any are classed as UN Hazard Class 1 (the explosives class) and you want to keep them on the premises**, you will need to register for a **Mode B Registered Premises** with your local authority under the Explosives Act 1875. The department dealing with registration varies from region to region, but it is usually the:
• fire brigade;
• trading standards; or
• environmental health

❑ **STEP B2: REGISTRATION:** The HSE recommend that, as a garage or workshop, you should register even if you don't plan to keep these devices, as delays in fitting them to the vehicle may mean they need to be kept on the premises, overnight, for example.

TOP TIP!

• **For airbags or seat belt pre-tensioners which are classed as UN Hazard Class 2 or UN Hazard Class 9**, the HSE recommend that you keep them under similar conditions to those required for Mode B registration.

❑ **STEP B3: STORING AIRBAGS AND SEAT BELT PRE-TENSIONERS:** You can buy cabinets or containers which meet the requirements for Mode B registration. In general terms, these requirements are for a substantial container which:
• has no exposed steel;
• is easy to keep clean; and
• can be closed and locked.
➔ You should keep the container away from:
• oils, paints and other flammable material;
• areas where hot work, such as welding or brazing, is taking place; and
• electricity cables, sockets, distribution boards etc.
➔ Also make sure the container is:
• secured to the wall or floor if possible; and
• kept dry at all times.

❑ **STEP B4: HANDLING AIRBAGS AND SEAT BELT PRE-TENSIONERS:** It is essential that the manufacturer's or supplier's information is checked before starting work on vehicles containing airbags, as procedural differences will occur from make to make.
➔ Never place your head or body close to the front of an un-deployed airbag, especially when fitting it, or removing it from a vehicle.

→ Always carry the airbag module with the trim cover facing away from you.
→ Never place an airbag module, or steering wheel assembly fitted with an airbag, face (trim side) down or with the trim against a hard surface.
→ Never attempt to repair or modify airbag modules.
→ Never expose airbag modules to excessive heat (over 90 ^{0}c), impact, electrical current (including static electricity) or radio transmitters.
→ Always use new components. Return any modules which are damaged or appear suspect to your supplier, **except** where the damage has resulted in the contents of the inflator cartridge being exposed or spilt, in which case obtain specialist advice from your supplier.
→ Return un-deployed airbags to your supplier using the packaging the replacement device is supplied in. If for any reason this packaging is not available, contact your supplier and ask them to provide you with it.
→ Airbags should only be deployed by appropriately trained personnel working to the manufacturer's procedures.
→ Seek the advice of your supplier before disposing of any deployed airbags and seat belt pre-tensioners. Some manufacturers advise that their deployed airbags or seat belt pre-tensioners can be disposed of, or recycled, as normal waste; others recommend that they are treated as hazardous waste.
→ It is illegal to dispose of explosives as normal waste and domestic/commercial waste bins **must not** be used for disposing of **un-deployed** airbags or seat belt pre-tensioners in Class 1.

❐ **STEP B5: TO SEEK MORE COMPREHENSIVE INFORMATION:** Comprehensive guidance for those handling, storing or transporting larger numbers of these devices is provided in the HSE publication: *The handling, storage and transport of airbags and seat belt pre-tensioners* HSG184 HSE Books 1998 ISBN 0 7176 1598 7.
→ HSE priced and free publications are available by mail order from: HSE Books, PO Box 1999, Sudbury, Suffolk CO10 6FS. Tel: 01787 881165 Fax: 01787 313995.
→ HSE priced publications (i.e. those for which a charge is made) are also available from good booksellers.
→ For other enquiries, ring HSE's InfoLine on 0541 545500, or write to HSE's Information Centre, Broad Lane, Sheffield S3 7HQ.

JOB 13: AIRBAG SYSTEM – *deactivate, reactive*.

DEACTIVATING THE AIRBAG SYSTEM

IMPORTANT NOTE: If the vehicle is fitted with a Peugeot alarm/immobiliser system then this system must be disabled before the airbag system – see *Chapter 10, FACT FILE: DISCONNECTING THE BATTERY*.

❐ **STEP 1:** Turn off the ignition, disconnect the battery and remove it from the vehicle so that there is no possibility of the battery leads accidentally contacting the terminals.

❐ **STEP 2:** Leave the vehicle for 30 minutes to ensure that any stored electrical energy in the airbag/pre-tensioner has been dispersed.

❐ **STEP 3:** If the vehicle body shell is to be welded, disconnect all airbag, airbag control unit, pyrotechnic seat belt pre-tensioner and control unit wiring harness leads.

RECONNECTING THE BATTERY

❐ **STEP 4:** As the battery is reconnected, there is a small risk that an airbag or seat belt pre-tensioner may deploy.

❐ **STEP 5:** Before reconnecting the battery, close the vehicle's doors and leave a window open by a small amount.

❐ **STEP 6:** Park the vehicle out of doors and make sure that no-one is standing closer than 10 metres to the vehicle. Reconnect the battery.
→ Open the driver's window and reach into the vehicle from outside when first switching on the ignition.

JOB 14: AIR BAGS – *replacement*.

SAFETY FIRST!

• We strongly advise that, if it is necessary to disconnect an air bag, unless you have the necessary understanding, expertise and safety equipment, the help of a Peugeot dealer or specialist is sought.

→ Air bag systems are activated by sensitive triggers and contain pyrotechnic devices. They can cause serious injury if triggered by mistake!

• You MUST read *Jobs 12 and 13* in this Chapter before carrying out the following work.

Chapter 14 Interior, Trim Job 14

FACT FILE

FACT FILE: HEADER

- Airbags are triggered by a frontal impact of around 20mph. They inflate at very high speed, and so no accessories should ever be mounted in the airbag inflation area.
- Passenger airbags inflate through the top of the dashboard, and nothing should ever be placed on that part of the dashboard.

Section A: Systems explained.

☐ **STEP A1:** The airbag system comprises the airbags themselves, a central control unit and the triggering mechanism.
→ The driver's airbag is situated in the steering wheel boss.
→ The presence of airbags should be indicated by the word 'AIRBAG' embossed in the trim.

☐ **STEP A2:** The airbags are triggered by capacitor discharge. Before working on or near them, disconnect the battery earth terminal and allow thirty minutes for the capacitor to discharge.

Section B: Airbag - remove refit.

See *Job 6* for information on the driver's airbag.

See *Job 3* for information on the side airbags.
→ The side airbags are built into the front seats and work on them should be entrusted to a specialist or Peugeot dealer.

PASSENGER AIRBAG

The passenger airbag is situated under a panel in the top of the dashboard.
→ The airbag is accessed through the glove compartment.

☐ **STEP B1:** Disconnect the battery negative (-) earth/ground terminal. See *Chapter 10, Electrical, Dash, Instruments, Fact File: Disconnecting the Battery* BEFORE doing so!
→ Wait at least thirty minutes before working on the airbag.

☐ **STEP B2:** Some dashboard components have to be removed to gain access to the airbag. They include the following - see *Job 9* for details.
→ Centre console – disconnect the airbag control unit wiring connector.
→ Audio unit.
→ Glove box.
→ Centre and passenger air vents.
→ Dashboard passenger side end cover.

☐ **STEP B3:** The passenger airbag wiring harness runs across the back of the dashboard.
→ Unclip the harness and disconnect the connector.

☐ **STEP B4:** The airbag and its panel are secured by four nuts and seven screws.
→ Remove the fixings, then carefully remove the airbag, taking care not to place strain on its harness.

☐ **STEP B5:** Refit as the reverse of removal.
→ Do NOT reconnect the battery until the airbag refitting is completed.
→ Reconnect the battery and switch on the ignition from OUTSIDE the vehicle, ensuring that no-one is near the airbags and seat belt pre-tensioning equipment.
→ Check that the airbag warning light operates correctly.
→ Then check for correct function of other electrical equipment.

Section C: Airbag control unit.

☐ **STEP C1:** Disconnect the battery negative (-) earth/ground terminal. See *Chapter 10, Electrical, Dash, Instruments, Fact File: Disconnecting the Battery* BEFORE doing so!
→ Wait at least ten minutes before working on the airbag control unit.

☐ **STEP C2:** Remove the centre console – see *Job 8*.

☐ **STEP C3:** Disconnect the wiring connectors.

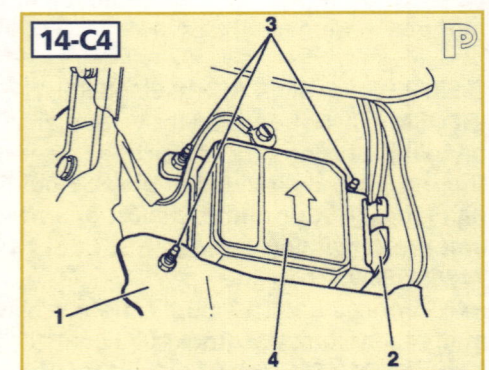

☐ **STEP C4:** Remove the securing nuts (**3**) and remove the airbag control unit (**4**).

☐ **STEP C5:** Refit as the reverse of removal.
→ Do NOT reconnect the battery until the airbag control unit refitting is completed.
→ Reconnect the battery and switch on the ignition from OUTSIDE the vehicle, ensuring that no-one is near the airbags and seat belt pre-tensioning equipment.
→ Check that the airbag warning light operates correctly.
→ Then check for correct function of other electrical equipment.

CHAPTER 15: WIRING DIAGRAMS

HOW TO USE PEUGEOT WIRING DIAGRAMS

We don't pretend to include every wiring diagram for every model of Peugeot covered in this manual. It simply can't be done in a single workshop manual.
• To show every wiring diagram for all of the vehicles covered by this manual would, we estimate, take well over a thousand pages!
• The wiring diagrams shown here are a selection aimed at the (generally more complex) later vehicles. We concentrate on providing you with a selection that might prove useful to you.
• This Chapter concentrates on explaining HOW to use the Peugeot wiring diagrams and shows you WHAT the various codes stand for. You can use this information to enable you to read the Peugeot wiring diagram if you need to purchase one.
• We also include a representative cross-section of typical wiring diagrams, some of which may contain information that is relevant to the vehicle you are working on.

TOP TIP!
❏ STEP 1: •
If you need a Wiring Diagram or Schematic Diagram specific to the vehicle you are working on, you should be able to buy a printed version of the diagram from your Peugeot dealership.
• Ask the Parts Department to order one for you.

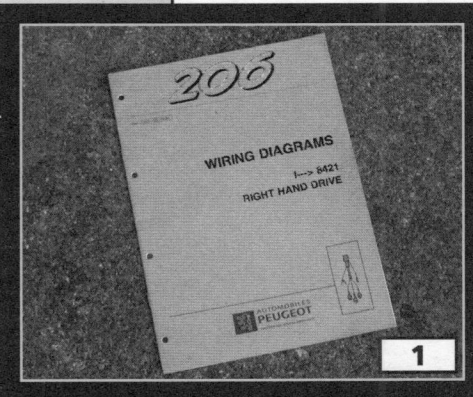

Part 1: Types of Drawing

Following Peugeot's own practice, we feature two types of drawing here - **Wiring Diagrams** and **Schematic Diagrams**.
➔ Peugeot also produce **Installation Diagrams** which indicate component locations, and locations of connectors and other associated electrical items.

❏ **STEP 2: WIRING DIAGRAMS:**
These are the features found on a wiring diagram:
➔ power supplies: +ve and -ve
➔ components (with references, function symbols, without internal electro-mechanical details)
➔ interconnections - connectors with references
➔ earth/ground points with references
➔ splices - with references
➔ harnesses - with references
➔ wire references

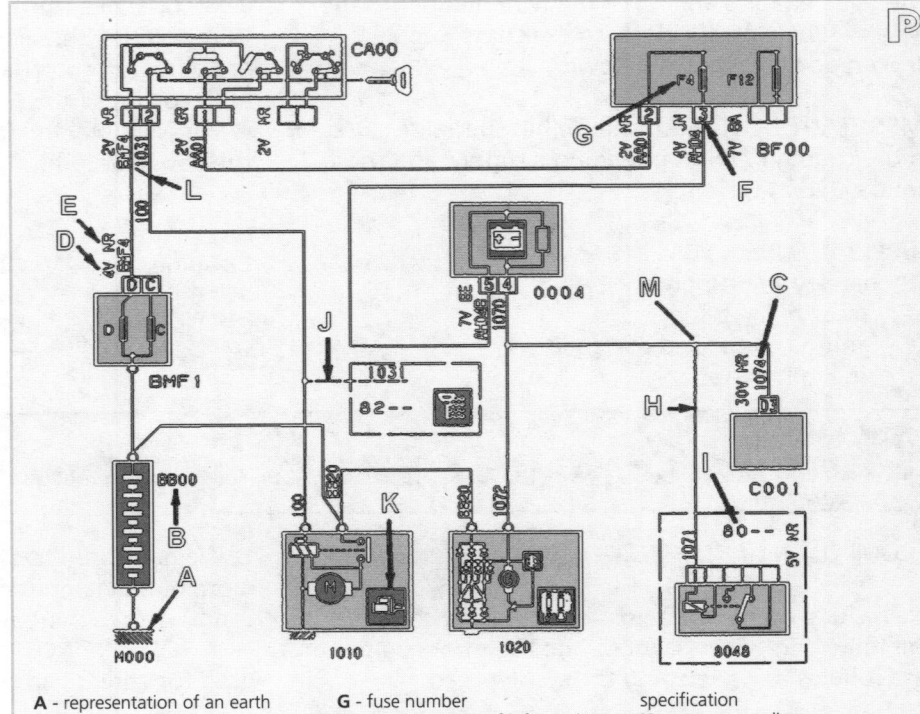

A - representation of an earth point
B - component number
C - wire number
D - connector socket number
E - connector colour
F - connector socket number
G - fuse number
H - representation of information going to another function
I - number of the function concerned
J - representation of a wire depending on vehicle specification
K - component diagram
L - matched wires
M - representation of a splice

15-1

N - harness identification
O - diagram of a fuse box
P - interconnection number
Q - number of interconnection ways
R - interconnection colour
S - representation of a partial interconnection
T - representation of a splice

3

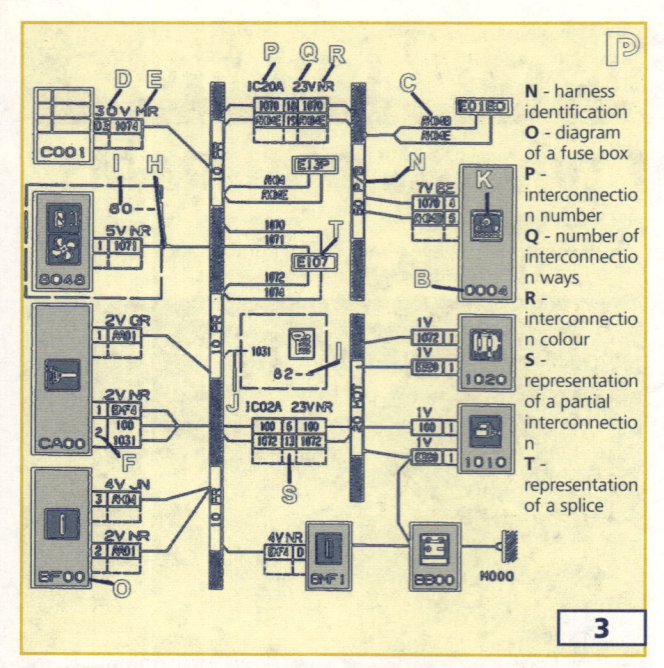

☐ **STEP 3: SCHEMATIC DIAGRAMS:** These are the features found on a schematic diagram:
➔ power supplies: +ve and -ve
➔ components - with references, function symbols and internal electro-mechanical details, except for electronics)
➔ connector sockets on components
➔ earth/ground points
➔ wire lines - with references

WIRE CODING

This code enables linking of the wire number to the type of supply or the electrical function. Supply is broken down as shown below:

IMPORTANT NOTE: Each vehicle has special features in the coding of wires providing a supply, and these are treated as variants.

SUPPLY BEFORE A FUSE:
BB - battery +ve supply
AA - accessory +ve supply
CC - ignition controlled +ve supply
VV - sidelight +ve supply
KK - +ve supply after ignition switched off
➔ Example: **BB2** (type of supply + wire identification number).

SUPPLY AFTER A FUSE:
B - battery +ve supply
A - accessory +ve supply
C - ignition controlled +ve supply
V - sidelight +ve supply
K - + ve supply after ignition switched off
➔ Example: **BO2A** (type of supply + fuse number + wire identification number, figure or letter).

OTHER SPECIFIC SUPPLIES:
M - earth/ground
D - screening
➔ Example: **M262** (type of supply + wire identification number, figure or letter).

OTHER CONNECTIONS BETWEEN COMPONENTS:
➔ The figures on the left repeat the number of the function concerned (see: coding of functions)
➔ The figures on the right represent the identification number in the function

ABBREVIATIONS:
➔ These abbreviations are quoted on the terminals of certain components, such as the ignition switch.
+ **BB** - battery +ve.
+ **AA** - accessory +ve.
+ **CC** - ignition controlled +ve.
+ **KK** - +ve after ignition-off.

WIRE COLOUR CODES
Wire colour abbreviations on the wiring diagrams are based (unsurprisingly) on the French word for each colour.
➔ For example, the French for 'yellow' is 'jaune', and the abbreviation for yellow is **JN**.

BA	White	**MR**	Brown	**VE**	Green
BE	Blue	**NR**	Black	**VI**	Mauve
BG	Beige	**OR**	Orange	**VJ**	
GR	Grey	**RG**	Red		Green/Yellow
JN	Yellow	**RS**	Pink		

Part 2: Componenets and Function Codes

COMPONENT AND FUNCTION CODES – *explained*.

We include a very large list of component codes on the following pages. Even so, the list is not complete and it helps to understand the system used.

FUNCTION CODES: The functions are grouped into eight 'families', as Peugeot call them.
➔ Where a code consists of four numbers, the first two numbers indicate the group shown below.

➔ We have used 'xx' to show that there may be two more numbers, subdividing the category into specific components - there is not room to list them all here.
➔ **IMPORTANT NOTE:** This coding system was not used for earlier vehicles, such as most 205s.

☐ 'FAMILY' 1: POWER UNIT:
10xx - starting, current generation
11xx - ignition system, pre - heating
12xx - 13xx - fuel system, fuel injection
14xx - engine diagnostics
15xx - cooling system
16xx - gearbox, drive shafts
17xx - engine electrical supply - accumulator

☐ 'FAMILY' 2: EXTERIOR LIGHTING AND SIGNALLING:
20xx - rear fog lights
21xx - stop lights
22xx - reversing lights
23xx - direction indicator, side repeater flashers, hazard warnings
24xx - running lights, headlight dim - dip (DIM - DIPS)
25xx - horns
26xx - headlights, tail lights, number plate lights, side lights and indicator lights

☐ 'FAMILY' 3: INTERIOR LIGHTING:
30xx - passenger compartment lighting
31xx - closed compartment lighting

☐ 'FAMILY' 4: DRIVER INFORMATION:
40xx - engine coolant and other water information, current generation
41xx - engine oil information
42xx - engine speed and engine air information
43xx - fuel and pre-heating information
44xx - brake information
45xx - suspension information
46xx - gearbox and transmission information
47xx - audible warning information
48xx - engine check information
49xx - doors etc. information

☐ 'FAMILY' 5: WIPE-WASH:
50xx - windscreen wipers
51xx - windscreen wash
52xx - rear screen wiper
53xx - rear screen wash
54xx, 55xx - headlight wipe - wash, headlight wash

☐ 'FAMILY' 6: ASSISTANCE MECHANISMS:
60xx - electric front windows
61xx - electric rear windows
62xx - central locking
63xx - electrically controlled seats
64 to 6469xx - electrically controlled mirrors
6470 to 6499xx - steering column
65xx - passive seat belts
66xx - headlight height correction
67xx - gearbox and transmission assistance
68xx - sun roof, rear quarters

☐ 'FAMILY' 7: DRIVER AIDS:
70xx - brakes
71xx - variable power steering
72xx - trip computer, clock
73xx - cruise control
74xx - ice warning
75xx - proximity detection
76xx - under inflation detection
77xx - suspension

☐ 'FAMILY' 8: DRIVING COMFORT:
80xx - heating/ventilation, air conditioning
81xx - heating equipment (heated rear screen, glass and mirrors, glass, cigar lighter)

82xx - coded anti-start
83xx - heated seats
84xx - radio, aerial, radio telephone
85xx - ice warning
86xx - anti-theft alarm system
87xx - electrically controlled blind

COMPONENT CODES:
→ All components have a four figure number, such as **4310**.
→ The first two numbers indicate the function.
→ The two following figures identify the component.

ENGINE- OR MODEL-SPECIFIC AREAS OF WIRING DIAGRAMS:
Where a part of a wiring diagram related only to specific engine or model type:
→ The specific section of the diagram is 'cordoned off' in a box with a broken line.
→ The engine or model number is shown in a tinted box.

LETTER PREFIXES:
Vxxxx: The numbers for indicator lamps are preceded by the letter **V** - for example, **V2610**. Where equipment supplies an electrical feed, the suffixes are:
→ **BB00:** battery
→ **BB10:** Battery +ve unit
→ **CA00:** Ignition switch
→ **BF00:** Fuse box
Cxxxx: Connectors which have a particular function (e.g. testing a function) are numbered as components with the letter C in front e.g.: **C1300**.
Mxxxx: is used for earth/ground points:
→ the letter **M** is used followed by an identifying number
→ examples: **M2A, M90C**
Exxxx: Splice numbering: The letter **E** is used followed by an identifying number
→ examples : **E028, E002**
→ An application of an alphabetical index if the splices are identical would be: **E005A**, and **E005B**.

NUMBERING OF INTERCONNECTIONS:
ICxx: The letters **IC** are used followed by a 2-digit identifying number.
→ Application of an alphabetical index if the interconnections are identical, e.g: **1C20, IC05A, IC05B**.

NUMBERING OF BRIDGE BLOCK CONNECTORS:
Bxxx: The letter **B** is used, followed by a 3 figure number, e.g: **B001**.
→ Application of an alphabetical index if terminals are identical e.g: **B003A, B003B**.

Part 3: Fuses

☐ **STEP 4:** See *Chapter 10, Job 8, Section J: Fuses* for information on fuse box locations.
➔ These are typical fuse box arrangements.
➔ On most models, there are also two more fuse boxes in the engine bay, a 'maxi-fuse' unit and one containing more regular fuses.

4

FUSE BOX IN PASSENGER COMPARTMENT			
Fuse No.	Amps	Components	Power source
F1	SH	Pretensioner unit/front airbags/side air bags/Built-in Systems Interface supply	ignition controlled +ve
F2	5A	Instrument panel	
F3		Free	
F4	5A	built-in systems interface	
F5		free	
F6	5A	engine management control unit/immobiliser	+ battery/ignition controlled +ve
F7	15A	free	
F8	10A	coolant temperature unit/instrument panel/hazard warning/clock /multifunction display/courtesy light	
F9	5A	built-in systems interface	
F10		free	
F11	10A	left-hand brake light/3rd brake light	ignition controlled +ve
F12	10A	right-hand brake light	
F13		free	+ battery
F14	30A	rear electric window	
F15	20A	luggage compartment illumination/tow-bar supply	
F16		free	
F17		free	
F18	10A	number plate light/lighter illumination/clock illumination/multifunction display lighting/instrument panel illumination/heater panel illumination/radio illumination/ashtray illumination/automatic transmission selector illumination	sidelights +
F19	5A	rear fog lights	+ rear fog light
F20		free	input/outlet
F21		free	
F22	10A	glove box illumination/map reading lamp/courtesy lamp/clock or multifunction display/instrument panel/on-board navigation system/rear electric window/rain sensor/charge warning light	accessories +ve
F23A	20A	lighter	accessories +ve
F23B	20A	lighter	+ battery
F24A	15A	radio	accessories +ve
F24B	20A	radio	+ battery
F25	20A	screen wiper/rear wiper	accessories +ve
F26		free	
F27	5A	built-in systems interface	
F28		free	
R1	5A		
R2	10A		
R3	30A		
R4	20A		
R5	15A		
MAXI-FUSES (IN ENGINE BAY)			
MF1	20A	lighting switch	+ battery
MF2	80A	passenger compartment fuse box (accessories +ve, ignition controlled +ve)	+ battery
MF3	40A	passenger compartment fuse box (+ve after ignition switched off)	+ battery
MF4	40A	passenger compartment fuse box (+ battery)	+ battery
FUSE BOX IN ENGINE BAY			
F1		free	+ battery
F2	30A	anti-lock brakes	+ battery
F3	30A	engine cooling system	+ battery
F4	30A	anti-lock brakes	+ battery
F5	30A	engine cooling system	+ battery
F6	15A	long-range headlights	+ battery
F7		free	+ battery
F8		free	+ battery
F9	10A	fuel pump	separate fuse
F10	15A	engine cooling system	separate fuse
F11	5A	oxygen sensor	separate fuse
F12	10A	left-hand main beam headlight	separate fuse
F13	10A	right-hand main beam headlight	separate fuse
F14	10A	left-hand dipped beam headlight	separate fuse
F15	10A	right-hand dipped beam headlight	separate fuse

Part 4: List of Component and Function Codes

TOP TIP!

- If the component or function number you require is not listed here, please read *Part 2: Components And Function Codes* for an explanation of how the codes 'work'.

B001 - mixed bridge block 1
BB00 - battery
BB01 - assembly battery rear
BB02 - assembly battery lower front
BB03 - assembly battery upper front
BB10 - battery + ve control unit
BF00 - fusebox (passenger compartment)
BF01 - fuse box (engine compartment)
BF02 - fuse box (luggage compartment)
BH12 - l2 fusebox (passenger compartment)
BH28 - 28 fuse box (passenger compartment)
BMF1 - maxi fuse unit
BMF2 - maxi fuse unit
BMF3 - maxi fuse unit
BMF4 - maxi fuse unit
BM27 - slave unit 27 engine fuses
BM34 - slave unit 34 engine fuses
BSI1 - intelligent slave unit
C00l - diagnostic connector
C002 - breakdown wire connector
C004 - instrument panel diagnostic connector
C1030 - test connector - engine running information
C1042 - general circuit breaker optional connector
C1100 - ignition test connector
C1105 - ignition suppression connector
C1110 - ignition adjustment connector for idle
C1200 - injection test connector
C1250 - emission control adjustment connector
C1260 - supply pump fuse holder connector
C1265 - carb. heating resistor fuse-holder connector
C1270 - EGR test connector
C1300 – injection/ignition test connector
C1310 - ignition/injection fuse holder connector
C1360 - oxygen sensor heater fuse holder connector
C1400 - TDC connector
C1450 - system development connector
C1500 - fan operation test connector
C1630 - BVA test connector
C1700 - electronic management test connector
C200 - caravan socket connector
C2310 - driving school dual control connector
C2600 - front fog-light fuse holder connector
C310 - caravan lighting battery positive supply connector
C4640 - fuse-holder connector for supply to chronograph
C6235 - door locking test connector
C6301 - test connector storing in memory seat
C6540 - pre-tensioning seat belts test connector
C6560 - test connector airbag
C6570 - test connector airbags + pre-tensioners
C6640 - ride height circuit bleeding connector
C6860 - electric hood test connector
C7000 - anti-lock brake test connector
C7001 - ABS power fuse holder connector
C7050 - traction control test connector
C7100 - variable power steering test connector
C7215 - multifunction screen diagnostic connector
C7710 - suspension test connector
C8000 - heater test connector
C8201 - coded anti-start device connector
C8400 - radio battery + ve connector
C8600 - test connector - anti-theft alarm system
C861 - connector fuel system anti-theft alarm system
C8630 - protection unit diagnostic connector
CA00 - ignition sw.
CP00 - socket 12v rear
CT00 - steering wheel rotary connector
DRA0 - shielded earth
ECV0 - assembly control on the steering wheel
MF175 - maxi fuse engine compartment 175A
PS00 - connector board
PSF0 - connection board - fuse box (passenger compartment)
PSF1 - connection board - fuse box (engine compartment)
PSF2 - connection board - fuse box (luggage compartment)
V0004 - stop warning light
V1000 - load warning light
V1001 - traction batteries correct charge light
V1002 - traction batteries discharged warning light
V1017 - 12v converter fault warning light
V1100 - ignition test warning light
V1150 - pre-heat warning light
V1200 - injection test warning light
V1203 - pump cut-off light
V1300 - engine diagnosis warning light
V1700 - temporary fault warning light
V1701 - forward drive warning light
V1702 - reverse drive warning light
V1703 - insulation fault warning light
V2000 - rear fog light warning light
V2010 - warning light front fog lights
V2300 - hazard warning light
V2310 - right or left flasher indicator light
V2320 - LH direction indicator warning light
V2330 - RH direction indicator warning light
V2600 - sidelight warning light
V2610 - dipped beam warning light
V2620 - main beam warning light
V2660 - front fog light warning light
V4010 - coolant low level warning light
V4017 - battery electrolyte level warning light
V4020 - engine coolant maximum temp. warning light
V4040 - screen wash fluid low level warning light
V4050 - water in diesel fuel warning light
V4110 - engine oil low pressure warning light
V4120 - engine oil low level warning light
V4130 - engine oil high temp. warning maximum
V4200 - choke warning light
V4205 - air cleaner blocked warning light
V4300 - low fuel level warning light
V4400 - parking brake warning light
V4410 - brake fluid low level warning light
V4420 - handbrake/low brake fluid level warning light
V4430 - brake pad wear warning light
V4440 - blown bulb warning light
V4600 - gear lever position warning light
V4610 - gearbox oil temp. warning light
V4700 - door open warning light
V4730 - seat belt buckled warning light
V4800 - catalytic converter overheating warning light
V6235 - deadlocking pilot light
V6560 - air bag warning light front
V6640 - ride height correction fluid low level warning light
V6700 - differential lock test warning light
V6709 - reduction gear change warning light
V7000 - ABS diagnostic warning light
V7001 - ABS operational indicator light
V7050 - traction control diagnostic warning light
V7060 - traction control operation light
V7310 - cruise control indicator light
V7700 - suspension diagnostic warning light
V8018 - additional heating low fuel level warning light
V8110 - heated rear screen indicator light
1000 - safety sw.(es) starting
1005 - starter inhibitor relay
1010 - starter
1020 - alternator
1030 - engine running signal relay
1040 - general maintenance relay
1041 - emergency stop sw.
1042 - general relay
1043 - re-setting push button
1044 - unit diode
1086 - alarm starter cut-off relay
1100 - distributor
1101 - engine coolant thermistor for advance module
1102 - advance module
1104 - advance correction solenoid
1105 - ignition amplifier module
1110 - ignition distributor

CHAPTER 15 Wiring Diagrams

15-5

CHAPTER 15 Wiring Diagrams

1115 - cylinder reference sensor
1120 - knock detector
1125 - accelerator pedal sw.
1127 - ignition supply relay.
1130 - ignition control unit
1131 - cylinder 1 ignition coil
1132 - cylinder 2 ignition coil
1133 - cylinder 3 ignition coil
1134 - cylinder 4 ignition coil
1135 - ignition coil
1136 - ignition coil capacitor
1140 - emission control module for carb.
1145 - throttle opening solenoid valve
1150 - pre-heat control unit
1155 - pre-heat relay
1156 - post-heat relay
1157 - post-heat thermal sw.
1160 - glow plugs
1161 - no.1 cylinder glow plug
1162 - no.2 cylinder glow plug
1163 - no.3 cylinder glow plug
1164 - no.4 cylinder glow plug
1190 - water circuit heater
1200 - fuel pump relay
1201 - injection pump relay
1202 - tachymetric relay
1203 - inertia sw.
1204 - impact safety relay
1205 - fuel pump fuse
1206 - decanting pump control unit
1207 - decanting pump
1208 - diesel injection pump (advance corrector, fuel cut-off solenoid)
1209 - scavenge pump
1210 - fuel pump
1211 - fuel gauge pump
1212 - air tank solenoid
1213 - air pump relay
1214 - econoscope
1215 - purge canister solenoid valve
1216 - canister simulation resistor
1217 - canister bleed cut-off solenoid
1218 - ignition advance cut-off solenoid
1219 - throttle potentiometer injection, auto. transmission
1220 - engine coolant temp. sensor
1221 - diesel thermistor
1222 - accelerometer
1223 - injection air solenoid valve
1224 - absorber closing solenoid valve
1225 - idling regulation stepper motor (MMBA)
1226 - idle regulation motor and idle sw.
1227 - fuel tank pressure sensor
1228 - idle regulation motor and idle sw. + Hall effect sensor
1229 - turbo regulator solenoid with variable resistance
1230 - supplementary air device
1231 - auto. transmission idling speed solenoid unit
1232 - idle maintaining solenoid valve
1233 - turbocharger pressure regulation solenoid valve
1234 - carb. damper solenoid valve
1235 - carb. breather solenoid valve
1236 - overrun cut-off solenoid valve
1237 - pulsair solenoid valve
1238 - 2 volume VASC solenoid
1239 - idling regulation solenoid valve
1240 - induction air temp. sensor
1241 - pulsair pump
1242 - pulsair relay
1243 - variable timing solenoid valve
1244 - EGR proportional solenoid valve
1245 - altitude sw.

1246 - EGR function supply relay
1247 - EGR coolant thermal sw.
1248 - EGR calibration resistor
1249 - load lever potentiometer (EGR)
1250 - EGR exhaust gas recycling control unit
1251 - EGR vacuum pump
1252 - diesel advance corrector relay
1253 - all or nothing solenoid valve (EGR)
1254 - EGR load lever sw.
1255 - fuel cut-off solenoid valve
1256 - advance solenoid valve (diesel)
1257 - - flow solenoid (diesel)
1258 - + flow solenoid (diesel)
1259 - + flow solenoid (diesel)
1260 - injector needle lift sensor
1261 - accelerator pedal position sensor
1262 - motorised butterfly
1265 - carb. heater thermal sw.
1266 - carb. heater relay
1269 - carb. heating resistor relay
1270 - carb. or throttle housing heater resistor
1271 - cut-off solenoid valve
1272 - cut-off solenoid assembly, carb. heater resistor
1273 - oil breather re-heat resistor
1275 - carb.
1280 - long 2 volume VASC solenoid
1281 - short 2 volume VASC solenoid
1301 - auto. transmission information relay (injection)
1302 - injection and supply relay
1303 - injection and ignition supply relay
1304 - engine management multi-function double relay
1305 - mixture potentiometer
1306 - shunt relay auto. gearbox
1307 - power multi-function double relay
1308 - engine oil pressure sensor
1309 - turbocharger air thermistor
1310 - air flow sensor
1311 - turbo pressure sensor
1312 - induction air pressure sensor
1313 - engine speed sensor
1314 - altitude sensor
1315 - injection resistor
1316 - throttle position sensor
1317 - diesel pump lever position sensor
1318 - throttle sw. unit
1319 - injection coding resistor
1320 - engine management control unit
1321 - sensor high pressure diesel
1322 - regulator high pressure diesel
1323 - high temp. sensor (exhaust gas)
1324 - proportional dosing solenoid valve
1326 - injection unit supply fuse
1327 - cam position sensor (diesel pump)
1328 - rotor position sensor (diesel pump)
1329 - slide position sensor (diesel pump)
1330 - injector
1331 - injector cylinder no. 1
1332 - injector cylinder no. 2
1333 - injector cylinder no. 3
1334 - injector cylinder no. 4
1335 - injector cylinder no. 5
1336 - injector cylinder no. 6
1337 - injector cylinder no. 7
1338 - injector cylinder no. 8
1339 - injector cylinder no. 9
1340 - injector cylinder no. 10
1342 - motor multi-function control unit
1345 - oxygen sensor heater relay
1348 - oxygen sensor heater fuse
1350 - oxygen sensor - front
1351 - oxygen sensor - rear
1400 - TDC sensor

1500 - fan relay
1501 - cooling fan fuse
1502 - left hand fan supply relay
1503 - right hand fan supply relay
1504 - left and right hand fan series supply relay
1505 - cooling fan thermal sw.
1506 - two-speed cooling fan resistor
1507 - fan control (coolant) temp. sender unit via ECU
1508 - low speed fan supply relay
1509 - high speed fan supply relay
1510 - fan
1511 - RH fan
1512 - LH fan
1515 - LH interference suppression filter
1516 - RH interference suppression filter
1520 - engine post-cooling thermal sw.
1525 - engine post-cooling relay
1526 - engine post-cooling time sw.
1530 - post-cooling device shunt
1550 - turbo coolant pump
1551 - turbo coolant pump fuse
1555 - turbo coolant pump control relay
1600 - selector lever position sw.
1601 - one-touch control lever sensor
1606 - parking position buzzer supply relay
1607 - auto transmission selector and display light supply relay
1613 - auto transmission engine speed sensor
1615 - pressure sensor auto. gearbox
1620 - vehicle speed sensor
1621 - vehicle speed sensor auto. gearbox
1625 - vehicle speed interface module
1630 - auto. transmission control unit
1632 - pedal position contact
1635 - auto. gearbox electro-hydraulic block
1636 - auto transmission position sensor
1637 - auto. gearbox kickdown sw.
1638 - auto transmission lever blocking actuator
1639 - accelerator pedal foot off contact
1640 - auto. transmission programme selector
1642 - gear lever blocking actuator control relay
1643 - key blocking actuator control relay
1644 - key blocking actuator
1700 - electric management control unit
1701 - temp. monitoring module -lower front battery voltage
1702 - temp. monitoring module -upper front battery voltage
1703 - temp. monitoring module -rear battery voltage
1704 - relay housing
1705 - electronic tool kit
1713 -accelerator potentiometer
1714 - energy gauge
1718 - electric motor cooling fan control thermistor
1722 - battery electrolyte cooling fan control thermistor
1725 - additional heating
1726 - additional heating fuel pump
1727 - traction battery coolant pump
1732 - battery heating relay
1733 - battery heating resistor
1740 - electric traction motor
1746 - electric motor cooling fan
1747 - charging socket
1748 - battery charging socket unit
0002 - lighting and signalling sw.
2000 - rear fog light sw.
2001 - lighting/wiping stalk
2002 - driving school buzzer (Germany)

2003 - driving school instructor's control unit
2004 - driving school jack socket (Germany)
2005 - rear fog light relay
2006 - driving school sw. (Germany)
2007 - driving school footwell lighting (Germany)
2010 - rear fog lights (left side)
2011 - rear fog lights centre
2015 - rear fog lights (right side)
2016 - rear fog lights control unit
2100 - stop light sw.
2110 - additional stop lights
2111 - additional stop lights (left side)
2112 - additional stop lights (right side)
2200 - reverse light sw.
2202 - reverse drive control sw.
2210 - LH reverse light sw.
2215 - RH reverse light sw.
2300 - hazard warning sw.
2305 - flasher unit
2310 - direction indicator sw.
2320 - LH front direction indicator light
2325 - RH front direction indicator light
2330 - LH rear direction indicator light (if separated)
2335 - RH rear direction indicator light (if separated)
2340 - LH side repeater flasher
2345 - RH side repeater flasher
2400 - sidelight day running lights line relay
2401 - dipped beam day running lights relay
2402 - shunt running light relay
2410 - dipped beam relay
2411 - dim-dip relay
2415 - dim-dip resistor
2500 - horn button
2501 - horn button in steering wheel
2505 - air horn compressor relay
2510 - air horn compressor
2520 - horns
2521 - low note horn
2522 - high note horn
2523 - pedestrian buzzer
2525 - air horn fuse
2530 - siren unit (police)
2531 - police siren sw.
2532 - day/night police siren sw.
2535 - siren speaker (police)
2600 - light rotator
2605 - dipped beam relay
2606 - main beam relay
2610 - LH headlight
2615 - RH headlight
2620 - front sidelights (left side)
2625 - front sidelights (right side)
2630 - LH tail light
2631 - RH tail light on boot lid
2632 - LH tail light on boot lid
2633 - number plate RH light
2634 - shunt jack socket
2635 - RH tail light
2636 - number plate light
2637 - jack plug for rotating light
2638 - rotating light
2639 - rotating light sw.
2640 - LH front door marker light
2641 - front right side marker
2642 - front left side marker
2643 - rear right side marker
2644 - rear left side marker
2645 - RH front door marker light
2650 - LH rear door marker light
2651 - police car bar across roof
2655 - RH rear door marker light
2656 - rear facing flashing stop lights
2657 - rear facing flashing stop lights central unit
2658 - rear roof light sw.
2659 - sw. orange light
2660 - front fog light sw.
2662 - front fog light inhibitor relay front
2665 - front fog light relay front
2670 - LH front fog light
2675 - RH front fog light
2680 - long range driving light sw.
2685 - long range driving light relay
2690 - left hand long range driving light
2695 - right hand long range driving light
3000 - door aperture sw.-front door (left side)
3001 - door aperture sw.-front door (right-side)
3002 - door aperture sw.-rear door (left side)
3003 - door aperture sw.-rear door (right side)
3004 - lighting timer unit
3005 - courtesy light timer relay
3006 - courtesy light sw.
3010 - front courtesy light
3012 - courtesy light (front LH)
3013 - courtesy light (front RH)
3015 - roof console + integral functions
3019 - rear courtesy light sw.
3020 - rear courtesy light
3022 - courtesy light (rear LH)
3023 - courtesy light (rear RH)
3024 - LH courtesy light
3025 - RH courtesy light
3029 - centre courtesy light sw.
3030 - central courtesy light
3031 - front RH reading light
3032 - front LH reading light
3033 - rear RH reading light
3034 - rear LH reading light
3035 - footwell illumination
3040 - LH front door tread light
3042 - LH rear door tread light
3045 - RH front door tread light
3047 - RH rear door tread light
3050 - lighting rheostat
3051 - heater control panel light
3052 - console light
3053 - cigar lighter light
3054 - ashtray light
3055 - radio cover control light
3056 - ashtray cover control light
3060 - vanity mirror light (driver's side)
3061 - vanity mirror light (passenger's side)
3065 - map reading light
3070 - selector lever light
3075 - ignition sw. light
3080 - police visor light
3085 - centre courtesy light sw. passenger white light
3086 - centre courtesy light sw. passenger blue light
3087 - parking lights sw.
3088 - parking lights relay
3100 - boot sw.
3105 - boot (or luggage compartment) light
3110 - glove box light sw.
3115 - glove box light
3120 - sw. engine
3121 - engine compartment light
3125 - luggage compartment light relay
3126 - luggage compartment light timer relay
0004 - instrument panel
4000 - instrument panel centralised electronic module
4010 - engine coolant level sw.
4015 - engine coolant level unit
4020 - engine coolant thermal sw.
4025 - temp. sensor - engine coolant thermal sw. (gauge)
4026 - coolant temp. gauge
4030 - coolant thermistor (gauge)
4035 - pre-warning heat sw.
4050 - water in fuel sensor
4060 - battery charge indicator
4100 - temp. gauge + engine oil level
4101 - engine oil temp. display
4102 - engine oil level gauge
4103 - temp. sensor engine oil
4104 - engine oil pressure sensor
4105 - engine oil pressure gauge
4106 - pressure sensor/oil pressure sw.
4110 - oil pressure sw.
4111 - temp. sensor + engine oil thermal sw.
4120 - engine oil level sensor
4130 - engine oil thermal sw.
4200 - choke sw.
4205 - air cleaner pressure sw.
4210 - tachometer
4240 - induction pressure sensor
4241 - turbocharge pressure gauge
4300 - low fuel level sw.
4310 - fuel gauge
4311 - electronic damping fuel pump
4315 - fuel gauge (transmitter)
4320 - tank cap present sw.
4330 - fuel flowmeter(trip computer)
4335 - fuel consumption interface unit
4340 - fuel consumption
4341 - current fuel consumption indicator
4400 - handbrake sw.
4401 - parking brake warning light diode
4402 - diode buzzer reverse
4405 - vacuum pressure sw.. control of brake servo vacuum
4410 - brake fluid level sw.
4420 - ABS warning light relay
4430 - front left brake pad wear contact
4431 - front right brake pad wear contact
4432 - rear left brake pad wear contact
4433 - rear right brake pad wear contact
4440 - bulb failure detection control unit
4445 - blown bulb relay (warning light)
4450 - brake warning light relay (Australia)
4500 - ride height correction fluid level sw.
4605 - selection or programme display
4610 - gearbox oil thermal sw.
4630 - speedometer
4635 - tachograph electronic converter
4700 - LH front door lock sw. (door open detection) (if not 3000)
4701 - RH front door lock sw. (door open detection) (if not 3001)
4702 - LH rear door lock sw. (door open detection) (if not 3002)
4703 - RH rear door lock sw. (door open detection) (if not 3003)
4704 - bonnet closed sw. (bonnet open detection)
4705 - boot lock sw. (boot open detection)
4710 - headlight flash relay
4715 - door open buzzer
4716 - parking brake position reminder buzzer
4720 - lights on buzzer relay
4725 - lights on + ignition key in buzzer relay
4730 - seat belt sw.
4735 - seat belt buzzer relay
4740 - overspeeding buzzer
4750 - anti-lock braking buzzer relay
4760 - ignition key in lock sw. (buzzer control)
4765 - ignition key in lock buzzer relay

CHAPTER 15 Wiring Diagrams

- 4790 - electric motor reminder buzzer
- 4800 - catalytic converter temp. sensor
- 4805 - catalytic converter temp. control unit
- 4900 - anomaly detector indicator
- 4905 - points matrix
- 4990 - charging flap open check contact
- 0005 - screen wiper sw.
- 5000 - windscreen wipe/wash sw. (if not 5)
- 5001 - rain sensor
- 5002 - rain sensor control relay
- 5003 - rain sensor speed control relay
- 5004 - auto. windscreen wiper control unit
- 5005 - windscreen wiper relay
- 5006 - front/rear wiper relay
- 5010 - windscreen wiper timer
- 5015 - windscreen wiper motor
- 5016 - parking stop unit
- 5020 - wash fluid heater
- 5021 - pipe heater
- 5100 - windscreen wash pump
- 5105 - heated windscreen wash jets
- 5110 - wash liquid level sensor
- 5115 - front/rear screen wash pump
- 5200 - tailgate wipe/wash control (if not 5)
- 5202 - rear screen wiper sw.
- 5203 - rear screen wash sw.
- 5205 - tailgate wiper relay
- 5210 - rear screen wiper timer
- 5211 - rear screen wiper motor (left side)
- 5212 - rear screen wiper motor (right side)
- 5215 - rear screen wiper motor
- 5300 - rear screen wash pump
- 5400 - headlight wash timer relay
- 5405 - headlight wash pump
- 5406 - headlight wash sw.
- 6000 - LH door LH window lift sw.
- 6001 - LH window lift front sw.
- 6002 - RH window lift front sw.
- 6005 - RH door RH window lift sw.
- 6010 - RH door LH window lift sw.
- 6015 - LH door RH window lift sw.
- 6016 - window lift circuit diode + sun roof
- 6020 - front window lift + sun roof relay
- 6021 - window lift relay
- 6025 - window lift + sun roof supply re-connection relay
- 6030 - one touch electric window control unit
- 6031 - passenger's one touch front electric window motor + control unit
- 6032 - driver's one touch front electric window motor + control unit
- 6033 - safety auto-reverse control unit
- 6034 - safety auto-reverse sensor
- 6035 - safety auto-reverse window motor (on the driver's side)
- 6036 - window lift control board rear-view mirror (on the driver's side)
- 6037 - window lift control board rear-view mirror (passenger's side)
- 6038 - safety auto-reverse window motor (passenger's side)
- 6040 - window lift motor (front LH)
- 6041 - sensor interior handle (on the driver's side)
- 6042 - sensor exterior door handle (on the driver's side)
- 6043 - sensor interior handle (passenger's side)
- 6044 - sensor exterior door handle (passenger's side)
- 6045 - window lift motor (front RH)
- 6100 - LH rear window lift rear sw.
- 6101 - right rear window lift unit + motor (one-touch)
- 6102 - left rear window lift unit + motor (one-touch)
- 6105 - RH rear window lift rear sw.
- 6110 - LH rear window lift front sw.
- 6115 - RH rear window lift front sw.
- 6120 - rear window lift inhibitor sw.
- 6121 - rear function locking relay
- 6122 - rear window lift inhibitor sw. + alarm cut-off
- 6125 - rear window lift relay
- 6126 - rear window lift relay on + aa
- 6130 - window lift motor (rear LH)
- 6131 - right rear window lift unit + motor
- 6132 - left rear window lift unit + motor
- 6133 - safety auto-reverse window motor rear LH door
- 6134 - safety auto-reverse window motor rear RH door
- 6135 - window lift motor (rear RH)
- 6200 - front LH door open sw.
- 6202 - front LH door lock assembly
- 6203 - diode sw. insulation front door/rear
- 6205 - front RH door open sw.
- 6207 - front RH door lock assembly
- 6210 - rear LH door open sw.
- 6212 - rear LH door lock assembly
- 6215 - rear RH door open sw.
- 6216 - boot lid open sw.
- 6217 - rear RH door lock assembly
- 6218 - RH rear hinged door-lock assembly
- 6219 - door unlocking safety relay
- 6220 - door locking sw.
- 6221 - RH rear hinged door locking sw.
- 6230 - infra red door locking receiver
- 6231 - high frequency receiver for central locking
- 6235 - central locking control unit
- 6237 - boot locking sw.
- 6240 - LH front door lock motor
- 6242 - front LH door deadlock motor
- 6245 - RH front door lock motor
- 6247 - front RH door deadlock motor
- 6250 - LH rear door lock motor
- 6252 - rear LH door deadlock motor
- 6253 - LH rear hinged door locking motor
- 6255 - RH rear door lock motor
- 6256 - rear door lock motor
- 6257 - rear RH door deadlock motor
- 6258 - RH rear hinged door locking motor
- 6259 - RH rear hinged door deadlocking motor
- 6260 - boot or tailgate lock motor
- 6261 - tailgate locking motor
- 6265 - fuel filler flap lock motor
- 6266 - charging flap locking motor
- 6300 - driver's seat sliding sw.
- 6301 - control unit for memorising seat and mirror positions
- 6302 - driver's seat adjustment assembly
- 6303 - passenger's seat adjustment assembly
- 6304 - unit position memorising passenger's seat
- 6305 - passenger's seat sliding sw.
- 6307 - keypad for memorising seat position
- 6308 - presence sensor
- 6310 - driver's seat raising sw.
- 6311 - sw. front seat driver's seat
- 6312 - sw. rear seat cushion driver's seat
- 6315 - passenger's seat raising sw.
- 6320 - driver's seat slide motor
- 6321 - slide position sensor (driver's seat)
- 6322 - height adjustment motor (driver's seat)
- 6323 - height adjustment motor (passenger's seat)
- 6325 - passenger's seat slide motor
- 6331 - driver's seat height position sensor
- 6332 - driver's seat cushion front height motor
- 6333 - seat cushion position sensor (driver's seat)
- 6334 - driver's seat cushion rear height motor
- 6335 - seat cushion position sensor rear driver's seat
- 6337 - passenger's seat cushion front height motor
- 6339 - passenger's seat cushion rear height motor
- 6340 - driver's seat backrest sw.
- 6341 - seatback position sensor (driver's seat)
- 6345 - passenger's seat backrest sw.
- 6346 - centre armrest sw.
- 6347 - centre armrest motor
- 6350 - driver's seat backrest inclination motor
- 6355 - passenger's seat backrest inclination motor
- 6360 - driver's seat adjustment relay
- 6365 - passenger's seat adjustment relay
- 6366 - slide high speed motor - passenger's seat
- 6367 - slide high speed motor - driver's seat
- 6370 - adjustment pump + solenoid valve assembly - driver's seat
- 6371 - passenger's seat backrest inflation contact
- 6372 - driver's seat backrest inflation contact
- 6373 - driver's seat front stop position micro sw.
- 6374 - seat back locked-position micro sw. - driver's seat
- 6375 - adjustment pump + solenoid valve assembly - passenger's seat
- 6376 - passenger's seat front stop position micro sw.
- 6377 - seat back folded position micro sw. - passenger's seat
- 6378 - seat back locked position micro sw. - passenger's seat
- 6379 - passenger's seat memorised position micro sw.
- 6380 - rear seat cushion adjustment sw.
- 6381 - rear seat adjustment motor
- 6382 - seat adjustment sw. rear RH
- 6383 - seat adjustment sw. rear LH
- 6384 - seat adjustment motor rear RH
- 6385 - seat adjustment motor rear LH
- 6386 - retractable head-rest sw. rear RH
- 6387 - retractable head-rest sw. rear LH
- 6388 - head-rest motor rear RH
- 6389 - head-rest motor rear LH
- 6390 - retractable head-rest sw., rear
- 6391 - seat adjustment assembly rear RH
- 6392 - seat adjustment assembly rear LH
- 6400 - driver's side rear view mirror control
- 6405 - passenger's side rear view mirror control
- 6406 - rear view mirror control
- 6407 - fold back rear view mirror unit
- 6410 - driver's side rear view mirror (electric mirror/heated mirror)
- 6415 - passenger's side rear view mirror (electric mirror/heated mirror)
- 6420 - sw. fold-back mirror
- 6421 - reverse indexing unit
- 6422 - reverse indexing sw.
- 6430 - electric interior mirror
- 6435 - anti-dazzle unit
- 6440 - electro chrome interior mirror
- 6470 - steering wheel adjustment sw.
- 6471 - steering wheel height adjustment motor

15-8

6472 - steering wheel depth adjustment motor
6500 - driver's passive restraint sw.
6505 - passenger's passive restraint sw.
6510 - driver's passive restraint control unit
6515 - passenger's passive restraint control unit
6520 - passive restraint time sw. relay
6530 - driver's passive restraint motor
6535 - passenger's passive restraint motor
6540 - driver's pre-tensioning seat belt control unit
6541 - passenger's pre-tensioning seat belt control unit
6542 - pre-tensioning seat belt control unit
6543 - presence detector passenger
6544 - presence detector rear RH
6545 - presence detector rear LH
6560 - control unit airbag
6561 - air bag auto interference suppression control unit
6562 - module airbag RH side
6563 - module airbag LH side
6564 - passenger's air bag module
6565 - driver's air bag module
6566 - relay air bag warning light
6567 - RH impact detector
6568 - LH impact detector
6570 - air bag and pre-tensioners control unit
6571 - unit airbag RH side
6572 - unit airbag LH side
6575 - driver's pre-tensioning seat-belt
6576 - passenger's pre-tensioning seat-belt
6577 - pre-tensioner rear LH
6578 - pre-tensioner rear RH
6579 - central rear pre-tensioner
6600 - headlight height adjustment control
6610 - LH headlight height adjustment motor
6615 - RH headlight height adjustment motor
6620 - vehicle height correction control fuse
6621 - vehicle height correction motor fuse
6625 - vehicle high position sw.
6630 - parking brake information relay (vehicle height correction)
6631 - brake pedal information relay (vehicle height correction)
6632 - hydraulic circuit fluid pressure sw.
6635 - vehicle height correction control sensor
6636 - vehicle height correction motor relay
6637 - vehicle height correction solenoid valve relay
6640 - vehicle height correction electric pump motor
6645 - vehicle height correction solenoid valve
6646 - vehicle height correction fluid level sw.
6700 - differential lock control sw.
6701 - control solenoid valve differential lock rear
6702 - control solenoid valve change to
6703 - control solenoid valve staying in
6705 - differential lock fuse
6706 - control relays change to
6707 - sw. change to
6709 - reduction gear change closing sw.
6710 - front differential lock position sw.
6711 - sensor closing change to
6712 - sensor toe-out differential lock rear
6715 - rear differential lock position sw.
6720 - differential lock control unit
6730 - front differential lock motor

6735 - rear differential lock motor
6740 - differential lock relay
6750 - controlled differential control unit
6755 - traction control cut-off sw.
6760 - controlled proportional differential solenoid
6800 - sun roof sw.
6801 - end of sliding travel sw. - sun roof
6802 - end of tilt travel sw. - sun roof
6803 - sun roof slide relay control
6804 - sun roof half travel control relay
6805 - sun roof relay
6806 - sun roof zero point sw.
6807 - sunroof relay in the sunroof assembly
6808 - sun roof intermediate position sw.
6810 - sun roof motor
6820 - sun roof assembly
6821 - safety auto-reverse sensor
6825 - sunroof infra-red transmitter
6826 - sunroof infra-red receiver
6830 - sunroof control unit
6840 - LH electric quarter light sw.
6842 - LH electric quarter light return sw.
6845 - RH electric quarter light sw.
6847 - RH electric quarter light return sw.
6850 - LH electric quarter light motor
6855 - RH electric quarter light motor
6860 - electric hood ECU
6861 - electric hood sw.
6862 - electric hood electric pump motor
6863 - rear section opening solenoid
6864 - rear section closing solenoid
6865 - electric hood closing solenoid
6866 - electric hood opening solenoid
6867 - cover opening solenoid
6868 - cover closing solenoid
6870 - electric hood electric pump motor relay
6871 - rear section ram sw.
6872 - electric hood ram sw.
6873 - cover ram sw.
6874 - electric hood sw.
6875 - electric hood buzzer
6876 - electric hood buzzer diode
6877 - boot open diode
7000 - front LH anti-lock brake sensor
7001 - power steering fluid pressure sw.
7005 - front RH anti-lock brake sensor
7010 - rear LH anti-lock brake sensor
7013 - gear lever neutral sw.
7014 - ABS gyrometric sensor
7015 - rear RH anti-lock brake sensor
7016 - ABS acceleration sensor
7017 - ABS control unit fuse
7018 - ABS control unit relay
7019 - idle maintaining simulation resistor
7020 - anti-lock brake control unit
7025 - ABS hydraulic unit (GPF)
7026 - brake assistance electric pump
7027 - ABS solenoids fuse
7028 - anti-lock braking system shunt
7029 - ABS pump fuse
7030 - electric pump unit
7040 - additional regulation unit (ARU)
7041 - additional regulation unit electrical board
7045 - clutch pedal information sw.
7046 - clutch position potentiometer
7048 - piloted brake servo
7049 - control unit piloted brake servo
7050 - traction control ECU
7055 - traction control hydraulic unit
7060 - traction control throttle actuator
7065 - traction control throttle potentiometer
7075 - traction control cut-off sw.

7076 - ABS sw. indicator light relay
7077 - hill holder cut-off sw.
7078 - hill holder buzzer
7080 - brake fluid level information diode
7090 - brake servo vacuum pump
7100 - power steering servo-regulator
7105 - variable power assisted steering control unit
7110 - power steering servo
7111 - proportional solenoid variable power-assisted steering
7112 - pressure sensor power steering
7115 - power steering control relay
7120 - converter during pressures
7121 - electric pump diode power-assisted steering
7125 - power steering power relay
7200 - trip computer-cruise control information relay
7205 - trip computer display sw.
7210 - trip computer
7215 - multifunction screen
7216 - keypad multifunction screen
7220 - clock
7222 - outside temp. sensor
7225 - clock + temp. display
7226 - exterior temp. display
7300 - cruise control sw.
7305 - cruise control sw.
7306 - cruise control override sw. (clutch)
7307 - cruise control override relay
7308 - cruise control safety sw. (brakes)
7309 - cruise control circuit shunt - engine check
7310 - cruise control unit
7311 - cruise control fuse
7312 - cruise control sw. indicator light circuit diode
7315 - cruise control vacuum pump breather assembly
7320 - cruise control override solenoid valve
7400 - external temp. display
7500 - control unit parking aid
7501 - laser distance guide
7502 - sw. laser distance guide
7503 - speaker parking aid
7504 - rear speakers parking aid
7505 - parking aid cut-off sw.
7506 - proximity sensor front LH exterior
7507 - proximity sensor front LH interior
7508 - proximity sensor front RH exterior
7509 - proximity sensor front RH interior
7510 - proximity sensor rear LH exterior
7511 - proximity sensor rear LH interior
7512 - proximity sensor rear RH exterior
7513 - proximity sensor rear RH interior
7514 - buzzer parking aid
7600 - under-inflation detector control unit
7605 - under-inflation detector re-initialisation sw.
7700 - steering wheel angle sensor
7704 - body height potentiometer
7705 - body height sensor
7706 - brake pressure sensor
7707 - accelerator pedal position sensor
7708 - front wheel movement sensor
7709 - rear wheel movement sensor
7710 - suspension sw.
7711 - front RH wheel movement sensor
7712 - front LH wheel movement sensor
7713 - rear RH wheel movement sensor
7714 - rear LH wheel movement sensor
7715 - suspension control unit
7716 - suspension solenoid valve (single or front)
7717 - rear suspension solenoid valve

CHAPTER 15 Wiring Diagrams

- 7718 - auto. roll correction solenoid
- 7719 - ADAC electro-hydraulic unit (active anti-roll)
- 7720 - front LH damper actuator
- 7721 - shock absorber auto anti-interference -front LH
- 7722 - ADAC control unit (active anti-roll)
- 7723 - ADAC acceleration meter (active anti-roll)
- 7725 - front RH damper actuator
- 7726 - damper auto anti-interference - front RH
- 7730 - rear LH damper actuator
- 7731 - shock absorber auto anti-interference -rear LH
- 7735 - rear RH damper actuator
- 7736 - shock absorber auto anti-interference -rear RH
- 7740 - suspension electro-hydraulic unit
- 7741 - front RH suspension solenoid valve unit
- 7742 - front LH suspension solenoid valve unit
- 7743 - rear RH suspension solenoid valve unit
- 7744 - rear LH suspension solenoid valve unit
- 7745 - vehicle height selector
- 7746 - piloted rear suspension pad solenoid valve
- 7747 - front suspension solenoid valve
- 7748 - rear suspension solenoid valve
- 7750 - suspension control board
- 7770 - hydraulic fluid level and/or pressure warning buzzer
- 8000 - air conditioning sw.
- 8001 - shunt air conditioning compressor relay
- 8004 - air conditioning cut-off control unit
- 8005 - air conditioning compressor relay
- 8006 - evaporator thermistor (if separated)
- 8007 - pressostat
- 8008 - air conditioning engine coolant temp. thermistor
- 8010 - air conditioning engine coolant temp. unit
- 8012 - air conditioning cut-off pressure sw.
- 8014 - idling stability solenoid valve
- 8015 - compressor cut-off relay controlled by coolant temp. unit
- 8016 - compressor cut off relay controlled by the injection ECU
- 8020 - air conditioning compressor
- 8022 - air conditioning coolant thermal sw.
- 8025 - heater panel (if separated)
- 8030 - passenger compartment air thermistor
- 8031 - coolant thermistor
- 8032 - outside air thermistor
- 8033 - sunshine temp. sender unit
- 8034 - air to footwell temp. sender unit
- 8035 - passenger compartment temp. electronic thermostat (if separated)
- 8036 - temp. display rheostat (if separated)
- 8037 - air vent temp. sender unit
- 8040 - blower speed rheostat (if separated)
- 8043 - RH blower control module
- 8044 - LH blower control module
- 8045 - blower control module (if separated)
- 8046 - blower motor resistor (if separated)
- 8047 - blower speed control (if separated)
- 8048 - blower relay
- 8050 - heater blower motor (if separated)
- 8051 - RH blower motor
- 8052 - LH blower motor
- 8060 - heater unit
- 8061 - heating unit relay
- 8065 - mixing flap motor
- 8067 - air inlet flap control
- 8068 - LH air inlet flap reduction motor
- 8069 - RH air inlet flap reduction motor
- 8070 - air inlet flap reduction motor
- 8071 - air distribution flap motor
- 8072 - ventilation flap motor
- 8073 - footwell/demisting flap motor
- 8074 - breaker valve
- 8080 - air conditioning ECU
- 8090 - compressor protection diode
- 8096 - additional heating operation information diode
- 8097 - fuel heating control sw.
- 8098 - additional heating
- 8100 - front cigar lighter
- 8105 - rear cigar lighter
- 8110 - heated rear screen sw.
- 8112 - rear screen demisting sensor
- 8115 - heated rear screen relay
- 8116 - rear screen heater time sw. relay
- 8118 - heated rear screen left
- 8119 - heated rear screen right
- 8120 - heated rear screen
- 8121 - rear screen de-misting motor
- 8125 - heated mirror driver's side (if separated electrical)
- 8130 - heated mirror passenger's side (if separated electrical)
- 8140 - heated windscreen
- 8141 - heated windscreen sw.
- 8145 - heated windscreen relay
- 8146 - heated windscreen timer unit
- 8200 - coded anti-start keypad
- 8201 - coded anti-start LED
- 8203 - relay circuit diode injection control unit supply
- 8205 - diagnostic indicator light circuit diode
- 8206 - coded anti-start device door circuit diode
- 8207 - coded anti-start relay for diesel pump
- 8208 - CAS control unit
- 8220 - analogue module transponder
- 8221 - control module transponder
- 8300 - driver's heated seat sw.
- 8301 - electrically heated seats control unit
- 8302 - driver's heated seat rheostat
- 8303 - passenger's heated seat rheostat
- 8305 - passenger's heated seat sw.
- 8306 - LH rear heated seat sw.
- 8307 - RH rear heated seat sw.
- 8308 - heated seat relay
- 8310 - heated seat (on the driver's side)
- 8311 - heated seat thermostat
- 8315 - heated seat (passenger's side)
- 8320 - heated rear seat
- 8402 - aerial lead
- 8403 - aerial filter
- 8404 - aerial
- 8405 - electric aerial
- 8406 - electric aerial module
- 8407 - duplexer
- 8408 - servo unit radio
- 8410 - radio
- 8411 - radio balance front left/right
- 8412 - radio balance front/rear
- 8413 - radio control
- 8415 - compact disc player
- 8416 - compact disc interface
- 8420 - front door speakers (on the driver's side)
- 8421 - front speakers
- 8422 - front door speakers left
- 8423 - front door speakers right
- 8425 - front door speakers (passenger's side)
- 8430 - speaker (rear LH)
- 8435 - speaker (rear RH)
- 8440 - LH front tweeter speaker
- 8442 - front LH mid range speaker
- 8443 - speaker boomer front LH
- 8445 - RH front tweeter speaker
- 8447 - front RH mid range speaker
- 8448 - speaker boomer front RH
- 8450 - LH rear tweeter speaker
- 8452 - rear LH mid range speaker
- 8453 - speaker boomer rear LH
- 8455 - RH rear tweeter speaker
- 8457 - rear RH mid range speaker
- 8458 - speaker boomer rear RH
- 8460 - headphone socket LH rear
- 8465 - headphone socket RH rear
- 8470 - police radio electrical supply front
- 8471 - police radio electrical supply 1 rear
- 8472 - police radio electrical supply 2 rear
- 8475 - radio telephone instrument panel
- 8480 - radio telephone transmitter-receiver
- 8481 - car-phone loudspeaker
- 8482 - car-phone microphone
- 8483 - car-phone on warning buzzer
- 8484 - car phone aerial
- 8485 - car-phone keypad
- 8500 - navigation control unit
- 8501 - aerial GPS
- 8502 - speaker navigation
- 8600 - anti-theft alarm system unit
- 8601 - anti-theft alarm key sw.
- 8602 - alarm ultrasonic unit
- 8603 - anti-theft alarm sw.
- 8604 - ultrasonic sensor
- 8605 - anti-theft alarm siren
- 8606 - anti-theft alarm system LED
- 8607 - ultrasonic transmitter
- 8608 - ultrasonic receiver
- 8609 - ultrasonic transmitter + alarm LED
- 8610 - anti-theft alarm system boot sw.
- 8611 - anti-theft alarm system bonnet sw.
- 8612 - RH rear hinged door alarm sw.
- 8613 - alarm rear LH door sw.
- 8614 - alarm rear RH door sw.
- 8615 - dipped beam supply relay for alarm
- 8616 - alarm relay
- 8617 - anti-theft alarm warning relay
- 8618 - anti-lifting contact
- 8630 - protection central unit
- 8700 - electric sun-blind motor
- 8701 - electric blind sw.
- 8702 - rear electric blind sw.
- 9000 - central unit
- 9005 - left front side light station
- 9010 - fan unit station
- 9015 - right front side light station
- 9020 - wipe/wash station
- 9025 - sensor information station
- 9030 - left front door station
- 9031 - equipment seat
- 9035 - instrument panel station
- 9040 - display station
- 9045 - passenger compartment station
- 9050 - right front door station
- 9055 - signalling sw. station
- 9060 - wiper sw. station
- 9065 - console station
- 9070 - towing station
- 9075 - left tail light station
- 9080 - tailgate station
- 9085 - right tail light station

CHAPTER 15 Wiring Diagrams 206

206 WIRING DIAGRAM: BATTERY, STARTER 'ALTERNATOR' POWER SUPPLY - typical.

15-11

Chapter 15 Wiring Diagrams 206

206 SCHEMATIC DIAGRAM: BATTERY, STARTER, ALTERNATOR, POWER SUPPLY - typical.

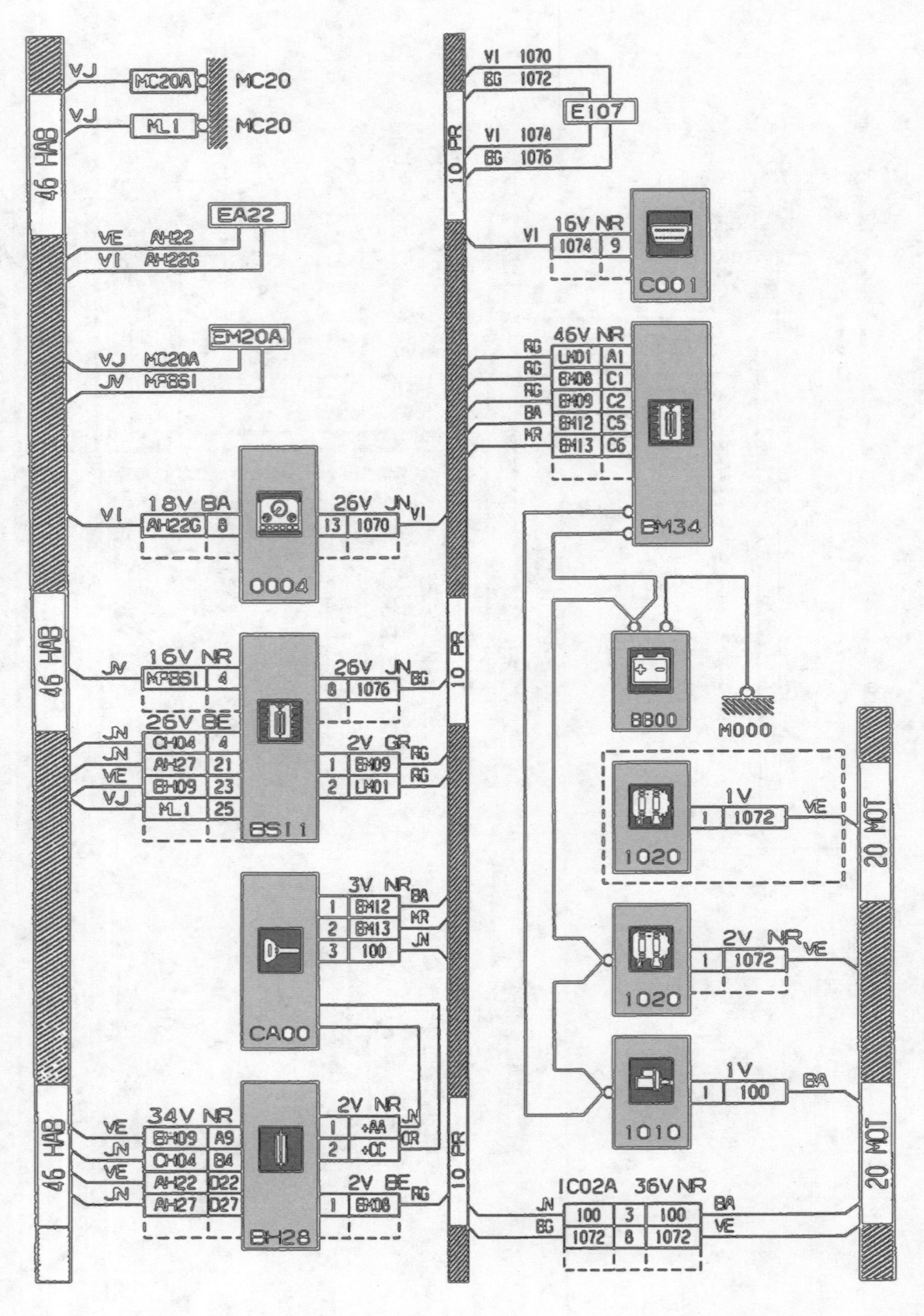

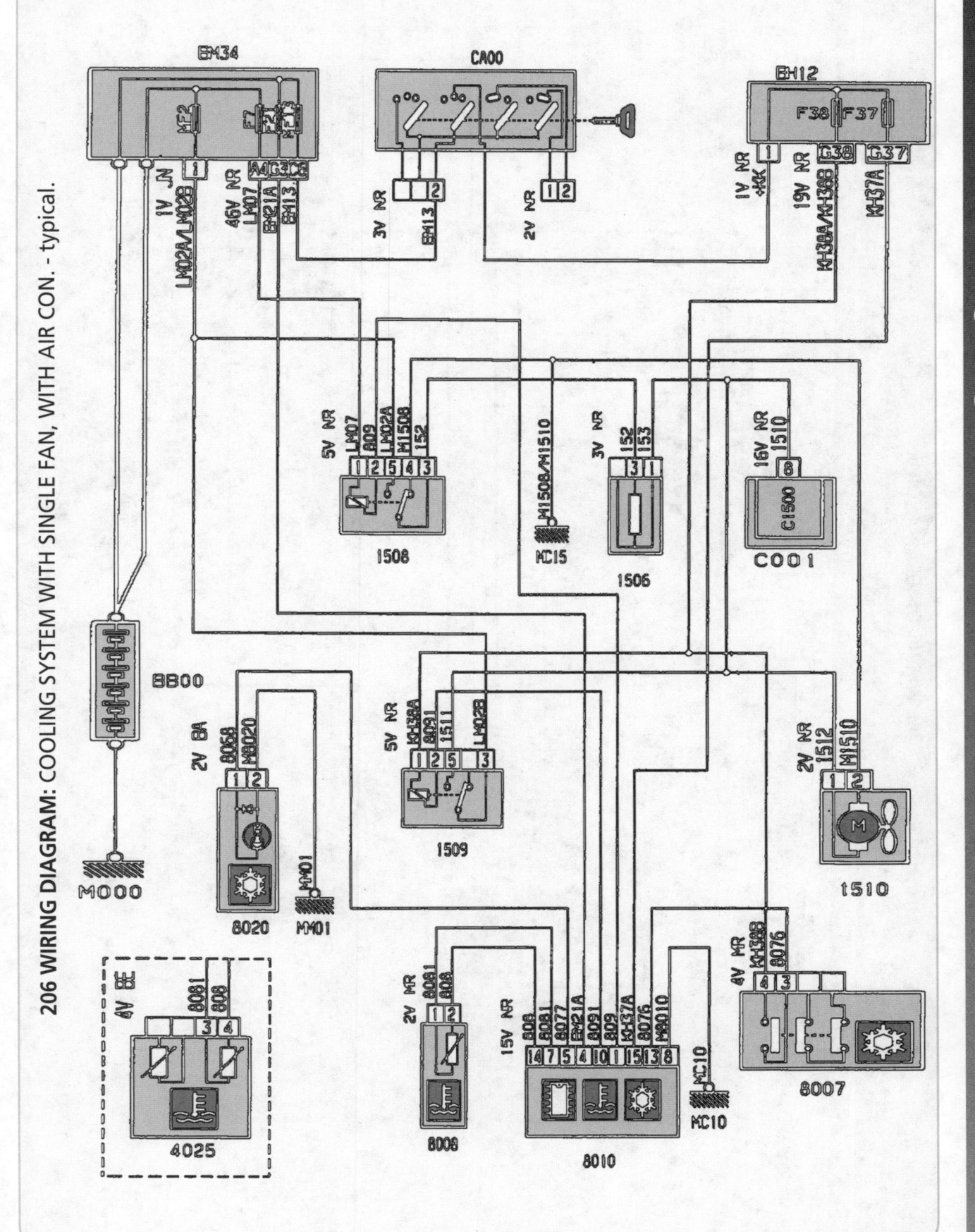

CHAPTER 15 Wiring Diagrams 206

206 WIRING DIAGRAM: COOLING SYSTEM WITH SINGLE FAN, WITH AIR CON. - typical.

15-13

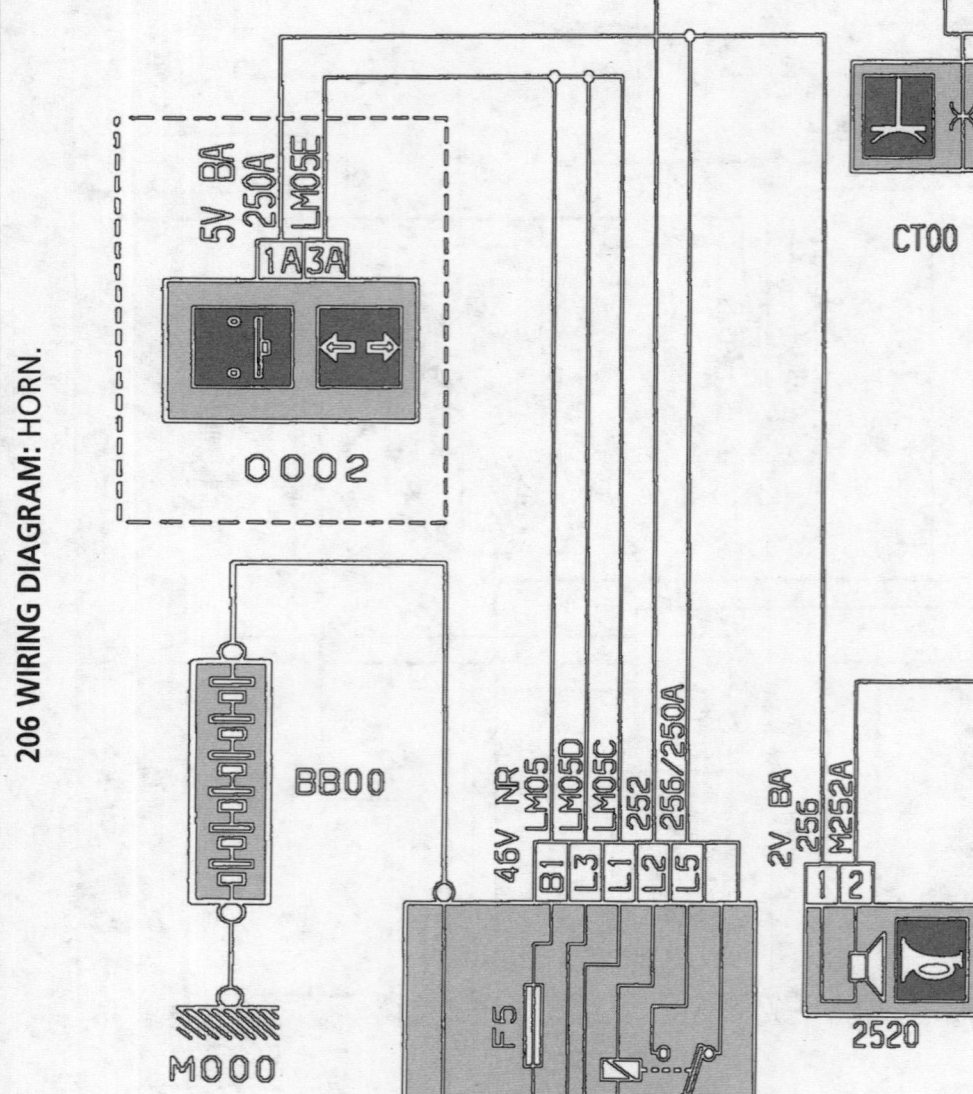

CHAPTER 15 Wiring Diagrams 206

206 WIRING DIAGRAM: HORN.

15-14

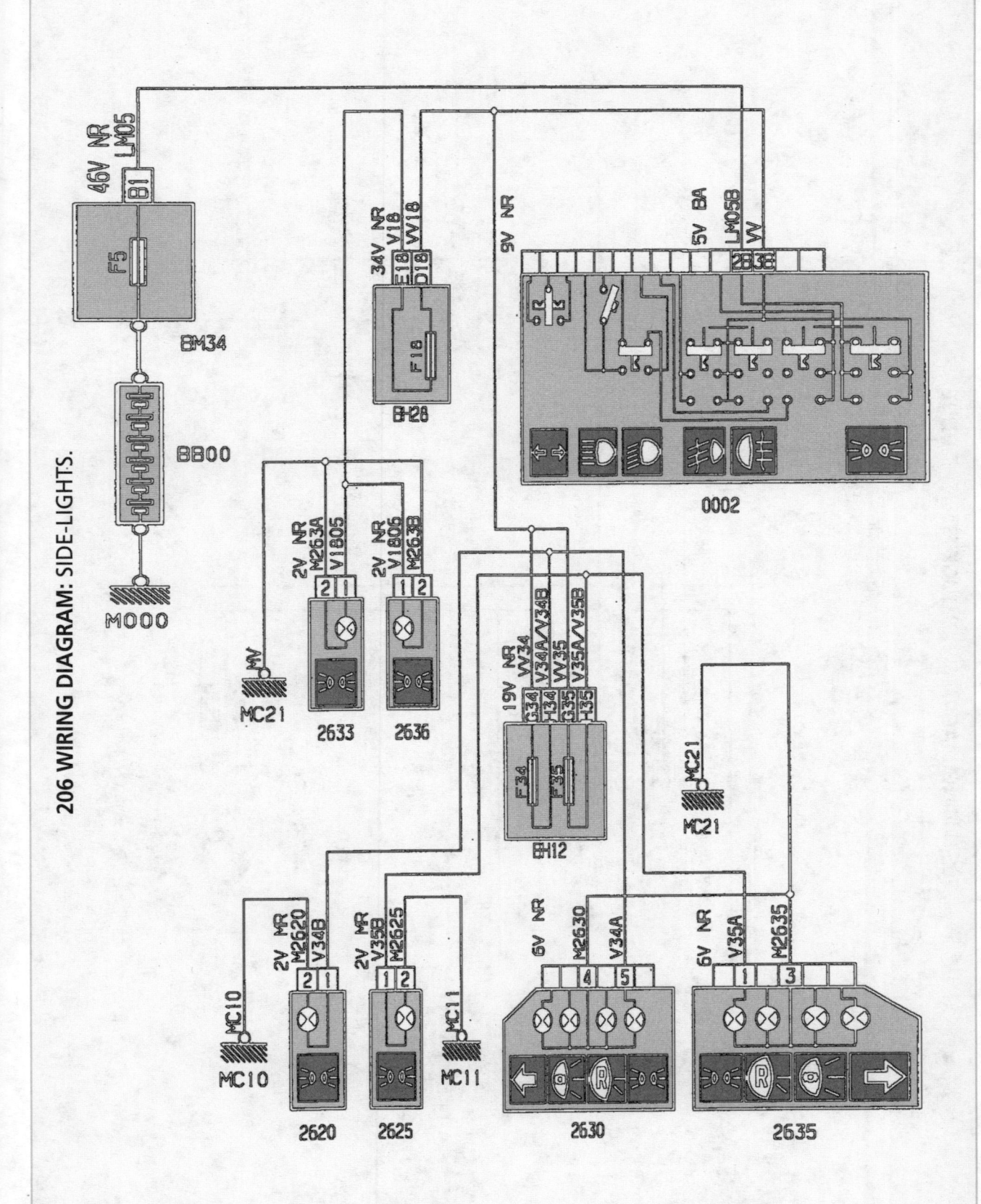

CHAPTER 15 Wiring Diagrams 206

206 WIRING DIAGRAM: SIDE-LIGHTS.

15-15

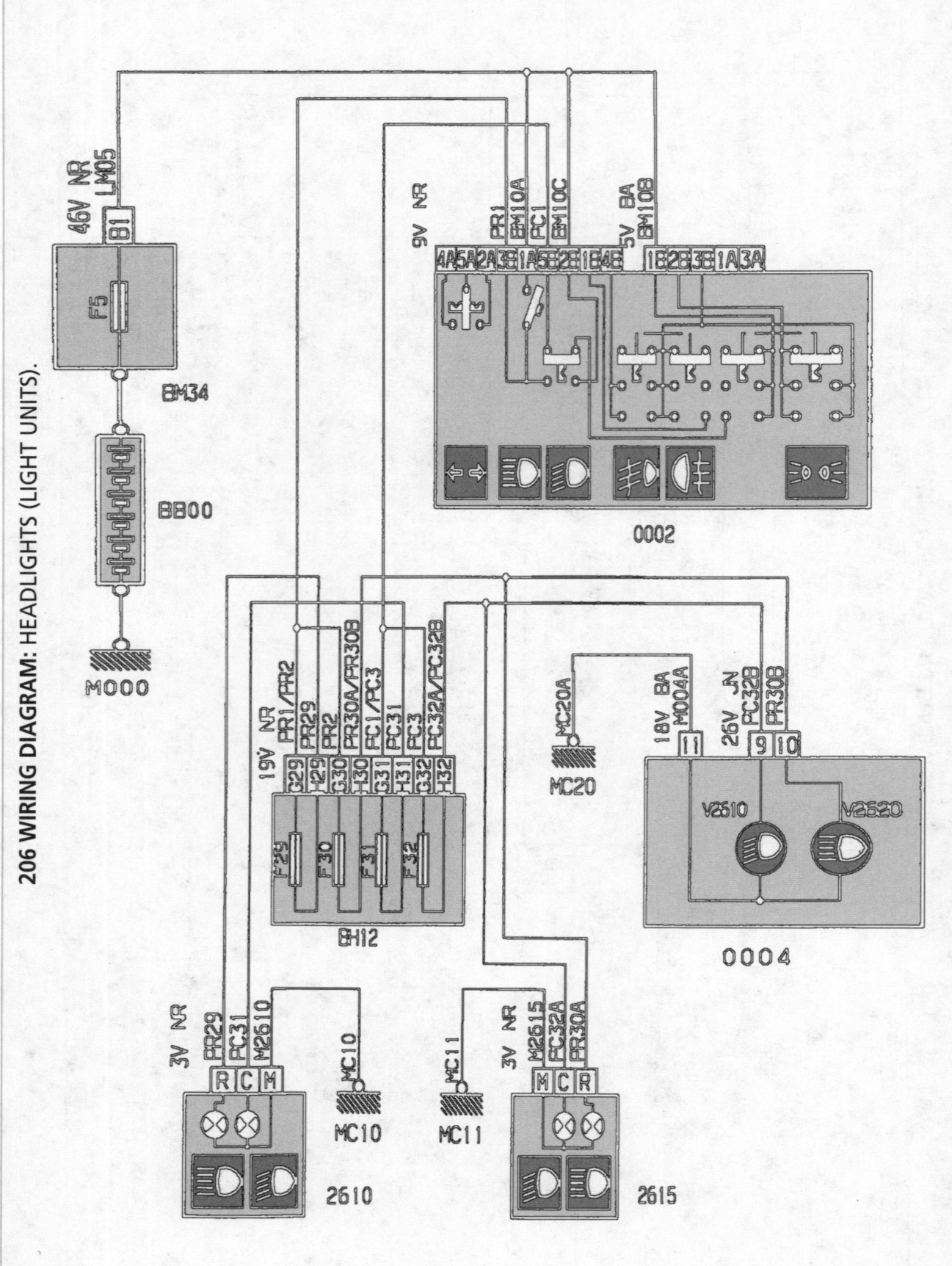

CHAPTER 15 Wiring Diagrams

206 WIRING DIAGRAM: HEADLIGHTS (LIGHT UNITS).

15-16

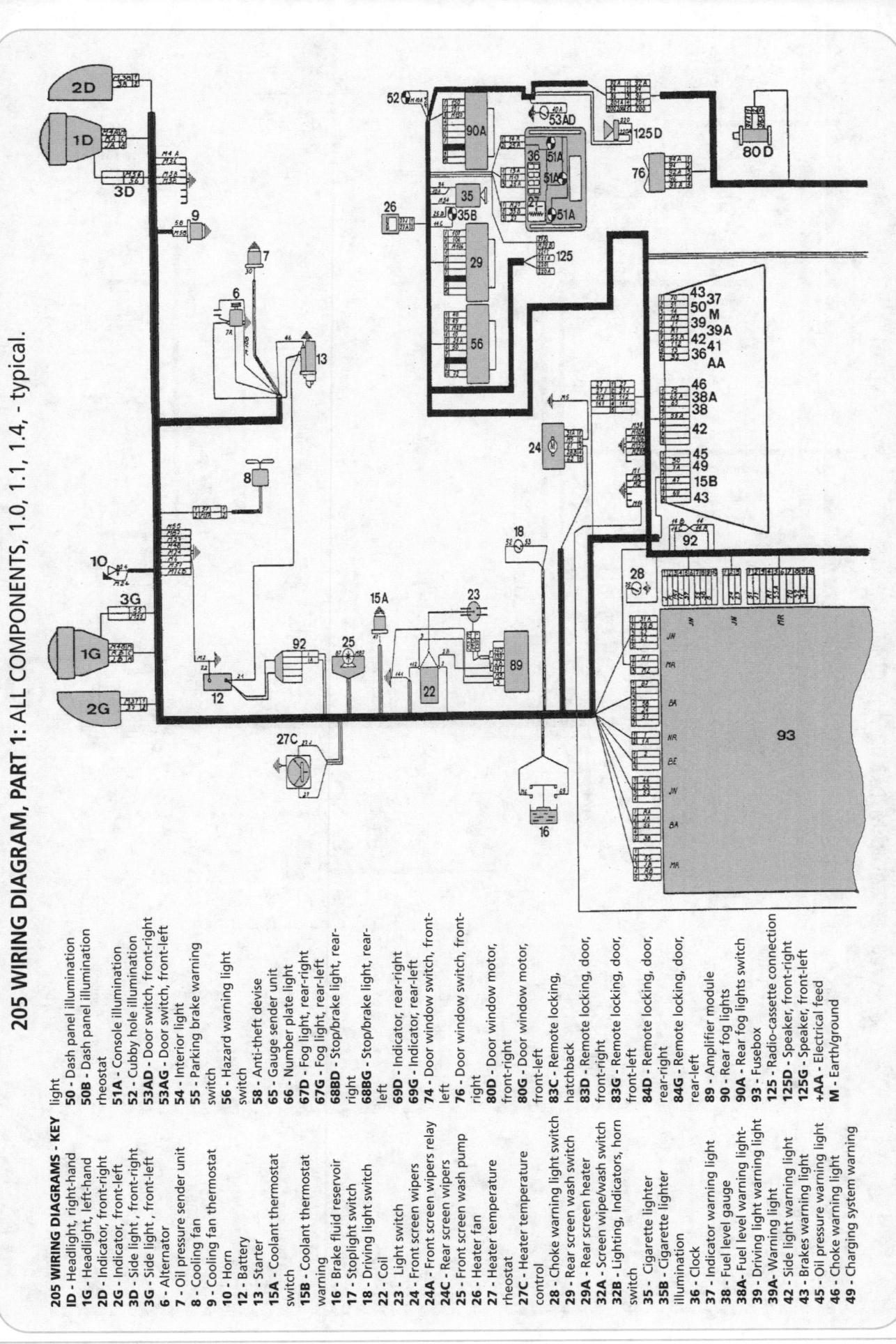

CHAPTER 15 Wiring Diagrams

205 WIRING DIAGRAM, PART 1: ALL COMPONENTS, 1.0, 1.1, 1.4, - typical.

205 WIRING DIAGRAMS - KEY

- 1D - Headlight, right-hand
- 1G - Headlight, left-hand
- 2D - Indicator, front-right
- 2G - Indicator, front-left
- 3D - Side light , front-right
- 3G - Side light, front-left
- 6 - Alternator
- 7 - Oil pressure sender unit
- 8 - Cooling fan
- 9 - Cooling fan thermostat
- 10 - Horn
- 12 - Battery
- 13 - Starter
- 15A - Coolant thermostat switch
- 15B - Coolant thermostat warning
- 16 - Brake fluid reservoir
- 17 - Stoplight switch
- 18 - Driving light switch
- 22 - Coil
- 23 - Light switch
- 24 - Front screen wipers
- 24A - Front screen wipers relay
- 24C - Rear screen wipers
- 25 - Front screen wash pump
- 26 - Heater fan
- 27 - Heater temperature rheostat
- 27C - Heater temperature control
- 28 - Choke warning light switch
- 29 - Rear screen wash switch
- 32A - Screen wipe/wash switch
- 32B - Lighting, Indicators, horn switch
- 35 - Cigarette lighter
- 35B - Cigarette lighter illumination
- 36 - Clock
- 37 - Indicator warning light
- 38 - Fuel level gauge
- 38A - Fuel level warning light
- 39 - Driving light warning light
- 39A - Side light warning light
- 42 - Side light warning light
- 43 - Brakes warning light
- 45 - Oil pressure warning light
- 46 - Choke warning light
- 49 - Charging system warning light
- 50 - Dash panel illumination
- 50B - Dash panel illumination rheostat
- 51A - Console illumination
- 52 - Cubby hole illumination
- 53AD - Door switch, front-right
- 53AG - Door switch, front-left
- 54 - Interior light
- 55 - Parking brake warning switch
- 56 - Hazard warning light switch
- 58 - Anti-theft devise
- 65 - Gauge sender unit
- 66 - Number plate light
- 67D - Fog light, rear-right
- 67G - Fog light, rear-left
- 68BD - Stop/brake light, rear-right
- 68BG - Stop/brake light, rear-left
- 69D - Indicator, rear-right
- 69G - Indicator, rear-left
- 74 - Door window switch, front-right
- 76 - Door window switch, front-left
- 80D - Door window motor, front-right
- 80G - Door window motor, front-left
- 83C - Remote locking, hatchback
- 83D - Remote locking, door, front-right
- 83G - Remote locking, door, front-left
- 84D - Remote locking, door, rear-right
- 84G - Remote locking, door, rear-left
- 89 - Amplifier module
- 90 - Rear fog lights
- 90A - Rear fog lights switch
- 93 - Fusebox
- 125 - Radio-cassette connection
- 125D - Speaker, front-right
- 125G - Speaker, front-left
- +AA - Electrical feed
- M - Earth/ground

15-17

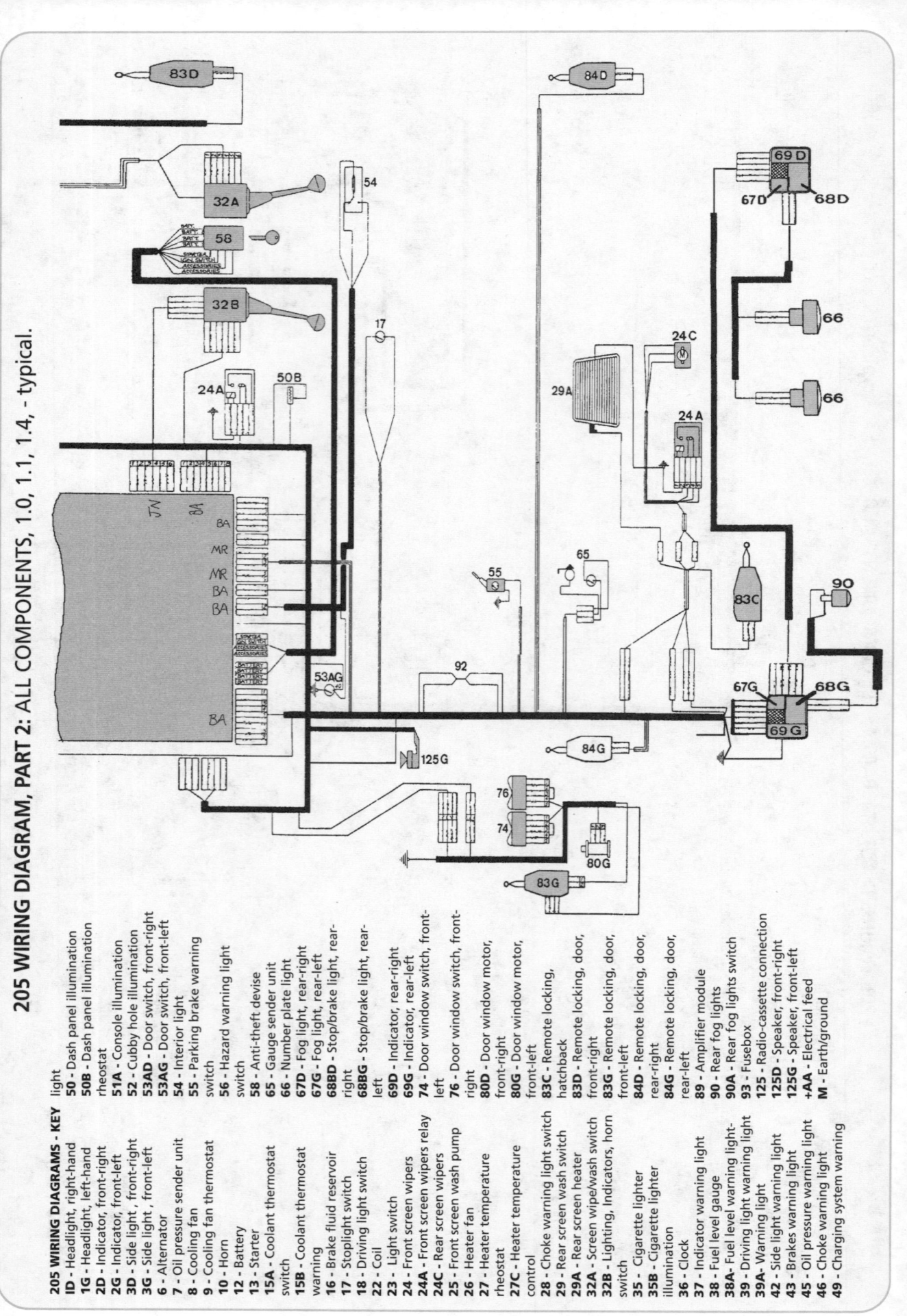

Chapter 15 Wiring Diagrams

205 WIRING DIAGRAM, PART 2: ALL COMPONENTS, 1.0, 1.1, 1.4, - typical.

205 WIRING DIAGRAMS - KEY

- 1D - Headlight, right-hand
- 1G - Headlight, left-hand
- 2D - Indicator, front-right
- 2G - Indicator, front-left
- 3D - Side light, front-right
- 3G - Side light, front-left
- 6 - Alternator
- 7 - Oil pressure sender unit
- 8 - Cooling fan
- 9 - Cooling fan thermostat
- 10 - Horn
- 12 - Battery
- 13 - Starter
- 15A - Coolant thermostat switch
- 15B - Coolant thermostat warning
- 16 - Brake fluid reservoir
- 17 - Stoplight switch
- 18 - Driving light switch
- 22 - Coil
- 23 - Light switch
- 24 - Front screen wipers
- 24A - Front screen wipers relay
- 24C - Rear screen wipers
- 25 - Front screen wash pump
- 26 - Heater fan
- 27 - Heater temperature rheostat
- 27C - Heater temperature control
- 28 - Choke warning light switch
- 29 - Rear screen wash switch
- 29A - Rear screen heater
- 32A - Screen wipe/wash switch
- 32B - Lighting, Indicators, horn switch
- 35 - Cigarette lighter
- 35B - Cigarette lighter illumination
- 36 - Clock
- 37 - Indicator warning light
- 38 - Fuel level gauge
- 38A - Fuel level warning light
- 39 - Driving light warning light
- 39A - Warning light
- 42 - Side light warning light
- 43 - Brakes warning light
- 45 - Oil pressure warning light
- 46 - Choke warning light
- 49 - Charging system warning light
- 50 - Dash panel illumination
- 50B - Dash panel illumination rheostat
- 51A - Console illumination
- 52 - Cubby hole illumination
- 53AD - Door switch, front-right
- 53AG - Door switch, front-left
- 54 - Interior light
- 55 - Parking brake warning switch
- 56 - Hazard warning light
- 58 - Anti-theft devise
- 65 - Gauge sender unit
- 66 - Number plate light
- 67D - Fog light, rear-right
- 67G - Fog light, rear-left
- 68BD - Stop/brake light, rear-right
- 68BG - Stop/brake light, rear-left
- 69D - Indicator, rear-right
- 69G - Indicator, rear-left
- 74 - Door window switch, front-left
- 76 - Door window switch, front-right
- 80D - Door window motor, front-right
- 80G - Door window motor, front-left
- 83C - Remote locking, hatchback
- 83D - Remote locking, door, front-right
- 83G - Remote locking, door, front-left
- 84D - Remote locking, door, rear-right
- 84G - Remote locking, door, rear-left
- 89 - Amplifier module
- 90 - Rear fog lights
- 90A - Rear fog lights switch
- 93 - Fusebox
- 125 - Radio-cassette connection
- 125D - Speaker, front-right
- 125G - Speaker, front-left
- +AA - Electrical feed
- M - Earth/ground

15-18

CHAPTER 15 Wiring Diagrams

106 WIRING DIAGRAM COOLING SYSTEM WITH SINGLE FAN - typical.

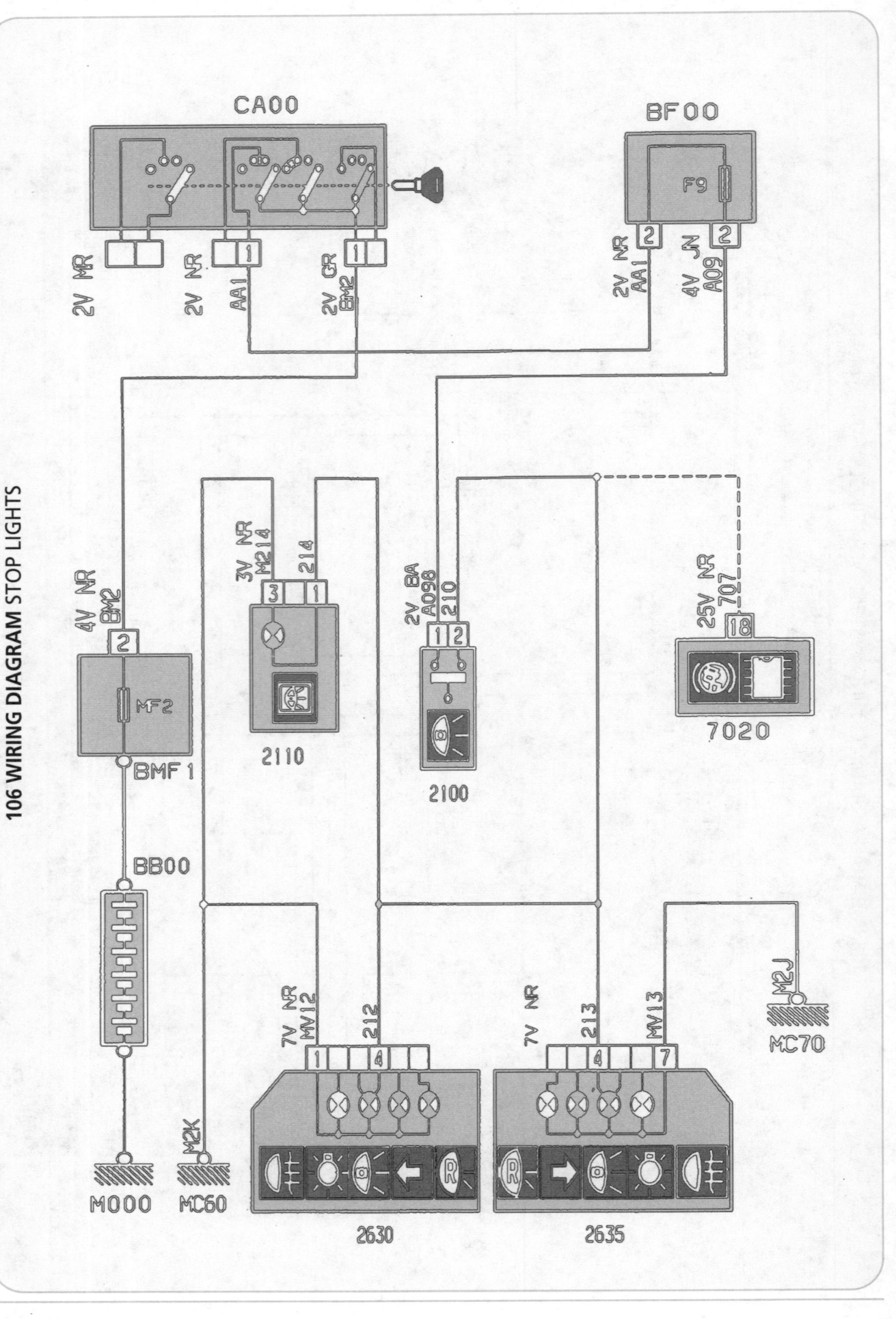

CHAPTER 15
Wiring Diagrams

106 WIRING DIAGRAM STOP LIGHTS

15-20

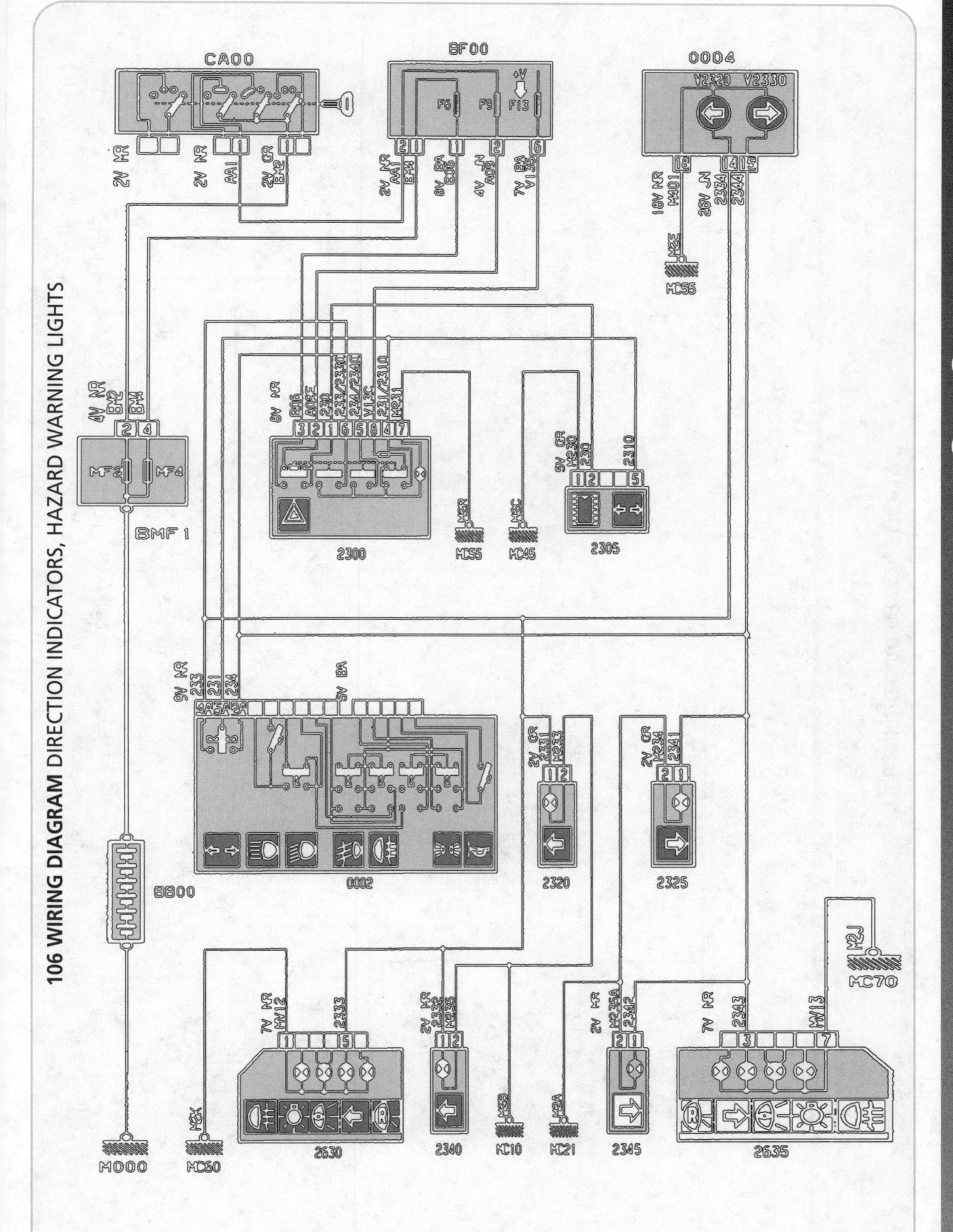

CHAPTER 15 Wiring Diagrams

106 WIRING DIAGRAM DIRECTION INDICATORS, HAZARD WARNING LIGHTS

Wiring Diagrams 106

15-21

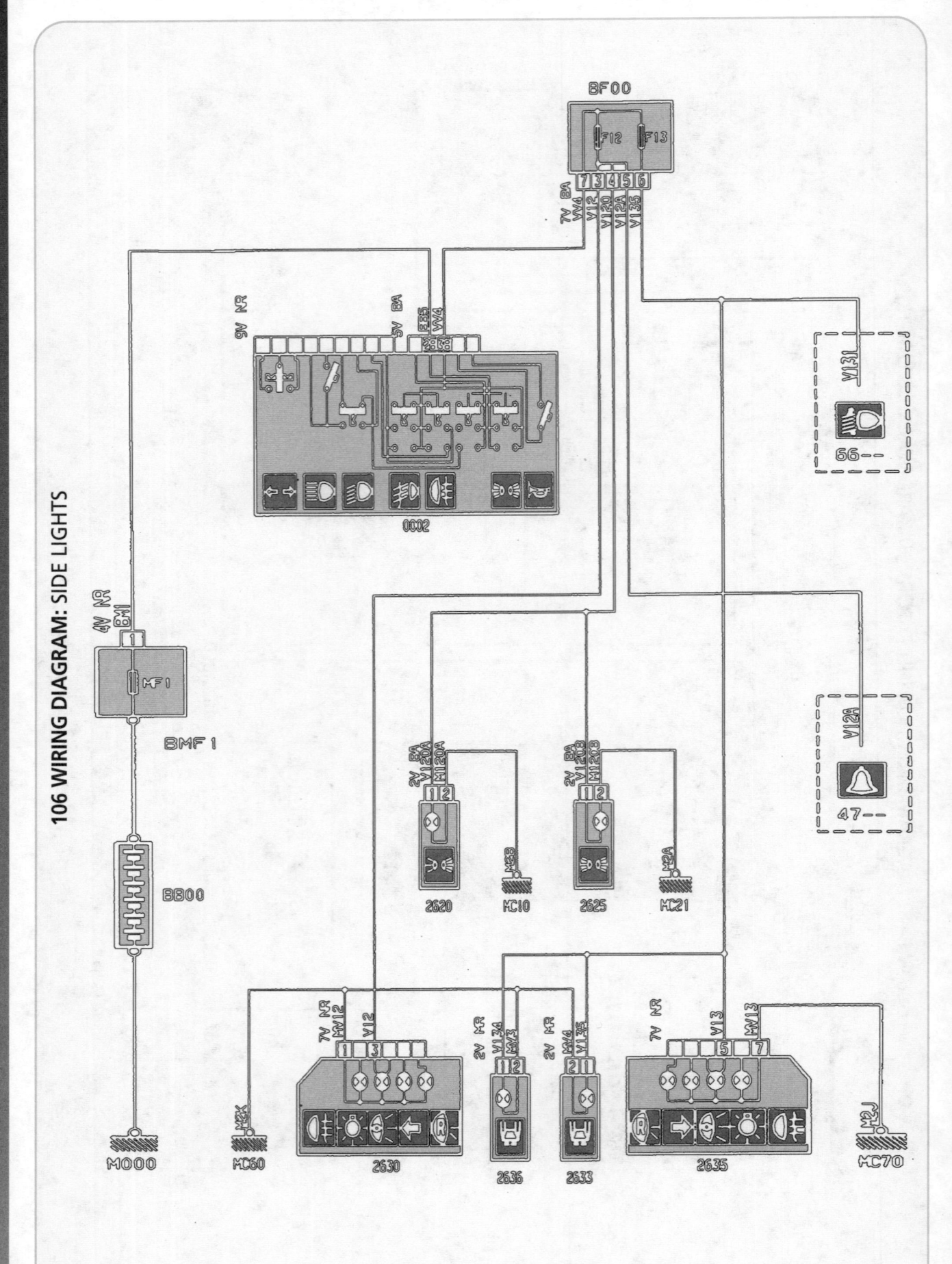

CHAPTER 15 Wiring Diagrams 106

106 WIRING DIAGRAM: SIDE LIGHTS

15-22

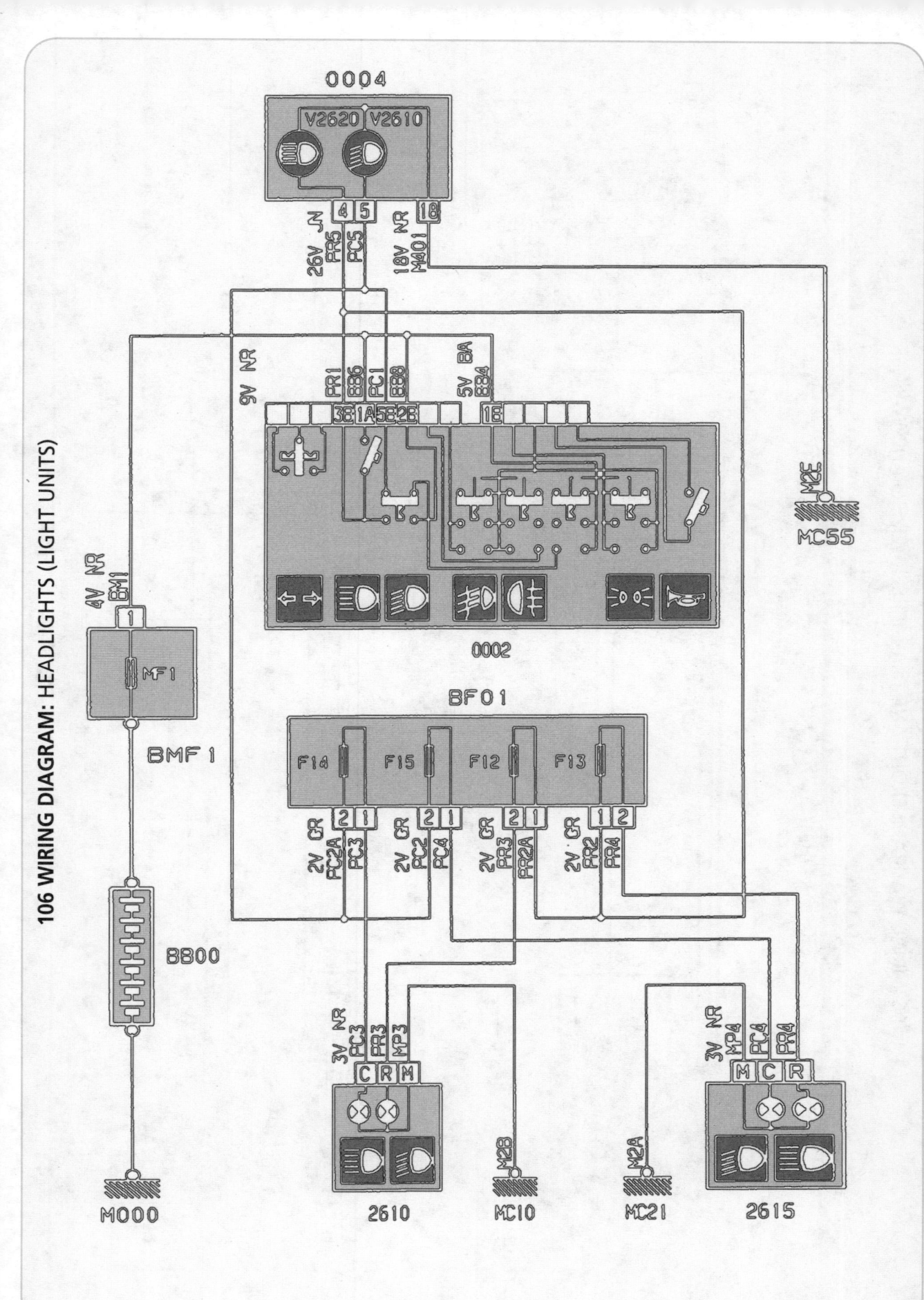

CHAPTER 15 Wiring Diagrams 106

106 WIRING DIAGRAM: HEADLIGHTS (LIGHT UNITS)

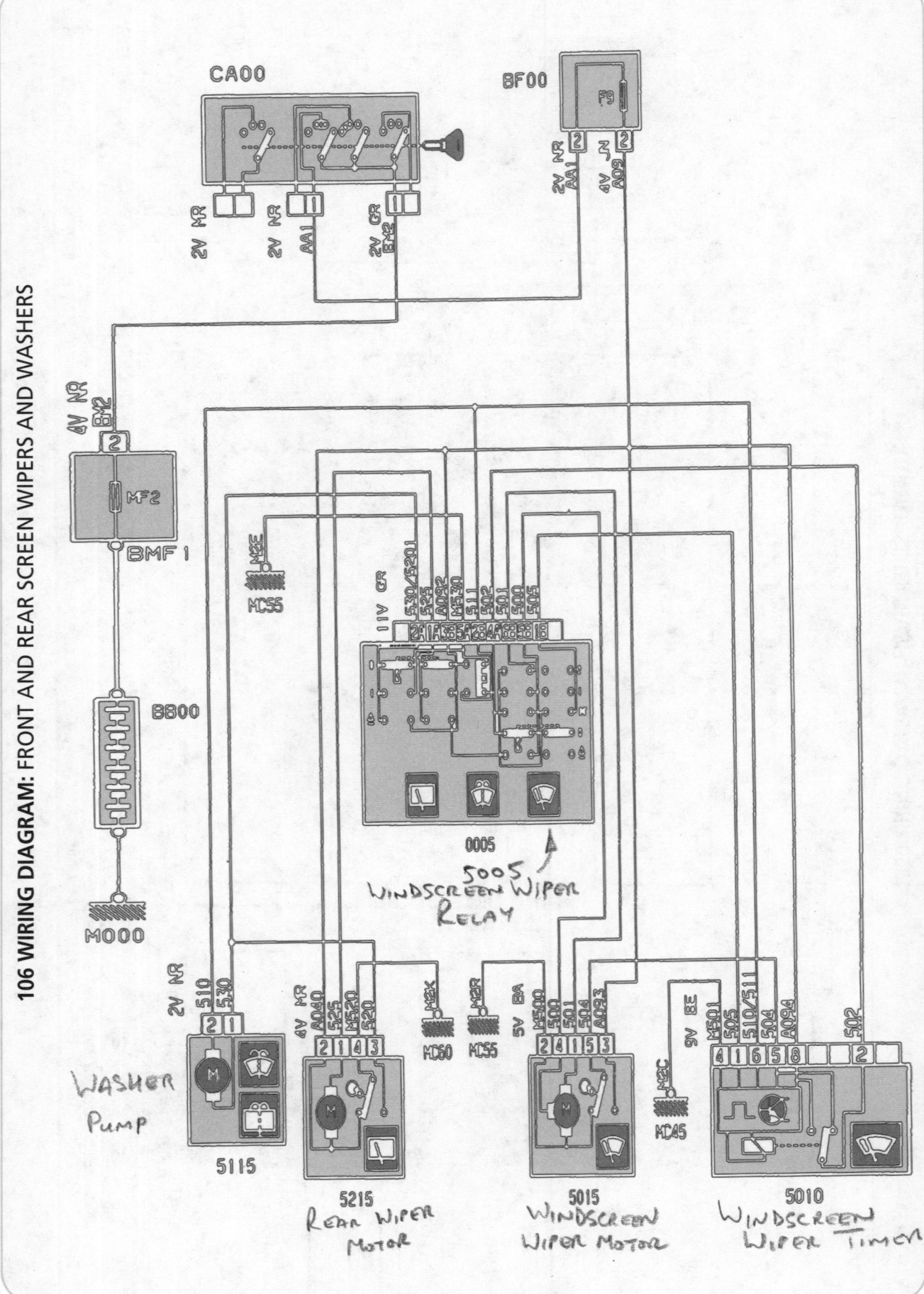

CHAPTER 15 Wiring Diagrams

106 WIRING DIAGRAM: FRONT AND REAR SCREEN WIPERS AND WASHERS

5005 WINDSCREEN WIPER RELAY

WASHER PUMP — 5115

5215 REAR WIPER MOTOR

5015 WINDSCREEN WIPER MOTOR

5010 WINDSCREEN WIPER TIMER

15-24

CHAPTER 15 Wiring Diagrams 306

306 WIRING DIAGRAM: BATTERY, STARTER, ALTERNATOR, POWER SUPPLY - TU engines with manual transmission

CHAPTER 15
Wiring Diagrams 306

306 SCHEMATIC DIAGRAM: BATTERY, STARTER, ALTERNATOR, POWER SUPPLY - TU engines with manual transmission

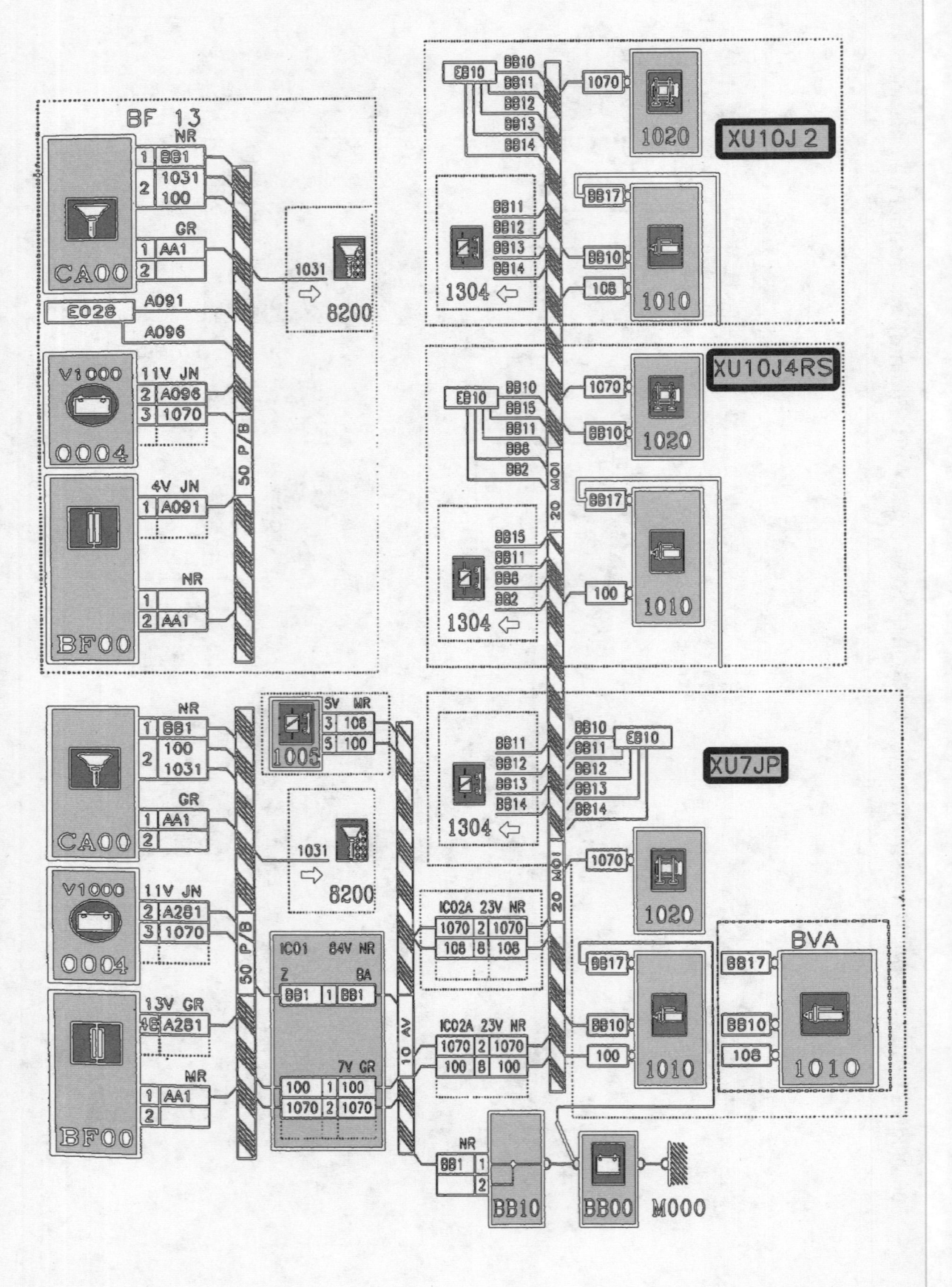

CHAPTER 15 Wiring Diagrams 306

306 WIRING DIAGRAM: HEADLIGHTS (LIGHT UNITS) - without dim-dip

CHAPTER 15 Wiring Diagrams 306

306 SCHEMATIC DIAGRAM: HEADLIGHTS (LIGHT UNITS) - without dim-dip

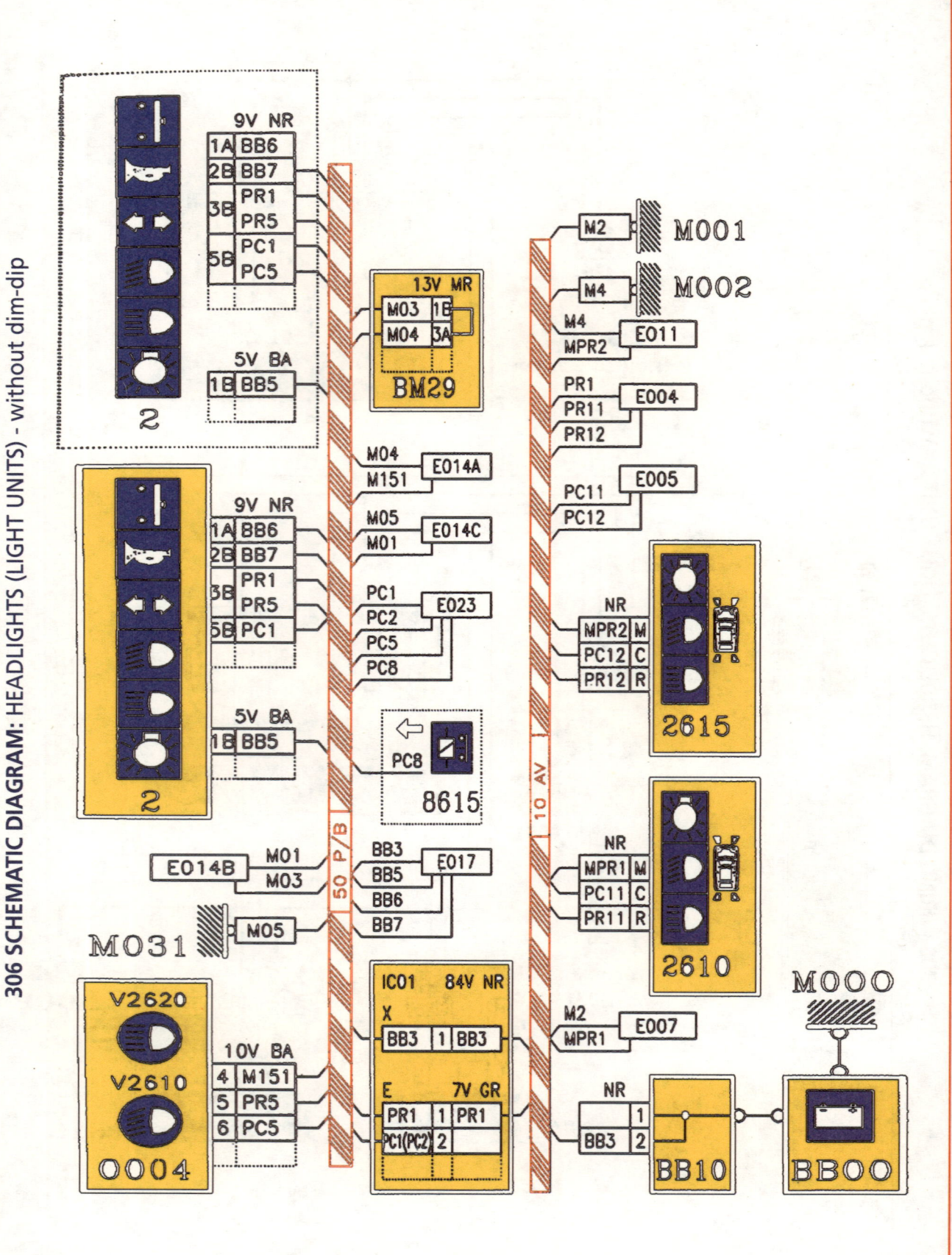

15-28

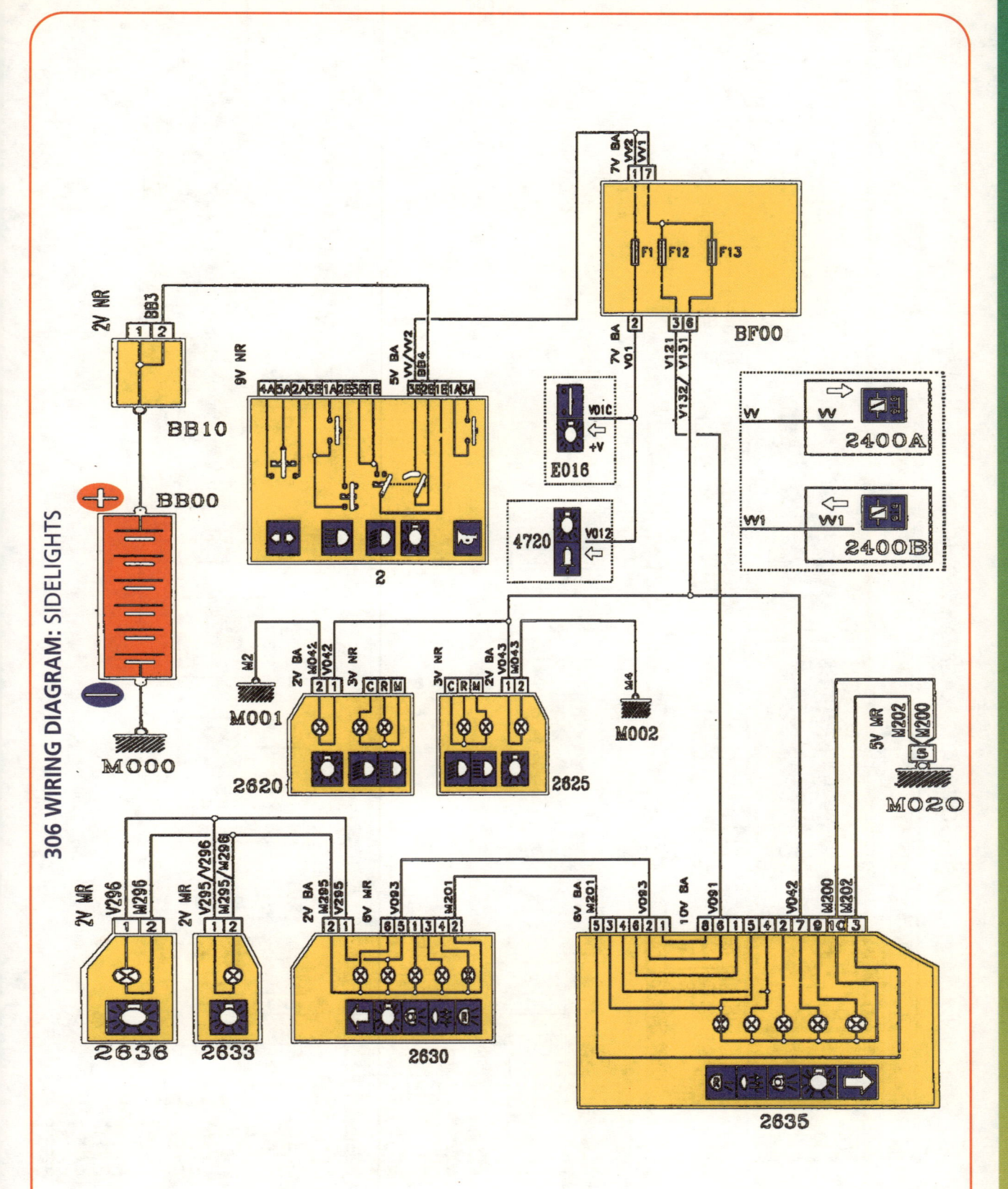

CHAPTER 15 Wiring Diagrams 306

306 WIRING DIAGRAM: SIDELIGHTS

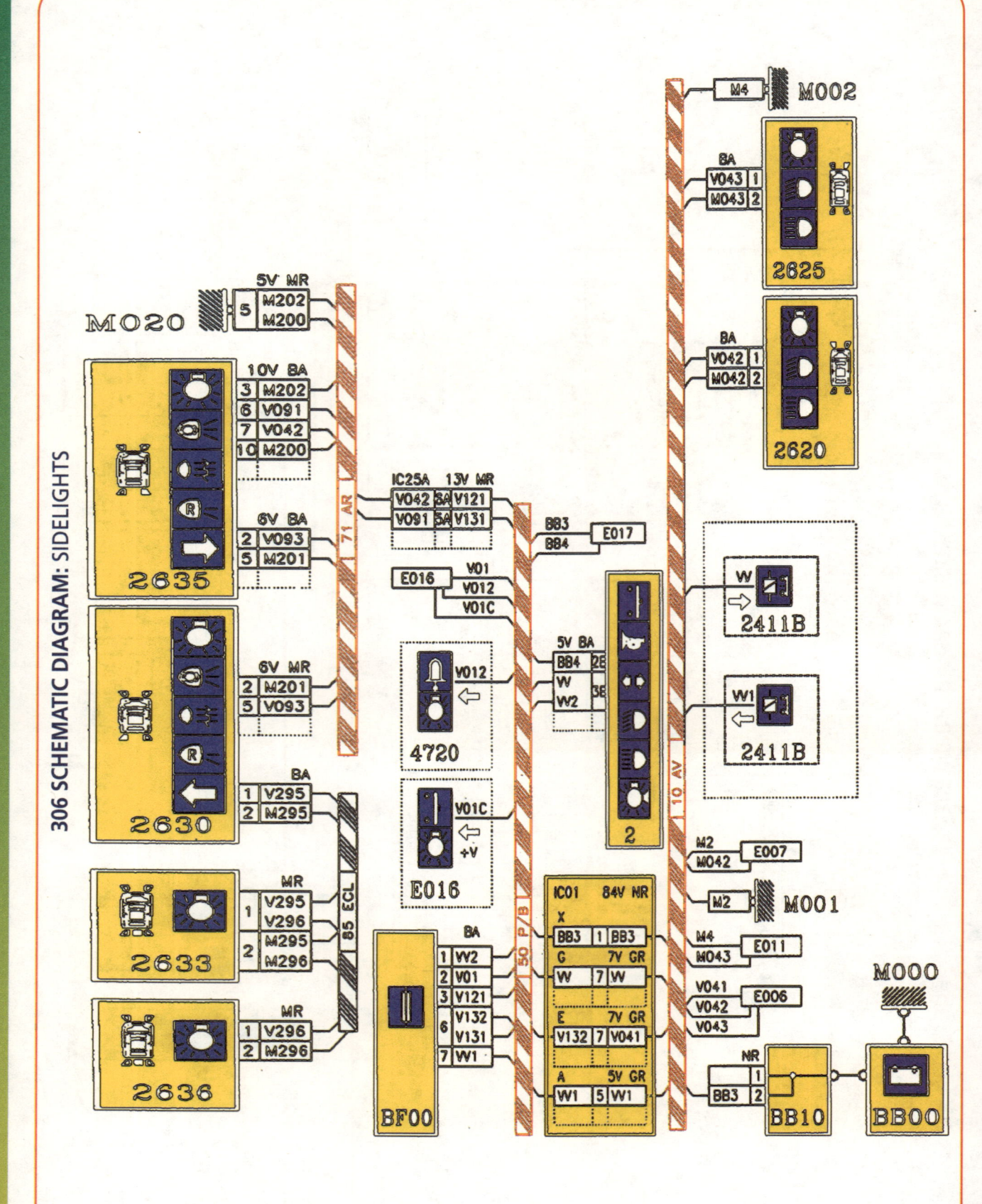

CHAPTER 15
Wiring Diagrams 306

306 SCHEMATIC DIAGRAM: SIDELIGHTS

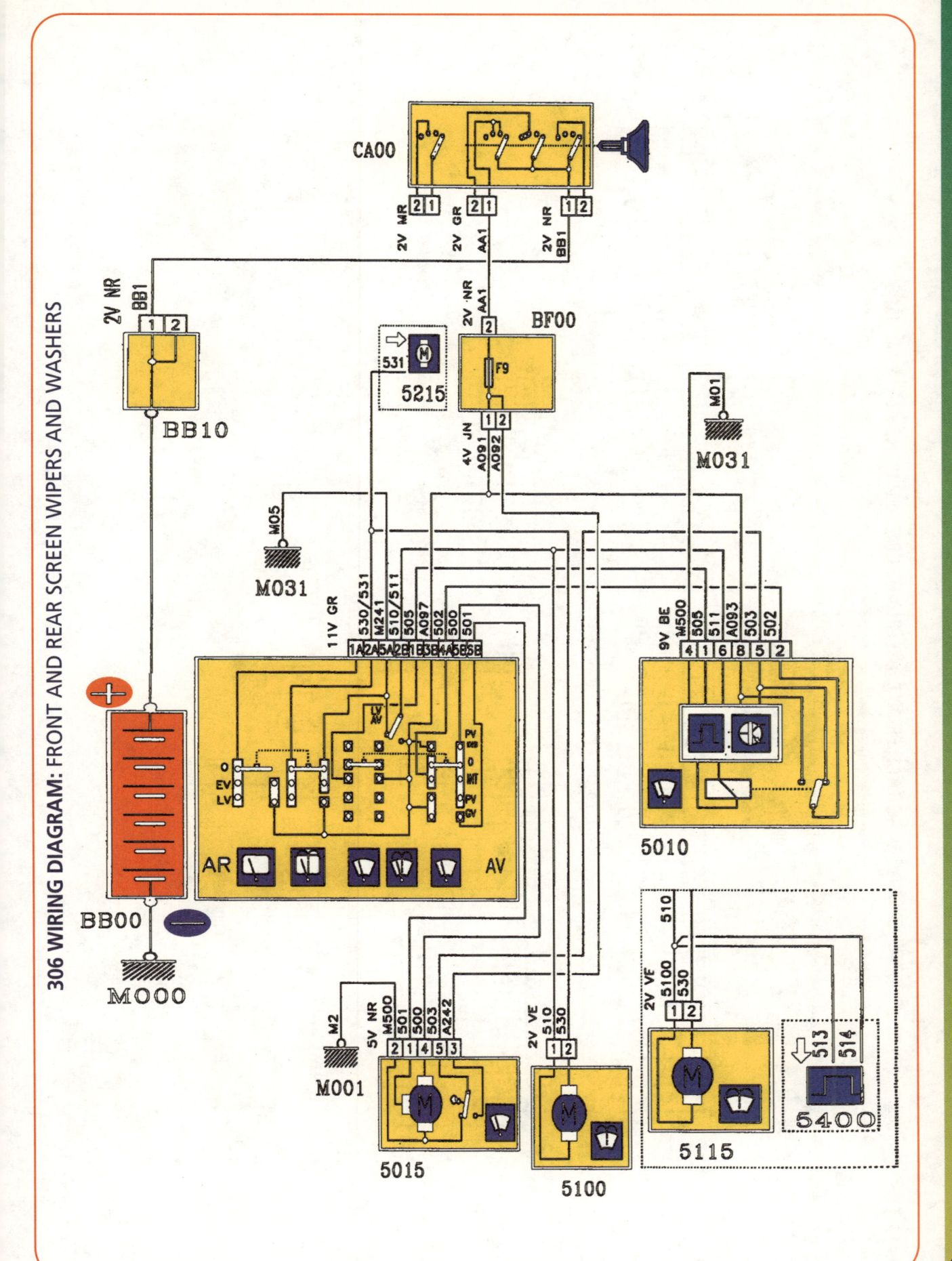

CHAPTER 15 Wiring Diagrams 306

306 WIRING DIAGRAM: FRONT AND REAR SCREEN WIPERS AND WASHERS

15-31

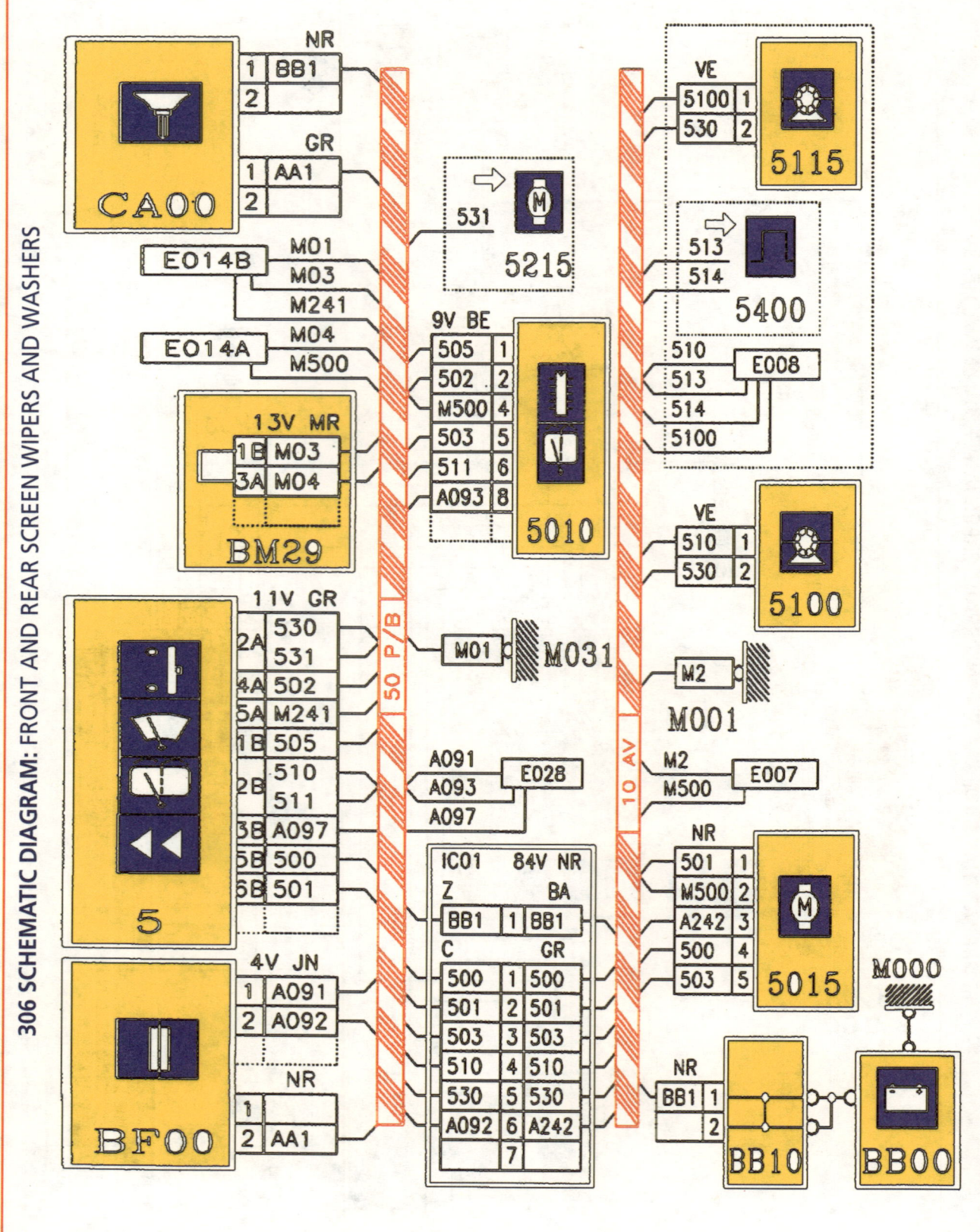

CHAPTER 15
Wiring Diagrams 306

306 SCHEMATIC DIAGRAM: FRONT AND REAR SCREEN WIPERS AND WASHERS

15-32

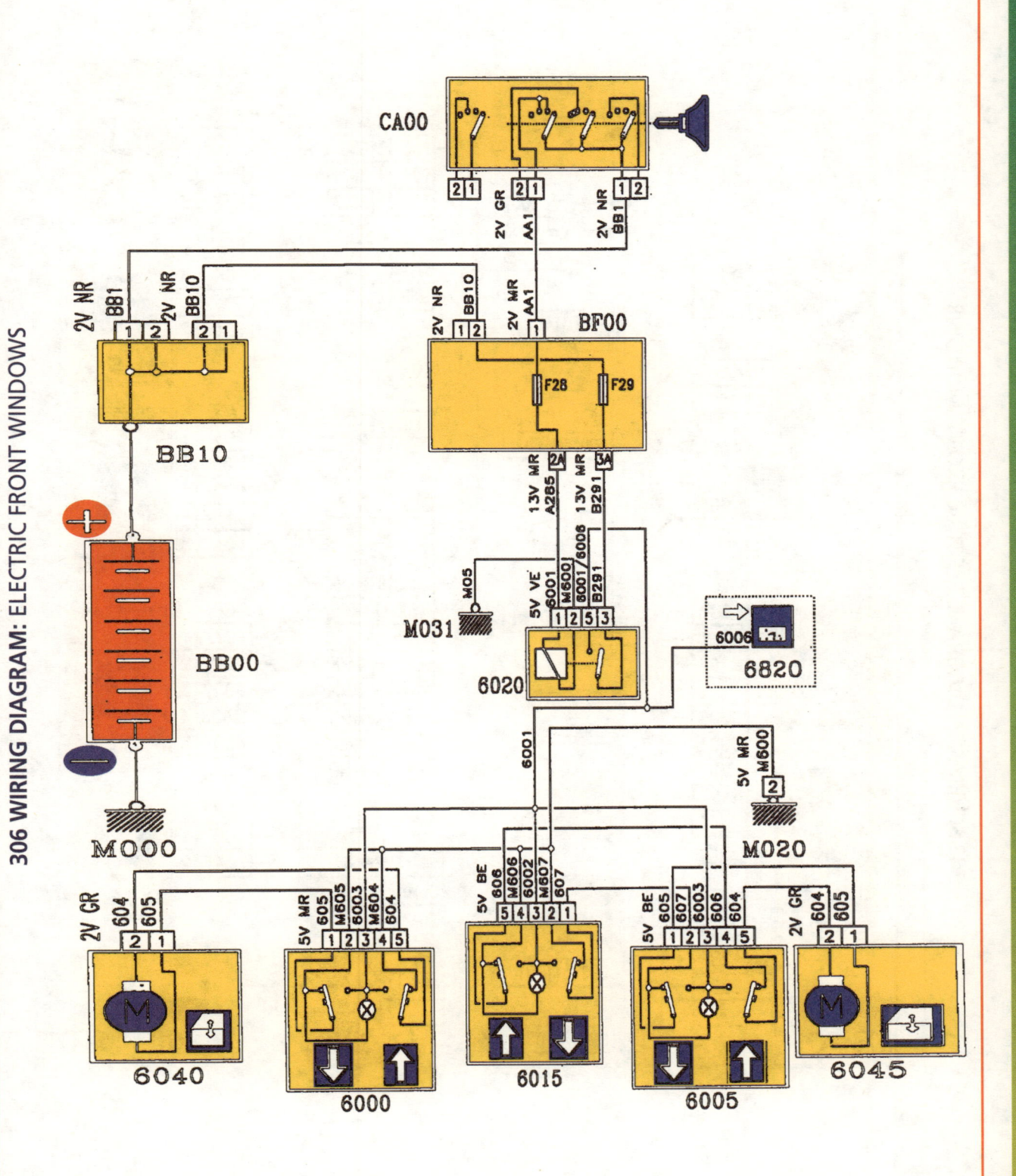

CHAPTER 15 Wiring Diagrams 306

306 WIRING DIAGRAM: ELECTRIC FRONT WINDOWS

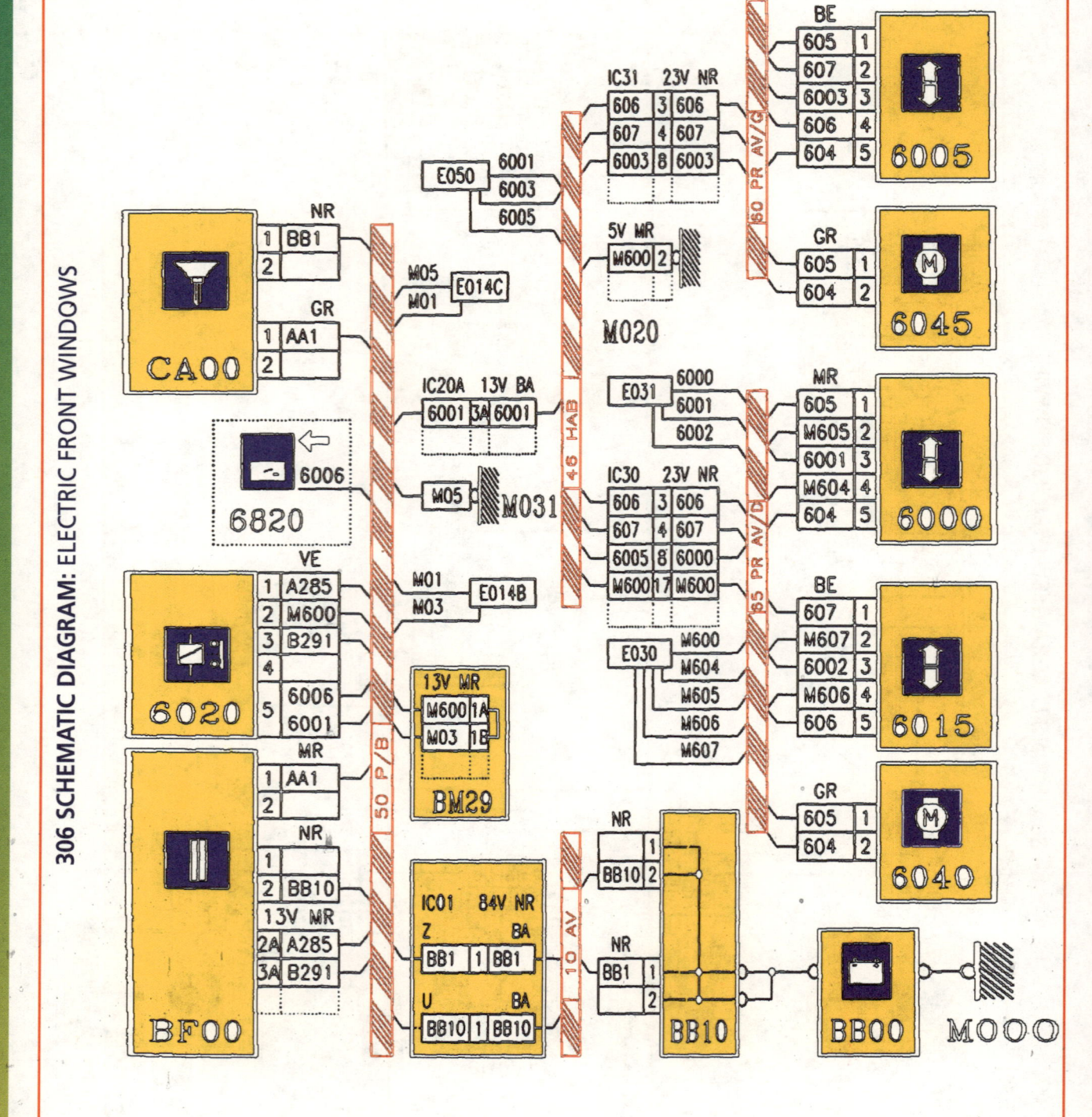

CHAPTER 15 Wiring Diagram 306

306 SCHEMATIC DIAGRAM: ELECTRIC FRONT WINDOWS

15-34

WADE TRAILERS

"We're delighted that Porter Colour Manuals choose to use a **Wade Trailers** car transporter! We're so confident ours are the best value-for-money trailers in the UK, we say - *"if you can find a better-built, better-specified trailer than we make - buy it!"*

"We're neither the cheapest nor the most expensive. We simply produce *quality* products, at *best-value* prices!"

Specialists in Van Trailers & Refridgerated Trailers.

WADE TRAILERS, Wade Yard, Wellesley Road, Clacton on Sea, Essex. CO15 3QF.
Phone: 01255 424924
Fax: 01255 424873 or 0845 3348 188

Visit us at: www.wade-trailers.co.uk

SPECIALISTS & SUPPLIERS

Autoclimate Ltd.
Battlefield Enterprise Park, March Way, Harlescott, Shrewsbury, SY1 3TE
Tel: 0800 542 9542.

Autoglass Ltd.
Autoglass operate the well-known, nation-wide call-out service for emergency glass replacement. Ring Freephone **0800 363 636** for details of your local branch.

Robert Bosch Ltd.
Broadwater Park, North Orbital Road, Denham, Uxbridge, Middx, UB9 5HJ
Tel: 01895 838 360

Castrol (UK) Ltd.
Castrol BSS, Pipers Way, Swindon, Wilts, SN3 1RE
Tel: 01793 512 712

Clarke International Ltd.
Hemnall Street, Epping, Essex, CM16 4LG
Tel: 01992 565 300

Dunlop Tyres Ltd.
Fort Dunlop, Birmingham, B24 9QT
Tel: 0121 384 4444

Hastings Direct
Conquest House, Collington Avenue, Bexhill-on-Sea, TN39 3NQ
Tel: 0800 00 1066

Hammerite Products Ltd.
Prudhoe, Northumberland, NE42 6LP
Tel: 01661 830 000

Potters Car Dismantlers
3 Sandy Lane, Titton, Stourport-on-Severn, Worcs, DY13 9PZ
Tel: 01299 823 134

Sykes-Pickavant Ltd.
Church Bridge Works, Walsall Road, Cannock, Staffs, WS11 3JR
Tel: 01253 784 800

Tecalemit Systems Ltd.
Estover Road, Plymouth, Devon, PL6 7PS
Tel: 01752 775 781

Wurth UK Ltd.
1 Centurion Way, Erith, Kent, DA18 4AE
Tel: 0870 5 98 78 41

Damaged Windscreen?

Windscreen damage the size of a 5p coin can mean an MOT failure

If you are fully comprehensively insured we can usually repair chipped glass

FREE OF CHARGE*

*With most leading insurers, there will be no insurance excess payment on a repair carried out by AUTOGLASS, for motorists with a fully comprehensive policy. This can be confirmed by checking your insurance policy.

24hrs MOBILE SERVICE
FREEPHONE FULLY GUARANTEED
ALL VEHICLE 0800 36 36 36
glass repair 7 DAYS WE COME
and replacement a week TO YOU!
www.autoglass.co.uk

AUTOGLASS
www.autoglass.co.uk
0800 36 36 36

AUTOGLASS® and The Device are registered Trade Marks of Carglass Luxembourg S.a.r.l. - Zug Branch and licensed to Autoglass Limited

WÜRTH — THE ASSEMBLY PROFESSIONALS

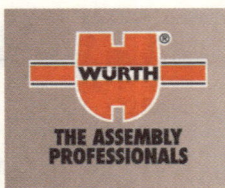

Würth UK Limited
1 Centurion Way
Erith
Kent
DA18 4AE

Tel. 0870 5 98 78 41
Fax. 0870 5 98 78 42

web: www.wurth.co.uk
email: sales@wurth.co.uk

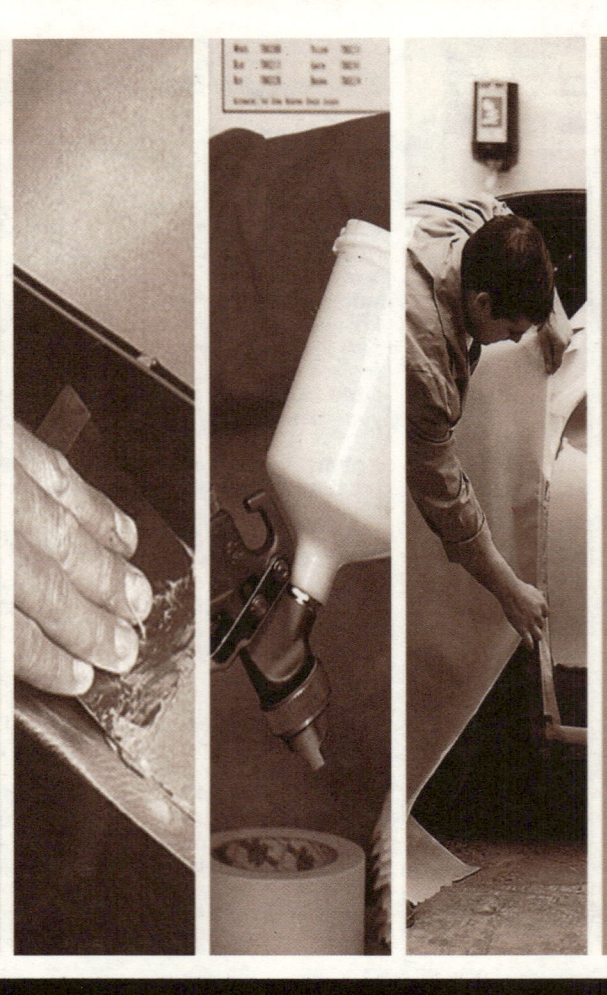

Würth UK has been supplying the automotive repair and refinishing trade for over 25 years. With over 7,000 product lines and over 250 sales consultants covering every inch of Great Britain, Würth UK are able to offer the highest level of service.

The product range includes hi-spec chemical products including additives, brake cleaner, carburettor cleaner, greases, lubricants, valeting sprays, screenwash and electrical cleaning, lubrication and protection sprays. Würth also stocks a full range of DIN and ISO standard fasteners, electrical terminals, bulbs and fuses, trim clips, and vehicle wire.

Würth products meet strict DIN standards and Würth have been ISO 9002 certified since 1996. Due to this high level of support and service, Würth are the preferred supplier to over 15 vehicle manufactures including BMW, Saab and Vauxhall, in excess of 30 dealer groups, and over 1000 independent vehicle repairers.

Simple Solutions in a Complex World

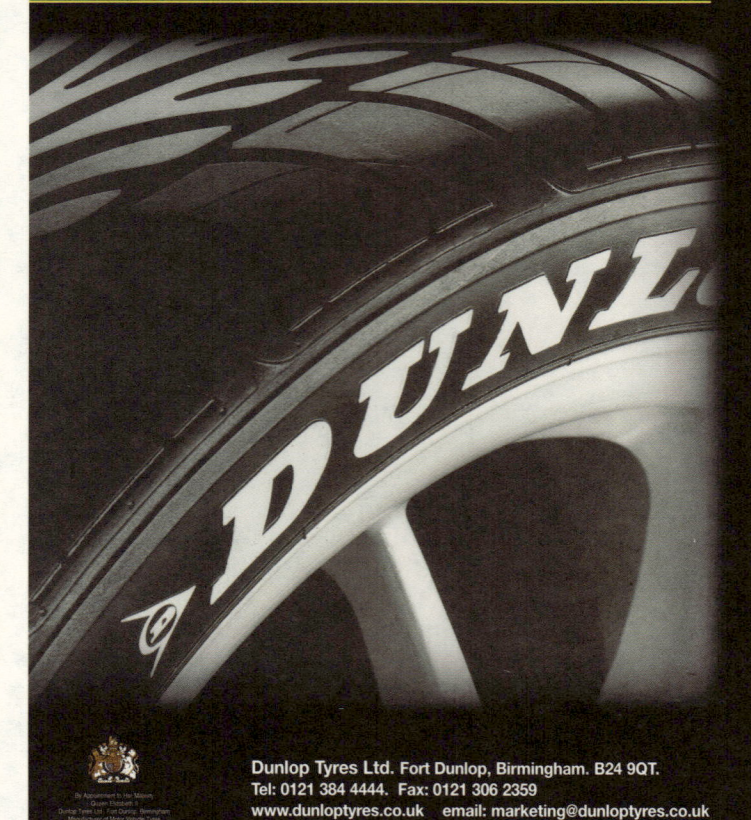

---

perfect grip

Continuous development,

rigorous testing, the very latest

technology and stringent

quality control.

The perfect combination.

Whatever you drive.

TESTED FOR THE UNEXPECTED.

DUNLOP — DRIVING TO THE FUTURE

Dunlop Tyres Ltd. Fort Dunlop, Birmingham. B24 9QT.
Tel: 0121 384 4444. Fax: 0121 306 2359
www.dunloptyres.co.uk   email: marketing@dunloptyres.co.uk

Leaders in Diagnostics Equipment

Sykes-Pickavant
Tel: 01922 702000

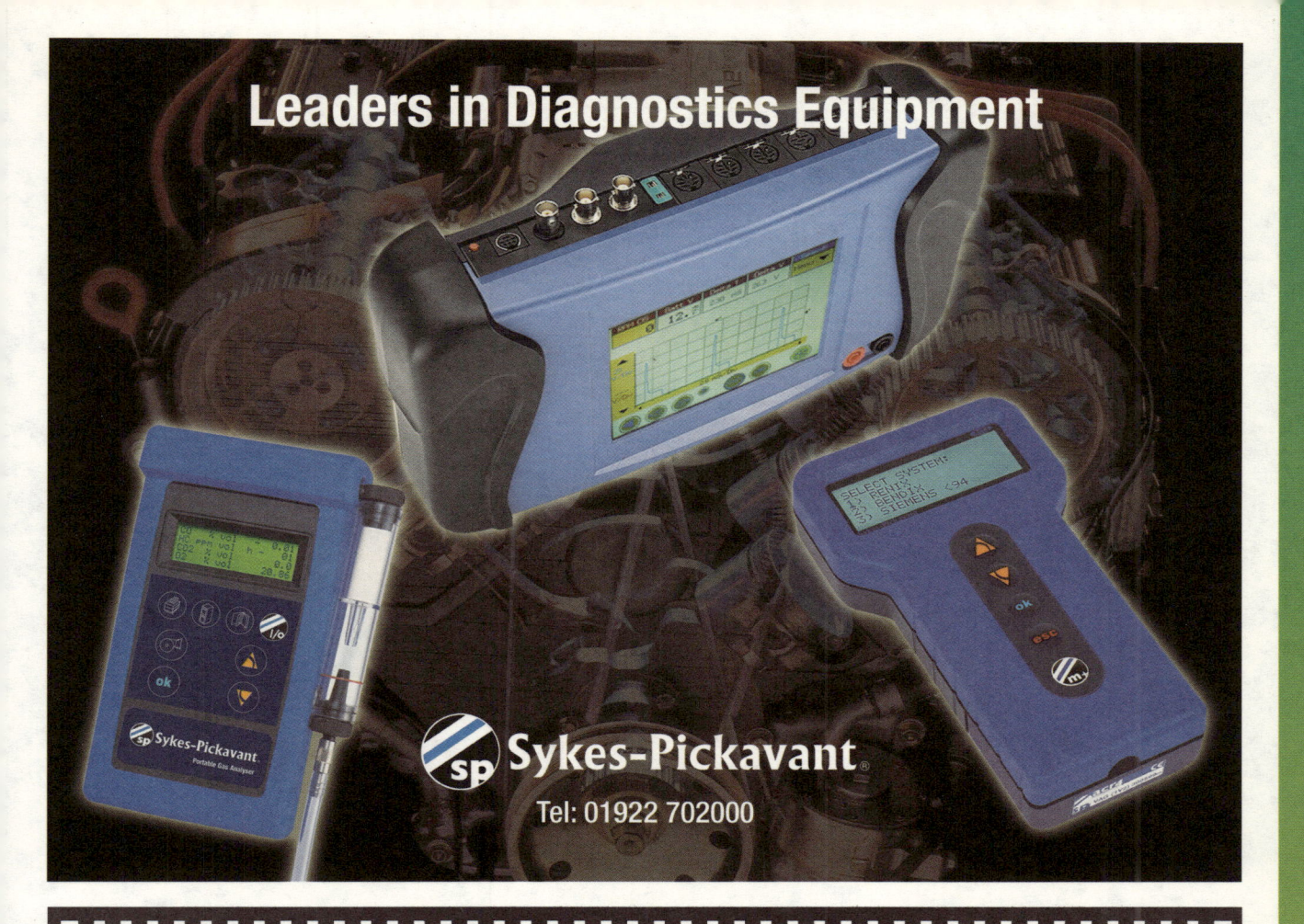

Battling for Cheaper Car Insurance?

A range of insurance products to meet your needs:

Car • Motorcycle • Home • Travel (annual and single trip)

Call Harry FREE on
0800 00 1066

- Monthly payment Option (written details on request)
- Range of discounts: security, low mileage vehicles, female drivers, married people and many more...
- Guaranteed service standards via our unique Customer Service Promise
- Insure online in no time - www.hastingsdirect.com

Mon-Fri 8am to 8pm; Sat 9am to 5pm

To help us continually improve customer service, calls may be monitored or recorded

Hastings DIRECT
0800 00 1066

Hastings Direct, Conquest House, Collington Avenue, Bexhill-on-Sea, East Sussex, TN39 3LW

With over 75 years of experience...

...Tecalemit Garage Equipment Co Ltd is the UK's longest established manufacturer of workshop equipment.

Tecalemit have a complete range of equipment covering MOT bays, 2 and 4 post lifts, tyre changers, wheel balancers, and emission products. We also have an extensive range of lubrication products.

We are the only UK based company with our own service operation. Nation-wide service engineers fully trained on Tecalemit products with genuine manufacturers spare parts.

Tecalemit Garage Equipment Co Ltd offer a complete service from workshop design, to delivery and installation, through the life time of your product.

"The name Tecalemit is synonymous with reliability, quality and above all service."

Wheel Balancers

Vehicle Lifts

Tyre Changers

MOT Bays

TECALEMIT

Sales: Tel. 01752 219111 Fax. 01752 219128 Email. sales@tecalemit.co.uk Web. www.tecalemit.co.uk
Service: Tel. 01752 219100 Fax. 01752 209320 Email. service@tecalemit.co.uk

---

New Castrol GTX reduces engine wear by 33%.*

The rest you don't need to know.

Castrol GTX
NEW Improved Formulation
33% Less Engine Wear*
15w 40
Ideal For Basic Engines
liquid engineering

*when compared to the leading competitors

Castrol

PORTER LEISURE MANUALS

Fix it yourself, keep it reliable
– and enjoy yourself,
with
Porter Leisure Manuals.

Great value at only £12.99*, from:

Porter Manuals. Little Hereford Street, Bromyard, Hereford, HR7 4DE, England.
Tel: 01 885 488 800. Fax 01 885 483 012
Visit us at www.portermanuals.com

*Price correct at going to press - subject to change.

PP VIDEO COLLECTION

We are proud to have been selected as the ONLY company with the rights to market Jaguar's great range of archive footage with the world famous 'leaping cat' logo.

JAGUAR

- One of the finest collections of action video tapes!
- Includes The Jaguar Cars Archive, The Dunlop Archive and official footage from Audi, Volkswagen and more.
- Classic motorsport from the 1900s to the '90s!

Jaguar Archive

XJ220 - The Official Story PPV3142 £12.98
Jaguar Victorious! PPV3143 £12.98
Jaguar Mk2 Building a Legend PPV3117 £12.98
The E-Type Jaguar Experience PPV3103 £12.98
The E-Type Jaguar Archive PPV3139 £12.98
The Jaguar V12 Archive PPV3138 £12.98
Jaguar Goes Racing PPV3152 £12.98

Classic Cars in Action

The Audi Quattro Experience PPV3120 £12.98
Audi Quattro The Official Story PPV3145 £12.98
Quattro Racing in the USA PPV3134 £12.98
Auto Union 1933-1940-the Official Story PPV3144 £12.98
The Story of Camaro SEV6014 £12.98
Classic Car Greats! Performance Cars PPV3114 £12.98
Ferrari Fever at the Nurburgring ESV4102 £12.98
Battle of the 'Bs PPV3104 £12.98 
Classic MG CC2001 £12.98
The MGB Experience PPV3101 £12.98
Mini Goes Racing PPV3129 £12.98
The Morgan Experience PPV3106 £12.98  
The Story of Mustang SEV6260 £12.98
The Porsche 911 Experience PPV3102 £12.98
The VW Beetle Experience PPV3119 £12.98  

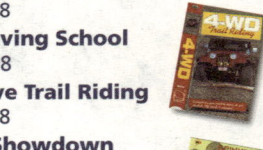

Classic Bike Videos

Classic 'Bike Grand Prix, 1994 ESV4110 £12.98
Motorcycle Racing Greats of 1951 PPV3116 £12.98
Motorcycle Racing Legends PPV3146 £12.98
Classic 'Bike Action 1953 & 1964 PPV3130 £12.98

Classic Race Archive Action

Pre-War Motor Racing PPV3105 £12.98
The Motor Racing Years - 1930s PPV3140 £12.98
The 1991 Mille Miglia ESV4101 £12.98
The 1993 Mille Miglia ESV4106 £12.98
The 1994 Mille Miglia ESV4108 £12.98
Vintage Formula Ones ESV4104 £12.98
Motor Racing '50s Style 1957 & 1958 PPV3115 £12.98
Motor Racing '60s Style 1960 & 1967 PPV3109 £12.98
Motor Racing '60s Style 1961 & 1962 PPV3107 £12.98
Motor Racing '60s Style 1963 & 1964 PPV3108 £12.98
Classic Saloon Car Racing '60s Style PPV3147 £12.98
The Phil Hill Story PPV3148 £12.98 
Motor Racing '70s Style PPV3121 £12.98
Classic Saloon Car Action '70s Style PPV3128 £12.98
Production Car Racing 1973, '74, '75 PPV3127 £12.98
Autocross '60s Style PPV3110 £12.98
Vintage Racing Greats 1965 & 1966 PPV3111 £12.98
Vintage Racing Greats 1969 & 1972 PPV3112 £12.98
Vintage Racing Greats 1973 & 1974 PPV3113 £12.98
Targa Tasmania 1995 PPV3151 £12.98
Targa Tasmania 1994 PPV3149 £12.98
Targa Tasmania 1993 PPV3132 £12.98
Targa Tasmania 1992 PPV3131 £12.98
La Carrera Pan-American 1990 ESV4105 £12.98
Gran Turismo ESV4103 £12.98 
1993 Production Car Championship PPV3135 £12.98
1992 Production Car Championship PPV3124 £12.98
1991 Production Car Championship PPV3125 £12.98
1990 Production Car Championship PPV3126 £12.98
1989 Production Car 25-hour Race PPV3123 £12.98
1988 Production Car 25-hour Race PPV3122 £12.98

Railway Tapes

Riding the Rails of the Texas State Railroad SEV2512 £12.98
Steam Engineer - More than Just a Job SEV2513 £12.98
Trams, Tracks and Trolleys PPV3141 £12.98

Other Titles

European Truck Trial 1994 ESV4109 £12.98
European Truck Trial 1993 ESV4107 £12.98
Off Road Driving School PPV3133 £12.98
4-Wheel Drive Trail Riding SEV2091 £12.98
Muscle Car Showdown SEV8028 £12.98   
Skill Guide to Gas Welding PPV3118 £12.98
Spinning Wheels: Cycle Sport '50s Style PPV3150 £12.98

Leisure Collection

The Good Sites Guide OIL104 £12.98
The Guide to Motorcaravanning OIL106 £12.98

All PP Video tapes should be available from your high street stockist but in case of difficulty, you can purchase them direct from PP Video by post, fax, telephone or web orders (quoting Visa or Mastercard number).

Porter Publishing Ltd, The Storehouse, Little Hereford Street, Bromyard, Hereford, HR7 4DE.
Tel: 01885 48 88 00 • Fax: 01885 48 30 12 • Web Site: www.portermanuals.com
Postage Rates: UK: £2.00 per tape • Europe: £4.00 per tape • Other Overseas: £6.00 per tape
Prices and postage rates may change.

INDEX

A
ABS brake, wheel sensors - check	12-25
ABS system - service operations	12-1
Accelerator cable - adjust, replace	9-23
Aerial/antenna - remove, refit	10-8
Air bags - replace	14-19
Air conditioning equipment	10-14
Airbag system - deactivate, reactivate	14-19
Airbags and pre-tensioners - essential safety first!	14-16
Alternator - remove, refit	10-2
Anti-roll bar and bushes, front - replace	11-19
Auto. Gear selector cable and handle - adjust, replace	7-8
Auto. Kickdown cable, 205/306 - adjust, replace	7-10
Auto. Transmission - remove, install	7-17
Auxiliary drive belt/s - check/adjust, replace	6-27

B
Bearing caps, OHC engine - remove	6-2
Bonnet/engine bay lid - remove, refit, adjusting	13-1
Bonnet/engine bay lid release - adjust, remove	13-2
Brake bleed	12-25
Brake caliper, front - remove, replace	12-10
Brake caliper, rear - replace	12-20
Brake disc pads, rear - replace	12-19
Brake disc, front - replace	12-11
Brake hoses	12-24
Brake pads - read this first! - applies to all types	12-3
Brake pads - specific types - remove replace	12-4
Brake pressure regulating valves - replace, adjust	12-20
Brake shoes, rear - check, replace	12-15
Brake types, rear, understanding	12-12
Brakes, systems explained	12-1
Bumpers, typical - remove, refit	13-7

C
Camshaft timing belt - check	6-15
Camshaft timing belt - replace, adjust, engine in vehicle	6-16
Camshaft timing belt - replace, adjust, engine out	6-23
Camshaft, TU engine - remove, replace	6-42
Camshaft, TUD engine - remove, replace	6-43
Camshaft, XU, XUD engines - remove, replace	6-43
Camshaft, XV, XW, XY engine - remove, replace	6-42
Capacities	1-6
Carburetor - adjust	9-15
Carburetor - remove, replace	9-17
Central locking	13-20
Central locking - replace components	10-14
Centre console - remove, replace	14-12
Choke cable - adjust, replace	9-25
Clutch cable - replace	7-3
Clutch cable, manually adjusted - adjust	7-3
Clutch replace, 205 with XV/XW/XY engines - dismantle, fit	7-18
Clutch replace, all other engines - dismantle, fit	7-20
Clutch, all types - inspect	7-20
Coolant - change	8-3
Coolant hoses - change	8-4
Coolant pump - remove, replace	8-12
Coolant temperature/level gauge senders - remove, replace	8-11
Cooling fan(s) - remove, refit	8-5
Cooling system explained	8-1
Crankshaft bearings, connecting rod bearings - remove	6-7
Cylinder block assembly - layouts	6-63
Cylinder block, TU & TUD engines - dismantle and reassemble	6-71
Cylinder block, XU & XUD engines - dismantle and reassemble	6-75
Cylinder block, XV/XW/XY engine - dismantle and reassemble	6-66
Cylinder head - lift and fit	6-3
Cylinder head - re-assembly	6-46
Cylinder head - refit	6-46
Cylinder head and combustion chambers	6-3
Cylinder head bolts - tighten, undo	6-2
Cylinder head gaskets	6-2
Cylinder head overhaul, read this first! - applies to all types	6-40
Cylinder head TU, TUD, XU, XUD engines - remove	6-36
Cylinder head types, understanding	6-13
Cylinder head, 'stuck' - free	6-3
Cylinder head, XV, XW, XY engines - remove	6-34

D
Dampers, rear - replace	11-21
Dashboard - remove, replace	14-13
Diesel engines accelerator, cold start cable - adjust, replace	9-37
Diesel engines diagnostic - carry out checks	9-29
Diesel engines fuel injectors and pipes - check, replace	9-33
Diesel engines fuel system and filters - bleed, change filters	9-38
Diesel engines preheat system - check, replace	9-35
Diesel engines systems - explained	9-29
Diesel engines turbocharger - replace	9-36
Diesel glow plugs - check, replace	10-14
Diesel injection pump - remove, refit, timing	9-29
Distributor - remove, refit	9-13
Door - remove, refit, adjust	13-11
Door lock/handle - remove, refit	13-14
Door mirror - replace	13-16
Door trim panel - remove, refit	14-3
Driveshaft - remove, refit	7-11
Driveshaft joint and gaiters– remove, replace	7-13

E
Electric fuel pump - replace	9-26
Engine - install	6-62
Engine - lift, moving	6-6
Engine and transmission - remove	6-53
Engine and transmission - separate, reconnect	6-60
Engine components - check, measuring for wear	6-9
Engine components, reassemble	6-10
Engine mounts - realign	6-79
Engine mounts - remove	6-80
Engine types, understanding	6-12
Engine, general procedures	6-1
Engine/transmission mounting types - overview	6-79
Engines - identification	6-63
Exhaust emissions	3-5
Exhaust system - replace	9-43

F
Front brake types, understanding	12-2
Front wing/fender, typical - replace	13-10
Fuel evaporative system	9-27
Fuel filter - injection engines	9-27
Fuel gauge sender unit - replace	9-43
Fuel injection systems - adjust	9-18
Fuel injection units - remove, replace	9-21
Fuel tank - remove, refit	9-41

INDEX

G
Gasket sealant	6-2
Gear lever - remove, refit	7-8
Gear lever and linkage - adjust, remove, refit	7-5
Gearbox, 4/5-speed, all other models - remove, install	7-15
Gearbox, 4/5-speed, XV/XW/XY engines - remove, install	7-15
Getting through the annual test	3-1

H
Headlight washer nozzles - remove, replace	8-13
Headlining	14-16
Heater matrix - remove, replace	8-13
Hub carrier, front - replace	11-16
Hub, brake drum and wheel bearings, rear – remove, replace, refit	11-27

I
Identification numbers	1-12
Ignition coil - replace	9-12
Ignition timing - check/set	9-9
Ignition, fuel systems diagnostics - carry out checks	9-5
Ignition, fuel, exhaust systems, petrol/gasoline engines - explained	9-3
Instrument panel - remove, refit	10-4
Interior mirror - remove, refit	14-11
Intermediate shaft bearing	7-14

L
Lambda sensor (engines with cat.) - testing, replace	9-14
Lights and fuses - replace	10-9
Luggage bay lid	13-5

M
Master cylinder - replace	12-21
Mechanical fuel pump - replace	9-25
Model changes	1-2

P
Parking brake cable - adjust, replace	12-18
Pedal boxes and cables - types	7-1
Pedal remove	9-44
Piston rings - fit	6-8
Pistons - remove, refit	6-8
Power steering pump - remove, refit	11-8
Power steering system - fill, bleed	11-9

R
Radiator - remove, clean, refit	8-8
Radio - remove and refit	14-16
Rear brake disc - replace	12-20
Repair data	1-9
Rocker shaft, XV, XW, XY & TU engines - overhaul	6-44

S
Safety first	2-1 to 2-4
Safety first!	6-1
Screen glass - replace	13-17
Screen washer pump - remove, replace	8-13
Seat belts - remove, replace	14-7
Seats, front - remove, replace	14-5
Seats, rear - remove, replace	14-6
Service data	1-7
Servicing	5-1
Servo - check, remove, refit	12-22
Servo vacuum pump, (diesel engines) - replace	12-25
Speedometer cable - remove, refit	10-5
Starter motor - remove, refit	10-3
Steering rack - remove, replace	11-6
Steering rack gaiter - replace	11-6
Steering wheel - remove, refit	11-4
Steering wheel - remove, refit	14-10
Steering, suspension systems explained	11-1
Strut, front - overhaul	11-14
Strut, front - remove, refit	11-12
Subframe, front - remove, refit	11-20
Sun roof	13-16
Suspension assembly, rear - dismantle, rebuild	11-23
Suspension assembly, rear - remove, refit	11-21
Suspension mounting bushes, rear - replace	11-22
Suspension, front, lower arm and balljoint - replace	11-9
Suspension, front, lower arm bushes - replace	11-12
Swirl chamber (diesel engines) - remove, replace	6-45

T
Tailgate / luggage bay lid handle, lock, lock motor and striker - remove, refit	13-5
Tailgate and strut - remove, refit, adjust	13-3
Thermostat - remove, test, replace	8-10
Thermostatic switch(es) - test, replace	8-10
Timing chain, XV, XW, XY engines - replace	6-25
Torque wrench settings	1-11
Track rod end - replace	11-4
Transmission oil cooler - remove, refit	7-11
Transmission remove, refit (with engine in car),	1-14
Trim and covers (typical) - remove, refit	13-11
Trim fixings, interior	14-2

V
Valve clearance (valve lash) - check, adjust	6-30
Valve guides - replace	6-45
Valve timing - locking camshaft and crankshaft	6-23
Valves - remove, reworking, refit	6-45
Valves and guides, exhaust and inlet - remove, replace	6-4
Valves, exhaust and inlet - grinding in	6-5
Vital statistics	1-4

W
Washer jet - remove, replace	8-13
Wheel arch liners and undertrays (typical) - remove, refit	13-7
Wheel bearings, front - replace	11-17
Wheel cylinder, rear - replace	12-18
Window winder mechanism, window glass - remove, refit	13-12
Wiper motor, front screen - remove, refit	10-5
Wiper motor, tailgate - remove, refit	10-6
Wiring diagrams	15-1
Workshop top tips!